Lecture Notes in Computer Science　8182

Commenced Publication in 1973
Founding and Former Series Editors:
Gerhard Goos, Juris Hartmanis, and Jan van Leeuwen

T0223912

Zhisheng Huang   Chengfei Liu
Jing He Guangyan Huang (Eds.)

Web Information Systems Engineering – WISE 2013 Workshops

WISE 2013 International Workshops
BigWebData, MBC, PCS, STeH, QUAT, SCEH, and STSC
Nanjing, China, October 13-15, 2013
Revised Selected Papers

 Springer

Volume Editors

Zhisheng Huang
Vrije University of Amsterdam
Amsterdam, The Netherlands
E-mail: huang@cs.vu.nl

Chengfei Liu
Swinburne University of Technology
Melbourne, VIC, Australia
E-mail: cliu@swin.edu.au

Jing He
Guangyan Huang
Victoria University
Melbourne, VIC, Australia
E-mail: {jing.he, guangyan.huang }@vu.edu.au

ISSN 0302-9743   e-ISSN 1611-3349
ISBN 978-3-642-54369-2   e-ISBN 978-3-642-54370-8
DOI 10.1007/978-3-642-54370-8
Springer Heidelberg New York Dordrecht London

Library of Congress Control Number: 2014931407

CR Subject Classification (1998): H.4, D.2, H.3, C.2, I.2, H.5

LNCS Sublibrary: SL 3 – Information Systems and Application, incl. Internet/Web
and HCI

Typesetting: Camera-ready by author, data conversion by Scientific Publishing Services, Chennai, India

Printed on acid-free paper

Springer is part of Springer Science+Business Media (www.springer.com)

Preface

Welcome to the proceedings of the Web Information Systems Engineering - WISE 2013 Workshops. The international conference series on Web Information Systems Engineering (WISE) aims to provide an international forum for researchers, professionals, and industrial practitioners to share their knowledge in the rapidly growing area of Web technologies, methodologies, and applications. The 14th WISE event (WISE 2013) was held in Nanjing, China, in October 2013. Previous WISE conferences were held in Hong Kong, China (2000), Kyoto, Japan (2001), Singapore (2002), Rome, Italy (2003), Brisbane, Australia (2004), New York, USA (2005), Wuhan, China (2006), Nancy, France (2007), Auckland, New Zealand (2008), Poznan, Poland (2009), Hong Kong, China (2010), Sydney, Australia (2011), and Paphos, Cyprus (2012).

The seven workshops of WISE 2013 reported on the recent developments and advances in contemporary topics in the related fields of: the big data problem on the Web (BigWebData 2013), mobile business (MBC 2013), personalization in cloud and service computing (PCS 2013), data quality and trust in dig data (QUAT 2013), e-health and social computing (SCEH 2013), semantic technology for e-health (STeH 2013), and semantic technology for smarter cities (STSC 2013).

Many colleagues helped towards the success of the above workshops. We would especially like to thank the Program Committee members and reviewers for their conscientious reviewing. We are also grateful to the WISE Society for generously supporting our workshops. We greatly appreciate Springer LNCS for publishing the WISE workshop proceedings.

December 2013

Zhisheng Huang
Chengfei Liu
Jing He
Guangyan Huang

Organization

Executive Committee

Workshops Co-chairs

Zhisheng Huang   Vrije University Amsterdam,
     The Netherlands

Chengfei Liu   Swinburne University of Technology, Australia

Publication Chair

Guangyan Huang   Victoria University, Australia

Challenging the Big Data Problem on the Web (BigWebData 2013)

Workshop Co-chairs

Alexey Cheptsov   University of Stuttgart, Germany
Guilin Qi   Southeast University, China
Zhisheng Huang   Vrije University Amsterdam, The Netherlands

The 4th International Workshop on Mobile Business (MBC 2013)

Workshop Co-chairs

Yi Zhuang   Zhejiang Gongshang University, China
Hua Hu   Hangzhou Dianzi University, China

Program Co-chairs

Jidong Ge   Nanjing University, China
Haiyang Hu   Hangzhou Dianzi University, China

The 6th International Workshop on Personalization in Cloud and Service Computing (PCS 2013)

Workshop Chair

Yanbo Han   North China University of Technology, China

Program Co-chairs

Jian Yu   Swinburne University of Technology, Australia
Zhuofeng Zhao   North China University of Technology, China

Publicity Chair

Chen Liu   North China University of Technology, China

Data Quality and Trust in Dig Data (QUAT 2013)

Workshop Honorary Chair

Bo Sundgren   Stockholm University, Sweden

Workshop Co-chairs

Deren Chen   Zhejiang University, China
William Song   Dalarna University, Sweden

E-Health and Social Computing (SCEH 2013)

Workshop Co-chairs

Jing He   Victoria University, Australia
Guangyan Huang   Victoria University, Australia

Semantic Technology for eHealth (STeH 2013)

Workshop Co-chairs

Huajun Chen   Zhejiang University, China
M. Scott Marshall   MAASTRO Clinic, The Netherlands
Zhisheng Huang   Vrije University Amsterdam, The Netherlands

Semantic Technology for Smarter Cities (STSC 2013)

Workshop Co-chairs

Tony Lee   Saltlux Inc., South Korea
Jun Fang   Northwestern Polytechnical University, China
Zhisheng Huang   Vrije University Amsterdam, The Netherlands

Program Committees

BigWebData 2013

Neil Audsley	University of York, UK
Michael Resch	University of Stuttgart, Germany
Bastian Koller	High-Performance Computing Center Stuttgart, Germany
Frank van Harmelen	Vrije University Amsterdam, The Netherlands
Haofen Wang	Shanghai Jiaotong University, China
Jianfeng Du	Guangdong University of Foreign Studies, China
Kewen Wang	Griffith University, Australia
Wei Hu	Nanjing University, China
Jeff Pan	University of Aberdeen, UK
Harold Boley	RuleML, Canada
Philip Moore	Birmingham City University, UK
Alexey Cheptsov	High-Performance Computing Center Stuttgart, Germany
Zhisheng Huang	Vrije University Amsterdam, The Netherlands
Guilin Qi	Southeast University, China

Industry Liaison Group

Andrey Sadovykh, Marcos Almeida, SOFTTEAM, France

MBC 2013

Patrick C.K. Hung	University of Ontario Institute of Technology, Canada
Dickson K.W. CHIU	Dickson Computer Systems, Hong Kong, SAR China
Jie Shao	The University of Melbourne, Australia
Samuel P.M. Choi	The Open University of Hong Kong, SAR China
Eleanna Kafeza	Athens University of Economics and Commerce, Greece
Baihua Zheng	Singapore Management University, Singapore
Edward Hung	Hong Kong Polytechnic University, SAR China
Ho-fung Leung	Chinese University of Hong, SAR China
Zakaria Maamar	Zayed University, UAE
Stefan Voss	University of Hamburg, Germany
Cuiping Li	Renmin University, China
Chi-hung Chi	National Tsing Hua University, Taiwan, China
Stephen Yang	National Central University, Taiwan, China

Ibrahim Kushchu   Mobile Government Consortium International,
                               UK
Hao Hu   Nanjing University, China
Junhua Ding   East Carolina University, USA
Yu Zhou   Nanjing University of Aeronautics &
                               Astronautics, China
Wei Song   Nanjing University of Science and Technology,
                               China
Yingzhou Zhang   Nanjing University of Posts and
                               Telecommunications, China
Keman Huang   Tsinghua University, China
Huiye Ma   CWI, The Netherlands
Pirkko Walden   Abo Akademi University, Finland
Raymond Wong   National ICT, Australia
Lidan Shou   Zhejiang University, China
Matti Rossi   Helsinki School of Economics, Finland
Achim Karduck   Furtwangen University, Germany
Xiangmin Zhou   CSIRO Canberra ICT Center, Australia
Hoyoung Jeung   EPFL, Switzerland
Zaiben Chen   The University of Queensland, Australia
Ruopeng Lu   SAP Research CEC Brisbane, Australia
Quanqing Xu   National University of Singapore, Singapore
Mohammed Eunus Ali   The University of Melbourne, Australia
Zhenjiang Lin   The Chinese University of Hong Kong,
                               SAR China

PCS 2013

Pengcheng Zhang   Hohai University, China
Zaiwen Feng   Wuhan University, China
Jinhua Xiong   Institute of Computing Technology, Chinese
                               Academy of Sciences, China
Bingxian Ma   University of Jinan, China
Talal H. Noor   The University of Adelaide, Australia
Yanhua Du   University of Science and Technology Beijing,
                               China
Chen Liu   North China University of Technology, China
Zhiyong Feng   Tianjin University, China
Zhuofeng Zhao   North China University of Technology, China
Hongbing Wang   Southeast University, China
Zhiming Ding   Institute of Software, Chinese Academy of
                               Sciences, China
Sen Su   Beijing University of Posts and
                               Telecommunications, China
Roland Wagner   Beuth University of Applied Science, Germnay

Raymond Wong	University of New South Wales, Australia
Lina Yao	University of Adelaide, Australia
Aviv Segev	KAIST, South Korea
Miao Du	Swinburne University of Technology, Australia
Zibin Zheng	The Chinese University of Hong Kong, SAR China
Qingtian Zeng	Shandong University of Science and Technology, China
Hong-Linh Truong	Vienna University of Technology, Austria
Qi Yu	Rochester Institute of Technology, USA
Mingdong Tang	Hunan University of Science and Technology, China
Chen Ding	Ryerson University, Canada
Jianwu Wang	University of California, San Diego, USA
Paolo Falcarin	University of East London, UK
Michael Mrissa	University of Lyon, France

QUAT 2013

Deren Chen	Zhejiang University, China
Xiaofeng Du	British Telecom, UK
Hasan Fleyeh	Dalarna University, Sweden
Johan Håkansson	Dalarna University, Sweden
Paul Johannesson	Stockholm University/KTH, Sweden
Yang Li	British Telecom, UK
Kami Makki	Lamar University, USA
Anders G. Nilsson	Stockholm/Karlstad University, Sweden
William Song	Dalarna University, Sweden
Yoshihisa Udagawa	Tokyo Polytechnic University, Japan
Xiaolin Zheng	Zhejiang University, China

SCEH 2013

Yanchun Zhang	Victoria University, Australia
Fernando Martin Sanchez	The University of Melbourne, Australia
Yong Tang	South China Normal University, China
Enhong Chen	University of Science and Technology of China
Hai Liu	South China Normal University, China
Xiaofei Zhou	Chinese Academy of Sciences, China
Lingling Zhang	Chinese Academy of Sciences, China
Lingfeng Niu	University of the Chinese Academy of Sciences, China
Zhiang Wu	Nanjing University of Finance and Economics, China
Xiaohui Liu	Brunel University, UK

Yingjie Tian	University of the Chinese Academy of Sciences, China
Haolan Zhang	NIT, Zhejiang University, China
Jie Cao	Nanjing University of Finance and Economics, China
Yong Shi	University of the Chinese Academy of Sciences, China
Bo Mao	Nanjing University of Finance and Economics, China

STeH 2013

Frank van Harmelen	Vrije University Amsterdam, The Netherlands
Yue Pan	IBM China
Annette ten Teije	Vrije University Amsterdam, The Netherlands
David Perez	UPM, Spain
Guoqian Jiang	Mayo Clinic College of Medicine, USA
Haofen Wang	Shanghai Jiaotong University, China
Zhiyuan Luo	Royal Holloway, University of London, UK
Jeff Pan	University of Aberdeen, UK
Jinsong Li	Zhejiang University, China
Mar Marcos	Universitat Jaume I, Spain
Yanchun Zhang	Victoria University, Australia
Siwei Yu	Wuhan University, China
Jinguang Gu	Wuhan University of Science and Technology, China
Jose Alberto Maldonado	Universidad Politecnica de Valencia, Spain
Xiaoli Hua	Wuhan Union Hospital, China
Huajun Chen	Zhejiang University, China
M. Scott Marshall	MAASTRO Clinic, The Netherlands
Zhisheng Huang	Vrije University Amsterdam, The Netherlands

STSC 2013

Spyros Kotoulas	The Smarter Cities Technology Center, IBM Ireland
Frank van Harmelen	Vrije University Amsterdam, The Netherlands
Yi Huang	Siemens, Germany
Haofen Wang	Shanghai Jiaotong University, China
Zhiqiang Gao	Southeast University, China
Alexey Cheptsov	High-Performance Computing Center Stuttgart, Germany
Jiancheng Weng	Beijing University of Technology, China
Ning Zhong	Maebashi Institute of Technology, Japan
Zengyu Duan	Tongji University, China
Dongyuan Yang	Tongji University, China

Wei Hu   Nanjing University, China
Qinghua Liu   Jiangsu University of Science and Technology,
                              China
Zhi Wang   Jiangsu University of Science and Technology,
                              China
Tony Lee   Saltlux Inc., Seoul, South Korea
Jun Fang   Northwestern Polytechnical University, China
Zhishen Huang   Vrije University Amsterdam, The Netherlands

Table of Contents

The 6th International Workshop on Personalization in Cloud and Service Computing (PCS 2013)

Data Quality and Trust in Dig Data (QUAT 2013)

E-health and Social Computing (SCEH2013)

Semantic Technology for eHealth (STeH2013)

Semantic Technology for Smarter Cities (STSC2013)

Large-Scale Complex Reasoning with Semantics: Approaches and Challenges

Grigoris Antoniou[1], Jeff Z. Pan[2], and Ilias Tachmazidis[1]

[1] University of Huddersfield, UK
[2] University of Aberdeen, UK

Abstract. Huge amounts of data are generated by sensor readings, social media and databases. Such data introduce new challenges due to their volume and variety, and thus, new techniques are required for their utilization. We believe that reasoning can facilitate the extraction of new and useful knowledge. In particular, we may apply reasoning in order to make and support decisions, clean noisy data and derive high-level information from low-level input data. In this work we discuss the problem of large-scale reasoning over incomplete or inconsistent information, with an emphasis on nonmonotonic reasoning. We outline previous work, challenges and possible solutions, both over MapReduce and alternative high performance computing infrastructures.

1 Introduction

We are in the middle of the big data revolution: huge amounts of data are published by public and private organizations, and generated by sensor networks and social media. Apart from issues of size, this data is often dynamic and heterogeneous. In addition, data as a resource has been identified, and is increasingly utilized to generate added value; we are heading towards a data economy.

The challenge of big data is about managing it, but even more so about making sense of it: we want to avoid drowning in the sea of data, identify and focus on important aspects, and uncover hidden information and value. The role of data mining in this context is clear, but we believe reasoning has also an important role to play: for decision making, decision support, and for uncovering hidden knowledge in data, e.g. by deriving high-level information from low-level input data. Semantics has also an important role to play, both for understanding the data and for facilitating the combination of data from heterogeneous sources. The potential of semantics and reasoning in the context of big data has been well realized and is being debated[1].

Big data poses great challenges to the reasoning and semantics communities, in terms of computational efficiency. The semantic web community has risen to this challenge through the use of mass parallelization and approximation, and a lot has been achieved. Considering parallelization, two techniques have been proposed in the literature, namely rule partitioning and data partitioning [15,23]. The former is based on the idea of assigning the computation of each rule to a node in the cluster, while the latter

---

[1] e.g. `http://lod2.eu/BlogPost/`
`1698-eswc-2013-panel-semantic-technologies-for-big-data-`
`analytics-opportunities-and-challenges.html`

Z. Huang et al. (Eds.): WISE 2013 Workshops 2013, LNCS 8182, pp. 1–10, 2014.

assigns subsets of the given dataset to each node in the cluster. Data partitioning, such as distributed summarization [1], proved to be more efficient as it allows more balanced distribution of the computation among nodes.

WebPIE [28] is a Web-scale parallel inference engine that performs forward chaining reasoning based on the MapReduce framework [7] under the RDFS and OWL *ter Horst* semantics. A set of algorithms is proposed, while arising challenges are addressed by introducing several optimizations. An extensive experimental evaluation over large real-world datasets and the LUBM^2 synthetic benchmark is presented, with parallel reasoning scaling up to 100 billion triples.

For the case of data partitioning, the degree of parallelization is strongly affected by the data distribution. In fact, Kotoulas et al. [16] pointed out that Semantic Web data follow a highly uneven distribution and addressed arising performance issues. MARVIN [17] introduces the *divide-conquer-swap* strategy, in which triples are being swapped between nodes in the cluster in order to achieve scalable and load-balanced reasoning. Inference results are gradually produced, while eventual completeness of the inference is guaranteed. Hogan et al. [12] introduces partial indexing techniques which are optimised for application of linear rules and which rely on a separation of schema triples from data triples. They evaluate their approach with LUBM(10) for RDFS, pD* (OWL Horst) and OWL 2 RL, demonstrating pragmatic distributed reasoning over 1.12 billion Linked Data statements for a subset of OWL 2 RL/RDF rules they argue to be suitable for Web reasoning.

Backward chaining reasoning over RDF/S data has recently been studied. The basic idea lies on the observation that schema triples are far less than instance triples. Thus, schema triples can be replicated to each processing node, while instance triples are traversed sequentially during the entailment. QueryPIE [27] optimizes the computation of backward reasoning by using the precalculated RDFS closure. The performance of QueryPIE has been tested on datasets of up to 1 billion triples.

4sr [21] performs backward chaining reasoning on top of 4store [11], which is an RDF storage and SPARQL query system. The system is evaluated on a server and a cluster configuration for up to 138M triples, with cluster configuration performing better for larger datasets. However, a preliminary evaluation in [22] reports scalability of up to 500M triples.

Despite their importance in addressing large-scale reasoning, these works addressed quite simple forms of reasoning: Datalog [2], and the aforementioned works on simple ontology/RDFS reasoning. In particular, all these works study monotonic forms of reasoning, and do not handle inconsistencies. Traditionally, the field of nonmonotonic reasoning addresses knowledge representation and reasoning issues related to incomplete and inconsistent information. Such imperfect information may naturally arise when information from independent sources is integrated. Indicative application scenarios of this kind of reasoning include:

- Decision making in smart environments [5].
- Rules with exceptions for decision making.
- Ontology evolution [9].
- Ontology repair [20].

---

^{2} http://swat.cse.lehigh.edu/projects/lubm/

Nonmonotonic approaches [4] and their adaptation to semantic web problems (e.g. [13,8,3]) have been traditionally memory based. But this approach cannot be maintained in the face of big data. This paper outlines challenges, early results and research plans related to the problem of large-scale reasoning with complex knowledge structures, in particular including inconsistencies.

2 MapReduce Framework Basics

MapReduce is a framework for parallel processing over huge datasets [7]. Processing is carried out in two phases, a map and a reduce phase. For each phase, a set of user-defined map and reduce functions are run in a parallel fashion. The former performs a user-defined operation over an arbitrary part of the input and partitions the data, while the latter performs a user-defined operation on each partition.

MapReduce is designed to operate over key/value pairs. Specifically, each Map function receives a key/value pair and emits a set of key/value pairs. All key/value pairs produced during the map phase are grouped by their key and passed to the reduce phase. During the reduce phase, a $Reduce$ function is called for each unique key, processing the corresponding set of values.

Probably the most well-known MapReduce example is the *wordcount* example. In this example, we take as input a large number of documents and the final result is the calculation of the number of occurrences of each word. The pseudo-code for the Map and $Reduce$ functions is depicted below.

```
map(Long key, String value):
    // key: position in document
    // value: document line
    for each (word w in value) do
        EmitIntermediate(w, "1");

reduce(String key, Iterator values):
    // key: a word
    // values : list of counts
    int count = 0;
    for each (v in values) do
        count += ParseInt(v);
    Emit(key, count);
```

Consider as input the lines "Hello world." and "Hello MapReduce.". During the map phase, each map operation gets as input a line of a document. The Map function extracts words from each line and emits that word w occurred once ("1"). Here we do not use the position of each line in the document, thus the *key* in Map is ignored. As mentioned above, the MapReduce framework will group and sort pairs by their key. The $Reduce$ function has to sum up all occurrence values for each word emitting a pair containing the word and the final number of occurrences for this word. The final result for each word will be <Hello, 2>, <MapReduce, 1> and <world, 1>.

3   Inconsistency-Tolerant Reasoning over MapReduce

3.1   Defeasible Logic

Early works on large-scale nonmonotonic reasoning studied defeasible logic [25,26], selected for its rather simple computational structure and its relative closeness to Datalog. The approach adopted the following idea: To perform reasoning in two stages, first calculate all applicable rules based on the current knowledge base and then apply the defeasible logic algorithm.

First stage. Consider the following rule set:

$$r1: R(X,Z), S(Z,Y) \Rightarrow Q(X,Y).$$
$$r2: T(X,Z), U(Z,Y) \Rightarrow \neg Q(X,Y).$$
$$r1 > r2.$$

and the following facts:

$$R(a,b) \quad S(b,b)$$
$$T(a,e) \quad U(e,b)$$

The Map function will transform each given fact and emit the following pairs:

$$<b, (a,R)> \quad <b, (b,S)>$$
$$<e, (a,T)> \quad <e, (b,U)>$$

The MapReduce framework will perform grouping/sorting resulting in the following intermediate pairs:

$$<b, <(a,R), (b,S)>>$$
$$<e, <(a,T), (b,U)>>$$

Finally, intermediate pairs will be processed in order to compute fired rules (in the form of <Literal, (knowledge, Fired rule ID)>). Thus, the reducer with key:

$$b \text{ will emit } <Q(a,b), (r1)>$$
$$e \text{ will emit } <Q(a,b), (\neg,r2)>$$

Second stage. Now, our knowledge base consists of:

$$R(a,b) \qquad S(b,b)$$
$$T(a,e) \qquad U(e,b)$$
$$<Q(a,b), (r1)> \quad <Q(a,b), (\neg, r2)>$$

The Map function will emit the following pairs:

$$<Q(a,b), (r1)> \quad <Q(a,b), (\neg, r2)>$$

since we need to apply the defeasible logic algorithm only for literals that are contained in the head of a rule, namely $Q(X,Y)$.

MapReduce framework will perform grouping/sorting resulting in the following intermediate pairs:

$$<Q(a,b), <(r1), (\neg, r2)>>$$

During the reduce phase, we apply the defeasible logic algorithm for each literal by taking into consideration our current knowledge for the literal. Thus, the reducer with key:

$$Q(a,b) \text{ will conclude } <Q(a,b), (\$)>$$

as $r1 > r2$.

However, this approach can only work for stratified theories because for the general case we need to compute and store both positive and negative conclusions. To understand this, let us briefly outline the basic idea of the defeasible logic algorithm. To prove a literal p positively $(+p)$ we need to consider all attacking rules r with head $\neg p$ and show that each such rule is either discarded or countered by a stronger rule for p. And to show that r is discarded with must find an antecedent (literal in the body) q for which we have established that it is not provable $(-q)$. $-q$ indicates finite failure to prove q. To derive such a conclusion we have to consider all rules with head q; in the simplest case it might be the case that all such rules are non-applicable (discarded).

So at the heart of the defeasible logic algorithm lie two principles: (a) that negative conclusions denoting finite failure to prove are proved and recorded; and (b) that to prove $-p$, all rules with head p must be considered. Since the MapReduce framework does not allow communication between nodes, all the available information, for a given literal p, must be processed by a single node, causing either main memory insufficiency or uneven load balancing decreasing parallelization. In addition, storing both positive and negative conclusions may become prohibiting on the Web-scale even for small datasets due to the huge amount of generated data.

While many rule sets and ontologies are stratified, the restriction is quite severe and in fact avoids most of the complexities in nonmonotonic reasoning. To overcome this restriction, current works seeks to develop an alternative characterization of defeasible logic, more tailored to being implemented with MapReduce. The main idea of is to transform the defeasible reasoning algorithm in order allow reasoning based exclusively on the positive derivation.

The new algorithm will allow the insertion of new knowledge to and the deletion of existing knowledge that is no longer supported from the knowledge base. Moreover, reasoning process will be divided into "derivation steps" and performed until no new conclusion is derived or no existing conclusion is retracted.

To better understand the new approach and its difference to the original defeasible logic algorithm, let us consider a simple example.

$$a$$
$$r1 : a \Rightarrow b$$
$$r2 : b \Rightarrow c$$
$$r3 : \quad \Rightarrow \neg c$$

Initially $r3$ is ready to fire, but is attacked by rule $r2$. However $+b$ has not been derived yet, so $r2$ can be discarded and $r3$ can fire to deduce $+\neg c$. Of course, at some stage in the derivation process, $+a$ and $+b$ will be derived. At that time, an inference rule retracting $+\neg c$ will be applied, as the attacking rule $r2$ is no longer discarded but fires.

So the big difference to the original defeasible logic algorithm is this: in the new approach, a conclusion $+p$ may be retracted when more conclusions are derived, whereas in the original algorithm $+p$ is derived once and for all. Thus seen, the new algorithm avoids the storage of negative derivation information $(-p)$ at the expense of allowing conclusions to be retracted at a later stage.

Obviously, this approach is unnecessarily inefficient for an in-memory solution, but it allows for a straightforward implementation using MapReduce. In each "derivation step", MapReduce regenerates the entire knowledge base. First, we calculate all the applicable rules given the current knowledge base and then perform defeasible reasoning in order to generate the new knowledge base. Although an in-memory solution could provide more optimal management of the knowledge base by applying only the computed changes during each step, a solution based on MapReduce is able to handle huge amounts of data and ensure scalability.

3.2   Well-Founded Semantics

One key difficulty in programming defeasible logic in MapReduce is the need to represent negative conclusions, as illustrated above. Therefore we have looked at another nonmonotonic reasoning approach that doesn't have this feature: Well Founded Semantics (WFS) of logic programs [19]. Indeed we have found a MapReduce based solution to computing WFS even in the nonstratified case, under some standard safety conditions. The main idea is to compute the WFS by applying the *alternating fixpoint procedure* [6].

This approach is based on the computation of two sets, namely an underestimate of true literals (K_i) and an overestimate of true and undefined literals (U_i). We perform reasoning adding (removing) gradually to the first (second) set of literals until no literal can be added to or removed from both sets. At this point we reach a fixpoint, namely we have a complete knowledge of which literals are true, undefined or false.

Earlier work [24] have addressed the computation of rules containing negative subgoals under the assumption of stratification. Our new approach calculates negative rules in a similar manner with respect to the MapReduce framework, but, without the restriction of stratification. For details on negative rules calculation over MapReduce readers are referred to [24].

Consider the following program P:

$$a \leftarrow c, \textbf{not } b.$$
$$b \leftarrow c, \textbf{not } a.$$
$$c \leftarrow d.$$
$$d.$$
$$e \leftarrow e.$$

We first compute the set K_0 which is the closure of the subprogram consisting only of positive rules, namely $K_0 = \{d, c\}$ (a and b belong to negative rules, while e cannot be inferred since it depends on itself). Consequently, each set U_i (correspondingly, K_i) is computed as the closure of the program P provided that for each applicable rule, none of the negative subgoals belongs to K_i (correspondingly, U_{i-1}). Thus $U_0 = \{d, c, b, a\}$ since a (as the negative subgoal "**not** a" in the second rule) and b (as the negative subgoal "**not** b" in the first rule) do not belong to K_0. We calculate K_1 and U_1 in the same fashion resulting in $K_1 = \{d, c\}$ and $U_1 = \{d, c, b, a\}$. Since $(K_0, U_0) = (K_1, U_1)$ we have reached a fixpoint, and thus, we can infer the following knowledge (where $BASE(P)$ is the Herbrand base of the program P):

> **true** literals = K_1 = {d,c}
> **unknown** literals = $U_1 - K_1$ = {b,a}
> **false** literals = $BASE(P) - U_1$ = {e,d,c,b,a} - {d,c,b,a} = {e}

In order to implement the new approach using the MapReduce framework we first need to compute the closure of the subprogram consisting only of positive rules, namely we perform reasoning until no new knowledge can be derived based on a positive rule. Once we have calculated K_0, the computation follows the following pattern. We calculate the closure of the given program by incrementally building the U_i (correspondingly, K_i) given a previously computed and unchangeable set K_i (correspondingly, U_{i-1}). While computing U_i (correspondingly, K_i), a rule is applicable if its positive part is supported by U_i (correspondingly, K_i) and none of the literals in its negative part is supported by the previously computed set K_i (correspondingly, U_{i-1}).

To detect that fixpoint is reached, we need to keep track of four sets, namely K_i, U_i, K_{i+1} and U_{i+1}, while reasoning for the step "$i + 1$". However, we need to check for fixpoints only at the end of each step, namely when both K_{i+1} and U_{i+1} are calculated. Given the four sets K_i, U_i, K_{i+1} and U_{i+1}, we can establish whether $(K_0, U_0) = (K_1, U_1)$ in one MapReduce pass. The intuition of the fixpoint lies on the fact that K_0 and K_1 contain the exact same literals, as do U_0 and U_1. We intend to verify, implement and evaluate this approach, while results in [24] indicate that our new approach will turn out to be scalable as well.

4   Inconsistency-Tolerant Reasoning: Beyond MapReduce

While the previous section has outlined MapReduce solutions for simple nonmonotonic approaches, there exist more complex solutions which are based on the idea that alternative world views (e.g. extensions [18] or answer sets [10]) are computed. Such approaches rely on the computation of alternative reasoning chains satisfying some properties of maximality and internal coherence. And if enriched with priority information, these reasoning chains are compared to identify the preferred chain(s).

In the area of the semantic web, such ideas lie at the heart of works on ontology evolution [14] and ontology repair [20]. Intuitively, ways of repairing violations of integrity rules are successively built - obviously there are often more than one possible ways to repair an integrity violation. In addition, the process is recursive as resolving one invalidity may cause new violations. Once alternative repairs are computed, they are compared w.r.t. a domain-dependent preference order to derive the optimal repair.

MapReduce is not well placed to generate good solutions to implementing this type of approaches. Intuitively, the difficulty can be described as follows: this type of

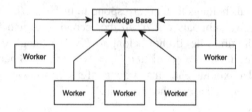

Fig. 1. Shared memory model

approaches need a certain degree of coordination between parallel tasks while the MapReduce framework does not allow communication between nodes during parallel computation (map and reduce phase). In addition, MapReduce is based on the idea that each node starts from the exact same initial state (source code and in-memory information) and operates on different data. However, problems such as ontology evolution require solutions that allow each node to have access to the whole dataset, starting from a different initial state (different violation resolution).

We can state it another way: MapReduce is known to be tailored towards "embarrassingly parallel" problems. For reasons we outlined above, we believe that these complex forms of reasoning do not fall under this category of problems. It follows that we need a different, more complex computational model to do this type of reasoning at large scale. A particular solution we envisage is based on the idea of parallel processes working on a shared memory.

As shown in Figure 1, a solution for ontology evolution can be based on a shared memory model. Initially, the knowledge base is loaded into the shared memory with each worker (computer) having access to the whole knowledge base. As our knowledge base may contain inconsistencies, we need to resolve all the violations resulting in a consistent knowledge base. However, our approach is based on a static knowledge base, namely instead of changing the knowledge base itself, each worker builds a solution by keeping track of only the required changes over the knowledge base.

In essence, we may represent all the possible solutions as a tree where each violation corresponds to node and each applied repair corresponds to an edge. By assigning different parts of the tree to each worker we reassure that each computer is working on a different solution. Since our new model allows communication between nodes, we can introduce several optimizations such as pruning techniques that will allow us to avoid computing the same set of repair actions. In addition, if the best solution is considered as the one with the least repairs applied and we have already found a solution at depth k we may prevent the rest of the workers to search for solutions at depth $k+1$.

Each worker has to be able to build its solution based on the repairs that are already applied and the violations that emerge due to the applied repairs. As the number of workers is far less than the number of potential solutions, each worker is assigned to a branch in the tree investigating which repairs may lead to a solution. We need to store all the solutions as in a second phase, they will be ordered based on given repair preferences in order to extract the optimal solution.

5   Conclusion

In this paper we discussed the problem of implementing complex forms of large-scale reasoning, capable of dealing with incomplete and inconsistent information. We explained some challenges and solutions for simpler forms of nonmonotonic reasoning based on MapReduce. In addition, we worked out some limitations of MapReduce for more complex forms of nonmonotonic reasoning, and proposed a new computational architecture tailored towards these kinds of reasoning.

We intend to implement and evaluate the reasoning methods we discussed over MapReduce or the new architecture. We will do so by running large-scale experiments with synthetic and real data. We expect to target real-world applications in domains such as smart cities and ambient assisted living.

References

1. Fokoue, A., Felipe Meneguzzi, M.S., Pan, J.Z.: Querying linked ontological data through distributed summarization. In: Proc. of the 26th AAAI Conference on Artificial Intelligence (AAAI 2012) (2012)
2. Afrati, F.N., Ullman, J.D.: Optimizing Multiway Joins in a Map-Reduce Environment. IEEE Trans. Knowl. Data Eng. 23(9), 1282–1298 (2011)
3. Antoniou, G., Bikakis, A.: DR-Prolog: A System for Defeasible Reasoning with Rules and Ontologies on the Semantic Web. IEEE Trans. Knowl. Data Eng. 19(2), 233–245 (2007)
4. Antoniou, G., Williams, M.A.: Nonmonotonic reasoning. MIT Press (1997)
5. Bikakis, A., Antoniou, G.: Contextual Defeasible Logic and Its Application to Ambient Intelligence. IEEE Transactions on Systems, Man, and Cybernetics, Part A 41(4), 705–716 (2011)
6. Brass, S., Zukowski, U., Freitag, B.: Transformation-based bottom-up computation of the well-founded model (1997)
7. Dean, J., Ghemawat, S.: MapReduce: simplified data processing on large clusters. In: Proc. of the 6th Conference on Symposium on Opearting Systems Design & Implementation, vol. 6, p. 10. USENIX Association, Berkeley (2004)
8. Eiter, T., Ianni, G., Lukasiewicz, T., Schindlauer, R.: Well-founded semantics for description logic programs in the semantic web. ACM Trans. Comput. Log. 12(2), 11 (2011)
9. Flouris, G., Konstantinidis, G., Antoniou, G., Christophides, V.: Formal foundations for RDF/S KB evolution. Knowl. Inf. Syst. 35(1), 153–191 (2013)
10. Gelfond, M.: Chapter 7 answer sets. In: van Harmelen, V.L., Porter, B. (eds.) Handbook of Knowledge Representation, vol. 3, pp. 285–316 (2008)
11. Harris, S., Lamb, N., Shadbolt, N.: 4store: The design and implementation of a clustered rdf store. In: 5th International Workshop on Scalable Semantic Web Knowledge Base Systems (SSWS 2009) (2009)
12. Hogan, A., Pan, J.Z., Polleres, A., Decker, S.: SAOR: Template Rule Optimisations for Distributed Reasoning over 1 Billion Linked Data Triples. In: Proc. of the 9th International Semantic Web Conference (ISWC 2010) (2010)
13. Knorr, M., Hitzler, P., Maier, F.: Reconciling OWL and Non-monotonic Rules for the Semantic Web. In: ECAI, pp. 474–479 (2012)
14. Konstantinidis, G., Flouris, G., Antoniou, G., Christophides, V.: A Formal Approach for RDF/S Ontology Evolution. In: ECAI, pp. 70–74 (2008)
15. Kotoulas, S., van Harmelen, F., Weaver, J.: KR and Reasoning on the Semantic Web: Web-Scale Reasoning (2011)

16. Kotoulas, S., Oren, E., van Harmelen, F.: Mind the data skew: distributed inferencing by speeddating in elastic regions. In: WWW, pp. 531–540 (2010)
17. Oren, E., Kotoulas, S., Anadiotis, G., Siebes, R., ten Teije, A., van Harmelen, F.: Marvin: Distributed reasoning over large-scale Semantic Web data. J. Web Sem. 7(4), 305–316 (2009)
18. Reiter, R.: A logic for default reasoning. Artif. Intell. 13(1-2), 81–132 (1980)
19. Ross, K.A.: The well-founded semantics for general logic programs. Journal of the ACM 38, 620–650 (1991)
20. Roussakis, Y., Flouris, G., Christophides, V.: Declarative Repairing Policies for Curated KBs. In: HDMS (2011)
21. Salvadores, M., Correndo, G., Harris, S., Gibbins, N., Shadbolt, N.: The design and implementation of minimal RDFS backward reasoning in 4store. In: Antoniou, G., Grobelnik, M., Simperl, E., Parsia, B., Plexousakis, D., De Leenheer, P., Pan, J. (eds.) ESWC 2011, Part II. LNCS, vol. 6644, pp. 139–153. Springer, Heidelberg (2011)
22. Salvadores, M., Correndo, G., Omitola, T., Gibbins, N., Harris, S., Shadbolt, N.: 4s-reasoner: Rdfs backward chained reasoning support in 4store. In: Web-scale Knowledge Representation, Retrieval, and Reasoning, Web-KR3 (September 2010)
23. Soma, R., Prasanna, V.K.: Parallel inferencing for owl knowledge bases. In: ICPP, pp. 75–82 (2008)
24. Tachmazidis, I., Antoniou, G.: Computing the stratified semantics of logic programs over big data through mass parallelization. In: Morgenstern, L., Stefaneas, P., Lévy, F., Wyner, A., Paschke, A. (eds.) RuleML 2013. LNCS, vol. 8035, pp. 188–202. Springer, Heidelberg (2013)
25. Tachmazidis, I., Antoniou, G., Flouris, G., Kotoulas, S.: Towards parallel nonmonotonic reasoning with billions of facts. In: KR (2012)
26. Tachmazidis, I., Antoniou, G., Flouris, G., Kotoulas, S., McCluskey, L.: Large-scale parallel stratified defeasible reasoning. In: ECAI, pp. 738–743 (2012)
27. Urbani, J., van Harmelen, F., Schlobach, S., Bal, H.: QueryPIE: Backward reasoning for OWL horst over very large knowledge bases. In: Aroyo, L., Welty, C., Alani, H., Taylor, J., Bernstein, A., Kagal, L., Noy, N., Blomqvist, E. (eds.) ISWC 2011, Part I. LNCS, vol. 7031, pp. 730–745. Springer, Heidelberg (2011)
28. Urbani, J., Kotoulas, S., Massen, J., van Harmelen, F., Bal, H.: Webpie: A web-scale parallel inference engine using mapreduce. Web Semantics: Science, Services and Agents on the World Wide Web 10 (2012)

Using Semantic Techology for Consistency Checking of Road Signs

Dongsheng Wang[1], Zhisheng Huang[2], Qinghua Liu[1], Xiaofei Zhang[1], Dan Xu[1], Zhi Wang[1], Ning Li[1], Jiangli Zhang[1], and Diming Zhang[1]

[1] Institute of Intelligent Transport System, School of Computer Science and Engineering, Jiangsu university of Science of Technology Zhenjiang, 212003, P.R. China
[2] Department of Computer Science, Vrije Universiteit Amsterdam, The Netherlands
{wds_ict,Giant_liu,tkh4,DMZhang}@163.com, huang@cs.vu.nl,
{julychang,cw,jiangli}@just.edu.cn, xudan.zj@gmail.com

Abstract. With the cities ever growing and evolving much faster than before, effectively managing road signs is a major problem, in particular checking the positioning and contents of road signs in compliance with related road sign regulations (RSRs) and validating if the newly built road signs are consistent with existing road signs according to RSRs. In this paper, we discuss challenges in developing road sign management system and propose a data integration solution which provides a basis for intelligent road sign management based upon the LarKC platform. We then present methods for automatically verifying road signs according to RSRs and simulating the process of generating new road signs when new roads are to be built. The proposed system can bring much convinence to decision makers and greatly decrease fees of the city operation.

Keywords: Semantic, Road Sign, LarKC, Consistency Checking.

1 Introduction

Big data refers to data sets that are too large and highly complex, traditional data processing technology has been unable to meet the demand of big data processing, and it is becoming a hot topic nowadays. With ever growing scales of semantic data such as Linked Geo Data [1], OSM[2], scalable semantic data processing is becoming an important branch of big data processing, while knowology mining and discovery based on the large scale semantic data sets is increasingly signicantly. We have oberverd this trend in a Semantic-enabled Road Sign Management (SeRSM) system, in which the above mentioned data sets and urban-related information are semantially integrated and road signs are intelligently managed based on the LarKC platform.

---

[1] http://www.linkedgeodata.org
[2] http://www.openstreetmap.org/

Z. Huang et al. (Eds.): WISE 2013 Workshops 2013, LNCS 8182, pp. 11–22, 2014.

LarKC[3] (the Large Knowledge Collider) is a massive data-oriented distributed incomplete reasoning platform [1] , in which semantic technology is used for massive knowledge representation, classification, reasoning, querying, and it has been widely used in the field of life sciences, biomedical, urban computing areas. The LarKC projects main goal is to develop a platform for reasoning using massive amounts of heterogeneous information. The platform has a pluggable architecture to exploit techniques and heuristics from diverse areas such as databases, machine learning and the semantic web.

With the cities ever growing and evolving much faster than before, there have been many new buildings (i.e., point of interest, POI in maps) and new roads are built. Accordingly, new road signs should be built while some old ones should be changed. Therefore, effectively managing road signs, in particular checking the positioning and contents of road signs in compliance with related road sign regulations (RSRs) and validating if the newly built road signs are consistent with existing road signs according to RSRs, is a major problem. In this work, we manually collect and maintain a database of all Zhenjiang (a city in Jiangsu province) road signs. And other urban-related information is from open and free sources. For example, The Open Street Map (OSM) provides free editable maps of the world, while Wikipedia and Baidu provide many POI descriptions.

There are some challenges in this work. The first challenge is to deal with heterogeneous data which has existed for a long time in many areas in computer science and engineering, e.g., database systems, multimedia applications, network systems, and artificial intelligence. Emanuele Della Valle [2] distingished three levels of heterogeneity: Representational Heterogeneity, Semantic Heterogeneity, and Default Heterogeneity. What we met in this work is representational heterogeneity which means semantic data are represented by using different specification languages.Semantic data in SeRSM are from different and independent data sources, which may be developed with traditional technologies and modeling methods (e.g., relational DBMS) or expressed with semantic" formats and languages (e.g., RDF/S, OWL, WSML); for example, geographic data are usually expressed in some geographic standard, road sign data are usually stored in databases, etc. The integration and reuse of those data, therefore, need a process of conversion/translation for the data to become useful together; Secondly, road sign regulations are traditionally readable for humans but not for computers, the problem that how to translate these rules into computer-understandable representation should be solved in advance to automatically verifies road signs; Additionally, when new roads are to be built, if system could recommend what road signs should be used and where to place them and whether some related old road signs should be updated according to new-built roads. Such simulation process would bring decision makers many conveniences and largely reduce risks of building road signs.

To deal with the frist challenge, we propose a data integration solution based upon the LarKC platform, which has been successfully applied in servral big data projects[3,4]. For the second challenge, Lee T K[5] and Zhisheng Huang[6] has

---

[3] http://www.larkc.eu/

used SPARQL and OWL Horst reasoning to validate if a sequence of road signs leads to a given address in Seoul road sign management system. In this paper, we classify road sign errors in real world into four types, and encode the checking rules and RSRs into SPARQL queries stored in configuration files, which makes the system very flexible. For the last challenge, we fistly use WKT (Well-known text)[7] to model the spatial geometry, then compute the qualitative spatial relation and junctions between roads and appropriate road signs are generated according to RSRs, the method used here is based upon mature theories about spatial geometry and does not require any human intervention, which is fitting to big data processing.

2   Verification of Road Sign According to RSRs

2.1   Types of Road Sign Errors

According to our investigation, there are serval types of road sign errors in real worlds, including:

(1) Information overloading. There too much informaiton are contained in one road sign panel, which may affect the quality of driver received information, and may lead to driving operational errors and safety issues. An example is shown in Figure 1.

(2) Unsuitable positioning. There several road signs are placed on one pole, which is difficult to warn drivers. An example is shown in Figure 2.

(3) Inconsistency of road signs. Road signs are not placed in the suitable poisitions according to RSRs or there are some contraditions between road signs. An example is shown in Figure 3.

(4) Irregular signs. Road sign panels shape or color is not consistent with some RSRs. An example is shown in Figure 4.

2.2   Road Sign Verification

The first three mentioned road sign errors can be resolved automatically by our proposed methods, but the last one error types should be solved by other techologies, for example, image processing, pattern recognition and so on. We will not talk about this in this paper.

As will be described in section 4, the road sign data and other related data are transformed into a uniformed representation, i.e., RDF, and they are managed by LarKC. The error-checking rules and road sign regulations are encoded into SPARQL queries and executed under the Owl Horst entailment regime including some axioms of rdfs:isa, rdfs:subClassOf and owl:sameAS. For examle, for the errror type 1, a SPARQL query is constructed as following:

Fig. 1. Information Overloading

Fig. 2. Unsuitability Apposition

Fig. 3. Inconsistency of road Signs

Fig. 4. Irregular Signs

```
SELECT ?RSP ? RoadORPoI
WHERE
{
      ?RSPlant rdf:type its:RoadSignPlant.
      ?RSPlant wgs:lat ?RSPlant_lat.
      ?RSPlant wgs:long ?RSPlant_long.
      ?RSPlant its:hasRs ?RSP.
      ?RSP rdf:type its:RoadSign.
      ?RSP its:RoadSignIndicate ?RoadORPoI
}
```

If the number of query result is bigger than a setted threshhold, which means
that too much information is contained contained in one road sign. For such
case, the system would give some warning information to the users.

For error type 2, a SPARQL query is constructed as following:

```
SELECT ?RSP ?RSPlant
{
      ?RSPlant rdf:type its:RoadSignPlant.
      ?RSPlant wgs:lat ?RSPlant_lat.
      ?RSPlant wgs:long ?RSPlant_long.
      ?RSPlant its:hasRs ?RSP.
      ?RSP rdf:type its:RoadSign.
}
```

Evéry road sign pole in the data base would be checked using above query, and ?RSPlant is the ID of the pole to be checked. If the number of query result of give road sign pole ID is bigger than a setted threshhold, which means that too many road sign panels are placed on one pole.

Most road sign errors are in type 3, i.e., position and naming of road signs are not consistent with RSRs. For example, there no road sign attention to children is placed aroud primary schools, kindergartens and so on, which contradicts with following RSRs rule:

(R1) In the vicinity of primary schools, kindergartens, Children's Palace, road sign attention to children should be placed;

For such errors, the above RSRs rule is firstly translated into two sparql queries as followings:

SPARQL query 1:

```
SELECT ?POI
{
      ?POI rdf:type POIType:Primary_education. // ontology is used here
}
```

SPARQL query 2:

```
SELECT ?RSP ?RSPlant_lat ?RSPlant_long ?POI ?POI_lat ?POI_long
{
    ?RSPlant rdf:type its:RoadSignPlant.
    ?RSPlant wgs:lat ?RSPlant_lat.
    ?RSPlant wgs:long ?RSPlant_long.
    ?RSPlant its:hasRs ?RSP.
    ?RSP rdf:type its:RoadSign.
    ?RSP its:label 'attention to children' 'xmls:string.
    ?POI wgs:lat ?POI_lat.
    ?POI wgs:long ?POI_long.
    ?POI its:label ?label 8mls:string.
    FILTER( abs(round(?RSPlant_lat-?POI_lat)) ≤0.01).
    //to make sure road sign is around the POI
}
```

Above two queries are iteratively excuted. In the first loop, the first query is excuted to get the result set of types of "Primary_education" POI (primary schools, kindergartens and Children's Palace are Subtypes of Primary education in Ontology). For each POI got from first loop, if result set of excuting the second SPARQL query is empty, then we can make the decision that this POI doesnt comply with the RSRs rule and should give some warning messages to users.

For some other complex RSRs rules, SPARQL queries may not work, plug-ins should be developed for LarKC. For example, following RSRs rule:

(R2) Reminders should be set around the roundabout ranged from 30m to 150m.

if roundabout or junctions on roads are not be labeled on the map, verifying these road signs may be impossible. So poisition and other information of these key points should be identified in advance to verifying related road signs, which can be implemented by plug-ins and workflows on the LarkC platform. We will not elaborate these content in this paper.

3   Road Sign Design and Update for New Roads

When new roads are to be built, SeRSM can also give advices to decision makers that what road signs should be added and where to place them, also it will warn that what old road signs should be updated because of building the new roads. On the system GUI, a start node and an end node of a new road can be selected to add on the map. Then you can select to build a new road from the start node to the end node.In this process, the system automatically computes all posibile juctions with existing roads. Then the system would give some recommdations about where to build new road signs and what content should be spcified in these road signs, which are to be consistent with existing road signs.The Simulation process allows an increased efficiency in the whole city as well as a decrease of the city operation fees.

3.1   Model the Spatial Geometry According to WKT

In order to compute the junctions between new road and existing ones, the original Map data are transformed into WKT formation,which is a text markup language for representing vector geometry objects on a map, spatial reference systems of spatial objects and transformations between spatial reference systems. In SeRSM, four kind of geometry objects are used, for example, POIs are represented by multiPoint, a way is represented by lineString, a road is represented by multilineString and so on.Geometric objects used in the road nets are as Figure 5.

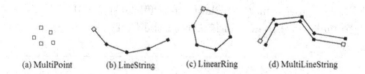

(a) MultiPoint   (b) LineString   (c) LinearRing   (d) MultiLineString

Fig. 5. Geometric objects used in the road nets

Some examples are as Figure 5.

3.2   Compute the Qualitative Spatial Relation between Roads

The qualitative spatial relations between roads is computed by the Dimensionally Extended nine-Intersection Model (DE-9IM)[8], which is a topological model and

绿茁路毒具势: MULTILINESTRING ((119.452675 32.19207, 119.45254 32.192265, 119.45248 32.192482, 119.45233 32.1932
*山西舘: MULTILINESTRING ((119.42033 32.2083, 119.42276 32.205692, 119.42033 32.2083, 119.42276 32.205692, 11'
东县舘: LINESTRING (119.44854 32.21796, 119.44867 32.2179, 119.44924 32.21763, 119.4512 32.21645, 119.45236 3:
連丙舘: MULTILINESTRING ((119.46243 32.194847, 119.46231 32.195103, 119.46223 32.19526, 119.462105 32.195477,
東嗣山舘: LINESTRING (119.44629 32.187477, 119.446075 32.18797, 119.44584 32.188335, 119.4455 32.188835, 119.4
北牛舘: MULTILINESTRING ((119.44062 32.199318, 119.43987 32.198685, 119.43873 32.197765, 119.43816 32.197468,
电力舘: MULTILINESTRING ((119.439354 32.205574, 119.43924 32.205826, 119.43905 32.20625, 119.43883 32.20677, 1
密陵舘: LINESTRING (119.504776 32.211502, 119.504715 32.211273, 119.50465 32.210995, 119.5042 32.20932, 119.5(
复山西舘: LINESTRING (119.41923 32.19715, 119.41986 32.19725, 119.421104 32.197292, 119.42474 32.197178, 119.4:
健富舘: LINESTRING (119.44062 32.199318, 119.44151 32.200035, 119.44238 32.200714, 119.44257 32.20086, 119.44:
怀山舘: LINESTRING (119.42344 32.204933, 119.42138 32.20337, 119.41901 32.201427, 119.41856 32.200882, 119.41:
乱江文认: LINESTRING (119.46412 32.168903, 119.463486 32.167686, 119.462105 32.165253, 119.46185 32.16445, 119
青门外大类: LINESTRING (119.45694 32.19733, 119.45692 32.19725, 119.45688 32.19719, 119.45683 32.197113, 119.45
昂山舘: MULTILINESTRING ((119.4761 32.220783, 119.47721 32.220585, 119.47751 32.22059, 119.47871 32.220604, 11
林海舘: LINESTRING (119.45257 32.191902, 119.45233 32.19207, 119.45215 32.192337, 119.45197 32.19254, 119.451:
*山北舘: MULTILINESTRING ((119.41417 32.21555, 119.41423 32.215332, 119.41436 32.21485, 119.41459 32.21429, 1:
九米山舘: MULTILINESTRING ((119.42474 32.197178, 119.42418 32.199875, 119.423965 32.200718, 119.42407 32.20157:
小角山舘: LINESTRING (119.47751 32.22059, 119.47762 32.220417, 119.47779 32.220165, 119.47797 32.21988, 119.47:
罗森舘: MULTILINESTRING ((119.460014 32.19858, 119.4602 32.199215, 119.4602 32.199215, 119.460205 32.19945, 1:
雄计舘: LINESTRING (119.4484 32.218, 119.44839 32.217903, 119.44836 32.217804, 119.44831 32.217583, 119.44825

Fig. 6. Example of spatial data

a standard used to describe the spatial relations of two regions (two geometries in two-dimensions, R2) and and was used as a basis for standards of queries and assertions in geographic information systems(GIS) and spatial databases.

In DE-9IM, a 3*3 intersection matrix with true/false domain is computed and geometry relations are clarified by matching the matrix with preseted binary classification schemes. In this paper, four geometry relations are used to describe relations between roads as shown in Figure 7.

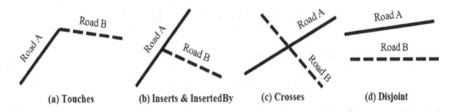

(a) Touches   (b) Inserts & InsertedBy   (c) Crosses   (d) Disjoint

Fig. 7. Relation types between roads

Some examples are as Figure 8. In the figure, name of roads are listed in the first row and the first column,and relations betweent roads are labeled on intersections.

3.3   Locate the Junctions and Generate Expected Road Signs

By using above mentioned method, we may know whether two roads are intersected with eachother and its Spatial Relation type, to lacate the junctions we can traverse all the points that constitute the roads, and common point(s) between two roads are recognized as junctions. However, there are typically no common points between new built roads and existing roads on the map, for such cases, methods from analytic geometry can be borrowed to compute the intersection points (junctions) between roads. As mentioned previously, roads

SFTR	解放路高架桥	中山西路	东吴路	运河路	黄鹤山路	北府路	电力路	谷阳路	...
解放路高架桥	equals	disjoint	disjoint	inserts	disjoint	disjoint	disjoint	disjoint	
中山西路	disjoint	equals	disjoint	touches	disjoint	disjoint	touches	disjoint	
东吴路	disjoint	disjoint	equals	disjoint	disjoint	disjoint	disjoint	disjoint	
运河路	insertedBy	touches	disjoint	equals	disjoint	disjoint	touches	disjoint	
黄鹤山路	disjoint	disjoint	disjoint	disjoint	equals	inserts	disjoint	disjoint	
北府路	disjoint	disjoint	disjoint	disjoint	insertedBy	equals	disjoint	disjoint	
电力路	disjoint	touches	disjoint	touches	disjoint	disjoint	equals	disjoint	
谷阳路	disjoint	disjoint	disjoint	disjoint	disjoint	disjoint	disjoint	equals	
...									

Fig. 8. Example of Relations between roads

are abstractly represented by line segments, the problem can be formalized as follows [9] :

Given two line segments, each line segments is defined by two points, i.e., $ls_1 = (x_1, y_1), (x'_1, y'_1)$; $ls_2 = (x_2, y_2), (x'_2, y'_2)$ We can firstly obtain the equation for line segments as follows:

$$l1 : y = \frac{y_1 - y'_1}{x_1 - x'_1} x + \frac{x_1 y'_1 - x'_1 y_1}{x_1 - x'_1} \tag{1}$$

$$l2 : y = \frac{y_2 - y'_2}{x_2 - x'_2} x + \frac{x_2 y'_2 - x'_2 y_2}{x_2 - x'_2} \tag{2}$$

$$ls_1 : min(x_1, x'_1) \leq x \leq max(x_1, x'_1) \tag{3}$$

$$ls_2 : min(x_2, x'_2) \leq x \leq max(x_2, x'_2) \tag{4}$$

And then compute the crossing point C as followings:

$$c_x = \frac{\frac{x_2 y'_2 - x'_2 y_2}{x_2 - x'_2} - \frac{x_1 y'_1 - x'_1 y_1}{x_1 - x'_1}}{\frac{y_1 - y'_1}{x_1 - x'_1} - \frac{y_2 - y'_2}{x_2 - x'_2}} \tag{5}$$

$$c_y = \frac{\frac{x_1 y'_1 - x'_1 y_1}{y_1 - y'_1} - \frac{x_2 y'_2 - x'_2 y_2}{y_2 - y'_2}}{\frac{x_1 - x'_1}{y_1 - y'_1} - \frac{x_2 - x'_2}{y_2 - y'_2}} \tag{6}$$

When junctions between roads are recognized, corresponding roads can be located on the map based on spatial relationships between junctions and roads. The Next step is to place appropriate road signs especially indicative ones around the junctions according to related RSRs. When the expected road signs are generated, it should be verified whether it is consistent with existing ones by methods described in section 2. It would give some warning information if existing road signs are found out to contradict with the new road signs.

4   System Architecture

A data integration solution for urban information is investigated to provide a basis for intelligent road sign management based upon the LarKC platform. The solution supports data modeling and the integration of massive amounts of linked geo-data, POI data, and road sign data, as well as scalable querying and reasoning. The data are integrated using the mediation ontology illustrated in Figure 9.

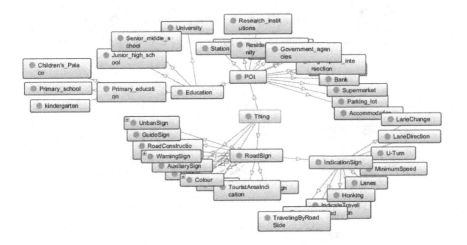

Fig. 9. Mediation ontology

Geographic data in SeRSM are defined primarily by three elements, i.e., node, way and relation, where each way element are modeled as a sequence of nodes, and a road on the map is composed of ways. Three types of node are modeled: (1) the generic nodes that can identify either a junction between multiple roads or just a point on a way; (2) the road sign (RS) nodes that indicate the presence of a road sign; (3) the Zhenjiang POIs (ZJPOI) that indicate POIs from Baidu Map and OSM. Node element corresponds to an actual node on the map which owns latitude and longitude information, so ways and roads represented by sequence of nodes will also have space trajectory information, which are benefitting to the modeling of urban road network and intelligent management of road signs. The architecture of SeRSM is shown in Figure 10.

As shown in figure2, the SeRSM system involves extremely large scale of semantic data. To easliy handle and reason upon them, the large scale of semantic data were converted to a uniform representation by runing some XSLT script programs or other techologies. The process is shown in Figure 11.

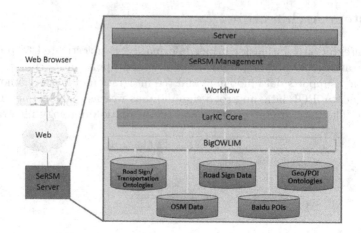

Fig. 10. Architecture of SeRSM

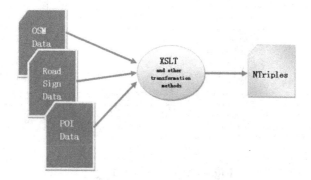

Fig. 11. Conversion of semantic data

5   Implementation (DEMO)

The data set we are manipulating contains about 3.9 million triples. 3 million triples describe the streets of Zhenjiang, and were directly extracted from OSM. 0.8 million triples describe POIs related to road signs and come from the Baidu map. 0.1 million triples describe road signs which are collected by our team members. 32 Chinese road sign regulations related to positioning and naming are encoded into SPARQL queries.User interface of SeRSM is shown in Figure 12.

In the SeRSM system, users use the web interface to post the operation requirements to the SeRSM server.Those operation requirements include road sign verification, simulations by selecting starting and ending node to build a new road and generating expected road signs, etc. Figure 13. is an examle of newly generated indicative road sign, in which the road signs location, remote, right and forward indications are specified. The SeRSM server sends the SPARQL queries to the SPARQL end point, which is launched by the SeRSM workflow on the LarKC platform.

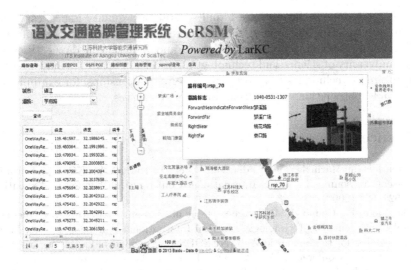

Fig. 12. UI of SeRSM

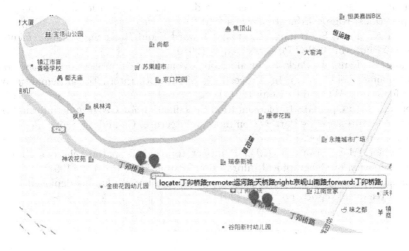

Fig. 13. Examle of newly generated road sign

6   Conclusion

In this paper we focus on presenting the challenges in developing road sign management system and propose a data integration solution which provides a basis for intelligent road sign management based upon the LarKC platform. We also propose methods for automatically verifying road signs according to RSRs and simulating the process of generating new road signs when new roads are to be built. The Simulation process allows an increased efficiency in the whole city as well as a decrease of the city operation fees.

In the work done so far we have found several data quality issues, especially there usually existing different names for the same POI present both in OSM and in Baidu map database, e.g., jiangkeda and jiangsu keji daxue (both for jiangsu university of science and technology). For this, in future we may use some semi-automatic techniques to assert owl: sameAs relationships, for example, full Names and abbreviations recognition for Chinese entities.

References

1. Fensel, D., van Harmelen, F., Andersson, B., et al.: Towards LarKC: a platform for web-scale reasoning. In: IEEE International Conference on Semantic Computing, pp. 524–529 (2008)
2. Della Valle, E., Celino, I., Dell Aglio, D., et al.: Urban Computing: a challenging problem for Semantic Technologies. In: 2nd International Workshop on New Forms of Reasoning for the Semantic Web (NEFORS 2008) co-located with the 3rd Asian Semantic Web Conference (ASWC 2008), Bangkok, Thailand (2008)
3. Della Valle, E., Celino, I., Dell'Aglio, D., et al.: Semantic traffic-aware routing using the larkc platform. IEEE Internet Computing 15(6), 15–23 (2011)
4. Huang, Z., Zhong, N.: Scalable semantic data processing-platform,technology and applications. Higher Education Press (2012)
5. Lee, T.K., Park, S., Huang, Z., et al.: Toward Seoul Road Sign Management on LarKC Platform. ISWC Posters&Demos (2010)
6. Huang, Z., Fang, J., Park, S., et al.: Noisy semantic data processing in Seoul road sign management system. In: Proceedings of the 10th International Semantic Web Conference (ISWC 2011), Bonn (2011)
7. Herring, J.R.: OpenGIS Implementation Specification for Geographic information - Simple feature access - Part 1: Common architecture. Candidate, Open Geospatial Consortium, Inc. (2006)
8. Egenhofer, M.J., Franzosa, R.D.: Point-set topological spatial relations. International Journal of Geographical Information System 5(2), 161–174 (1991)
9. Huang, Z., et al.: D4.7.3 Final evaluation and revision of plug-ins deployed in use-cases. Technical report, pp. 10–11 (2011)

HG-Bitmap Join Index: A Hybrid GPU/CPU Bitmap Join Index Mechanism for OLAP

Yu Zhang[1,2], Yansong Zhang[1,3,*], Mingchuan Su[1,2], Fangzhou Wang[1,2], and Hong Chen[1,2]

[1] School of Information, Renmin University of China, Beijing 100872, China
[2] DEKE Lab, Renmin University of China, Beijing 100872, China
[3] National Survey Research Center at Renmin University of China, Beijing 100872, China
Zhangys_ruc@hotmail.com

Abstract. In-memory big data OLAP(on-line analytical processing) is time consuming task for data access latency and complex star join processing overhead. GPU is introduced to DBMSs for its remarkable parallel computing power but also restricted by its limited GPU memory size and low PCI-E bandwidth between GPU and memory. GPU is suitable for linear processing with its powerful SIMD(Single Instruction Multiple Data) parallel processing, and lack efficiency for complex control and logic processing. So how to optimize management for dimension tables and fact table, how to dispatch different processing stages of OLAP(Select, Project, Join, Grouping, Aggregate) between CPU and GPU devices and how to minimize data movement latency and maximize parallel processing efficiency of GPU are important for a hybrid GPU/CPU OLAP platform. We propose a hybrid GPU/CPU Bitmap Join index(HG-Bitmap Join index) for OLAP to exploit a GPU memory resident join index mechanism to accelerate star join in a star schema OLAP workload. We design memory constraint bitmap join index with fine granularity keyword based bitmaps from TOP K predicates to accurately assign specified GPU memory size for specified frequent keyword bitmap join indexes. An OLAP query is transformed into bitwise operations on matched bitmaps first to generate global bitmap filter to minimize big fact table scan cost. In this mechanism, GPU is fully utilized with simple bitmap store and processing, the small bitmap filter from GPU to memory minimizes the data movement overhead, and the hybrid GPU/CPU join index can improve OLAP performance dramatically.

Keywords: OLAP, hybrid GPU/CPU platform, star join, bitmap join index.

1 Introduction

Moore's law drives hardware techniques move forward. First, the frequency of computer kept increasing until power wall became bottleneck, and then the cores increased gradually in general purpose CPU from dual core to deca-core processor (contains ten cores e.g. Intel Xeon E7-8870). Compared with larger and larger memory size(Max Memory size of TBs), more cores are required for in-memory big data

---

* Corresponding author.

Z. Huang et al. (Eds.): WISE 2013 Workshops 2013, LNCS 8182, pp. 23–36, 2014.

with larger bandwidth for just-in-time applications. In another way, many-core co-processors such as GPGPU and Intel Xeon Phi™ Coprocessor 5110P can provide more simple processing cores and higher memory bandwidth as shown in table 1.

Table 1. Multi-core and many-core processors

Type	Xeon E7-8870	Xeon Phi 5110P	Tesla K20X
Core/thread	10 /20	60/240	2688 CUDA cores
Frequency	2.40 GHz	1.053 GHz	732MHz
Memory	4096GB(maximum)	8GB	6GB
Memory type	DDR-3	GDDR5 ECC	GDDR5
Memory bandwidth	30 GB/s	320 GB/s	249.6 GB/s

(http://www.intel.com.cn, http://www.nvidia.com)

GPU memory is much smaller but much faster in throughput than CPU memory. In table 1, nowadays GPU memory bandwidth exceeds 200GB/s. But limited GPU memory makes data intensive applications transfer large dataset from memory to GPU. Data movement overhead between GPU and CPU memory is much costly: in real system, the PCI-E×16 Bus can achieve a throughput of around 4GB/s, for moderate computer, this throughput may be around 2GB/s which is far below the bandwidth of CPU memory. So we have two choices for GPU: one is to utilize GPU as an off-board co-processor on the condition that GPU processing profit outperforms data movement overhead, and as the PCI-E throughput increases the performance profit rises up automatically. The other is focusing on the locality of GPU memory to make critical processing stage GPU memory resident, and make GPU as a key accelerator in whole query process.

Behind the large web application such as E-business is big data warehouse. It is essential for the backend data warehouse to provide real-time processing to create new value. In data warehousing workload, query cost mainly lies on two operations: one is sequential scan on big fact table with high memory bandwidth consuming; the other is star join between fact table and multiple dimension tables under foreign key references. Join index[1] is a kind of index for join relation between tables, and bitmap join index[2] is commonly employed in data warehouse to reduce both join cost and fact table scan cost, but state-of-the-art in-memory analytical database such as MonetDB[3], VectorWise[4], SAP HANA[5] etc. have not announced to support in-memory bitmap join index for analytical workload. Bitmap join index can map dimensional attributes to fact table bitmaps, joins can be dramatically reduced by bitmap filters. For complex queries, more dimensions involve more candidate bitmap join index processing overhead. This kind of sequential bitwise operation is suitable for GPU's powerful SIMD processing, and the operation only output a small bitmap for low percent of fact table, this can reduce query cost.

We propose a lightweight bitmap join index on hybrid GPU/CPU platform, GPU is used as bitmap join index container and engine, GPU memory is carefully used to hold the most frequently accessed bitmaps, bitmap operations are performed with low latency by GPU parallel processing power, the small bitmap filter is piped to CPU database engine to drop most useless processing cost.

In this paper, our contributions include two folds:

- A keywords based GPU bitmap join index for global database
- A cost model for hybrid GPU/CPU platform based OLAP query processing

The key issues for GPU bitmap join index lies on how to manage bitmap join index with different cardinalities and different size in limited GPU memory and how to update index from main-memory to GPU memory. We propose a cost model for hybrid GPU/CPU platform to figure out key performance bottlenecks and how to leverage the overhead by distributing processing stages to different storage and processing platform.

The related work is presented in Sec.2. GPU bitmap join index is discussed in Sec.3. Sec.4 shows the results of experiments. Finally, Sec.5 summarizes the paper.

2   Related Work

2.1   OLAP Query Processing

Multiple joins, especially hash join[6,7,8] for the equal-join between primary-foreign key pairs, seriously affect OLAP performance. In CPU architecture, cache locality is essential for join performance. Radix-Decluster[9] is proposed to improve cache hit ratio by cache conscious radix partition. It is widely accepted in database and is also adopted in GDB[10,11] as a GPU hash join solution. The latest research discovered that partition based hash joins sounds good for multicore parallel processing but the answer is not exactly[12]. In OLAP scenario, star join requires multiple pass data partition and parallel join operations, and join stream materialization between two parallel joins are space and time consuming workloads. Furthermore, partitioning needs large swap memory and more logical controls. This is not suitable for GPU. So, for star join processing on GPU, simple one-pass parallel scan based star join is the best candidate.

Invisible join[13] scans each foreign key column with probing in dimension hash table to generate join result bitmap, and then performs a bitwise AND operation on these bitmaps to produce star join result bitmaps. DDTA-JOIN[14] uses surrogate key as offset address of column in star schema and can avoid materializing fact table bitmaps for star join. It is a bitmap and vector based star join algorithm, the one-pass scan based OLAP makes it suitable for multicore/many core processing. It is also proved to be higher performance than hash join based OLAP engines.

As in-memory analytical database becomes larger and larger, foreign keys in big fact table are also big data for limited GPU memory, so moving foreign keys from memory to GPU memory to perform foreign key join[15] becomes the main bottleneck. DMA(Direct Memory Access) and asynchronous bulk implementation can help some but the bandwidth between the GPU and host main memory restricts sending foreign key columns for efficient GPU processing.

2.2   Bitmap Join Index

Bitmap join index can dramatically reduce big fact table scan cost and useless joins between dimension tables and fact table. It is organized as a B+-tree for low cardinality attribute, bitmaps which represent join positions in table to be joined are leaf nodes.

Bitmap join index can be created for single column, multiple columns, columns from different tables, even columns without direct join relations.

The bitmap join index prefers to low cardinality columns for space efficiency, but low cardinality means that the selectivity of each member is higher than high cardinality column. Index is tradeoff between space and performance. [16] proposed bitmap join index selection strategy based on cost models of bitmap join index storage, maintenance, data access and join without indexes. Bitmap join index size can be accurately computed with cardinality and rows in fact table, and selectivity in each bitmap is accurate for evaluating data access cost. Selecting indexing attributes is key issue. Many data mining algorithms[17,18,19] are applied for choosing better indexing candidate attributes. A fine granularity bitmap join index mechanism is essential for improving space efficiency and index effectiveness.

The frequency of indexed members may vary with different workloads, a dynamic index update mechanism is required for space constrain bitmap join index especially for a GPU memory resident bitmap join index with limited size. The existing researches usually focused on how to develop a GPU based general purpose index, such as B+-tree index and hash index, GPU bitmap join index is still uncovered.

3   Hybrid GPU/CPU Bitmap Join Index

3.1   Architecture of Hierarchical Bitmap Join Index

Bitmap join index is efficient for OLAP workload, query involved predicates in dimensions or hierarchies can be mapped to bitmaps to identify join result without real join operations. But bitmap join index is space consuming index with big cardinality for each member in indexed columns producing one bitmap equal to the length of table to be joined. For the join example $D \bowtie F$, D_i is the column to be indexed, $\mid D_i \mid$ is the cardinality of D_i, N is the rows of table F, then bitmap join index size S can be calculated as $S = \mid D_i \mid \times N/8$(Bytes). OLAP is multidimensional model based, and queries commonly involve many dimension columns in different dimension tables. So, bitmap join indices cover a large range of predicate candidates and need large storage space.

For in-memory OLAP workloads, memory is more expensive than disk, so raw data should be resident in memory as much as possible to improve memory utilization. So bitmap join indexes must be space constraint for specified memory quotas, this constraint means that only specified m bitmaps can be memory resident from different disk resident bitmap join indices. Bitwise operations on large bitmaps are also costly(hundreds of ms) in memory resident processing scenario. While GPU is much superior in bitmap processing(hundreds of μs). Compared with existing data-move-process-move style join processing, bitmap join index is GPU resident, local processing, minimizing data movement and eliminating the vast majority of tuple joins in big fact table(the least selectivity 0.00000076% in Star Schema Benchmark, http://www.cs.umb.edu/~poneil/StarSchemaB.PDF). So we use GPU as bitmap join index processer to improve star join performance in a hybrid GPU/CPU platform, and this hybrid platform can adapt to the nowadays low PCI-E throughput circumstance.

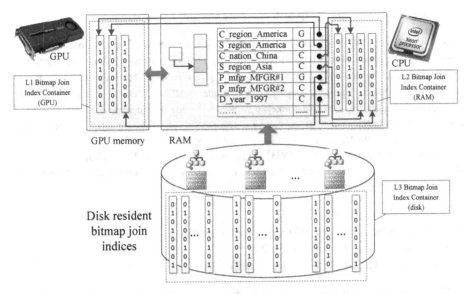

Fig. 1. Hybrid GPU/CPU Bitmap Join Index Architecture

We have three hierarchies for bitmap join indices storage: GPU memory, main-memory(RAM) and disk. Creating more bitmap join indices can better improve query processing performance but consuming more space for the large amount of candidate bitmaps. According to Power law, only small proportion of all the candidate bitmaps is frequently accessed. So we propose a hierarchical bitmap join index mechanism for hybrid GPU/CPU platform in figure 1.

Bitmap join indices are managed with 3-level container. Traditional bitmap join indices are created on disk to support a large join bitmap candidate set. The disk resident bitmap join indices are used as L3 level bitmap join index container. Bitmaps are organized with column granularity. By analyzing keyword logs in query statements, we choose TOP K frequent bitmaps from different bitmap join indices as global bitmap join index. The K bitmaps are further divided into two sets: one is memory resident, the other is GPU memory resident. GPU memory resident bitmap join index is L1 bitmap join index contianer with highest processing power and a few GB memory size; memory resident bitmap join index is L2 bitmap join index container for specified memory quotas with relative lower bitmap processing performance. This hierarchical bitmap join index mechanism includes the following modules:

- Keyword log derived from query statements to record keyword frequency
- TOP K keyword mining for GPU/CPU bitmap join index candidates
- Bitmap join index updating mechanism in hybrid GPU/CPU platform
- Bitmap storage and compression
- Bitwise operation in hybrid GPU/CPU platform

3.2   Keyword Log and TOP K Keywords Mining

In a typical query, **WHERE** clause comprises with two types of conditions: equal join conditions and predicates. Predicates commonly include attribute name and predicate expression like the following query "SELECT d_year, c_nation, SUM(lo_revenue-lo_supplycost) AS profit FROM date, customer, supplier, part, lineorder WHERE lo_custkey=c_custkey   AND lo_suppkey=s_suppkey   AND lo_partkey=p_partkey   AND lo_orderdate=d_datekey   AND c_region='AMERICAN'   AND s_region='AMERICAN'   AND (p_mfgr='MFGR#1' OR p_mfgr='MFGR#2') GROUP BY d_year, c_nation ORDER BY d_year, c_nation"

Keywords are extracted from **WHERE** clauses except equal join clauses no matter they are from fact table, dimension tables or which attributes they belong. Keywords are organized with uniform name, for example:

- d_year=1993⇨d_year_1993
- lo_discount between1 and 3⇨lo_discount_between_1_3
- lo_quantity < 25⇨lo_quantity_ <_25
- s_region = 'AMERICA'⇨s_region_AMERICA

The principle of uniform keyword name is: table name(in short)_attribute name_operator(equal can be neglected)_key(between operator has another key).

Keywords derived from query are piping to keyword log with timestamp, uniform keyword, count, ..., to maintain a keyword access history information. LRU or frequent keywords mining can be employed to identify TOP K frequent keywords as bitmap join index candidates.

We can also use counter list as a lightweight TOP K keywords identification method. Each keyword in counter list denotes one counter in specified time window. So we can maintain a frequency list for continuous periods, recency can also computed with latest frequency items. We also set up a weighted frequency model based on frequency list and selectivity:

- $F=a_0+2^{-1}a_1+2^{-2}a_2,...,2^{-n}a_n$, where a_i is the ith frequency of time window$_i$, frequency reduces as time window get old, and the latest windows have higher effectiveness for the weighted frequency;
- let $Fw=f(s)\times F$, where s represents selectivity of keyword varies from 0 to 1, $f(s)$ generates a selectivity weight to encourage high selective keywords to be indexed(we set $f(s)=1+(1-s)/5$ to generate a maximal 1.2 weight for high selective keyword). So, weighted frequency Fw can represents frequency, recency and selectivity.

We use TOP K method to create K candidate keywords; K is configured according to RAM quotas and GPU memory for bitmap join index. Let G_m denotes GPU memory size(byte), C_m denotes assigned memory size(byte), K is calculated as:

$$K=K_G+K_C= 8\times G_m/N+8\times C_m/N$$

The first K_G keywords are in L1 GPU memory bitmap join index and the next K_C keywords are in L2 RAM bitmap join index.

3.3   Adaptive Bitmap Join Index Update

L3 disk resident bitmap join indices are maintained by users with "create index..." or "drop index..." SQL commands. L1 and L2 level bitmap join index is a subset(K members) of superset(union all bitmap join indices). We use a triplet group to manage L1 and L2 level bitmap join index:

Keyword_Bitmap_Join_index<keyword, flag, bitmap>, where *keyword* is the uniform keyword name, *flag* is "G" or "C" to identify whether bitmap for current keyword is GPU resident or memory resident, *bitmap* denotes the address or array name for join bitmap. *Keyword_Bitmap_Join_index* can be further simplified as key/value store without *bitmap* when we use uniform keyword name as bitmap name both in main-memory and GPU memory.

We invoke keyword log mining periodically to update TOP K frequent keyword candidates to make bitmap join index more efficient. The latest TOP K keyword candidates may change some join bitmaps by upgrading from low level container to higher level or degrading from higher level to low level container. If some keywords from non-indexed columns are frequently used, new disk resident bitmap join index should be created to enlarge bitmap join index candidate set.

Keyword_Bitmap_Join_index can be organized with hash table or other structure to support efficient access by keyword.

3.4   Bitmap Store in GPU

In SSB workload, the selectivity in each dimension table is much higher than typical OLTP workload(varies from 6/7 to 1/1000). Due to high dimension characteristic, the overall selectivity is low(varies from 3.4% to 0.00000076%). GPU memory holds two types of bitmaps: one is join bitmaps from bitmap join indices, the other is bitmap filter for join bitmap bitwise operation result. The join bitmaps should be uncompressed to perform an equal length bitwise operation with vector based SIMD(Single Instruction Multiple Data) operation, the high selective bitmap filter can be compressed to minimize transfer overhead from GPU memory to main memory.

[20] proposed GPU based WAH(word aligned hybrid) bitmap compression with machine word length value. As the selectivity of filter is extreme low, we use a lightweight compression method like VOID in MonetDB, each "1" position in the bitmap is recorded in a W-bit array(position array). The compression ratio can be calculated as: $C_{ratio}=\eta \times N \times W/N=\eta \times W$, where η denotes selectivity of '1', W denotes array width(bits), $W=log_2N$. Considering the CPU cost for non-padding W-bit array, we only use fixed length of standard data type as *byte*(8-bit), *short*(16-bit) and *int*(32-bit). For example, in an OLAP workload with 600,000,000(SSB dataset, SF=100), W is set with 32. We can see in table 2 that only when selectivity goes below 3.1%(1/32) can position array compression gains benefits. For most low selectivity bitmap filters, position array compression can reduce data movement overhead.

Let $B_{GPU2RAM}$ denotes bandwidth(bytes/s) between GPU and memory, the transfer latency from GPU to RAM can be evaluated by:

$$T_{GPU2RAM}=4 \times \eta \times N/B_{GPU2RAM}$$

Table 2. Compression ratio of bitmap filter

Query	selectivity	compress ratio	$T_{GPU2RAM}(ms)$	Query	selectivity	compress ratio	$T_{GPU2RAM}(ms)$
Q1.1	1.90%	60.80%	18.24	Q3.2	0.14%	4.48%	1.344
Q1.2	0.07%	2.24%	0.67	Q3.3	0.01%	0.32%	0.096
Q1.3	0.01%	0.32%	0.10	Q3.4	0.00008%	0.00243%	0.001
Q2.1	0.80%	25.60%	7.68	Q4.1	1.60%	51.20%	15.360
Q2.2	0.16%	5.12%	1.54	Q4.2	0.46%	14.72%	4.416
Q2.3	0.02%	0.64%	0.19	Q4.3	0.01%	0.32%	0.096
Q3.1	3.40%	108.80%	32.64	AVER	0.66%	21.12%	6.34

For a moderate PCI-E channel with 2.5GB/s bandwidth/throughput, we can evaluate ideal $T_{GPU2RAM}$ with position array compression in SF=100 SSB dataset in table 2.

3.5   Bitmap Join Index Based OLAP

We show how the hybrid bitmap join index improves OLAP performance in figure 2. SQL statement is parsed to derive uniform keywords from predicate expressions, by probing in *Keyword_Bitmap_Join_index* hash table to locate indexed bitmaps to construct a predicate tree in the right of figure 2. GPU resident keyword bitmaps are marked with dark color, and memory resident keyword bitmaps are marked with white color. The whole predicate tree is divided into three region: R1, R2 and R3. R1 is GPU resident predicate sub-tree, R2 is hybrid predicate sub-tree, and R3 is memory resident sub-tree. R1 is processed by GPU, R2 is pruned for its OR operator span GPU and memory bitmaps, the GPU bitmap filter is transferred to memory to perform R3 process in final stage. If R2 is all memory resident keywords, R1 and R2 processing can be performed in parallel.

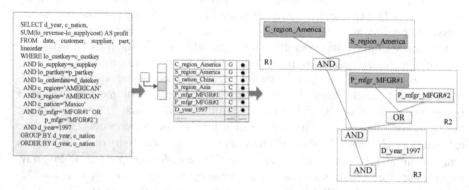

Fig. 2. Bitwise operation for query predicates

For the case in figure 2, if all predicates locate bitmaps in either GPU or memory, the join with supplier can be removed by bitmap filtering of 's_region_AMERICA' because there is no grouping attributes on supplier table, and join with part table can also be removed for the same reason. So bitmap join index simplifies 5-table star join to 3-table star join.

3.6   Cost Model

For a hybrid GPU/CPU OLAP platform with bitmap join indices, an OLAP query can be divided into several stages:

- Pre-process. SQL statement is parsed to derive uniform keywords to locate join bitmaps in L1 and L2 bitmap join index containers.
- Bitmap processing. Bitwise operations on GPU and CPU can be performed in parallel; the processing time can be overlapped.
- GPU bitmap filter transferring. Transferring GPU bitmap filter to memory with compressed position array.
- Bitwise operation between GPU bitmap filter and CPU bitmap filter for final join filter.
- Filtering fact table for re-written SQL processing.

The total processing cost T_{total} can be modeled as:

$$T_Q = Max(T_{GPU\_bitwise} + T_{CPU\_bitwise}) + T_{GPU2RAM} + T_{final\_bitwise} + T_{Q'\_proc}$$

In order to minimize query processing latency T_{total}, we should improve bitmap *hit ratio* of GPU bitmap join index. In ideal cost model, query predicates can all be located in GPU memory, then GPU is a full speed join accelerator. The cost model can be simplified as:

$$T_Q = T_{GPU\_bitwise} + T_{GPU2RAM} + T_{Q'\_proc}$$

For high selective queries, GPU bitwise operation is very efficient with microseconds latency, data movement latency is minimized by position array compression for minimal data size, and query processing with CPU also benefits from high selective filtering for minimal big table scan cost and less join cost.

4   Experiments

Our experiments are conducted on a HP ProLiant BL460c G7 server with two Intel® Xeon® Processor E5645 (6-core, 12M Cache, 2.40 GHz), 48GB memory and 300G 10Krpm 2.5' SAS hard disk. The OS version is ubuntu-11.10-server-amd64, with gcc version 4.3.4. We use SSB(a formal schema of TPC-H) dataset with SF=100. With standard SSB data generator, the row number of fact table is 600,000,000, and four dimension tables only occupy 0.84% in total size. 13 queries involve from 1 to 4 dimensions. We load fact table into array oriented column store to provide positional scan according to keyword bitmap filter.

4.1   Bitmap Join Index Based OLAP

For we have less information about bitmap join index from existing research work, we first develop experiments to measure the improvement of bitmap join index for in-memory OLAP.

We have developed C++ based DDTA-JOIN as column analytical engine for in-memory OLAP, we use column store and column processing like open-source

MonetDB, DDTA-JOIN uses a directly dimensional tuple access by mapping foreign key to array offset of dimensional column to reduce hash join cost, the costly star join is simplified as star filtering on bitmaps with specified positions. We further design bitmap join index to evaluate the performance improvement of bitmap join index.

Table 3. Bitmap join index DDTA-JOIN performance

ms	DDTA-JOIN	Bitmap join index DDTA-JOIN					
		bitmaps	Bitwise	BIndex Join	Total	Improvement	selectivity
Q1.1	1891.61	1	0	1169.27	1169.27	62%	15.1342%
Q1.2	888.669	1	0	110.86	110.86	702%	1.3087%
Q1.3	824.195	2	153	26.11	179.11	360%	0.2881%
Q2.1	1471.48	2	153.03	660.68	813.71	81%	0.8052%
Q2.2	1006.2	2	170.6	132.09	302.69	232%	0.1568%
Q2.3	984.181	2	159.13	18.87	178	453%	0.0220%
Q3.1	4544.22	3	204.42	3545.98	3750.4	21%	3.6745%
Q3.2	1027.4	3	208.29	180.21	388.5	164%	0.1479%
Q3.3	900.072	3	198.31	8.59	206.9	335%	0.0058%
Q3.4	915.074	3	211.7	2.89	214.59	326%	0.0001%
Q4.1	2334.07	3	217.13	1217.9	1435.03	63%	1.6241%
Q4.2	1455.5	4	259.54	402.59	662.13	120%	0.3962%
Q4.3	1124.59	3	213.07	188.32	401.39	180%	0.0380%
Aver	1489.79		165.25	589.57	754.81	238.42%	1.82%

We can see in table 3 that bitmap join index can efficiently improve OLAP performance from average processing time 1489.79ms to 754.81ms, the average processing latency reduces 50%. For CPU, bitwise operation is costly for $O(n)$ complexity and CPU bound. In low selectivity queries such as Q2.3, Q3.3, Q3.4 and Q4.3, bitwise operation cost dominates the total cost. With bitmap filter, DDTA-JOIN is much faster than standard DDTA-JOIN. If we compare DDTA-JOIN column with BIndex Join column, we can get maximal speedup ratio of 702% in Q1.2 and average speedup ratio of 238%. These experimental results prove that filtering big fact table and pruning unnecessary joins can improve OLAP performance dramatically.

Now let's focus on bitwise latency again. Bitwise operation is simple for large amount of rows but needs a high bandwidth and powerful SIMD. It is very suitable for GPU.

4.2   GPU as Bitmap Join Index Accelerator

From the detail information of table 3, bitwise overhead comes to be new bottleneck, especially for low selectivity queries. Fortunately, bitwise operation on bitmap join index is linear and simple processing adapt to GPU's high SIMD processing power. Furthermore, the GPU memory resident keyword based bitmap join index mechanism support local processing and only outputs very low selectivity bitmap filter with efficient position array compression. Both the local processing latency and PCI-E transfer latency are minimized.

We use a moderate GeForce 610M GPU as bitmap join index accelerator. The GPU supports CUDA 2.1, designed with 1GB DDR-3 on-board memory, 48 CUDA cores, processor core clock is 1.48Ghz, each block supports 1024 threads, and bandwidth between GPU memory and main-memory is about 2.5GB/s. This GPU is not the latest powerful GPU but a moderate GPU for common configuration. We design experiment to show that on the key processing bottleneck, a moderate GPU can outperform multicore processor.

Each query involves 2-3 selective bitmaps to speedup query processing. Even a low end GPU is far superior to multicore CPU on bitwise operation for bitmaps. Table 4 shows the results of GPU bitwise latency.

Table 4. GPU bitmap join index processing latency(*ms*)

Query	Bitwise	Transfer	Total	Query	Bitwise	Transfer	Total
Q1.1	0.000	31,08	31.08	Q3.2	0.027	1.64	1.66
Q1.2	0.000	13.11	13.11	Q3.3	0.027	0.22	0.25
Q1.3	0.000	2.89	2.89	Q3.4	0.027	0.16	0.19
Q2.1	0.027	8.00	8.02	Q4.1	0.027	15.98	16.01
Q2.2	0.026	1.73	1.75	Q4.2	0.027	4.03	4.05
Q2.3	0.026	0.39	0.41	Q4.3	0.027	0.56	0.59
Q3.1	0.027	29.67	29.70	AVER	0.021	8.419	8.440

Compared with table 3 we can see that GPU is average 240 times faster than CPU, bitwise operation on big bitmaps only cost less than 30 *μs* latency. Due to the very low selectivity of result bitmap filter and position array compression, even the low bandwidth can support very low bitmap join index result transfer latency at several *ms*. As a result, a moderate GPU bitmap join index accelerator can provide less than 10 *ms* level response.

Table 5. GPU bitmap join index DDTA-JOIN

ms	DDTA-JOIN	GPU Bitmap join index DDTA-JOIN					
		bitmaps	Bitwise	BIndex Join	Total	Improvement	selectivity
Q1.1	1891.61	1	31.076	1169.27	1200.35	58%	15.1342%
Q1.2	888.669	1	13.1118	110.86	123.972	617%	1.3087%
Q1.3	824.195	2	2.8909	26.11	29.0009	2742%	0.2881%
Q2.1	1471.48	2	8.0247	660.68	668.705	120%	0.8052%
Q2.2	1006.2	2	1.754	132.09	133.844	652%	0.1568%
Q2.3	984.181	2	0.4118	18.87	19.2818	5004%	0.0220%
Q3.1	4544.22	3	29.695	3545.98	3575.68	27%	3.6745%
Q3.2	1027.4	3	1.6633	180.21	181.873	465%	0.1479%
Q3.3	900.072	3	0.2512	8.59	8.8412	10080%	0.0058%
Q3.4	915.074	3	0.19082	2.89	3.08082	29602%	0.0001%
Q4.1	2334.07	3	16.0077	1217.9	1233.91	89%	1.6241%
Q4.2	1455.5	4	4.0528	402.59	406.643	258%	0.3962%
Q4.3	1124.59	3	0.5893	188.32	188.909	495%	0.0380%
Aver	1489.79		8.44	589.57	598.01	3862.27%	1.82%

4.3   Performance of Hybrid Processing Engine

Updating table 3 with CUDA programmed GPU bitmap join index processing, we can further reduce index processing overhead. The average bitmap join index processing latency has reduced from 165.25 *ms* to 8.44 *ms*, the total processing latency also reduces from 754.81 *ms* to 598.01 *ms*, the average improvement remarkably increases from 238.42% to 3862.27%. Especially for low selectivity queries, bitmap join index overhead is no longer bottleneck for overall performance, and the improvements also increase rapidly.

In table 6, the VectorWise, original DDTA-JOIN algorithm, CPU based bitmap join index DDTA-JOIN and GPU based bitmap join index DDTA-JOIN algorithms are all compared to analyze how and when GPU bitmap join index accelerator can gain largest benefits.

DDTA-JOIN has comparable performance in SSB with improved foreign key mapping instead of hash join to gain better performance. GPU bitmap join index is a tradeoff between performance and space. In experiments, we measure the maximal accelerating benefit by assume that all involved keywords have join bitmaps in GPU memory, but that is the ideal scenario. With 100GB dataset, 600,000,000 rows need about 70MB for each bitmap, nowadays GPU can hold about 100 join bitmaps, only high selective and high frequent keywords should create GPU bitmap join index.

Table 6. GPU bitmap join index DDTA-JOIN

ms	VectorWise	DDTA-JOIN	BJIDDTA-JOIN	GBJIDDTA-JOIN	improvement of GPU/CPU	selectivity
Q1.1	846.00	1891.61	1169.27	1200.35	-2.59%	15.1342%
Q1.2	604.00	888.67	110.86	123.97	-10.58%	1.3087%
Q1.3	581.00	824.20	179.11	29.00	517.60%	0.2881%
Q2.1	2876.00	1471.48	813.71	668.70	21.68%	0.8052%
Q2.2	2641.00	1006.20	302.69	133.84	126.15%	0.1568%
Q2.3	2326.00	984.18	178.00	19.28	823.15%	0.0220%
Q3.1	5116.00	4544.22	3750.40	3575.68	4.89%	3.6745%
Q3.2	3451.00	1027.40	388.50	181.87	113.61%	0.1479%
Q3.3	2631.00	900.07	206.90	8.84	2240.18%	0.0058%
Q3.4	1018.00	915.07	214.59	3.08	6865.35%	0.0001%
Q4.1	4730.00	2334.07	1435.03	1233.91	16.30%	1.6241%
Q4.2	3999.00	1455.50	662.13	406.64	62.83%	0.3962%
Q4.3	8088.00	1124.59	401.39	188.91	112.48%	0.0380%
Aver	2992.85	1489.79	754.81	598.01	838%	

We can see in table 6 that selectivity higher than 10% gains limited improvement. Cache line is 64 bytes, for *int* type column scan, when selectivity is higher than 4/64, no cache lines can be skipped to reduce memory bandwidth consumption. When selectivity is lower than 1/16(6%), unnecessary cache line accesses can be skipped. We can see from table 6 that when selectivity is lower than 10%, bitmap join index can gain high benefit, and when selectivity is even lower than 1%, GPU bitmap join index accelerating effectiveness is encouraging. For low selectivity queries such as Q1.3, Q2.3, Q3.3, Q3.4 and Q4.3, GPU based bitmap join index can greatly reduce index processing latency and overall query processing latency.

As a summary, bitmap join index is effective for in-memory OLAP, but we also have to consider some rules:

- Low cardinality columns are space efficient for bitmap join index but the high selectivity of each bitmap brings limited performance improvement.
- OLAP is multidimensional processing with bitmap join indices from different dimension tables, if multiple frequent but high selectivity bitmaps can generate overall low selectivity bitmap filter, these bitmaps are to be hold.
- Frequent keywords in different high cardinality columns are useful, keyword based global bitmap join index instead of column based bitmap join indices is necessary.

5   Conclusions

State-of-the-art GPU is powerful with local memory but has bottleneck on low PCI-E throughput. OLAP query can be considered as extracting small multidimensional dataset from big data cube for aggregate, the small dataset retrieval process can be either performed by traditional star join or supported by bitmap join index. Star join in GPU is still a hard work for both data movement overhead and multiple parallel join processing. The existing researches usually focus on two table join, the partition overhead in star join will be even higher. We propose GPU bitmap join index mechanism because bitmap join index is efficient to process star join with simple bitmap processing with controlled memory assignment. The GPU can also be used as pluggable bitmap join index accelerator for exiting OLAP system with a loose API for additional big table filtering service.

Acknowledgements. This work is supported by the Basic Research funds in Renmin University of China from the central government(12XNQ072, 13XNLF01), the Graduate Science Foundation of Renmin University of China (13XNH217).

References

1. Valduriez, P.: Join Indices. ACM Trans. Database Syst. 12(2), 218–246 (1987)
2. http://docs.oracle.com/cd/B10500_01/
   server.920/a96520/indexes.htm
3. Boncz, P.A., Kersten, M.L., Manegold, S.: Breaking the memory wall in MonetDB. Commun. ACM 51(12), 77–85 (2008)
4. Zukowski, M., Boncz, P.A.: Vectorwise: Beyond Column Stores. IEEE Data Eng. Bull. 35(1), 21–27 (2012)
5. http://www.sap.com/solutions/technology/
   in-memory-computing-platform/hana/overview/index.epx
6. DeWitt, D.J., Katz, R.H., Olken, F., Shapiro, L.D., Stonebraker, M., Wood, D.A.: Implementation techniques for main memory database systems. In: SIGMOD, pp. 1–8 (1984)

7. Kitsuregawa, M., Nakayama, M., Takagi, M.: The effect of bucket size tuning in the dynamic hybrid GRACE hash join method. In: VLDB, pp. 257–266 (1989)
8. Nakayama, M., Kitsuregawa, M., Takagi, M.: Hash-partitioned join method using dynamic destaging strategy. In: VLDB, pp. 468–478 (1988)
9. Manegold, S., Boncz, P.A., Nes, N.: Cache-Conscious Radix-Decluster Projections. In: VLDB 2004, pp. 684–695 (2004)
10. He, B., Yang, K., Fang, R., Lu, M., Govindaraju, N.K., Luo, Q., Sander, P.V.: Relational joins on graphics processors. In: SIGMOD Conference 2008, pp. 511–524 (2008)
11. He, B., Lu, M., Yang, K., Fang, R., Govindaraju, N.K., Luo, Q., Sander, P.V.: Relational query coprocessing on graphics processors. ACM Trans. Database Syst. 34(4) (2009)
12. Blanas, S., Li, Y., Patel, J.M.: Design and evaluation of main memory hash join algorithms for multi-core CPUs. In: SIGMOD Conference 2011, pp. 37–48 (2011)
13. Abadi, D.J., Madden, S., Hachem, N.: Column-stores vs. row-stores: how different are they really? In: SIGMOD Conference, pp. 967–980 (2008)
14. Zhang, Y., Wang, S., Lu, J.: Improving performance by creating a native join-index for OLAP. Frontiers of Computer Science in China 5(2), 236–249 (2011)
15. Pirk, H., Manegold, S., Kersten, M.: Accelerating foreign-key joins using asymmetric memory channels. In: Proceedings of International Conference on Very Large Data Bases (VLDB 2011), pp. 585–597 (2011)
16. Aouiche, K., Darmont, J., Boussaid, O., Bentayeb, F.: Automatic Selection of Bitmap Join Indexes in Data Warehouses. CoRR abs/cs/0703113 (2007)
17. Bellatreche, L., Missaoui, R., Necir, H., Drias, H.: Selection and Pruning Algorithms for Bitmap Index Selection Problem Using Data Mining. In: Song, I.-Y., Eder, J., Nguyen, T.M. (eds.) DaWaK 2007. LNCS, vol. 4654, pp. 221–230. Springer, Heidelberg (2007)
18. Bellatreche, L., Missaoui, R., Necir, H., Drias, H.: A Data Mining Approach for selecting Bitmap Join Indices. JCSE 1(2), 177–194 (2007)
19. Hamid Necir, A.: data mining approach for efficient selection bitmap join index. IJDMMM 2(3), 238–251 (2010)
20. Andrzejewski, W., Wrembel, R.: GPU-WAH: Applying GPUs to Compressing Bitmap Indexes with Word Aligned Hybrid. DEXA (2), 315–329 (2010)

Semantic and Qualitative Spatial Reasoning Based Road Network Modeling

Xiaofei Zhang[1], Zhisheng Huang[2,1], Ning Li[1],
Dan Xu[1], Zhi Wang[1], and Qinghua Liu[1]

[1] Jiangsu University of Science and Technology, Zhenjiang, China
julychang@just.edu.cn
[2] Vrije University of Amsterdam, The Netherlands
huang@cs.vu.nl

Abstract. Road Network Modeling is a fundamental issue for urban computing and uses massive primitive geospatial data retrieved from Geographic Information Database. The modeling for road network is extremely complicated because of the scalable and reticular relations between the roads in the city. In this paper, we propose an approach of qualitative spatial relation and semantic web based predication for road network modeling, and define five spatial relation predicates according to the notions in point-set topology for better representing the spatial relation between roads. The roads and junctions in road network are modeled as standardized well-known text literals, and deterministic spatial realtions are calculated by spatial relation reasoning. Then, all road network elements and their relations are stored as RDF triples into LarKC, a platform for scalable semantic data processing and reasoning. In this paper, we show that the triplized road network data stored in semantic web repository is very convenient for spatial information quering and junction type calculation.

Keywords: road network, spatial relation predicates, point-set topology, LarKC.

1 Introduction

Road Network Modeling is a fundamental issue for Urban Computing which is an emerging field of study that focuses on technology applications in public environments. The road length all over the world has totally reached 102,260,304 kilometers in 2008 and are still increasing fast these years. A large number of geographic database has been used to store spatial data of the roads up to date. The relations' number between roads is exponential compared to the number of roads and has become an incredible big digit. If the deterministic spatial relation can be calculated and stored in geographic information system, it will be more efficient to query the roads which have specified spatial relation with others, or some roads which share the same junction.

Big geographic data has been provided on the Web and become available data sets for road network modeling. OpenStreetMap[1] is one of the free datasets

---

[1] http://www.openstreetmap.org/

Z. Huang et al. (Eds.): WISE 2013 Workshops 2013, LNCS 8182, pp. 37–47, 2014.

available which include worldwide geographic data. It defines element Node and Way to represent geographic point and line respectively, and can be retrieved as linked data provided on LinkedGeoData[2] which is a large spatial knowledge base derived from OpenStreetMap. The contents in OpenStreetMap and LinkedGeo-Data are equivalent and provide adequate two-dimensional geospatial data. A third optional dimension, altitute, just as latitude and longitude for locating a spatial point, can also be recorded.

Even these geographic dataset provide enough coordinate information for the spatial features, they don't contain explicit spatial relations between them. Region connection calculus [1] are widely used to represent qualitative sptaial relation between two regions. 9-Intersection Model was developed by Clementini and others[2][3], based on the seminal works of Egenhofer and others[4][5] ,and was used as a basis for standards of queries and assertions in geographic information systems (GIS) and spatial databases were introduced. These spatial relation information is not only useful, but also big because the underlying geographic data is large-scale. If this useful and big spatial relation information can be stored explicitly in geographic information system, it will be convenient for some applications to query according to spatial relationship.

In this paper, we propose an approach of qualitative spatial relation reasoning which comes from a major brunch of spatial-temporal study. The qualitative aspects of road network are abstracted in terms of notions in point-set topology theory. The elements of road network are modeled as standardized well-known text, which is a text markup language for representing vector geometry objects in map. Five common binary spatial relation predicates between roads are also defined here, which include Touches, Joins, JoinsedBy, Crosses and Disjoint. Each relation can be denoted by a four-tuple, according to the relation between two geometries' interior and/or bounday. These four-tuple spatial relations are later extended as 9 intersection model[6], for easier calculating spatial relation by some application interface like GeoSPARQL[7].

After getting the spatial relation between roads, we also use point-set theory to calculate the intersection between roads which have spatial relation except Disjoint. The common point set shared by roads is the junction between them and are modeled as POINT literal or MultiPoint literal of well-known text. We also give a practial algorithm to calculate the type of junction by spatial relation between junction and related roads. All road network elements and their relations are stored as RDF triples into LarKC, a platform for scalable semantic data processing and reasoning[3], at last. This explicit triplized spatial knowledge provides an efficient way for geographic information application to query later.

OpenStreetMap currently lacks of practical sources and devices to provide the altitude of a given spatial point. It is limited for us to process spatial data assuming they are on the same plane and focus on at-grade road junction, instead of grade-separated road junction. Because of the big amount of available

---

[2] http://www.linkedgeodata.org/
[3] http://www.larkc.eu

geographic data and extremely heavy spatial reasoning, some new computing architecture should be adopted for massive geographic data processing.

The remainder of this paper is organized as follows: Section 2 introduces the method about how to model road network elements, including road and junction. Section 3 gives an approach to represent spatial relation between roads and five predicates are defined based on point-theory topology. We apply it on some data from geographic database and discuss about the result. In Section 4, we design an algorithm which is still based on point-set topology to calculate the type of junction and has a contrast with the geographic landform. The conclusion is given in Section 6 and future researches are also discussed based on the previous results.

2   Road Network Spatial Structure

2.1   Road Network Elements

Road Network is the network of motorways, trunk roads and principle roads that serve the country's strategic transport needs. Road Networks, roads, and junctions are examples of natural language terms whose semantics can be described by affordances of their referents[8].

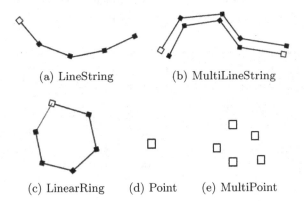

(a) LineString   (b) MultiLineString

(c) LinearRing   (d) Point   (e) MultiPoint

Fig. 1. Typical Geometry Objects Type

The most important objects to construct road network are roads and junctions in a city. These objects will be represented as different geometry objects shown in Fig 1. The white dot represents the first node of a sequence while the dark ones do not. A road is a route or way on land between two places, which has been paved or otherwise improved to allow travel by some transport. We model the road which has one roadway as a LineString in Fig 1(a), and the road with two roadways as MulitLineString which has and only has two LineString shown in Fig 1(b). As a special case, ring road is modeled as LinearRing shown in Fig 1(c). More complicated road which has fork is not considered in this paper. A junction is a location where vehicular traffic going in different directions can proceed in a controlled manner designated to minimize accidents. We model the junction as Point, as in Fig 1(d) or MultiPoint, as in Fig 1(e) according to how many intersected points between roads.

2.2 Types of Junctions

Two different types of junction between roads exist according to whether the relative roads are at grade or not. One type is interchange and the other is intersection. Interchange are junctions where roads pass above or below one another, preventing a single point of conflict by utilizing grade separation and slip roads. The terms motorway junction and highway junction typically refer to this layout. Intersections do not use grade separation and road cross directly. Forms of these junction types include Roundabouts and traffic circles, priority junctions, and junctions controlled by traffic lights or signals.

In this paper, we focus on the secondary type of junction which may be explicit or implicit. The explicit intersection is a Node element which has a special tag indicating that the node has contributed to constructing different ways. Instead of having correspond Node element in OpenStreetMap, the implicit intersection has an implicit spatial point due to the intersected road trajectories. This problem is due to quality issues in the OpenStreetMap data set, so not all the junctions are explicitly stated.[9] These implicit junctions can be calculated by the following sptial topological reasoning approach.

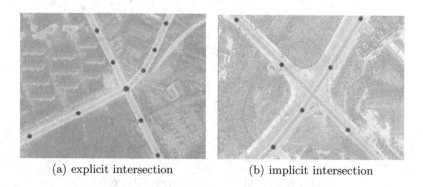

(a) explicit intersection   (b) implicit intersection

Fig. 2. Intersection in OpenStreetMap

3 Spatial Relations between Roads

3.1 Point-Set Topology

Point-set topology is the branch of topology which studies preperties of topological spaces and structures defined on them. A topology on X, which is a set, is a collection A of subsets of X that satisfies the following three conditions:

(1) the exmpty set and X are in A,
(2) A is closed under arbitrary unions,
(3) A is closed under finite intersections.

A topological space is a set X with a topological A on X. The sets in a topology on X are called open sets, and their complements in X are called closed sets. The collection of closed sets satisfies the following conditions:

(1) contains the empty set and X,
(2) is closed under arbitrary intersections,
(3) is closed under finite unions.

The notion of interior, boundary, and closure used in point-set theory are defined as follows[4]:

Interior: Given $Y \subset X$, the interior of Y, denoted by Y°, is defined to be the union of all open sets that are contained in Y.

Boundary: The boundary of Y, denoted by ∂Y, is the intersection of the closure of Y and the closure of the complement of Y.

Closure: The closure of Y, denoted by $\overline{Y}$, is defined to be the intersection of all closed sets that contain Y.

3.2 Approach for Describing Topological Spatial Relations

Binary topological relationships may be defined in terms of the boundaries and interiors of the two objects to be compared. A formalism is developed which identifies 16 potential relationships[10]. Our approach describes the topological spatial relations between two subsets, road A and road B, of a topological space X is based on a consideration of the four intersections of the boundaries and interior of the two sets A and B, i.e., $\partial A \cap \partial B$, $A^\circ \cap B^\circ$, $\partial A \cap B^\circ$, and $A^\circ \cap \partial B$. The topological spatial relation between two sets is preserved under homeomorphism of the underlying space X.

Some comlete and orthogonal predicates should be defined to describe the spatial relation knowledge between roads. In point-set topology theory, 57relations between two lines, 33 of them can be realized between simple lines[6]. And 8 spatial popularly used spatial relations derived from DE-9IM[11] are widely used and have been adopted in OGC GeoSPARQL specification[7] as the Simple Features Topological Relations. The explicitly stated predicates in GeoSPARQL can not provide complete and orthogonal topological relations between roads. This problem will be solved by defining five dedicated topological predicates as depicted in Fig 3.

We use tuple with four elements to describe a topological spatial relation. Each element of the tuple correspond to different set intersection combination between two geometries. The four elements are interior-interior intersection, interior-interior intersection, boundary-interior intersection, and interior-boundary intersection respectively. The sixteen possibilities from those combinations are summarized in Table 1:

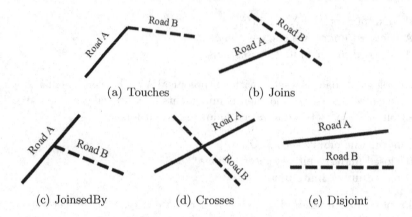

(a) Touches   (b) Joins

(c) JoinsedBy   (d) Crosses   (e) Disjoint

Fig. 3. Five Spatial Relation between Rods

Table 1. 16 Possible Combinations and Their Semantic

Relations	$A° \cap B°$	$A° \cap \partial B$	$\partial A \cap B°$	$\partial A \cap \partial B$	Semantic
R0	$\neg\emptyset$	$\neg\emptyset$	$\neg\emptyset$	$\neg\emptyset$	
R1	$\emptyset$	$\neg\emptyset$	$\neg\emptyset$	$\neg\emptyset$	
R2	$\neg\emptyset$	$\emptyset$	$\neg\emptyset$	$\neg\emptyset$	
R3	$\neg\emptyset$	$\neg\emptyset$	$\emptyset$	$\neg\emptyset$	
R4	$\neg\emptyset$	$\neg\emptyset$	$\neg\emptyset$	$\emptyset$	Touches
R5	$\emptyset$	$\emptyset$	$\neg\emptyset$	$\neg\emptyset$	
R6	$\emptyset$	$\neg\emptyset$	$\emptyset$	$\neg\emptyset$	
R7	$\emptyset$	$\neg\emptyset$	$\neg\emptyset$	$\emptyset$	
R8	$\neg\emptyset$	$\emptyset$	$\emptyset$	$\neg\emptyset$	
R9	$\emptyset$	$\emptyset$	$\emptyset$	$\neg\emptyset$	
R10	$\neg\emptyset$	$\emptyset$	$\neg\emptyset$	$\emptyset$	Joins
R11	$\emptyset$	$\emptyset$	$\neg\emptyset$	$\emptyset$	
R12	$\neg\emptyset$	$\neg\emptyset$	$\emptyset$	$\emptyset$	JoinsedBy
R13	$\emptyset$	$\neg\emptyset$	$\emptyset$	$\emptyset$	
R14	$\neg\emptyset$	$\emptyset$	$\emptyset$	$\emptyset$	Crosses
R15	$\emptyset$	$\emptyset$	$\emptyset$	$\emptyset$	Disjoint

As depicted in Table 1, the first 10 combinations has a spatal semantic Touches in terms of practical connection between roads' geometry trajectory. R10 and R11 hava a semantic of Joins which means one road's boundary is conneted to other's interior. R12 and R13 are symmetrical to R10 and R11 respectively, named JoinsedBy, which means one road's interior is connected by other's boundary. R14's spatial semantic is typical Crosses, which indicates two roads intersect in both interior. The last relation combination, R15, which holds great majority in practical scenes, means two roads have no intersection.

The examples in Fig 4 are not complete and considering more complecated roads which are strictly modeled as a MultiLineString containing two, and only

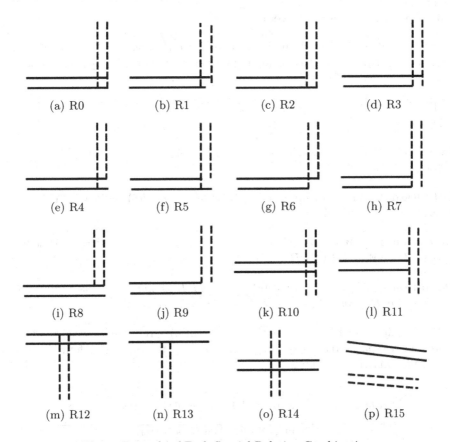

Fig. 4. Example of Each Spatial Relation Combination

two LineString. Each example intuitively exhibits the spatial relation between roads and its spatial semantic. If the spatial relaiton is considered as a predicate in Semantic Web, then the real line and dotted line represent subject and object respectively. Some extreme occasion may happen, as an example, spatial relation combination R14 donot really mean Crosses because of poor geographic data quality. This problem is not the key component considered in this paper.

A set is either empty or non-empty, therefore, it is clear that these sixteen topological spatial relations provide complete coverage, that is, given any pair of sets of A and B in X, there is always a topological spatial relation associated with A and B, exactly one of the sixteen spatial relations can occur between two sets. Depending on various restrictions on the sets and underlying topological space, the actual set of existing topological spatial relations may be a subset of the sixteen in the table. For general poin-sets in the plane $\mathbb{R}^2$, all sixteen topological spatial relations can be realized(figure1).

3.3 Spatial Relation between Roads

Our object of road network modeling is to reason topological spatial relations that occur between lines. The complete and orthogonal spatial relation between roads are defined as follows:

Definition 1. *A Joins B if and only if $A° \cap \partial B = \emptyset$ and $\partial A \cap B° \neq \emptyset$ and $\partial A \cap \partial B = \emptyset$*

Definition 2. *A is JoinsedBy B if and only if $A° \cap \partial B \neq \emptyset$, $\partial A \cap B° = \emptyset$ and $\partial A \cap partial B = \emptyset$*

Definition 3. *A and B Crosses with each other if only if $A° \cap B° \neq \emptyset$, $A° \cap \partial B = \emptyset$, $\partial A \cap B° = \emptyset$ and $\partial A \cap \partial B = \emptyset$*

Definition 4. *A and B Disjoint with each other if only if $A° \cap B° = \emptyset$, $A° \cap \partial B = \emptyset$, $\partial A \cap B° = \emptyset$ and $\partial A \cap \partial B = \emptyset$*

Definition 5. *If the relation between A and B is neither Joins, JoinsedBy, Crosses, nor Disjoint, then A and B Touches with each other.*

In this paper, for better calculating the qualitative relation between roads for more general spatial reasoning purpose. We extend the tuple with four elements to DE-9IM matrices in Tab 2.

Table 2. Five Predicates and Their DE-9IM Matrice's Pattern

Predicate	Corresponding DE-9IM Matrice's Pattern
Touches	$\begin{bmatrix} 0 & 0 & * \\ 0 & 0 & * \\ * & * & * \end{bmatrix}$ or $\begin{bmatrix} 0 & 0 & * \\ 0 & \emptyset & * \\ * & * & * \end{bmatrix}$ or $\begin{bmatrix} \emptyset & 0 & * \\ 0 & 0 & * \\ * & * & * \end{bmatrix}$ or $\begin{bmatrix} 0 & \emptyset & * \\ 0 & 0 & * \\ * & * & * \end{bmatrix}$ or $\begin{bmatrix} 0 & 0 & * \\ \emptyset & 0 & * \\ * & * & * \end{bmatrix}$ or $\begin{bmatrix} \emptyset & 0 & * \\ 0 & \emptyset & * \\ * & * & * \end{bmatrix}$ or $\begin{bmatrix} 0 & \emptyset & * \\ \emptyset & 0 & * \\ * & * & * \end{bmatrix}$ or $\begin{bmatrix} \emptyset & \emptyset & * \\ 0 & 0 & * \\ * & * & * \end{bmatrix}$ or $\begin{bmatrix} \emptyset & 0 & * \\ \emptyset & 0 & * \\ * & * & * \end{bmatrix}$ or $\begin{bmatrix} \emptyset & \emptyset & * \\ \emptyset & 0 & * \\ * & * & * \end{bmatrix}$
Joins	$\begin{bmatrix} 0 & 0 & * \\ 0 & \emptyset & * \\ * & * & * \end{bmatrix}$ or $\begin{bmatrix} \emptyset & 0 & * \\ 0 & 0 & * \\ * & * & * \end{bmatrix}$
JoinsedBy	$\begin{bmatrix} 0 & 0 & * \\ \emptyset & \emptyset & * \\ * & * & * \end{bmatrix}$ or $\begin{bmatrix} \emptyset & 0 & * \\ \emptyset & \emptyset & * \\ * & * & * \end{bmatrix}$
Crosses	$\begin{bmatrix} 0 & \emptyset & * \\ \emptyset & \emptyset & * \\ * & * & * \end{bmatrix}$
Disjoint	$\begin{bmatrix} \emptyset & \emptyset & * \\ \emptyset & \emptyset & * \\ * & * & * \end{bmatrix}$

4   Experiment and Evaluation

We take Zhenjiang city as an example, there are 66 roads in OpenStreetMap. So the relation number between roads is the combination C_2^n and totally 2145. By using DE-9IM matrices defined in Table 2, we find there are 26 pairs of Crosses relations, 50 pairs of Touches relations, and 86 pairs of Joins/JoinsedBy relations in Fig 5. It is reasonable that disjoint relations hold absolutely large proportion in that most roads have no intersection with each other.

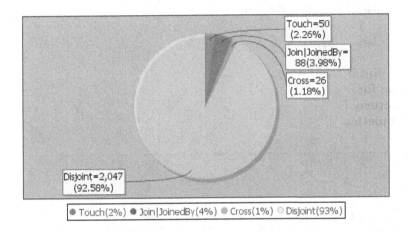

Touch=50
(2.26%)

Join|JoinedBy=
88(3.98%)

Cross=26
(1.18%)

Disjoint=2,047
(92.58%)

● Touch(2%) ● Join|JoinedBy(4%) ● Cross(1%) ○ Disjoint(93%)

Fig. 5. Statistics of Roads' Relation in Zhenjiang

By calculating the binary spatial relations between roads, we also can get the geometry points of the junctions. If the binary spatial relation between A and B is not Disjoint, then the set C, where $C = A \cap B$, is the points belonging to the junction between the two roads. At last, we get many points belonging to different junction. Some junction point is the same or quite near according to some threshold value, so these junction should be merged and it implies that some roads, more than three, share the same junction.

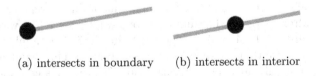

(a) intersects in boundary   (b) intersects in interior

Fig. 6. Spatial Relation between Junction and Road

After merging the junctions which share the same points, we use the points to judge the junction type. If a junction has an intersection with the boundary of a road, the road must join to other roads at this junction. Otherwise, if a junction has an intersection with the interior of a road, the road must be divided by the junction. As an example, a junction, represented as P, is shared by road A_0, A_1, $\cdots$, A_n. The branches number of P, represented as variable T, can be calculated by the following prodecure:

function RETURNJUNCTIONTYPE(P, A)
    $T \leftarrow 0$
    for $i = 0 \rightarrow n$ **do**
        if $P \cap \partial A_i \neq \emptyset$ **then**
            $T+ = 1$
        else if $P \cap A_i^\circ \neq \emptyset$ **then**
            $T+ = 2$
        else
            continue
        end if
    end for
    return T
end function

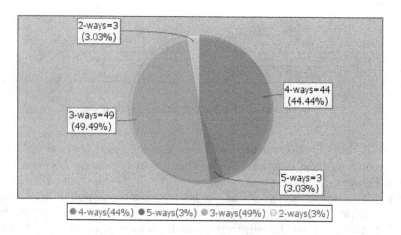

Fig. 7. Statistics of Junctions' Type in Zhenjiang

We use this algorithm to calculate the junctions of Zhenjiang city, which has 101 junctions after merging. The numbers of 2-ways, 3-ways, 4-ways, and 5-ways junctions are 3, 49, 44, and 3 respectively in Fig 7. The number of 3-ways junctions is even more than the one of 4-ways junctions. This result reflects the fact that too many hills in Zhenjiang city, and relative roads can not be easily extended.

5   Conclusions

A formal definition of spatial relation between roads has been given and it is more suitable than RCC-8 and 9-Intersection Model. RCC-8 does not have eqivalent predicate as Joins or JoinsedBy defined in this paper. While 9-Intersection Model covers all topological relation, it still does not provide explicit predicates for some useful relation combination. By asserting these spatial relations between roads, it is more efficient to query big geographic information.

The geographic data of Zhenjiang used in the experiment is about 33,000 triples, and the spatial reasoning time is acceptable. While facing some big data of giant city, like Shanghai whose geographic data in OpenSteetMap is approximately 1,000,000 triples, the spatial reasoning time is extremely consuming and unlikely estimated. We do need some new computing architecture to overcome the spatial reasoning problems on big geographic data. Some new computing technology like distributed reasoning approach is promising and we will adopt it for big geographic data reasoning in the future work.

Junctions and their relative roads can be calculated by the procedure presented in this paper and stored as semantic data in LarKC. This knowledge is very useful for road's relation querying, and can also be used to calculate the roadsigns by quantitative reasoning on road's boundary and the junction. The quantitative reasoning approach will be discussed in later paper.

References

1. Randell, D.A., Cui, Z., Cohn, A.G.: A spatial logic based on regions and connection. In: KR 1992, pp. 165–176 (1992)
2. Clementini, E., Di Felice, P., van Oosterom, P.: A small set of formal topological relationships suitable for end-user interaction. In: Abel, D., Ooi, B.C. (eds.) Advances in Spatial Databases, pp. 277–295. Springer, Heidelberg (1993)
3. Clementini, E., Sharma, J., Egenhofer, M.J.: Modelling topological spatial relations: Strategies for query processing. Computers & Graphics 18(6), 815–822 (1994)
4. Egenhofer, M.J., Franzosa, R.D.: Point-set topological spatial relations. International Journal of Geographical Information System 5(2), 161–174 (1991)
5. Egenhofer, M.J., Herring, J.: A mathematical framework for the definition of topological relationships. In: Fourth International Symposium on Spatial Data Handling, Zurich, Switzerland, pp. 803–813 (1990)
6. Egenhofer, M.J., Herring, J.: Categorizing binary topological relations between regions, lines, and points in geographic databases. The 9, 94–1 (1990)
7. Consortium, O.G., et al.: Ogc geosparql-a geographic query language for rdf data. OGC Candidate Implementation Standard (2012)
8. Scheider, S., Kuhn, W.: Road networks and their incomplete representation by network data models. In: Cova, T.J., Miller, H.J., Beard, K., Frank, A.U., Goodchild, M.F. (eds.) GIScience 2008. LNCS, vol. 5266, pp. 290–307. Springer, Heidelberg (2008)
9. Lee, T.K.I., Park, S., Huang, Z., Della Valle, E.: Toward seoul road sign management on larkc platform. In: ISWC Posters&Demos (2010)
10. Egenhofer, M.J.: A formal definition of binary topological relationships. In: Litwin, W., Schek, H.-J. (eds.) Foundations of data organization and algorithms. LNCS, vol. 367, pp. 457–472. Springer, Heidelberg (1989)
11. Strobl, C.: Dimensionally extended nine-intersection model, de-9im (2008)

A System to Generate Mobile Data
Based on Real User Behavior

Runqiang Du[1], Jiajin Huang[1], Zhisheng Huang[2],
Hui Wang[1], and Ning Zhong[1,3]

[1] International WIC Institute, Beijing University of Technology, China
[2] Knowledge Representation and Reasoning Group, Vrije University Amsterdam,
The Netherlands
[3] Department of Life Science and Informatics, Maebashi Institute of Technology,
Maebashi 371-0816, Japan
hjj@emails.bjut.edu.cn, huang.zhisheng.nl@gmail.com,
zhong@maebashi-it.ac.jp

Abstract. Mobile data generated by a mobile phone in a GSM network
can indirectly reflect the change of a user's positions. However, it is
difficult to get these data due to the privacy issue. The generation of
simulated mobile data provides an alternate method to solve the problem.
This paper designs a system called a generation system of mobile data
based on real user behavior. This system can simulate the communication
events to generate mobile data and extract the trajectory points of users'
past activities with some appropriate semantic annotations.

1   Introduction

A mobile phone has become an indispensable tool of human life. The mobile
positioning data in a GSM network reflect the user's behavior objectively. As a
mobile phone on a specific route always tends to change the base station nearly at
the same position, the position data of a mobile phone in a GSM network reflect
the user's behavior. Since the switching of location and time of base station (or
cell) can reflect a mobile phone user's location and time information, we can make
full use of them to identify the stay points of the user's trajectories. Combining
with the information of traffic zones, we can also calculate the amount of each
traffic zone and other traffic parameters between one traffic zone and another
one; in addition, according to the stay points of a user's trajectories, we can
obtain the user's travel destination, and then analyze the user's travel chain and
so on.

Firstly, in fact, mobile data are crucial for the mobile communication operators, mainly because they involve users' privacy. These sensitive personal information will not be easily available for scientific research. Secondly, in technical
aspects, all of the users' location information is not always associated with trading purpose, therefore, mobile service providers generally only store those data
for transaction purpose. Large amounts of data need to take up a lot of storage
space, although we can get continuous positioning information from the base

Z. Huang et al. (Eds.): WISE 2013 Workshops 2013, LNCS 8182, pp. 48–61, 2014.

station directly, such as downloading data directly into a portable computer or hard disk. Thirdly, there is also a problem about itself, even if we have obtained mobile data from mobile communication operators. The mobile positioning data are often lack of available semantic annotations, the results of data analysis cannot be compared with real users' activities and the reliability of the algorithms cannot be verified.

These problems make the research on mobile data very difficult, so simulated mobile data will become an important data source. The Generator for Spatio-Temporal Data (GSTD) [1,2] is one of the most well known in the related literatures. GSTD can be seen as a general synthetic spatio temporal data generator. Since it is not directed to a particular application field, it aims at representing object general movements behaviors. [3] provided a system called CENTRE(Cellular Network Trajectories Reconstruction Environment) based on the spatio-temporal data generator GSTD [1,2], and was able to randomly generate movement data by simulating different movement behaviors specified by some user preferences, defining user defined topologies and cellular network requirements. Moreover, such data are referenced on a geographic scenario which provides further constrains and background knowledge. [4] used a simulator tool to emulate a corridor in an inter-urban area covered by cellular network. This corridor has a set of cells and LAs, which are spread along the road. Each cell covers a road link, along which the simulated vehicle types are traveling. For simplicity, the traffic in each direction is analyzed independently. The simulator creates a set of vehicles with mobile phones on-board traveling along the studied highway. The input data required by the simulator tool are a simulation scenario and a set of simulation parameters that define the experiment. The scenario is composed of different types of data: road network description, LAs and cells (GSM network description) and traffic demand data. These two literatures have simulated the real users' behavior in the real world. The users' behavior is divided into two categories, people walking and people on vehicle. The simulation parameters have been set up according to the real situation in the real world, such as the settings of a few simple buildings and roads. However, the behaviors of people and vehicles are too random, without purpose, non-authenticity and the situation relative to the environment in the real world is far cry, the simulated mobile data is inadequate for scientific research.

For the existing problems about the simulation of mobile data, we combine with the electronic map of reflecting the real geographical environment of human lives, set the simulation area, divide the simulation area into cells and location areas by the cell and location area division of real GSM coverage area, simulate common people's behavior of the real life, extract the mobile users' trajectory points from the electronic map and simultaneously add some appropriate semantic annotations for each trajectory point, reappear/reproduce the users' past activities through these orderly trajectory points and simultaneously add some mobile communication events randomly to produce corresponding mobile data, establish a system called A System to Generate Mobile Data Based on Real User Behavior. The simulated mobile data are basically consistent with the generation of mobile phone data in a real GSM network. Furthermore, they contain the corresponding semantic annotations. Therefore, it is entirely available for the research of mobile data, such as the identification of stay point, the analysis of travel purpose, the prediction of users' behavior.

The remainder of this paper is organized as follows: We describe the principle of mobile data generation in Section 2. Then we present a detailed description on the Generation System of Mobile Data Based on Real User Behavior in Section 3. In Section 4, we provide an example of the simulation process of mobile data in detail. In Section 5, we used the simulated mobile data to do an experiment on the identification of stay point of mobile phone trajectory. Finally, we conclude our work and discuss promising future research directions in Section 6.

2   The Principle of Mobile Data Generation

In this section we first give the foundations about mobile phone trajectories when needed to understand our approach, and then review existing approaches to semantic annotation.

Now and in the near future, the most used worldwide telecommunication network for mobile phones is still GSM (Global Systems for Mobile Communications), so in this section we only focus our attention on GSM rather than other novel kinds of network such as UMTS (Universal Mobile Telecommunications System). UMTS and GSM system uses a similar structure, including the Radio Access Network (RAN), Core Network (CN). By the research on the generation of mobile data in GSM will make us understand the UMTS well.

First of all, the concepts of LAs and cells will be explained concisely. In a GSM network, the coverage area, where the network provides services for its subscribers or mobile phones, is divided into smaller areas of hexagonal shape, referred to as cells. Each cell is defined as an area in which an antenna (or base station) is installed and the subscribers can communicate with the antenna. In other words, a cell is served by a base station. In urban areas, cells are close to each other and small in area whose diameter can be down to hundred meters, while in rural areas the diameter of a cell can reach kilometers. An LA (Location Area) is a geographic area consisting of a set of cells, which is set for locating a particular mobile phone in case of a call to the mobile phone. As we know, the subscribers with phones are moving and there have no permanent connections between the phones and the network. So when there is a call to the mobile phone, the network obtains the location area where the mobile phone is staying from a two-level hierarchical database, which is made up of the visitor location register (VLR) and the home location register (HLR) and employed to record the locations of mobile phones.

Secondly, the process that the network records the locations of mobile phones by VLR and HLR will be presented briefly. According the GSM, a mobile phone corresponds with the network by sending or receiving signal, and the signal sent by the mobile phone contains the location information which LA and cell the mobile phone is staying in. The location information will be recorded in the HLR and the VLR when the network receives the signal sent by the mobile phone. The signal will be generated by one of the following events:

- The mobile phone is switched on or switched off;
- The mobile phone receives or sends a short message;
- The mobile phone places or receives a call (both at the beginning and end of the call);
- The mobile phone connects the Internet (for example, browsing the web);
- The mobile phone moves into a cell belonging to a new LA, as is called Normal Location Updating;
- The mobile phone during a call is entering into a new cell, as is called Handover;
- The timer set by GSM comes to an end when there is no any event mentioned above happened to the mobile phone, as is called Periodical Location Updating.

Finally, we will give the reason that mobile phone data can reflect the behaviors of people. When the subscribers are moving and entering into a new LA, the location information must be updated. Moreover, the happen of some events of communicating increases the times updating the location information of mobile phone. So the mobile phone data can represent the trajectory of the subscribers.

3   Overview of Our System

In this section, we will introduce the Generation System of Mobile Data Based on Real User Behavior in detail. Our system can be divided into four parts. In the first part, we set a virtual mobile phone communication network environment. In the second part, we collected the detailed statements of users' past travel activities. In the third part, we extracted the trajectory points of users' past travel activities and simultaneously added some semantic annotations at each trajectory point. In the fourth part, we describe the simulation of the users' past travel activities and the generation of simulated mobile data.

3.1   The Settings of a Virtual Mobile Communication Network Environment

In the real world, people generally stay in the coverage of GSM network. GSM network records the mobile data that reflect the users's behavior. In this paper, in order to make the communication network environment of the users'activities close to the real, we adopt four steps to set a virtual mobile communication network environment for our system, as follows: The first step is the setting of scope of simulation area. The simulation area is only limited to a part or the entire scope of the city, so it is not too large. As the base stations are generally located in the spherical surface of earth, the simulation area is not a strict plane. If we regard the simulation area as a plane, it will have a little impact on the

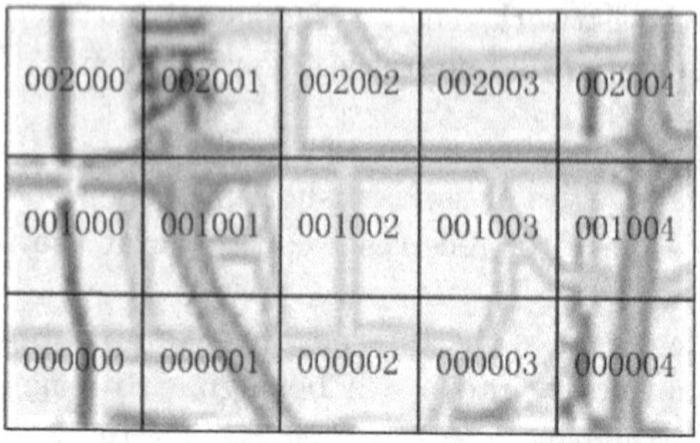

Fig. 1. The schematic diagram of the division of cell and location area

analysis of results. In this paper, we set the scope of within the Fourth Ring in Beijing as the simulation area.

The second step is the setting of a coordinate system for the simulation area. The simulation area does not contain 0,180 degree longitude line and 0 degree latitude line. So the most northern latitude line called Lat_{max}, the most southern latitude line called Lat_{min}, the most western longitude line called $Lngt_{min}$ and the most eastern longitude line called $Lngt_{max}$ are treated as the boundary lines for the simulation area. we only illustrates this condition as example, therefore, the others will not be analyzed. Here we consider the crossing point of $Lngt_{min}$ and Lat_{min} (namely, the coordinate $(Lngt_{min}, Lat_{min})$) as the origin, $Lngt_{min}$ line as the horizontal axis, Lat_{min} line as the vertical axis.

The third step is the division of cell for the simulation area. The simulation area is regarded as a coverage area of GSM and will be divided into cells and the location areas. As the real distribution of cell (or base station) and location area is unknown, we need to make two assumptions here. 1) In GSM, as the radiation range of a base is general a polygon area, we assume that it is a square area and its width is 250m here(As the actual coverage of a base has a great relationship with power control and the number of users, it is generally 200-300m in the urban areas). 2) Four adjacent cells closely form a location area. As shown in Figure 1, it is the schematic diagram of the division of cell and location area.

The fourth step is to calculate parameters related to cells and location area. The parameters include the ID, center coordinate, and boundary coordinate of a cell. By using a distance formula in Google API, we calculate the length XL on the X-axis and the length YL on the Y-axis for the simulation region. Let N_x and N_y be the number that we divide the XL and YL respectively, and then we have $N_x = XL/W$ and $N_y = YL/W$ where W is a unit of the coordinate axis scale. As mentioned above, W could be set by 250m similar to the radiation range of a base. Let the X-axis and Y-axis direction in the coordinate of a cell be id_x and id_y, respectively. We can define the ID of a cell by six numbers in which id_x and id_y occupy the first and last three numbers respecitvely. We call the id CellID. The range covered by a cell could be denote by the center coordinate and boundary coordinate. The longitude and latitude of center coordinate are denoted by $Lngt_{center}$ and Lat_{center} respectively which are written by

$$Lngt_{center} = Lngt_{min} + id_x * P_x + P_x/2 \qquad (1)$$

$$Lat_{center} = Lat_{min} + id_y * P_y + P_y/2 \qquad (2)$$

where P_x and P_y are the step coordinate on the the X-axis and the Y-axis as shown in Equation (3) and (4), respectively.

$$P_x = (Lngt_{max} - Lngt_{min})/N_x \qquad (3)$$

$$P_y = (Lat_{max} - Lat_{min})/N_y \qquad (4)$$

Besides, the boundary of CellID is written by $(Lngt_{min} + id_x * P_x, Lngt_{min} + (id_x + 1) * P_x, Lat_{min} + id_y * P_y, Lat_{min} + (id_y + 1) * P_y)$.

3.2   The Collection of Users' Past Travel Activities

The past travel activities reflects the users' real-life behavior and can be divided into eight major city activities, including Home, Work, Primary school, Secondary school, College or University, Shopping, Culture and Entertainment, Life. The behavior of different groups (e.g. workers, students, etc.) may show different patterns, therefore, we can collect the past travel activities of different groups as the basis dataset of human activities in the real world.

The collection of the users' past travel activities can be accomplished by three methods. The first collection method is to ask users to complete the questionnaire. For example, we can conducted a questionnaire of their usual trip chain for the working-class on the bus or on their way to home, such as the home location, bus routes, workplace, working hours. The second collection method is similar to the first one by completing the network questionnaire. The two collection methods in practice will generally encounter some difficulties. In order to protect their private information or save their precious time, the users may politely refuse to fill out the questionnaire. The third collection method, we can assume some users' real trip chains. For example, the trip chain "home-work-shopping-home" shows that a user moves from home to office, then from office to a downtown shopping mall, finally go back home.

3.3   The Extraction of Trajectory Points and the Addition of Semantic Annotations

The map is a microcosm of the real world and related with people's daily lives closely. The network map (e.g. the Baidu map, the Google map, etc.) service with its real-time, a large amount of information, rich features becomes an extension of the traditional map, therefore, you can query the streets, shopping malls, real estate location and also find your nearest all restaurants, schools, banks, parks, etc. The network map in a more intuitive, concise and abundant elements reflecting human life environment can be regarded as the virtual real environment of human activities, therefore, the collection of extracting the orderly trajectory points of users' travel path from the map can be used to represent the trajectory of users' past travel activities.

Based on the Baidu map, we have made a web application about the extraction of those orderly right trajectory points of user's past travel activities and the addition of some appropriate semantic annotations for each trajectory point. When we extract the trajectory points from the map (or add markers) sequentially, some appropriate semantic annotations will be also added to represent the user's current behavior. The users' current state contains two states, including Staying and Moving. Moving contains four modes, including walking, by car, by bus, on the subway.

When we add semantic annotations to some trajectory points, we adopt the following three principles: 1)Here the state of each trajectory point represents the state that the user moves to the next trajectory point on the path rather than the current state of the user. If the user is in Staying, we can set the corresponding stay time not for zero minutes. If the user is in Moving, we can set the corresponding stay time for 0 minutes. 2)Travel purpose (e.g. Sightseeing, Shopping, Work, School, Home, etc.) also can be regarded as semantic annotations to be added. 3)In addition, when the users' trajectory points at trajectories are related to a special travel purpose, we also will add appropriate semantic annotations of travel purpose to those trajectory points. In this paper about the application of the identification of stay point of trajectory, we regard these trajectory points overall as a stay point.

In one word, a trajectory is made up of a sequence of semantic annotation geographic points. As shown in [1], the semantic annotation geographic points that can be summarized by the septuple (Id, Lngt_value, Lat_value, Trans_style, Is_stop, Stay_time, Travel_purpose) called Instance, where Id is generated in order, Lngt_value and Lat_value represent the current position, Trans_style represents in which style that the user is going to travel, Is_stop represents whether the user stayed here for a special purpose or not, Stay_time represents that how long the user stayed, Travel_purpose represents the purpose that User_id travels. In practice, for the convenience of description, we regard (id = i, Lngt_value Lat_value, Trans_style, Is_stop, Stay_time, Travel_purpose) as Instance (i) and the properties of Instance(i) can be obtained by Instance(i).property respectively.

3.4   The Simulation of Users' Past Activities and the Generation of Simulated Mobile Data

Another application is based on those orderly right trajectory points to simulate the users' past travel activities, simultaneously add some communication events randomly to produce the simulated mobile data.

According to the principle of mobile data generation, we produce the simulated mobile data. Follow the storage format of mobile data of the China Mobile, our data are also stored in text format. As shown in [3], the simulated mobile data can also be summarized by the eightfold (User_id, Time_stamp, Lngt_value,

Lat_value, Event_id, Reserved1, CellID, Stop_tag) called Log where User_id is a number that we used to distinct different users, Time_stamp represents the time that communication event was occurring, Lngt_value and Lat_value represent the center coordinate of the cell that User_id belongs to, Event_id and Reserved1 represent the type of communication event, CellID represents the number that User_id belongs to, Stop_tag represents whether User_id is stay here for a special purpose or not.

The communication event, namely Event_id and Reserved1, is generated by two generators (functions) which can generate the number from 0 to 9. For example, Event_id is number 5 and Reserved1 is number 1, which represents the generation of the communication event of receiving a short message, simply called "5-1"; Event_id is number 5 and Reserved1 is number 2, which represents that no communication event is generated. The event list was sort out during the generation of mobile data, as shown in table 1. Take into account the relationship of mutual restriction of different event types, we set the following rules: "0-0" and "0-1", "2-0" and "2-1" are in pairs; In the process of "0-0", "2-0", "2-1" and "5-0" will not happen; In the process of event "2-0", "0-0", "0-1" and "5-0" will not happen; In the process of "2-0" and "0-0", while the user passes through the cell or location area, "7-0" and "7-1" will happen; Not in the process of "2-0" and "0-0", while the user passes through the LA, "4-0" will happen; Here we set the time of Periodical Location Updating for 20 minutes, therefore, every 20 minutes "4-1" will happen. Based on the above rules, we make an event generator called Event Generator. For various travel styles, the

Table 1. Event list

EventID	Reserved1	Description
5	0	send a short message
5	1	receive a short message
7	0	switch between cell and cell(within BSC)
7	1	switch between BSC and BSC
4	0	Normal Location Updating
4	1	Periodical Location Updating
4	2	switch on
4	4	switch off
0	0	at the beginning of receiving a call
0	1	at the end of receiving a call
2	0	at the beginning of placing a call
2	1	at the end of placing a call

users' moving speed is different. For each travel style we will adopt a proprietary random number generator to generate the speed within the scope of the corresponding style. Based on this approach, we constructed a Speed Generator. When we input the parameter for travel style, it can generate a random speed within the scope of the corresponding style. In real life, the users' moving speed varies with the change of real road conditions. Therefore, the moving

Table 2. Speed indicators

Number	Travel_style	Speed/km · h^{-1}
a	walking	0 ~ 5
b	by bicycle	5 ~ 20
c	by bus	15 ~ 50
d	by car	40 ~ 180
e	by subway	80 ~ 200

speed between one Instance and another one by Speed Generator generates a random speed to simulate the change of real road conditions. Here is speed reference table about several common modes of transportation, as shown in table 2. In order to facilitate understanding and calculation of Instance, we add Speed_value and Arrive_time to the Instance and extend the Instance to nine. The Instance becomes (id, Lngt_value, Lat_value, Travel_style, Speed_value, Arrive_time, Is_stop, Stay_time, Trip_purpose). Speed_value is a random speed value generate by the Speed Generator based on the input parameter Trans_Style. We assumed that Instance(1).Arrive_time is the starting time of simulation, namely, the switch on time of the user' mobile. The distance between one Instance and the next one is the straight-line distance. Therefore, Instance (2).Arrive_time is the sum of Instance (1).Stay_time and the time that the user moves from Instance(1) to Instance(2). Do the same analogy, Instance(i+1).Arrive_time = Instance(i).Arrive_time + Instance(i).Stay_time + distance / Speed_value, among the distance for the coordinate distance between Instance(i) and Instance(i+1) that we can refer to Google API. The users' trajectories are the sequential lines of connecting all Instances. These crossing points between the sequential lines and cell or location area and the arriving time for each crossing point can be obtained by geometric calculation sequentially. Therefore, we define every crossing point as CrossPoint, which contains User_id, Lngt_value, Lat_value, Before_cell, After_cell, Is_innerCell, Is_innerLA, Travel_time, Arrive_time, Travle_style ten elements, in which User_id is the user' ID, Lngt_value and Lat_value represent the coordinate of CrossPoint, Before_cell is the former cell of the Crosspoint, After_cell is the latter cell of the Crosspoint, Is_innerCell for "true" represents the switch between one cell and another one within LA, Is_innerCell for "false" represents the contrary, buy Is_innerLA for "true" represents the switch between one location area and another one, but Is_innerLA for "false" represents the contrary. When the user passes through the CrossPoint, the Event Generator will generate corresponding communication event based on the properties of CrossPoint.

The process can be shown in Algorithm 1. The getuserlocation method is used to calculate the cell which the user' positioning location belongs to instantly; When the user' positioning location is at the boundary among two adjacent cells, the users' positioning location belongs to the next cell that the user will step in. All records of the mobile data are generated in chronological order. The first record corresponds to the switch on event of user's mobile at the time denoted by Instance(1).Arrive_time and positioning location denoted by the center of the

---

Algorithm 1. the Generation of Simulated Mobile Data

Input: A Instance sequence S, Start time, CELLS, Event Generator
  //Instance is the User_id's current instance of the evolving
  //CELLS is a collection of all cells
Output: LOGS[]
  //LOGS[] is an ordered array of Logs that were generated by our system.
  LOGS.add(User_id, Time_stamp, a.Lngt_value, a.Lat_value, 4, 2, Stop_tag)
  //Instance(1)∈cell(a), a∈CELLS, a.Lngt_value and Lat_value is the center of a,
  //Time_stamp=Instance(1).Start_time, Stop_tag=Instance(1).Is_stop
   For k ⟵ 1 to (| S |-1) do
   T=Instance(k+1).Arrive_time+Instance(k+1).Stay_time-Instance(k).Arrive_time
   For t ⟵ 1 to T do
   Event event ⟵ Event Generator
   //Event is a class and contains Event_time, Event_location, Event_type and Re-
   served1.
   //event is an example.Event_time=Instance(1).Arrive_time+t.
   Event_location=getuserlocation(Instance(k), Instance(k+1), t)
   LOGS.add(User_id, Event_time, a.Lngt_value, a.Lat_value, Event_type, Reserved1,
   Stop_tag)
   //Instance(k)∈cell(b),b∈CELLS,b.Lngt_value and b.Lat_value is the center of
   b,Stop_tag= Instance(k).Is_stop
   LOGS.add(User_id, Time_stamp, c.Lngt_value, c.Lat_value, 4, 4, Stop_tag)
   //Instance(| S |)∈cell(c), c∈CELLS, Time_stamp=Instance(| S |).Start_time +
   Instance(| S |), c.Lngt_value and c.Lat_value is the center of c, Stop_tag=Instance(|
   S |).Is_stop.

---

cell of Instance(1). This system will generate a series of communication events generated by Event Generator for the moving user. The last record corresponds to the switch off event of user' mobile at the time denoted by the sum of Instance (| S |).Arrive_time and Instance (| S |).Stay_time.

Above all, this system can simulate the user's travel process and simultaneously use Event Generator to generate the random mobile communication events. In the total process, the system will record all the events to produce the mobile data.

4   An Example

In this section, we use an example to demonstrate the process, including supposing the user's past activities, extracting trajectory points and adding semantic annotations, the simulation of the user's past activities and the generation of simulated mobile data.

The user's past activities is generated by supposing the possible behavior of different groups. For example, we suppose a student visit the Palace Museum from Beijing University of Technology to the Subway Station of TIAN'ANMEN East. The travel route is the shortcut route that we query the Baidu map from the Internet, namely, he takes the bus 605, 985, 973, 988, 621 or 30 about 6 stations to BAWANGFEN North, walks to the subway station of DAWANGLU, takes No.1 subway towards PINGGUOYUAN direction, gets off from the subway station of TIAN'ANMEN East, then walks to the Palace Museum. The time arrangement often need to set some random value based on the actual situation. Here we supposed that he set up at half past seven, spends 25 minutes on washing, walks to the canteen and spends 20 minutes on eating breakfast, walks ten minutes to reach the bus station, waits the bus about 3 minutes, takes bus to BAWANGFEN South station, walks 8 minutes to reach DAWANGLU subway station, waits 3 minutes, takes the subway to TIAN'ANMEN East, walks to the ticket office and spends ten minute on queuing up for ticket, then enters into the Palace Museum. For each iconic point it costs him a random tour time, such as 5-20minutes range. We follow the supposed process of the user's past activities, extract the trajectory points by the way of adding markers sequentially in the user's travel route on the map and simultaneously add some appropriate semantic annotations for each trajectory point, such as Travel_style, Is_stop, Stay_time, Travel_purpose and so on. Figure 2 is a whole view of the overall trajectories of visiting the Palace Museum. Figure 3 is the schematic diagram of the record sheet of trajectoy points.

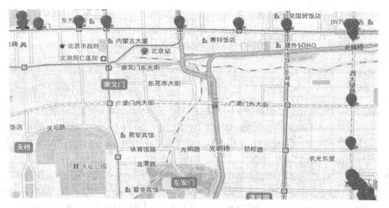

Fig. 2. The overall trajectories of visiting the Palace Museum

Mobile Number: 000001   Date: 20110910   Start Time: 063000

The Table of Mobile Record

Option	Id	Longitude	Latitude	Travel Style	IsStop	Stay Time (Minute)	Travel Purpose
○	1	116.488286	39.880171	Walk ▼	True ▼	60	Tourism ▼
○	2	116.488194	39.879648	Walk ▼	True ▼	10	Tourism ▼
○	3	116.487242	39.879548	Walk ▼	True ▼	2	Tourism ▼
○	4	116.48681	39.879946	Walk ▼	True ▼	1	Tourism ▼
○	5	116.486806	39.881102	Walk ▼	True ▼	1	Tourism ▼
○	6	116.485759	39.88197	Walk ▼	True ▼	1	Tourism ▼
●	7	116.484592	39.881968	Walk ▼	True ▼	1	Tourism ▼

Save

Fig. 3. The record sheet of trajectory points

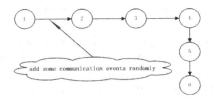

Fig. 4. The simulation of the users' past trajectories

	A	B	C	D	E	F	G	H
1	IMSI	Time	Longitude	Latitude	EventID	Reserved1	CellID	Tag
2	000001	20110901081603	116.4891842	39.87762482	2	1	88049	TRUE
3	000001	20110901081613	116.4891842	39.87762482	2	0	88049	TRUE
4	000001	20110901081625	116.4891842	39.87762482	2	1	88049	TRUE
5	000001	20110901081629	116.4856477	39.88301471	5	1	87051	FALSE
6	000001	20110901081634	116.4856477	39.88301471	5	0	87051	FALSE
7	000001	20110901081654	116.4856477	39.88301471	2	0	87051	FALSE
8	000001	20110901081709	116.4856477	39.88301471	2	1	87051	FALSE

Fig. 5. Some examples of mobile data

Figure 4 is a schematic diagram of the simulation of the users' past trajectories. Those endpoints of each segment represent the user's trajectory points and the user is moving among them. In the moving process, the Event Generator can generate some communication events randomly. We can calculate the user' positioning location or the cell that the user belongs to at any time. All communication events can be recorded by the record of mobile data.

Above all, we can generate the simulated mobile data, as shown in Figure 5.

5   An Application of the Stay Point Identification

In the extraction process of trajectory points of users' past activities, we add the semantic annotation of Is_stop to the stay points that the user stay there for some purposes. As the simulated mobile data have the tag of Is_stop, we can use them to do the experiment on the stay point identification of mobile phone trajectory and verify the merits of the algorithms that we designed.

The identification of stay points of a trajectory is a key step for the analysis of users' behaviors and the result of identification has an important influence on the analysis of travel style, travel purpose, recommend friends [5], location prediction [6] and so on. As the positioning accuracy of GPS data is higher than that of mobile data, the identification of stay point of GPS trajectory usually use clustering, multi-split and so on. The identification of stay point of mobile trajectory is mostly based on [5], uses the stay time that user had stayed in a cell (the difference between last communication time and the first communication in the coverage area of a base station) as a constrain to decide whether the cell is a stay point or not. Only when the difference is bigger than the time threshold, we think the cell is a stay point [7,8,9]. This conventional method is easy to cause normal switch or error switch to identify stay point. The main reason is that most take the geographical characteristics of trajectory into consideration while ignore the background geographic information of trajectory.

For the existing problem of the identification of stay point, our proposed method introduces the concept of functional areas [10], which combines the users' trajectories and background geographic information together. By considering the overall activities of the users in a particular functional area, this method can judge whether the user is here to stay for a special purpose or not. The experiment on the identification of stay point for labeled mobile data proved that this method can avoid the misjudgment of normal switching, error switching. This method of identification of stay point is more general. The definition of scope of stay point is also a collection of cells that a continuous trajectory involves in a functional area instead of a small range (the coverage of a single base station).

6   Conclusions and Future Work

This system provides a mobile data generator based on user real behavior. Particularly, the simulated mobile data is suited for the algorithm of identification of stay point, the analysis of origin-destination, the prediction of location and so on. We have demonstrated how to use the simulated mobile data to identify stay points.

As the system only considers the switch that happens at cell boundary and ignore the fake position switching caused by the normal or error switching, the conditions of normal switching, such as better cell switching, load switching, switching of poor quality, emergency switching; the conditions of error switching such as fast-moving switching, ping-pong switching. Therefore, the actual switching location may not happen at near the border of cell. Furthermore, those normal switching, error switching also happen. The fake position switching in real mobile data is ubiquitous and in the future we will try to take it into consideration in the simulation process.

In addition, surfing the Internet with mobile possess the advantages of ease, anytime, anywhere etc. It has become increasingly widespread and an important way of access the Internet in modern life. The positioning data of surfing the Internet with mobile is not considered in this paper, therefore, it also needs to be considered in future work.

Acknowledgements. The research was supported by International Science & Technology Cooperation Program of China (2013DFA32180), National Science Foundation of China (61272345) and the CAS/SAFEA International Partnership Program for Creative Research Teams.

References

1. Pfoser, D., Theodoridis, Y.: Generating semantics-based trajectories of moving objects computers. Environment and Urban Systems 27(3), 243–263 (2003)

2. Theodoridis, Y., Silva, J.R.O., Nascimento, M.A.: On the generation of spatiotemporal datasets. In: Güting, R.H., Papadias, D., Lochovsky, F.H. (eds.) SSD 1999. LNCS, vol. 1651, pp. 147–164. Springer, Heidelberg (1999)
3. Giannotti, F., Mazzoni, A., Puntoni, S., Renso, C.: Synthetic generation of cellular network positioning data. In: Proceedings of the 13th ACM International Workshop on Geographic Information Systems, pp. 12–20 (2005)
4. Caceres, N., Wideberg, J.P., Benitez, F.G.: Deriving origin-destination data from a mobile phone network. IET Intelligent Transport Systems 1(1), 15–26 (2007)
5. Zheng, Y., Zhang, L.Z., Ma, Z.X., Xie, X., Ma, W.Y.: Recommending friends and locations based on individual location history. ACM Transactions on the Web 5(1), 247–256 (2011)
6. Ying, J.J.C., Lee, W.C., Weng, T.C., Tseng, V.S.: Semantic trajectory mining for location prediction. In: Proceedings of the 19th ACM International Symposium on Advances in Geographic Information Systems, pp. 34–43 (2011)
7. Lu, E.H.C., Tseng, V.S., Yu, P.S.: Mining cluster-based temperal mobile sequential patterns in location-lased service environments. IEEE Transaction on Knowlegde and Data Engingering 23(6), 914–927 (2011)
8. Monreale, A., Pinelli, F., Trasarti, R., Giannotti, F.: WhereNext: a location predictor on trajectory pattern mining. In: Proceedings of the 15th ACM SIGKDD International Conference on Knowledge Discovery and Data Mining, pp. 637–646 (2009)
9. Ying, J.J.C., Lu, E.H.C., Lee, W.C., Weng, T.C., Tseng, V.S.: Mining user similarity from semantic trajectories. In: Proceedings of the 2nd ACM SIGSPATIAL International Workshop on Location Based Social Networks, pp. 19–26 (2010)
10. Yuan, J., Zheng, Y., Xie, X.: Discovering regions of different functions in a city using human mobility and POIs. In: Proceedings of the 18th ACM SIGKDD International Conference on Knowledge Discovery and Data Mining, pp. 186–194 (2012)

Introducing a New Scalable Data-as-a-Service Cloud Platform for Enriching Traditional Text Mining Techniques by Integrating Ontology Modelling and Natural Language Processing

Alexey Cheptsov[1], Axel Tenschert[1], Paul Schmidt[2], Birte Glimm[3], Mauricio Matthesius[4], and Thorsten Liebig[5]

[1] High-Performance Computing Center Stuttgart, Nobelstr. 19,
70569 Stuttgart, Germany
`{cheptsov,tenschert}@hlrs.de`
[2] Institute of the Society for the Promotion of Applied Information Sciences at the Saarland University, Martin-Luther-Str. 14, 66111 Saarbrücken, Germany
`Paul.Schmidt@iai-sb.de`
[3] University of Ulm, Institute of Artificial Intelligence, 89069 Ulm, Germany
`birte.glimm@uni-ulm.de`
[4] Objectivity, Inc., 3099 North First Street, Suite 200 San Jose, CA 95134 USA
`mmatthesius@objectivity.com`
[5] derivo GmbH, James-Franck-Ring, 89081 Ulm, Germany
`liebig@derivo.de`

Abstract. A good deal of digital data produced in academia, commerce and industry is made up of a raw, unstructured text, such as Word documents, Excel tables, emails, web pages, etc., which are also often represented in a natural language. An important analytical task in a number of scientific and technological domains is to retrieve information from text data, aiming to get a deeper insight into the content represented by the data in order to obtain some useful, often not explicitly stated knowledge and facts, related to a particular domain of interest. The major challenge is the size, structural complexity, and frequency of the analysed text sets' updates (i.e., the 'big data' aspect), which makes the use of traditional analysis techniques and tools impossible. We introduce an innovative approach to analyse unstructured text data. This allows for improving traditional data mining techniques by adopting algorithms from ontological domain modelling, natural language processing, and machine learning. The technique is inherently designed with parallelism in mind, which allows for high performance on large-scale Cloud computing infrastructures.

Keywords: Data-as-a-Service, Text Mining, Ontology Modelling, Cloud computing.

1 Introduction

The modern IT technologies are increasingly getting data-centric, fostered by the broad availability of data acquisition, collection and storing platforms. The concepts

Z. Huang et al. (Eds.): WISE 2013 Workshops 2013, LNCS 8182, pp. 62–74, 2014.

of linked and open data have enabled a principally new dimension of data analysis, which is no longer limited to internal document collections, i.e., "local data", but comprises a number of heterogeneous data sources, in particular from the Web, i.e., "global data". However, existing data processing and analysis technologies are still far from being able to scale to demands of global and, in case of large industrial corporations, even of local data, which makes up the core of the "big data" problem. With regard to this, the design of the current data analysis algorithms requires to be reconsidered in order to enable the scalability to big data demands. The problem has two major aspects: (1) the solid design of current algorithms makes the integration with other techniques that would help increase the analysis quality impossible, and (2) sequential design of the algorithms prevents porting them to parallel computing infrastructures and thus do not fulfil high performance and other QoS user requirements.

Text analytics is an important application area of data mining algorithms. At the same time, it is one of the applications impacted worst by the big data aspect: along on the Web there are several tens of billions web pages, which might be potentially related to the search context. Also on intranets of large and medium size companies there are a huge number of stored documents, e.g., as Word documents, Excel tables, emails, etc., which frequently need to be analyzed. The main purpose of such an analysis is to get a deeper insight into the content of textual information collected in documents in order to obtain some useful, often not explicitly stated knowledge and facts, related to a particular search query. However, automatic knowledge extraction from large text collections, also considering external data sources (e.g., Wikipedia), is a nontrivial and very challenging task. It requires the availability of high performance computing facilities as an "on demand" infrastructure as well as an experimental platform for implementing and later on for running interdisciplinary text analysis algorithms in the way that ensures fulfilment of both quality and efficiency requirements. Unfortunately, existing approaches seem to be neither efficient enough to ensure a proper quality of results (in terms of analysis automation, performance, etc.) nor scalable to catch up with the big data requirements.

In this paper, we suggest and discuss a new technique to develop innovative applications for information retrieval from unstructured text corpora allowing for the determination of causal inter-contextual relations between the analyzed text entities (i.e., documents, web pages, etc.). The main innovation of the technique consists in enabling an interdisciplinary approach that allows traditional data mining algorithms to be enhanced towards incorporation of domain-specific ontology modelling methods as well as template-based, self learning natural language processing technologies in order to ensure a fully automated, reliable, and efficient information retrieval. The technique is inherently designed in a parallel fashion, which allows it to scale well on high performance computing infrastructures, such as Cloud computing. Apart from this, the use of a Cloud also offers a solution for the data privacy problem – whereas the critical (in terms of security and privacy restrictions) data will be processed on Private Cloud infrastructures, the use of Public Cloud resources will be restricted to the processing of publically available and accessible data.

The paper is organized as follows. Section 2 gives an overview of state-of-the-art R&D activities in the related areas, namely, ontology modelling and semantic techniques, data mining and machine learning, natural human language understanding, and scalable data management. Section 3 introduces our approach to combine the above-mentioned techniques in a text analysis platform. Section 4 discusses the cloud-based architecture of the platform. Section 5 introduces two typical application scenarios that can take advantage of the proposed technique. Section 6 summarizes the main ideas of the paper and draws up a conclusion.

2   Related Work and Progress the Beyond State-of-the-Art

This section provides an overview of the technologies related to the topic of our research as well as an introduction of major enhancements and improvements targeted by our new analysis approach.

2.1   Parallelization and Scale-Up Technique for Data-Centric Processing

The big data problem represents several challenges to the efficient use of existing popular information retrieval platforms for text data such as SMILA [1] or GATE [2], mainly related to scaling up their algorithms to meet rapidly growing data demands. Due to a high complexity of the problem, current approaches to information retrieval focus on very restricted domains. Those challenges have been addressed by partially parallelizing computationally expensive parts of the text processing workflows. Being an obvious solution, this is not sufficient to meet the increasing big data demands. Instead of a top-down parallelization approach, which is currently followed by most of the analysis systems, whereby the parallelization begins at the application level and very rarely reaches the processing algorithms, the basic support of parallel processing should be provided in a bottom-up way. This means the parallelisation should already be included in the design of the underlying processing algorithms, in order to provide extensive support for developing highly parallel and thus efficient applications. In our research, we follow the second way – by reconsidering the basics of text processing algorithms, we aim to develop an innovative platform that will incorporate best practices of the currently available tools and techniques and also consider relatively recent developments in service-oriented data processing (e.g., SOA4ALL project [3]) and large-scale semantic web reasoning (e.g., LarKC project [4]).

In terms of the parallelization technology, Hadoop (a Java-based implementation of MapReduce of Yahoo [5]) is currently enjoying a prominent position in data-centric distributed and parallel computing. However, the bottom-up development approach, followed by us, puts very strict requirements on the platform in order to ensure a "near peak performance" utilization rate of the computing facilities by parallel programs, which Hadoop cannot meet due to the service-oriented and Java-based architecture design. With regard to this, a use of alternative approaches, such as Message-Passing Interface (MPI) or Partitioned Global Address Space (PGAS), is becoming the latest trend. However, the major challenge for applying these parallelization techniques is constituted by a Java programs' execution environment (Java Virtual Machine, or JVM), which is extensively used for implementing data-centric applications nowadays. Whereas the abstraction to the underlying hardware architecture, offered by JVM, simplifies the application development for the users, the access to special hardware's features, such as cluster's high-bandwidth and low-latency network interconnect (e.g., Infiniband), is only possible through virtualized interfaces, which thus considerably limits the performance.

Nevertheless, the latest advances of such tools as ompiJava [6], which is an implementation of Java bindings for Open MPI [7], along with the promises of ongoing projects, such as JUNIPER [8], which aims to develop an efficient PGAS-based parallelization model for Java applications, offer a promising outlook on the perspectives of using both MPI and PGAS technologies complementary to Hadoop in data-centric parallel applications design.

2.2 Ontology Modelling and Semantics Analysis

Information Retrieval (IR) powered by Ontology Modelling Modelling (OM) has been investigated in several previous research works. For example, the approach introduced in [9] discusses an application from the Business Intelligence domain that allows for automatic extraction of facts by using domain-specific OM. Existing frameworks, such as the above-discussed SMILA, also allow for the integration of ontologies. To the best of our knowledge, the ontologies are, however, mainly used as data stores rather than for supporting the knowledge extraction by inferring implicit knowledge. An approach with a deeper integration of ontologies is proposed in [10], where the results of IR are purely based on OM; the approach does not consider learning methods, though.

Compared to existing alternatives, our approach takes the advantage of OM (along with decision making algorithms) to constitute the core of a model-based, intelligent (i.e., self-learning) knowledge extraction platform. The approach suggests that IR of domain knowledge should be conducted in a semi-automated way by using "seed patterns" (see Section 4 for more details) through machine learning instead of being manually created. Domain knowledge is used to identify antagonisms in the learned facts as well as to revise the ontology. The problem of the ontologically "clashing" and mismatching concepts is resolved by a decision-making system, which refines the ontology based on deductive reasoning algorithms, e.g., the one described in [11]. However, there is a clear need for such algorithms to be optimized and improved in order to address the big data scale, which involves, e.g., the computation of disjoint ontology classes or domains in an incremental and parallel fashion as described in [12].

2.3 Data Mining and Machine Learning

Data Mining (DM) is the technique of automatic information extraction from structured and unstructured machine-readable data sources, often accompanied by natural language processing algorithms. A prominent example of the domain that has been revolutionized by DM is Business Intelligence, which allows companies to define their market strategy in a tight alignment with the current business goals and company's profile. In this relation, traditional statistical methods as well as manually created rules are extensively used. Unfortunately, the classical DM methods are only capable of identifying the statistical significance between the commonly collocated terms, e.g., *Barack Obama, Angela Merkel, state heads*. Therefore the meaning behind these collocated concepts remains uncovered and the relationship to the other concepts cannot be discovered.

One of the most promising concepts to deal with this problem is the use of Machine Learning (ML) in order to improve the extraction of new facts and generalization of the already extracted ones based on the predefined patterns and examples (also called "seeds"). NELL [13] is one of the pilot projects investigating the ability of ML algorithms to improve the IR quality on the web scale. NELL crawls over the sites on the Web, identifies newly appeared concepts (e.g., *persons, cities*) and retrieves the relationship between them (e.g., the *city* in which the *person was born*). The knowledge extraction is performed in a completely automated way. The major disadvantage of this approach is a poor ability to tackle with noisy and non-trustful data, which is often referred as a semantic drift [14], which leads to the propagation of the non-credible facts to the newly learned fact base. On a small scale of data, the negative impact of the semantic drift can be overcome by constant monitoring and controlling the quality of the information extraction process by a human, i.e., a specialist of the problem domain. However, this makes neither meeting ad-hoc solutions nor scaling to big data demands technically possible.

Our suggested approach to overcome this limitation is to use the domain-specific OM algorithm to evaluate and control the ML process. The first proof-of-concept prototype, discussed in [15], reveals a positive impact of such an integrated "ML-over-OM" approach. By optimally balancing the OM workflow on the parallel hardware resources, which should be achieved by means of the techniques discussed in Section 2.1, we expect to scale up the ML algorithm to the real complexity, i.e., web-scale, use cases.

2.4   Language Processing

Natural Language Processing (NLP) is an important technique for text-based analytics and has found a wide application in a number of scientific and technological domains. As an example, NLP has been extensively used and proved successful for a long time in language checking, language quality control, information retrieval (amongst others [16]), machine translation and many others. At the same time, NLP is also much affected by the big data problem. The major challenge is not only the size (the length of a single document as well as the size of the document collection), but also the heterogeneous nature of language (ranging from a free-style email communication to semi-structured Wikipedia articles). In order to sufficiently address these challenges, the NLP technology should be designed in a highly scalable manner. Modern hybrid methods that allow linguistic analysis techniques to be combined with the corpus-based processing [17][18] offer a promising vision on how the high scalability can be achieved. However, these methods are pretty shallow in terms of the depth of semantics to be retrieved. Therefore a combination with the machine learning techniques discussed in Section 2.3 would be of an enormous advantage. Moreover, the integration with ontology modelling methods will allow further components of an IR workflow to use the NLP techniques, e.g., for named entity recognition (retrieval of names related to persons, organizations, places, vehicles, etc.), sentiment analysis (e.g., by means of special forms of text mining), extraction of relationships between the objects, etc.

2.5   Scalable Data Management

The advances of modern large-scale infrastructures, such as Cloud computing, offer an extensive computing power to conduct challenging experiments quickly. However, the computation-centric orientation leads to a very high complexity of the data-centric application scenarios implementation. Data management services, such as Amazon S3, which are mature and well-established on the market, are very limited as far as efficient processing of stored data is concerned. This would be crucial for any integrated text analytics platform as the example in [19] indicates. Highly-optimized high performance computing systems are also characterized by extremely poor support offered to data-centric processing algorithms, which is the case when the major challenge of the application is constituted by the size of data rather than the complexity of the processing algorithm itself.

From the technology perspective, relational databases are typically used for storing textual data. This is also the case for the above-discussed SMILA and Gate frameworks. Additionally, XML databases may be used on top of relational databases for managing the ontology as well as the indexing system, which somewhat speeds up the rate of data access and, consequently, the overall performance. Despite being efficient and robust for small-scale data, this approach does not scale well on the big data range. Moreover, relational database technologies are not very suitable to be applied for statistical algorithms required for the text analysis, which is due to the need of processing sparse matrices.

The shortcomings of relational databases in their application to text analysis algorithms can be overcome by using graph data bases, such as InfiniteGraph [20] – a distributed graph database tailored to store and process structured and linked data, implemented in the Java language. Indeed, the use of graph data structures for representing textual and ontological concepts offers a lot of opportunities in terms of performance and scalability improvement as compared to traditional, relational database approaches. Moreover, the exceeding horizontal scalability features of graph databases offer a good basis for the deployment on parallel computing resources. However, the major challenge of integrating graph databases into the existing text analysis platforms is constituted by the solid design of those frameworks, which makes the seamless integration impossible and requires the underlying algorithms to be redesigned.

3 Approach to Enrich Data Mining by Enabling Ontology Modelling and Natural Language Processing

The state-of-the-art analysis, briefly summarized in Section 2, reveals that the traditional approaches to text mining stand to benefit from enrichment by innovative ontology modelling and natural language processing techniques. This would not only improve the quality of the analysis, thus increasing its practical value for a number of data science domains, but also enable the application to problem sizes on big data scale. The suggested workflow of the typical information retrieval process can be summarized as shown in Fig. 1.

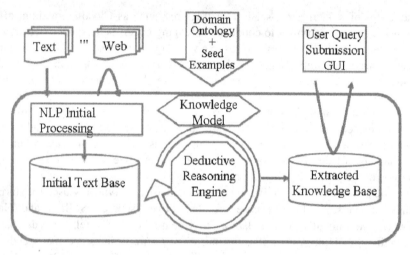

Fig. 1. Schema of the workflow combining data mining, deductive reasoning, natural language processing, and ontology modelling methods to improve the information retrieval from text corpora

As a preparatory step, the analyzed document corpus is uploaded to a document base, which can be done either by users manually or also performed automatically by the analysis platform. For the latter purpose, the platform offers a special service that crawls the internet pages that are in scope of the research, downloads them, recognises the text format and stores the extracted text in the base. A set of smart converters for the most wide-spread document formats, e.g., doc, pdf, html, etc., are provided by the platform as well. The analysis begins with the identification of sentences as well as principal lexical forms in them, supported by computer linguistic and natural language processing (NLP) methods, as discussed in Section 2.4. At the next phase, a bootstrapping analysis mechanism is used to identify new terms (e.g., Persons) as well as relations (e.g., role in the company) that constitute the basic knowledge model of the whole text corpus. The process is then iteratively repeated and at each step the knowledge model is enhanced and extended with the new set of terms (such as other persons), definitions, and relations. The key role during this process is taken by a deductive reasoning algorithm, used for checking the semantic consistency of the retrieved statements. The latter is performed based on a domain-specific ontology schema. The schema is produced from the domain ontology, enhanced by the analysis of seed examples, as described in Section 2.3. The major advantage of the ontology-based reasoning algorithm is that it allows for a certain level of automation of the knowledge retrieval processes and does not require any human inspector as in case of the traditional knowledge discovery methods. The growing algorithmic complexity, caused by the need to make reasoning over the initial data corpus at each iteration of the analysis, is supposed not to have any considerable impact on the computational performance of the analysis due to enabled inherent parallel implementation of the reasoning algorithm, leveraging the high performance computing resources, see Section 4 for details on the platform's system organization.

4   Analytics Platform's Architecture Design

The practical realisation of the analysis approach discussed in Section 3 requires an elastic (in terms of offered resources) and rich (in terms of ensured data services quality) infrastructure, where the data should be collected and analysed in a centralised way, as well as a software platform that leverages the infrastructure's storage and computing facilities to solving on-demand (in terms of the needed scale and performance) data analytics tasks. Text analysis is a typical task that can be offered as a service – the users are interested in the information contained in the data rather than the data themselves. Therefore, the suggested text analysis platform's architecture is conceptualized according to the "Data-as-a-Service" (DaaS) system organization (see Fig. 2). It is worth mentioning, that our notion of DaaS-based cloud

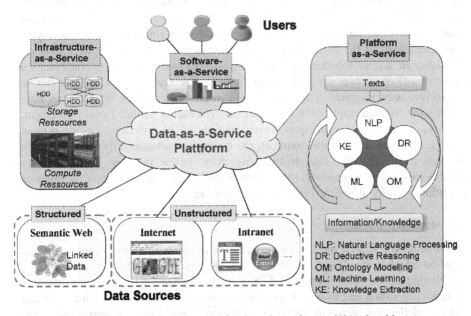

Fig. 2. Data-centric cloud model for the enhanced text mining algorithm

model is a little bit broader than the one given by Wikipedia [21] and assumes a consolidated service stack built on top of the infrastructure (IaaS), data analysis platform (PaaS) and user-centric application (SaaS) services. Following subsections discuss some distinctive features of the suggested data-centric cloud architecture design with regard to the analysis platform, infrastructure, and user-centric services.

Analysis Platform

The interdisciplinary nature of the integrated text mining approach, as discussed in Section 3, fosters the collaboration between independent groups of data scientists, each working on a corresponding part of the text mining workflow, whether it is natural language processing, deductive reasoning, ontology modelling, machine learning, or knowledge extraction. Thus, the main task of the platform is to provide means for developing services that implement the certain component's functionality by ensuring the needed level of interoperability between the loosely coupled services in order to be integrated in a common application, i.e., a workflow. Furthermore, the services can incorporate previously developed services, which have been designed in a way that allows their easy adoption by the upper-level services. In particular, such an approach has been investigated and successfully implemented in the LarKC project [3], whereby applications are developed as a workflow that is constructed of several services (or plug-ins, in the LarKC terminology) connected through a common data- and workflow management system. A "Data-as-a-Service" concept, as suggested by us, extends the basic principals of LarKC by providing such an analysis platform as a service, which means that all the essential components of the platform's software stack, such as execution runtime, database, web services host, workflow manager, etc., are permanently deployed on the cloud. The platform's advantage from the service-oriented design is manifold: (1) it does not introduce any additional requirements to the configuration of the user's underlying software or hardware layers – the client part of the cloud platform is constituted by light-weight web services, accessible via a plain schema (typically XML-based) from any internet- (in case of a public cloud) or intranet (in case of a private cloud) connected device; (2) it can be relatively easily migrated to another cloud-based infrastructure in order to help meeting the concrete application's requirements (including Service Level Agreement, security, costs, etc.) or even spawn over multiple cloud providers, i.e., be offered through a federated cloud environment; (3) it matches automatically the application demands to the available infrastructure resources, so that the users do not need to make the allocation themselves; (4) it exploits the inherent parallelism of the analysis algorithms to fully utilize the infrastructure capacities.

Infrastructure

An on-demand infrastructure provisioning is one of the key features of the suggested cloud-based platform design. Depending on the concrete application scenario, the underlying hardware can virtually scale to meet the application demands, e.g., the size of data to be stored and analyzed, as well as to satisfy the predefined functional and Quality of Service requirements, such as the maximal query answering time, the number of parallel processed of user queries, etc. The infrastructure consists of three basic types of resources: compute cluster, storage disc farm, and local area network (LAN). Compute clusters offer hardware for performing computation, i.e., CPUs and RAM, loosely connected to each other by means of a (e.g., TCP-IP based) LAN, or, in case of supercomputers, through a high-speed network like Infiniband or Gigabit Ethernet. Some cluster nodes might be equipped with a local disk, however a more common case is when all nodes are getting access to a shared storage, available through a networked file system, such as Lustre. The main task of the cloudware is thus to manage all those hardware resources constituting the cloud infrastructure among the user experiments, or jobs, which is done by means of a cloud resource manager. Resource manager is an interactive service, having a role of the infrastructure frontend with regard to the platform's system software.

User-centric Software

The use of the cloud platform by the users is facilitated by user-centric software, which includes interfaces to submit and control experiments, analyse results, etc. For this purpose, a set of intuitive general-purpose web services has been designed. Depending on the use case scenario, these services can be extended to meet user and application specific requirements.

5   Use Case Scenarios

This section presents two exemplary applications of the proposed text mining platform. The aim is to demonstrate the advantages of the platform with regard to typical analysis scenarios from science and industry. None of the scenarios could have been implemented with the existing tools so far.

5.1   Open Media Data Analytics on the Web

The everyday work of journalists and news agencies is largely influenced by the availability of free media data, published on the internet. The market success of a media platform is largely dependent on the timeframe between the news' arrival and their releasing in both internet and traditional (printed) media. The crucial point here is that the newly arrived information has to be validated with respect to its truthfulness and actuality before being published. Having a high performance contextualization platform, which would enable information extraction from all those large-sized, heterogeneous, and unstructured data sources, would be of a great advantage for journalists.

As an example, let's suppose a journalist has to take a decision about publishing a news item about some recent political event. The news might be outdated, come from an unreliable source, or might contain knowingly false statements, such as the wrong political allegiance or affiliation of the news's protagonist. Therefore, the information contained in this news must be validated according to other related news, e.g., the previously published ones, as well as publically available information from the internet. The analysis platform would automatically identify the information from the sources related to this news, categorize it, extract the main statements as well as the context they are used in (e.g., sentiments), etc. This helps greatly and serves as a recommendation for the publication. Moreover, the platform will allow the journalist to essentially extend the scope of news by considering other related events and articles. Considering the size of the analyzed data as well as the availability of near real time requirements for the discussed application scenario, this is a typical big data task that obviously requires such a platform as suggested in this paper. The research has already attracted attention of key players on the media market, such as Deutsche Welle. The potential end users of this technology are newspapers, radios, TV channels, and journals.

5.2   Strategic Business Decision Making in Enterprises

Intelligent taking of strategic business decisions is an important task for many enterprises that are planning or/and optimizing their research and prototyping activities towards achieving the identified innovation and technology management aims. For example, before reorienting its main production line to producing electrical vehicles instead of petrol or gas ones, car manufactures like BMW would need to analyze the results of a huge number of reports, studying the impact of this strategic decision from very different perspectives, including the technological, economical, and social ones. Successfully conducting this task often involves an extensive analysis of the internal document collections, such as marketing studies, technical reports, instruction manuals, technical email discussions, forums, trackers, and other textually captured and stored documents, whose aggregated volume can easily reach the size of several Petabytes. The role of the platform in the decision making process is not only to identify the documents related to a particular query as well as to retrieve the useful information contained in those document, but also to enrich this formation with other knowledge coming from external, usually unstructured, data sources, e.g., from the Internet, in order to build a knowledge base to be used for the internal planning of the enterprise's strategy.

Unfortunately, a trivial syntactic look-up (e.g., via Google Search Appliance) has proved ineffective for such kind of search, since it only returns co-occurrences and does not retrieve the relationship between the searched terms and events. The suggested platform improves this kind of analysis by integrating enterprise-related domain knowledge regarding the search directly into the knowledge extraction process in the form of ontologies. The use of learning and reasoning during the knowledge extraction process further improves the amount and quality of the gained knowledge. Hence, the platform will retrieve knowledge for the concrete search from unstructured, distributed and heterogeneous big data in order to provide a highly-structured, comprehensive knowledge base, aligned with the current situation at the enterprise, in order to support meeting ad-hoc operative decisions.

6 Conclusion and Outlook

The paper introduced the results of an interdisciplinary research (spanning over information retrieval and analysis, semantic technologies, computational linguistic, data management, and high performance computing domains) aimed to elaborate a new technique to information and knowledge extraction from text corpora that fall within the scope of the big data aspect, i.e., the analysis of heterogeneous, unstructured, and large-sized data. The major motivation for the research lies in an increasing inability of the traditional techniques to address the big data challenges in textual data processing, as reported by numerous scientific and industrial research communities. The elaborated approach suggests enriching the traditional text mining techniques by integrating ontology modelling and natural language processing algorithms. The major benefits of the integrated approach can be summarized in the following points: (1) full automation of the knowledge extraction process thanks to adopting a domain ontology based deductive reasoning algorithm; (2) very high quality of the retrieved information thanks to the iterative, self-learning analysis method; (3) applicability to a wide range of data sources thanks to adaptive NLP methods; (4) short time-to-market and high cost effectiveness during adoption by the new application domains.

The approach should be implemented and deployed in a data-centric cloud environment, conceptualized in a way conforming to the "data-as-a-service" paradigm. The cloud services, implementing the elaborated algorithms, will be designed considering the most promising parallelization techniques, such as MapReduce, MPI, PGAS, etc., in order to ensure a high efficiency of the developed software when running in high performance computing and cloud environments.

The future research will concentrate on the following actions: (1) further elaboration of the interdisciplinary analysis approach in cooperation with providers of the identified use case; (2) more precise assessment of the performance and scalability promises, enabled by the new approach; (3) implementation of a platform's prototype; (4) spreading out the data-as-a-service innovations for implementing data-centric algorithms in diverse science and technology communities; (5) validation of the software implementing the elaborated algorithms in a cloud computing environment.

References

1. SMILA Framework Website,
   http://www.eclipse.org/smila/
2. GATE Projekt Website, http://gate.ac.uk/
3. Cheptsov, A.: Semantic Web Reasoning on the Internet Scale with Large Knowledge Collider. International Journal of Computer Science and Applications, Technomathematics Research Foundation 8(2), 102–117 (2011)
4. Pedrinaci, C., Lambert, D., Maleshkova, M., Liu, D., Domingue, J., Krummenacher, R.: Adaptive Service Binding with Lightweight Semantic Web Services. In: Dustdar, S., Li, F. (eds.) Service Engineering. European Research Results. Springer, Heidelberg (2010)

5. Dean, J., Ghemawat, S.: MapReduce - simplified data processing on large clusters. In: Proc. OSDI 2004: 6th Symposium on Operating Systems Design and Implementation (2004)

6. Cheptsov, A., Koller, B.: Message-Passing Interface for Java Applications: Practical Aspects of Leveraging High Performance Computing to Speed and Scale Up the Semantic Web. International Journal on Advances in Software 6(1&2), 45–55 (2013)

7. Gabriel, E., et al.: Open MPI: Goals, concept, and design of a next generation MPI implementation. In: Kranzlmüller, D., Kacsuk, P., Dongarra, J. (eds.) EuroPVM/MPI 2004. LNCS, vol. 3241, pp. 97–104. Springer, Heidelberg (2004)

8. Cheptsov, A., Koller, B.: JUNIPER takes aim at Big Data. inSiDE - Innovatives Supercomputing in Deutschland 11(1), 68–69 (2011)

9. Saggion, H., Funk, A., Maynard, D., Bontcheva, K.: Ontology-based Information Extraction for Business Intelligence. In: Aberer, K., Choi, K.-S., Noy, N., Allemang, D., Lee, K.-I., Nixon, L.J.B., Golbeck, J., Mika, P., Maynard, D., Mizoguchi, R., Schreiber, G., Cudré-Mauroux, P. (eds.) ASWC 2007 and ISWC 2007. LNCS, vol. 4825, pp. 843–856. Springer, Heidelberg (2007)

10. Yildiz, B.: Ontology-Driven Information Extraction. In: Wien, T.U (Hrsg.) (2007)

11. Langbein, J.: Concept and implementation of a self-learning, ontology-based retrieval of entities and relations in natural language texts (2012) (in German)

12. Glimm, B.H.: A Novel Approach to Ontology Classification. Journal of Web Semantics. Science, Services and Agents on the World Wide Web 14(84-101) (2012)

13. Movshovitz-Attias, D., Cohen, W.W.: Bootstrapping Biomedical Ontologies for Scientific Text using NELL. In: BioNLP 2012 (2012)

14. Carlson, A., Betteridge, J., Hruschka, E., Mitchell, T.: Coupling Semi-Supervised Learning of Categories and Relations. In: Proceedings of the NAACL HLT Workshop on Semi-Supervised Learning for Natural Language Processing (2009)

15. Carnegie Mellon University: Read the Web (2012), http://rtw.ml.cmu.edu/rtw/

16. Deriu, U., Lehmann, J., Schmidt, P.: Creation of a technique ontology based on filtered language technologies. In: Proceedings Knowtech, Bad Homburg (2009) (in German)

17. Jurafsky, D., Martin, J.: Speech and Language Processing, Upper Saddle River, New Jersey (2009)

18. Manning, C., Schütze, H.: Foundations of Statistical Natural Language Processing. MIT Press (2004)

19. Goodman, E.L., Mizell, D.: Scalable In-memory RDFS Closure on Billions of Triples. In: Proceedings of the 4th InternationalWorkshop on Scalable SemanticWeb Knowledge Base Systems, Shanghai, China (2010)

20. InfiniteGraph Website, http://www.objectivity.com/infinitegraph

21. Data-as-a-Service Wikipedia Entry, http://en.wikipedia.org/wiki/Data_as_a_service

Towards Fine-Grained Verification
of Application Mobility

Yu Zhou[1,2], Yankai Huang[1], Jidong Ge[2,3], and Jun Hu[1]

[1] College of Computer Science and Technology
Nanjing University of Aeronautics and Astronautics, 210019 Nanjing, China
[2] State Key Lab. for Novel Software Technology
Nanjing University, 210093 Nanjing, China
[3] Key Lab. for Intelligent Perception and Systems for High-Dimensional Information,
Nanjing University of Science and Technology, 210000 Nanjing, China
{zhouyu,huangyankai}@nuaa.edu.cn, gjdnju@163.com, hujun@nuaa.edu.cn

Abstract. Component mobility introduces additional complexity for
software engineers along with the convenience it brings to the end-users.
The provision of detailed formal analysis can help to reduce the potential risks for the application design. In the paper, we propose a novel
approach to facilitate fine-grained verification for component mobility
based on Bogor, in which the domain specific knowledge can be embedded and provided as the first class entity. The customization helps to
reduce the generated state space compared with others based on general-
purpose model checkers. The experiment demonstrates the efficiency and
feasibility of our approach.

Keywords: mobility, verification, model checking.

1 Introduction

The vision of pervasive environment brings about a paradigm shift to the user-
centric model, while the associated network intensive and computation intensive
characteristics provide the necessary infrastructure to materialize this vision.
On top of these infrastructures, application migration with users is an effective
ways to hide the uneven conditioning of the environments and provide seamless
services with the least interruption to the end-users [13].

Mobile conditions would inevitably introduce uncertainty to the running applications, e.g., different server configurations, multi-version middleware APIs,
cross-organization policies. Therefore developers need to equip the applications
with some degree of context-awareness capabilities which inevitably increases
the design complexity. To answer the challenge, various approaches have been
proposed [14]. However, most of the work tackle the problems from the technical perspective, for example, agent-based approaches [15], middleware-based
approaches [10]. But few of them address the issue from modeling perspective.
This imbalance motivates us to provide modeling and analyzing support for
application mobility. We agree with the fact that the mobility-enactment mechanism is important, but we also believe that design phase support is a key factor

Z. Huang et al. (Eds.): WISE 2013 Workshops 2013, LNCS 8182, pp. 75–83, 2014.
© Springer-Verlag Berlin Heidelberg 2014

to improve the system quality. Specifically, existing work mainly leverage graph transformation based approaches to specify and validate the design [3,16]. This is mainly because that visually modeling methods have a natural correspondence with the software components. The problem is that the lack of fine-grained verification support hampers the applicability of these models. In this paper, different from using the traditional graph based tools, we try to exploit the domain-specific knowledge of application mobility and embed them into the verification engine. Based on the highly modular architecture of model checker–Bogor [6], the domain specific concepts are provided as the first-class primitives for modeling, which not only facilitate the following analysis but also help reduce the state space compared with other general purpose model checkers.

The rest of the paper is structured as follows. Section 2 gives brief technology background of Bogor. Section 3 illustrates our approach with an example. Section 4 presents the evaluation and comparison with other approaches. Section 5 discusses some related work and Section 6 draws an conclusion.

2   Background

Bogor [6] is a popular highly modular model checker developed by Kansas State University. The framework provides direct support for modern language features as well as convenient extensibility.

Listing 1.1. BIR extension example for resource management modeling

```
1   system ResourceExample{
2       extension Set for mypackage.myextensions.SetModule{
3           typedef type<'a>;
4           expdef Set.type<'a> create<'a>('a ...);
5           expdef 'a selectElement<'a>(Set.type<'a>);
6           expdef boolean isEmpty<'a>(Set.type<'a>);
7           actiondef add<'a>(Set.type<'a>, 'a);
8           actiondef remove<'a>(Set.type<'a>, 'a);
9       }
10      record Resource{boolean isFree;}
11      record Memory extends Resource{}
12      Set.type<Resource> resourcePool;
13      main thread MAIN(){
14          loc loc0:
15          do{
16              resourcePool := Set.create<Resource>(new Memory);
17          }goto loc1:
18          ...
19      }
20  }
```

The input is specified in the format of Bandera Intermediate Representation (BIR), which was originally designed to be an intermediate language used for translating Java programs to the input language of other existing model checkers, e.g., SPIN [7]. Thus it can directly support modelling of threads, Java locks and a bounded form of heap allocation etc. On the other hand, Bogor was designed with a highly modular architecture and it provide utilities to add new types, expressions, and commands according to users' needs. Because of this feature, users can customize according to the domain knowledge by implementing the correspondent extensions. In this way, the irrelevant states which would be generated otherwise to the properties being checked can be avoided.

Listing 1.1 illustrates how to extend the BIR language and model a resource management scheme. Line 2-9 describes the *set* extension defined by users. The generic style guarantees the reusability in case of multiple element data types. There are three kinds of extension definition for BIR: the first is *type extension* (line 3); the second kind is *expression extension* (line 4-6); the last kind is *action extension* (line 7-8). Line 10-11 describes two *record* types. Line 13-19 describes a running unit of Bogor, where *main thread* indicates the entry point. The atomic statement is labeld by keyword *loc*. Multiple threads can be interleaved for execution. For space limitation, details of these extensions are not listed here, but interested readers can refer to [6] for a complete presentation.

The user is responsible to give the implementation of the extension including each action and expression declared. Bogor provides a well-defined architecture to ease this process. By inheriting several abstract classes and implementing some interfaces, user-defined modules can be incorporated into the model checker and the extensions can be provided as the primitives for the modeling process.

By default, Bogor can check embedded assertions or whether the input model contains deadlock. If the model violates the assertion or contains deadlock, a counter example with error traces will be given. Moreover, Bogor also supports the verification against properties specified by Linear Temporal Logic (LTL). The highly customizable characteristics of Bogor and the support of LTL are two key factors of our approach which allows for a detailed property specification as well as a reduction of unnecessary state space.

3 Our Approach

Application mobility mechanisms are usually adaptive and very flexible to meet different requirements. Taken popular Model-View-Controller (MVC) architectural pattern [4] compliant applications as an example, there are several mobility strategies, i.e., state migration, user interface migration, or even whole application migration. The final choice actually depends on the context after the application is deployed. Thus we need to provide modeling support for both application as well as context. In design phase, the modeling language needs to provide high level abstract, but not unnecessary detailed constructs. In light of this, for simplicity, we make some assumptions on the application mobility. Application consists of a set of loosely coupled components. There is a specific application mobility manager, which is responsible for scheduling the mobility event and keeping the states. Moreover, we does not take into consideration of cross-organization boundaries during modeling.

For mobile applications, since the components are loosely coupled. Each component may have some dependencies on others or some requirements on the resources. This could be naturally modeled by a reference type: *record*. Thus at least five pieces of information are needed for the component, i.e., ownership, user's id, location's id, dependencies, and resource requirements. The former three parts can be easily represented via native primitives, but the last two requires some further reference types to model, since multiple dependencies and resource requirements are possible in many cases. And the sequence of these dependencies and requirements are not important, the *set* data type is of our natural choice. Besides, since not all components are inherently movable, for example, database component, we need to add a flag to indicate.

Different from implementation languages, we do not require design models have the ability to migrate across platforms. Instead, we use the mobility manager, i.e., *MobiManager* to keep track of the component place information and mimic the migration behavior. In real cases, sensors detect the user's move and announce the latest location to the mobility manager. Mobility manager will then check the context and decide the corresponding component to migrate with the users to the new destination. To model this process, we simply let user send a message to the mobility manager through a channel, stating the user id and the destination information. Mobility manager will non-deterministically decide which part of the application in case of multiple options available.

As aforementioned, we can reuse the *set* extension to model the notion of *component* as in Listing 1.2. In applications, specific component can inherit (or *extend* in terms of Bogor) this general construct.

Listing 1.2. BIR extension example for resource management modeling

```
1        record  component{
2             string  ownership;
3             int  userId;
4             string  locId;
5             boolean  movable;
6             Set.type<string> dependencies;
7             Set.type<string> rscReq;
8        }
```

We use the extension of channel in Bogor to model the notification of mobility event. Since Bogor's extension facility provides an open-ended mechanism for adding any number of domain-specific abstractions, the properties are usually only concerned with a channel's abstract states. Therefore, the extension allow us to hide the implementation-level states and not to be exposed in the model state space. After receive the event, the manager will update the corresponding component information. Since component has a set of dependencies and resource requirements, if the destination environment fails to satisfy such requirements, the manager will not initiate migration activity.

Listing 1.3 illustrates the mobility manager extension. Line 1 defines the name of the extension (i.e., *MobiManager*), together with the implementation semantics (i.e., *myPackage.MobiManagerModule.java*). Line 2 defines a generic non-primitive type parameterized by *¿'a¿*. Line 4-6 defines two expressions. The first one is a create expression, which takes the set of possible locations and application components as the arguments and returns an instance of the mobility manager. The second one is the channel instantiation expression, by which an instance of the communication with the mobility manager can be derived. Since both of these two expressions have no side effect and have no impact on the state space, we define them as expressions. The case is similar in Line 8, in which a guard expression is defined to return a Boolean value based on the mobility request message sent through the channel. Line 7 and 9 define two actions, i.e., *notify* and *move*. The former action mimics the sensor's detection of mobility event and report to the mobility manager, while the latter one mimics the scheduling decision of the manager based on the received message. Obviously these two behaviors are relevant with the model's state space, therefore we define them as actions. In the semantic implementation part, both expression and action definitions need to be materialized in the form of class member functions.

Listing 1.3. Mobility manager extension constructs

```
1   extension MobiManager for myPackage.MobiManagerModule{
2       typedef type<'a>;
3
4       expdef MobiManager.type<'a> create<'a>(set.type<Location>,
5                                   set.type<component>);
6       expdef channel<'a> getChannel(MobiManager.type<'a>);
7       actiondef notify<'a>(channel<'a>, 'a);
8       expdef boolean guard<'a>(MobileManager.type<'a>, 'a);
9       actiondef move<'a>(MobieManager.type<'a>, Location);
10  }
```

4   Case Study

In this section, we use a scenario to illustrate the aforementioned approach and present our preliminary performance evaluation. The example is taken from a popular follow-me like application category widely studied in pervasive environments [8].

A MVC pattern compliant application consists of three essential components, i.e., UI (view), Database (Model), and Logic (controller). Database is bounded with a static container and not movable. UI can migrate with users to provide seamless service. But UI component needs some resources and has some library

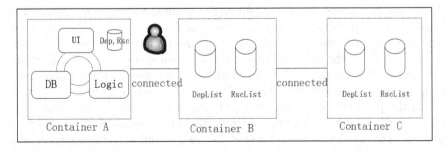

Fig. 1. Scenario illustration

dependencies which are assumed to be provided by the host container. Logic is also movable, but the host container should provide authentication module to guarantee the data access security.

As an initial configuration, we set up three distributed containers with different resource allocations as described by Figure 1. User is free to move across containers. The latest location can be notified to the mobility manager via a message channel. The application firstly run in Container A. Except that the DB component is fixed, the other two are free to move based on the user's location, but each has a separate requirement list of resources and dependencies for the host container.

Based on the above statements, we model the system using the previously defined extensions and data structures. Listing 1.4 gives an excerpt of the model.

Listing 1.4. Example modelling excerpt

```
1    //define the application component instances, three locations,
2    //messages and their member values;
3    Component UI, Logic, DB;
4    record Message{string userId; string locName;}
5    record Location {string locId; set.type<string> depList;
6                     set.type<string> rscList;}
7    Location containerA, containerB, containerC;
8    ...
9
10   set.type<componet> application := set.create<component>(UI,Logic,DB);
11   set.type<Location> containers :=
12      set.create<Location>(containerA, containerB, containerC);
13   //define active user thread;
14   active thread process(){
15     MobiManager.type<Message> mgr;
16     Channel.type<Message> chan;
17     Message msg;
18     loc loc0:
19       do{  mgr := MobiManager.create<Message>(application, containers);
20            chan := MobiManager.getChannel<Message>(mgr);   }goto loc1;
21     loc loc1:
22       do{  msg := {"user", "containerB"};
23            MobiManager.notify(chan, msg);   }goto loc2;
24     loc loc2:
25       when MobiManager.guard(mgr, msg) do{
26          MobiManager.move(mgr, containerB);
27       }return;
28   }
29   ...
```

Based on the model, we can conduct fine-grained verifications besides the normal deadlock detection, assertion violations. For example, one of the interested properties we want to verify is, given the design, whether it is always true that wherever the user goes, the UI component will eventually migrate to the corresponding container. We use R to predicate user's location container, and Q to denote the predicate that UI migrates to user's container. Written in LTL, the property is the following P_1: $\Box(Q \vdash \Diamond R)$. We use the above two property verification to evaluate the performance of our approach compared with general-purpose model checkers. Specifically, we use Spin as the comparison, and translate the model to its input language *promela*. To scale up, we use the number of containers as the parameter. The experiment is conducted on a PC with

Table 1. Performance comparison of our approach with Spin based approach (In the bracket, left is the result of our approach, and right is of Spin-based approach. NA denotes Not Available, OM denotes Out of Memory.)

(Parameter)	States	Memory(MB)	Time(sec)
3	(216, 329)	(23, 65)	(2.1, 1.3)
4	(438, 752)	(39, 127)	(3.2, 4.8)
6	(1025, 3162)	(46, 638)	(16.7, 103)
10	(20438, NA)	(125, OM)	(153.2, NA)

an Intel i5-2.5GHz CPU with 4GB RAM running Windows XP. The comparison is summarized in Table 1.

The comparison result above demonstrates the customized approach leveraging on domain knowledge can significantly reduce the state space and thus enhance the verification efficiency. We can also verify other properties, for example whether it is always true DB component will not migrate to other containers. Written in LTL, the property P_2 is: $\Box DBatContainerA$. But for space limitations, the performance evaluation is not included.

5 Related Work

Application mobility is an important topic in pervasive computing. Most of work investigate the problem from the perspective of enabling techniques, especially focusing on the context-aware mobility. Representative examples include [1,5,12]. In [1], authors proposed a decentralized supporting platform named "A2M" for application mobility. Based on the framework, an example application capable of moving between heterogeneous devices was implemented to provided a seamless video playing experience. In [5], an agent based mobile application framework which provides the opportunity for applications to better adapt their interface tot he new environment was proposed, in which agent functions similar to the mobility coordinator modeled in our paper. Xu et al. [12], proposed a task migration mechanism in the OSGi Framework named ScudOSGi which focues on context-driven migraiton and local facilities rebinding. All these approaches did not provide direct support for design-phase modeling and analysis.

In [2,3], Baresi et al. illustrates the applicability of graph transformation based modeling tools to analyze the service oriented systems. In order to exploit graphical notations, the model is first translated into a transition system based on which the verification is conducted. The translation process per se is non-trivial and error prone, since there are often cases that no exact equal constructs can be found in the source and target languages. Moreover, the work did not cover the application mobility domain. In [16], a graph transformation based modeling approach for modeling component migration was proposed. Global topology styles were modeled as attributed type graphs and speific application deployment structure as instance graphs. By leveraging third party tools, such as AGG [11], consistency checking can be automated. Although the approach provides some level of formal analysis, the tool itself lacks support for detailed property specification, thus insufficient to conduct fine-grained analysis. In [9], the authors proposed a translation based approach to verify layered graph transformation specification models. Generally left hand side of product rules are translated into the guards, and the right hand side of product rules are translated into the actions. The work alleviate the inability of popular graph modelling tools for verification, but again does not address the application migration domain.

6 Conclusions

In this paper, we presented a novel approach to verify fine-grained application mobility in pervasive environments. We studied the domain-specific concerns and embed them into the highly customizable model checker Bogor. These concerns become the first class primitives to construct the models during design phase. Developers can not only conduct general validation activities, e.g., deadlock-free, but also other fine-grained properties specified by LTL. To the best of our knowledge, this is the first work to leverage domain specific knowledge to verify design artifacts of mobile applications. The preliminary performance result demonstrates the feasibility of our approach.

For the current work, we made strong assumptions over the low-level hardware architectures and cross organizational boundaries. In the future, we would like to embed the guarantees from the middleware layer and integrated into our approach, we also plan to incorporate some process scheduling models used by the application servers and complement our verification framework with extensions to provide direct modeling support.

Acknowledgments. The work was partially funded by the Chinese Fundamental Research Funds for the Central Universities under grant No.NS2012135, No.NZ2013306, the NSF of China under grant No.61202002, No.61100039, Natural Science Foundation of Jiangsu Province (No. BK20131277), and Key Lab. of Intelligent Perception and Systems for High-Dimensional Information No.309201 30122005.

References

1. Åhlund, A., Mitra, K., Johansson, D., Åhlund, C., Zaslavsky, A.: Context-aware application mobility support in pervasive computing environments. In: Proceedings of the 6th International Conference on Mobile Technology, Application & Systems, p. 21. ACM (2009)
2. Baresi, L., Heckel, R., Thöne, S., Varró, D.: Modeling and validation of service-oriented architectures: application vs. style. In: ACM SIGSOFT Software Engineering Notes, vol. 28, pp. 68–77. ACM (2003)
3. Baresi, L., Heckel, R., Thöne, S., et al.: Style-based modeling and refinement of service-oriented architectures. Software & Systems Modeling 5(2), 187–207 (2006)

4. Curry, E., Grace, P.: Flexible self-management using the model-view-controller pattern. IEEE Software 25(3), 84–90 (2008)
5. David, F.M., Donkervoet, B., Carlyle, J.C., Chan, E.M., Campbell, R.H.: Supporting adaptive application mobility. In: Meersman, R., Tari, Z. (eds.) OTM-WS 2007, Part II. LNCS, vol. 4806, pp. 896–905. Springer, Heidelberg (2007)
6. Dwyer, M.B., Hatcliff, J., et al.: Bogor: an extensible and highly-modular software model checking framework. In: ACM SIGSOFT Software Engineering Notes, vol. 28, pp. 267–276. ACM (2003)
7. Holzmann, G.J.: The model checker spin. IEEE Transactions on Software Engineering 23(5), 279–295 (1997)
8. Li, J., Bu, Y., Chen, S., Tao, X., Lu, J.: Followme: on research of pluggable infrastructure for context-awareness. In: 20th International Conference on Advanced Information Networking and Applications, AINA 2006, vol. 1, IEEE (2006)
9. Rafe, V., Rahmani, A.T., Baresi, L., Spoletini, P.: Towards automated verification of layered graph transformation specifications. IET Software 3(4), 276–291 (2009)
10. Ranganathan, A., Chetan, S., Campbell, R.: Mobile polymorphic applications in ubiquitous computing environments. In: The First Annual International Conference on Mobile and Ubiquitous Systems: Networking and Services, MOBIQUITOUS 2004, pp. 402–411. IEEE (2004)
11. Taentzer, G.: Agg: A graph transformation environment for modeling and validation of software. In: Pfaltz, J.L., Nagl, M., Böhlen, B. (eds.) AGTIVE 2003. LNCS, vol. 3062, pp. 446–453. Springer, Heidelberg (2004)
12. Xu, Y., Li, S., Pan, G.: Scudosgi: enabling facility-involved task migration in osgi framework. In: Fourth International Conference on Frontier of Computer Science and Technology, FCST 2009, pp. 125–131. IEEE (2009)
13. Yu, P., Cao, J., Wen, W., Lu, J.: Mobile agent enabled application mobility for pervasive computing. In: Ma, J., Jin, H., Yang, L.T., Tsai, J.J.-P. (eds.) UIC 2006. LNCS, vol. 4159, pp. 648–657. Springer, Heidelberg (2006)
14. Yu, P., Ma, X., Cao, J., Lu, J.: Application mobility in pervasive computing: A survey. Pervasive and Mobile Computing (2012)
15. Zhou, Y., Cao, J., Raychoudhury, V., Siebert, J., Lu, J.: A middleware support for agent-based application mobility in pervasive environments. In: 27th International Conference on Distributed Computing Systems Workshops, ICDCSW 2007, p. 9. IEEE (2007)
16. Zhou, Y., Yan, X., Huang, Z.: A graph transformation based approach for modeling component-level migration in mobile environments. In: 2012 IEEE 36th Annual Computer Software and Applications Conference Workshops (COMPSACW), pp. 152–157. IEEE (2012)

Matrix Factorization for User Behavior Analysis of Location-Based Social Network

Xiang Tao, Yongli Wang, and Gongxuan Zhang

School of Computer Science and Technology,
Nanjing University of Science and Technology, Nanjing 210094, China
taoxiangxiang610@gmail.com, {yongliwang,gongxuan}@njust.edu.cn

Abstract. The online social network services have been growing rapidly over the past few years, and allows user to share location information by the GPS enabled mobile device. The information about the location can reflect social characteristic and record behaviors tracks of users. For location information has an impact on user behavior analysis of location-based social network, this paper proposed a new matrix factorization for user behavior analysis in location-based social network. The matrix model is based on the information of the user and location. Considering that large data sets and the problem of matrix sparsity would significantly increase the time and space complexity, matrix factorization was introduced to alleviate the effect of data problems, combining with the key information about the user in a social network. In order to evaluate the proposed method, we crawl live data from the Foursquare social network. The experimental results show that the proposed method is effective in solving the problem of matrix sparsity which has large data sets, and improving the accuracy of user behavior analysis.

Keywords: Matrix factorization, Location based service, Social network, Behavior analysis.

1   Introduction

Nowadays, with the development of Web 2.0 technologies, online social network services, such as Facebook, Foursquare, Renren, Micro-channel and so on, have had its own space in the Internet market rapidly. The user can create personal information, share pictures and videos, exchange feelings and experience with others in social network by using smart phones and other network approach. Recent research [1] shows that the number of visitors of social network has reached 25% of Internet traffic and 2/3 users of worldwide web are using social network. Besides, GPS has bought new opportunity for online social network services. Users can locate their positions by smart phones and other network which with GPS.

Location-based Social Network integrates the mobile Internet and social network services. It supports users to record freely, share location and any other information at any time. Users can update their locations synchronously through social network services when location information changes, and thus strengthen contact with their

Z. Huang et al. (Eds.): WISE 2013 Workshops 2013, LNCS 8182, pp. 84–97, 2014.

friends conveniently. Using social network services, users often hope that the system can recommend some friends who have the same hobbies or recommend some places they are interested around them. However, social network in China and foreign countries seldom involves these services. In order to realize these recommended services, they have to analyze user behavior in real location so that they can know the hobbies, social attributes and so on by users. As a result, the analysis of user behavior plays a key role in realizing these recommended services.

This thesis is based on matrix factorization to analyze user behavior of Location-based Social Network. Combining real information with virtual social network information of users is to promote the quality of recommended services. The meaning of this thesis is as follows: first, establish matrix model according to the user and location, and analyze real behaviors of users by using the algorithm of matrix factorization. Second, propose that combine real behavior with virtual social network, analyze the similarity of behaviors between users simultaneously, recommend some users who are similar to present users and places they are interested to present users.

The rest of this paper is organized as follows. Section 2 introduces some relative work. Section 3 gives the relative definition and model. Section 4 describes the similarity analysis algorithm of location-based social network services. Section 5 demonstrates the effectiveness of our approach by carrying out experiments on a data set. And section 6 concludes this paper.

2   Related Work

Many contributions, which focus on analyzing user behavior, have been made recently. Guy et al. [2] figured out a kind of analysis method which based on variety of aggregate information between users, but the first thing is that the users have known each other already, consequently, it doesn't adapt to finding new friends in social network. Terveen et al. [3] worked out a kind of framework of social matching, aimed at analyzing the level of matching between users according to their location.

Nisgav et al. [4] proposed that they could calculate users' similarity by using user query category. However, the query category didn't get used widely for Location-based Social Network mainly depends on smart phone. Besides, they didn't consider the location information.

With the continuous development of GPS and WI-Fi, the social network can provide specific location information of users and analyze the users' behavioral trajectory through GPS log. Chen et al. [5] figured out a raw-GPS route tracking method and used GPS route for semantic analysis. Krumm et al. [6] forecasted user's destination in one journey by analyzing statistics of GPS. And a kind of extended sequential patterns was proposed by Gonotti et al. [7] to analyze movement locus. Literature [8] said to identify User Associations according to access tracks of users. Literature [9] said to calculate similarity of user's behavioral trajectories through GPS log. First, figure out the location of the user access point and clustering these location points. Then, match the access sequence to calculate the similarity. Location services social networking sites, Foursquare, classify location statistics semantically. And study users' semantic similarity on location by using classified information of location was said in [10]. GPS log can track the users' behavioral trajectory continuously while location-based social networking cannot. The reason is that only users reach the specific location can they check in and the information could be some arbitrariness.

These analysis methods haven't combined existing user information on an online social network with real user location information. These two parts of information are both indispensable and play very important roles in analyzing the similarity of user behavior. Considering present situation, this thesis combines virtual network with real society of users to analyze user behavior, to get further information about the similarity between user behaviors and to recommend according to historical behavior and user behavior similarity of users.

3   Model and Definition

Currently, online social network is prevailing. A lot of users send their location information by registration and fill their basic information, such as Age, Sex, and publish content, make comments on others' content in social website. You can abstract key words for this kind of information. This chapter analyzes location-based user similarity through establishing social network model at first. Then it analyzes social-network-based user similarity. Last, combine real information and virtual social network information about users and promote the quality of recommended services.

3.1   Location-Based Social Network Services Model

When a user is in location-based social network and reaches a certain geographic position in the real world, he can make registration in social website by using mobile phone and some other devices.

Definition 1. Registration Tuple: sign once containing the information of users, locations and the time of user access locations. It can be expressed by Triples< UserId, LocationId,Time >.

Definition 2. Access Matrix: establish matrix R according to the times that user collection visit location collection. Each row in the matrix represents a user and each column represents a position. Each value r_{ij} in the matrix is defined as the times of the user i visited position j. That is to say, the more value of r_{ij} is, the more times the visit is, the more interests user has. On the contrary, the less value of r_{ij} is, the less interests user has.

$$
R_{(n\times m)} = \begin{bmatrix}
r_{11} & r_{12} & \cdots & r_{1j} & \cdots & r_{1m} \\
r_{21} & r_{22} & \cdots & r_{2j} & \cdots & r_{2m} \\
\cdots & \cdots & \cdot & & & \cdots \\
r_{i1} & r_{i2} & \cdots & r_{ij} & \cdots & r_{im} \\
\cdots & \cdots & & \cdot & & \cdots \\
r_{n1} & r_{n2} & \cdots & r_{nj} & \cdots & r_{nm}
\end{bmatrix}
$$

Among these, letter i is the number of users and letter j is the number of positions, and each value r_{ij} in the matrix is defined as the times of user i visits position j.

You should decompose the matrix in order to analyze the feature information of user and location. SVD is a common way of matrix factorization. It decomposes a matrix R, which is $n\times m$, into three matrices. Among the formula R=U×S×V, U is an orthogonal matrix in $n\times n$; the V is an orthogonal matrix in m×m; S is a diagonal matrix in n×m. Elements on the diagonal is in descending order from top to bottom, that is to say, $S = diag(\sigma_1, \sigma_2, ..., \sigma_m)$ and it must be under the circumstance of $\sigma_1 \geq \sigma_2 \geq ... \geq \sigma_m \geq 0$, elements which are not on the diagonal are all be 0, and all σ_m are in descending order, called singular value. Retain k largest singular value and get a new diagonal matrix S_k, accordingly, dimensions of U,S,V changes into $n\times k$, $k\times k$, $k\times m$, then get a similarity matrix $R_k = U_k \times S_k \times V_k$, $R_k \approx R$ of original matrix R. The value of k in this method is not easy to select: if k is small, it will be easy to lose important information and structures of original data; if big, it can't reach the lower dimension and easy to over-fitting the training data.

What is different from the traditional method SVD is that this method looks for a low-rank matrix X to approximate the original matrix R. And $X = P \times Q^T$, users characteristic matrix $P \in C^{n\times f}$, position characteristic matrix $Q \in C^{m\times f}$, f means number of features, generally speaking, f<<r, r is the rank of the original matrix R, and $r \leq \min(n, m)$.

Definition 3. Location Eigenvector: vector in the number l line of matrix Q means eigenvector of position l. It expressed by q_l to measure the extent of these characteristics the position l possesses. Value in the vector can be positive or negative.

Definition 4. Users Eigenvector: vector in the number u line of matrix P means eigenvector of user u. It expressed by p_u to measure the degree of likeness of user u for the position corresponding feature.

Definition 5. Estimated Interest Value: you can figure out estimated interest value of user u for position l by the inner product of p_u and q_l, $\hat{r}_{ul} = q_l^T p_u$.

3.2   User Similarity Analysis of Location Services

According to access matrix of user-location, eigenvector of all the users and locations can be got by using decomposition method. Dimension of q_l is f, each dimension value of q_l measures extent of each characteristic the position l possesses. Dimension of p_u is f, each dimension value of p_u measures the degree of likeness of user u for position corresponding feature. For example, a and b are different users, their eigenvectors are p_a and p_b, and dimensions are both f. Each dimension means different likeness of users, a and b, refer to corresponding position characteristic.

Definition 6. Location-based User Similarity: there are two different users, a and b, calculate similarity of dimensional space f by using method cosine similarity. Calculation of the following formula:

$$simbl(a,b) = \cos(p_a, p_b) = \frac{p_a \cdot p_b}{\|p_a\| * \|p_b\|}$$

3.3   User Similarity Analysis of Online Social Network Services

Definition 7. Users Keyword Information Set: abstract related keyword information according to information in virtual social network and describe the characteristics of the information. A collection of these keywords is called users keyword information set. This set is denoted as $U = \{ch_1, ch_2, ch_3, ..., ch_n \mid n \in N\}$, and ch_i is keyword of number i.

Keyword information set of any user a can be expressed by the following formula $U_a = \{ch_i, ch_j, ..., ch_m \mid 1 \leq i < j < m \leq n\} \subset U$.

Different keyword information can be discretized by different approaches. (1) For basic social network of users', like sex and age, zero represents male and one female, zero means age from zero to ten, one means age from eleven to twenty and so on, which ten years is a section. (2) For content in social network which is made by users or reviewed by others, filter this information and select keyword. One means users hold this keyword and zero means not. Lastly, statistics all critical information and get users' keyword information set. For instance, users' keyword information set is made up of basic information and content information. Basic information includes sex, age and major and content information includes going travelling, excising, watching movie, reading books, going shopping and eating food. U represents users' keyword information set. If {male, 23, computer, going travelling, watching movie, reading books.} is keyword information set of use a, it can be considered as multidimensional space and be expressed by vector $(0,2,1,1,0,1,1,0,0)$, each value in the vector corresponds to each element in the set U.

Definition 8. Users Keyword Vector: discrete users' keyword information and mapped to multidimensional space, and then get vector, that's the Users Keyword Vector.

Definition 9. Users Keyword Information Similarity: similarity of any vector $a(a_1, a_2, ..., a_n)$ and $b(b_1, b_2, ..., b_n)$ in n-dimensional space can be got by calculating Euclidean distance between corresponding points. That is to say,

$$simbn(a,b) = 1 - \frac{\sqrt{(a_1 - b_1)^2 + (a_2 - b_2)^2 + ... + (a_n - b_n)^2}}{Dis_{max}}$$

, and Dis_{max} is the maximum distance that any two users can produce. The greater the distance is, the smaller the similarity is; on the contrary, the smaller the distance is, the greater the similarity is.

3.4   Users Similarity Analysis of Location-Based Social Network Services

Location service and social network are two different kinds of aspects which are abstracted from characteristics of users. Ways to measure and calculate these characteristics are different. Two kinds of consolidation methods need a normalization process in order to combine two different measurement methods. For any two users a and b, the value of $simbl(a,b)$ and $simbn(a,b)$ are in the interval [0, 1]. The definition, $sim(a,b) = t \times simbl(a,b) + (1-t) \times simbn(a,b)$ and $0 \leq t \leq 1$, is to describe the similarity between a and b. It reflects the likeness of users for the location attribute of reality, simultaneously; it reflects keyword information of users in virtual social network. At last, recommend resources according to similarity of users' preference. Identify the previous k most similar users and recommend them and their locations to the current user.

4   Users Similarity Algorithm of Location-Based Services Social Network

What we can know from the previous chapter is that we have to find a low-rank matrix X to approach to the original matrix R as much as possible if we want to decompose access matrix R.

Theorem 1. User feature matrix P multiplied by position feature matrix Q is low-rank matrix X, and it can approach to the original matrix R as much as possible.

Proof: you need to minimize the following loss function for approaching.

$$L(x) = \sum_{ul} (r_{ul} - x_{ul})^2 \tag{1}$$

Formula (1) can be changed into the formula (2) according to user eigenvector and location eigenvector.

$$L(q,p) = \sum_{ul} (r_{ul} - q_l^T p_u)^2 \qquad (2)$$

Formula (2) should be adding the regularization term in order to prevent small date from appearing over fitting, and then you can get formula (3).

$$L(q,p) = \sum_{ul} (r_{ul} - q_l^T p_u)^2 + \lambda(\| q_l \|^2 + \| p_u \|^2) \qquad (3)$$

λ is a regularization parameter. Minimize formula (3) by adopting a stochastic gradient descent method and figure out partial derivatives of p_u and q_l respectively. Then you'll get

$$p_u \leftarrow p_u + \gamma(e_{ul} \cdot q_l - \lambda \cdot p_u),$$
$$q_l \leftarrow q_l + \gamma(e_{ul} \cdot p_u - \lambda \cdot q_l) \qquad (4)$$

λ is a regularization parameter; γ is the step gradient descent. The error can be figured out by using formulas. You can obtain eigenvectors, and get matrix X through updating constantly.

Algorithm steps are as follows: first, initialize all vectors p_u, q_l and assign f-dimensional vectors p_u and q_l at random. For any known access record r_{ul} of the training set, calculate $\hat{r}_{ul} = q_l^T p_u$, and you'll get $e_{ul} = r_{ul} - \hat{r}_{ul}$. Then update each dimension on the basis of a formula (4) until figure out root-mean-square error ($RMSE$: $\sqrt{\sum_{(u,l) \in TestSet} (r_{ul} - q_l^T p_u)^2 / |TestSet|}$) convergence or enough iterations and end iteration.

Algorithm 1. MFBOL (*Matrix Factorization Based On Location*)
Input: access matrix R,   number of features f
Output: user eigenvector, location eigenvector

Description of the algorithm
1: Initialize   pu ,ql   = Random (-0.01,0.01)
2: for   count = 1,..., k   do
3:      for   u = 1,...,n   do
4:          for   all   l ∈ S(u) do
5:              $\hat{r}_{ul} = q_l^T p_u$
6:              $e_{ul} = r_{ul} - \hat{r}_{ul}$
7:          for   i = 0,1,...f-1   do
8:              $p_{ui} \leftarrow p_{ui} + \gamma(e_{ul} \cdot q_{li} - \lambda \cdot p_{ui})$
9:              $q_{li} \leftarrow q_{li} + \gamma(e_{ul} \cdot p_{ui} - \lambda \cdot q_{li})$
10: return

Algorithm 2. QUS (Query User Similarity)
Input: inquiry two users a and b
Output: the similarity between a and b

Description of the algorithm
1: *Initialize* $a(a_1, a_2, a_3, ..., a_n)$, $b(b_1, b_2, b_3, ..., b_n)$

2: $simbn(a,b) = 1 - \dfrac{\sqrt{(a_1-b_1)^2 + (a_2-b_2)^2 + ... + (a_n-b_n)^2}}{Dis_{max}}$

3: $simbl(a,b) = \cos(p_a, p_b) = \dfrac{p_a \cdot p_b}{\|p_a\| * \|p_b\|}$

4: $sim(a,b) = t \times simbl(a,b) + (1-t) \times simbn(a,b)$

5: *return*

Analysis of Algorithm Complexity

(1) Algorithm of MFBOL: since the access matrix is a very big and sparse matrix model, supposing that the number of users is n, the number of positions is *m* and the number of access record is e in access matrix. Adjacency table storage can be adopted because of e<<n*m. It can save space and accelerate the traverse speed. The complexity of the initialization vector in the first line is O(f * (n + m)) and the complexity of all access records from the third to sixth line traverse again is O(n + e). And k-times loop iteration and updating of f-dimensional vectors make the complexity of process from the third to ninth line be O(k * f * (n + e)).

In summary, the complexity of algorithm of MFBOL is O(f * (n + m) + k * f * (n + e)).

(2) Algorithm of QUS : when inquire similarity between any two users, keyword information set and the complexity of processing eigenvector are both O(1), obviously, the complexity of algorithm of QUS is O(1).

5   Experimental Results and Analysis

5.1   Experimental Environment and Datasets

In this paper, experiment analyzes the effectiveness of user similarity calculation to testify the quality of recommending the service. The experimental environment of this paper is as follows:

Table 1. Experimental environment

Operating System	Ubuntu 10.04
Kernel Version	2.6.32-33
CPU	Intel(R) Xeon(R) CPU E5620 2.40GHz
Memory	12GB
Hard Disk	250GB
NIC	Intel(R) PRO/1000MT
Development of Language	Java 1.6,Python 2.7
Development Tools	Vim7.2,Eclipse3.3.2

5.2   Experimental Performance Analysis

Seven hundred users who sign frequently are selected in this experiment to calculate user similarity for most users in social network website are not active. Find out the most similar user for each user on the basis of the similarity between two of them. Jaccard coefficient is a popular method of computing user similarity and analyzing two users' overlap on common attributes. It is a ratio of the intersection's and the union's elements' number on two users' attributes. Compare precision of method Jaccard with the method mentioned in this paper by calculating the basic indicators of information retrieval system, like precision, recall and F-measure. The location $Top\text{-}K$ is selected when calculate.

Among the formula $Precision = \dfrac{\left| f(u) \cap f(u_r) \right|}{\left| f(u_r) \right|}$, $f(u)$ is number of species of

user u in location $Top\text{-}K$; u_r is the most similar user of user u. This formula means the ratio of user u and u_r intersection number of species occupy the u_r's location Top-K of number of species;

$Recall = \dfrac{\left| f(u) \cap f(u_r) \right|}{\left| f(u) \right|}$, this formula means ratio of user u and u_r intersection

number of species occupies the u's location Top-K of number of species;

$F\text{-}measure = \dfrac{2 * Precision * Recall}{Precision + Recall}$, F-Measure is the weighted harmonic

mean of Precision and Recall

   Experiment 1: in algorithm of MFBOL, selection of number of features f is very important. This paper chooses $f=30$, $f=50$, $f=100$, $f=200$ respectively, and adapts RMSE as metrics. Parameter $\gamma = 0.003, \lambda = 0.04$. The results shown in Figure 1: with the addition of f, the value of RMSE becomes smaller, however, the consumption of time and space increase at the same time.

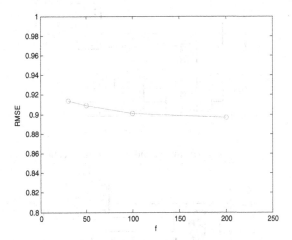

Fig. 1. The number of feature affects on RMSE

Experiment 2: we can know that a better experimental result can be got when $f=50$. And later experiments can all adapt $f=50, \gamma = 0.003, \lambda = 0.04$. Experiment 2 is focused on uncertainty of t in formula $sim(a,b) = t \times simbl(a,b) + (1-t) \times simbn(a,b)$. Calculate Precision, Recall and F-measure of 700 users' *Top-10* respectively according to the value of t. And then take the average of them, and the results are shown in Figure 2.

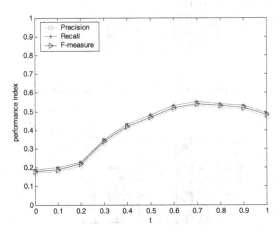

Fig. 2. The performance index of different t at Top-10 locations

Experimental result shows that the value of Precision, Recall and F-measure are the optimal when t is about 0.7. Clearly, location information in reality and key information in virtual social network are both fundamental to similarity analysis.

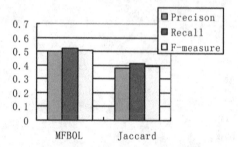

(a) The performance index of Top-5 locations

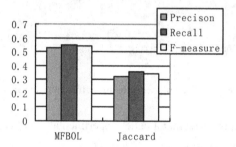

(b) The performance index of Top-10 locations

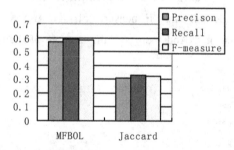

(c) The performance index of Top-20 locations

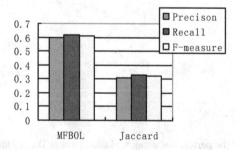

(d) The performance index of Top-30 locations

Fig. 3. The performance index of different Top-K locations

Experiment 3: the value of t is 0.7 in fixed similarity calculation. Calculate Precision, Recall and F-measure of 700 users' *Top-10* respectively according to the value of *Top-K*, take the average of them and the results are shown in Figure 3.

Experiment 4: experiment 3 only uses location *Top-K* to calculate the similarity between users. Experiment 4 tells that use *Top-K* superior to using all access location. In order to indicate users visit *Top-K* occupying the most users' access record, TopKCover(k) can be defined to express the ratio of accessing *Top-K*. Among the

$$
formula\, TopKCover(k) = \frac{\sum_{u \in U} \frac{TopK(u)}{Total(u)}}{|U|}
$$
, U is user-selected collection, TopK(u)

is the times of user u visiting location Top-K and Total(u) is the number of visit of user u.

Figure 4: the coverage of users Top-5 was 34%, users Top-10 46% and users Top-20 55%.

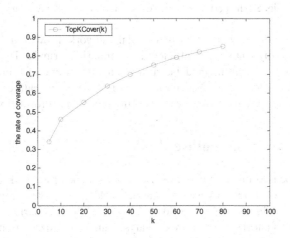

Fig. 4. The rate of coverage of use's Top-K locations

Figure 5: three measurement methods begin to decline after location *Top-50*. The results show that use of Top-K is better than using all access records.

5.3   Experimental Results

The above experimental analysis shows that this thesis provides a more accurate method to calculate similarities between users. It doesn't only take advantage of the conditions of users' access location information in reality, but key information of users in virtual social network. Access conditions of users in reality are focused on in previous studies; as a result, some other information of users is omitted. In order to

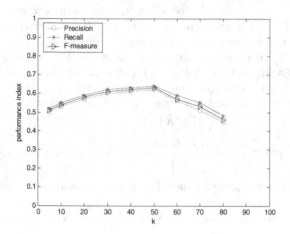

Fig. 5. The performance index at different Top-K locations

testify that key information on virtual social network is also important to user similarity analysis by changing coefficient t in similarity formula. The method in this thesis is more precise than method Jaccard. Change the value of k in *Top-K* and get *Top-K* main access locations. And it can completely reflect features of user access location and achieve the performance of ignoring secondary information.

6   Conclusions and Future Work

This thesis is focused on studying similarity between social network users according to characteristic of location-based social network services and proposes a study method which combines virtual world and reality. User similarity is measured by means of matrix factorization, discrete analysis and normalized. Experiments show that the model and algorithm which proposed in this thesis are applicable to users' similarity analysis in location services social network. The future research work is mainly focused on how to update the access matrix, eigenvectors and get more critical information of users.

Acknowledgement. The authors wish to thank the reviewers for their valuable comments and suggestions. This work is supported in part by National Natural Science Foundation (No.61272420), Jiangsu Province Natural Science Foundation of major projects (BK2011022), Natural Science Foundation of Jiangsu Province (BK2011702), the Fundamental Research Funds for the Central Universities (No.30920130112006), Jiangsu Province Blue Project Innovation team, Nanjing science and technology project (No.020142010), Nanjing University of Science and Technology in 2009 Zijin Star project funding.

References

1. Benevenuto, F., Rodrigues, T., Cha, M., et al.: Characterizing user behavior in online social networks. In: Proceedings of the 9th ACM SIGCOMM Conference on Internet Measurement, pp. 49–62. ACM, New York (2009)
2. Guy, I., Ronen, I., Wilcox, E.: Do you know?: recommending people to invite into your social network. In: International Conference on Intelligent User Interfaces, pp. 77–86 (2009)
3. Terveen, L.G., McDonald, D.W.: Social matching: A framework and research agenda. ACM Trans. Comput. -Hum. Interact., 401–434 (2005)
4. Nisgav, A., Patt-Shamir, B.: Finding similar users in social networks: extended abstract. In: 21st Annual ACM Symposium on Parallel Algorithms and Architectures, pp. 169–177 (2009)
5. Chen, Y., Jiang, K., Zheng, Y., Li, C., Yu, N.: Trajectory simplification method for location-based social networking services. In: International Workshop on Location Based Social Networks, pp. 33–40 (2009)
6. Krumm, J., Horvitz, E.: Predestination: Inferring destinations from partial trajectories. In: 8th International Conference on Ubiquitous Computing, pp. 243–260 (2006)
7. Giannotti, F., Nanni, M., Pinelli, F., Pedreschi, D.: Trajectory pattern mining. In: 13th ACM SIGKDD International Conference on Knowledge Discovery and Data Mining, pp. 330–339 (2007)
8. Hung, C.-C., Chang, C.-W., Peng, W.-C.: Mining trajectory profiles for discovering user communities. In: Proceedings of the 2009 International Workshop on Location Based Social Networks, pp. 1–8. ACM, New York (2009)
9. Li, Q., Zheng, Y., Xie, X., et al.: Mining user similarity based on location history. In: Proceedings of the 16th ACM SIGSPATIAL International Conference on Advances in Geographic Information Systems, pp. 1–10. ACM, New York (2008)
10. Lee, M.-J., Chung, C.-W.: A user similarity calculation based on the location for social network services. In: Yu, J.X., Kim, M.H., Unland, R. (eds.) DASFAA 2011, Part 1. LNCS, vol. 6587, pp. 38–52. Springer, Heidelberg (2011)

Understanding User Behavior through URL Analysis in Sina Tweets

Youquan Wang[1], Haicheng Tao[1], Jie Cao[2,1,*], and Zhiang Wu[2]

[1] College of Computer Science and Engineering,
Nanjing University of Science and Technology, Nanjing, China
[2] Jiangsu Provincial Key Laboratory of E-Business,
Nanjing University of Finance and Economics, Nanjing, China
{youq.wang,haicheng.tao}@gmail.com, Jie.Cao@njue.edu.cn,
zawuster@gmail.com

Abstract. As the popularity of online social networks, the user behavior in cyber-world might probably become a mirror of the user in physical world. Therefore, understanding online user's behavior is an interesting yet challenging task. This paper aims to analyze URLs in Sina tweets, the largest Chinese Twitter, to facilitate the understanding of the user behavior. In particular, we first provide some statistics data to show the global behavior. Then, we take a close look to users who publish similar URLs frequently to track their abnormal behaviors. By observing the contents and publishing time of these users, we classify users with commercial purposes into several types, and thus showcase some interesting cases to validate our classification.

Keywords: Online Social Networks, Chinese Twitter, URL Analysis, User Behavior.

1 Introduction

Online Social Networks (OSNs) like Twitter, Flickr and YouTube have become extremely popular, and attracts much more attention [1, 2, 3]. Numerous of users on those OSNs platform are constantly emerging. Twitter, the world-wide most influential OSNs platform, has more than 500 million registered users. Sina Weibo, the Chinese largest OSNs platform, launched by blogging service provider Sina since August 2009. Through those OSNs platform, users can make friends with common interests, disseminate information, share pictures and videos, and many more [4]. However, lots of users might make use of OSNs to attain their specific purposes, among which a number of users indeed have commercial or even malicious intents. For example, some users often publish advertisements, and some users even diffuse links to phishing websites. Therefore, to analyze the contents published by users in order to understand their behaviors undoubtedly is an interesting yet challenging issue.

---

* Corresponding author.

Z. Huang et al. (Eds.): WISE 2013 Workshops 2013, LNCS 8182, pp. 98–108, 2014.

URL links contained in user contents are a special type of data [5]. Many users with commercial or even malicious purposes depend on these URL links. For instance, user contents with advertisement intent might probably contain URL of online shops, and user contents with phishing or malicious intents often contain mendacious URL linked to banks or URL for downloading or loading the malware. In this paper, we focus on analyzing URL links contained in user contents, and thus attempt to understand user behaviors. In particular, we provide some statistics data to show global behaviors, and then we take a close look to users who publish similar URLs frequently to track their abnormal behaviors. By observing the contents and publishing time of these users, we classify users with commercial and malicious purposes into several types, and thus showcase some interesting cases to validate our classification.

The remainder of this paper is organized as follows. In Section 2, We reviews the related work. In Section 3, we briefly introduce background knowledge about Sina Tweets and data pre-processing. In Section 4, Some statistical analysis on the content of URLs, and utilize the classification of URLs in tweets are conducted. Section 5 make some case studies on user behavior with commercial intents. We finally present conclude our work in Section Section 6.

2   Related Work

To date, a large number of studies on analyzing micro-bloging have been proposed. As one of the most popular OSNs, Twitter has gained the particular attention. Kwak et al. conducted a series of studies about the topological characteristics of Twitter and its power as a new medium of information sharing [6]. It is observed that the majority (over 85%) of topics are headline or persistent news in nature by classifying the trending topics based on the active period and the tweets. Zubiaga et al. provided an efficient way to immediately and accurately categorize trending topics without the assistance of external data [7]. They defined a typology to categorize the triggers that caused Twitter's trending topics happening: news, current events, memes, and commemorative. For the Chinese twitter, Yu et al. studied the key topics trending on Sina Weibo and compared them with the observations on Twitter [8]. They found a vast difference in the content shared between Sina Weibo and Twitter, for example: jokes, images and videos sharing and percentage of retweets. Chen et al. also have shown that the following preference of Sina Weibo users is more concentrated and hierarchical than Twitter [9].

Recently, more and more research efforts have been devoted to analyze URLs in tweets due to the special role of URLs in tweets. Antoniades et al. studied the contents to which short URLs pointed, including the following aspects: how they are published, their popularity and activity over time, as well as their potential impact on the performance of the web on Twitter, owly and bitly [10]. Rodrigues et al. analyzed URLs shared on Twitter to show that users who are geographically close to each other are more likely to share the same URL [11]. Moreover, the malicious URLs in Twitter, particularly including the phishing

URLs, have been attracted attention, and thus some detection methods beyond blacklists learning are proposed. Ma et al. used automated URL classification and statistical methods to discover the tell-tale lexical and host-based properties of malicious Web site URLs [12]. Chhabra et al. used the blacklisted phishing URLs from PhishTank, linked these URLs to bit.ly and analyzed phishing shortened URLs orig-inating from Twitter [13]. Cui et al. explored the features of the malicious URLs and propose to classify them into four spam categories [14] in on English (Twitter) and Chinese (Sina Weibo) messages. These studies indeed shade light in our work to investigate the user behavior reflected by URLs and the characteristic of users who often publish malicious URLs on Chinese Twitter.

3   Data Collection

Our data collection spans three months of Sina micro-blogging starting on 1st June and lasting until 1st September 2012. During this time we gathered over 19,760 users and 1,374,657 tweets or retweets, and over 153,781 URLs were issued by 14,446 users. Note that our data is collected by Sina public APIs, and thus only part of tweets/retweets rather than all of the data during three months can be collected.

3.1   Background on Sina Tweets

Sina Microblog (`http://weibo.com`), the biggest online Twitter in China, was released by the Sina corporation in August 2009. By the end of 2012, the number of registered users in Sina Microblog reached over 300 million, and over 1000 tweets were generated per minutes on average. A tweet is a colloquialism which is limited up to 140 characters. Although the tweet might contain text, pictures, videos and links, since the focal point of this paper is links, we omit other media types but only use text in tweets to validate our analysis. To facilitate the posting of URLs in these length-restricted tweets, URL shortening services are commonly used. All links posted in tweets are automatically converted to short URLs. A short URL contains around 20 characters to an arbitrary URL, and the redirection service in browser is invoked once a short URL is accessed.

A user profile on Sina Microblog is made up of the user's name, a brief description of the user, the list of the user's followers and followees. There are three types of user accounts on Sina Microblog: regular users, verified users, and expert (star) users [15]. A verified user typically represents a well known public figure or organization in China. Besides posting Tweets, there are other two commonly used methods to release messages. The first one is "retweeting" which means re-broadcasting some else's messages to one's followers. Another one is "comment" which cannot be rebroadcasted to the user's followers.

3.2   Data Pre-processing

Almost all of the Microblog systems have employed URL shortening services, which makes Internet users easy sharing web addresses by providing a short

equivalent one [12]. For example: a URL link `http://item.taobao.com/`
`item.htm?spm=686.1000925.1000774.71&id=16170479963` which is submitted
to Sina micro-blogging `t.cn` will return the following URL to the user:
`t.cn/zWNOO5y`, and `t.cn` has been used as Sina Weibo's official URL shortening
domain name since March 2011. It makes Internet users especially convenient for
various OSNs, such as Twitter and Sina Weibo, which severely limit the length
of characters that can be used in a posted message.

In order to identify user behavior behind short URLs, we collect short URLs
by matching the HTTP header "http://t.cn/" that were posted on Sina Weibo.
The short URL cannot provide us any semantic information for analysis. Hence
we need to resolve the short URLs to orininal URLs firstly. A tool called `S_to_L`
based on the PHP script was designed to resolve it by sending web requests to
target short URLs and recovering the domain of original URLs. The key technology behind `S_to_L` is the permanent redirection mechanism named "HTTP 301
Moved Permanently". We set the waiting time to be 60 seconds, which means if
there is no response during the waiting period, redirection fails and thus a null
URL is recorded.

4   Analysis on the Content of URLs

In this section, we conduct a statistical analysis on the content of URLs to show
the popular URLs and their categories. Moreover, by utilizing the classification
of a navigation site, URLs in tweets are automatically classified into several
types, which provides us some interesting observations.

4.1   Statistics on the Frequencies of URLs

In the experimental dataset, we have totally extracted 192,074 short URLs from
tweets, and finally obtain 153,781 long URLs by our `S_to_L` tool. We then aggregated different URLs of the same website, for example, URLs ended by `sina.com`,
`sina.cn`, and `weibo.com` were from Sina, and URLs ended with `taobao.com` and
`tmall.com` were from Taobao. By ranking the aggregated URLs, we obtain a list
of popular URLs in tweets, and the top-25 popular websites is tabulated in Table 1. As can be seen, tweets in Sina Microblog contain a large number of URLs
linked to itself, and Taobao is ranked second, since lots of online shop owners posted advertisements through the freely-used microblog system. We further
note that links of social websites take up a large percentage, especially video-
sharing social websites such as `Youku` and `Tudou`, since people enjoy to share
videos he/she felt interesting. Many all-around portals such as `qq`, `163`, and
`Sohu` also account for a large share.

Given links of Sina makes up over 40% of all URLs, we then take a close
look at the types of sub-domains in Sina. We manually classify the sub-domains
frequently appearing in Sina into 10 categories. For example, `blog.sina.com` and
`weibo.com` fall into the category of social media. Fig. 1 shows the statistic results
on the categories of Sina. We can see that social media holds the overwhelming

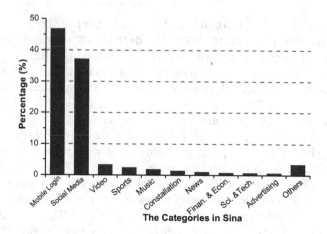

Fig. 1. The category of Sina website

Table 1. The top-25 popular URLs in Sina tweets

Rank	Name	#URL	Pct.	Description
1	sina( )	66629	43.33%	Comprehensive Portal
2	taobao( )	6283	4.09%	C2C E-commerce
3	youku( )	5991	3.9%	A Chinese Video Hosting Service Website
4	tudou( )	3229	2.1%	A Chinese Video Hosting Service Website
5	douban( )	2568	1.67%	A Chinese SNS Website
6	jiepang( )	2082	1.35%	A Chinese SNS Website for Mobile Devices
7	163( )	1880	1.22%	Comprehensive Portal
8	inewscrunch( )	1225	0.8%	News Comprehensive Portal
9	qq( )	1169	0.76%	Comprehensive Portal
10	ifeng( )	1138	0.74%	Comprehensive Portal
11	instagram	957	0.62%	An Online Photo-sharing Websites
12	sohu( )	923	0.62%	Comprehensive Portal
13	tuding001( )	895	0.58%	Video-sharing Website
14	xiami( )	887	0.58%	An online music-sharing Website
15	baidu( )	880	0.57%	Search Engine for Websites, Movies, and Images
16	meilishuo( )	707	0.46%	C2C E-commerce
17	renren( )	703	0.46%	Social Medial,The Facebook of China
18	yinyuetai( )	657	0.43%	A MV Sharing Website
19	changba( )	647	0.42%	Mobile Application of KTV Social Network
20	56.com(56)	640	0.42%	A Chinese Video Hosting Service Website
21	pomoho( )	615	0.4%	A Video Sharing Website
22	itunes	599	0.39%	A Media Player and Media Library App
23	weatherweibo( )	465	0.3%	Weather Social Network
24	dianping( )	374	0.24%	A City Life Consumption Guide Website
25	ku6( )	361	0.23%	A Chinese Video Hosting Service Website

quantity, and "Others" means subsidiaries of Sina and its sub-websites except ones mentioned before.

It is interesting to note that there are quite a lot of URLs about sports shown in Fig. 1, since London's 2012 Olympic Games was taking place during the time period of the data set. To illustrate this, we extracted the contents of tweets containing URLs on sports, and generated a tag cloud using words in these tweets, as shown in Fig. 2. Note that since the contents are composed of Chinese words, we translated them into English in Fig. 2. As we can see, "YangSun",

Fig. 2. A tag-cloud for sports category

"DanLin", "Gold", "Records" and "Medals" occurred frequently in the URLs about sports. Chinese weibo users mainly focused on the tags mentioned before because Yang Sun became the first Chinese man ever to win an Olympic gold medal in swimming and broke the world record in the 1500 metres freestyle and also Dan Lin became the first men's singles player to retain the Olympic gold medal by winning in 2008 and defending his title in 2012.

We then turn to observe URLs in Taobao and find that all URLs, without exception in the scale of our investigation, are ended by `item.taobao.com`, `detail.tmall.com`, and `shopXXX.taobao.com`. These URLs link to the description of commodities, online shops, and other advertising campaigns. This implies that the advertising behavior in tweets cannot be neglected.

4.2 The Categories of URLs

From the Section 4.1, we can get the URLs of which the number exceeds 100. To automatically classify the URLs into different categories, we mined the label of category and its URL list from the Web navigation of Baidu[1]. Then by aggregating sub-domains of the selected URLs, the statistics of the categories can be found in Fig. 3.

As shown in Fig. 3(a), Social Media was referenced more than four times Video's amount which is the second largest category. Also interestingly, SCi. & Tech. got more numbers than Finan. & Econ. from all URLs, but Comparing with the Sina's statistics in Fig. 1, it seems that Weibo users are more likely to read science and technique articles from other comprehensive portals such as 163 than Finance and Economic articles.

In Fig. 3(b), we can see that Taobao dominates the E-commerce part, because it is the largest C2C E-commerce company in China. Meanwhile, Meilishuo and

---

[1] http://site.baidu.com.cn/

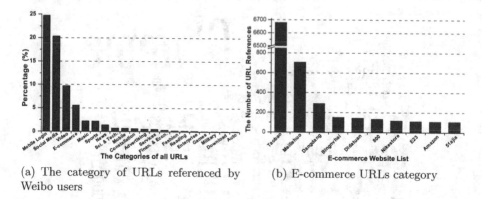

(a) The category of URLs referenced by Weibo users

(b) E-commerce URLs category

Fig. 3. The category of URLs referenced by Weibo users and E-commerce URLs category

Bingnvhai took a large proportion in the E-commerce website list, thus we can infer that female should be the largest group and the prime target of advertisements in the E-commerce Business.

5   Case Study on User Behavior with Commercial Intents

Sina Weibo announced cross-platform strategic partnership with Qihoo 360 in 2012, which provides intelligent malicious URLs detection methods for recognition of phishing and fraudulent websites[2]. Therefore, a large number of websites with phishing and malicious URLs have been filtered by 360. However, there are still a sea of users, i.e., online shop owners, frequently publishing advertisement URLs. This is largely due to the fact that publishing advertisements in Sina Weibo is free! Therefore, we here explore several case studies on users with commercial intents.

Based upon our observations and analysis, we have found two kinds of commercial users that are deserved to be noted, i.e., *Advertisers* and *Water Army*. The characteristics of two types of users are summarized in Table 2. The advertisers tend to post same URLs with same or very similar contents. By observing their posting time, we found a sub-class of advertisers can post their tweets in a very-short time span or even at the same time. So we infer this sub-class of advertisers are "Robots". Another sub-class of advertisers manually posted their advertisements in a random time span.

The water army is a special type of users in China, and it is often described as "*paid* users inspired by companies to post comments and articles in online communities with the agenda of influencing other users' opinions toward events, people or products [16]". Apart from paid posters, another type of water army named *reward* posters usually provide some opportunities such as traveling abroad or

---

[2] http://ir.360.cn/phoenix.zhtml?c=243376&p=irol-newsArticle&ID=1655823&highlight=

Table 2. The characteristics of users with commercial intents

User Category		Users	Contents	URLs	Time-span
Advertisers	Robots	same	same	same	short
	Manual Posters	similar/different	same/similar	same/similar	random
Water Army	Paid Posters	different	same/similar	same/similar	short
	Reward Posters	different	different or similar	same/similar	not very long

sending gifts to attract the attention of users. As can be seen from Table 2, though there might be big diversities in users, contents, and time-span, URLs will often be same or similar since the target of the water army is to popularize products/services of the same company.

5.1 Examples of Advertisers

We first give two examples of advertisers: *robots* and *manual posters*, respectively. Fig 4 shows an example of robots. In Fig 4, a verified user about Dawei tattoo of Nanjing in Sina Weibo is referred, and there are same contents about the address and the telephone of their company with same URLs at the same time. To make their tweets get more attentions, they just copy and paste existing posts to increase the total number of posts, which works like a robot doing the same thing over and over again.

Fig 5 shows the example of manual posters. These posters usually work for a online shop in C2C e-commerce website or a private enterprise with a entity shop. As we can see from Fig 5, a wedding photography studio is mentioned, and similar contents with same URL are posted. It is a clear indication of manual poster, which attempts to persuade potential customers to purchase or buy a product or service by posting tweets in Sina Weibo.

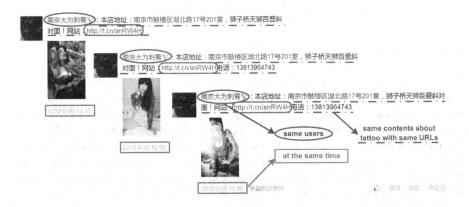

Fig. 4. An example of robot

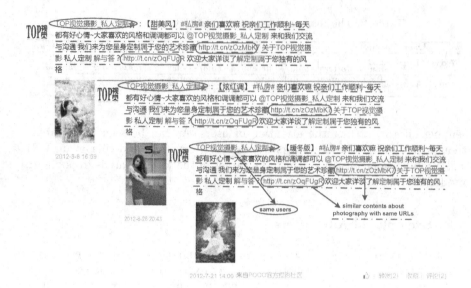

Fig. 5. An example of manual poster

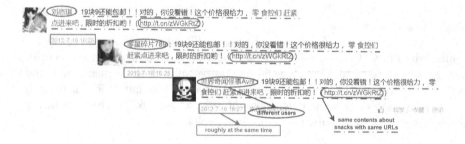

Fig. 6. An example of paid poster

5.2   Examples of the Water Army

Here, we also showcase two examples of water army, *paid posters* and *reward posters*, respectively. The major characteristic of a paid poster is that different users tweet same or similar contents with same URLs. Paid poster usually tweet same or similar contents with same URLs roughly at the same time. Fig 6 are typical paid posters hired by food company for sales promotion. In order to make their products more popular, the companies will hire hundreds of paid posters to tweet their products within a short period of time, and so the posting times of these tweets are very close to each other.

Reward advertising is a common business strategy, and we define Reward advertising which is used in OSNs platform as reward poster. As we can see in Fig 7, each advertisement about Haggen-Dazs claimed buying the product will win an opportunity for traveling abroad freely. The reward posters tweet different

Fig. 7. An example of reward poster

contents with same URLs. In this way, Haggen-Dazs company promotes their products with minimal cost.

6   Conclusion and Future Work

In this paper, we study user behaviors through URL analysis about Sina tweets. Some statistics about user global behavior are provided. To analyze the users who often post similar URLs, we classify users into two categories: advertisers and water army according to their commercial intents, and showcase some interesting cases. A robustness method for detecting advertisers and water army would be finished in our future work.

Acknowledgments. This research is supported by National Natural Science Foundation of China under Grants 61103229 and 71072172, National Key Technologies R&D Program of China under Grant 2013BAH16F03, and Industry Projects in the Jiangsu S&T Pillar Program under Grants No. BE2011198.

References

[1] Ritter, A., Mausam, Etzioni, O.: Open domain event extraction from twitter. In: Proc. of the 18th ACM SIGKDD International Conference on Knowledge Discovery and Data Mining (KDD 2012), pp. 1104–1112 (2012)

[2] Cha, M., Mislove, A., Gummadi, K.P.: A measurement-driven analysis of information propagation in the flickr social network. In: Proc. of the 18th International Conference on World Wide Web (WWW 2009), pp. 721–730 (2009)

[3] Zhou, J., Li, Y., Adhikari, V.K., Zhang, Z.: Counting youtube videos via random prefix sampling. In: Proc. of the 11th ACM SIGCOMM Conference on Internet Measurement (IMC 2011), pp. 371–379 (2011)

[4] Benevenuto, F., Rodrigues, T., Cha, M., Almeida, V.: Characterizing user behavior in online social networks. In: Proc. of the 9th ACM SIGCOMM Conference on Internet Measurement (IMC 2009), pp. 49–62 (2009)

[5] Kandylas, V., Dasdan, A.: The utility of tweeted urls for web search. In: Proc. of the 20th International Conference on World Wide Web (WWW 2011), pp. 1127–1128 (2011)

[6] Kwak, H., Lee, C., Park, H., Moon, S.: What is twitter, a social network or a news media? In: Proc. of the 19th International Conference on World Wide Web (WWW 2010), pp. 591–600 (2010)

[7] Zubiaga, A., Spina, D., Fresno, V., Martínez, R.: Classifying trending topics: A typology of conversation triggers on twitter. In: Proc. of the 20th ACM International Conference on Information and Knowledge Management (CIKM 2011), pp. 2461–2464 (2011)

[8] Yu, L., Asur, S., Huberman, B.A.: What trends in chinese social media. In: Proc. of the 5th SNA-KDD Workshop 2011 on Social Network Mining and Analysis, SNA-KDD 2011 (2011)

[9] Chen, Z., Liu, P., Wang, X., Gu, Y.: Follow whom? chinese users have different choice. CoRR abs/1212.0167 (2012)

[10] Antoniades, D., Polakis, I., Kontaxis, G.: we.b: The web of short urls. In: Proc. of the 20th International Conference on World Wide Web (WWW 2011), pp. 715–724 (2011)

[11] Rodrigues, T., Benevenuto, F., Cha, M.: On word-of-mouth based discovery of the web. In: Proc. of the 11th ACM SIGCOMM Conference on Internet Measurement (IMC 2007), pp. 381–396 (2007)

[12] Ma, J., Saul, L.K., Savage, S., Voelker, G.M.: Beyond blacklists: Learning to detect malicious web sites from suspicious urls. In: Proc. of the 15th ACM SIGKDD International Conference on Knowledge Discovery and Data Mining (KDD 2009), pp. 1245–1254 (2009)

[13] Chhabra, S., Aggarwal, A., Benevenuto, F., Kumaraguru, P.: Phi.sh/$ocial: The phishing landscape through short urls. In: Proc. of the 8th Annual Collaboration, Electronic Messaging, Anti-Abuse and Spam Conference (CEAS 2011), pp. 92–101 (2011)

[14] Cui, A., Zhang, M., Liu, Y., Ma, S.: Are the urls really popular in microblog messages? In: Proc. of the 1st IEEE International Conference on Cloud Computing and Intelligence Systems (CCIS 2011), pp. 1–5 (2011)

[15] Wu, X., Zhang, X.: Micro-blog in china: Identify influential users and automatically classify posts on sina micro-blog. J. Ambient Intell. Human Comput. (2012), doi:10.1007/s12652-012-0121-3

[16] Chen, C., Wu, K., Srinivasan, V., Zhang, X.: Battling the internet wa-ter army: Detection of hidden paid posters. CoRR, vol. abs/1111.4297 (2012)

Towards Evaluating the Performance of Higher Education: From a Non-financial Perspective

Wenyun Yao[1,2], Xin Xu[2], and Wenlei Chen[2]

[1] School of Business, Nanjing University, Nanjing, China
[2] School of Accounting, Nanjing University of Finance and Economics,
Nanjing, China
{yaowenyun9999,jyxx.0306}@163.com,
yzcwl1115@hotmail.com

Abstract. In recent years, most of the research efforts on performance evaluation of higher education in China are barely based on the financial data, but lack of considering the non-financial data. However, evaluating the performance from non-financial perspective will be an interesting yet challenging task, due in large part to the complexity and qualitative property of the non-financial data. In this paper, we employ the multiple linear regression model for incorporating the non-financial data into the performance evaluation. Our results show that institutes of high education can increase the utilization efficiency of financial capital and thus improve the performance by controlling the scale of the school as well as optimizing both human and material resources. Therefore, our results imply that colleges and universities should pay attention to the management of human resources, the degree of utilization of material resources, and the proper control of the scale, in order to construct a better performance evaluation system at the university level.

Keywords: Non-financial Information, High Education, Performance Evaluation, Multiple Linear Regression.

1 Introduction

Recent years have witnessed an increasing advance of the strategy of rejuvenating the country through science and education. The government continues to increase the investments on higher education every year. The scale of education has extended steadily, and the focus turns from the macro increments of financial investment in higher education to the efficiency of management of the universities. To date, a great deal of research has been devoted to theories and practices of performance evaluation index and system in higher education. However, these research efforts are mostly based on financial data, but lack of taking the non-financial data into consideration.

Lots of evidences have shown the non-financial data is the necessary yet important supplements to the financial data, having the potential to provide more comprehensive and broader information. Zhou et al. introduced non-financial

Z. Huang et al. (Eds.): WISE 2013 Workshops 2013, LNCS 8182, pp. 109–119, 2014.

information as a tool to assess value creation, explored the inner workings of an organization in depth and provided the reference for studying the performance evaluation system of higher education from the non-financial perspective [1]. Wang et al. investigated the financial early-warning system, combined the financial ratio with non-financial information, in order to expand the information content of early-warning model and improve the accuracy of early warning [2]. At present, non-financial information is widely used for value measurement and financial early warning, which shades light in our research on evaluating the performance of higher education from the non-financial perspective.

Along this line, we first propose three hypotheses based on the extensive survey on current literatures. We then collect data from 85 colleges/universities in Jiangsu province during 2008 to 2010 as our source data, and thus conduct the statistical analysis and the multiple linear regression analysis to validate the proposed hypotheses. Last but not the least, we present several countermeasures and suggestions for higher schools to enhance their performances.

The remainder of this paper is organized as follows. In Section 2, we present three hypotheses. In Section 3 and Section 4, we introduce the analysis methods and results, respectively. Based on our analysis results, several countermeasures and suggestions are given in Section 5. We finally conclude this paper in Section 6.

2   Literature and Hypotheses

Under the background of the continuing improvement of the system evolution and reform in higher education, the efficiency of university management should not only be related to teaching quality, but also to social efficiency. This paper starts from the perspective of non-financial information, chooses the key research on the feasibility of utilizing scale of university and the utilization of human and material resources, as the index of performance evaluation system in higher education. The purpose of this paper is to increase the interest in the utilization of non-financial information, in addition to the analysis of financial information, to realize the optimal allocation of resources and produce maximal operational efficiency in higher education.

2.1   The Impact from the Economies of Scale

In the theory of neoclassical economics, economies of scale is described as: when the enterprises is at the initial stage of production expansion, operational efficiency is greater with increasing scale; when the production scale has reached a certain size, declined efficiency will be resulted by continually increasing the scale, which is called diseconomies of scale [3]. As early as 1920s, Koos discussed the relationship between cost of higher education and the scale, by applying economies of scale to the education area [4]. Andrew D.Colegrave (2008)and Margaret J.Gile used the method of mathematical regression to investigate the cost of running universities. The regression outcome shows that variation in costs is significantly influenced by the university's scale. According to the factor analysis of economies of scale [5], Wang Rui found it contributing to the enhancement of publicity and overall comprehensiveness, which increase the core competence for the university in the world [6]. However, the scale expansion is limited. Further increase in scale may leads to a loss in the education function as a result of diseconomies of scale [7]. Based on the above analysis, this paper proposes the fowling assumptions:

Hypothesis 1. *The performance of higher education tends to be in direct proportion to the mediate scale of universities/colleges.*

2.2   The Impact from the Human Resource

In the 1960s, US economics Theodore W.Schults have initially built the framework of human capital theory and education economic theory [8,9]. Human resource is the resource that makes university more competitive. He also pointed to the fact that faculty quality and ability are great contributing factors to the educational efficiency [10]. If the university is short of high quality faculty, it will lead to lower operational efficiency and higher finical cost [11], even its hardware is first-class. Moreover, when human resource is incorporated into the system of performance evaluation in higher education, it could attract great attention to the efficiency of human resource utilization, and its dynamic role in determination of the distribution of funds. In summary, this paper gives a following hypothesis:

Hypothesis 2. *The performance of higher education tends to be in direct proportion to the expenses on human resources of universities/colleges.*

2.3   The Impact from the Material Resource

Material resource provides the essential material base for the study, work and life of college teachers and students, and is the physical form of teaching activity funds. Only by fully utilizing the material resource for personnel cultivation, can institutes of higher education convert material resource to financial resource, so as to improve its efficiency in the use of funds [12]. Bian etc pointed out that university financial performance evaluation only embodies the financial resource into the evaluation index system, but neglect the management and use of human and material resource [13]. This phenomenon has negative influence on the effective allocation of funds between human, finance and material, which result in the inefficiency and lower level of higher education performance. In management of university material resource, it should be scientific, open-sourced and economical in order to maximize the effective use of financial and material resources. We therefore come up with the following hypothesis:

Hypothesis 3. *The performance of higher education tends to be in direct proportion to the expenses on material resources of universities/colleges.*

3   Data Collection and Model Design

In this section, we describe our experimental data first, and thus present variable selection as well as the hypotheses testing model.

3.1   Data Collection

We collect data from 85 colleges/universities in Jiangsu province during 2008 to 2010 as our source data. Each record corresponding to a college or university contains the basic information of this school, the expenditure and income of this school. In particular, the basic information about the school includes the number of teachers and students, area, permanent assets, the scale of library, etc. The expenditure is classified in terms of usage, i.e., construction, wage and allowance for teachers, all kinds of equipments, etc. The income data consists of the financial aid from the government, donation, operating income, etc. Among 255 records of 85 colleges/universities in 3 years, we finally obtain 174 records, since other records have missing values or abnormal data.

3.2   Variable Selection and Hypotheses Testing Model

As the aforementioned three hypotheses, three kinds of variables are presented for further analysis. The detailed information of variables is shown in Table 1.

1. **Variables to be explained.** These variables are used to measure the performance of higher schools, and thus three different expenses are utilized here, i.e., the expenses on education, on human resources, and material resources.
2. **Explanatory Variables.** This kind of variables is used to explain or impact the performance of higher schools, i.e., variables to be explained. It might contain the asset size, the scale of teachers and students, and the scale of library facilities.
3. **Control Variable.** To eliminate the difference between operating condition and funding profile of university, we define the control variable to indicate the nature of university, i.e., academy and vocational school.

   To sum up, our task is to estimate the first kind of variables based on the second kind of variables and under the control of the third kind of variable. Regression is a predictive modeling technique where the target variable to be estimated is *continuous*. Obviously, the expense used for measuring the performance is a continuous variable, which essentially agrees with the regression model. Meanwhile, the regression has been successfully applied to a wide range of applications, including predicting a stock market index using other economic indicators, forecasting the amount of precipitation in a region based on characteristics of the jet stream, projecting the total sales of a company based on the amount spent for advertising, and estimating the age of a fossil according to the amount of carbon-14 left in the organic material [14,15].

   In light of these applications, we employ the Multivariate Linear Regression (MLR) technique to estimate the performance of the higher education. First of

Table 1. The Detailed Description of Variables

Variable name		Variable symbol	Variable definition
Explained variable	education spending	Scale	Housing construction expenditure +Major repair expenditure + capital construction expenditure + Wage subsidy expenditure + Goods and services expenditure
		Human	Salary welfare spending + Personal and family aid spending
		Material	goods and services + Special public spending
Explanatory variable	asset size	Area	School area(square meter)
		Asset	Fixed assets gross (thousand yuan)
		Building	Houses and buildings (thousand yuan)
	scale of the teachers and students	Master	The master number
		Undergraduate	Undergraduate number
		Teacher	Teacher number
	library facility expenditure	Book	Book number +E-book number
		Equipment	Purchase of special equipment (thousand yuan)
Control variable	University nature	Property	Regular college take 1, non-regular college take 0

all, we have to construct *target functions* mapping the attribute to be estimated into the explanatory variables (a.k.a. observations). We define three target functions on Scale S, Human H, and Material M as follows.

$$Scale = \beta_0 + \beta_1 Area + \beta_2 Asset + \beta_3 Building + \beta_4 Master \quad (1)$$
$$+\beta_5 Undergraduate + \beta_6 Teacher + \beta_7 Book + \beta_8 Property + \varepsilon_S,$$

$$H = \beta_0 + \beta_1 Master + \beta_2 Undergraduate + \beta_3 Teacher + \beta_4 Property + \varepsilon_H, \quad (2)$$

$$M = \beta_0 + \beta_1 Book + \beta_2 Equipment + \beta_3 Property + \varepsilon_M. \quad (3)$$

Table 2. Descriptive Statistical Analysis on Variables

Variable symbol	Minimum	Maximum	Mean value	Standard deviation
Scale	38493.00	1092651.00	267344.31	1.95E5
Human	24604.00	491634.00	115464.24	1.00E5
Material	8559.00	433650.00	99051.12	88528.46
Area	36155.00	1610516.00	391337.56	2.69E5
Asset	68732.00	3753651.00	831520.11	6.35E5
Building	30126.00	2648001.00	558416.01	4.21E5
Master	0.00	11704.00	838.83	2017.17
Undergraduate	903	2644.70	12541.97	4962.42
Teacher	184	4971	1133.96	985.98
Book	241	766332	151229.86	1.97E5
Equipment	0.00	67914	13776.96	14289.40

The goal of MLR is to find target functions that can fit the input data with minimum errors. We select squared error as our error function as shown in Equ. 4.

$$SquaredError = \sum_i (y_i - f(x_i))^2. \tag{4}$$

4   Analysis Results

4.1   Descriptive Statistics Analysis

Here, we show the descriptive statistics analysis on selected variables. The results are tabulated in Table 2. The first observation is that the operating condition differs too much among different schools. For instance, the standard deviation of "Asset" and "Area" reached 635,000 and 269,000, respectively. Another observation is that the proportions of human and material accounting for scale expenditure are 43.19% and 37.05%, respectively. This implies it is necessary to extract human and material factors separately for further analysis. Moreover, it is worth to pay attention to the proportion of fixed assets expenditure accounting for other individual expenditure, which shows its large capital and reflection in performance system.

4.2   Multivariate Linear Regression Analysis

The analysis results by the MLR model are displayed in Fig. 1. Note that "*", "**", "***" represent the significance of coefficient at level of 10%, 5%, 1%, respectively Firstly, the five among seven measures for scale, except "school building area" and "house", have significantly positive coefficients with the overall performance. This roughly validates the *Hypothesis* 1. Three indexes

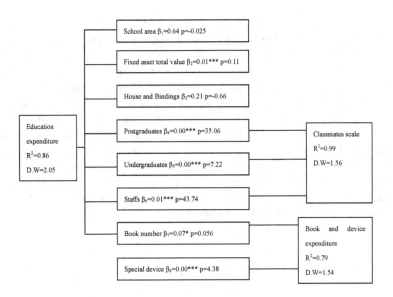

Fig. 1. Analysis results of MLR model

of postgraduates, undergraduates and staffs measuring human resource are all through the examination at 1% significance, which obviously illustrates the positive relationship between human resource and performance, and thus proves the *Hypothesis* 2. *Hypothesis* 3 is also proved by testing the significance of booking number and special device that are positively at the level of 10% and 1%.

5   Countermeasures and Suggestions

On the basis of our analysis results, here we present several countermeasures and suggestions for enhancing the performance evaluation systems of high schools and the performance evaluation in terms of non-financial data.

5.1   Enhancing the Performance Evaluation Systems

Optimize the Scale. Fig. 2 demonstrates great importance attached to the influence of university scale on performance level of higher education. It proves the conclusion proposed in [16], that is, university scale's expansion is beneficial for the resource utilization as the scale increased and average cost declined, accordingly generate economic benefit. On the other hand, the phenomenon of neglect of economic performance will be derived by means of poor management and inconsistent organization, leading to the waste of education resource. As a result, the optima point of scale should be explored in order to optimize the recourse and increase the level of education performance.

Improve the Utilization of Human and Material Resources. The outcomes of study indicate that taking full advantage of human and material resources could enhance the utilization efficiency of university funds, which signifies good evaluation criteria for education performance. On one hand, human resource is the main part of fund use and subjective initiative, can not only increase the use of funds, but also increase the capital inflow by using scientific achievements. On the other hand, material resource is the physical form of university monetary capital, reflecting the occupancy and consumption of materialized labor. Only by fully utilizing every university owned material resources, can we maximize the efficiency in teaching, research and personal achievements. If books and devices are under utilized or left unused, the negative result will cause waste and inefficient utilization of other resources, resulting in the decline of performance level as an undesired effect.

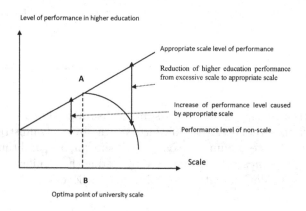

Fig. 2. Impact of the university scale on the performance of higher education

Construct Accountability Mechanism of Performance. In public higher education, there is increased attention of the public to universities that performance generated by public finance is not clearly defined and measured, leading to the increasing targeting of universities for accountability. The United States as one of the countries began to enforce accountability mechanism of performance in the 1990s, believing monitoring and investigation into university operating efficiency could improve and advance the development of performance evaluation system in higher education. If the responsibility is not clearly defined, the first priority would be on how to spend the public funds for education, but not how to adopt reasonable measures to enhance the efficiency of fund utilization. Consequently, we must establish responsibility mechanism and carry out university accountability, so that the public can not only clearly evaluate the results of fund usage and judge whether it meets the estimated goals, but also integrate the results of the evaluation with the responsibility and accountability mechanisms.

Table 3. Non-financial Evaluation System of the Performance

First index	Second index	Third index
Teaching performance evaluation index	Human resource	Student-teacher ratio
		Staffs ratio
	Material resource	Occupied area
		Total fixed assets value
		Book number
	Financial resource	Revenue growth of education fund
		Spending growth of education fund
Research performance evaluation index	Cultivate talents	Student employment rate
		Postgraduate entrance rate
	Scientific research	Number of published paper
		Number of research award
		Conversion rate of research application
Use efficiency of raised fund indicator	Raise ability	National and local fund
		Self-raised fund
	Financial ability	Asset-liability ratio
		Financial ratio
Benefits of industry indicator	Ability to social contribution	Elasticity for financial expenditure of higher education to GDP
	Ability to social production	Technology transfer income
		University-enterprise cooperation industrial investment yields
Student satisfaction indicator	Teaching level	Ratio of doctor and postgraduate in full time teacher Ratio of profess in full time teacher
	Operating condition	Education expenditure per student Dormitory area per student Book per student Experimental occupancy and sport filed area per student
	Quality level of student	Graduate rate One-time employment rate Postgraduate entrance rate

5.2 Enhancing the Performance Evaluation in Terms of Non-financial Data

The development of institutions of higher education demands a serious of resource integration activities, such as the integration of the finance and education resources. When estimating education performance, we must pay more attention on non-financial information in addition to strengthening financial management, adjust policy in a timely fashion and increase the utilization efficiency of resources as a whole. The factors contributing to education performance in higher education are both economic and social. How to incorporate the non-financial indexes into the assessment system and increase its role in the evaluation process is a difficult part in the current performance system and requires urgent attention.

As a result of the above conclusion, this paper puts forward the suggestions below regarding the performance evaluation system in higher education. As illustrated in Table 3, we established five indicators that are: teaching performance indicator, research performance indicator, utilization efficiency of raised fund indicator, benefits of industry indicator and student satisfaction indicator. They additionally can be separated to second and third simple index that cover comprehensively all the aspects of achievement and outcomes and measure the level of education performance by integrated comparison.

The purpose of higher education operation is primarily aimed at meeting the demands of teaching activities, which are the foundation of launching other operational activities. Under the socialism market economy system, it is required that institutes of higher education have to achieve the best possible operational effectiveness to accommodate needs of economic development and in the meantime create social benefits. The fund utilization efficiency is not only related to the economic aspect but also to social and cultural aspects. In addition, we pay close attention to explaining how non-financial indexes get into the evaluation system and exert influence. Currently, there is a lack of consideration in applying non-financial index in the performance evaluation system. We proposed that only by combining the non-financial index with financial index, can we improve the quality of performance evaluation system, enhance the accuracy of assessed outcome, and reasonably allocate limited resources in order to promote optimal operating efficiency in higher education.

6   Concluding Remark

In this paper, we explore how to evaluate the performance of high schools in terms of non-financial data. Tapping on the extensive survey on current literatures, three hypotheses are sketched out. We then collect sampling data from 85 colleges/universities in Jiangsu province during 2008 to 2010 as our source data, and thus conduct the statistical analysis and the multiple linear regression analysis to validate the proposed hypotheses. Last but not the least, we present several countermeasures and suggestions for higher schools to enhance their performances.

Acknowledgments. This research was partially supported by University Philosophy and Social Science Fund of Educational Commission of Jiangsu Province (No. 2013SJB6300038), Postdoctoral Foundation of Jiangsu Province (No. 1101057C), the Research Fund for Nanjing University of Finance and Economics (No. A2011018) and the Priority Academic Program Development of Jiangsu Higher Education Institutions.

References

1. Zongjun, W., Yingping, X., Xiaolan, D.: Non-financial Information and Financial Warning. Value Engineering (2006) (in Chinese)
2. Weihua, Z.: Research on Non-financial Information and Enterprise Value Relevance, Hu Nan University (2007) (in Chinese)
3. Marshall, A.: The Principles of Economics (1890)
4. Koos, L.V.: The Junior-College Movement. Ginn and Company (1925)
5. Colegrave, A.D., Giles, M.J.: School Cost Functions: A Meta-Regression Analysis. Economics of Education 6 (2008)
6. Rui, W.: Thought on Scale Efficiency of Chinese University. Information Technology (2007) (in Chinese)
7. Weiqiao, L.: Research on Use Efficiency of Human Resouce of Higher Education in Liao Ning Province. Journal of An Shan Normal College (2007) (in Chinese)
8. Schultz, T.W.: Reflections on Investment in Man. Journal of Political Economy 70 (1962)
9. Schultz, T.W.: Resources for Higher Education: An Economist View. Journal of Political Economy 76 (1968)
10. Maishan, W.: Education Investment and Research Output. He Bei Science and Education Press (1996) (in Chinese)
11. Ming, Z., Bihui, Z.: Empirical Research on Financial Performance Evaluation of Chinese University on the Basis of Non-financial Information. Educational Technology (2008) (in Chinese)
12. Chunhui, W.: The Analysis of Improving the Access to Material Resource Use in the University of Inner Mongolia. Journal of Inner Mongolia Institute of Finance and Economics (2011) (in Chinese)
13. Jihong, B., Lei, Z.: The Construction of Performance Budget System of University Human Resource. Communication of Finance and Accounting (2009) (in Chinese)
14. Zhiang, W., Junjie, W., Jie, C., Dacheng, T.: HySAD: A Semi-Supervised Hybrid Shilling Attack Detector for Trustworthy Product Recommendation. In: The 18th ACM SIGKDD Conference on Knowledge Discovery and Data Mining (KDD 2012), Beijing, China, pp. 985–993 (August 2012)
15. Jie, C., Zhiang, W., Junjie, W., Hui, X.: SAIL: Summation-bAsed Incremental Learning for Information-Theoretic Text Clustering. IEEE Transactions on Cybernetics 43(2), 570–584 (2013)
16. Weifang, H., Xiaohao, D.: Scale Profit Theory and Education Structure Adjustment. Journal of Higher Education (1997) (in Chinese)

Dynamically Predicting the Deadlines in Time-Constrained Workflows

Xiaobo Guo [1,2], Jidong Ge [1,2,3,*], Yu, Zhou[1,4], Haiyang Hu[1,5], Feng Yao[1,2],
Chuanyi Li[1,2], and Hao Hu[1]

[1] State Key Laboratory for Novel Software Technology, Nanjing University, China, 210093
[2] Software Institute, Nanjing University, Nanjing, China 210093
[3] Key Laboratory of Intelligent Perception and Systems for High-Dimensional Information,
Ministry of Education, Nanjing University of Science and Technology, Nanjing, China
[4] College of Computer Science and Technology,
Nanjing University of Aeronautics and Astronautics, 210019 Nanjing, China
[5] School of Computer, Hangzhou Dianzi University, Hangzhou, China, 310018
gjdnju@163.com

Abstract. In order to predict workflow's deadline, and improve the efficiency of the entire workflow management, this paper proposes an efficient method to dynamically predict the deadline of time-constrained workflows. This method improves the lack of the existing method in which all the paths in selection structures were assigned the same deadline. We apply LMST-invariant decomposition to decompose the selection structures of the workflow. With the checkpoints which are inserted on selection activities, we propose an efficient method to timely predict the workflow's deadline. This method is more suitable for the practical application.

Keywords: Workflow, Time Constrained, Deadline, Critical Path, Dynamically Predicting.

1   Introduction

Workflow technology commonly used in the management of enterprise business processes, Process Modeling Language (PML) is the key component of workflow management system. Petri net is the popular model for the formal modeling of workflow process [1]. Time management is a crucial part of workflow management system. Handling Time and time constraints are very important aspects in business processes planning and management. Thus, time management is the important function which workflow management system should provide. Huifang Li *et al.* [2] summarized the developing trends of time management in workflow system. The key problems of time management in workflow systems are estimating the start time and end time of the activities, and checking the satisfaction of temporal constraints. Jianqiang Li *et al.* [3, 4] and Eder *et al.* [5, 6] proposed methods for define and model

---

* Corresponding author.

Z. Huang et al. (Eds.): WISE 2013 Workshops 2013, LNCS 8182, pp. 120–132, 2014.
© Springer-Verlag Berlin Heidelberg 2014

time-constrained workflow. Marjanovic [7] proposed dynamic verification method for time-constrained workflow. The issue of deadline constraint in workflow management has been researched by many people. Son *et al.* [8], [9], [10] proposed a method to find out the critical path in a workflow based on the defined workflow control structure. Huifang Li *et al.* [11] proposed a deadline assignment and monitoring method based on the critical path for time management in time-constrained workflows.

Most of the above mentioned works are based on static analysis in the modeling phase. However, under the run-time environment, the workflow time management should put more emphasis on workflow system performance and throughput[9]. Considering the load of workflow system, there will be some process instances in the waiting queue and cannot be executed. So when the waiting process instances are executed, and when the running process instances are finished, the prediction of workflow's deadline will become particularly important, since this is an important measurement for system throughput. However, due to the existence of selection structure in the process definition, the process instance deadline cannot be easily predicted.

In order to predict process instance's deadline, we should obtain a sequence of activities which have longest execution time, and is also called *critical path*. However, the traditional critical path algorithm does not apply to the workflow which has selection structure. In this paper, we use a novel method to calculate the critical path of the workflow which has selection structure. We propose a method based on LMST-invariant to decompose the selection structures and divides the workflow model into several subnets, then calculate each subnet's critical path. Applying the concept of the selection activity and adding the *checkpoints* on the selection activities, we propose an efficient method to dynamically predict the workflow's deadline, and make it more suitable for practical applications.

The remainder of the paper is organized as follows: In Section 2, we describe the time-constrained workflow. Section 3 proposes the critical path method for workflow which has selection structure. Section 4 presents the dynamically predicting Deadline of Instance in Runtime. Section 5 gives a case study and analysis. Finally, conclusions are drawn in Section 6.

2 Time Constrained Workflow Model

In this paper, by adding time parameters to traditional Petri net, we define the time-constrained workflow nets.

Definition 1 (Time Constrained Workflow net, *abbr.* TCWF-net). Time constrained workflow net is a 4-tuple $= (P, T, D, F)$. P is the place set, and T is transition set, and $F \subseteq (P \times T) \cup (T \times P)$ is the arc set (flow relations). D are the time parameters.

$TCWF = (P, T, D, F)$ should satisfy the following two conditions:

(1) (P, T, F) is a WF-net [1].

(2) $D : T \to N$, denotes the anticipated execution time of the transition. □

In time-constrained Petri Net (TCWF-net), the transitions represent the activities of workflow process, while the tokens and the places represent the enabled conditions of the process activities. A time-constrained workflow should satisfy soundness [1], which is originated by Aalst and viewed as a notion of correctness of workflow process model. In this paper, there are three control structures in time-constrained workflow, such as sequence structure, selection structure and concurrent structure.

There is an example of time-constrained workflow net shown in Fig.1, the data behind of transition name represents the anticipated execution time of the transition.

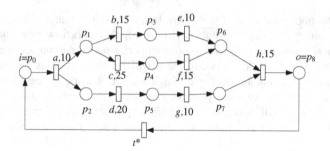

Fig. 1. An example: a time constrained workflow net

3   The Solution of Workflow's Critical Path

Traditional critical path method does not support the selection structure of the workflow. However, to predict the business instance's deadline, we should find a path with the longest execution time which is calculated by critical path method. Therefore, finding the critical path of the workflow is essential. Son *et al.* [8] proposed ICSF (Innermost Control Structure First) algorithm to decompose the selection structures. Based on the four basic workflow control structures: Sequence, AND, OR and LOOP , the algorithm uses a set of reduction rules to calculate the critical path of the process, and uses the well-formed workflow structure called nested workflow to transform and simplify workflow model and to calculate the execution time of the workflow instance. The longest execution path of each control block can be calculated as the sub-critical paths of a workflow because a workflow is viewed as a sequence of control blocks. Therefore, ICSF can find out the sub-critical path with the longest execution time in each control block and then combines these sub-critical paths to make the total critical path. The ICSF algorithm includes two steps: 1. if innermost control structure is a LOOP, we transform the LOOP into a sequence. 2. If the innermost control structure is an AND or an OR, we will calculate its longest execution path as the sub-critical path. After applying these steps, we can obtain a workflow control structure with n branches composed of only SEQUENCE control structures. Because the control structure is corresponding to the control block, the sub-critical path of the control block is the longest average execution path of the control structure.

Son *et al.* [8] considers that the longest execution path of each control block is to the part of the critical path of a workflow because a workflow is a sequence of control blocks. However, Son's method is only suitable to static analysis. In the actual runtime environment, because the workflow business instance may select different selection structures, the algorithm is not suitable for run-time environment.

When a process instance is running, because of the business requirement, it will execute different selection branches. Therefore the execution time of each process instance is different. When calculating the critical path of the workflow model that has selection structure, firstly, we must decompose the selection structure. So we can use a method to decompose a workflow model into a set of subnets which does not contain selection structure. Secondly, we calculate the critical path of each subnet. The concept of the critical path may be more useful because it can be utilized in run-time workflow management.

3.1   Decompose Selection Structure by LMST-Invariant Decomposition

The selection structures of workflow model are decomposed by LMST-Invariant. An LMST-invariant means an actually sound execution branch, and there exists a firing sequence from initial state to final state, LMST-invariant can decompose a sound workflow net into several subnets, and each subnet does not contain selection structure. In this section, we will introduce the concept of LMST-Invariant, and give an example to show how LMST-invariant can decompose a workflow net into subnets.

Definition 2 (Incidence Matrix, T-invariant).
   (1)   A Petri $PN=(P, T, F)$ can be represented by an incidence matrix,
         $PN : (P \times T) \rightarrow \{-1,0,1\}$, which is define by

$$PN(p,t) = \begin{cases} -1 & if \ (p,t) \in F \\ 0 & if \ (p,t) \notin F \wedge (t,p) \notin F \ or \ (p,t) \in F \wedge (t,p) \in F \\ 1 & if \ (t,p) \in F \end{cases}$$

   (2)   For the Petri net $PN=(P, T, F)$, A T-invariant of a net $PN=(P, T, F)$ is a rational-valued solution of the equation $PN \cdot Y = 0$. The solution set is denoted by $J = \{J_1, J_2, ..., J_n\}$. In essence, a T-invariant J_k is a T-vector, as a mapping $J_k : T \rightarrow Z$. A T-invariant J_k is called semi-positive if $J_k \geq 0$ and $J_k \neq 0$. A T-invariant J_k is called positive if $\forall t \in T : J_k(t) > 0$. $\| J_k \|$ denotes the set of transitions t satisfying $J_k(t) > 0$. A Petri net is called covered by T-invariants iff there is a positive T-invariant $J_k > 0$.

   (3)   Minimal invariants: A semi-positive T-invariant J_k is minimal if no semi-positive T-invariant J_x satisfies $J_x \subset J_k$. Every semi-positive invariant is the sum of minimal invariants. If a net has a positive invariant, then every invariant is a linear combination of minimal invariants.

   (4)   Fundamental property of T-invariant: Let (PN, M_0) be a system, and let J_k be a T-invariant of PN, then the Parikh vector $\vec{\sigma}$ is a T-invariant iff $M \xrightarrow{\sigma} M$ (i.e., iff the occurrence of σ reproduces the marking M).   □

For the particularity of invariants of the workflow net and the relations between invariants and the liveness and boundedness of Petri net, the soundness [1] property of workflow net can be analyzed by invariants. In this paper, according to the particularity of workflow nets, we propose LMST-invariants.

Definition 3 (T-invariants of Workflow net). Let $PN=(P, T, F)$ be a workflow net. $t*$ is the additional transition to connect source place i and sink place o. $\overline{PN} = (P, T \cup \{t*\}, F \cup \{(o, t*), (t*, i)\})$ is the extended workflow net of PN. J_k is a T-invariant of $\overline{PN}$. J_k is called legal if $J_k(t*) = 1 \wedge J_k \geq 0$. J_k is called LMST-invariant (Legal Minimal Semi-positive T-invariant), if $J_k(t*) = 1 \wedge J_k \geq 0$ and is a minimal T-invariants of $\overline{PN}$. An LMST-invariant J_k of $\overline{PN}$ means an actually sound execution branch, and there is a firing sequence $(\sigma = u_1 u_2 ... u_n t*) \wedge$ $(u_x \in T)$, corresponding to J_k such that $[i] \xrightarrow{u_1} M_1 \xrightarrow{u_2} M_2 \longrightarrow ... \xrightarrow{u_{n-1}}$ $M_{n-1} \xrightarrow{u_n} [o] \xrightarrow{t*} [i]$. Let $\pi(\sigma)$ be a function to record the occurrence times of each transitions over the sequence, then $\pi(\sigma) = J_k$. $\pi(\sigma, t) = J_k(t)$ denotes the times of transition t fired in the sequence σ.

According to Definition 2, the Incidence Matrix of $\overline{PN}$ in Fig.1 is shown in Fig.2. The decomposition results by LMST-invariants are $J_1 = [1,1,0,1,1,0,1,1,1]$, $J_2 = [1,0,1,1,0,1,1,1,1]$, $\|J_1\| = \{a, b, d, e, g, h, t^*\}$, $\|J_2\| = \{a, c, d, f, g, h, t^*\}$.

	a	b	c	d	e	f	g	h	t*
p_0	-1	0	0	0	0	0	0	0	1
p_1	1	-1	-1	0	0	0	0	0	0
p_2	1	0	0	-1	0	0	0	0	0
p_3	0	1	0	0	-1	0	0	0	0
p_4	0	0	1	0	0	-1	0	0	0
p_5	0	0	0	1	0	0	-1	0	0
p_6	0	0	0	0	1	1	0	-1	0
p_7	0	0	0	0	0	0	1	-1	0
p_8	0	0	0	0	0	0	0	1	-1

Fig. 2. The Incidence Matrix of $\overline{PN}$ in **Fig.**1

Definition 4 (The Decomposition Based on LMST-invariants [12]). Let $PN = (P, T, F)$ be a workflow net. $\overline{PN} = (P, T \cup \{t^*\}, F \cup \{(o, t^*), (t^*, i)\})$ is its extended workflow net, and J_k is an LMST-invariant of $\overline{PN}$, then the subnet decomposed from J_k is denoted $PN \mid_{J_k} = (P_{J_k}, T_{J_k}, F_{J_k})$, where:

(1) $T_{J_k} = \|J_k\| \setminus \{t^*\}$,

(2) $P_{J_k} = \{p \in {}^\bullet T_{J_k} \mid p \in P\} \cup \{p \in T_{J_k}{}^\bullet \mid p \in P\}$,

(3) $F_{J_k} = \{(p, t) \mid p \in P_{J_k} \wedge t \in T_{J_k} \wedge (p, t) \in F\} \cup \{(t, p) \mid p \in P_{J_k} \wedge t \in T_{J_k} \wedge (t, p) \in F\}$. □

According to the above conclusions, a workflow net which satisfies soundness [1] can be decomposed by LMST-Invariant, The decomposition results by LMST-invariants from Fig.1 are shown in Fig.3.

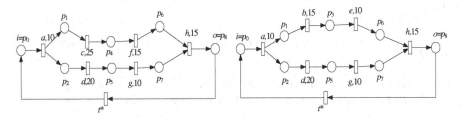

Fig. 3. The decomposition results by LMST-invariants from Fig.1

Definition 5 (Business Instance). Each subnet decomposed by LMST-invariant (removing transition t^*) can be considered as the actual process instance which running in the workflow environment. Because the choice of selection branch is related to the business execution of process, so we define the subnets decomposed by LMST-invariants as business instances.   □

According to Fig.3, we can obtain two business instances, which are $I_1 = \{a,c,d,f,g,h\}$ and $I_2 = \{a,b,d,e,g,h\}$. The number of business instances depends on the number of selection places and selection branches, which are usually not large.

3.2   The Critical Path and Completion Time of Business Instance

Since the business instances are decomposed by LMST-invariant, we can use CPM to calculate the critical path of each business instance. In traditional CPM, the time parameters are attached to the arc of model. While in workflow net, the time parameters are attached to the transition. Therefore, some changes should be taken to solving this problem. Section 5 will give an example to show this new method.

Definition 6 (Pre-activity and Post-activity). Let t_1 and t_2 are two transitions in the workflow net $PN= (P, T, F)$, $p \in P, (t_1, p) \in F$ and $(p, t_2) \in F$, so t_1 is the pre-activity of t_2, and t_2 is the post-activity of t_1.   □

With Definition 6 and the workflow model (see Fig.3), we can get the following table from business instance $I_1 = \{a,c,d,f,g,h\}$ (see Table 1).

Table 1. Information about each activity

Activity	a	c	d	f	g	h
Duration	10	25	20	15	10	15
Pre-Activity	ϕ	a	a	c	d	f, g
Post-Activity	c, d	f	g	h	h	ϕ

Definition 7 (Earliest Start Time of Activity, Latest Start Time of Activity).
$EST(a_i)$ denotes the Earliest Start Time of Activity, and $LST(a_i)$ denotes the Latest
Start Time of Activity, which are calculated separately by the formula as following:

$$EST(a_i) = \begin{cases} \max\{EST(a_j)+D(a_j)\mid a_j = a_i.pre-activity\} & (a_i.pre-activity \neq \varnothing) \\ 0 & (a_i.pre-activity = \varnothing) \end{cases}$$

$$LST(a_i) = \begin{cases} \min\{LST(a_j)-D(a_i)\mid a_j = a_i.post-activity\} & (a_i.post-activity \neq \varnothing) \\ EST(a_i) & (a_i.post-activity = \varnothing) \end{cases}$$

If there is a path from initial place i to final place o, all activities on this path satisfy $\forall t \in T, EST(t) = LST(t)$, then this path is the *critical path* of the business instance. The *completion time* of the business instance is the latest start time of end
activity plus its time parameter.

With the data of table 1, according to Definition 7, we can get the following table:

Table 2. The $EST(a_i)$ and $LST(a_i)$ of each activity for $I_1 = \{a,c,d,f,g,h\}$

a_i	a	c	d	f	g	h
$EST(a_i)$	0	10	10	35	30	50
$LST(a_i)$	0	10	20	35	40	50

We get $EST(a)=LST(a)$, $EST(c)=LST(c)$, $EST(f)=LST(f)$, $EST(h)=LST(h)$ in table 2.
Therefore, the critical path of the business instance is $\{a, c, f, h\}$.and the execution
time of the business instance is 65(50+15), the earliest start time of each activity is
$a(0)$, $c(10)$, $f(35)$, $h(50)$.

4   Dynamically Predicting Deadline of Instance in Runtime

In section 3, we can obtain a set of business instances by LMST-invariant decomposition, and then apply CPM to calculate the critical path and the completion time of
each instance. But the static analysis of workflow model definition can't reflect the
real run-time state of the process. When the process instance is loaded by workflow
engine, we don't know which series of selection branch will be executed. So it won't
give the administrator effective feedback. We put more emphasis on monitoring the
runtime instantiation, getting runtime feedback during monitoring. Monitoring
process needs some additional means. Therefore, we should add *checkpoint* mechanism to monitor the execution, predict deadline based on the selected process's execution branch. For example, Liu and Chen et al. [13], [14], [15] use the *checkpoint* to
dynamically monitor and adjust the temporal consistency states of scientific
workflows in runtime.

The *Checkpoint* is added to activity in workflow system in order to administrate
during run time. In traditional workflow system, checkpoint is a common fault-
tolerant technology. It saves the present running state of system (such as instance
variable, execution context). When detecting an error, process will go back to
previous checkpoint and restart tasks.

In the QoS management of workflow system, the role of checkpoint is more outstanding. Chen *et al.* [14] has discussed the method about using temporal checkpoint to monitor temporal consistency. Analyzing the feedback of checkpoint on activity, it is easy to see whether the process violate the temporal consistency or not.

Therefore, checkpoint is not only a fault-tolerant technology, but also a mean of monitoring. Inserting checkpoint on activity can help monitoring the running process effectively. This article also introduces checkpoint mechanism, which is used to monitoring the running process and to predict the deadline of process instance.

4.1   Selection Strategy of Checkpoint

It's important to select proper checkpoint in applying checkpoint mechanism to workflow system. Too many or too few checkpoints all have their own defects. If the checkpoints are too many, the execution of checkpoint will be frequent, and will bring the system additional consumption. While if the checkpoints is too few, it won't monitor the operation of system effectively, thus can't give administrator enough feedback.

The checkpoint selection strategy needs thorough consideration. If we set checkpoint at every activity, it will better monitor the running state of process instance and predict the deadline of instance, but it will also result in more cost.

Definition 8 (Selection Activity). The selection activities are the post-transitions of the selection place, i.e., $t \in p \bullet \cap |p \bullet| \geq 2$ ($|p \bullet|$ is the number of post-transitions of place p). □

In Fig.1, the post-activity of selection place p_1 are c, b, so according to Definition 8, the selection activity of this workflow model are c, b, its selection activity set is. $\{c, b\}$. The scale of selection activity depends on the number of selection place in business process and the number of post-activity of selection place. The selection places in workflow model won't be too much, so the scale of selection activities won't be too large.

In the run-time of workflow instance, if there is no selection structure, the deadline will be determined when the process instance starts. But when the process instance has selection structures, the deadline of process instance becomes uncertain. We don't know which serial of selection branches of the process instance will be executed.

When a workflow model contains selection structure, we can't predict the deadline when the process instance starts. But once a branch is executed after selection place, other branches which are based on this selection place will not be executed. For example, based on the business instances in Fig.3, when the process instance starts at the time point t, the deadline of this process instance has two possible values: $t+65$, $t+55$, while the selection activity c starts, another branch $\{b, e\}$ will not be executed. Therefore, even if the process instance does not finish, we can know the deadline of the process instance is $t+65$.

According to this idea, the selection strategy of checkpoint is arranged on the post-activities of the selection places. After solving the problem of checkpoint selection, we have a problem that how to predict deadline based on the feedback by checkpoint monitoring. The principle of prediction is to judge which business instance fits the process instance based on present selection activities and execution log. It's a matching procedure. But if we compare the activity log with business instance activity one by one, it will take long time. So, it's necessary to optimize the matching process.

Definition 9 (Combined Selection Activities). The Combined Selection Activities are the Selection Activity set of in a business instance, which is a subnet decomposed by LMST-invariants (see Definition 5). □

A business instance differs from the other business instances according to its combined selection activities. A business instance can be represented by its combined selection activities.

We propose Algorithm 1 which makes a mapping from business instance to combined selection activities. Suppose that the number of business instance decomposed by LMST-invariant is m, the activity number of a business instance is n, which equal to the activity number of subnet decomposed by LMST-invariant. The number of selection activities is k, According to the loop structure of Algorithm 1. The time complexity of this algorithm is $O(m \times n \times k)$. The number m, n depend on the scale of workflow model. In most cases, these three numbers are not large; it won't take long time to run this algorithm. Therefore, the time token by this algorithm won't affect the prediction algorithm.

Algorithm 1: A mapping from business instance to combined selection activities

```
Input:
Set_bi: the set of business instances
Set_sa: the set of selection activities
Output:
Set_csa: the set of combined selection activities
Begin
Set_csa = ø; /*Initialize an empty set */
for instance in Set_bi do
    /*Initialize a combined selection activities*/
    csa = ø;
    for activity in Set_sa do     /*whether a selection ac-
tivity is in business instance*/
        if activity ⊆ instance then
    /*add an activity into an combined selection activities*/
            csa += activity;
        end if
    end for
    /*add combined selection activities into a set*/
    Set_csa += csa;
end for
return Set_csa;
end
```

4.2   Predicting Deadline of Process Instance by its Execution Record

The workflow engine will save the finished activities of working process instance in the logs. For example, a process instance will save $\{a\}$ after activity a finished, after activity c finished, the log is saved as $\{a, c\}$. This execution sequence is called process instance execution log. At the same time, the workflow engine will also save present running activity, if this activity is a selection activity. The checkpoint attached will be activated to execute prediction algorithm, calculate the deadline of this business instance. Since not every activity execution will activate prediction algorithm, only selection activities will activate prediction algorithm so that this mechanism is more effective.

We will propose the algorithm of deadline prediction (see Algorithm 2). The number of finished activities of this process instance is l, and the number of selection activities is m, according to the loop structure of step 1. The time complexity of this algorithm is $O(l \times m)$. In Step2, the number of combined selection activities is l, the number of selection activity which contained by combined selection activities is p, and the number of selection activity is q. The time complexity of the prediction algorithm is $O(n \times p \times q)$. According to the above analysis, the value of n, p is not very large, what's more, the value of q is less than or equal to p. So the consumption of the algorithm does not affect on deadline prediction much.

Algorithm 2: Prediction Algorithm
Input:
curAct: current running selection activity
log: process instance execution log
Set$_{sa}$: the set of selection activities
ts: the instance start time
Set$_{csa}$: the set of combined selection activities
map: a map which key is the combined selection activities
and value is the execution time of this business instance
Output:
Set$_{dp}$: deadline predictions of the instance
Step1: Extract selection activity from the process instance execution log
Set$_{act}$ += curAct;
for activity in log **do**
    if activity $\subseteq$ Set$_{sa}$ **then**
    /*if an activity belongs to selection activities*/
    Set$_{act}$ += activity;
  end if
end for
Step2: According to the selection activities of this
process instance, matching combined selection activities
Set$_{dp}$ = ∅;/*Initialize an empty deadline prediction set */
for csa in Set$_{csa}$ **do**
  if Set$_{act}$ $\subseteq$ csa **then**{
    deadline = map[csa] + ts;
    Set$_{dp}$ += deadline;
  }
end for
return Set$_{dp}$;

5   Case Study

As shown in Fig.4 is a time-constrained workflow net, it can be decomposed into 4 subnets by LMST-invariant which shown in Fig.5. So this workflow model has 4 business instances, which are $I_1=\{a,c,d,f,e,h\}$, $I_2=\{a,c,d,g,e,h\}$, $I_3=\{a,b,d,f,e,h\}$, $I_4=\{a,b,d,g,e,h\}$ respectively. According to the algorithm of critical path in section 3.2, we can obtain the completion time of four business instance are 100, 95, 97, 92 respectively.

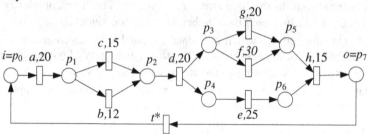

Fig. 4. An example: a time constrained workflow net

Based on Definition 5, the selection activity set of this workflow model is $\{c, b, f, g\}$. According to Algorithm 1, the combined selection activities of I_1 is $\{c, f\}$, of I_2 is $\{c,g\}$, of I_3 is $\{b,f\}$, and of I_4 is $\{b,g\}$. With the static analysis of workflow model, the results include the business instances of workflow model, selection activity set and the set of combined selection activities.

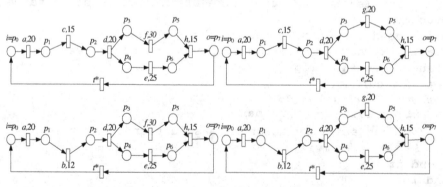

Fig. 5. The decomposition results by LMST-invariants from Fig.4

Suppose the present time is t, process instance is loaded and run by workflow engine. The deadlines of the process instances are four discrete values. They are $\{92+t, 95+t, 97+t, 100+t\}$, which can only predict the minimum and maximum deadline of this process instance at most. When activity a is finished, p_1 select the execution of selection activity c, and the checkpoint attached to selection activity c will activate Algorithm 2, i.e., selection activity=$\{c\}$. The corresponding combined selection activities are $\{c, f\}$, $\{c, g\}$. We can obtain two possible deadlines $\{95+t, 100+t\}$. After activity c is finished, the execution of activity d does not activate prediction algorithm, because activity d is not a selection activity. When activity d is finished, p_3 select selection activity g to execute, and the checkpoint attached to selection activity g activate algorithm 2, i.e., selection activity=$\{c, g\}$. The corresponding combined selection activities are only$\{c, g\}$, and we obtain the only one deadline $\{95+t\}$. Even though the whole process instance is not finished, we can calculate the deadline of process instance in advance.

6   Conclusions

In the related work, Son *et al.* presented the ICSF algorithm to predict the deadline of a Petri-based time-constrained workflow, based on the four basic workflow control structures: Sequence, AND, OR and LOOP. The ICSF algorithm uses the well-formed workflow structure called nested workflow to transform and simplify workflow model and calculate the execution time of the workflow instance [8], [9]. However, with regard to the selection structure, the algorithm only takes the longest alternative branches to calculate the critical path, which cannot adapt to the dynamics and uncertainty of runtime process instance deadline. In this paper, we use a novel method to calculate the critical path of the workflow which has selection structures. By LMST-invariant decomposition, the method decomposes the selection structure and divides the workflow model into several subnets, then, calculates each subnet's critical path. We introduced the concept of selection activity. With the checkpoints which are inserted on selection activities, we proposed an efficient method to timely predict the workflow's deadline, which can be used to improve the utilization of time resource and monitor workflow system performance and throughput. This method can improve the efficiency of process management for time-constrained workflow management system.

Acknowledgments. This work was supported by the National Natural Science Foundation, China (No.61100039, 61003019, 91318301, 61272188, 61202002, 61003024), the 973 Program (2009CB320702), the Natural Science Foundation of Jiangsu Province (No.BK20131277), the Key Laboratory of Intelligent Perception and Systems for High-Dimensional Information (Nanjing University of Science and Technology), Ministry of Education (No.309201301222005), Natural Science Foundation of Zhejiang Province (No. LY12F02005), and Chinese Fundamental Research Funds for the Central Universities at NJU and NUAA (No.NS2012135, No.NZ2013306).

References

1. van der Aalst, W.M.P.: The application of Petri nets to workflow management. Journal of Circuits Systems and Computers 8(1), 21–66 (1998)
2. Li, H.F., Fan, Y.S.: Overview on Managing Time in Workflow Systems. Journal of software 13(8), 1552–1558 (2002)
3. Li, J.Q., Fan, Y.S., Zhou, M.C.: Performance modeling and analysis of workflow. IEEE Transactions on Systems, Man, and Cybernetics, Part A 34(2), 229–242 (2004)
4. Li, J.Q., Fan, Y.S., Zhou, M.C.: Timing constraint workflow nets for workflow analysis. IEEE Transactions on Systems, Man, and Cybernetics, Part A 33(2), 179–193 (2003)

5. Eder, J., Panagos, E., Pozewaunig, H., et al.: Time management in Workflow system. In: Proceedings of the 3rd International Conference on Business Information Systems (1999)
6. Eder, J., Panagos, E., Rabinovich, M.I.: Time constraints in workflow systems. In: Jarke, M., Oberweis, A. (eds.) CAiSE 1999. LNCS, vol. 1626, pp. 286–300. Springer, Heidelberg (1999)
7. Marjanovic, O.: Dynamic verification of temporal constraints in production workflows. In: Proceedings of the 11th Australian Database Conference, pp. 74–81. IEEE (2000)
8. Son, J.H., Kim, J.H.: Finding the critical path in a time constrained workflow. In: Proceedings of the Seventh International Conference on Real-Time Systems and Applications, Cheju Island, South Korea, pp. 102–107. IEEE Compute Society (2000)
9. Son, J.H., Kim, J.H., Kim, M.H.: Deadline allocation in a time-constrained workflow. International Journal of Cooperative Information Systems 10(4), 509–530 (2001)
10. Son, J.H., Kim, J.H., Kim, M.H.: An effective static deadline assignment method in workflow systems. In: Proceedings of the Fifth Joint Conference on Information Sciences, pp. 433–436. Duke University, Atlantic (2000)
11. Li, H.F., Feng, F.J.: Management and Dynamic Monitoring of Deadlines in Time-Constrained Workflows. Transactions of Beijing Institute of Technology 31(8), 938–943 (2011)
12. Ge, J.D., Hu, H., Lu, J.: A Transformation Approach from Workflow Net to PERT Diagram Based on Invariants. Acta Electronica Sinica 36(5), 893–898 (2008)
13. Chen, J., Yang, Y.: Adaptive selection of necessary and sufficient checkpoints for dynamic verification of temporal constraints in grid workflow systems. ACM Transactions on Autonomous and Adaptive Systems 2(2) (2007)
14. Chen, J., Yang, Y.: Temporal dependency-based checkpoint selection for dynamic verification of temporal constraints in scientific workflow systems. ACM Transactions on Software Engineering and Methodology 20(3) (2011)
15. Liu, X., Yuan, D., Zhang, G.F., et al.: The Design of Cloud Workflow Systems: Springer Briefs in Computer Science. Springer (2012)

A Task Selecting Algorithm for Personal Schedules in Workflow Systems

Huan Yang[1,2], Jidong Ge[1,2,3,*], Quanjiang Yu[1,2], Chuanyi Li[1,2],
Zhihong Zhao[1,2], Hao Hu[1], and Bin Luo[1,2]

[1] State Key Laboratory for Novel Software Technology, Nanjing University, China, 210093
[2] Software Institute, Nanjing University, Nanjing, China 210093
[3] Key Laboratory of Intelligent Perception and Systems for High-Dimensional Information,
Ministry of Education, Nanjing University of Science and Technology, Nanjing, China
gjdnju@163.com

Abstract. In personal schedules for workflow systems, a participant may be assigned a lot of tasks in a work cycle or work period. However, the cycle may not be long enough such that all the assigned tasks can be scheduled within it, i.e. there does not exist a task sequence containing all the tasks so that any two tasks do not overlap and the makespan does not exceed the work cycle. So we can filter out some tasks to make up a task subsequence based on certain strategy. The participant executes these selected tasks in the work cycle and achieves the best working efficiency. The strategy can be either maximum task amount completed in the cycle or maximum working time during the period. This paper proposes an algorithm solving this problem with experimental result showing good performance.

Keywords: Personal Schedules, Work Cycle, Task Selecting.

1 Introduction

Many scheduling algorithms for workflow systems concentrate on minimizing the makespan. They aim at reducing the costs and flow times and increasing the quality of service or productivity by information technology [1]. Great effort has been made to classic scheduling problems such as job shop, flow shop, open shop, mixed shop, permutation flow shop [2],[3], static or dynamic project and resource constrained project in single or multiple modes [4],[5],[6]. These effort gave birth to various algorithms either newly proposed or borrowed from other fields including critical path method (CPM), program evaluation and review technique (PERT), genetic algorithms (GA) [7], simulated annealing (SA) [8],[9], ant colony optimization (ACO)[10], [11], etc.

However, all the algorithms above solve the scheduling problems from the projects' point of view and pay little attention to the participants. In fact, many activities in work

---

* Corresponding author.

Z. Huang et al. (Eds.): WISE 2013 Workshops 2013, LNCS 8182, pp. 133–143, 2014.

flow systems are accomplished by participants. When a participant receives dozens of tasks from different work flows, a personal scheduling is needed. Personal scheduling is somewhat similar to project scheduling. Eder *et al.* [12] proposes a personal scheduling algorithm making use of statistical data called probabilistic timed graph to generate a personal schedule for a participant. When execution durations of tasks overlap, the algorithm delays or brings forward some tasks according to certain strategy to maximize the target function.

But it is not the case that the personal scheduling algorithms always work. When a participant is assigned so many tasks in a work cycle that it is not possible to schedule all the tasks into a sequence within the cycle, an alternative way is to select some of the tasks to make up a subsequence based on some strategy such that the tasks in the subsequence do not overlap each other. The strategy can be either maximum working time or maximum tasks amount, where the former means that the sum of the execution duration of the tasks in the subsequence is maximized and the latter the number of tasks in the subsequence maximized. In other words, the maximum working time makes the participant busiest in the work cycle while the maximum tasks amount requires the participant to accomplish the most tasks during the work duration.

This paper proposes an algorithm corresponding to the problem mentioned above and presents the reader the experimental result showing good performance of the algorithm. The rest of the paper is organized as follows: In section 2, some basic definitions and notations on tasks are given. In section 3, we describe the problem in detail using both natural and formalized language. Section 4 analyzes the problem and presents the concrete content of the algorithm. Section 5 is the experimental result and section 6 the conclusion.

2   Definitions and Notations

Definition 1 (Task). A task T consists of two elements: s and e, denoted as $T = [s, e]$, where $s \in N \wedge e \in N \wedge s < e$, N is the natural numbers set. s and e are the start time and finish time of the task, respectively. The execution duration of task T is defined as $ED(T) = e - s$.

Temporal Relations. Temporal relationship between two tasks T_i and T_j must be one of the seven expressions displayed in Table 1. It is described by Allen's interval logic [4]. The third case defines overlap, but without loss of generality, we define overlap between T_i and T_j as the common part of their execution duration, denoted as $T_i \cap T_j$. Specially, when T_i meets T_j, we define $T_i \cap T_j = \varnothing$.

Table 1. Temporal relations between two tasks

Temporal Relation	Time Relation	Graphical Illustration	Overlap
T_i before T_j	$s_i < e_i < s_j < e_j$	T_i T_j	$T_i \cap T_j = \varnothing$
T_i meets T_j	$s_i < e_i = s_j < e_j$	T_i T_j	$T_i \cap T_j = \varnothing$
T_i overlaps T_j	$s_i < s_j < e_i < e_j$	T_i T_j	$T_i \cap T_j = [s_j, e_i]$
T_i starts T_j	$s_i = s_j < e_i < e_j$	T_i T_j	$T_i \cap T_j = T_i$
T_i during T_j	$s_j < s_i < e_i < e_j$	T_i T_j	$T_i \cap T_j = T_i$
T_i finishes T_j	$s_j < s_i < e_i = e_j$	T_i T_j	$T_i \cap T_j = T_i$
T_i equals T_j	$s_i = s_j < e_i = e_j$	T_i T_j	$T_i \cap T_j = T_i$

Definition 2 (Time Interval). A time interval is period of time denoted by $TI = [s, e]$, where $s \in N \wedge e \in N \wedge s < e$, N is the natural numbers set. s and e represent the start and end of the interval respectively. The length of time interval TI is defined as $ED(TI) = e - s$.

Definition 3 (Before Relation). Given two tasks T_i and T_j, if $e_i \leq s_j$ (the first case in Table 1), we denote it as $T_i \prec T_j$. This means that T_i finished before T_j starts.

Definition 4 (Within Relation). Given two tasks T_i and T_j, if $s_j \leq s_i \wedge e_i \leq e_j$ (the fourth, fifth, sixth and seventh cases in Table 1), we denote it as $T_i \subset T_j$. It means that execution duration of T_i is within that of T_j.

Definition 5 (Total Time and Total Number). $TS = \{T_1, T_2, ..., T_n\}$ is a set of tasks, $n \in N^+$. Define $TT(TS) = \sum_{i=1}^{n} ED(T_i)$ as the sum of the execution durations of all tasks in TS, namely total time of the task set. Define $TN(TS) = |TS|$ as the total number of tasks in TS.

3   Description of the Problem

A participant is assigned *n* tasks in a work cycle. The amount of tasks is too large for the personal scheduling algorithms to schedule them within the cycle, because the participant is not able to deal with two or more tasks at the same time and tasks are not allowed to be interrupted while being processed.

An alternative way is to filter out some of the tasks to make up a subsequence and execute them without changing the start time. This means that no selected tasks should be delayed or advanced. It is also required that the selected tasks must not overlap each other.

When selecting tasks, two strategies are available. One is to make the participant work for the most time during the cycle while the other one makes the participant accomplish as many tasks as possible within the cycle. Take Fig. 1 for example. A participant is assigned 9 tasks in the work cycle [0, 60]. If he/she chooses to excecute {T6, T7, T5}, he/she will work for (13 - 4) + (44 -16) + (55 - 50) = 42 time units. It's the longest time he/she can work in the cycle because no other subsequence exceeds it in term of execution duration. For example, consider the subsequence $\{T_6, T_8, T_9, T_5\}$, the sum of execution duration is (13 - 4) + (34 - 19) + (49 - 37) + (55 - 50) = 41 time units which is less than that of the former. And if he/she chooses to execute {T6, T1, T2, T3, T5}, he/she will finish the most number of tasks in the work cycle because no other subsequence can exceed it in term of task amount.

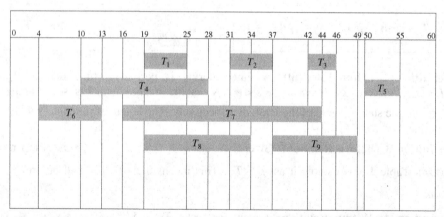

Fig. 1. An example for the problem: The vertical lines mark the start or end time of tasks

In formal language, the problem can be described like follows: Given a task set $TS = \{T_1, T_2, ..., T_n\}$, try to find a task set *MS* such that

(1) $MS \subseteq TS \wedge (\forall T_i, T_j \in MS, i \neq j, T_i \cap T_j = \varnothing)$,

(2) $\neg \exists MS' s.t. (MS' \subseteq TS \wedge (\forall T_i, T_j \in MS', i \neq j, T_i \cap T_j = \varnothing)$

   $\wedge f(MS') > f(MS)), f \in \{TT, TN\}$

Condition (1) ensures that the selected tasks do not overlap each other. Condition (2) guarantees that *MS* is the best solution: when $f = TT$, *MS* is the longest working time set; when $f = TN$, *MS* is the most number of task set.

4   Problem Analysis and Solution

We use the branch-and-bound method to solve the problem. Firstly, we sort the tasks by the start time in ascending order. Take Fig. 1 for example and we can get the sorted tasks as shown in Fig. 2.

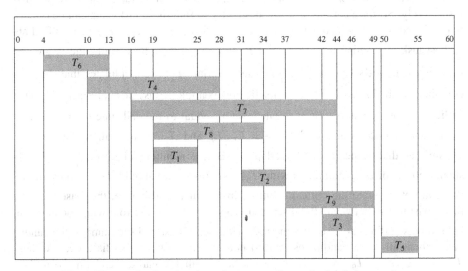

Fig. 2. The result of sorting the tasks in ascending order by their start time

For special use, all the start and end time (or time points) are collected. And for those tasks that have identical start time, we store them in a list. As shown in Fig. 3, 16 time points are collected and sorted in ascending order. Tasks having identical start time are stored in a list, like T_1 and T_8.

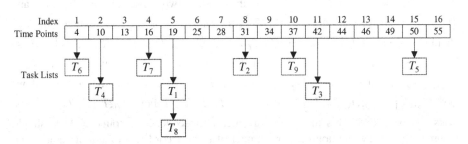

Fig. 3. The collected time points and task lists storing tasks with identical start time

Now, let's consider how to search two tasks that can be combined to make up a subsequence. That means the two tasks must not overlap each other. Take T_6 in Fig. 2 for example. T_7, T_8, T_1 can be combined with T_6 because of no overlap, thus forming three cases: $\{T_6, T_7\}$, $\{T_6, T_8\}$ and $\{T_6, T_1\}$. T_2, T_9, T_3, T_5 should not be directly combined with T_6 because the combination $\{T_6,T_2\}$, $\{T_6,T_9\}$, $\{T_6,T_3\}$ and $\{T_6,T_5\}$ can not be the optimal solution. The reason is following. Between T_6 and T_2, we have T_1 that does not overlap T_6 or T_2; so if we insert T_1 into the subsequence $\{T_6,T_2\}$ and get a new subsequence $\{T_6,T_1,T_2\}$, then either the execution duration sum or the task number of the latter is more than that of the former respectively. So for a certain task, we should try to find those tasks that can be directly combined with it, which can be realized by following: for task T_i, we first find an earliest task T_j satisfying $T_i \prec T_j$, then all those tasks whose start time is greater than or equal to the start time of T_j and overlap T_j are candidates that may be combined with T_i, including T_j itself. For example, consider again task T_6. The earliest task whose start time is greater than or equal to the end time of T_6, is T_7. Then candidate tasks are T_7, T_8, T_1, T_2 T_9 and T_3 because their start time is greater than that of the T_6 and overlap T_6. But, as mentioned before, T_2,T_9,T_3,T_5 should not be directly combined with T_6. As a result, we should discard those tasks that can not generate the optical solution. Just as analyzed before, the reason is that there exist tasks "between" the discarded tasks and T_i. So the following method can help the discarding: at first, find the task with the earliest end time among the candidates; then, all those candidates that do not overlap it should be discarded. Among T_7, T_8, T_1, T_2 T_9 and T_3, T_1 is the task with the earliest end time and T_2, T_9 and T_3 do not overlap it, indicating that they three should be discarded.

With the help of the analysis above, we can find the possible subsequences using the method below:

Firstly, use a virtual task $T_0 = [-1,-1]$ as the initial task. T_0 is contrary to the definition of task, but it is very useful to our algorithm. From T_0, we know that T_6 and T_4 can be combined with T_0 directly, thus getting two subsequences: $\{T_0,T_6\}$ and $\{T_0,T_4\}$. Then for subsequence $\{T_0,T_4\}$, the latest task is T_4, with which only T_2 should be combined. So we get $\{T_0,T_6\}$ and $\{T_0,T_4,T_2\}$. For $\{T_0,T_4,T_2\}$, whose latest task is T_2, T_9 and T_3 can be added to it, hence we get $\{T_0,T_6\}$, $\{T_0,T_4,T_2,T_9\}$ and $\{T_0,T_4,T_2,T_3\}$. For $\{T_0,T_4,T_2,T_3\}$, T_5 can be added and we get $\{T_0,T_6\}$, $\{T_0,T_4,T_2,T_9\}$ and $\{T_0,T_4,T_2,T_3,T_5\}$. For $\{T_0,T_4,T_2,T_3,T_5\}$, no tasks can be added. This means that a longest subsequence is found and we should compute the total execution time or number of tasks according to the requirement and check whether the subsequence is "better" than the best one currently found. The process above should be repeated until no new subsequences are found.

Given a task set $TS = \{T_1,T_2,...,T_n\}$, $n \in N^+$, and a strategy target $f \in \{TT,TN\}$, try to find the subsequence $MTS \subseteq TS$ such that $f(MTS)$ is maximum.

Let $TPS = \{t_1, t_2, t_3, ..., t_m\}$ be a time points set, $t_i \in N$ for $i = 1, 2, ..., m$, as shown in Fig. 3. No matter when, the elements in TPS are sorted in ascending order. Or in formal language, if $t_i, t_j \in TPS$ and $i < j$, then $t_i < t_j$. Let operator $TPSGetIndex(t)$ be the operation of returning the index of time point t in TPS.

Let $TLS = \{(t_1, \{T_{1,1}, T_{1.2}, ..., T_{1,m_1}\}), (t_2, \{T_{2,1}, T_{2.2}, ..., T_{2,m_2}\}), ..., (t_m, \{T_{m,1}, T_{m.2}, ..., T_{m,m_m}\})\}$ be task lists, t_i is a time point and $\{T_{i,1}, T_{i.2}, ..., T_{i,m_1}\}$ is a task list, as shown in Fig. 3. TLS stores tasks with identical start time in corresponding list, namely, $\forall i \in \{1, 2, ..., m\}$, $t_i = s_{i,1} = s_{i,2} = ... = s_{i,m_i}$, $s_{i,j}$ is the start time of task $T_{i,j}$. No matter when, the elements in TLS is sorted in ascending order by t_i. Let operator $TLSAdd(T)$ be the operation of adding task T to the list in which it should be according to its start time. Let operator $TLSGet(i)$ be the operation of returning the task list in index i. Let operator $TLSGetFirstNonemptyList(i)$ be the operation of returning the first nonempty task list, searching from index i.

Let $Stack$ be a stack containing task subsequences. Let operator $StackPush(\{T_1, T_2, ..., T_n\})$ be the operation of pushing a task subsequence into the stack and $StackPop(Stack)$ returning the subsequence on the top and removing it.

Let operator $GetRandomTask(\{T_1, T_2, ..., T_n\})$ be the operation of returning a random task from the task set $\{T_1, T_2, ..., T_n\}$. Let operator $GetLatestFinish(\{T_1, T_2, ..., T_n\})$ be the operation of returning the task with the biggest end time and $GetEarliestFinish(\{T_1, T_2, ..., T_n\})$ returning the task with the smallest end time. Abstract the process above, the algorithm is shown following:

Algorithm 1 Maximum Working Time / Task Count (MTT/MTC).

---

1   task **var**:
    earliestFinish, *latestFinish*, *aTask*
2   task subsequence **var**:
    currentSequence
3   task set **var**:
    firstNomemptyList, *combinableTasks*
4   int **var**:
    index, *startIndex*, *endIndex*
5    $TPS \leftarrow \varnothing$
6    $TLS \leftarrow \varnothing$
7    $MTS \leftarrow \varnothing$
8    $Stack \leftarrow \{[-1, -1]\}$
9   *combinableTasks* $\leftarrow \varnothing$
10   **for** each $T_i \in TS$ **do**
11   **if** $s_i \in TPS$ **then**
12       $TPS \leftarrow TPS \cup \{s_i\}$

13	$TLS \leftarrow TLS \cup \{(s_i, \varnothing)\}$
14	**end if**
15	**if** $e_i \in TPS$ **then**
16	$TPS \leftarrow TPS \cup \{e_i\}$
17	$TLS \leftarrow TLS \cup \{(e_i, \varnothing)\}$
18	**end if**
19	**end for**
20	**for** each $T_i \in TS$ **do**
21	$TLSAdd(T_i)$
22	**end for**
23	**while** $Stack \neq \varnothing$ **do**
24	$currentSequence \leftarrow StackPop(Stack)$
25	$latestFinish \leftarrow GetLatestFinish(currentSequence)$
26	$index \leftarrow TPSGetIndex(e_{latestFinish})$
27	$firstNomemptyList \leftarrow TLSGetFirstNonemptyList(index)$
28	**if** $firstNomemptyList = \varnothing$ **then**
29	**if** $f(currentSequence) > f(MTS)$ **then**
30	$MTS \leftarrow currentSequence$
31	**goto** 23
32	**end if**
33	**end if**
34	$aTask \leftarrow GetRandomTask(firstNomemptyList)$
35	$startIndex \leftarrow TPSGetIndex(s_{aTask})$
36	$endIndex \leftarrow TPSGetIndex(e_{aTask})$
37	**for** each $j \in \{startIndex, startIndex + 1, ..., endInde - 2, endIndex - 1\}$ **do**
38	$combinableTasks \leftarrow combinableTasks \cup TLSGet(j)$
39	**end for**
40	$earliestFinish \leftarrow GetEarliestFinish(combinableTasks)$
41	**for** each $T_i \in combinableTasks$ **do**
42	**if** $earliestFinish \cap T_i = \varnothing$ **then**
43	$combinableTasks \leftarrow combinableTasks \setminus \{T_i\}$
44	**end if**
45	**end for**
46	**for** each $T_i \in combinableTasks$ **do**
47	$StackPush(\{currentSequence \cup \{T_i\}\})$
48	**end for**
49	**end while**

The codes from Line 10 to Line 19 collect all the time points and sort them, costing $O(n \log_2 n)$ time complexity. The codes from Line 20 to Line 22 build the task lists in $O(n)$ time. The rest lines enumerate all possible subsequences, and its time complexity is dependent on how the tasks overlap: The codes from Line 25 to Line 33 check if any tasks can be added to the current subsequence, if no tasks can be added, compare the current subsequence with the current best solution; The codes from Line 34 to Line 39 find the candidate tasks that may be combined with *latestFinish*; The codes from Line 40 to Line 45 remove all the tasks that should not combine with *latestFinish* directly; The codes from Line 46 to Line 48 generate new subsequences and push them into the stack.

5   Experimental Result

The algorithm is implemented in Java programming language in our experiment. It is executed on a computer with a CPU of 2.5 GHz and a physical memory of 4 GB. There is no doubt that the number of tasks is a significant factor that affects the performance of the algorithm. So we consider the task count from 10 to 100, because the number of tasks that a participant is assigned is usually much less than 100. We assume a work cycle of [0, 1000]. And for full check on the performance of the algorithm, we do not generate tasks very arbitrarily. When generating a bat of tasks, a percentage is used. The percentage is the ratio of the maximum execution duration to the work cycle. For example, if the percentage is 0.2, then the execution duration of any task in this bat should not exceed 1000*0.2=200 time units. This is for testing the time and memory consumption of the algorithm in different amount of branches.

Table 2. Experimental result for the algorithm. The percentage in the first column is the ratio of the maximum execution duration to the work cycle. For example, if the percentage is 0.2, then the execution duration of any task in this bat will not exceed 1000*0.2=200 time units. The numbers 10, 20, ..., 100 in the second row is the number of tasks. The unit of the value in table body is millisecond.

Percentage	Task Amount									
	10	20	30	40	50	60	70	80	90	100
0.1	10	8	33	94	144	214	2899	3377	16758	107653
0.2	4	4	4	5	17	49	119	113	1450	3703
0.3	3	4	4	4	5	11	22	45	40	375
0.4	3	4	4	4	5	6	9	16	31	223
0.5	4	4	3	4	4	4	6	8	8	20
0.6	4	4	3	4	4	5	4	6	4	14
0.7	4	3	4	4	3	4	4	5	7	8
0.8	8	4	4	3	4	4	5	5	5	7
0.9	3	4	3	4	3	3	4	4	4	5
1	4	4	3	4	4	4	7	11	7	8

The experimental result is shown in Table 2. The result indicates that with the increasing of the task amount and the decreasing of the percentage, the time costs increases extremely quickly. Intuitively, the smaller the percentage is, the smaller possibility two tasks will overlap, leading more branches; also, more tasks bring more branches. Meanwhile, Table 2 shows an important conclusion: the percentage is the main factor that affects the performance. Only when the percentage is between 0.1 and 0.3, the influence of the task amount is obvious. Besides, the memory consumption keeps between 50 and 300 mega bytes during the whole execution of the algorithm, usually about 140 mega bytes. This is due to the use of stack, which makes the algorithm run on depth-first search instead of breadth-first search and saves memory space.

6   Conclusions and Future Work

The experimental result above shows that the MTT/MTC algorithm performs well when used to find the task subsequence with the most execution duration sum or task amount. This indicates that when a participant is assigned dozens of tasks within a work cycle and scheduling algorithms fail to schedule all the tasks within the cycle, the MTT/MTC algorithm is able to find a task subsequence for the participant to execute according to the requirement, thus improving the working efficiency.

This paper proposes a new idea in job scheduling: when a bat of tasks is assigned to some participant in a work cycle, instead of scheduling all the tasks by delaying or advancing some tasks, we turn to selecting some of them for executing because scheduling algorithms may not work due to the work cycle limit.

While finishing this algorithm, we are also thinking about how to improve it. We notice that the problem can be divided into some sub-problems recursively and many braches in the algorithm are repeatedly used when considering how to combine tasks. This means that dynamic programming may be applied to solve this problem and our future work is to study the application of it.

Acknowledgments. This work was supported by the National Natural Science Foundation, China (No.61003024, 61100039, 61003019, 91318301, 61272188, 61202002), the 973 Program (2009CB320702), the Natural Science Foundation of Jiangsu Province (No.BK20131277), the Key Laboratory of Intelligent Perception and Systems for High-Dimensional Information (Nanjing University of Science and Technology), Ministry of Education (No.30920130122005), Natural Science Foundation of Zhejiang Province (No. LY12F02005), and Chinese Fundamental Research Funds for the Central Universities at NJU.

References

1. Li, H.C., Yang, Y.: Dynamic checking of temporal constraints for concurrent work-flows. Electronic Commerce Research and Applications 4, 124–142 (2005)
2. Karger, D., Stein, C., Wein, J.: Scheduling Algorithms, CRC Handbook of Computer Science. CRC Press (1997)

3. Brucker, P.: Scheduling Algorithms, 5th edn. Springer (2007)
4. Li, H.C., Yang, Y., Chen, T.Y.: Resource constraints analysis of workflow specifications. The Journal of Systems and Software 73, 271–285 (2004)
5. Sprecher, A., Drexl, A.: Multi-mode resource-constrained project scheduling by a simple, general and powerful sequencing algorithm. European Journal of Operational Research 107, 431–450 (1998)
6. Mori, M., Tseng, C.C.: A genetic algorithm for multi-mode resource constrained project scheduling problem. European Journal of Operational Research 100, 134–141 (1997)
7. Hartmann, S.: Project Scheduling with Multiple Modes: A Genetic Algorithm. Annals of Operations Research 102, 111–135 (2001)
8. Józefowska, J., Mika, M., Różycki, R., Waligóra, G., Węglarz, J.: Simulated Annealing for Multi-Mode Resource-Constrained Project Scheduling. Annals of Operations Research 102, 13–155 (2001)
9. Bouleimen, K., Lecocq, H.: A new efficient simulated annealing algorithm for the resource-constrained project scheduling problem and its multiple mode version. European Journal of Operational Research 149, 268–281 (2003)
10. Gajpal, Y., Rajendran, C.: An ant-colony optimization algorithm for minimizing the completion-time variance of jobs in flowshops. International Journal of Production Economics 101, 259–272 (2006)
11. Rajendran, C., Ziegler, H.: Two ant-colony algorithms for minimizing total flowtime in permutation flowshops. Computers & Industrial Engineering 48, 789–797 (2005)
12. Eder, J., Pichler, H., Gruber, W., Ninaus, M.: Personal Schedules for Workflow Systems. In: van der Aalst, W.M.P., ter Hofstede, A.H.M., Weske, M. (eds.) BPM 2003. LNCS, vol. 2678, pp. 216–231. Springer, Heidelberg (2003)

Entity Identification in Deep Web

Fangjiao Jiang, Yuehong Meng, Mingsheng Wei, and Quanbin Li

School of Physics and Electronic Engineering
Jiangsu Normal University
Jiangsu, China
{jiangfj,mengyh,weims,liqb}@jsnu.edu.cn

Abstract. The Web has been rapidly deepened with the prevalence of databases online. From different Web sources, the records usually use different representations to refer to the same real world entity. Therefore, there is a high demand for identifying these entities from multiple Web databases in many Web application, e.g., comparison shopping. In this paper, we propose an effective entity identification approach which is based on a similarity function. Moreover, we develop query-based dynamic weight techniques in our approach. Experimental results show that our approach can effectively discover the records representing the same entity in the real world.

Keywords: Deep Web, dynamic attribute weight, similarity function, entity identification.

1 Introduction

The Web has been rapidly deepened with the prevalence of databases online, which are also called Hidden or Deep Web. Data sources on the Deep Web are mostly structured with a 3.4 ratio outnumbering unstructured sources and span well across all subject domains. Today, this high qualified and diverse information is playing an important role in our lives. However, Web databases provide dynamic query-based data access through their query interfaces instead of static URL links the Web Pages in the Surface Web provide, which makes the traditional search engine do not work well. It is thus essential to build a system which can help users to access the information from Web databases effectively and efficiently as traditional search engine does to the Surface Web.

In brief, the goal of Web database integration is to provide an uniform interface which helps the user to submit his/her queriesand then access the data from numerous Web databases automatically. While integrating data from different sources, heterogeneity often occurs when the records use different representations to refer to the same real-world entity. Therefore, there is a high demand for identifying these entities from multiple Web databases. For example, a comparison-shopping system needs to collect the price and other information of the same product from multiple providers. Such kind of applications requires that the collected data be entity identified so that they can be appropriately organized for subsequent analysis.

Z. Huang et al. (Eds.): WISE 2013 Workshops 2013, LNCS 8182, pp. 144–152, 2014.

Example 1 *It is a typical scenario that a user wants to purchase a book with lowest price among book sources. Fig. 1 shows a portion of a sample result page from three online bookstores, gobookshopping.com, abebooks.com and amazon.com, in response to the same query Stephenie over the Author field. We can figure out that the 1st record in Fig.1(a) and the 1st record in Fig.1(b) refer to the same book, because they have the same title and the same author which are very important for a book, even if these records are not identical.*

(a)   (b)

Fig. 1. The Example of the Same Entities from Different Web Databases

Therefore, before these query results returned from multiple Web databases to the user, one of the main task of integration system is to match records representing the same entity, although they return from different databases in the presence of mismatched information. There have been many techniques proposed for solving the entity identification problem [1]. And developing accurate and efficient techniques for entity identification has emerged as an important problem. Accuracy means the correctness of the result, i.e., whether the record representing the same entity can be identified correctly, which is the basic and main goal of the entity identification. Efficiency refers to the computation complexity of the entity identification algorithm which is essential to large-scale data sets. In Deep Web scenario, these two problems also exist. In particularly, since the data is large-scale, on-the-fly and query-dependent, these two problems become more difficult to address.

How to improve the computational efficiency of entity identification algorithms for the large-scale records from Web databases?

How to define the distance metric for the on-the-fly and query-dependent recorders from Web databases?

The first is to apply a computationally efficient approach instead of a nested-loop approach between each pair of records which is the need of $O(n^2)$ pairs of comparison for a data set of records. The second is to combine field-level similarity metrics with appropriate weights according to user query to determine overall similarity between two records. In this paper, we mainly focus on the second challenge. Our extensive experiments using real data sets show that our solution has very good accuracy for entity identification.

The rest of this paper is organized as follows. Section 2 reviews previous related work. Section 3 defines a similarity function based on static attribute weight. Section 4 explores the dynamic attribute weight based on the user query for entity identification. In Section 5, we report our experimental results. Section 6 concludes the paper.

2   Related Works

There have been many methods and tools developed for entity resolution (see[2], [3] for surveys). The presented methods of entity identification can be divided into two categories: Some approaches rely on training data to learn how to match the records. Others rely on domain knowledge or on generic distance metrics to match records.

Probabilistic Matching Models [4], [5]Supervised and Semi-Supervised Learning [6], [7], Active-Learning-Based Techniques [8],[9],[10] require some training data or some human effort to create the matching models. In Deep Web scenario, since the data can only be obtained via query, it is a partial and biased part of a full dataset. Therefore, the representative data for training is absent. This makes the supervised, active learning and other techniques which need training data are not appropriate. One good way of avoiding the need for training data is to define a similarity metric [11],[12] for records. Using the similarity metric and an appropriate matching threshold, it is possible to match similar records, without the need for training.

Some techniques have been applied for similarity metric: Character-based similarity metrics [13], Token-based similarity metrics [14], Numeric Similarity Metrics [15]. While multiple methods exist for detecting similarities of string-based data, the methods for capturing similarities in numeric data are rather primitive.

3   Similarity Function

In this section, we firstly describe techniques that will be applied for matching attribute with string data and numeric data in the entity identification context. In most real-life situations, the records consist of multiple attributes, making the entity identification problem much more complicated. In this section, we also propose the method that is used for matching records with multiple attributes.

3.1   Similarity Metrics of Attribute Value

Consider two relations R and S that share a set of attributes $A_1, \ldots, A_k$, Each attribute has a metric Mi that defines the difference a value of $R.A_i$ and a value of $S.A_i$. There are many ways to define the similarity metric at the attribute level. In this paper, We take two character-based similarity metrics: Edit distance and

Q-gram distance, and one token-based similarity metric: Atomic strings distance for textual similarity. Since the methods for capturing similarities in numeric data are rather primitive, we define a similarity metrics called Range distance for numeric similarity.

Edit distance: Given two strings s_1 and s_2, their edit distance is the minimum number of edit operations (insertions, deletions, and substitutions) of single characters that are needed.

Q-gram distance: Given a string s and an integer q, the set of Q-grams of s, denote G(s) is obtained by sliding a window of length q over the characters of string s. The q-gram distance between two strings s_1 and s_2 is defined as follows:

$$S(a_i) = 1 - \frac{|G(s_1) \cap G(s_2)|}{|G(s_1) \cup G(s_2)}$$ (1)

Atomic strings distance: An atomic string is a sequence of alphanumeric characters delimited by punctuation characters. Given two strings s1 and s2, their atomic strings distance is the number of their matching atomic strings divided by their average number of atomic strings.

Range distance: Given two numbers n1 and n2, denote R(n1) is the range from 0 to n1, and denote R(n2) is the range from 0 to n2 , The Range distance between two numbers n1 and n2 is define as follows:

$$S(a_i) = 1 - \frac{|R(s_1) \cap R(s_2)|}{|R(s_1) \cup R(s_2)}$$ (2)

3.2   Similarity Function

Different attribute may have different importance when we decide whether two records represent the same entity. If we know about this, using a set of pre-defined basis similarity measures and the weight of each attribute, a single composite similarity function over one pair of records r_j and r_k could be identified as follows.

$$S(r_j, r_k) = \sum_i w_i * S(a_i)$$ (3)

In which w_i denotes the importance of attribute i, $S(a_i)$ denotes the value similarity of attribute i between record r_j and r_k .

$$S(r_j, r_k) = \begin{cases} \geq \delta & \text{Yes} \\ < \delta & \text{No} \end{cases}$$ (4)

If most of their attributes are similar of two records, it is likely that the two records are duplicate. Therefore, we define that when the composite similarity is larger than the specified threshold, the pair of records represent the same entity.

4   Dynamical Attribute Weight

In section 3, we described methods that can be used to match individual fields
of a record. Moreover, we defined a single composite similarity function over
one pair of records to identify the same entity in real world. However, since
all the data of the Web database could not be accessed, the access of weights of
attributes will be much more complicated. In this section, we propose a sampling
method for entity identification with appropriate attribute weights based on the
user query.

4.1   Query-Dependent Sampling

The only way to access the data from Web databases is submitting queries on
the interface. Due to the restricted nature of the interface, it is challenging to
produce samples that are truly uniform.

Example 2 *In Academic Papers domain, because the topics that every Author
focuses on are so different, the Attribute Word Distributions of the corresponding results on attribute Title by submitting the query probes on the attribute
Author are usually quite different. So Attribute Correlation of Title and Author
is relatively strong. However, if we submit different values on attribute Year,
the Attribute Word Distributions of the different returned results on attribute
Title are very similar because the topics usually change very slowly each year.
Therefore, the Attribute Correlation of Title and Year is relatively weak.*

Consequently, the task is to produce samples that have small skew, i.e., samples that deviate as little as possible from uniform distribution. In this paper,
we apply attribute-correlation-based sampling approach [16] for approximate
information of the Web Database.

After discovering the least correlative attribute $Attr_i$, we submit some query
probes on $Attr_i$ to the Web databases and collect the returned results on attribute $Attr_u$ as the attribute-level sample of $Attr_u$, which is the approximate
random sample. Then we analyze the distribution of attribute values. More diverse the attribute values are, more distinguishing the specific attribute value is.
We adopt standard error to represent the diverse of attribute values.

4.2   Record-Frequency-Based Weight

In information retrieval, we consider idf as an important factor for the term
weight. Here, we view every record as a short document with several phrases,
in which each phrase is a value of one field. More frequent the records contain
different values of a field; less important this field will be in differentiating the
different records.

Therefore, we compute the weight of the field associated with the record frequency information.

$$ifw_i = log(N/rf) \tag{5}$$

where N is the number of all the records in the Web database, rf is the number of different values of the field. Therefore, in order to compute the appropriate attribute weight, we need all the record of the Web Database, which can reflect the true distribution of the attribute values. However, as we mentioned in section 1, usually, we do not know all the information which only be access via the user query. As mentioned in section 4.1, we can access the better sample on each attribute by Query-dependent Sampling approach.

4.3   Query-Based Tuning Weight

When we give the queries on different attributes or different attribute combinations, the distribution of attribute values are quietly different. For example, if the query is on Price attribute, the values on this attribute of every returned record are the same. Obviously, the value of Price attribute is no longer distinguishing for entity identification. Moreover, if an attribute is correlation with the attribute that the user cares more about and submits the query on, the distribution of this attribute values will be less diverse. Therefore, the attribute weight will change according to user query. Correlation of each attribute pair can be calculated that was introduced in our prior work[16]. Based on the Attribute Correlation (AC), we adjust the weight as follows.

$$w_i = ifw_i * \prod_j (1 - AC(a_j, a_i)) \tag{6}$$

where a_j is the attribute that the user submit their query on. If the query refers to several attributes, we take every AC between attribute j and attribute i into consideration.

5   Experiments

In this section, we first describe our experiments as well as the data sets and then introduce our evaluation. Finally, we report the experimental results.

5.1   Experimental Setup

To evaluate the effectiveness of our approach in identifying the entities, we select 40 Web databases as our data sets which cover four domains: Movies, Books, Jobs and houses. For each domain, we collect 10 Web databases for integration. We invite forty users with different professions and different ages to behave as buyers. Each of them issue 5 queries on the integrated interface of each domain respectively. For returned results of each query, we use our approach to identify the same entity pairs from different Web Databases.

5.2   Experimental Evaluation

We evaluate the entity identification results by three popular measures: precision, recall and F1-measure, where precision is defined as the proportion of correctly identified entity pairs, i.e., two records matching the same entity, to candidate pairs returned from multiple Web databases, recall is the proportion of correctly identified record pairs to all correct entity pairs, and F1-measure is the harmonic average of precision and recall. They are defined as follows.

$$precision = \frac{N_C}{N_A} \tag{7}$$

$$recall = \frac{N_C}{N_T} \tag{8}$$

$$F1 - measure = \frac{2 * precision * recall}{precision + recall} \tag{9}$$

where N_C denotes correctly identified entity pairs, N_A denotes all identified entity pairs, and N_A denotes all correct entity pairs.

5.3   Experimental Results

We report the precision, recall and F1-measure using dynamic attribute weight and static attribute weight for entity identification. Table 1 shows the experimental results when the threshold is equal to 0.85. The accuracy of entity identification using dynamic attribute weight method is much higher than that using static attribute weight method.

Table 1. Accuracy Comparison of Dynamic and Static Attribute Weight

Domain	weight	precision	recall	F1-measure
Movie	Dynamic	0.944	0.907	0.925
	Static	0.902	0.862	0.882
Book	Dynamic	0.956	0.912	0.933
	Static	0.921	0.861	0.89
Job	Dynamic	0.912	0.873	0.892
	Static	0.877	0.821	0.848
House	Dynamic	0.923	0.901	0.912
	Static	0.889	0.843	0.865

Different similarity threshold may affect the accuracy of entity identification. In Figure 2, we investigate the change of the precision, recall and F1-measure. When the threshold is below 0.8, the precision grows greatly, while the recall decreases with the threshold increasing. On the other hand, it can be seen that the growth of the precision increases gently while the recall decreases quickly when the threshold is above 8.5. Therefore, in experiments, we select the threshold between 0.8 and 0.9.

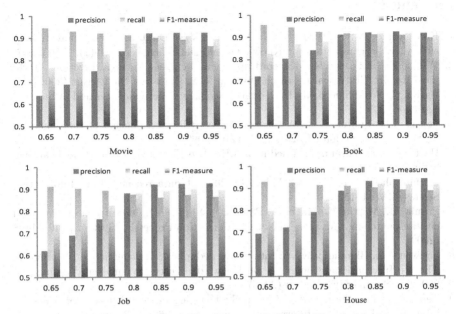

Fig. 2. Accuracy Sensitivity to Different Threshold

6   Conclusion

In this paper, we studied entity identification problem in Deep Web scenario. We introduced a novel entity identification approach for return results over Web database. We firstly gave a similarity function based on static attribute weight. Then we analyzed the characteristics of Deep Web and take the user query into consideration. We explored a dynamic attribute weight approach based on user query. To evaluate the effectiveness of our approach, we performed experiments over 40 Web databases as our data sets which cover four domains: Movies, Books, Jobs and houses. The experimental results indicated that the accuracy of our approach is higher than that of the static attribute weight approach. How to improve the computational efficiency of entity identification algorithms for the large-scale records from Web databases is another challenge problem. We will address it in the future work.

Acknowledgments. This research was supported by the grants from Natural Science Foundation of Jiangsu Higher Education(No: 12KJB520004) and Project Funded by the Priority Academic Program Development of Jiangsu Higher Education Institutions (PAPD).

References

1. Elmagarmid, A.K., Ipeirotis, P.G., Verykios, V.S.: Duplicate record detection: A survey. IEEE Transactions on Knowledge and Data Engineering 19(1), 1–16 (2007)
2. Winkler, W.E.: Overview of record linkage and current research directions. Technical Report, Statistical Research Division, U.S. Bureau of the Census (2006)
3. Batini, C., Scannapieco, M.: Data quality: Concepts, methodologies and techniques. Springer (2006)
4. Fellegi, I.P., Sunter, A.B.: A theory for record linkage. Journal of the American Statistical Association 64(328), 1183–1210 (1969)
5. Hastie, T., Tibshirani, R., Friedman, J.H.: The Elements of Statistical Learning. Springer (2001)
6. Cochinwala, M., Kurien, V., Lalk, G.: Efficient data reconciliation. Information Sciences 137, 1–15 (2001)
7. Pasula, H., Marthi, B., Milch, B., Russell, S., Shpitser, I.: Identity uncertainty and citation matching. Advances in Neural Information Processing Systems, 1401–1408 (2002)
8. Sarawagi, S., Bhamidipaty, A.: Interactive deduplication using active learning. In: The 8th International Conference on Knowledge Discovery and Data Mining, pp. 269–278. Springer, Edmonton (2002)
9. Tejada, S., Knoblock, C.A., Minton, S.: Learning object identification rules for information integration. Information Systems 26(8), 607–633 (2001)
10. Tejada, S., Knoblock, C.A., Minton, S.: Learning domain-independent string transformation weights for high accuracy object identification. In: The 8th International Conference on Knowledge Discovery and Data Mining, pp. 350–359. Springer, Edmonton (2002)
11. Guha, S., Koudas, N., Marathe, A., Srivastava, D.: Merging the results of approximate match operations. In: The 30th International Conference on Very Large Databases, pp. 636–647. Springer, Toronto (2004)
12. Koudas, N., Marathe, A., Srivastava, D.: Flexible string matching against large databases in practice. In: The 30th International Conference on Very Large Databases, pp. 1078–1086. Springer, Toronto (2004)
13. Navarro, G.: A guided tour to approximate string matching. ACM Computing Surveys 33(1), 31–88 (2001)
14. Monge, A.E., Elkan, C.P.: The field matching problem: Algorithms and applications. In: The Second International Conference on Knowledge Discovery and Data Mining, pp. 267–270. AAAI Press, Portland (1996)
15. Agrawal, R., Srikant, R.: Searching with numbers. In: The 11th International World Wide Web Conference, pp. 420–431. ACM, Honolulu (2002)
16. Jiang, F., Meng, W., Meng, X.: Selectivity estimation for exclusive query translation in deep web data integration. In: Zhou, X., Yokota, H., Deng, K., Liu, Q. (eds.) DASFAA 2009. LNCS, vol. 5463, pp. 595–600. Springer, Heidelberg (2009)

Situation-Aware Data Service Composition
Based on Service Hyperlinks

Chen Liu[1], Jianwu Wang[2], and Yanbo Han[1]

[1] Cloud Computing Research Center, North China University of Technology, Beijing, China
[2] San Diego Supercomputer Center, UCSD, U.S.A.
liuchen@ncut.edu.cn,jianwu@sdsc.edu,hanyanbo@ncut.edu.cn

Abstract. Today, it is a big challenge to support on-demand Web data combination in accordance with situation changes. This paper proposes a service hyperlink model to describe loose data dependencies between data services. Service hyperlinks can be automatically discovered using semantic matching techniques, and then be utilized via an automatic algorithm to efficiently compose data services to respond situation changes. Analyses and applications show the feasibility of our approach.

Keywords: Data Service; Service Hyperlink; Automatic Composition; Situational Integration.

1 Introduction

Situational applications are essentially "good enough" software, which are developed fast, easy-to-use, uncomplicated and serve a unique set of requirements[1]. As business requirements keep changing, situational applications have to evolve to accommodate these changes [1] [2]. When it comes to the data integration applications, traditional approaches face great challenges [3]. They need to be flexible enough and quickly adapted to embrace ever-changing situations.

Recently, the concept of "data as service" or "data service" is proposed to offer a unified access to diverse Web data, provide semantically richer view and advanced querying functionality [4]. Composition of such data services is essentially a new way to integrate data through combining service interfaces [5]. A key challenge is how to quickly and flexibly compose data services to respond situation changes.

Traditional automatic service composition approaches can be referenced for data service composition [6]. However, current approaches still are not flexible enough to handle lasting situation changes. For example, many automatic composition approaches need to pre-define a global ontology, which provides unified and consistent semantic descriptions for all services to be composed [7-8]. The biggest obstacle of these approaches is how to flexibly adapt global ontology in accordance with situation changes. It is very hard and costly, especially in an open environment like Web.

---

[1] Situational application, http://en.wikipedia.org/wiki/Situated_software

Z. Huang et al. (Eds.): WISE 2013 Workshops 2013, LNCS 8182, pp. 153–167, 2014.

Inspired by Web hyperlink, on top of our previous data service model [5][9], this paper proposes a new abstraction to model linkages between services, called **Service Hyperlink,** and a corresponding approach, named **DASA**, to automate data service composition process. Our main contributions include two parts. First, DASA does not require the pre-establishment of a global ontology. With the techniques of P2P semantic matching, the necessary knowledge for each service linkage in a composition process is decentralized and recorded in a service hyperlink. Second, DASA can handle situation changes through supporting users to easily express and flexibly update their requirements by drawing visualized tables. An automatic algorithm is developed to generate subsequent composition plans to reach updated goals.

2   Running Example and Problem Analysis

Criminal investigation is a typical scenario of situational data integration across multiple organizations. When a vicious injury case happens, police officers need to infer and determine suspects via available clues. The task, shown in Fig. 1, is to find possible relations between victims and suspects. With the investigation goes on, more clues are discovered. They can help the police narrow down the scope of suspect candidates. However, to make full use of them, data integration approaches need to be flexible enough to adapt to situation changes, which often means updated integration requirements and more involved data sources.

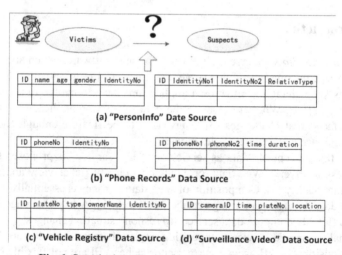

Fig. 1. Sample data sources for data service composition

For example, it is usually a good start to investigate relatives and recent contacts of victims because most crimes are done by acquaintances. To get required data, shown in part (a) and (b) of Fig. 1, several data sources are involved, which are provided by the civil affair agency and a mobile telecommunication company, respectively. Shortly after the case happens, police officers discover that there are two related crime scenes. The first scene is far from the second one. Therefore, police officers infer that the criminals probably use a vehicle. Then they decide to trace suspicious vehicles through investigating surveillance videos and take them as a breakthrough point.   As part (c) and (d) of Fig. 1 show, this means two new data sources are involved, which are provided by the local transportation management agency.

The above scenario illustrates the problem this paper tries to solve: how to easily and quickly compose data services in accordance with situation changes? The paper focuses on how to handle changes of integration requirements. For example, in the above scenario, at the beginning, the police wants to integrate the data source (a) and (b) in Fig. 1 to mine the social relationships of the victims. Next, after new clues are discovered, integration requirements are updated to make vehicle information involved.   It also cause that more data sources like (c) and (d) in Fig. 1 are involved.

3   Data Service Model

The paper adopts our previously proposed data service model [4][8]. In this model, nested relation [9] is the unified data model for common kinds of data sources, such as XML, HTML and relation tables. Nested relation allows relations to have relation-valued attributes.

Definition 1 (Nested Relation): A nested relation consists of its schema and instances. The attributes and relations are **elements** of the schema. Let A be the universal set of attribute names and relation names.

- A **relation schema** is the form of $R(S)$ where $R \in A$ is the relation schema name and S is a list of the form $(A_1, A_2, ..., A_m)$, where each A_i is (i) either an atomic attribute or (ii) a relation schema of a sub-relation. Here, we call $(A_1, A_2, ..., A_m)$ as the root elements of a relation schema $R(S)$.
- An **instance** of schema $R(S)$ is an ordered m-tuple in form of $(a_1, a_2, ..., a_m)$ such that (i) a_i is a primary data value if A_i is an atomic attribute, or (ii) a_i is an instance of A_i if A_i is a relation scheme.

Definition 2 (Data Service): A data service is a tuple with five elements: $ds=$ *<uri, name, i_params, o_schema, o_instance_list>*, where:
- *uri is the universal identifier of the data service;*
- *name* is the name of the data service;
- *i_params* is the input parameter set of a service;

Table 1. Visualized Operators Of Nested Tables

Object	Operators	Semantics
Table	CreateTable	create a new table with a unique table name
	RenameTable	rename a table
	AddSubTable	copy a table and make it a sub-relation of an element in a new table
	Filter	filter a table by some pre-defined conditions
Column	CreateColumn	create a column from a table
	RenameColumn	rename a column from a table
	AddColumn	copy a column and make it an attribute of an element in a new table
	DeleteColumn	delete a column from a table

- *o_schema* is the data schema of the service's output represented as the nested relational schema defined in Def. 1;
- *o_instance_list* is the runtime instance list of a data service, which is a list of nested relation instances in Def. 1 in accordance with the o_schema.

Furthermore, a data service is associated and configured with a presentation view, which is a nested table. Nested table provides a spreadsheet-like end-user programming environment and is intuitive and easy for users to manipulate and analyze business data [8]. A set of operators for visually handling nested tables is also defined in our previous work [4]. Table I shows some commonly used operators.

For example, as shown in Fig. 1, the relational tables of *PersonInfo* and *Phone Record* data source cover data about the basic information of a person, her mobile phone number and her phone records. Across these tables, a data service *PhoneRecords queryPhoneRecords(string startTime, string endTime)* can be provided. With it, users can easily retrieve all phone records by giving a time interval. As Fig. 2 shows, the output of *queryPhoneRecords* service can be transformed and represented as a nested relation and a corresponding nested table.

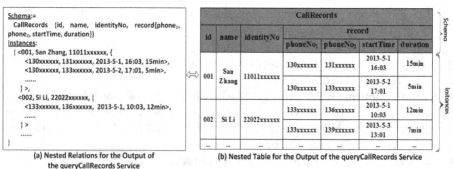

(a) Nested Relations for the Output of the queryCallRecords Service

(b) Nested Table for the Output of the queryCallRecords Service

Fig. 2. A sample of nested relations and its corresponding nested table

4   Data Service Composition Approach

Rationales of our DASA approach are shown in Fig. 3. Based on the above-mentioned data service model, various data sources can be modeled and accessed via a unified service interface. All underlying data services are registered into a centralized service registry for better management and maintenance.

With our previously developed tools [5], at the beginning, users need to draw two tables to represent the start and the goal respectively. An example can be found in Fig. 5. These tables can be updated when situation changes. Possible composition plans can be automatically computed and recommended with the algorithm 1 in Section 6 after the goal change each time.

Note that involved data sources could be very different, even cross several domains. Pre-establishment of global domain ontology is practically impossible. Hence, the DASA approach tries to decompose the necessary domain knowledge into small

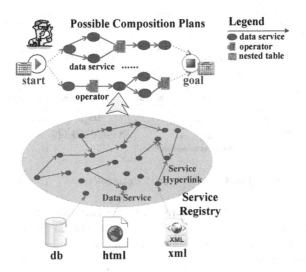

Fig. 3. Rationales of the DASA approach

pieces, called as *service hyperlink*, which records data correlations between two data services. Service hyperlinks can be automatically detected and generated by analyzing and mining semantic relationships between data service schemas. They are locally established in a peer-to-peer pattern and can be reused in future service compositions.

5   Service Hyperlink

5.1   Service Hyperlink Model

Given two data services ds_1 and ds_2, if input or output of a service is fully or partially semantically matched with another service, we say there is a data correlation relation between them. DASA distinguishes two kinds of data correlations. The first one is between output and input of two data services. It can help users compose and invoke them in sequence. The second one is between the service outputs. It can help users aggregate the outputs in order to combine the corresponding Web data. We define data correlation as a set of data mappings in Def. 3 and Def. 4. Based on them, the service hyperlink is defined in Def. 5. Fig. 4 gives two service hyperlink examples with different kinds of data mappings.

Definition 3 (Output-Input Data Mapping): Given two data services ds_1 and ds_2, S is the output schema of ds_1, I is the input parameters of ds_2, an Output-Input data mapping between an element e in S and a parameter p in I can be defined as a 4-tuple <$e, p, rel, confidence$>, where:

- e: an element of output schema of ds_1;
- p: an input parameter of ds_2;
- rel: semantic relationship between e and p, which will be defined in Def. 6;
- *confidence:* a confidence value in [0, 1] that e and p have the given relationship.

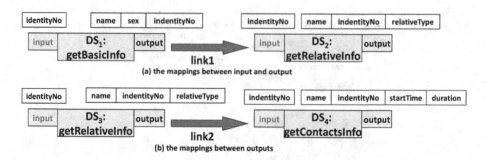

Fig. 4. Service hyperlink examples

Definition 4 (Output-Output Data Mapping): Given two data services ds_1 and ds_2, S_1 and S_2 are the output schema of ds_1 and ds_2 respectively, an Output-Output data mapping between two elements e_1 and e_2 in S_1 and S_2 can be defined as a 4-tuple $< e_1, e_2, rel, confidence>$, where:

- e_1, e_2: two elements belong to output schema S_1 and S_2 respectively;
- rel: semantic relationship between e_1 and e_2, which will be defined in Def. 6;
- $confidence$: a confidence value in $[0, 1]$ that e and p have the given relationship.

Definition 5 (Service Hyperlink): A service hyperlink is a 5-tuple: $<id, S_s, S_t, oi\_mappings, oo\_mappings >$, where:

- id: a unique identifier for a service hyperlink;
- Ss, St: source and target data service;
- $oi\_mappings$: a set of Output-Input mappings between output of S_s and input of S_t;
- $oo\_mappings$: a set of Output-Output mappings between outputs of S_s and S_t

5.2   Automatic Generation of Service Hyperlinks

As analyzed in Section 1, it is usually impractical to pre-establish a global domain ontology that suits the needs of all data services. DASA regards involved data services as independent peers. Each data service organizes related data in accordance with its own data schemas. Data mappings between two data services are locally detected and recorded as a service hyperlink.

To specify data mappings in Def. 3 and 4, we define six types of semantic relationships. Here, in a matching process, the input parameters and output schema elements of a data service are called in a joint name: **entity**. The definition of semantic relationships is based on the comparisons of entity intentional domains, i.e. the set of real world objects that they represent [11].

Definition 6 (Semantic Relationship): Given two entities e_1 and e_2, $Dom(e)$ represents the intentional domain of an entity, the possible semantic relationships are:

- equivalence($\doteq$): $e_1 \doteq e_2$ iff $Dom(e_1) = Dom(e_2)$;
- subset-subsumption ($\subseteq$): $e_1 \subseteq e_2$ iff $Dom(e_1) \subset Dom(e_2)$;
- superset-subsumption: ($\supseteq$): $e_1 \supseteq e_2$ iff $Dom(e_1) \supset Dom(e_2)$;

- overlapping $(⋒)$: $e_1 ⋒ e_2$ iff $Dom(e_1) \cap Dom(e_2) \neq \phi$ and e_1 and e_2 do not have equivalence, subset-subsumption or superset-subsumption relationship;
- disjointness $(\perp)$: $e_1 \perp e_2$ iff $Dom(e_1) \cap Dom(e_2) = \phi \wedge \exists e_3 (Dom(e_1) \cup Dom(e_2) \subset Dom(e_3))$;
- incompatibility $(\not\approx)$: $e_1 \not\approx e_2$ iff $Dom(e_1) \cap Dom(e_2) = \phi \wedge \not\exists e_3 (Dom(e_1) \cup Dom(e_2) \subset Dom(e_3))$;

DASA uses the lexical knowledge to automatically detect data mappings, which is the knowledge about the words used in describing entities. A linguistic-based matcher is developed to use an electronic lexicon WordNet [12] as common knowledge to calculate the terminological relations between entity names. In the thesaurus, terms are semantically grouped using terminological relations according to their meanings.

Table 2. Terminological relations and corresponding Similarity Weight

Terminological Relation	Weight	Comments
Synonym	1	two words are synonym
Hypernymy/ Hyponymy	0.8	one word has a broader, more general meaning than the other word
Meronymy/ Holonymy	0.6	one word is part of the other word
Antonymy	0	two words are antonymy
Unrecognized	0.4	two words do not have any above-mentioned relations

Similar with the P2P semantic technique in H-Match algorithm [13], we pre-assign a weight, shown in Table 2, to each terminological relation in order to calculate the similarity value between two entities. For single terms that can be found in Wordnet, the similarity value is the weight based on their terminological relation. For compound terms like *IDCardNo* and *IdentityCardNo*, which usually cannot be directly found in Wordnet, the matcher will first divide them into a set of simple terms, such as {ID, Card, No} and {Identity, Card, No}. Then, it tries to find the highest-strength terminological relationships between terms in the different sets by looking them up in thesaurus. The product of weights of these discovered terminological relationships will be the similarity value between the two compound terms. Based on the similarity value, the matcher can discover the semantic relationship between elements. The main idea is to divide similarity values into several intervals. By judging which interval the similarity value falls into, as Table 3 shows, the semantic relationship can be discovered.

Table 3. Intervals and corresponding Semantic relationships

Similarity Value Intervals	Semantic Relationship
(0.8, 1]	equivalence($\doteq$)
(0.6, 0.8]	subset/superset subsumption ($\subseteq$)
(0.4, 0.6]	overlapping ($⋒$)
(0.2, 0.4]	disjointness ($\perp$)
[0, 0.2]	incompatibility ($\not\approx$)

When a new service is added into the registry, the above matching algorithm is invoked so that service hyperlinks will be automatically detected. Note that the matching algorithm cannot guarantee 100% correctness of discovered data mappings. Therefore, incorrect service hyperlinks might be detected. We allow users to manually correct the service hyperlinks before they are used for service composition.

6   Automatic Data Service Composition with Service Hyperlinks

6.1   Data Service Composition

Fig. 5 shows two sample nested tables that are the start and the goal of a service composition, respectively. These two nested tables are also encapsulated as special data services, which do not have input parameters and return all contents in the table as outputs.

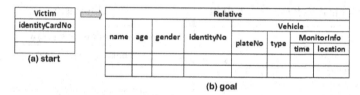

Fig. 5. A sample of start and goal of a composition process

Definition 7 (Data Service Composition Plan): Let S be the available data service set; H be the underlying service hyperlinks; s and g are two special data services predefined by users, which denote the start and the goal of the composition process respectively; A data service composition plan is defined as a path from s to g which satisfy the following predicate logic:

$$\exists\, S' \subseteq S, S' = \{s_1, s_2, \ldots, s_t, \ldots, s_n\}, H' \subseteq H, H'$$
$$= \{link_1, link_2 \ldots, link_t, \ldots, link_{(n-1)}\} : s_1 = s, s_n = g, s_t$$
$$= op_i\big(s_{(t-2)}, s_{(t-1)}, link_{(t-1)}\big) \; or \; s_t = op_j\big(s_{(t-1)}, link_{(t-1)}\big)$$

where:
- op_i: a recommended unary/binary operator in Table I for just s_i, or both s_i and s_{i+1};
- s_i and s_{i+1} : two data services need to be invoked, s_{i+1} is the follow-up service of s_i, in which s_0 is the start service s, s_n is the goal service g;
- $link_i$: a service hyperlink between s_i and s_{i+1} .

Def. 7 gives the formal definition of a data service composition in DASA. As this definition shows, the goal of whole composition process is to find a path to reach the goal defined by users. However, in many cases, it may be too ideal to achieve a composite data service which is exactly the same as the goal predefined by users. Therefore, we relax this constraint by finding a composite data service which can fully cover the users' goal. For example, shown in Fig. 6, the suspect information in part (b) can cover the part (a). The definition about coverage degree can be found in Def. 8. If the coverage degree is equal or greater than 1, we say a service can fully cover the other service.

Suspect			
name	age	gender	identityNo

(a) suspect information

Suspect				Relative	
name	age	gender	identityNo	identityNo	relation

(b) suspect information with relatives

Fig. 6. Two possible goals about suspect information

Definition 8 (Coverage Degree): Let S_1 and S_2 are the output schemas of two data service ds_1 and ds_2, E_1 and E_2 are their corresponding entity set, the coverage degree denotes the degree how much ds_1 will be covered by ds_2, which is defined as:

$$c(ds_1, ds_2) := |E_1 \div E_2|/|E_1| \text{ ,where:}$$

- $E_1 \div E_2 = \{e | e \in E_1 \wedge \nexists e_i(e_i \in E_2 \wedge e \doteq e_i)\} \, (i = 1..|E_2|)$

For example, as Fig 6 shows, the entity set of part (a) is *suspect{name, age, gender, identityNo}*; the entity set of part (b) is *suspect{name, age, gender, identityNo, Relative{identityNo, relation}}*. According to Def. 8, we can calculate that the coverage degree is 1, which means part (a) is fully covered by part (b).

6.2   Service Operator Recommendation

As explained above, proper service operators might be needed to connect services, which will be part of service composition plan. So we explain how to recommend service operators first. Here, we assume that e_1 and e_2 are two elements from two schemas of current service and its follow-up service. We will introduce the recommendation rule for each possible semantic relationship between them, and discuss how to achieve the combination with the help of the rules.

(1) $e_1 \doteq e_2$

This means e_1 and e_2 refer to the same real world object set and they should be combined into one element. For example, attribute *identityNo* and *identityNumber* are equivalent although they have different names. In this case, operator *RenameColumn* will be recommended.

(2) $e_1 \subseteq e_2$ or $e_1 \supseteq e_2$

This means the set of real world objects referred by e_1 should be the subset or superset of e_2. According to the type of e_1 and e_2, the recommendation rules are:

- If $e_1 \subseteq e_2$, e_1 is an attribute and e_2 is a sub-relation, then recommend operator *addColumn(e_2, e_1)*;
- If $e_1 \subseteq e_2$, e_1 is a sub-relation and e_2 is a sub-relation, then recommend operator *addSubTable(e_2, e_1)*;
- If $e_1 \subseteq e_2$, e_1 is an attribute and e_2 is an attribute, then recommend two sequential operators: *createColumn(e_2, newCol)→addColumn(e_2, newCol, e_1)*;
- If $e_1 \subseteq e_2$, e_1 is an sub-relation and e_2 is an attribute, then recommend two sequential operators: *createColumn(e_2, newCol)→addSubTable(e_2, newCol, e_1)*;

(3) $e_1 \pitchfork e_2$

This means the set of real world objects, referred by e_1 and e_2, may have something in common but not completely the same. In this case, the recommendation rule is to split the element e_1 and e_2 into three disjoint elements e_1-$(e_1 \cap e_2)$, $e_1 \cap e_2$ and e_2-$(e_1 \cap e_2)$. Besides, a common parent element will also be defined.

(4) $e_1 \perp e_2$

This means e_1 should be a sibling of e_2. In this case, the recommendation rule is to add element e_2 to be e_1's sibling. Assume the parent element of e_1 is e_1', then operator $AddColumn(e_1', e_1, e_2)$ will be recommended.

(5) $e_1 \ncong e_2$

This means the set of real world objects, referred by e_1 and e_2, are completely disjointed. In this case, the recommendation rule can be defined as follows. Assume the parent element of e_1 and e_2 are e_1' and e_2', if $e_1'=/\ni e_2'$, then operator $AddColumn(e_1', e_1, e_2)$ will be recommended.

6.3   Automatic Data Service Composition Algorithm

We develop an algorithm to automatically get all possible composition plans in Def. 7 to reach user's goal. Note that user's goal can be updated in accordance with situation changes. If the goal changed, the following algorithm will be re-invoked to compute the updated composition plans and recommend to users. Users can choose and alter the resulted plans on their own needs. Our algorithm is designed to be recursive. For each iteration, based on the chosen data service in the last iteration, it will infer the follow-up data service and decide how to compose them. To be uniform, we also define a new operator *invoke*, which simply means the invoking of a follow-up service based on the current service. With the corresponding service hyperlinks, the output of current service will be automatically transformed and fill into the corresponding input parameters of the follow-up service.

Algorithm 1. The automatic data service composition algorithm

---

Function: ADSC;

Input: a start data service *(cur_ser)*, a goal data service *(goal_ser)*;

Output: a set of possible composition paths from the source to the target;

---

1. set *outputSet* = ∅
2. get follow-up services *FS* for the current data service by looking up service hyperlinks;
3. for each service *p_next_ser in FS*
4.   if the corresponding hyperlink is output-output mappings, then recommend operators in table I for *(cur_ser, p_next_ser)*, else recommend the operator *invoke(cur_ser, p_next_ser)*;
5.   call operators in step 3 and result in a new data service *tmp_ser*;
6.   calculate coverage degree *c(goal, tmp_ser)*;
7.   if *c(goal, tmp_ser)>1*, then find a composition plan and add it to *outputSet*;
8.   else if *p_next_ser* does not have service hyperlinks or its follow-up services have been already invoked before, return *outputSet*;
9.   *outputSet = outputSet* ∪ ADSC *(p_next_ser, goal_ser)*;
10. endfor
11. return *outputSet*;

In Line 1-2, the algorithm initiate the output set and first searches all related services for the source data service based on service hyperlinks.
Line 3-10 looks for all possible composition plans defined in Def. 7. Line 4-5 tries to generate a new composite data service by composing the current data service and its follow-up data service. This new composite service will be taken as the current service in the next iteration. Line 6-7 judges whether a possible composition plan has been found. In Section 6.1, according to the relaxed constrains about the goal, if we find a composite data service which has fully covered the goal, then we think an approximate solution has been found.

Line 8 shows one exit conditions for the algorithm. If no more hyperlinks can be found or these hyperlinks have been used in prior composition, this algorithm exits with the current output set. Or it will recursively call itself with the input parameters new composite service and the final goal.

7   Application

We illustrate our DASA approach with the scenario described in Section 2, where more than 30 data services from 3 different organizations are provided. Some of these data services are listed in Table 4.

Table 4. Invovled Data Service Examples

Organization	Name	Function	Comments
Civil Affair Agency	*PersonInfo getBasicPersonInfo (String IDCardNo)*	get basic person information by his identity card No.	return a set of <name, age, gender, IDCardNo>
	String getRelation (String IDCardNo₁, String IDCardNo₂)	return relative relation of two people	return relative relation like "father-son", "mother-son"
	List getRelativesInfo(String IDCardNo)	query relative information of a person	return a set of <name, age, gender, IDCardNo>
Mobile Telecommunication Company	*String getPhoneNumber(String IDCardNo)*	query mobile phone number of a person	return the mobile phone number
	String getRegisterInfo(String phone)	query registered person for a given phone number	return the identity card no for a person
	List queryPhoneRecordsByIdentityID (String IDCardNo, Time start, Time end)	query call records for a person in a given time interval	return a list of <phone1, phone2, start, duration>
Local Transportation Management Agency	*List getVehicleRegistry(String IDCardNo)*	query registered vehicle information for a person	return a list of <id, plateNo, type, ownerName, IDCardNo >
	List getMonitorInfo(String crossNo, Time start, Time end)	query monitor information for a vehicle in a given time interval	return a list of <time, plateNo>

Based on data services listed in Table IV, we will explain how to solve the problem in Fig. 5 with Alg. 1.

(1) First, users draw two nested tables as start and goal of the composition process, shown in part (a) and part (b) in Fig 5 respectively. These two nested tables will be encapsulated as two special data services: *getVictimID* and *getSuspectRelatives*.

(2) According to the output schema of *getVictimID* service, several possible links can be found:

- *getVictimID →getRelativesInfo (linked by the idCardNo attribute)*
- *getVictimID →getRelation (linked by the idCardNo attribute)*
- *getVictimID →getPhoneNumber (linked by the idCardNo attribute)*
- *getVictimID →getVehicleRegistry (linked by the idCardNo attribute)*

(3) According to Def. 8, we can calculate the coverage degree for each possible follow-up service. For example, we will calculate the degree which *getRelativesInfo* service covers the goal service. Note that the entity set of goal service *getSuspectRelatives* has 11 entities, which are *Relative{name, age, gender, identityNo, Vehicle{plateNo, type, MonitorInfo{time, location}}}*; the entity set of *getRelativesInfo* have five entities, which are *Relative {name, age, gender, IDCardNo}*. So its cover degree is 5/11. After calculating coverage degrees for all possible follow-up services, we can find that the *getRelativesInfo* service have the maximum degree to cover the goal. Therefore, it will be chosen and invoked.

(4) After invoking *getRelativesInfo* service, several possible links can also be found:

- *getRelativesInfo →getRelation (linked by the idCardNo attribute)*
- *getRelativesInfo →getPhoneNumber (linked by the idCardNo attribute)*
- *getRelativesInfo →getVehicleRegistry (linked by the idCardNo attribute)*

Like step (3), we can calculate the coverage degree for each possible follow-up service and find the service *getVehicleRegistry* which have the maximum coverage degree. Note that these are two kinds of data mappings between these two services, which will lead to possible composition paths. For the Ouptut-Output link, according to Section 6.2, DASA can recommend *renameColumn* and serials of *AddColumn* operators to combine output of these two services and result in a new temporal service. Then, taken this service as input, the algorithm will enter the next round of iteration until all possible composition plans are found.

8   Related Work

8.1   Automatic Service Composition

Current automatic service composition can be roughly classified into two categories [14]. The first one is AI-planning based approaches [15-16]. In these approaches, service composition can be seen as a planning problem where each service corresponds to actions as well as the initial and goal states are suitably defined to correspond to the composition requirements. The second one is template-based approaches [17-18]. They try to customize and instantiate outlines of abstract workflows (or templates) to obtain an executable workflow for specific requirements.

The DASA approach belongs to the first category. But it tries to avoid a main drawback of such approaches. Most of the above planning approaches assume the closed-world assumption wherein the environment is assumed to be unchanged. It is usually not the case for an open environment like the Web.

8.2   Service Link

In recent years, there has been a few works on service link. For example, Radetzki et al. propose adaptors, which are reusable software components developed to realize data matching and transformation among resources [19]. Gu et al. propose a service data link model, which is a service relationship among schema. It can describe service data correlations, which are data mappings among the input and output attributes of services [20]. Zhao et al. propose a HyperService approach to provide a much more flexible way to link and explore existing services for solving various situational problems [21]. With the HyperService approach, a group of relevant services are dynamically searched, ranked and recommended for facilitating future navigations.

The above-mentioned works provide good foundations for our service hyperlink model. Different from current works, our service hyperlink tries to model two different kinds of data mappings for services, which are Output-Input and Output-Output data mappings. These mappings can be used for different purposes. Output-Input mappings can help users compose services. Output-Output mappings can help users aggregate output schema of data services. Besides, a service hyperlink is designed to decentralize and load knowledge fragment that is necessary for service compositions. It can be easily reused in many different service compositions.

9   Conclusion

Based on our previous data service model, this paper proposes a service hyperlink model to describe loose data dependencies between data services as well as a corresponding service composition algorithm. The main contribution is that it is flexible and can respond to situation changes. The proposed service hyperlinks are designed to load decentralized knowledge fragment for a composition process. They can be easily reused in many different data service compositions and decrease the complexities of them. In future works, we plan to take more optimization techniques such as selecting top-k composition plans during the running of algorithm. Besides, we plan to do more experiments for further evaluation of our algorithm.

Acknowledgements. The research work is supported by the Scientific Research Common Program of Beijing Municipal Commission of Education (Research on a User-oriented Approach to Visualized Aggregation of Data Services, No. KM201310009003) and Doctoral Initial Funding of North China University of Technology (Research on Service Hyperlink Modeling Approach to Enabling Situational Integration of Multi-source Data).

References

[1] Altinel, M., Brown, P., Cline, S., Kartha, R., Louie, E., Markl, V., Mau, L., Ng, Y.H., Simmen, D., Singh, A.: Damia: a data mashup fabric for intranet applications. In: Proceedings of the 33rd International Conference on Very Large Databases, Vienna, Austria, pp. 1370–1373 (2007)

[2] Jhingran, A.: Enterprise information mashups: Integrating information, simply. In: Proceedings of the 32nd International Conference on Very Large Databases, Seoul, Korea, pp. 3–4 (2006)

[3] Halevy, A., Rajaraman, A., Ordille, J.: Data integration: The teenage years. In: Proceedings of the 32nd International Conference on Very Large Data Bases, pp. 9–16 (2006)

[4] Carey, M.J., Onose, N., Petropoulos, M.: Data services. Communications of the ACM 55(6), 86–97 (2012)

[5] Han, Y., et al.: Situational data integration with data services and nested table. Service Oriented Computing and Application, 1–22 (2012)

[6] Syu, Y., et al.: A survey on automated service composition methods and related techniques. In: Proceedings of the 9th IEEE International Conference on Services Computing (SCC 2012), pp. 290–297 (2012)

[7] Menascé, D.A., Casalicchio, E., Dubey, V.: A Heuristic Approach to Optimal Service Selection in Service Oriented Architectures. In: Proceedings of the 7th International Workshop on Software and Performance (2008)

[8] Kaijun, R., Nong, X., Jinjun, C.: Building Quick Service Query List Using WordNet and Multiple Heterogeneous Ontologies toward More Realistic Service Composition. IEEE Transactions on Services Computing 4, 216–229 (2011)

[9] Wang, G., Yang, S., Han, Y.: Mashroom: End-user mashup programming using nested tables. In: Proceedings of the 18th International Conference on World Wide Web, pp. 861–870 (2009)

[10] Makinouchi, A.: A consideration of normal form of notnecessarily-normalized relations in the relational data model. In: Proceedings of the 3rd VLDB Conference (Tokyo), pp. 445–453 (1977)

[11] Magnani, M., Rizopoulos, N., Mc.Brien, P., Cucci, F.: Schema integration based on uncertain semantic mappings. In: Delcambre, L., Kop, C., Mayr, H.C., Mylopoulos, J., Pastor, Ó. (eds.) ER 2005. LNCS, vol. 3716, pp. 31–46. Springer, Heidelberg (2005)

[12] Miller, A.G.: WordNet: A lexical database for English. Communications of the ACM 38(11), 39–41 (1995)

[13] Castano, S., Ferrara, A., Montanelli, S.: H-match: An algorithm for dynamically matching ontologies in peer-based systems (2003)

[14] Agarwal, V., et al.: Understanding approaches for web service composition and execution. In: COMPUTE 2008, New York, NY, USA (2008)

[15] Blythe, J., et al.: The Role of Planning in Grid Computing. In: Proceedings of International Conference on AI Planning and Scheduling (2003)

[16] Srivastava, B.: Automatic Web Services Composition Using Planning. In: Proceedings of KBCS, Mumbai, pp. 467–477 (2002)

[17] Chun, S.A., Atluri, V., Adam, N.R.: Policy-based Web Service Composition. In: Research Issues on Data Engineering: Web Services for e-Commerce and e-Government Applications, RIDE (2004)

[18]   Sirin, E., Parsia, B., Hendler, J.: Template-based Composition of Semantic Web Services. In: AAAI Fall Symposium on Agents and the Semantic Web, Virginia, USA, pp.
85–92 (2005)
[19]   Radetzki, U., Leser, U., et al.: Adapters, shims, and glue-service interoperability for in
silico experiments. Bioinformatics 22(9), 1137–1143 (2006)
[20]   Gu, Z., Xu, B., Li, J.Z.: Service data correlation modeling and its application in data-
driven service composition. IEEE Transactions on Services Computing 3(4), 279–291
(2010)
[21]   Zhao, C., Ma, C., Zhang, J., et al.: HyperService: Linking and exploring services on the
web. In: IEEE International Conference on Web Services (ICWS), pp. 17–24 (2010)

Research on Service-Content-Based Web Service Selection Method

Bingxian Ma[1,2,*] and Jipeng Cui[1,2]

[1] Shandong Provincial Key Laboratory of Network based Intelligent Computing,
Jinan 250022, China
[2] School of Information Science and Engineering, University of Jinan, Jinan 250022, China
ise_mabx@ujn.edu.cn, 117478009@qq.com

Abstract. Web service composition focuses on combining existing web services into more sophisticated ones to provide more powerful functionality. Web service selection during functionally similar services is a critical issue in web service composition. This paper proposes a method for web service selection based on content of service. Firstly, content of service is defined formally and its property is given. What go after are the content of service initialization and its update. Also, a scoring method is established to evaluate each web service according to content of service and user requirements and then decide whether this web service is reasonable for selection. At last, an example is given to illustrate the whole idea.

Keywords: Web service composition, web service selection, service content, scoring method.

1   Introduction

Web services can be described, published, located, and accessed over a network basing on open standards. Actually, the functionality of a single web service is limited, so a number of single web services are combined together to meet complex application level requirements. This process is known as web service composition, which has gained a considerable momentum as a means to create and streamline business-to-business collaborations within and across organizational boundaries [1].

When dealing with web service composition, a key issue is how to select web services for composition, given a great number of functionally similar web services. Current jobs on web service selection mainly considers QoS (quality of service), and they tend to build up a scientific way to select web services based on QoS. In [2], the authors propose a predictive QoS model to work out workflow QoS automatically. In [3], the authors address the problem by maximizing user satisfaction which is presented using utility functions over QoS items. Paper [4] treats the problem as a multi-objective global optimization problem, and takes advantage of the combination of the modified simplex method and the heuristic enumerate method. In [5], a global optimal algorithm based on particle swarm optimization (PSO) is presented to resolve web service selection with QoS; it produces a set of optimal Pareto with constraint principle by optimizing multi QoS parameters simultaneously.

Z. Huang et al. (Eds.): WISE 2013 Workshops 2013, LNCS 8182, pp. 168–180, 2014.
© Springer-Verlag Berlin Heidelberg 2014

Web service selection is expected to find out the most proper web services for composition. Web service selection based on QoS is conspicuously reasonable and relative studies on it are fruitful, but it is not enough, especially when users' requirements for the content of service are considered.

Generally, semantic web technologies, such as OWL-S [6] (Web ontology language for services) can be used to describe the detailed content information of web services. The work of paper [7] and [8] are based on the OWL-S description of web services, where the authors use Service Profiles and Prediction to depict the content of services. But there are some problems. We cannot expect that all web services are described using OWL-S; moreover, the description is not well-formed and is only for a specific web service, but in practice we usually hope that information of a set of similar web services can be described uniformly.

The purpose of this paper is to focus on the content of service, based on which a whole idea to address web service selection problem is provided. Firstly, a formally definition of CoS (content of service) is given, and its property is discussed to differentiate it from QoS. What follows is the initialization and update of CoS; a scoring method which makes use of the CoS information for web service selection is established afterwards.

The remainder of this paper is organized as follows: Section 2 defines CoS and its properties. Section 3 presents the initialization and update of CoS. Section 4 describes the scoring method for web service selection based on CoS. Section 5 illustrates the whole idea with an example. Finally, the conclusion and discussion is given in Section 6.

2   From QoS to CoS

To simply the discussion, we will first introduce the concept of abstract service class, which is proposed in paper [9] as follows:

Define set $S_{service}$ as a union of abstract web service classes. Each abstract service class $S_j \in S_{service}$ is used to describe a set of functionally-similar web services. Next we will distinguish between the following two concepts [9]:

- An abstract web service composition, which can be defined as an abstract representation of a composition request $CS_{abstract} = \{S_1, S_2 ... S_n\}$. $CS_{abstract}$ describes the required abstract service classes.

- A concrete web service composition, which can be defined as an instantiation of an abstract web service composition. This can be obtained by binding each abstract service class in $CS_{abstract}$ to a concrete web service s_j, $s_j \in S_j$.

Conspicuously, the process of web service selection is the transportation from abstract web service composition to concrete web service composition. We confine this process so that we will only take the content of service into consideration during web service selection.

2.1 The Definition of CoS

As shown in [10], a web service S can described as S = {Func, QoS}, where Func is the set of functionality of S, and QoS represents the non-functional properties of S. Here Func gives an overall description of the function of web service S, but fails to provide any detailed information.

Let us illustrate this with a room-booking web service, ws = {$Func_{room}$, QoS_{room}}. $Func_{room}$ tells its consumers something as 'this web service is used for room-booking', which is a general idea. But what kind rooms can it provide? How about the prices? Is there anything special about the rooms? Such questions cannot be answered.

To address these problems, content of service (CoS) is introduced now to depict detailed functional information of a web service by obtaining and keeping some of its run-time information. The concept of CoS is defined as follows:

Definition 1 Suppose WS is a web service, the CoS of WS is a 2-tuple:

CoS_{WS} = (S_j, item_list), where S_j is the abstract service class that WS belongs to; item_list is a list of items with the following form:

item_list = ($item_1$, $item_2$...$item_N$), where N is the total number of items and $item_i$ is the ith item in item_list.

Each item in item_list shows detailed information about certain aspects of the functionality of WS. Still we take a room-booking web service for example. The CoS of room-booking web service might have the following form of item_list,

item_list$_{room-booking}$= (room_type, air_conditioner, wakeup_serv, room_price), where the first item points out what kind of room it can provide, the last item specifies the corresponding price, and the second and third items depict some special information.

Both the items and the total number N are determined by S_j, so it is not hard to see that the form of CoS of a web service is determined by its abstract service class.

2.2 The Predefined Uniform CoS

Web services of the same abstract service class share the same form of CoS, we use the concept 'predefined uniform CoS' to describe the shared form of CoS of web services from the same abstract service class.

For abstract service class S_j, we predefine how many items in item_list$_j$ and what each item is; thereby we obtain the predefined uniform CoS_j for S_j.

If we eventually decide that there are N_j items in item_list$_j$, then these items can be listed in Table 1 as follows:

Table 1. Item_list of CoS_j

item_name	$item_1$	$item_2$	....	item $_{Nj}$
value1	v_{11}	v_{12}	....	v_{1Nj}
value2	v_{21}	v_{22}	....	v_{2Nj}
value3	v_{31}	v_{32}	....	v_{3Nj}
....				

We can see from Table 1 that each item has a number of values. Because items are not independent, these values can only be given in the form of value vectors. For example, value1 = $(v_{11}, v_{12}... v_{1Nj})$ is a value vector for item_list$_j$. Generally, each value vector has exactly N_j values for all N_j items, respectively.

For any web service WS form S_j, we use a set, called vector_set$_{WS}$, to store all its vector values. The CoS of WS from S_j can be denoted as CoS$_j$ (WS),

$$CoS(i) = (S_j, item\_list_j(WS)),$$

Here item_list$_j$(WS) characterizes item_list$_j$ with value vectors from vector_set$_{WS}$.

For each item in item_list$_j$, there are only three possible date types:

(1) String. All items with data type String have enumerable values.

(2) Boolean. All items with data type Boolean have an alternative of value 0 and 1.

(3) Decimal. All items with data type Decimal have decimal values.

Of all items in item_list$_j$, we define item$_1$ as primary_item. The primary_item is the most significant item in item_list$_j$, and it serves as an index for each value vector in vector_set.

For simplicity, we arrange items in item_list$_j$ in such sequence: what comes first is the primary_item; items with Boolean values follow closely; Decimal items are located at the end.

In the predefined uniform CoS$_j$, primary_item and Boolean items are of great importance. The values of primary_item are enumerable and formatted, so other values cannot be set to primary_item. Given a primary_item, the value combinations of Boolean items form a classification of value vector modes, with each combination corresponding to a unique mode. Each item_list$_j$ can have at most as many value vectors as the number of modes; this assumption is essential when we deal with CoS initialization and its update.

Take the room-booking web service for example; its predefined uniform CoS has item_list as follows: item_list$_{room-booking}$= (room_type, air_conditioner, wakeup_serv, room_price), with room_type as primary_item, air_conditioner and wakeup_serv Boolean items, and room_price Decimal items. Under the primary_item, there are totally four value combinations of Boolean items; they are (1, 0), (1, 1), (0, 1), (0, 0), respectively. Each combination represents one value vector mode, so there are four modes in all, which means that we can store at most four value vectors for item_list$_{room-booking}$ under the given primary_item, with one for each mode. For example, given the primary_item 'single-room', we might store four value vactors for item_list$_{room-booking}$ as follows when dealing with CoS initialization and update:

$$item\_list_{room-booking}(1) = (sing\text{-}room, 1, 1, 200);$$
$$item\_list_{room-booking}(2) = (sing\text{-}room, 1, 0, 200);$$
$$item\_list_{room-booking}(3) = (sing\text{-}room, 0, 1, 200);$$
$$item\_list_{room-booking}(4) = (sing\text{-}room, 0, 0, 200).$$

2.3   Properties of CoS

QoS properties are suitable for all kinds of web services. Paper [11] gives a form of QoS as qos = (T, C, Rep, R), where T is the response time, C is the cost, Rep is the reputation and R is the reliability of a web service. Clearly, this form of QoS can be used to describe any kinds of web services; they all response in a finite time, cost the users some money, and perform a degree of reputation and reliability. Needless to say, all web services share a uniform QoS.

But things are quite different when we turn to CoS, which does not have a uniform description for web services from different abstract service classes. Generally, CoS_j, for abstract service class S_j, has the following properties:

(1) abstract-service-class-related. As discussed above, $CoS_j = (S_j, item\_list_j)$. The abstract-service-class-related property states that S_j determines the total number of items in the item_list$_j$ and what each item is.

(2) item-dependent. For two items in item_list$_j$ = (item$_1$, item$_2$...item$_N$), say, item$_s$ and item$_t$ (s≠t), they are correlated in some way. So the change of one item might affect the others.

(3) incommensurable. We call this incommensurability between items of CoS from different abstract service classes. As a matter of incommensurability, the items of CoS from different abstract service classes cannot be simply combined together, even if they have got the same name.

(4) changeable. Only web service providers and user feed-backs have got the chance to change the item contents in CoS; the change of item contents usually comes with the update or improvement of a certain web service.

With these properties, we know that CoS is abstract-service-class-related, with items dependent, incommensurable and changeable. These properties are of great significance for web service selection based on CoS.

3   CoS Initialization and Update

Given the predefined uniform CoS_j for abstract service class S_j, web service providers are required to provide information of CoS in forms of value vectors. We will record these value vectors for each web service as its initialization of CoS. This happens when providers register their web services. Fig. 1 shows this process.

After initialization, each web service has got its initialized CoS. Something subtle will happen, however, if the providers would not like to provide any initialization information or if the initialized CoS should be changed. To address this problem, CoS update is adopted.

Fig. 2 shows the update of CoS for a certain web service from abstract service class S_j.

CoS update can be done by both web service providers and authorized web service users. To update the CoS information of a certain web service, providers and users are

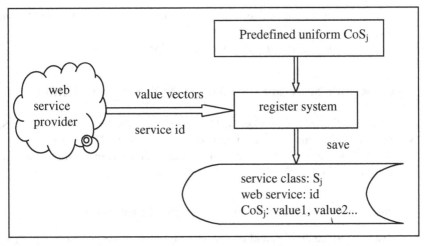

Fig. 1. CoS initialization by web service provider

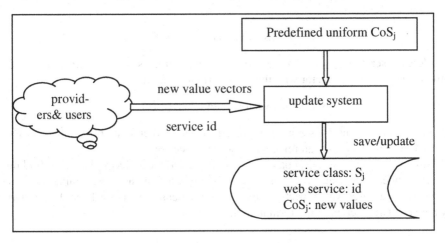

Fig. 2. Update of CoS by users and providers

required to provide new value vectors, according to which the update system would record new information or renew old information of CoS. Here is how the update system works:

Suppose there are M value vectors stored in vector_set$_{WS}$, then on a newly coming value vector v,

Step1: get the primary_item of v, say, v.primary_item;

Step2: get the set of all value vectors, say, set$_{ready}$, with the same primary_item as v.primary_item;

Step3: examine whether the mode of v is contained in set$_{ready}$; if so, go to Step4; if not, go to Step5;

Step4: renew the values in the ith value vector using values in v; go to Step6;

Step5: add the newly coming value vector to vector_set$_{WS}$; execute M=M+1; go to
     Step6;
Step6: return the updated vector_set$_{WS}$ and set size M; update complete.

4   Web Service Selection Based on CoS: A Scoring Method

So far, we have introduced what CoS is, CoS properties, predefined uniform CoS,
value vectors, primary_item, and CoS initialization and update. We will now go on
working with web service selection problem: to establish a scoring method for web
service selection based on CoS.

4.1   Detailed Description of Web Service Selection Based on CoS

Given an abstract service class S_j and its predefined uniform CoS$_j$, suppose that there
are K web services from S_j. Then the CoS of the ith web service from S_j is denoted as
CoS$_j$ (i),

$$CoS(i) = (S_j, item\_list_j(i)), 1 \leq i \leq K$$

We use user_value_vector to denote users' requirements for web service contents;
obviously it is a value vector with the same form as item_list$_j$:

$$user\_value\_vactor = item\_list_j (user)$$

Here item_list$_j$ (user) is a user-characterized value vector; it sufficiently and formally figures out user's requirements for web service contents.

Now web service selection based on CoS can be addressed as follows: To find out
a web service WS where item_list$_j$(WS) has the same or the most similar value as
compared with user_value_vector. Next, we will discuss how to evaluate the similarity between two vectors of the form item_list$_j$.

4.2   Evaluation of Similarity between Two Vectors

For abstract service class S_j and predefined uniform CoS$_j$, suppose there are N_j items
in item_list$_j$,

$$item\_list_j = (item_1, item_2...item_{Nj})$$

Suppose there are two different value vectors of the form item_list$_j$,

$$vector_1 = (v_{11}, v_{12}...v_{1Nj})$$

$$vector_2 = (v_{21}, v_{22}... v_{2Nj})$$

We define item_match_degree(i) to show the similarity of the ith item of two value
vectors:

(1) If the date type of the ith item is String, then it has only enumerable values,

$$item\_match\_\deg ree(i) = \begin{cases} 1, & \textit{if two values are the same} \\ 0, & \textit{otherwise} \end{cases}$$

(2) If the data type of the ith item is Boolean, then

$$item\_match\_\deg ree(i) = \begin{cases} 1, \textit{if two values are both 1 or both 0} \\ 0, \textit{otheriwse} \end{cases}$$

(3) If the data type of the ith item is Decimal, we denote the two decimal values as d_1 and d_2, respectively, and we can assume without losing generality that d_1 is not greater than d_2, then

$$item\_match\_\deg ree(i) = \begin{cases} 1, & \textit{if } d_1 = d_2 \\ d_1 / d_2, & \textit{if } d_1, d_2 > 0 \textit{ and } d_1 \neq d_2 \\ d_2 / d_1, & \textit{if } d_1, d_2 < 0 \textit{ and } d_1 \neq d_2 \\ 0, & \textit{else} \end{cases}$$

The vector_match_degree(vector$_1$, vector$_2$) is defined to show the similarity between vector$_1$ and vector$_2$. It can be computed using the following code:

```
vector_match_degree(vector_1, vector_2) = 0;
i=1;
if (item_match_degree(i) == 0)
   return vector_match_degree(vector_1, vector_2);
else {
   vector_match_degree(vector_1, vector_2) =1;
   for (i=2; i<=N_j; i++) {
   vector_match_degree(vector_1, vector_2) +=
item_match_degree(i);
         }
   vector_match_degree(vector_1, vector_2)
= vector_match_degree(vector_1, vector_2)/N_j;
   return vector_match_degree(vector_1, vector_2);
}
```

The vector_match_degree(v_1, v_2) can be written in formula as follows:

$$vector\_match\_\deg ree(v_1, v_2) = \frac{item\_match\_\deg ree(1)}{N_j} \times \sum_{i=1}^{N_j} item\_match\_\deg ree(i) \qquad (1)$$

4.3   Web Service Selection Based on CoS

Suppose there are N abstract service classes in an abstract web service composition, and the jth abstract service class, S_j, has M_j function similar web services. The predefined uniform CoS_j has T_j items for its item_list$_j$. For the kth web service from S_j, there are R_k value vectors in its vector_set, and the mth vector is vec(j, k, m)

User' requirements for content of web services from S_j can be written as vec$_j$(user), and it has the same format as vec (j, k, m). The score of a web service composition can be defined as follows:

$$score(CS) = \sum_{j=1}^{N} vector\_match\_degree(vec(j,k,m), vec_j(user)), \ 1 \leq k \leq M_j, 1 \leq m \leq R_k \qquad (2)$$

The vector_match_degree(vec(j, k, m), vec$_j$ (user)) can be computed by formula (1).Here is some explanation about this formula. For abstract service class S_j, if we choose the kth web service for composition based on the match degree between vec$_j$(user) and the mth value vector vec(j, k, m), we will get a web service composition with score(CS).

Our concern on web service selection based on CoS is to maximize the score(CS) and determine which web service is best to choose for each abstract service class. From the definition of score(CS), it is clear that if we could always select a web service with the greatest score for each service class, we will eventually obtain a web service composition with the greatest score(CS).

The following code shows the process of web service selection based on CoS using a scoring method:

```
score_CS = 0;
vec_degree = 0;
serv_degree = 0;
for (int j=1; j<=N; j++)
{
  for (int k=1; k<=M_j; k++)
  {
    for (int m=1; m<=R_k; m++)
    {
      if(m==1)
        vec_degree=vector_match_degree(vec(j, k, m),
                    vec_j(user));
      else
      {
        vec_degree=MAX(vec_degree,
        vector_match_degree(vec(j, k, m), vec_j(user)));
      }
    }
    if (k==1)
    {
      serv_degree=vec_degree;
      id_array[j]=1;
    }
    else
```

```
{
  if (serv_degree<vec_degree)
  {
    serv_degree=vec_degree;
    id_array[j]=k;
  }
}
}
score_CS += serv_degree;
}
```

Here is some explanation about the code above. The ids of web services to be selected are initialized as 1s and stored in an array called id_array. It has N elements, each of which represents the selected web service for an abstract service class. The vec_degree is used to record the maximum of vector_match_degree of the same web service; the serv_degree is used to record the maximum of vec_degree of web services from the same abstract service class; the score_CS is used to record the score(CS) for web service selection.

The returned array id_array consists of all web services selected, and the corresponding score_CS is the maximum of score(CS). Thus we have completed web service selection based on CoS. In the next section, we will illustrate the whole idea with an example.

5   Example

Assume that tour_service (abstract web service composition) contains three abstract service classes, which are hotel_service, transport_service, and dinning_service, respectively. That is,

tour_service = (hotel_service, transport_service, dining_service).

The item_list of predefined uniform CoS for these three abstract service classes are shown in Table 2, Table 3, and Table 4, respectively.

Table 2. Item_list of CoS for hotel_service

item_name	room_type	room_price	wakeup_serv	air_conditioner
value1	single-room			
value2	double-room			
value3	standard-room			
value4	deluxe-room			

For hotel_service, room_type is the primary_item, and it is enumerable. Initialization information for room_type has only four choices: single-room, double-room, standard-room, and deluxe-room. The room_price item is decimal; wakeup_serv and air_conditioner have Boolean data type, and their values can only be 0 or 1.

Table 3. Item_list of CoS for transport_service

item_name	tranport_type	t_price	time_consume
value1	taxi		
value2	bus		
value3	bicycle		

For transport_service, transport_type is the primary_item whose initialization information can only be selected among taxi, bus, and bicycle. The t_price item and time_consume item are decimal.

Table 4. Item_list of CoS for dinning_service

item_name	dinning_style	cost	package_support	free_tableware
value1	western-style			
value2	fast-food			
value3	buffet			
value4	local-delicacy			

For dinning_service, dinning_style is the primary_item, and it has only four possible values: western-style, fast-food, buffet, and local-delicacy. The cost item is decimal; package_support and free_tableware have Boolean data type, and their values can only be 0 or 1.

We have got 20 web services for abstract service class hotel_service, 24 for transport_serivce, and 17 for dining_service. The item_list of CoS for each web service WS is initialized with value vectors which are stored in vector_set(WS).

Suppose that users' requirements for the content of service are given in the following three vectors:

$$user\_value\_vector_{hotel} = (standard\text{-}room, 160, 1, 1)$$

$$user\_value\_vector_{transport} = (taxi, 45, 50)$$

$$user\_value\_vector_{dinning} = (local\text{-}delicacy, 300, 0, 1)$$

Then after running on our system using scoring method, the returned results are as follows:

$$id\_array = [5, 21, 14], score\_WS = 2.08$$

That is to say, we select the 5th web service for hotel_service, the 21st for transport_service, and the 14th for dinning_service. The final web service composition gets the maximum of score(WS), with value 2.08.

6   Conclusion and Discussion

This paper focuses on the content of web service (CoS) to address web service selection problem. CoS can be seen as a supplement for the functionality of web services, and it has four important properties. Web services from the same abstract service class share the same form of CoS, which is called predefined uniform CoS. CoS initialization and update, the evaluation of similarity between two vectors, and even the implementation of scoring method are all on basis of predefined uniform CoS. By evaluating the similarity between user_value_vector and value vectors of web services, a scoring method is implemented. The process of scoring is the process of web service selection based on CoS.

Our work mainly considers the content of web services for web service selection, and we finally get a web service selection with maximum of score (CS). We are now devoted to taking QoS into consideration, and trying to work out an effective method for CoS-and-QoS-based web service selection.

Acknowledgement. This work was supported by National Natural Science Foundation of China (60903099), the Excellent Young and Middle-Aged Scientist Award Grant of Shandong Province of China (BS2009DX012), and A Project of Shandong Province Higher Educational Science and Technology Program (J09LG14).

References

1. Li, W., Yanxiang, H.: A Web Service Composition Algorithm based on Global QoS Optimizing with MOCACO. In: 2010 ISECS International Colloquium on Computing, Control, and Management, CCCM (2010)
2. Jorge, C., Amit, S., John, M.: Quality of Service for workflows and Web Service Processes. Journal of Web Semantics 1(3), 281–338 (2004)
3. Zeng, L., Benatallah, B., Ngu, A.H.H., Dumas, M., Kalagnanam, J., Chang, H.: QoS-aware middleware for Web services composition. IEEE Transactions on Software Engineering 30, 311–327 (2004)
4. Wan, L., Gao, C., Xiao, W., Su, L.: Global optimization method of Web service composition based on QoS. Computer Engineer and Applications 24 (2007)
5. Hong, X., Zengzhi, L.: A Particle Swarm Optimization Algorithm for Service Selection Problem Based on Quality of Service in Web Services Composition. Journal of Beijing University of Posts and Telecommunications 32(4), 63–67 (2009)
6. W3C. OWL-S: Semantic markup for Web services [EB/OL] (November 22, 2004), http://www.w3.org/Submission/OWL-S/
7. Li-mou, X., Ke-yin, J., Hui, Y., Shuang-quan, T.: Matchmaking of Web Service Based on the OWL-S Service Model. Computer Engineering & Science 29(8), 64–67 (2007)
8. Paolucci, M., Kawamura, T., Sycara, K., et al.: Semantic matching of Web services capabilities. In: Proceeding of the First International Web Conferences (ISWC), Sardinia, Italy, June 10-12, pp. 333–347 (2002)

9. Alrifai, M., Risse, T., Dolog, P., Nejdl, W.: A Scalabel Approach for QoS-based Web Service Selection. In: Feuerlicht, G., Lamersdorf, W. (eds.) ICSOC 2008. LNCS, vol. 5472, pp. 190–199. Springer, Heidelberg (2009)
10. Yanping, C., Zengzhi, L., Zhisheng, G., Qinxue, J., Chuang, W.: Service Selection Algorithm Based on Quality of Service and Its Implementation for Web Services Composition. Journal of Xi' an Jiaotong University 40(8), 897–900 (2006)
11. Zheyuan, J., Jianghong, H., Zhao, W.: An Optimization Model for Dynamic QoS-Aware Web Services Selection and Composition. Chinese Journal of Computers 32(5), 1014–1025 (2009)

A Petri Net Based Execution Engine
for Web Service Composition

Kai Xu[1,2] and Bingxian Ma[1,2,*]

[1] Shandong Provincial Key Laboratory of Network based Intelligent Computing, Jinan, China
[2] School of Information Science and Engineering, University of Jinan, China
890318xu@163.com, ise_mabx@ujn.edu.cn

Abstract. Based on the Petri net description of web service composition, control structures within web service composition, registration information of web services, demand parameters validation, parameters converting among web services through reflection mechanism, output parameters checking and conflict resolution through reflection mechanism are studied. Afterwards, this paper designs and carries out a Petri-net-based execution engine for web service composition. Execution engine will invoke atomic web services corresponding to transitions selected to fire simultaneously, and it will feed back the dynamic execution information to Petri net. Then, execution engine will adjust state of Petri net according to web services execution, selects transitions to fire again with transitions firing rules. Repeating the above process until the execution of web service composition is done. All these will push forward the application of Petri net in service oriented computing.

Keywords: Petri net, web service composition, reflection mechanism, execution engine.

1   Introduction

Web services are designed mainly to share heterogeneous data on the web. Sometimes a simple web service can not satisfy complex user demands, so web services should be combined to provide more powerful functions. In recent years, many works have been done on web services composition, and they mainly base on BPEL (Business Process Execution Language) [1], OWL-S (Ontology Web Language for Services) [2], and Petri net [3]. BPEL and OWL-S do not provide validation mechanism for composite service model and cannot be analyzed online. Both BPEL and OWL-S supply a GUI (graphic user interface) for design, but they cannot validate the whole process of web service composition. When designing web services, BPEL rely on large quantities of primitive activities and structural activities, both of which easily lead to what is called the explosion of space. Moreover, BEPL use elements such as If and If_Else to choose web services for execution in a selection structure context. However, these elements, which can make use of xpath expression, support numeric expression, equation and comparison computation through imbedded functions yet might be in dilemma when facing complex selection. OWL-S adds intelligence to web services, but it

Z. Huang et al. (Eds.): WISE 2013 Workshops 2013, LNCS 8182, pp. 181–193, 2014.
© Springer-Verlag Berlin Heidelberg 2014

encounters setbacks in actual application, since the semantic web is still not widely used. Petri net has a solid mathematical foundation and has a capability to describe distributed systems and concurrent systems. Many works have been done to model and analyze web service composition with Petri net: [5] utilized a functional valida-tion to check the seamless connectivity between individual services to be composed and to represent services' interdependency in a Petri Nets with reachability analysis and each service's semantic description; [6] used time Petri net as a formalism to simulate and validate web service composition; [7] used the means of dynamic execu-tion reasoning and data flow analysis of Petri net to construct seamlessly Add/Remove recovery behavior for composition transaction.

However, as we can see, related works mainly focus on web services modeling and analyze properties of web service composition with Petri net, but fail to study the construction of Petri net for web service composition online and the corresponding execution engine.

Based on Petri net description of web service composition, we design and carry out a Petri net based execution engine for it. In our design, Petri net can not only simulate the whole process of web service composition with token flows but also provides a validation mechanism using reach-ability graph. Moreover, with places used for web service parameters, transitions for execution, and tokens for ready-or-not state of pa-rameters, the complexity of web service composition files is reduced dramatically in web services designing. In the context of selection structure, reflection mechanism is used for automatic selection of web services; the reflection mechanism allows design-ers to establish flexible programs for web service selection, thus it is qualified to deal with sophisticated user requirements.

The remainder of this paper is organized as follows: Section 2 describes web ser-vice composition with Petri net and studies control structures within web service composition. Section 3 presents the registration and execution of web services based on Petri net. The design and implement of execution engine is given in Section 4. Section 5 provides a specific example. Finally, we summarize the whole idea of this paper and outlook further works in section 6.

2   Modeling Web Service with Petri Net

2.1   Petri Nets

Definition 1[3]: A triple $N = (S,T;F)$ is a Petri net, if and only if:

(1) $S \cup T \neq \varnothing$

(2) $S \cap T = \varnothing$

(3) $F \subseteq (S \times T) \cup (T \times S)$

(4) $dom(F) \cup cod(F) = S \cup T$

S is a set of places; T is a set of transitions; F is a set of flow relations between places and transitions.

Definition 2[3]: Petri net system is $\Sigma = (S,T;F,M)$. Mapping: $M : S \to \{0,1,2,\cdots\}$ is a marking of Petri net Σ.

Definition 3[3]: Firing rule of transitions in Petri net system:

(1) For transition $t \in T$, if $\forall s \in S : s \in {}^{\bullet}t \to M(s) \geq 1$, then t can fire, denoted by $M[t>$.

(2) If $M[t>$, t can fire in marking M. When t fires, a new marking M' is obtained (denoted by $M[t>M'$),

$$M'(s) = \begin{cases} M(s)-1, & \text{if } s \in {}^{\bullet}t\text{-}t^{\bullet} \\ M(s)+1, & \text{if } s \in t^{\bullet}\text{-}{}^{\bullet}t \\ M(s), & \text{others} \end{cases}$$

2.2   Petri net of Web Service Composition

Definition 4:   A Petri net corresponding to Web service composition is a 6-tuple $CWS = (P,T;F,W,K,M)$. Where:

(1) $P = P^W \cup P^D \cup P^A$. P^W is a set of places which represents parameters of Web services; P^D is a set of places which represents demand parameters of users. If multiple Web services combine into a new service, the input parameters of the new Web service are demand parameters; P^A is a set of places which assist the process of Web service composition.

(2) T is the set of transitions that represents atomic web services within the web service composition.

(3) F represents the set of the relationships between web services and their input or output parameters.

(4) M, K, W are the same as those defined in P/T system [3].

Parameters of web services correspond to place elements of Petri net. The number of tokens in a place represents whether the corresponding parameter is ready, with 1 for ready and 0 for not ready. Atomic web service execution corresponds to the firing of transition. The relationship between parameters and services is the flow relations F in definition 4.

We use PNML [8] to describe Petri net. The location of IP address service [9] is taken as an example, and its Petri net is shown in figure 1:

theIpAddress   **getCountryCityByIp**   **getCountryCityByIpResult**

Fig. 1. The location of IP address service

The corresponding PNML is:

```
<place id="theIpAddress">
  <name><value></value></name>
```

```
<initialMarking><value>1</value></initialMarking>
</place>
<transition id="getCountryCityByIp">
  <name><value>67</value></name>
</transition>
<arc source="theIpAddress" target="getCountryCityByIp">
  <inscription><value>1</value></inscription>
</arc>
```

2.3   Control Structures within Web Service Composition

Generally there are four control structures within web service composition: they are sequence structure, concurrency structure, selection structure, and loop structure, respectively. Figure 2 shows the corresponding structures. In sequence structure, the relationship between T1 and T2 is sequence; in concurrency structure, the relationship between T4 and T5 is concurrency, and the relationship between T8 and T9 is selection; T11 and T12 are in a loop structure, which can be constructed with selection structure.

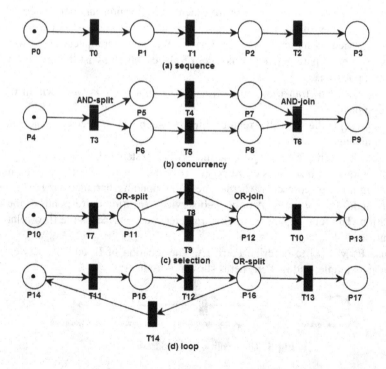

Fig. 2. Control structures

3   Registration and Execution of Web Service

3.1   Registration Information of Web Service

Atomic web services and web service composition registration information is stored and used for the execution of web service composition.

Table 1 shows key registration information of atomic web services. The Field ID stores the unique identification of atomic web services. The Field inputParam stores the input parameters of atomic web services, including both names and types. The Field outputParam stores the output parameters of atomic Web services, also with names and types included. The Field wsdl stores WSDL (Web Services Description Language) [10] of atomic web services. The Field namespace stores the namespace of atomic web services.

Table 1. Registration information of atomic web service

Field name	Example of field value
ID	67
method	getCountryCityByIp
inputParam	[{"name":"theIpAddress","type":"string"}]
outputParam	[{"name":"getCountryCityByIpResult","type":"string"}]
wsdl	http://webservice.webxml.com.cn/WebServices/IpAddressSearchWebService.asmx ?wsdl
namespace	http://WebXml.com.cn/

Table 2. Registration information of composite web service

Field name	Example of field value
ID	3
pnml	petriOfWS\Travel.xml
demandParam	[{"name":"startCity","type":"string","regularExpression":"","desc":"city of depar-ture"},{"name":"lastCity","type":"string","regularExpression":"","desc":"destinition"},{ "name":"theDate","type":"string","regularExpression":"","desc":"the date"}]
outputParam	[{"name":"travelResult","type":"string"}]
convertClassAndMethod	[{"id":67,"covertClassName":"","convertMethod":""},{{"id":24,"covertClassName ":"covertClass3","convertMethod":"convert24"}]
selectivePlaces	[{"place-Id":"startCity","selectClassName":"selectClass3","selectMethod":"selectStartCity"}]

Table 2 shows key registration information of web service composition, where the Field ID stores the unique identification of web service composition, the Field pnml stores the directories of corresponding PNML files, and the Field demandParam stores the demand parameters of users, including names, types, regular expressions and descriptions. Moreover, the Field outputParam stores the output parameters of web service composition, with names and types included. The Field convertClassAndMethod stores information used for converting parameters among atomic services; the information is mainly about names of converting methods and their corresponding classes. Finally, the Field selectivePlaces stores information for selecting the firing transition in the context of selection structure, and it depicts the names of OR-Split places, names selecting methods and those of corresponding classes.

3.2   Converting Parameters among Atomic Web Services

In general, a web service composition is created based on business association and data association and includes multi-atomic web services. As atomic web services may be delivered by different developers and published in different servers, their parameters may diverse. If the web service composition is based on data association, we should consider the matching of parameters among different atomic services. Here we propose a method for converting parameters among services based on reflection mechanism. In order to realize the conversion, we need to do some preparing work as follows:

(1) Create Java codes for converting parameters methods according to actual situation of web service composition.

(2) Fill in the field convertClassAndMethod, which is defined in table 2, with converting parameters methods and the corresponding classes.

For example, suppose that the given field convertClassAndMethod in table 2 is:

[{"id":67,"covertClassName":"","convertMethod":""},{{"id":24,"covertClassName":"covertClass2","convertMethod":"convert24"}}]. Here the value of "id" serves as the unique identification of atomic web service; the value of "covertClassName" is the name of converting parameters methods; the value of "convertMethod" is the name of corresponding classes. It is not necessary to convert parameters when value of "convertMethod" is empty; otherwise, the parameters should be converted.

Algorithm 3-1 should be operated early before invoking atomic web services.

Algorithm 3-1: Parameters Converting Algorithm

Input: ID of current web service composition; ID of atomic web service; parameters of current atomic service

Output: parameters converted

Step0: Get the value of the field convertClassAndMethod in table 2 from database. For the current atomic service, get the name of converting parameters method and its corresponding class;

Step1:   **If**   the name of converting parameters method is empty   **then**
                Return the parameters of current atomic service directly;

Step2:   **If**   the name of converting parameters method is not empty   **then**
                Call the converting parameters method through reflection mechanism and return the parameters converted.

3.3   Output Parameters Checking

Sometimes, the output parameters of a web service might fail to meet user demands even if it is successfully invoked. The invoking result of a web service could be listed as follows: (1) Fail, when there are no returned output parameters; (2) Succeed, when the output parameters meet user demands; (3) Succeed, when the output parameters fail to meet user demands.

Knowledge frame for web services is introduced to facilitate the out put parameters checking, and it has three components which are described as follows:

Name of knowledge frame: output parameter;

Items count of output parameter;

Regular expression of each item of output parameter.

The knowledge frame should be established when a web service composition is created. The second component of knowledge frame, say, the items count of output parameter, is represented by an interval. For example, the closed interval [1, 3] means that items count of the output parameter is between 1 and 3, with both 1 and 3 included. Once a web service is invoked, following steps should be operated:

Step0: Extract the invoking result of the web service; create the knowledge frame according to the invoking result.

Step1: Decide whether the knowledge frame created in step0 meets the knowledge frame that has been established early when the web service is created, that is, whether items count of output parameter falls in the interval; decide whether each item of output parameter matches the regular expression.

Step2: If the knowledge frame obtained from step0 and that established at the beginning completely match, the invoking result is accepted. Otherwise, the output parameters do not meet user demands, thus the exception state of the web service is set.

3.4   Execution of Atomic Web Service

According to its Petri net model, when an atomic web service is invoked, its execution can be described as follows:

Step0: Get ID of atomic web service from corresponding transition;

Step1: Get input parameters from input places of corresponding transition;

Step2: Convert parameters;

Step3: Set the state of atomic web service to 'running', splice SOAP message and send it to the server by HTTP POST; wait until the atomic service returns SOAP message and then get the output parameters by analyzing received SOAP message;

Step4: Check output parameters;

Step5: Write output parameters back to the output places of corresponding transition and add one token to each of its output places.

If all steps above are finished successfully, the atomic web service has finished; exception happens otherwise, in which case we set the state of the atomic web service to 'exception'.

4   Petri Net Based Execution Engine for Web Service Composition

Figure3 shows execution engine architecture. Here is how execution engine works. Firstly, execution engine validates demand parameters of web service composition that users input, and gets initial marking for Pets net of web service composition. Secondly, execution engine detects transitions that enabled with transitions firing rules, deletes transitions in the selection structure through conflict resolution algorithm and selects transitions to fire. Execution engine will invoke web services corresponding to transitions selected to fire simultaneously and feed back the dynamic execution information to Petri net. Execution engine will adjust the state of Petri net according to web services execution, and selects transitions to fire according to transitions firing rules. Repeat this procedure until web service composition is finished.

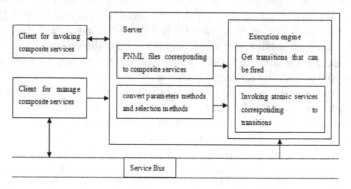

Fig. 3. Execution engine architecture

4.1   Parameter Validation

Execution engine requires necessary parameters at the beginning of web service composition execution. The types and grammars of demand parameters may correspond to specific requirements. Web service execution may fail if execution engine dose not validate them. Execution engine uses regular expressions to validate grammars. The field demandParam in table 2 stores types and regular expressions of demand parameters. For example, the parameter telephone number of the query phone number service [9] is:

{"name":"phoneNum","type":"string","regularExpression":"^(1)\\d{10}$","desc":"t elephone number "}. The corresponding value of the key "regularExpression" represents that phone number starts with 1 and has 11 digits.

4.2   Conflict Resolution

All transitions within a selection structure of web service composition may be enabled in some state, but only one of these transitions can eventually be fired in practical. The competition for firing among enabled transitions triggers conflict, and we can add control in the face of conflict.

In order to realize the control of selection, we extend PNML of web service composition by adding a port label to arc elements:

```
<arc source="startCity" target="getStation">
  <inscription><value>1</value></inscription>
  <port>1</port>
</arc>
```

Selection has two modes: artificial selection and automatic selection. Artificial selection needs user participation, and the execution engine requires user to select which transition to fire within the selection structure. For automatic selection, execution engine will select transition to fire in the selection structure through reflection mechanism automatically.

For automatic selection, the Java codes of selection methods should be clear created according to actual demand while web service composition is created. The selection methods return an integer whose name is "port". The returned integer corresponds to the value of extended port label of PNML. Execution engine will compare the returned integer of selection method with the value of extended port label. In a selection structure context, the post-transition of the arc element whose port label is matched will be selected and other transitions in the selection structure will be deleted. The Field selectivePlaces in table 2 stores information such as OR-split places, names of selection methods and corresponding classes, for example, [{"placeId":"startCity","selectClassName":"selectClass3","selectMethod":"selectSt artCity"}]. If the value of key selectMethod is empty, the selection mode is artificial selection. Otherwise, the selection is an automatic selection. Execution engine will select transitions to fire according to algorithm 4-1.

Algorithm 4-1 conflict resolution

Input: ID of current composite service; current PNML document; set of transitions that are enabled

Output: Set of transitions to fire

Step0: Analyze the PNML file; get set P' of all places with tokens in current PNML file.

Step1: For   each place p in set P' Do
        If   p is not an OR-split place   Then
           Delete p from collection P';

Step2: For   each place p in set P' Do
  2.1: Get all the successor transitions of p; put the transitions into a new set T';
  2.2: For   each transition t in set T' Do
        If   t is not enabled   Do
           Delete all the successor transitions of p from the set of transitions that are enabled, delete p from set P, go to step2, break;

Step3: For each place p in set P' Do
  3.1: Determine mode of selection according to field selective places as in table 2;
  3.2: If selection mode is artificial selection   Then
        Let user select which transition to be fire: execution engine gets the port corresponding to user's selection, select the transition to fire according to the port, and delete other transitions in the selection structure from the set of transitions that are enabled;
  3.3: If selection mode is automatic selection   Then
        Call the selection method through reflection mechanism, execution engine gets result port of selection method, select the transition to fire according to the port, delete other transitions in the selection structure from the set of transitions that are enabled;

Step4: Return current set of transitions that are enabled.

4.3   Running of Execution Engine

Execution engine will run the following steps when a web service composition is invoked:

Step0: Read the information of the demand parameters from database; send request to user for the values of demand parameters; get the values of demand parameters after user has input them;

Step1: Set the state of all atomic Web services to 'waiting'; read the directory of PNML file; load PNML file; write the values of demand parameters to the corresponding places and add one token to the corresponding places;

Step2: create set T' to store the enabled transitions; get all enabled transitions from current PNML document according to firing rule of transitions; put the obtained transitions into set T';

Step3: If set T' is not empty, resolve Conflict for T' with algorithm 5-1;

Step4: If   set T' is not empty   Then

    4.1: set the state of the corresponding atomic web services to 'ready';

    4.2: For   transition t in set T'   Do

        Decrease one token in input places of t;

    4.3: For   transition t in set T'   Do

        Create threads to execute the corresponding Web services according to set T' (When the execution of each web service is finished, go to step2, find and execute the successor Web services that can execute);

Step5: While   count of Threads for Web services' execution not equals 0 Do

        Do nothing;

Step6: Get the results from current PNML document according field outputParam of table 2;

5   Example

Here we give a web service composition whose main function is to query the information of weather and select the pattern of travel according to the obtained weather condition. There are six web services [9] within the web service composition: they are for querying the information of weather (getReginProvince, ID=1, no input) for all supported provinces, the information of all supported cities (getSupportCityString, ID=2) according to the code of province, the information of weather according the code of city (getWeather, ID=3), the information of flight(getDomesticAirlinesTime, ID=4), the information of train (getStationAndTimeByStationName, ID=5) and the information of transit(GetTransferInfoByStation, ID=6), respectively.

Firstly, the developer creates its Petri net model of the web service composition as in figure 4, writes the information of web service composition into PNML and uploads the PNML file to server.

Places corresponding to parameters of services (P") are as follows: place provinceList(list of provinces' name and code), place cityList(list of cities' name and code), place weather and weather01(weather information), place startCity(start city), place endCity(destination), place theDate(travel date), place travelInfo(travel information), place transferInfo(transit information).

Places corresponding to demand parameters of users (P^D) are as follows: place province (name of province), place startCity, place endCity, place theDate, place endStation.

Place which assists the process of web service composition (P^A) is place auxiliary01.

Then, developer designs converting parameters methods, selection methods, and knowledge frames for web service composition. Write the information of demand parameters, PNML directory, and information of output parameters to database in the form of table 2.

We take getSupportCityString service as example to show the method for converting parameters. Parameter "provinceList" stores all the names of supported provinces and corresponding codes. Parameter "province" stores the name of province that user wants to query. The getSupportCityString service needs a code of province for its input parameter. So the main function of converting parameters method is to query the code of the province from the parameter "provinceList" by the parameter "province".

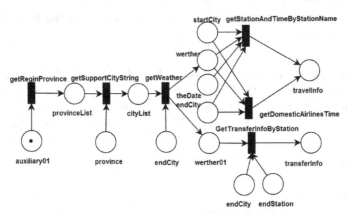

Fig. 4. The Petri net corresponding to the composite service

From figure 4, we can see the relationship between "getDomesticAirlinesTime" service and "getStationAndTimeByStationName" service is selection. The main function of the selection method is to select proper travel pattern by specific weather condition.

The output parameter of getSupportCityString service, which meets demands of users, is a one-dimensional array of strings. Each item in the array stores the name and code of a province, such as: "Shandong:3119". If too many users call the service, the server will return the string of "Non-commercial users cannot access with high speed". The resulting knowledge frame is:

Name of knowledge frame: proper output parameter of getSupportCityString

Items count of output parameter: $[1, +\infty]$

Regular expression of each item of output parameter: $^\wedge$\w+:[0-9]+$

If the system starts with following inputs: startCity:Beijing, province:Shandong, endCity:Jinan, endStation:University of Jinan, theDate:2013-07-27.

We get web service execution sequence as follows: getReginProvince, getSupport-CityStr, getWeather, getStationAndTimeByStationName&GetTransferInfoByStation.

Finally, we obtain the web service composition results: The weather of Jinan (thunderstorms), train information of Beijing to Jinan, transit info of Jinan Station to university of Jinan.

6   Conclusion and Further Work

We have studied Petri net model of web service, running of web service and implement of Petri net based execution engine for web service composition. Based on parameters validation, parameters converting among atomic web services, output parameters checking, and conflict resolution, the execution engine will run according to Petri net model of web service established on firing rule of transitions, monitor web service execution and feed back the dynamic execution information of web services to the Petri net.

Our further work is the system optimization and exception handling during the running of execution engine.

Acknowledgement. This work was supported by National Natural Science Foundation of China (60903099), the Excellent Young and Middle-Aged Scientist Award Grant of Shandong Province of China (BS2009DX012), and A Project of Shandong Province Higher Educational Science and Technology Program (J09LG14).

References

1. BPEL (July 2013),
   http://www.eclipse.org/bpel/
2. OWL-S (July 2013), http://www.w3.org/Submission/OWL-S/
3. Wu, Z.: Introduction to Petri Nets, pp. 1–103. Mechine press, Beijing (2006)
4. PIPE (July 2013), http://sourceforge.net/projects/pipe2/
5. Yoo, T., Jeong, B., Cho, H.: A Petri Nets based functional validation for services composition. Expert Systems with Applications 37, 3768–3776 (2010)
6. Valero, V., Cambronero, E.M.: A Petri net Approach for the design analysis of Web services Choreographies. The Journal of Logic Algebraic Programming 78, 359–380 (2009)
7. Mei, X.-Y., Li, S.-X., Huang, C.-Q., Zheng, X.-L.: An Execution Semantic Analysis Method for Composition Transaction. Acta Electronica Sinica 7, 1386–1396 (2012)
8. Billington, J., et al.: The Petri Net Markup Language: Concepts, technology, and tools. In: van der Aalst, W.M.P., Best, E. (eds.) ICATPN 2003. LNCS, vol. 2679, pp. 483–505. Springer, Heidelberg (2003)
9. http://webservice.webxml.com.cn/ (July 2013)
10. WSDL, http://www.w3.org/TR/wsdl (July 2013)

11. Ding, Z., Shen, H., Kandel, A.: Life Fellow, IEEE. Performance Analysis of Service Composition Based on Fuzzy Differential Equations. IEEE Transaction on Fuzzy Systems 2, 164–178 (2011)
12. Du, Y., Li, X., Xiong, P.C.: A Petri Net Approach to Mediation-Aided Composition of Web Services 4, 429–435 (2012)
13. Ma, B., Xie, N.: From OWL-S to PNML+OWL for Semantic Web Services. In: 2010 Second International Conference on Computer Modeling and Simulation, vol. 4, pp. 326–328. IEEE, Beijing (2010)
14. Zhang, Z.-M., Ma, B.-X., Xiang, D.-M.: Creation and Description of Web Service Based on Petri Nets. Journal of System Simulation 7, 19–25 (2011)
15. Xiang, D.-M., Ma, B.-X., Zhang, Z.-M.: Automatic Sharing Synthesis of Petri Nets based on Semantics. Journal of System Simulation 11, 2237–2242 (2012)
16. JSON, http://www.json.org/ (July 2013)

A Method of Optimizing Multi-tenant Database Query Access

Haitham Yaish[1,2], Madhu Goyal[1,2], and George Feuerlicht[2,3]

[1] Centre for Quantum Computation & Intelligent Systems
[2] Faculty of Engineering and Information Technology
University of Technology, Sydney
P.O. Box 123, Broadway NSW 2007, Australia
[3] Faculty of Information Technology,
University of Economics, Prague, Czech Republic
haitham.yaish@student.uts.edu.au, madhu@it.uts.edu.au,
george.feuerlicht@uts.edu.au

Abstract. Multi-tenant database is a new cloud computing paradigm that has recently attracted attention to deliver database functionalities for multiple database users to create, store, and access their databases over the internet. However, such approach raises an issue in database performance, due to the fact that the multi-tenant database is shared between multiple tenants. Therefore, this contemporary database requires a special query method to optimize different query retrievals for multiple tenants who are using the same resources of a single multi-tenant database. In this paper, we are proposing a multi-tenant query optimization method based on multi-tenant database schema called Elastic Extension Tables (EET). This method estimates the cost of different query execution plans, to determine the optimal plan. Then uses this plan to execute a tenant's query by using a code base solution that converts multi-tenant queries into traditional database queries and executes them by using a query optimizer of any Relational Database Management System (RDBMS).

Keywords: Cloud Computing, Software as a Service, SaaS, Query Optimizer, Multi-tenancy, Multi-tenant Database Schema, Elastic Extension Tables.

1 Introduction

Organisations often spend large amounts of their time, resources and money managing and supporting information stored in their on-premises databases, to ensure that the right information is available when it is needed. According to statistics, data management cost is 5 to 10 times more than the data gain cost [1], [10]. Therefore, it is widely agreed that this is a significant issue for organisations in general and for small and medium size organisations in particular. Subsequently, the multi-tenant database is considered the solution for this issue because it provides database features like data definition, storage and retrieval which can be accessed from the service providers' premises on a subscription basis over the internet [11].

Z. Huang et al. (Eds.): WISE 2013 Workshops 2013, LNCS 8182, pp. 194–212, 2014.

The majority of modern Relational Database Management Systems (RDBMS) like Oracle, SQL Server [12], and PostgreSQL [4] have a query optimizer to optimize the query execution of a single-user database. Nevertheless, the multi-tenant database requires a special query optimizer method which plays a vital role in improving the multi-tenant query processing and solves the issues of multi-tenant database, which are including isolating tenant's data statistics, retrieving tenant's queries in a timely and cost efficient manner, and making the best use of multi-tenant database resources. Salesforce [14], [15] states that modern database query optimizers are designed for single-user databases and they are not suitable for multi-tenant database, and because they are not taking in consideration the unique characteristics of each tenant's data, such as indexes and the gathered statistics for all tenants instead of specific statistics for a particular tenant, which in return is leading to incorrect assumptions and query plans of tenants' data. Therefore, the multi-tenant database requires a special query optimizer with special query execution plans.

Cost effective scalability is very significant for multi-tenant applications. The maximum number of tenants that can be supported by a multi-tenant application can be increased as long as the resources increased while keeping the performance metrics of each tenant at an acceptable level. In terms of scalability, scale-out approach is more efficient than scale-up approach [9], [13]. The same case can be applied for the multi-tenant database. However, before we can start thinking to scale-out or scale-up multi-tenant database to optimize its performance, the multi-tenant database performance should be optimized in each single server instance by applying a proper multi-tenant query optimizer, then any of the scale-out or the scale-up approaches can be applied afterwards. Accordingly, we will focus in this paper on how to optimize multi-tenant query performance in a single server instance and scalability will be out of this paper scope. Nevertheless, we will focus on scalability in the future work.

There are various models of multi-tenant database designs and techniques, which have studied and implemented to overcome multi-tenant database challenges [2],[3],[5],[8],[16]. Nevertheless, these techniques are still not overcoming multi-tenant database challenges [6]. Based on this analysis, we have proposed a novel multi-tenant database schema design to create and configure multi-tenant applications, by introducing an Elastic Extension Tables (EET), which consists of Common Tenant Tables (CTT), Virtual Extension Tables (VET), and Extension Tables (ET) [16]. This design enables tenants creating and configuring their own virtual database schema including a required number of tables and columns, a virtual database relationship with any of CTTs or VETs, and assigning suitable data types and constraints for columns during multi-tenant application run-time execution [16]. Also, we have proposed a multi-tenant database proxy service, called EET Proxy Service (EETPS) which based on EET multi-tenant database schema. This service combines, generates, and executes tenants' queries by using a code base solution that converts multi-tenant queries into traditional database queries and executes them in any RDBMS by using its traditional query optimizer [17].

The main contribution of this paper is proposing a multi-tenant optimization method called Elastic Extension Tables Query Optimizer (EETQO). This method optimizes the query access of the proposed Elastic Extension Tables Proxy Service (EETPS) through estimating the cost of different query execution plans, and then determining the optimal query execution plan based on the estimated cost and the structure of the given query. Moreover, we verified the practicability of applying the multi-tenant optimization method on EETPS by executing different types of queries.

The rest of the paper is organized as follows: section 2 reviews the related work, section 3 describes EET, section 4 describes the EETPS, section 5 proposes our optimization method which called EETQO, section 6 describes the single table algorithm of EETPS, section 7 gives our experimental results, and Section 8 concludes this paper and descries the future work.

2   Related Work

Monitoring the performance of executing queries in RDBMS by database administrators is costly and difficult. Therefore, the Query Optimizer module emerged to improve manual tuning of queries to automatic query optimization [12]. The Query optimizer is a query processing technique which uses statistical properties to select an efficient execution query plan [7]. There are a large number of related works, which have done on the query optimizer for single-user database including Oracle, SQL Server [12], PostgreSQL [4], and others. These query optimizers are suitable for single-tenant applications but not for multi-tenant applications.

Salesforce [15] states that modern databases query optimizers like the ones described earlier designed for single-tenant applications. However, these query optimizers are not suitable for the multi-tenant environment. The Salesforce Query optimizer considers accessing data partitions that contain tenants' data rather than an entire table or index, accessing statistics of tenants, and group and user-level for each virtual multi-tenant object. This query optimizer considers the user who is executing a given application function by using related tenant-specific metadata with system pivot tables to build and execute optimized database queries. Moreover, Salesforce uses other types of statistics to help with any particular queries like custom indexes to reveal the total number of not null and unique values in the corresponding field, and histograms for pick list fields, which reveal the cardinality of each list value. However, when statistics are not helpful to generate optimal query a FallbackIndex pivot table is used efficiently to find the requested results as a secondary search mechanism, instead of returning a disappointed error message.

In this related work section, we have listed different single-tenant database query optimizer works which are suitable for a single-user database schema, but not for multi-tenant database schema. Moreover, we discussed how Salesforce optimizes its multi-tenant database which based on a multi-tenant database schema that consists of a set of metadata, universal data table, and pivot tables. Salesforce proposed a multi-tenant optimization method that based on their multi-tenant data storage. Whereas in this paper we propose a multi-tenant optimization method, that based on EET multi-tenant database schema that we proposed in a previous work [16].

3   Elastic Extension Tables

The multi-tenant database schema is a new way of designing and creating a multi-tenant database which consists of three types of tables. The first type is Common Tenant Tables (CTT), which are shared between tenants who are using a single instance of the multi-tenant database. These are physical relational tables, which can be applied to any business domain database such as Customer Relationship Management (CRM), Accounting, Human Resource (HR), or any other business domain. The second type is Virtual Extension Tables (VET), which eligible tenants extending on the existing business domain database, or having their own configurable database through creating their virtual database structures from scratch by creating (1) virtual database tables, (2) virtual database relationships between the virtual tables, and (3) other database constraints. The third type is Extension Tables (ET), which consists of eight tables that are used to construct VETs [16]. The data architecture details of these eight tables are listed below and shown in Fig. 1.

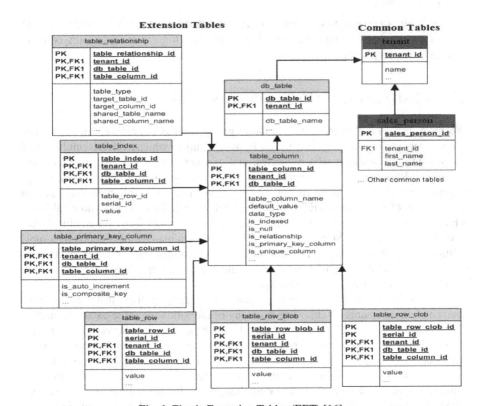

Fig. 1. Elastic Extension Tables (EET) [16]

- **The db_Table Extension Table:** This table allows a tenant creating virtual tables and giving them unique names.

- **The table_column Extension Table:** This table allows a tenant creating virtual columns for a virtual table stored in the "db_table" extension table.

- **The table_row Extension Tables:** The row extension tables store records of virtual extension columns in three separate tables. These tables are separated in order to store small data values in the "table_row" extension table such as NUMBER, DATE-and-TIME, BOOLEAN, VARCHAR and other data types. Whereas the large data values stored in two other tables. The first one is the "table_row_blob" extension table, which stores a uniform resource locator (URL) for the Binary Large Objects (BLOB). The second one is the "table_row_clob" extension table, which stores Character Large Objects (CLOB) values for virtual columns with TEXT data type.

- **The Table_relationship Extension Table:** This table allows tenants creating a virtual relationship for their virtual tables with any of CTTs or VETs.
- **The table_index Extension Table:** This table is used to add indexes to virtual columns, which reduce the query execution time when a tenant retrieves data from database tables.
- **The table_primary_key_column Extension Table:** This table allows tenants creating single or composite virtual primary key for virtual extension columns which are stored in the "table_column" extension table.

4   Elastic Extension Tables Proxy Service

We have proposed a multi-tenant database proxy service to combine, generate, and execute tenants' queries by using a code base solution which converts multi-tenant queries into traditional database queries, and execute these traditional database queries in any RDBMS [17]. This service has two objectives, first, to enable tenants' applications retrieve table rows from CTTs, retrieve combined table rows from two or more tables of CTTs and VETs, or retrieve table rows from two or more tables of VETs. Second, to spare tenants from spending money and efforts on writing Structured Query Language (SQL) queries and backend data management codes by simply calling functions from this service, which retrieves simple and complex queries including join operations, union operations, filtering on multiple properties, and filtering of data based on sub queries results.

This service gives tenants the opportunity of satisfying their different business needs and requirements by choosing from any of the following three database models. First, the Multi-tenant relational database: This database model allows tenants using a ready relational database structure for a particular business domain database without any need of extending on the existing database structure, and this business domain database can be shared between multiple tenants and differentiate between them by using a Tenant ID. This model can be applied to any business domain database like: CRM, Accounting, HR, or any other business domains. Second, the Combined multi-tenant relational database and virtual relational database: This database model allows tenants using a ready relational database structure of a business domain with the ability of extending on this relational database, by adding more virtual database tables, and creating virtual relationships between them to combine the virtual tables with the existing relational database structure. Third, the Multi-tenant virtual relational database: This database model allows tenants using their own configurable database through creating their virtual database structures from scratch, by creating virtual database tables, virtual database relationships between the virtual tables, and other database constraints to satisfy their special business requirements for their business domain applications.

The EETPS provides functions which allow tenants building their web, mobile, and desktop applications without the need of writing SQL queries and backend data management codes. Instead, EETPS retrieves their data by simply calling these functions, which return a two dimensional array (Object [n] [m]), where n denotes the number of array rows that represents a number of retrieved table rows, and m denotes the number of array columns that represents a number of retrieved table columns for a particular virtual table. This two dimensional array stores the virtual table row in a structure, which is similar to any physical table row structured in any physical database table, and in return will facilitate accessing virtual tuples from any VET. These functions designed and built to retrieve tenants' data from the following tables:

- One table, either a CTT or a VET.
- Two tables, which have one-to-one, one-to-many, many-to-many, or self-referencing virtual relationships. These relationships can be between two VETs, two CTTs, or one VET and one CTT.
- Two tables which may have or not have a relationship between them, by using different types of joins including left join, right join, inner join, outer join, left excluding join, right excluding join, and outer excluding join. The join operation can be used between two VETs, two CTTs, or one VET and one CTT.
- Two tables or more, which may have or not have a relationship between them, by using the union operator that combines the result-set of these tables whether they are CTTs or VETs.
- Two or more tables, which have a relationship between them, by using filters on multiple tables, or filtering the data based on the results of sub queries.

Moreover, the EETPS functions have the capabilities of retrieving data from CTTs or VETs by using the following query options: specifying query SELECT clause, specifying query WHERE clause, specifying query LIMIT, using single or composite primary keys, retrieving BLOB and CLOB values, logical operators, arithmetic operators, aggregate functions, and mathematical functions.

5   EET Query Optimizer Method

The overview of the EET Query Optimizer (EETQO) Architecture is shown in Fig.2. This query optimizer has four aims: gathering statistics of virtual rows, which a query can potentially access, finding the fastest path to execute a query, estimating the cost of different query execution plans, and determining the optimal plan for execution. Then the determined optimal execution plans will be used in the EETPS [17], which constructs and generates multi-tenant queries, and executes them in RDBMS by using its traditional query optimizer. The following seven points show the components of EET Query Optimizer Architecture and how they are orchestrating with EETPS and EET.

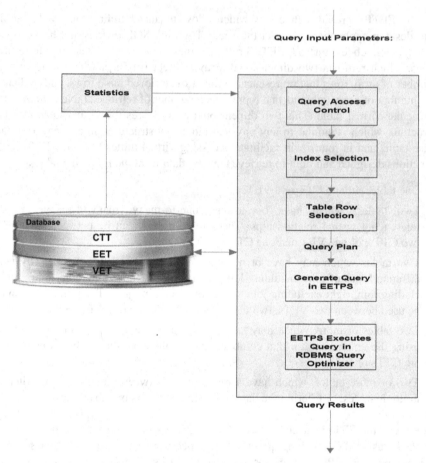

Fig. 2. Overview of EET Query Optimizer Architecture and how it is orchestrated with EETPS and EET

5.1   Query Access Control

This is the first component that has to be executed in the EETQO, which controls the access of multi-tenant data in CTTs and VETs. As long as CTTs and VETs are using "tenant_id" to isolate tenant data in EET multi-tenant database and divide it into partitions, then each tenant will have his/her own partitions to store their own data. Moreover, these partitions can be divided by tenants' users according to some access control permissions which can be granted to these users. These access control permissions are stored in the database, and before executing the users' queries these permissons will be checked to optimize the query execution by generating the optimal query structure, which in return reduces the query execution time.

In this component, we applied two methods to control tenants' users in the multi-tenant EET, which in return allows EETQO determining the optimal query execution plan that reduces the cost of query execution. These methods are listed below:

Accessing Table Columns. This method allows tenants granting users permissions to access some or all columns of a CTT or a VET. These permissions can restrict tenants' users from accessing some or all columns of a table. In addition, they can help EETQO to decide the optimal query execution plans, by knowing whether a user can access all, some, or none of table columns. In this method, the query optimization occurs in two cases. The first one, when a user cannot access any of a table columns, in this case the query will not be executed. The second one, when a user can access some of the table columns. In this case, the data will be retrieved from some of the table columns by generating a query structure which is different from the query structure that needs extra execution time to retrieve data from all the table columns.

Accessing Table Rows. This method allows tenants granting users permissions to access some or all rows of a CTT or a VET. These permissions can restrict tenants' users from accessing some or all rows of a table. These permissions help the EETQO to choose the optimal query execution plan based on the number of rows which can be accessed by a user, and generating a query structure to retrieve data from some of the table rows, which is different from the query structure that needs extra execution time to retrieve all the table rows.

In summary, the EETQO method allows choosing the optimal execution plan between different query execution paths based on tenants' users and the different columns and rows which they can access. This selected plan reduces the overhead on the multi-tenant EET and accelerates their query execution time.

5.2   Index Selection

This is the second component that has to be executed in the EETQO, which checks whether a VET has virtual indexes that estimate the cost and choose the optimal execution plan between different query execution paths. These virtual indexes are related to virtual columns of a VET, and they are typically stored in the "table_index" extension table. This extension table stores three types of indexes:

Primary Key Index. This index is typically created for a single primary key column by having a single primary key index, or composite primary key columns by having multiple primary key indexes for a VET.

Foreign Key Index. This index is typically created for a single foreign key column, or for composite foreign key columns in a VET.

Custom Index. This index can be created for any virtual column of a VET which is used often as a selective filter in a tenant query. The virtual column should be other than the primary key and the foreign key columns.

When tenants create a VET and assign to it any of the three indexes listed above, and then this VET can have three cases to retrieve rows. The first case is retrieving rows from a VET by specifying primary keys. The second case is retrieving rows from a VET by specifying table row IDs which are stored in the "table_row" extension table. The third case is retrieving VET rows without specifying any primary keys or row IDs. These three cases can construct a SELECT clause and a WHERE clause in the query to retrieve data from a VET based on the following six execution plans:

Primary Key. This execution plan does not use indexes; instead, it uses the following filters to execute a query: tenant ID, user ID, VET ID, and specific Primary Keys.

Row ID. This execution plan does not use indexes; instead, it uses the following filters to execute the query: tenant ID, user ID, VET ID, and specific Row IDs.

Full Table. This execution plan does not use indexes or any other filters except the standard filters which are: tenant ID, user ID, and VET ID.

A Percentage of Custom Index. This execution plan uses a percentage of a custom index, tenant ID, user ID, VET ID, and a value belongs to the custom index which filters the query.

All of Custom Index. This execution plan uses all the indexes of a custom index, tenant ID, user ID, VET ID, and a value belongs to the custom index which filters the query.

None of Custom Index. This execution plan uses none of the indexes of Custom Index, tenant ID, user ID, VET ID, and a particular value which relates to the custom index.

The EET multi-tenant database schema, allows each tenant having a unique data structure, tables, columns, and column constraints. These characteristics work side by side with the above listed index execution plans to support multi-tenant query execution strategies of the EETQO.

5.3   Table Row Selection

This is the third component that has to be executed in the EETQO. In EET that we have proposed [16], there are three row extension tables that store rows of virtual extension columns. These tables store three different data types; therefore they are separated in order to store small data values in the "table_row" extension table, and large data values in the other two tables. The first one is the "table_row_blob" extension table that stores all BLOB, and the second one is the "table_row_clob" extension table that stores CLOB values. More details of these row tables presented in section 3. The reason behind separating these three tables is to reduce the impact of BLOB and CLOB values from slowing down virtual schema queries [16].

It is not always the case that all the tables in the virtual database will have BLOB and CLOB data types. Therefore, this function will eliminate searching in "table_row_blob", and "table_row_clob" extension tables, if a table has not got any BLOB or CLOB columns, or if a table has got BLOB or CLOB columns, but these columns are not part of the query SELECT clause or WHERE clause.

The Table Row Selection method helps the EETQO in two aspects. The first aspect is checking whether a table has a CLOB or BLOB data types, if any of them exists then the query will retrieve rows from "table_row" extension table, and both or either "table_row_blob" or "table_row_clob" extension tables. Otherwise, the query will retrieve rows from only "table_row" extension table. The UNION operator keyword is used to combine the result-set of three SELECT statements of the three row tables if the VET only contains BLOB and/or CLOB. However, if the VET does not contain BLOB and CLOB then the UNION operator will not be used in the query. This approach minimizes the runtime optimization overhead on the EETQO by avoiding using the UNION operator keyword unless it is necessary.

The second aspect is separating the data which stored in the three row extension tables, by storing small data values in the "table_row" extension table and large data values in two others extension tables the "table_row_blob" and the "table_row_clob". This approach minimizes the runtime optimization overhead on the EETQO, by minimizing the size and the stored content of the "table_row" extension table that stores most of the tenants' data, and by accessing the BLOB and the CLOB data only on demand.

5.4 Statistics

The concept of statistics in modern RDBMS is gathering the amount and the type of data which is stored in the database. These statistics estimate the cost of different query execution plans which determine the optimal one. In multi-tenant databases, the statistical concept is slightly different from the single-tenant database. In the multi-tenant database there are two ways of gathering statistics, the first way is by differentiating between tenants' rows, by gathering statistics for each tenant. The second way is by gathering statistics of rows that are accessible by a user who is granted an access to view a query result based on groups and/or roles which are assigned to the user.

5.5 Multi-tenant Database

The EETQO is based on retrieving data stored in EET multi-tenant database schema that consists of three types of tables CTT, VET, and ET that presented in section 3.

5.6 Generate Query

After executing the EETQO and finding the best execution plans, the EETPS is invoked to generate a virtual multi-tenant query based on the selected query plans which decided on the components of the Multi-tenant EETQO.

5.7   Execute Query

The EETPS executes multi-tenant database query according to the best and lowest cost execution plan that was selected from the query optimizer components. Then this multi-tenant query get converted into a traditional database query and executed in RDBMS by using its traditional query optimizer.

6   Single Table Algorithm of EETPS

In this section, we are exploring a sample algorithm from EETPS, which retrieves data from CTT and VET. This algorithm is used to generate the queries that are added in the Appendix section, and these queries are used in the experiments which are presented in section 7. There are four different cases in this algorithm that retrieve data from VETs. The first case is retrieving rows from a VET by specifying some primary keys. The second case is retrieving rows from a VET by specifying some table row IDs which are stored in 'table_row' extension table. The third case is retrieving data from a VET by specifying one or more custom indexes. The fourth case is retrieving all rows of CTT or VET. In this section, we will explore the main algorithm of the Single Table Algorithm, and a sample subsidiary algorithm which represents the second case that mentioned in this paragraph. However, the first, the third, and the fourth cases details are not listed in this paper due to the space limit.

6.1   Main Single Table Algorithm

This main algorithm is outlined in Program Listing 1. The input parameters of this algorithm are passed from the tenant by invoking the Single Table function from EETPS. One of these algorithm input parameters is used to determine which of the above mentioned four cases will be used to retrieve the query statement, and then this query statement will be executed in a RDBMS to return SQL query results from "table_row", "table_row_blob", and "table_row_clob" extension tables, then store these results in a set, and finally, the virtual columns set will be stored in an array.

Definition 1 (Single Table Main Algorithm). T denotes a tenant ID. B denotes a table name. λ denotes a set of table row ID values. Ω denotes a set of primary key values. S denotes a string of the SELECT clause parameter. W denotes a string of the WHERE clause. F denotes the first result number of a query LIMIT. M denotes the maximum amount of the query LIMIT which will be retrieved. Q denotes the table type whether it is a CTT or a VET. I denotes a set of table_row_id values, which represent indexes for a VET, and they are retrieved from the table_index extension table. C denotes a set of retrieved rows from a CTT. V denotes a set of retrieved rows from a VET. θ denotes a string of the select statement. Φ denotes a two dimensional array that stores the retrieved rows.

Input. T, B, λ, Ω, S, W, F, M and Q.
Output. Φ.

```
1. if Q = CTT then   /* Retrieve data from CTT */
2.    C ← retrieve rows from B table by using T, Ω, S, W, F,
      and M query filters
3. else  /* Retrieve data from VET */
4.    if Ω ≠ null then  /* The first case */
5.       V ← retrieve rows from B table by using T, Ω, S, W, F,
         and M query filters
6.    else if λ ≠ null then     /* The second case */
7.       θ ← tableRowQuery(T, B, λ, S, W, F, M)  /* Program
         Listing 2 */
8.       V ← execute θ in DBMS
9.    else
10.      I ← retrieve the custom indexes of B table from ta-
         ble_index extension table
11.      if I ≠ null then  /* The third case (Custom Index) */
12.         θ ← tableRowQuery(T, B, I, S, W, F, M)  /* Program
            Listing 2 */
13.         V ← execute θ in DBMS
14.      else /* The fourth case */
15.         V ← retrieve rows from B table by using T, S, W, F,
            and M query filters
16.      end if
17.   end if
18. end if  /* End of retrieving data from VET */
19. if Q = CTT then
20.    Φ ← C
21. else
22.    Φ ← V
23. end if
24. Return Φ
```
[1] The program listings of single table algorithm.

6.2   Table Row Query Algorithm

This subsidiary query algorithm is used to retrieve rows for a tenant from a VET. The database query used in this algorithm uses UNION operator keyword to combine the result-set of three SELECT statements for three tables: "table_row", "table_row_blob", and "table_row_clob". That is if the VET only contains BLOB and/or CLOB. However, if the VET does not contain BLOB and CLOB then the UNION operator will not be used in the query. This subsidiary algorithm is outlined in Program Listing 2.

Definition 2 (Table Row Query Algorithm). T denotes a tenant ID. B denotes a table name. λ denotes a set of table row ID values. S denotes a string of the SELECT clause parameter. W denotes a string of the WHERE clause. F denotes the first result number of the query LIMIT. M denotes the maximum amount of the query LIMIT which will be retrieved. θ denotes a string of the select statement. R denotes the data types of the VET's columns. If R equals 1, this means that the VET does not contain BLOB or CLOB values. If R equals 2, this means that the VET contains CLOB values. If R equals 3, this means that the VET contains BLOB values. If R equals 4, this means that the VET contains BLOB and CLOB values.

Input. T, B, λ, S, W, F, and M.
Output. θ.

```
1. R ← retrieve the columns' data types of B table from the ta-
   ble_column extension table
2. θ ← SELECT tr.table_column_name, tr.value, tr.table_row_id,
   tr.serial_id FROM table_row tr WHERE tr.tenant_id = T AND
   tr.db_table_id = B AND tr.table_row_id IN (λ) AND ta-
   ble_column_id in (S) AND W
3. if R = 3 ∨ R = 4 then
4.     θ ← θ ∪ UNION SELECT trb.table_column_name, trb.value,
       trb.table_row_blob_id, trb.serial_id FROM table_row_blob
       trb WHERE trb.tenant_id = T AND trb.db_table_id = B AND
       trb.table_row_blob_id IN (λ)
5. else if R = 2 ∨ R = 4 then
6.     θ ← θ ∪ UNION SELECT trc.table_column_name, trc.value,
       trc.table_row_clob_id, trc.serial_id FROM table_row_clob
       trc WHERE trc.tenant_id = T AND trc.db_table_id = B AND
       trc.table_row_clob_id IN (λ)
7. end if
8. θ ← θ ∪ ORDER BY 3, 4 LIMIT M OFFSET F
9. Return θ
```

[2] The program listings of table row query algorithm.

7   Performance Evaluation

After developing the EETPS [17], we applied on this service the EETQO method that we present in this paper, and we carried out three types of experiments to verify the practicability of applying the EETQO on the EETPS. We have evaluated the response time through accessing the EETPS which converts multi-tenant queries into traditional database queries, instead of accessing the database directly, and execute the traditional database queries in any RDBMS.

7.1   Experimental Setup

The EETQO was implemented in Java 1.6.0, Hibernate 4.0, and Spring 3.1.0. The database is PostgreSQL 8.4 and the application server is Jboss-5.0.0.CR2. Both of database and application server is deployed on the same PC. The operating system is Windows 7 Home Premium, CPU is Intel Core i5 2.40GHz, the memory is 8 GB, and the hard disk is 500 GB.

7.2   Experimental Data Set

The EETPS has designed and developed to serve multiple tenants on one instance application. Nevertheless, in this paper the aim of the experiments is evaluating the performance after applying the EETQO method on the EETPS for one tenant. Typically, multi-tenant databases store massive data volumes across multiple servers to optimize the performance of data retrieval. However, before we can start thinking to scale-up or scale-out multi-tenant database to optimize its performance, the multi-tenant database performance should be optimized in each single server instance by applying a proper multi-tenant query optimizer, then either of the scale-up or the scale-out approaches can be applied afterwards. In this experiment, we used one machine and invoked the Main Single Table function of the EETPS (presented in section 6) to retrieve a 100 of rows from the 'product' VET, which is shown in Fig. 3. There are 200,000 rows stored in this table which belongs to a tenant whose "tenant_id" equals 1000, and the "db_table_id" of this table equals 16. All the queries, which are implemented in these experiments, are filtered by "tenant_id", "db_table_id", and all the filters which will be specified in the experiments. We executed our experiments for one tenant because, in the multi-tenant database, each tenant's data is isolated in a table partition. Thus, these experiments can evaluate the effectiveness of retrieving data for each single tenant from the multi-tenant database by using EETQO. These experiments are divided into three types sharing the details of this data set. The queries of these experiments are shown in the Appendix section, and they are structured based on the algorithm that we propose in this paper and the proposed EETPS [17]. The three experiments are listed below:

Accessing Data from Table Columns Experiment (Exp.1). In this experiment, we executed Query 1 (Q1) and Query 2 (Q2) to benchmark the query execution time difference between a tenant's user who can access data from all of the table's columns by executing Q1, and another tenant's user who can access data from only three out of eight columns of the same table by executing Q2.

Accessing Data from Table Rows Experiment (Exp.2). In this experiment, we executed Query 1 (Q1) and Query 3 (Q3) to benchmark the query execution time difference between a tenant's user who can access data from all of the table's rows by executing Q1, and the same user if he can access 10% of the table's data, which equals approximately 20,000 rows by executing Q3.

Accessing Data from Filters and Indexes Experiment (Exp. 3): This experiment is divided into six sub experiments including:

- **None of Custom Index Experiment (Exp. 3.1):** In this experiment, the aim is to filter a query by having a query filter on the "standard_cost" column of the table. This filter contributes in retrieving all the rows which have a standard cost value greater than 9000 ("standard_cost" > 9000). Also, we assume here that the tenant did not create a custom index to tune the query execution, and no any other index of the table is used to execute Q1.

- **A Percentage of Custom Index Experiment (Exp. 3.2):** In this experiment, the aim is to have the same assumption of using the standard cost filter which we mentioned in Exp. 3.1. However, in this experiment we created a custom index to tune the query execution. Accordingly, in this experiment the custom indexes of "standard_cost" column will be used to execute Q3, and only a particular percentage of the table rows, which match the filter criteria will be retrieved.

- **All of Custom Index Experiment (Exp. 3.3):** The aim of this experiment is to benchmark the effectiveness of using all the table indexes in Query 4 (Q4), by using the same standard cost filter which we assumed in Exp. 3.1.

- **Full Table Experiment (Exp. 3.4):** The aim of this experiment is to benchmark the effectiveness of not using any query filters or indexes filters in Query 5 (Q5).

- **Primary Key Index Experiment (Exp. 3.5):** The aim of this experiment is to benchmark the effectiveness of filtering Query 6 (Q6) by using three values of the primary key "product_id" including 101, 102 and 103, and without using any indexes or query filters.

- **Row ID Experiment (Exp. 3.6):** The aim of this experiment is to benchmark the effectiveness of filtering Query 7 (Q7) by using three values of the "table_row_id" including 22, 23 and 24, and without using any indexes or query filters.

We have included Exp. 3.4, Exp. 3.5, and Exp. 3.6 in Exp. 3 to compare the query execution time of these experiments with the other experiments (Exp. 3.1, Exp. 3.2, and Exp. 3.3) of the Custom Index.

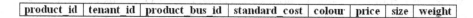

product_id	tenant_id	product_bus_id	standard_cost	colour	price	size	weight

Fig. 3. The columns of the 'product' table

7.3   Experimental Results

Accessing Table Columns Experimental Results. Typically, users are granted access to table columns from the application level because in a single-user database users are not granted database access on the column level. Whereas, the EETQO method, is granting users a database access on the column level. This capability reduces the query execution time in the multi-tenant database. The experimental study of Exp.1 is showing that the execution time of Q1 for a user who can access fewer numbers of columns of a table is less than the execution time of Q2 for a user who can access all the table columns. The details results of this experiment are shown in Fig. 4 and Table 1.

Accessing Table Rows Experiment Result. Typically, users cannot be granted a database access to table rows from the database. Whereas, the EETQO method, is granting users a database access on the row level. This capability reduces the query execution time in the multi-tenant database. The experimental study of Exp. 2 is showing that the execution time of Q3 for a user who can access a percentage of a table rows is less than the execution time of Q1 for a user who can access all the table rows. The details results of this experiment are shown in Fig. 5 and Table 1.

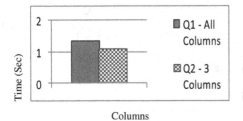

Fig. 4. Accessing Data from Table Columns Experiment (Exp.1)

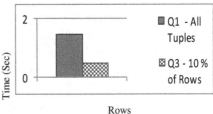

Fig. 5. Accessing Data from Table rows Experiment (Exp.2)

Table 1. The query execution time of Experiment 1 (Exp. 1) and Experiment 2 (Exp2)

Experiment	Query executed	Time in seconds
Exp. 1	Q1	1.35
Exp. 1	Q2	1.10
Exp. 2	Q1	1.45
Exp. 2	Q3	0.48

Accessing Data from Query Filters and Indexes Experiment. The experimental study of Exp. 3 is showing that the average execution time for Q5, Q6, and Q7 equals approximately 240 milliseconds. Further, the execution time of Q3 is approximately one time greater that Q5, Q6, and Q7. Whereas, the execution time of Q1 is approximately two times higher than Q5, Q6, and Q7, and finally, the execution time of Q4 is the highest one. It is approximately 3 times higher than Q5, Q6, and Q7. Exp. 3.4, Exp. 3.5, and Exp. 3.6 verified the practicability and the advancements of EET database structure [16], by executing the query of these experiments in a short time. Whereas Exp. 3.1, Exp. 3.2, and Exp. 3.3 compared the difference between three Custom Index cases including None of Custom Index (Q1), A Percentage of Custom Index (Q3), and All of Custom Index (Q4). The interpretation of these three experiments leads to the following conclusions: First, if a tenant wants to filter a query by using a column value not indexed, and other than a primary key and a foreign key, then the EETQO chooses the execution plan of a None of Custom Index (Q1). Second, if a tenant wants to use the same column mentioned in the first point, and this column is a Custom Index, then the EETQO chooses the execution plan of the Percentage of Custom Index (Q3). The last conclusion is that the EETQO will never choose the execution plan of the All of Custom Index (Q4) because the query execution cost of this query is high in comparison with the execution plan of a None of Custom Index (Q1) and the Percentage of Custom Index (Q3). The details results of this experiment are shown in Fig. 6 and Table 2.

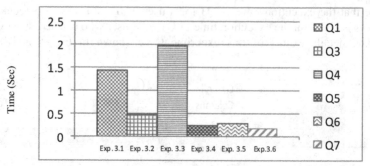

Showing Exp3.1 -3.6 from left to right

Fig. 6. Accessing Data from Filters and Indexes Experiment (Exp. 3)

Table 2. The query execution time of Experiment 3 (Exp. 3)

Experiment	Query executed	Time in seconds
Exp. 3.1	Q1	1.45
Exp. 3.2	Q3	0.48
Exp. 3.3	Q4	1.99
Exp. 3.4	Q5	0.25
Exp. 3.5	Q6	0.29
Exp. 3.6	Q7	0.18

8   Conclusion

In this paper, we have proposed a multi-tenant query optimizer method called Elastic Extension Table Query Optimizer (EETQO), which estimates the cost of different query execution plans to determine the optimal query execution plan. This query optimizer method reduces the query execution time of EETPS, which is accessing data from EET multi-tenant database schema. Moreover, we carried out three types of experiments and we verified the practicability of applying the EETQO on the EETPS.

The first experiment verified that the cost of executing a query in a multi-tenant database for a user who can access some numbers of columns of a VET is less than the cost of executing the same query for a user who can access all the VET columns. The second experiment verified that the cost of executing a query in a multi-tenant database for a user who can access a percentage of a VET rows is less than the cost of executing the same query for a user who can access all the VET rows. The third experiment verified the practicability and the advancements of the EET database structure. Further, it led to a conclusion that the cost of executing a query from a VET by using all the indexes of that VET is high in comparison with the cost of executing the same query without using any index. Nevertheless, we found that the least cost of the query execution is when a query uses a custom index with a percentage of a VET indexes.

In our future work will focus on enhancing our EETQO by adding more methods to determine the optimal query execution plans. Also, caching the frequently used queries effectively to speed up the EETQO processing time, and reduce the consumption of the EET database resources. In addition, we will focus on the scalability of the proposed EET, EETPS, and EETQO.

References

1. Alzain, M.A., Pardede, E.: Using Multi Shares for Ensuring Privacy in Database-as-a-Service. In: System Sciences, pp. 1–9. IEEE Press, Hawaii (2011)
2. Aulbach, S., Grust, T., Jacobs, D., Kemper, A., Seibold, M.: A Comparison of Flexible Schemas for Software as a Service. In: Proceedings of the 35th SIGMOD International Conference on Management of Data, pp. 881–888. ACM, Rhode Island (2009)
3. Aulbach, S., Grust, T., Jacobs, D., Kemper, A., Rittinger, J.: Multitenant Databases for Software as a Service: Schema Mapping Techniques. In: Proceedings of the 34th SIGMOD International Conference on Management of Data, pp. 1195–1206. ACM, Vancouver (2008)
4. Dash, D., Alagiannis, I., Maier, C., Ailamaki, A.: Caching All Plans With Just One Optimizer Call. In: Data Engineering Workshops, pp. 105–110. IEEE Press, California (2010)
5. Du, J., Wen, H.Y., Yang, Z.J.: Research on Data Layer Structure of Multitenant E-commerce System. In: IEEE 17th International Conference on Industrial Engineering and Engineering Management, pp. 362–365, Xiamen (2010)
6. Elmore, A.J., Das, S., Agrawal, D., El Abbadi, A.: Towards an Elastic and Autonomic Multitenant Database. In: Proceedings of NetDB Workshop, Athens (2011)
7. Farahani, M.G., Sharifnejad, M., Shari, M.: An Enhanced Tuple Routing Strategy for Adaptive Processing of Continuous Queries. Journal of Information and Communication Technologies, 3146–3150 (2006)
8. Foping, F.S., Dokas, I.M., Feehan, J., Imran, S.: A New Hybrid Schema-sharing Technique for Multitenant Applications. In: Fourth International Conference on Digital Information Management, pp. 1–6. IEEE Press, Michigan (2009)
9. Gao, B., An, W., Sun, X., Wang, Z.H., Fan, L., Guo, C.J., Sun, W.: A Non-intrusive Multitenant Database Software for Large Scale SaaS Application. In: e-Business Engineering, pp. 324–328. IEEE Press, Beijing (2011)
10. Hacig, H., Iyer, B., Li, C., Mehrotra, S.: Executing SQL Over Encrypted Data in the Database-service-provider Model. In: SIGMOD, pp. 216–227. ACM, Madison (2002)
11. Mateljan, V., Cisic, D., Ogrizovic, D.: Cloud Database-as-a-Service (DaaS) - ROI. In: Proceedings of the 33rd International Convention, pp. 1185–1188. IEEE Press, Opatija (2010)
12. Raza, B., Mateen, A., Sher, M., Awais, M.M., Hussain, T.: Autonomic View of Query Optimizers in Database Management Systems. In: Software Engineering Research, Management and Applications, pp. 3–8. IEEE Press, Montreal (2010)
13. Wang, Z.H., Guo, C.J., Gao, B., Sun, W., Zhang, Z., An, W.: A Study and Performance Evaluation of The Multi-tenant Data Tier Design Patterns for Service Oriented Computing. In: e-Business Engineering, pp. 94–101. IEEE Press, Xi'an (2008)
14. Weissman, C., Moellenhoff, D., Wong, S., Nakada, P.: Multi-tenant Database System. U.S.Patent 8,280,874 (October 2, 2012)
15. Weissman, C.D., Bobrowski, S.: The Design of The Force.com Multitenant Internet Application Development Platform. In: Proceedings of the 35th SIGMOD International Conference on Management of Data, pp. 889–896. ACM, Rhode Island (2009)

16. Yaish, H., Goyal, M., Feuerlicht, G.: An Elastic Multi-tenant Database Schema for Software as a Service. In: Ninth IEEE International Conference on Dependable, Autonomic and Secure Computing, pp. 737–743. IEEE Press, Sydney (2011)
17. Yaish, H., Goyal, M., Feuerlicht, G.: Proxy Service for Multi-tenant Database Access. In: The International Cross Domain Conference and Workshop, pp. 101–117, Regensburg (2013)

A   Appendix: Description of the Experiments Queries

Q1   SELECT tr.table_column_id, tr.value, tr.table_row_id, tr.serial_id FROM table_row tr WHERE tr.tenant_id =1000 AND tr.db_table_id = 16 AND tr.table_row_id IN (SELECT distinct tr.table_row_id **FROM table_row** tr WHERE tr.tenant_id = 1000 AND tr.db_table_id = 16 AND tr.table_column_id = 50 **AND (cast (value as numeric) > '9000'**)) ORDER BY 3, 4 LIMIT 800 OFFSET 0

Q2   SELECT tr.table_column_id, tr.value, tr.table_row_id, tr.serial_id FROM table_row tr WHERE tr.tenant_id =1000 AND tr.db_table_id = 16 **AND tr.table_column_id in (47, 48, 49)** AND tr.table_row_id IN (SELECT distinct tr.table_row_id **FROM table_row** tr WHERE tr.tenant_id = 1000 AND tr.db_table_id = 16 AND tr.table_column_id = 50 **AND (cast(value as numeric) > '9000'**)) ORDER BY 3,4 LIMIT 800 OFFSET 0

Q3   SELECT tr.table_column_id, tr.value, tr.table_row_id, tr.serial_id FROM table_row tr WHERE tr.tenant_id =1000 AND tr.db_table_id = 16 AND tr.table_row_id IN (SELECT distinct tr.table_row_id **FROM table_index** tr WHERE tr.tenant_id = 1000 AND tr.db_table_id = 16 AND tr.table_column_id = 50 **AND (cast (row_value as numeric) > '9000'**)) ORDER BY 3, 4 LIMIT 800 OFFSET 0

Q4   SELECT tr.table_column_id, tr.value, tr.table_row_id, tr.serial_id FROM table_row tr WHERE tr.tenant_id =1000 AND tr.db_table_id = 16 AND tr.table_row_id IN (SELECT distinct tr.table_row_id FROM table_row tr WHERE tr.tenant_id = 1000 AND tr.db_table_id = 16 AND tr.table_column_id = 50 **AND (cast (value as numeric) > '9000'**)) **AND tr.table_row_id IN (SELECT distinct tr.table_row_id FROM table_index tr WHERE tr.tenant_id = 1000 AND tr.db_table_id = 16**) ORDER BY 3, 4 LIMIT 800 OFFSET 0

Q5   SELECT tr.table_column_id, tr.value, tr.table_row_id, tr.serial_id FROM table_row tr WHERE tr.tenant_id =1000 AND tr.db_table_id = 16 ORDER BY 3, 4 LIMIT 800 OFFSET 0

Q6   SELECT tr.table_column_id, tr.value, tr.table_row_id, tr.serial_id FROM table_row tr WHERE tr.tenant_id =1000 AND tr.db_table_id = 16 AND tr.table_row_id IN (SELECT DISTINCT tr.table_row_id FROM table_row tr WHERE tr.tenant_id = 1000 AND tr.db_table_id = 16 **AND ((tr.table_column_id =47 AND tr.value ='101') OR (tr.table_column_id =47 AND tr.value ='102') OR (tr.table_column_id =47 AND tr.value ='103'))**) ORDER BY 3,4

Q7   SELECT tr.table_column_id, tr.value, tr.table_row_id, tr.serial_id FROM table_row tr WHERE tr.tenant_id =1000 AND tr.db_table_id = 16 **AND tr.table_row_id IN (22, 23, 24)** ORDER BY 3, 4

Cloud-Based Massive Electricity Data Mining and Consumption Pattern Discovery

Ming Chen[1,2], Maoyong Cao[1], and Yan Wen[1]

[1] Shandong University of Science and Technology, Qingdao, Shandong, China
[2] State Grid Corporation of China, Qingdao power supply company, Qingdao, Shandong, China
cmtop@163.com, my-cao@263.net, wenyan84@hotmail.com

Abstract. With the development of the power systems in China, there is large volume of basic electricity consumption data accumulated. Mining these data to discover possible consumption patterns and group the users in a more fine-grained way can help the State Grid Corporation to understand users' personalized and differentiated requirements. In this work, an algorithm called TMeans is proposed to mine the electricity consumption patterns. TMeans improves the classical K-Means algorithm by presenting a set of static and dynamical rules which can dynamically adjust the clustering process according to the statistical features of the clusters, making the process more flexible and practical. Then a MapReduce-based implementation of TMeans is proposed to make itself capable of handling large volume of data efficiently. Through experiment, we first demonstrate that the consumption patterns can be effectively discovered and can be refined to very small granularity through TMeans, and then we show that the MapReduce-based implementation of TMeans can efficiently speed up the clustering process.

Keywords: electricity consumption pattern, cluster, cloud, map-reduce, massive data.

1 Introduction

Smart Grid is a modernized electrical grid that uses information and communication technology to gather and act on information, such as information about the behaviors of suppliers and consumers, in an automated fashion to improve the efficiency, reliability, economy, and sustainability of the production and distribution of electricity [1]. Intelligent electrical information collection and analysis is one of its key tasks. With the development of the national power systems in China, there is large volume of basic electrical data accumulated, like voltage, load, current, etc. In recent years, the data volume takes a sharp increase owning to the refined metering facilities in Smart Grid. Qingdao, a city in China with a 7 million populations, can generate the electrical data up to 3.1G in a day. These data are not only massive, highly-concurrent and disperse, but also have potential correlations among them, such as users' electricity consumption habits. Mining these data to discover possible consumption patterns and group the users in a more fine-grained way can help the State Grid Corporation to

Z. Huang et al. (Eds.): WISE 2013 Workshops 2013, LNCS 8182, pp. 213–227, 2014.

understand users' personalized and differentiated requirements, and to provide a grounded foundation for the electricity delivery patterns and the price policies [2]. To this end, this work tries to mine consumption patterns from massive electrical data. It has the following challenges: 1) How to develop a mining algorithm that can discover electricity consumption patterns effectively? 2) The traditional data mining methods have limited capabilities in processing massive data, so how to improve the existing methods to make it scalable to large volume of dataset?

The basic idea is quite straightforward—to use clustering techniques to partition the electricity users into different clusters and to make the process paralleled executed. This work is organized as follows: section 2 is the related work, section 3 is the mining algorithm, section 4 is the map-reduce-based implementation of TMeans, section 5 is the experiments and section 6 is the conclusion.

2   Related Work

K-Means is the most classical algorithm, however its two main drawbacks make itself limitedly practical, one is the need to define the number of divisions precisely beforehand and the other is the random selected initial centers, which might lead to different results. ISODATA[3] and K-Means++[4] are two algorithms that work on these issues. However, these works are based on a set of data constraints that needs to be quantified by the user, which is not flexible or practical. Meanwhile, most of current mining methods have efficiency issues when handling large volume of data. So in order to reduce the processing time of clustering algorithms or the storage space needed, there emerges lots of new approaches, including the sequential methods [5] in which data loading and computing are executed at the same time to decrease the demands for memories; sampling methods [6] in which records are selected and clustered to represent the whole data package, and so on. In recent years, the novel cloud computing technologies [7,8] have brought new opportunities to speedup clustering algorithms. The Hadoop Map-Reduce paradigm [9] can make the algorithms execute on multiple distributed processors in a paralleled way to gain considerable speedup.

Currently, the State Grid is grouping users based some common knowledge of their domains, and conducts differentiated management using qualitative analysis. Refined consumption pattern discovery and analysis have not been fully studied. In recent years, lots of domestic and overseas scholars study on this area. In [10] Beckel tried to use classification methods to identify useful properties that are inferable from electricity consumption data, like the size of the house and the number of persons living in, so that relevant services can be provided. In [11] Chicco proposed a clustering approach based on the support vectors and a Gaussian kernel, which is less computationally intensive and has a good performance especially for identifying the outliers. In [12] De Silva identified the voluminous, fast-paced, transient and stream-like properties of the data generated by electricity meters, which is not able to be handled by conventional approaches. So he proposed ISPC framework to incorporate interim summarization and incrementally characterizes patterns in stream data and correlates them across time.

To handle the massive electricity consumption data, lots of researchers use cloud computing technologies to improve current power system infrastructures. In [13] Zhu proposed a cloud based resource management system CCRMP to increase the resource utilization of data recovery center and the efficiency of complex data recovery process, with the help of virtualization of server and storage, resource consolidation, allocation and modeling. In [14] Mu discussed the feasibility and necessity of adopting clouding computing to power system applications, it presents that there are five layers of clouds needed in the power systems, they are infrastructure cloud, data management cloud, simulation cloud, cooperation cloud and consulting services cloud, Mu also presented the principles for implementing these clouds. In [8] Zhang implemented K-means algorithm in a cloud environment to help to analyze the power users' behaviors, and the results showed an apparently speedup.

The above related works present the needs to mine the consumption patterns and category users from the massive data. Existing works do not combine them effectively. In this work, we first propose a refinement of the K-Means algorithm called TMeans to improve K-Means by making a set of static and dynamical rules to enable the clustering process dynamically adjusted according to the statistical characteristics of the clusters. And we also proposed a MapReduce-based implementation to make TMeans efficiently executed.

3   Discovery of Electricity Consumption Pattern

3.1   Electricity Consumption Model

The characteristics of electricity consumption can be described using many metrics, like voltage, current, load (product of voltage and current), power used, and the peak-to-valley ratio, etc. Voltage and load are two fundamental and representative dimensions among them. The power systems collect the information at set intervals (often once an hour) to form a discrete time-series. To simplify the problem and make it conform to the real data format, we model this time-series as a linear multi-dimensional vector, i.e., the consumption data for a day is modeled as a vector $C=<V_1, W_1, V_2, W_2, \ldots, V_k, W_k>$, where V_i and W_i are the voltage and load value for the ith interval, $1<=i<=k$, and k is the number of intervals within a day. Meanwhile, we are concerned about the periodical consumption patterns, which cannot be precisely reflected by just using one day's data, so we use statistical values for voltage and load: EV_i and EW_i, where EV_i is the mean value of a particular user's voltage for every same interval i within long-term continuous dates, EW_i means that for the load dimension. So the electricity consumption vector for a user can be represented as $EC=<EV_1, EW_1, EV_2, EW_2, \ldots, EV_k, EW_k>$. If the data are sampled every hour, then $k=24$, and if the sample rate is every 2 hours, then $k=12$.

Above vector cannot be directly used in the clustering process, as voltage and load are not based on the same scale, which might affect the distance measurements, so we use the following equations to normalize the vectors.

Let $EC = [x_1, x_2, ..., x_k]$,

Then $T = [t_1, t_2, ..., t_k]$, where $t_i = \dfrac{x_i - \min(x_i)}{\max(x_i) - \min(x_i)}, i = 1, 2, ..., k$,   (eq. 1)

3.2   Electricity Consumption Pattern Mining Algorithm—TMeans

K-Means is most classical clustering algorithm, and it has two main drawbacks, one is the need to define the number of divisions k precisely beforehand, and in most cases, the exact value of k cannot be provided, and even worse, the value of k needs to be determined during the clustering process. The other is that the randomly selected initial centers might lead to different results. ISODATA and K-Means++ are two representative algorithms that work on the issues. ISODATA introduced two operations— merge and split. K-Means++ pre-selected some initial centers. However, these works are based on a set of data constraints that needs to be quantified by the user, which is not flexible or practical. So we propose the TMeans (Tuning Means) to make some improvement on these issues.

TMeans has the following steps:

1.   For a dataset with N samples, pre-select initial cluster centers of size C: $z_1, z_2, ... z_C$, the value of C will be adjusted during the clustering process. This step is like in the K-Means++ algorithm, i.e., the initial centers are selected as follows:

 a) Randomly pick one sample as the seeded center;

 b) For each sample x_i, compute its nearest seeded center D_i, then compute

   the sum of all samples to their centers $S = \sum\limits_{i=1}^{N} D_i$.   (eq. 2)

 c) Select next seeded center: let ran be a random value in $(0, S)$, repeat this equation ran-= D_i, until $ran<0$, then x_i is the next center.

 d) Repeat step b) and c) until C initial centers are found.

2.   TMeans will evaluate current clustering results based on some metrics. If the number of samples in a cluster is larger than the upper bound N_U, which means there are too many samples in the cluster, or the standard deviation of a cluster is larger than its upper bound SD_U which means the samples in this cluster is too sparse, there will be a splitting operation. On the contrary, if the number of samples in a cluster is less than the lower bound N_L, which means there are too few samples in the cluster and the cluster need to be merged into other clusters, or the distance between two clusters is smaller than its lower bound D_L, which means the clusters are closely related and they need to be merged.

3.   Splitting   Operation: split   current   center z_j into   two   centers: $z_j^- = z_j - \alpha * SD_j$ (eq. 3) and $z_j^+ = z_j + \alpha * SD_j$ (eq. 4), where $0 < \alpha \le 1$, and

$SD_j = \sqrt{\dfrac{1}{N_j} \sum\limits_{i=1}^{N_j} (x_i - z_j)^2}$ (eq. 5) is the standard deviation of the original cluster, N_j is the

number of samples in this cluster.

4. Merge operation: compute the distance between each cluster center pair, and select the smallest one, if it is smaller than the lower bound D_L, then merge the two clusters. If the number of samples in a cluster z_j is smaller than the lower bound N_L, selected its closest center z_i, then merge z_j into z_i. The new center is

$$z^* = (N_i z_i + N_j z_j) / (N_i + N_j) \text{ (eq. 6)}.$$

5. The above steps will iterate until one of the following conditions are met:

    a) The target function $E_C = \sum_{i=1}^{C} \sum_{p \in C_i} (p - z_i)^2$ (eq. 7), which is the sum of the deviation for all the clusters, no longer decreases.

    b) The cluster centers of two iterations are the same, which means the divisions won't change any more.

    c) The number of iterations has reached its upper bound.

It can be seen from above steps that the execution of the algorithm relies on the bounds of the metrics, including the upper and lower bound of the cluster size N_L and N_U, and the upper bound of the standard deviation of the cluster SD_U, and the lower bound of the cluster distance D_L. For users, it is hard to determine meaningful values for these metrics. In this work, we propose a set of rules to dynamically determine the value of above metrics and to guide the clustering process. These rules are based on the statistical characteristics of the clusters and can be divided into static and dynamic rules. The former ones are provided by the global distribution of the samples, regardless how the samples are related with clusters, and the latter ones are provided by the distribution of samples in clusters, which change a lot during the clustering iterations. Specifically, we have:

Static Rules:

1. If the standard deviation of all the samples is $SD = \sqrt{\dfrac{1}{N} \sum_{i=1}^{N} (x_i - \overline{X})^2}$ (eq. 8),

where $\overline{X} = \dfrac{1}{N} \sum_{i=1}^{N} x_i$, then the upper bound of the standard deviation for each cluster is SD.

2. If the average distance between all the samples is

$$D = \sqrt{\dfrac{2}{N*(N-1)} \sum_{i=1}^{N-1} \sum_{j=i+1}^{N} (x_i - x_j)^2} \text{ (eq. 9)}, \text{ then the lower bound of the cluster distance}$$

is D.

3. If the number of all the samples is N, then the upper and lower bound of the number of samples in each cluster is $k_1 * N / C$ and $(N / C) / k_2$, where k_1 and k_2 are tuning indices and $k_1, k_2 > 1$ (the same hereinafter).

Dynamic Rules:

4. If the average standard deviation for all the clusters is $SD_C = \dfrac{1}{C} \sum_{j=1}^{C} SD_j$

,where z_j is the center for a cluster and $SD_j = \sqrt{\dfrac{1}{N_j} \sum_{i=1}^{N_j} (x_i - z_j)^2}$ is the standard ldeviation for the cluster, C is the number of clusters and N_j is the number of samples in this cluster, then the upper bound of the standard deviation for a cluster is $k * SD_C$, where $k > 1$.

5.   If the average distance between clusters is $D_C = \dfrac{2}{C*(C-1)} \sum\limits_{i=1}^{C-1} \sum\limits_{j=i+1}^{C} D_{ij}$,

where z_i and z_j are two cluster centers, and $D_{ij} = \sqrt{(z_i - z_j)^2}$ is their distance, then the lower bound of the cluster distance is D_C / k, where $k > 1$.

6.   If the average number of samples in all clusters is $N_C = \dfrac{1}{C}\sum\limits_{j=1}^{C} N_j$, where N_j is

the number of samples in a cluster, then the upper and lower bound of the number of samples in a cluster are $k_1 * N_C$ and N_C / k_2, where $k_1, k_2 > 1$.

For rules 1 and 2, we did quite a number of experiments to demonstrate that:

- If the standard deviation for a cluster is larger than the standard deviation of all the samples, then find one sample in this cluster that is farthest from its center, we can always reposition this sample to other clusters to decrease its standard deviation until all clusters met the requirement that rule 1 states. This means for a good clustering process, the standard deviation for all the samples can be used as the upper bound for that of the clusters;

- If the distance between two clusters is smaller than the average distance between all the samples, then find one sample in one of cluster that is closest to the other cluster, we can always reposition this sample to other clusters to increase the distance between the two clusters until all clusters met the requirement that rule 2 states. This means for a good clustering process, the average distance between all the samples can be used as the lower bound for the cluster distances.

This two empirical findings form the ground for rules 1 and 2. Their proof is left as our future work. For static rules 3, we only need to show that the average number of samples in all clusters is N / C which is straightforward. The dynamic rules 4~6 are based on the idea that one particular value cannot be too far away from the average measures. The tuning indices k, k_1, k_2 determine the strictness of the rules. The larger the tuning indices, the less strict the results are, and in practical terms, $k=2$ is a reasonable value. It is much easier to define the indices than the metrics of N_L, N_U, SD_U, D_L. Among above rules, the ones based on the standard deviation and cluster distances have higher priorities than those based on the number of samples, due to possible unbalanced sample distributions and outliers.

4   The Implementation of TMeans Based on MapReduce

To make TMeans efficiently executed, we implement TMeans based on Hadoop MapReduce, which includes three map-reduce phases, i.e., the data compressing phase, the cluster center initialization phase and the clustering phase, shown in Figure.1. The input data are partitioned into multiple sets, each of which is sent to each map function. The first phase compresses the long-term electricity consumption data for a specific user into a 24-hour data. The map function for this phase takes data for a certain period to calculate the number of days, the sum of voltage and load, as described in section 2.1, and the reduce function will calculate the average value for the voltage and energy. After data normalization, the vectors used as the input for the latter two phases are constructed. As the simplicity of this phase, we will not discuss it in details. The second phase takes the approximate number of clusters and calculates the initial cluster centers in an incremental manner. There are a number of iterations before all the initial centers are selected out. The third is the main clustering phase. There also need a few iterations of map and reduce in this phase. The input file keeps unchanged for the above phases, as the iterations are about how to tuning the centers and related metrics, and do not influent the input data. The involved global variables are listed below which can be easily accessed through all the phases:

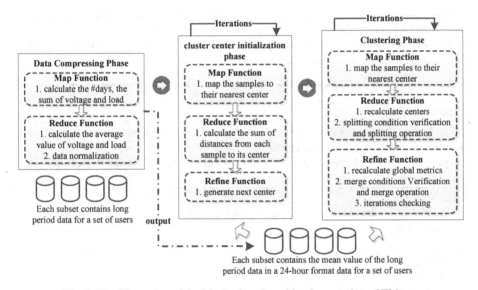

Fig. 1. The illustration of the MapReduce-based implementation of TMeans

Centers is the array of cluster centers; *SD* is the standard deviation of all the records; *D* is the average distance between all the records; *Nc* is the average size of all clusters; SD_C is the average standard deviation of all clusters; D_C is the average distance between all clusters; E_C is the deviation sum for all the clusters. Following are details of the phases.

1.   Cluster Center Initialization Phase

At the beginning of this phase, the global variable *Centers* contains only one random selected element.

The *Map* function maps the records onto their closest center. The input takes the offset of the record from the start of the input file as the key and the record as the value.

Map Function

Input: *key* is the offset of the record, *value* is the record
Output: *key'*: the center which the record is mapped onto, *value'*: the record and its distance to the center

BEGIN:
$\quad$ minDistance = MAX;
$\quad$ center=Centers[0];
$\quad$ minDistance = $\min_{c_i \in Centers}(value, c_i)$
$\quad$ *key'*=center;
$\quad$ *value'*=value + minDistance; // string construction
$\quad$ output<*key'*, *value'*> pair
END

The **Reduce** function takes the output of the map functions and calculates the sum of distances from the records to their centers.

Reduce Function

Input: **key** is the cluster center; **value** is an array containing all the records in this cluster and their distances to the center.
Output: **key'** is the cluster center; **value'** contains all the records of this cluster and the sum of their distances to the center.

BEGIN:
$\quad$ Initialize an **array** to store the records of the center;
$\quad$ sum_distance = $\sum_{v_i \in value} v_i.distance$

$\quad$ key' = key;
$\quad$ value' = array + sum_distance
$\quad$ output <key', value'> pair.
END

After the reduce function there is an additional global **Refine** function which takes the output of reduce functions to generate next center.

Refine Function

Input: an **array** containing <*key, value*> pairs, where *key* is the center, and *value* contains the **records** of this center and their sum of distances(***sum_distance***) to the center.

BEGIN:
$\quad$ sum = $\sum_{p_i \in array} p_i.value.sum\_distance$;

$\quad$ ran = random(0, *sum*);

```
FOR each p in array
   FOR each r in p.value.records
      ran -= r.;
      IF ran<=0
         centers.add(r);
      END IF
   END FOR
END FOR
END
```

2. Clustering Phase

The *Map* function in this phase is much the same with that in the cluster center initialization phase, except for that there is no need to maintain the distances, so we will not discuss it in details here.

The *Reduce* function takes the output of the map function to form a cluster. It recalculates the clustering centers and other cluster related metrics, and determine the conditions for the splitting operation. Because above tasks involve only one cluster, it can be executed in the reduce function, while merge operation involves more than one clusters, so it will be executed afterwards.

Reduce Function

Input: *key* is the center; *value* is an array containing all the records of the center.
Output: *key'* is the same as key; *value'* is the same as value.

BEGIN:

$$sum = \sum_{v \in value} v \quad //sum;$$

$$sd = \sqrt{\frac{1}{|value|} \sum_{x \in value} (x - key)^2} \quad //standard\ deviation;$$

$$ds = \sum_{x \in value} (x - key)^2 \quad //deviation\ sum;$$

//splitting
IF (|value| >> Nc || sd >> SDc || sd > SD)
$center\_1 = key - \alpha * sd;$//Equation
$center\_2 = key + \alpha * sd;$//Equation
centers.remove(center);
center.add(center_1);
center.add(center_2);
END IF
    $key' = key;$
    $value' = value + |value| + sd + ds;$ // string construction
END

There is also an additional global *Refine* function to recalculates the global metrics such as the average standard deviation for all the clusters. It also verifies the conditions for merge operation, and do the merge task if satisfied. Finally it determines where the iterations are terminated and if not then starts a new one.

Refine Function

Input: an **array** containing **<key, value>** pairs, where **key** is the cluster center, and **value** contains the **records** of the center, the **size**, the standard deviation(**sd**), and the deviation sum (**ds**) of the cluster.

BEGIN:

    Initialize a two dimensional **dist** to store distances of clusters;

    FOR ($i = 0$; i < *array*.length ; i++)

        FOR (j=i; j<*array*.length)

$$dist[i][j] = dist[j][i] = \sqrt{(array[i].key - array[j].key)^2}$$

        END FOR

    END FOR

    IF ($N_i \ll N_C \| N_j \ll N_C$)

        D_{ij}= closest_cluster_distance(i/j); // i/j means i or j, not i divided by j

        merge = true; //false initially

    END IF

    D_{ij}= min (*array*); //select the clusters with the smallest distance;

    IF ($D_{ij} \ll D_C \| D_{ij} < D \|$ merge == true)

$$center\_m = \frac{|array[i].value|*array[i].key + |array[j].value|*array[j].key}{|array[i].value| + |array[j].value|}$$

        centers.remove(*array*[i].*key*);

        centers.remove(*array*[j].*key*);

        centers.add(*center_m*);

        update_distance();

    END IF

    //recalculate the global variables, the global standard deviation *SD* and record distance *D* will stay the same

$$SD_C = \frac{1}{|array|} \sum_{a \in array} a.value.sd$$

$$D_C = \frac{2}{|array|(|array|)-1} \sum_{i=1}^{|array|} \sum_{j=i+1}^{|array|} dist[i][j]$$

$$N_C = \frac{1}{|array|} \sum_{a \in array} a.value.size$$

$$E_C = \sum_{a \in array} a.value.ds$$

    Verify whether the iterations are terminated.

END

---

5 Experiments

In this section, we conduct two kinds of experiments to evaluate 1) how TMeans performs on clustering the electricity consumption data, 2) the efficiency of the MapReduce-based implementation of TMeans.

The data source used in this work is from the real electricity consumption data in Qingdao State Grid Corporation. The data is sampled every hours in recent six months for all the users (2013-6-1~2013-7-1). The data size is 3.1G, including around 2 million users. Thanks to the advanced electric data metering equipment, the data can be specific to single household, or a particular line of a user.

The experiments were run on a cluster of computers, each of which has two 2.8 GHz cores and 4GB of memory. Hadoop version 1.2.0 and Java 1.6.23 are used as the MapReduce system for all experiments.

5.1 Clustering of Electricity Consumption Data

In this experiment, we set the approximate number of clusters to evaluate how TMeans helps to find the electricity consumption patterns for all the industrial users, and the initial number of clusters is set to 10. Under the settings, we have the statistical characteristics for each cluster shown in Figure 2 and 3 (The clusters are not shown in one figure because of the scaling problem of y-axis). The x-axis represents the time intervals, and the y-axis is the mean value of load for each cluster. The clusters correspond to the series. The analysis for the results is shown in Table. 1. We also randomly select a number of samples to calculate the clustering accuracy and recall rate, and the experiments show that the accuracy can reach to 91.3%, and the recall rate can reach to 89.7%. This experiment demonstrates that, through clustering, the consumption patterns can be refined to very small granularity, and be used in various situations.

5.2 Paralleled Clustering Algorithm Efficiency

In this section, we conduct a set of experiments to evaluate the performance of TMeans and its MapReduce-based implementation in handling large volume of data. The experiments are based on increasing dataset sizes and number of paralleled nodes, the selected dataset is same as in section 4.1, and we use simple duplicate policy if the size needs to expand.

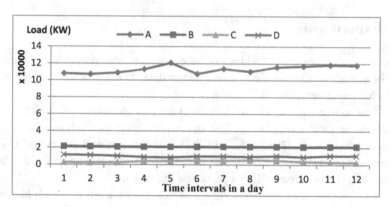

Fig. 2. Mean load value for each cluster (1)

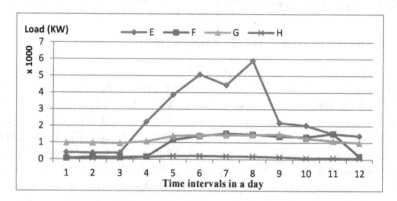

Fig. 3. Mean load value for each cluster (2)

Table 1. The clusters and their characteristics

Clus-ters	User categories in the cluster	Characteristics
A	The Iron making Industry	The load keeps very high because this is a very intensive consumption industry.
B	Refining Oil Industry Chemical Materials Manufacturing	The load keeps high and is relatively stable during all day; These two kinds of industries cannot be differentiated as their behaviors are similar
C	Textile Dyeing	The load is relatively low during the night time. In the rest time of the day, the load is significantly higher and show regular changes.
D	Water Transport	Load is relatively stable.
E	Equipment Manufacturing Industry	The load is significantly high at the daytime and reaches its peak value in the afternoon which is its intensive operating time.

Table 1. (*continued*)

F	Commodity Wholesale	The load has a very obvious trend. It's quite high at the work time 8:00--22:00 and quite low the rest of the day.
G	Broadcasting	The load also has an obvious trend. It is significantly higher at 8:00--18:00, during which the communications are quite intensive. And in the rest time of the day, the load is relative low.
H	Retail	The load also has an obvious trend. It is quite low at night, and start to increase in the morning, and reach its peak value at noon.

The result is shown in Figure 5 and Figure 6. Figure 5 shows how the dataset size relates with the efficiency when the number of nodes is fixed (1 node vs. 4 nodes), and we can see from this figure that when the data size keeps increasing, the unparalleled implementation underwent a sharp increase in execution time, while the paralleled one is performing quite better. Figure. 6 shows how the combination of dataset size and number of nodes relates with efficiency of the paralleled implementation. As the result shows, TMeans has a very good speedup

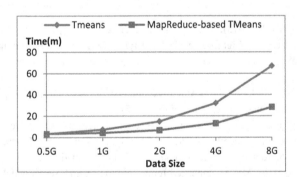

Fig. 4. The run time of TMeans and its MapReduce-based implementation

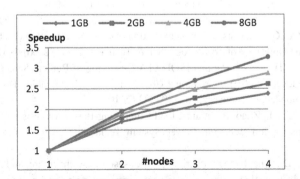

Fig. 5. The speedup ratio of MapReduce-based TMeans implementation

performance. Ideally, the speedup ratio and the number of nodes should present a linear relationship: a system with m times the number of nodes yields a speedup of m, but because of the file access and communication cost, the linear speedup is hard to achieve. Through these two experiments, we have shown that the MapReduce-based implementation can efficiently speed up the clustering process.

6   Conclusion

In this work, to mine electricity consumption patterns and category users from massive consumption data, we proposed the TMeans algorithm and its MapReduce-based implementation. TMeans improves the classical K-Means clustering algorithm and presents a set of static and dynamical rules which enable the clustering process dynamically adjusted according to the statistical features of the clusters. The MapReduce-based implementation of TMeans can handle large volume of data efficiently. Through experiments, we demonstrate the effectiveness of TMeans and the efficiency of its MapReduce-based implementation. In the future, we'd like to verify the proposed algorithms theoretically, and to apply the results to production environments.

References

[1]   Smart Grid (July 20, 2013), http://en.wikipedia.org/wiki/Smart_grid
[2]   Firth, S., Lomas, K., Wright, A., et al.: Identifying trends in the use of domestic appliances from household electricity consumption measurements. Energy and Buildings 40(5), 926–936 (2008)
[3]   Ball, G.H., Hall, D.J.: ISODATA, a novel method of data analysis and pattern classification. Stanford Research Inst., Menlo Park (1965)
[4]   Arthur, D., Vassilvitskii, S.: k-means++: The advantages of careful seeding. In: Proceedings of the Eighteenth ACM-SIAM Symposium on Discrete Algorithms, pp. 1027–1035. Society for Industrial and Applied Mathematics (2007)
[5]   Keogh, E., Pazzani, M.: An enhanced representation of time series which allows fast and accurate classification, clustering and relevance feedback. In: Proceedings of the 3rd International Conference of Knowledge Discovery and Data Mining, pp. 239–241. The Association for the Advancement of Artificial Intelligence, New York (1998)
[6]   Zhao, G., Qu, G.: Analysis and implementation of CLARA algorithm on clustering. Journal of Shandong University of Technology: Sci. & Tech. (2), 45–48 (2006) (in Chinese)
[7]   Li, B., Zhao, H., Lv, Z.: Parallel ISODATA Clustering of Remote Sensing Images Based on MapReduce. In: 2010 International Conference on Cyber-Enabled Distributed Computing and Knowledge Discovery, pp. 380–383 (2010)
[8]   Zhang, S., Liu, J., Zhao, B., et al.: Cloud Computing-Based Analysis on Residential Electricity Consumption Behavior. Power System Technology 37(6), 1542–1546 (2013) (in Chinese)
[9]   Borthakur, D.: The hadoop distributed file system: Architecture and design. Hadoop Project Website (2013), http://hadoop.apache.org/common/docs/

[10] Beckel, C., Sadamori, L., Santini, S.: Towards automatic classification of private households using electricity consumption data. In: Proceedings of the Fourth ACM Workshop on Embedded Sensing Systems for Energy-Efficiency in Buildings, pp. 169–176. ACM (2012)

[11] Chicco, G., Ilie, I.S.: Support vector clustering of electrical load pattern data. IEEE Transactions on Power Systems 24(3), 1619–1628 (2009)

[12] De Silva, D., Yu, X., Alahakoon, D., et al.: A data mining framework for electricity consumption analysis from meter data. IEEE Transactions on Industrial Informatics 7(3), 399–407 (2011)

[13] Zhu, Z., Gu, Z., Wu, J., et al.: Application of cloud computing in electric power system data recovery. Power System Technology 36(9), 44–50 (2012) (in Chinese)

[14] Mu, L., Cui, L., An, N.: Research and practice of cloud computing center for power system. Power System Technology 35(6), 171–175 (2011) (In Chinese)

Modelling Web Service Personalization with Rule Nets

Wei Wang[1], Sheng Zong[2], Jian Yu[3], and Sira Yongchareon[4]

[1] School of Digial Information Technology
ZheJiang Technical Institute of Economics, Hangzhou 310018, China
wangw_me@163.com
[2] Cooperation Communication Operating and Support Centre,
China Telecom, Hangzhou 310006, China
zs1929@163.com
[3] School of Computing and Mathematical Sciences,
Auckland University of Technology, Auckland 1010, New Zealand
jian.yu@aut.ac.nz
[4] Department of Computing,
Unitec Institute of Technology, Auckland, NZ
syongchareon@unitec.ac.nz

Abstract. Web service personalization is an important research topic in the area of service-oriented computing which has the potential to bring more service value to end users that are fit for individual user's particular needs. In this paper, we propose *Rule nets*, which is based on PrT (Predicate/Transition) nets. Rule nets has the capability to model a wide spectrum of rules for expressing personalization needs. There rules then can be woven to a business process to bring flexible personalization features to this process. The woven process can be expressed as a PrT net suitable for formal analysis and simulation using existing Petri net tools.

Keywords: Web service personalization, Petri nets, business rules, Business process modelling.

1 Introduction

Personalization in the area of service-oriented computing is emerging as an important topic with the transformation of Internet and Web from traditional linking and sharing of computers and documents (i.e., "Web of Data") to current connecting of people (i.e., "Web of People") [1,2] , reflected by the popularity of social networks such as Facebook and Linkedin.

To implement web service personalization, a major hurdle to cross is to ensure that personalization features of a service can be well modelled and integrated in a web services, for example, a BPEL web service process. However, the personalization logic encoded in a service processes is often hard-coded and difficult to change.

Z. Huang et al. (Eds.): WISE 2013 Workshops 2013, LNCS 8182, pp. 228–238, 2014.
© Springer-Verlag Berlin Heidelberg 2014

In this paper, we use business rules to model the personalization logic of a web service process, and then use Predicate/Transition nets (PrT nets) [3], a kind of widely used high-level Petri nets, to model both business processes and business rules, and then use an aspect-oriented mechanism to weave them into a coherent PrT net. The rationale behind our approach is that Petri nets have long been recognised as a valuable tool for modelling business processes [4], and PrT nets are suitable for dealing with logic and rules [5]. Our modelling approach features the following benefits. Firstly, a unified language is used to formally specify the software design instead of ad-hoc mixing of process specification and personalization specification. Secondly, in our approach, the modularity of the personalization logic is well-kept which eases the maintenance and evolution of the design specification.

The rest of this paper is organised as follows: Section 2 briefly review business rules and how to use them to express personalization logic.

Some fundamental concepts and definitions that underpin the discussion throughout the paper. Section 3 defines rule nets and explains how to model business rules with rule nets. Section 4 specifies the PrT net-based aspect and the weaving mechanism. Finally, Section 5 discusses and concludes the paper.

2 Business Rules and Personalization

In this section, we briefly review the concepts of business rule and aspect-orientation. Some example rules and aspects used throughout the paper are also discussed.

According to the Business Rules Group [6], a business rule is a statement that defines or constrains some aspect of a business. It is intended to assert business structure or to control the behaviour of the business. In [9], business rules are classified into four types as the following:

- A *constraint rule* is a statement that expresses an unconditional circumstance that must be true or false.
- An *action-enabler rule* is a statement that checks conditions and initiates some actions upon finding the conditions true.
- A *computation rule* is a statement that checks a condition and when the result is true, provides an algorithm to calculate the value of a term.
- An *inference rule* is a statement that tests conditions and establishes the truth of a new fact upon finding the conditions true.

For instance, a travel-package-requesting scenario could have the following business rules [7]:

R_1(*constraint rule*): a vacation request must have a departure airport and a destination airport.

R_2(*action-enabler rule*): if no flight is found, do not look for accommodation.

R_3(*computation rule*): if more than 2 persons travel together, give 10% discount to the total price.

R_4(*inference rule*): if a customer is frequent customer, he gets a discount of 5%.

The reason that why R_4 is an inference rule is that to resolve what is a frequent customer, we need another two rules:

R_5 (*constraint rule*): if a customer has bought more than 5 travel packages, he is a frequent customer.

R_6 (*constraint rule*): if a customer has bought products for a sum exceeding 4000 euros, he is a frequent customer.

Clearly all the above discussed four types of business rules can be used to declarative express individual user's personalization logic.

3   Rule Nets

In this section, we formally define rule nets, and then demonstrate how to use rule nets to model the four types of rules discussed in Section 2.

3.1   PrT Nets

Since rule nets are a sub-set of PrT nets, here we first give the structural definition of PrT nets for the self-containness of this paper.

Definition 1 (PrT nets). *A PrT net N is a tuple (P, T, F, Σ, L, φ, M_0) [9], where:*

- *P is a finite set of predicates, T is a finite set of transitions ($P \cap T = \emptyset$, $P \cup T = \emptyset$), and $F \subseteq (P \times T) \cup (T \times P)$ is the set of arcs. (P, T, F) forms a directed net.*
- *Σ is a finite set of constants, operations, and relations.*
- *L is a labelling function on arcs. Given an arc $f \in F$, the labelling of f, L(f), is a set of labels, which are n-tuples of individuals and variables where n is the arity of the predicate connected to the arc.*
- *φ is a formula inscription function on transitions. Given a transition $t \in T$, $\varphi(t)$ is a logical formula built from variables and the individuals, operations, and relations in structure Σ, where variables occurring free in a transition have to occur at an adjacent input arc of the transition.*
- *$M_0 = \bigcup_{p \in P} M_0(p)$ is the initial marking, where $M_0(p)$ is the set of tokens residing in predicate p. Each token is a tuple of constants or structured terms constructed from the constants and operations in Σ.*

For the convenience of discussion, we also define the following concepts:

- The preset of an element x is: $^\bullet x = \{y|(y, x) \in F\}$.
- The postset of an element x is: $x^\bullet = \{y|(x, y) \in F\}$.
- The input predicates of a net N is: $inP(N) = \{p \in P|^\bullet p = \emptyset\}$.
- The input transitions of a net N is: $inT(N) = \{t \in T|^\bullet t = \emptyset\}$.
- The output predicates of a net N is: $outP(N) = \{p \in P|p^\bullet = \emptyset\}$.
- The output transitions of a net N is: $outT(N) = \{t \in T|t^\bullet = \emptyset\}$.

3.2   Rule Nets

Definition 2 (Rule nets). *A PrT net $N = (P, T, F, \Sigma, L, \varphi, M_0)$ is a rule net if and only if:*

- *There is one source place $i \in P$ such that $^\bullet i = \emptyset$.*
- *There is one sink place $o \in P$ such that $o^\bullet = \emptyset$.*
- *Every node $x \in P \cup T$ is on a path from i to o.*

Note that the above definition is adapted from the definition to Workflow nets [8]. So all the structural analysis approaches for Workflow nets can also be applied to rule nets.

Syntactically, we classify the transitions in a rule net with three stereotypes:

- An *action transition* T_A represents a business activity, e.g., get flight.
- A *computation transition* T_C represents the specific action of assigning variables with arithmetic expressions, e.g., assigning $price \times 90\%$ to the variable *price*.
- And a *dummy transition* T_D does nothing.

Transition stereotypes provide additional information to a net at the business level; they do not change the behavioural semantics of rule nets.

Definition 3 (Constraint nets). *A constraint net is a rule net with only one dummy transition t, and $\varphi(t) \neq \emptyset$.*

To model a constraint rule, we use a dummy transition with its inscription representing the constraints. For example, R_1 *(A vacation request must have a departure airport and a destination airport)* can be modelled as the constraint net in Fig. 1.

Fig. 1. Constraint net R_1

Definition 4 (Action-enabler nets). *An action-enabler net is a rule net containing at least one action transition t, and $\varphi(t) \neq \emptyset$.*

To model an action-enabler rule, we use an action transition to represent the business activity, and the inscription of this transition representing the enabling condition. For example, R_2 *(If no flight is found, do not look for accommodation)* can be modelled as the action-enabler net in Fig. 2.

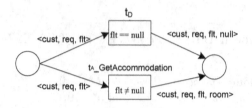

Fig. 2. Constraint net R_2

Definition 5 (Computation nets). *A computation net is a rule net with only one computation transition.*

For example, R_3 *(If more than 2 persons travel together, give* 10% *discount to the total price)* can be modelled as the computation net in Fig. 3. Note that the computation expression is reflected in the name of the transition.

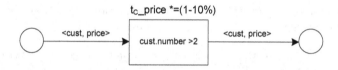

Fig. 3. Computation net R_3

Definition 6 (Inference nets). *An inference rule is created by composing two rule nets with AND-JOIN, OR-JOIN, or SEQ-JOIN*[1].

Intuitively, if we connect two rule nets with AND-JOIN, then the composed rule net means the conjunction of the two rules; if we connect two rule nets with OR-JOIN, then the composed rule net means the disjunction of the two rules. As shown in Fig 4, supposing o_1 and o_2 are the sink places (or the consequents) of two rule nets, then the conjunction of the two rule nets is depicted in Fig 4.a, which means that the predicate o is determined by o_1 *AND* o_2; while the OR-JOIN of the two rules is depicted in Fig 4.b, which means that the predicate o is determined by o_1 *OR* o_2. Note that AND-JOIN and OR-JOIN are also two workflow patterns defined in [8].

The sequential join of two rule nets means that the resolve of one rule net depends on the consequents of the other rule net. The SEQ-JOIN operation fuses the source place of the dependent net with the sink place of the independent rule net. Usually, an inference net can be built first by introducing the net representing the final goal, and then introducing the rules backwards with the SEQ-JOIN

---

[1] For space limitations, here we only informally introduce the three operators of rule nets.

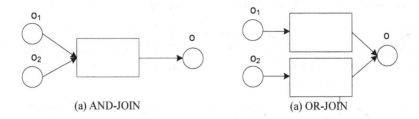

Fig. 4. The AND-JOIN and OR-JOIN of two rule nets

operation based on the cause-effect relations until all the newly introduced rules are resolvable.

Taking R_4(textitif a customer is frequent, he qualifies for a discount of 5%) as an example, to resolve the meaning of frequent, we need another two rules: R_5(if a customer has bought more than 5 travel packages, he is a frequent customer), and R_6(if a customer has bought products for a sum exceeding 4000 euros, he is a frequent customer). Fig. 5.a, b and c are the rule nets for R_4, R_5 and R_6 respectively. Because R_4 depends on the consequent of R_5 or R_6, we use OR-JOIN to compose them and then use SEQ-JOIN to connect the combined consequent to the rule net of R_4 to form a complete inference rule net as depicted in Fig. 5.d. Looking closely, we can find that R_4 is represented by a computation net, and R_5 and R_6 constraint nets. So an inference net is in fact the composition of other forms of rule nets. With this example, we also demonstrate the power of PrT nets in modelling complex rules.

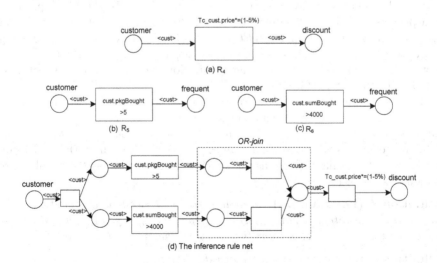

Fig. 5. The inference rule derived from R_4, R_5, and R_6

4   Weaving Rule Nets into Process Nets

Corresponding to rule nets, we use the term process nets to call the PrT nets representing business processes. For example, Fig. 6 is the process net N for the travel package request process described in Section 2.

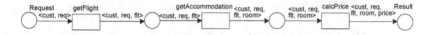

Fig. 6. Travel package request process net N

Just like aspect-oriented programming, we use *pointcut* to select a transition as join point. Without losing generality, every pointcut can only select one transition to simplify the definition of weaving. The advices are represented by rule nets. A rule net can be weaved into a process net either *before*, *after*, or *around* a pointcut/transition. Another important concept is context net, for exposing context of the process net to the rule net. It is interesting to note that the process net and its rule nets could be authored independently, which reflects the modular feature of aspect-orientation. To weave them smoothly, we use context net to put them in the same context and mediate possible parameter inconsistencies. For example, the input parameters for the transition $N.getFlight$ is a structure $< Customer, Request >$, but its constraint net R_1 accepts $< Request >$ as input. Finally, we can wrap up pointcuts, advices, and context net into an *aspect*.

To demonstrate our idea, before formally defining the above concepts, we give an example on how to weave the rule net R_1 before $N.getFlight$. Fig. 7 presents an aspect asp_rule_1. The context net is built first by introducing the preset of the pointcut, i.e. transition $N.getFlight$, as initial context, and then splitting the request to match the input of the advice net, finally merging the results and transferring them back to the cutting point. Note that we use round rectangle to represent the net R_1 for simplicity.

Fig. 8 is the resulting net after we weave asp_rule_1 into N. This net is built simply by putting the context net and the process net together, and then deleting the arcs between the cutting point and its preset because it is a *before* cut. Note that elements with the same names are merged to reflect the expansion of context. The formal definitions on weaving business processes and rules, are given as the following.

Definition 7 (Pointcuts). *A pointcut over a PrT net N is a transition in N. The syntax is: pointcut $< N.transition >$; For brevity, a pointcut has the same name as its transition. This transition is called the cutting transition.*

Definition 8 (advices). *An advice has the form:*
advice $< adviceName >$ before$|$after$|$around $< cutName >:< R >$;
Where R is a rule net, which is also called the advice net of this advice. So there are three types of advice: before advice, after advice, and around advice.

Aspect asp_rule$_1$ {
  pointcut N.getFlight;
  advice a_checkRequest before N.getFlight: R$_1$;
  R$_1$:

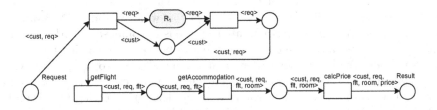

P$_{a1}$ checkRequest   **P**$_{a2}$

<req>   req.deptPort ≠ null && req.arrPort ≠ null   <req>

context(a_checkRequest): N$_{c1}$;
  N$_{c1}$:

<req>   R$_1$ <req>

<cust, req>   <req>

N.Request   <cust>   <cust>   <cust, req>

N.getFlight

Fig. 7. Aspect asp_rule$_1$

<req>   R$_1$ <req>   <req>

<cust, req>   <cust>   <cust>

<cust, req>

Request   getFlight   getAccommodation   <cust, req,   <cust, req,   calcPrice   <cust, req,   Result
<cust, req, flt>   <cust, req, flt>   flt, room>   flt, room>   flt, room, price>

Fig. 8. Resulting net of weaving N and asp_rule$_1$

Definition 9 (contexts). *A context has the form:*
$context(< adviceName >) :< Net >$; *For brevity, a context has the same name as its associated net.*
Depending on the type of the related advice, a context net has the following constraints.

– *Before advice:* $\bullet pointcut \subseteq inP(contextNet) \& pointcut \in outT(contextNet)$.
– *After advice:* $pointcut \in inT(contextNet) \& N.t_i^\bullet \subseteq outP(contextnet)$.
– *Around advice:* $\bullet pointcut \subseteq inP(contextNet) \& pointcut^\bullet \subseteq outP(contextNet)$.

These constraints ensure that the weaving of a process net and a context net always produces another consistent process net.

Definition 10 (Aspects). *A PrT net-based aspect A is a 3-tuple (Pcut, Adv, Ctx) where Pcut is a set of pointcuts, Adv is a set of advices, and Ctx is a set of contexts.*

Definition 11 (Net weaving). *The weaving of a process net N and an aspect A is defined as[2]:*

---

[2] We use $N.x$ to represent component x of N.

- For every before advice adv_i, its cutting transition $N.t_i$, and its context net N_{ci}, the weaving of adv_i and N is a new PrT net N_w:
  $N_w.X = N.X \cup N_{ci}.X$, where $X \in \{P, T, L, \varphi, M_0\}$,
  and $N_w.F = N.F \cup N_{ci}.F \setminus N.{}^\bullet t_i \times N.\{t_i\}$.
- For every after advice adv_i, its cutting transition $N.t_i$, and its context net N_{ci}, the weaving of adv_i is a new PrT net N_w:
  $N_w.X = N.X \cup N_{ci}.X$, where $X \in \{P, T, L, \varphi, M_0\}$,
  and $N_w.F = N.F \cup N_{ci}.F \setminus N.\{t_i\} \times N.{}^\bullet t_i$.
- For every around advice adv_i, its cutting transition $N.t_i$, and its context net N_{ci}, the weaving of adv_i and N is a new PrT net N_w:
  $N_w.X = N.X \cup N_{ci}.X$, where $X \in \{P, L, \varphi, M_0\}$,
  and $N_w.T = N.T \cup N_{ci}.T \setminus N.\{t_i\}$
  and $N_w.F = N.F \cup N_{ci}.F \setminus N.{}^\bullet t_i \times N.\{t_i\} \setminus N.\{t_i\} \times N.{}^\bullet t_i$.

From Definition 11, we can infer that weaving N with a before advice is to compose N with the context net of the before advice and deleting the arcs between the cutting transition and its preset, just as what we did in the example shown in Fig. 7. Weaving N with an after advice is to compose N with the context net of the after advice and deleting the arcs between the cutting transition and its postset. Finally, weaving N with an around advice is to compose N with the context net of the around advice, and deleting the cutting transition and its arcs. The reason why we let around weaving delete the cutting transition is that the semantics of the cutting transition will be reiterated in the advice net if necessary.

The above weaving definition assumes that a process net does not share names with advice nets. This assumption can be relaxed by either renaming or following a naming convention [10]. If more than two advices are related to one cutting transition, a weaving sequence may be necessary. Because around weaving deletes the cutting transition, it should always be put in the last. And we should prevent relating more than two around advices to a transition.

5   Discussion and Conclusion

PrT nets are a high-level formalism of Petri nets suitable for modelling, analysing, and simulating the behaviour of software systems. In [5], the authors proposed an efficient reachability analysis technique for PrT nets based on the compact structure of planning graphs. Prod [11] is another tool for reachability analysis. In [12], PrT nets are translated to Promela, the input language of model checker Spin, and various temporal properties can be checked automatically. As far as the graphical editor is concerned, SEA [13] is an integrated environment for visual modelling and simulating PrT nets that runs on Solaris. Recently, Rock et al. extend the Petri Net Kernel tool [14] to support the graphical modelling and invariants computation of PrT nets [15].

The stream of work that is particularly relevant to our work is composing PrT nets from an aspect-oriented point of view, and weaving rules with processes. As far as we know, only Xu et al. proposed an aspect-oriented PrT net model

[14]. In their work, advice nets and the base net are woven in a tightly coupled fashion: they must share the same variable type at the cutting point. Instead, we use context nets to allow a flexible weaving. Also their model is not intuitive in terms of the concept mapping between aspect-oriented programming and aspect-oriented PrT nets. The important concepts of advice type, i.e. *before*, *after*, and *around* are lost in their model.

In this paper, we have presented Rule nets, a special PrT nets used to express the personalization rules of web services. PrT nets as a kind of Petri nets are suitable for process modelling. Its logic aspect also makes it a good candidate for modelling rules. We defined a kind of special PrT, the rule nets, to model the four types of business rules. Corresponding to the principle of aspect oriented programming, we defined the net-based aspect and the weaving mechanism to integrate rules nets and process nets. The woven net not only keeps the modularity of rules, but also is ready for analysis and simulation by various PrT techniques and tools. We view our work presented in this paper as a first step towards a formalised model-driven approach of developing flexible personalised web services. Our future work includes elaborating the composition of rule nets, providing an integrated graphical environment for the modelling, weaving and analysis of rule nets, automatic translation from personalization rules to rule nets.

References

1. Han, J., Han, Y., Jin, Y., Yu, J.: Personalized active service spaces for end-user service composition. In: IEEE International Conference on Services Computing SCC, pp. 198–205 (2006)
2. Yu, J., Wang, J., Han, Y., Yang, S., Zhang, L.: Developing End-User Programmable Service-Oriented Applications with VINCA. In: Workshop on Web Logistics (2004)
3. Genrich, H.J.: Predicate/Transition Nets. In: Brauer, W., Reisig, W., Rozenberg, G. (eds.) APN 1987. LNCS, vol. 254, pp. 207–247. Springer, Heidelberg (1987)
4. van der Aalst, W.M.P., van Hee, K.: Workflow Management: Models, Methods, and Systems. MIT Press, Cambridge (2002)
5. Xu, D., Yin, J., Deng, Y., Ding, J.: A Formal Architecture Model for Logical Agent Mobility. IEEE Trans. on Software Engineering. 29(1), 31–45 (2003)
6. The Business Rules Group: Defining Business Rules, What Are They Really? http://www.businessrulesgroup.org
7. Charfi, A., Mezini, M.: Hybrid Web Service Composition: Business Processes Meet Business Rules. In: 1st International Conference on Service Oriented Computing ICSOC, pp. 30–38 (2004)
8. van der Aalst, W.M.P., van Hee, K.: Workflow Management: Models, Methods, and Systems. MIT Press, Cambridge (2002)
9. von Halle, B.: Business Rules Applied: Building Better Systems Using the Business Rules Approach. Wiley (2001)
10. Xu, D., Nygard, K.E.: Threat-Driven Modeling and Verification of Secure Software Using Aspect-Oriented Petri Nets. IEEE Trans. on Software Engineering 32(4), 265–278 (2006)
11. PROD: An Advanced Tool for Efficient Reachability Analysis, http://www.tcs.hut.fi/Software/prod/

12. Ding, J., Dai, Z., Wang, J., He, X.: Formally Modeling and Analyzing a Secure Mobile Agent Finder. In: 2005 IEEE International Conference on Systems, Man and Cybernetics, pp. 47–52 (2005)
13. SEA: The System Engineering and Animation Environment, http://jerry.c-lab.de/sea/
14. Petri Net Kernel, version 2.2, http://www.informatik.hu-berlin.de/top/pnk/index.html
15. Röck, A., Kresman, R.: On Petri Nets and Predicate-Transition Nets. In: 2006 International Conference on Software Engineering Research and Practice, pp. 903–909 (2006)

Conceptual Graph: An Approach to Improve Quality of Business Services Modeling

Xiaofeng Du[1] and William W. Song[2,*]

[1] British Telecom, Ipswich, UK
[2] Informatics, Business & Technology Studies, Dalarna University, Borlänge, Sweden
wso@du.se

Abstract. Business development or renovation is to introduce newer, more efficient routines and processes through redesign or re-engineering of businesses, which form a set of business patterns. Business patterns encapsulate the best solutions for business practices and tasks confirming business strategies of the enterprise. Nowadays, services with SOA (Service oriented-Architecture) become more and more important in implementing and supporting business routines and processes. An enterprise that can encapsulate their SOA solutions into patterns will make the business more agile and effective. However, with the SOA solutions to automation of locating relevant instance services for its business patterns with minimum human intervention one has to look into the semantic and operational difference between the description of a business pattern and that of an instance service—a gap between the two levels of semantic descriptions. In this paper, we propose a conceptual modeling method to address how to bridge the gap, by a semantic service description for usage contextual approach formalized with the conceptual graphs formalism.

Keywords: Web Services, service composition, conceptual graphs, business process modeling and patterns.

1 Introduction

In an enterprise, business routines and processes form a foundation for its businesses. Business development within the enterprise relies heavily on its innovation, i.e. newer, or further re-designed, and more effective routines and processes. In other words, business is a set of routine-based operations and innovation is a move from the set of original routines to a set of innovative routines. Business patterns encapsulate the best practice solutions for business tasks. They are the best practices within an enterprise or across enterprises. Business patterns help an enterprise to run their business smoothly and effectively and quicken restructuring process to meet new business demands.

Business patterns under Service Oriented Architecture (SOA) [2] are enterprise-focused best practice with SOA based solutions. These patterns include the solutions

---

* Corresponding author.

Z. Huang et al. (Eds.): WISE 2013 Workshops 2013, LNCS 8182, pp. 239–251, 2014.

for business under the SOA infrastructure and the technologies for these solutions that have been accumulated over the years. These patterns help an enterprise to understand and analyze complex business problems, break them down into smaller functions, and modularize them into services for future (re)use. The SOA provides the architecture for agile service construction. In other words, it is how an enterprise can quickly reconstruct their business to meet the new demands. If an enterprise can encapsulate their SOA solutions into patterns, it can make business more agile and business solutions more flexible.

However, under the SOA infrastructure, it is difficult to connect and match an instance service (i.e. a concrete, executable web service) into a suitable business pattern without a large amount of manual work. One reason is that the description of a business pattern and its requirements is entirely different from the description of an instance service: the former is at a high level and business oriented whereas the latter at low level and technical oriented [12]. Therefore, system developers or business process designers are required to work as an in-between to translate the descriptions from one level to another in order to locate suitable concrete services to meet business demands. Obviously, we need to bridge this gap between the two types of descriptions. Currently, once a new business pattern is developed and adopted, a manual process is carried out to decompose the pattern into some sub-components, create a set of relevant business processes, and connect (embed) relevant instance services into the business processes. This process greatly reduces the efficiency of business processes reforming. An ideal situation is, when a new business pattern is adopted, a set of related instance services will be automatically or semi-automatically located and embedded into the pattern with its related business processes. However, how to realize this process is a challenge. In the following, we discuss how the problems we need to address in order to bridge the gap.

Service Description Does not Take into Account Business Context. The existing Web services description standards, such as WSDL, are technical focused standards. They describe the technical details and specifications of Web services' interfaces so that programmers can use them to develop services for applications. However, the technical based description is not sufficient and rich in semantics for them to directly match with the business requirements specified in a business pattern (where a business process is a part) without service developers' interferences. Because of this gap between technical descriptions and abstract business requirements, human's interpretation is required for a service to be linked and embedded into a business pattern.

Inter-service Relationships Are not Sufficiently Addressed. More often than not, a service needs to work together with other services to provide a richer functionality for a more complex task, and hence services need to interact with one another as a whole to supply a better business solution. Moreover, understanding interaction (operational relationships) of a service with other services is a better way to understand and interpret this service at both conceptual and technical levels. This kind of interactions between services is termed as inter-service relationships. Currently, none of the existing web services description standards, such as WSDL, addresses this aspect of business semantics for Web services. If inter-service relationships are maintained in the service description, it will be much more efficient and effective to correlate services in a business pattern or process.

In this paper, we propose a novel approach to bridging the gap between business pattern/process descriptions and the instance service descriptions. In this approach, we describe instance services in terms of not only the technical specifications, but also their usage contexts. The usage contextual information is like a puzzle from the perspective of the existing service description frameworks since it tries to identify what kind of business cases, i.e. a usage context, in which an instance service typically participates and within which how this instance service is conceptually related to other instance services in terms of business processes and situations. Therefore to include the usage context information of an instance service in its semantic description, it will make it conceptually more convenient and accurate for service discovery, composition, and scheduling through giving a business pattern and process. A usage context of instance services is defined according to the conceptual graphs (CGs) formalism [13], a conceptual modeling system focusing on formal representation of concepts, relationships between concepts, and behaviors of concepts and relationships. A conceptual graph can conveniently describe an application domain of interest and represent it in a logically formal way so that a knowledge base can be built to manage, process, and reason about the information gathered. We use CGs to represent the semantic meaning of both business patterns and instance services. Through the operations and reasoning facilities provided by the CGs formalism, such as graph matching, projection, generalization, and specialization [13], a given business pattern or process's requirement can be identified and located, and matched to instance services directly.

The rest of the paper is organized as follows. In the next section, we discuss general relationships from business pattern, and business process, to services in order to identify why an enterprise expects to shorten the lead time by flexibly integrate services, of their own or from other enterprises via the web, into their business pattern and how this can be done. Then in section 3, we introduce the concept of contextual usage scenario, discuss its conceptual modeling constructs, and define them with Sowa's Concept Graph (CG). Based these definitions we discuss further how services are represented in a simplified version of CG, i.e. S-CG. In section 4, we propose a graph match method together with an algorithm used for locating relevant services when given a business pattern and a graph similarity computation for refining the match of CG and S-CG. It is obvious that this paper can only report a small part of our research on Business Patterns-Usage Scenarios-Concept Services and thus in section 5, we will conclude the paper in section 5 by pointing out what are out next steps of investigation in this direction.

2   Business Pattern, Business Process and Web Services

In order to better understand the problem, it should be made clear what the relationships between business patterns, business processes, and instance services are and where the problem is. In this section, we discuss how these different aspects are related to each other.

Human beings have been doing business and trading for thousands of years. Most of the types of business we are doing today are well tried out and adopted over years. A concept of business pattern is introduced to capture and model such best practices and successful experiences in businesses [11]. In other words, business patterns are built on the business experiences and activities proven successfully in the past. Business patterns provide guidelines that can be used to conduct business activities such as initialize businesses, decompose large organizations into a number of value-adding enterprises, and decompose the value-adding enterprises into a number of value-adding business processes [11].

According to the granularity of business patterns, we can use a hierarchical structure to represent business patterns. At the top level of the hierarchy, business patterns define the type of businesses. Russell et al. [11] listed some of the top layer business patterns, such as Manufacturer, Service Creator, and Reseller. At the middle level of the hierarchy, business patterns define how a business is organized, i.e. the enterprise structures. Endrei et al. [7] pointed out some patterns at this level, such as self-service patterns, extended enterprise patterns, and collaboration patterns. At the low level of the hierarchy, business patterns define how business services are delivered. The business patterns at this level are also called business processes. Typical examples of business patterns at this level include online shopping process, credit card validation process, and stock control process. Finally, for a given business pattern and business process, a set of instance services need to be identified for an actual implementation. That is, at the bottom level of the hierarchy are the instance services that implement the business patterns and business processes. The business pattern hierarchy also represents a decomposition process, from high-level business requirements, to enterprise components, business processes/workflows, and to low level instances services that ultimately fulfill and deliver the business services.

The layered business model, proposed in [12], focuses on the decomposition of business tasks to services through analysis of business workflows. The first layer from the top is the Business Layer, which describes what types of business an organization does. The second layer is the Enterprise Layer, which describes how a business is organized into value-adding enterprises and the interactions among them in order to achieve business goals. The third layer is the Workflow (Process) Layer, which describes workflows/business processes for delivering business services. The fourth layer is the Service-flow Layer, which describes how a workflow or process's relevant instance services interact in order to achieve the desired goals. The key difference between the above two models lies in that the latter considers workflows to be used as service flows.

The descriptions for the top three layers of the business model are normally represented in business terms, such as online shopping orders, ticket booking services, and broadband network enabling requests. They are formally defined using conceptual modeling (CM) and knowledge representation (KR) methods, such as ER model [4], CGs, and OWL [10]. The components (instance services) from the bottom layer of the business model, i.e. the Service-flow Layer, are described in technical terms, such as method interfaces, data types, pre-conditions, post-conditions, and etc. From the viewpoint of conceptual modeling, this business model can be divided into two key layers: a conceptual layer where business requirements and tasks are described using business terms, such as business patterns and business processes, and a technical layer where components are described using technical specifications, such as instance services. Obviously, it is difficult to match one of these two types of description into another. That is to say, there is a gap, i.e. a grey area, existing in the diagram that we would like to bridge – a set of matching links to be found. Usually, it is service developers who are making the matching, e.g. transforming one business task into an instance service or mapping a service into a component of business workflow. In this paper, we propose a conceptual modeling method that support to cover this grey belt by semantically enhancing the conceptual description of both business patterns and services by introducing the concept of service usage context and applying Concept Graph.

3   Service Usage Context and Service Conceptual Graphs

As a function unit, an instance service needs to interact with other (instance) services and entities (e.g. organizational components) in order e.g. to take inputting parameters, perform its function, and deliver outputs to other functional units. Entities that interact with instance services are organizational components such as service users or other business components from other enterprises. In a given business domain, we instance services together with their interactions with other services can be classified into categories (business patterns) in terms of their usage scenarios, with which business requirements and tasks are achieved. Each scenario in which a service works demonstrates a way of using the service.

Our research aims to extract, from the contextual usage scenarios of a business, the concepts representing services, entities, and the relations representing their interactions, and hence to construct the conceptual usage scenario (schema or graph) of a concept service implemented by this instance service in a business domain. A concept service is a node (conceptual expression of the service) in the service ontology, which forms a part of the domain ontology (other parts of the ontology are e.g. organizational ontology and personal ontology). Each conceptual usage scenario (CUS) of a service (concept service) describes the conceptual relationships between this service (implemented by the instance service later) to the other services and entities, altogether being used to achieve the business task or provide a business service collaboratively. If a business organization possesses a collection of conceptual usage scenarios (CUSes) in which an instance service can participate, i.e. the schemata of its concept service, we will be able to understand how this service is conceptually used in the business domain or how it is conceptually related to other concept services and entities. This is called its usage context, denoted to be *T-Context*.

Obviously the concepts in a *T-Context* of a concept service include concept services and type definitions that are defined in the domain ontology. There are two types of conceptual relations between service concepts in a *T-Context*: hierarchical conceptual relations generally representing one concept service belongs to another concept service, e.g. Bus ⊑ Travel_Service[1], and horizontal conceptual relations generally representing a sequential order between the two concept services, e.g. *requires*(Payment_Service, Card_Number_Validation_Service).

Theoretically, in an extreme case, when a service is applicable in an open domain rather than a specific business domain, it may be able to participate in a large or even infinite number of business scenarios, i.e. its concept service may theoretically have a large or infinite number of conceptual relations with other concept services or entities. In this case, the *T-Context* of this service could be infinitely large. However, in reality the *T-Context* of a service has not to be infinite in order to describe this service. According to the schemata definition given in [13], to define the meaning of a concept it is not necessary to enumerate all its schemata. Instead we consider its typical schemata which are sufficient to be used to define its meaning. For example, even though people may use a hammer as a paperweight, it is not the typical function of a hammer and without enumerating all the usage cases it is still necessarily clear to know the meaning of a hammer (as a concept) by using its typical schemata of its functions. In our case of instance services, as long as the *T-Context* of a concept service covers the most typical usages (i.e. use cases) of the service, it is sufficient. In an enterprise, services are normally provided in a closed business domain (i.e. the local business area) and their capabilities are defined, developed, and manageable by the enterprise [14]. In this case, the problem of an infinite *T-Context* for a concept service does not exist.

As the *T-Context* of an instance service consists of a collection of conceptual usage scenarios, before formally defining *T-Context*, we first give the definition of a conceptual usage scenario. Given a business domain, let $\mathcal{O}$ be a domain ontology, $\mathcal{O}_c$ ⊆ $\mathcal{O}$ be the whole collection of concepts from $\mathcal{O}$, $\mathcal{R}$ be a set of labels representing the conceptual relations among services and entities in the business domain, a conceptual usage scenario is defined as follows.

Definition 1. Given a concept service $c_s \in \mathcal{O}_c$, a conceptual usage scenario $\varphi(c_s)$ of c_s is a pair (G, l), where:

$G = (V, E)$ is a directed labelled graph; and

$l:V \cup E \rightarrow \mathcal{O}_c \cup \mathcal{R}$ is a labelling function that labels each vertex in V with concept name, so that $V = \{v_i \mid v_i \in \mathcal{O}_c, 0 < i\}$, and each edge in E with predefined relations to indicate the relationship between concepts.

Fig. 1 illustrates a simple conceptual usage scenario about "Money Transfer". In the diagram the concept service "Money Transfer" is related to other concept services in the domain, including "Financial Service", "Currency", "Currency Conversion", and "Bank Service". This conceptual usage scenario example describes the process of how a "Money Transfer" service is performed through a scenario (also called conceptual context) in the given business domain.

---

[1] Here we use the symbol from Description Logic [1].

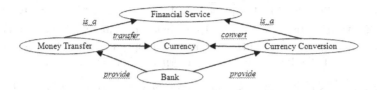

Fig. 1. A fragment of the conceptual usage scenario of a service concept – Money Transfer – and its connections to other concept services and entities.

The *T-Context* of a service is defined to be a collection of conceptual usage scenarios in which the conceptual relations of this concept service with other concept services and entities are described.

Definition 2. Given a concept service $c_s \in \mathcal{O}_c$, its *T-Context* is a set of conceptual usage scenarios $T(c_s) = \{\varphi_1(c_s), \varphi_2(c_s), ..., \varphi_n(c_s)\}$, whose element satisfies the following two conditions:

$c_s \in (\varphi_1(c_s).V_1 \cap \varphi_2(c_s).V_2 \cap ... \cap \varphi_n(c_s).V_n)$; and

$\forall \varphi_i(c_s), \varphi_j(c_s) \in T(c_s), \varphi_i(c_s) \not\subset \varphi_j(c_s) \land \varphi_j(c_s) \not\subset \varphi_i(c_s)$.

Here c_s is called the *owner concept service* of $T(c_s)$ and the instance services of c_s the *owner instance services* of $T(c_s)$.

For each instance service in a service repository, its concept service together with the conceptual relations between this concept service and the other concept services can be seen as a segment (centered on this concept service) of a knowledge base and all the services in the repository apparently form this knowledge base of services, whereas the *T-Context* can be seen as a mechanism of partitioning the knowledge base and assigning partitions to their relevant services. In an enterprise, its knowledge base partitioning is extra useful to the process of creating business services based on the enterprise's existing and potential capabilities and functions. It is the advantage of knowledge base partitioning in an enterprise that when a new business pattern or business process is introduced, the capabilities and relevant instance services in the enterprise required to implement the pattern or process can be located, with conceptual ease, by matching the requirements for the new business pattern to the concept services defined by *T-Context* and *T-Context* is extendable with new business services, since we only need to add new conceptual usage scenarios to *T-Context* of the related instance services.

In the previous definitions of conceptual usage scenarios, we use logic expressions. In the actual semantic description for concept and instance services, *T-Context* is represented using service conceptual graphs (S-CG), an extension to and simplification of the Concept Graphs (CG) formalism [13] for the reasons that CG provides both conceptual, graphical expressions for conceptual modeling and logic based, formal expressions for knowledge base implementation and reasoning. An S-CG is a simplified CG, which does not contain co-reference links and nested context [13]. Similar to the definition of CG, an S-CG is also defined over a *support*

$\mathcal{J} = (T_C, T_R, \mathcal{G}, \tau)$. For further explanation of *support*, readers are referred to [3]. Regarding the definition of S-CGs, T_C includes domain concepts and concept services; $\mathcal{G}$ includes the individuals of domain concepts and the instance services of concept services. In the following, we give a formal definition for S-CGs.

Definition 3. An S-CG gs, defined over a *support* $\mathcal{J}$, is a binary $((C_{gs} \cup R_{gs}, E_{gs}), l_{gs})$, where,

$(C_{gs} \cup R_{gs}, E_{gs})$ is a bipartite graph, where, C_{gs} and R_{gs} are node sets, respectively of concept nodes and relation nodes, and E_{gs} is a set of edges; and

l_{gs} is a labelling function of nodes and edges. A concept node $c_{gs} \in C_{gs}$ is labeled by an ordered pair $(type(c_{gs}), marker(c_{gs}))$, where $type(c_{gs}) \in T_c$, $marker(c_{gs}) \in \mathcal{G} \cup \{*\}$. A relation node $r_{gs} \in R_{gs}$ is labeled by $type(r_{gs})$, where $type(r_{gs}) \in T_R$. The edge labeling is omitted in S-CG.

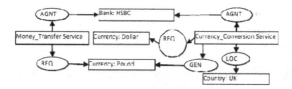

Fig. 2. An example of an S-CG, representing the fragment of the scenario in Fig. 1

Fig. 2 illustrates an S-CG for the usage scenario of a money transfer service. In this S-CG, two concept services are considered: the Money_Transfer Service and the Currency_Conversion Service. The other concept services or entities, such as "Currency", "Bank", and "Country", in the S-CG, are related to these two concept services. For example, the Money_Transfer service is provided by the entity Bank (the concrete performer is HSBC) and it requires the entity Currency (its unit is Pound). The second service Currency_Conversion, located (LOC) in the entity Country (the instance is UK), is also provided by the entity Bank, and it requires (REQ) Currency (Dollar) and generates (GEN) Currency (Pound). These relation nodes, such as "AGNT", "REQ", "GEN", and "LOC", describe relationships between these concepts.

A more complicated S-CG that describes a complicated scenario can be either created based on a complex business service or generated dynamically by joining simple S-CGs. Reader is referred to [6] and [5] for how to embed an S-CG into existing service descriptions.

4   Determination of Relevant Services by S-CGs

The requirements and specifications of a business pattern or process are usually described using business terms in natural language. However, in order to computing the matching between a business pattern and an S-CG schema, we need to have both expressed in a formal, logic form. Now, by applying the methods proposed in [15] and [8], a natural language description or statement can be converted into CGs. After the conversion, the business pattern and process can be directly matched with T-Context so that the related instance services can be located since the T-Context of a service is also represented in S-CG. The T-Context information embedded in S-CGs has provided, at a conceptual level, the information of which kind of business scenarios an instance service can participate in. By computing the similarity between the CGs generated from the business patterns and processes and the S-CGs in the instance service descriptions, we can determine which instance services are most relevant to the required business patterns. In the following, we discuss how the similarity between the S-CGs for services and the CGs for business patterns are computed.

An instance service can be considered to be relevant and irrelevant to a business pattern. Recall that a business pattern can be represented as a Concept Graph (CG) and a concept service with its instance services can be represented as a Concept Graph for Services (S-CGs) in section 3. Now the location of a concept service in a business pattern is turned into a graph-match computation, i.e. matching an S-CG into CG. Therefore, how a service is relevant to the specification of a business pattern becomes how the S-CG of this service matches the CG of the business pattern. There are six situations in which an S-CG's corresponding services can be considered as relevant to the specification of a business pattern.

- **Exact match**: The CG of a business pattern is exactly matched into one or more the S-CGs. That is, for an instance service $s \in$ S-CG, $\mathcal{T}(s) \subseteq$ CG.
- **Projection**: The CG of a business pattern is a projection on one or more S-CGs. Here the projection of a CG on an S-CG represents a mapping of a concept service (not an instance service) in the CUS of the pattern to be identified in the S-CG.
- **Composite projection**: The CG of a business pattern is a projection on a set of joint S-CGs, i.e. a new S-CG that is generated by joining the existing S-CGs.
- **Overlap**: The CG of a business pattern overlaps the concepts and/or relations in one or more S-CGs.
- **Concept match**: The CG of a business pattern has only its concept nodes matched to one or more S-CGs' concept nodes.
- **Relation match**: The CG of a business pattern has only its relation nodes matched to one or more S-CGs' relation nodes.

In the above six situations, the relevance degree of services to business patterns decreases gradually from "Exact match" to "Relation match". For a semi-automatic process of graph-match computation for CG and S-CG, we develop an algorithm, which can categorize the instance services in the repository into different relevance situations. Then, based on each situation, we further refine the results of the graph matching through performing the CG similarity computation, which yields an actual similarity degree of the instance services in its S-CGs to the business pattern in CGs. The algorithm is shown in Listing 1. The relevance degrees are from 1 representing "Exact match" to 6 representing "Relation match". In order to improve performance, "Composite projection" is checked in the last step and only on the services that are confirmed as relevant ones because, if a set of S-CGs have no common concepts with the query CG, the derived graphs from them will not contain a projection of that CG of the business pattern.

```
List relevantServices = null;
CG q = query.CG;
S = {s₁, s₂, ..., sₙ}; //the service repository
for each s∈ S do
{      if projectionCheck(q, s.S-CG) = = true then
       {              if exactMatch(q, s.S-CG) = = true then
                      {              s.setRelevanceLevel(1);
                                     relevantService.add(s);
                                     continue;
                      }
                      else
                      {              s.setRelevanceLevel(2);
                                     relevantService.add(s);
                                     continue;
                      }
       }
       if overlapCheck(q, s.S-CG) = = true then
       {              s.setRelevanceLevel(4);
                      relevantService.add(s);
                      continue;
       }
       if commonConceptCheck(q, s.S-CG) = = true then
       {              s.setRelevanceLevel(5);
                      relevantService.add(s);
                      continue;
       }
       if commonConceptCheck(q, s.S-CG) = = true then
       {              s.setRelevanceLevel(6);
                      relevantService.add(s);
                      continue;
       }
}
if compositeProjectionCheck(q, relevantServices.S-CGList) = = true then
{      List participatedSerivces = compositeProject.getServices()
       for each s∈ participatedSerivces do
       {              if s.getRelevanceLevel() != 1 or s.getRelevanceLevel() != 2 then
                             s.updateRelevanceLevel(3);
       }
}
```

Listing 1. Relevance classification algorithm

The actual similarity degree is then computed between the relevant instance services' S-CGs to determine which one does match in the business pattern the best. We use the method to compute the CG similarity proposed by Montes et al. [9]. The similarity between two CGs, u and v, consists of a concept similarity S_c and a relation similarity S_r. The actual similarity degree formula, having been extended to meet the different situations discussed above, is given in the formula (1).

The first condition in the formula (1) applies when two CGs have only common concept nodes, i.e. the "Concept match" situation. The second condition applies when two CGs have only common relation nodes, i.e. the "Relation match" situation. The third condition applies when two CGs overlap, i.e. the "Overlap" situation. However, the "Projection", and the "Composite Projection" situations are special cases of overlapping, thus the last condition is also applicable in these situations.

$$Sim = \begin{cases} S_c = 2\left(\sum_{c \in \bigcup o}(weight(c) \times \beta(\pi_u c, \pi_v c))\right)\Big/\left(\sum_{c \in u}weight(c) + \sum_{c \in v}weight(c)\right) & if\ S_r = 0\ and\ S_c \neq 0 \\[2ex] S_r = \dfrac{2m(o)}{m_c(u) + m_c(v)} & if\ S_c = 0\ and\ S_r \neq 0 \\[2ex] S_c \cdot S_r & if\ S_c \neq 0\ and\ S_r \neq 0 \end{cases} \quad (1)$$

The $\beta(\pi_u c, \pi_v c)$ function in the formula (1), calculating the semantic similarity between the two concepts $\pi_u c$ and $\pi_v c$, is defined in the formula (2).

$$\beta(\pi_u c, \pi_v c) = \begin{cases} 1 & if\ type(\pi_u c) = type(\pi_v c)\ and\ referent(\pi_u c) = referent(\pi_v c) \\ depth/(depth+1) & if\ type(\pi_u c) = type(\pi_v c)\ and\ referent(\pi_u c) \neq referent(\pi_v c) \\ 2d_c/(d_{\pi_u c} + d_{\pi_v c}) & if\ type(\pi_u c) \neq type(\pi_v c) \end{cases} \quad (2)$$

The first condition in the formula (2) indicates that the two concepts are exactly the same. The second condition indicates that the two concepts have the same type but refer to different instances, where *depth* represents the number of levels in the ontology that contains both concepts. The third condition indicates that the two concepts have different types, where, d_c represents the distance from the least common super-type of $\pi_u c$ and $\pi_v c$ to the root of the ontology; $d_{\pi_u c}$ and $d_{\pi_v c}$ represent the distances from $\pi_u c$ and $\pi_v c$ to the root of the ontology.

5   Conclusion

Business patterns provide business with agility and reliability to quickly reform in order to catch market trends, especially under the SOA infrastructure. However, one problem a business has to face is that large amount of manual work is required when locating suitable instance services for newly introduced business patterns or reformed processes. The reason is that the description of a business pattern is entirely different from the description of an instance service. In this paper, we have chosen to address this problem and propose a "Pattern-Scenario-Service" method to bridge the gap of the description of these different layers in business processes.

We introduced the relationships between business patterns, business processes, and instance services in order to identify the problem and proposed a service description approach to tackling the gap. In this approach, each instance service is described with not only technical terms, but also the T-Context information that explains how the service should be used in terms of business cases. The advantage of T-Context is that it adds conceptual semantics into technical description. Through T-Context and its representation – S-CGs, a business pattern or processes described using business terms can be directly matched with technically described instance services.

We have developed a pilot system to test the theory and method. However, a huge number of services are available now on the web and enterprises are intending to make full use of them. For out next step of study, we aim at the following three aspects of this investigation: 1) filtering the web services to make a business oriented classification for them so that a semantic richer description framework will be developed to meet the needs of different business requirements and patterns; 2) assessing the system, in terms of its performance and scalability, when it is applied in a relatively larger scale of business cases, for example, an SME, with a dynamic adjustment of services on their availability; and 3) optimizing the algorithm (described in section 4) for a quick yet semantic retained CG match method that can support direct mapping between the users' requirements (to business patterns) and the enterprises' available services.

References

1. Baader, F., Horrocks, I., Sattler, U.: Description logics for the semantic web. KI - Künstliche Intelligenz 16(4), 57–59 (2002)
2. Bieberstein, N., Bose, S., Fiammante, M., Jones, K., Shah, R.: Service-Oriented Architecture Compass: Business Value, Planning, and Enterprise Roadmap, vol. 19. IBM Press (2005)
3. Chein, M., Mugnier, M.L.: Conceptual Graphs: Fundamental Notions. Revue d'Intelligence Artificielle 6(4), 365–406 (1992)
4. Chen, P.P.: The Entity-Relationship Model: Toward a Unified View of Data. ACM Transactions on Database Systems 1, 9–36 (1976)
5. Du, X., Munro, M., Song, W.W.: CbSSDF: A Two Layer Conceptual Graph Description for Web Services. Accepted by the Int'l Journal on Information Systems Modelling and Design (2011)
6. Du, X., Song, W., Munro, M.: A Method for Transforming Existing Web service Descriptions into an Enhanced Semantic Web service Framework. In: Proc. of 17th International Conference on Information System Development, Paphos, Cyprus, Paphos, Cyprus, August 25-27 (2008)
7. Endrei, M., Ang, J., Arsanjani, A., Chua, S., Comte, P., Krogdahl, P., Luo, M., Newling, T.: Patterns: Service-Oriented Architecture and Web Services. International Business Machines Corporation. IBM RedBooks, International Business Machines Corporation (2004)
8. Mann, G.A.: Assembly of Conceptual Graphs from Natural Language by Means of Multiple Knowledge Specialists. In: Pfeiffer, H.D., Nagle, T.E. (eds.) Conceptual Structures: Theory and Implementation. LNCS, vol. 754, pp. 232–275. Springer, Heidelberg (1993)
9. Montes-y-Gómez, M., Gelbukh, A., López-López, A., Baeza-Yates, R.: Flexible Comparison of Conceptual Graphs. In: Mayr, H.C., Lazanský, J., Quirchmayr, G., Vogel, P. (eds.) DEXA 2001. LNCS, vol. 2113, pp. 102–111. Springer, Heidelberg (2001)
10. RDF: Resource Description Framework (RDF) Model and Syntax Specification, W3C (1999), http://www.w3.org/TR/PR-rdf-syntax/
11. Russell, C., Barnsley, P., Holladay, M.: Business Patterns within Telecommunications. The Journal of Production Planning and Control 12(2), 188–197 (2001)

12. Song, W.: Business Process and Integration Model: an Approach to Guide Constructing Service Flows. In: Proceeding of the IASTED Int'l Conf. on Web Technologies, Calgary, Canada, July 17-19 (2006)
13. Sowa, J.F.: Conceptual Structures: Information Processing in Mind and Machine. Addison-Wesley, Canada (1984)
14. Strang, C.J.: Next generation systems architecture — the Matrix. BT Technology Journal 23(1) (January 2005)
15. Strzalkowski, T.: A Fast and Robust Parser for Natural Language. In: The 14th Int'l Conference on Computational Linguistics (COLING 1992), Nantes, France, pp. 198–204 (1992)

Making Recommendations on Microblogs through Topic Modeling

Chaochao Chen, Xiaolin Zheng*, Chaofei Zhou, and Deren Chen

Department of Computer Science, Zhejiang University,
310027 HangZhou, ZheJiang, P.R. China
{zjuccc,xlzheng,cfzhou,drchen}@zju.edu.cn

Abstract. The large-data era has made microblogs important platforms
for propagating and searching for information. Analyzing microblog content with topic models facilitates the search for users and microblogs of
interest from a vast amount of information. However, traditional topic
model doesn't work well on microblog because these blogs are short and
have irregular writing patterns. Considering that microblog have obviously concentration on the field and time they were posted, we propose
a microblog recommender approach called time-field latent Dirichlet allocation (TF-LDA), which effectively makes topics more discriminative
and thus improves recommender performance. An experiment shows that
user and microblog recommendations based on TF-LDA increases accuracy compared with those based on traditional topic models.

Keywords: microblog, topic model, recommendation, field time.

1 Introduction

Microblogs have become a significant platform for users to propagate and search
for information, and it's also becoming a platform of big data. It's fatal important for microblog users to find interesting information from vast amounts of
information. Microblog users demand system recommendations of more highly
similar microblogs. However the existing microblog platforms primarily make
recommendations based on user social graphs [1] and thus do not meet the
personal requirement of users because such platforms cannot filter information
based on user interest.

To resolve this problem efficiently, we propose an approach based on topic
modeling to analyze microblog content. Traditional topic models cannot be effectively used for microblogs because microblogs are short (often allowing only
140 words) and exhibit noise-like irregular writing patterns [2]. Therefore, we
propose TF-LDA, an enhanced version of LDA. We make recommendations on
microblogs according to a well-trained TF-LDA model, including recommendations on users with interests similar to the target user and microblogs which the
target user is interested in.

---

* Corresponding author.

Z. Huang et al. (Eds.): WISE 2013 Workshops 2013, LNCS 8182, pp. 252–265, 2014.
© Springer-Verlag Berlin Heidelberg 2014

The paper is structured as follows: Section 2 reviews related literature on topic models and microblogs. Section 3 describes the framework for recommending users and microblogs. Section 4 describes the recommendation problem with microblogs and proposes our TF-LDA. Section 5 describes the experiments and analyzes the experimental results. Section 6 concludes the paper with a discussion of future work.

2 Related Work

Topic models have been widely used in data mining and analysis. Before topic models were developed, the vector space model [3] and language model [4] had been used to mine and process textual information. To enhance the ability to express text, Deerwester [5] proposed latent semantic analysis (LSA), a linear algebra-based dimensionality reduction technique for mining information that focuses on basic linguistic notions, such as synonymy and polysemy. Utilizing advances in probability and statistics, Hoffman [6] developed probabilistic LSA (pLSA), a probabilistic modeling of text. After that, Blei [7] proposed latent dirichlet distribution (LDA), perhaps the most common topic model currently in use, as a generalized pLSA and has thereby accelerated the development of topic models.

Many topic models based on LDA have been proposed. Blei and Lafferty [8] proposed the correlated topic model, in which topic proportions are correlated via logistic normal distribution. Griffiths [9] proposed hidden Markov model-LDA, a generative model that can capture the interaction between short- and long-range dependencies between words. Other topic models based on LDA include dynamic topic models [10], supervised topic models [11] and syntactic topic models [12].

Studies on microblog platforms have primarily analyzed the social and community structures of microblog users. Java [13] studied the topological and geographical properties of Twitter social networks and found that people use microblogging to talk about their daily activities and seek or share information. Daniel [14] analyzed the influence of tweet topics on user interaction to determine if the social aspect dominates the topic during interaction. Wu [15] proposed the XinRank algorithm to identify the influential users of Sina. Naaman [16] classified Twitter users into two according to the content of their tweets: "informers", who post messages that are informational in nature, and "meformers", who typically post messages about themselves or their thoughts.

Recommender systems in the microblog field have drawn significant attention recent years. Chen [17] proposed an algorithm (an extension of PageRank) that uses user influence to recommend users in Sina microblogs. Li [18] proposed a hybrid recommender system that combines collaborative and content-based filtering to determine user preference to make recommendations in Tencent microblogs. Wu [19] presented a microblog recommendation system to predict the top K Twitter users who will retweet or mention a focal user in the future.

Studies of topic models in the microblog field remain limited. Hong [20] applied the topic model to Twitter and proposed three methods (MSG, USER, and

TERM) to predict popular Twitter messages and classify Twitter users and messages. Among these methods, USER is the most effective because it trains LDA on aggregated user profiles. Ramage [1] presented a scalable implementation of labeled LDA [21] that maps the content of the Twitter feed onto certain dimensions. Zhou [22] proposed two methods based on LDA to make recommendations in microblogs.

In this paper, we propose TF-LDA, an LDA enhancement that effectively makes topics more discriminative and thus improves recommender performance. Therefore, TF-LDA can be used to make recommendations in microblogs.

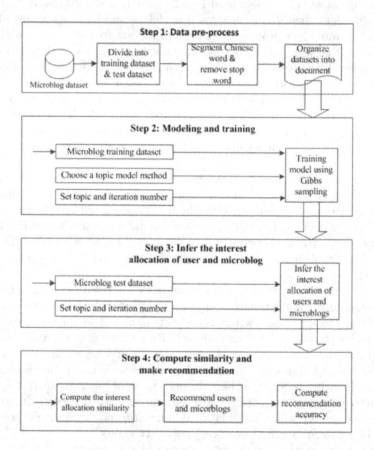

Fig. 1. Framework for user and microblog recommendation

3   Framework for Recommending Users and Microblogs

The proposed TF-LDA method can be used to make recommendations in microblogs, including recommendations of users with interests that match those of the target user and microblogs which the target user is interested in. The recommendation process is divided into the following steps:

Step 1: The crawled microblog data set is divided into training and test data sets. These data sets are preprocessed by segmenting Chinese words and removing stop words. The data sets are organized into LDA input documents.

Step 2: A topic modeling method is chosen, the topic and iteration numbers are set, and Gibbs sampling is used to train the model by using the training data set.

Step 3: The trained model is used to infer the topic distributions (i.e., interest distributions) of users and microblogs in the test data set.

Step 4: The similarity in interest distribution between users as well as between users and microblogs is computed. Users with similar interests and microblogs which users are interested in are recommended. The recommendation accuracy is computed.

The framework for user and microblog recommendation is shown in Fig. 1.

4   User and Microblog Recommendation

4.1   Problem Definition

Definition 1: Microblog field. Sina[1] microblog divide popular certified users into different fields, such as entertainment, sports, and military. We define the microblog field as $F = \{ F_1, F_2, ..., F_L\}$, where $|F_i|$ denotes the number of users in the i-th microblog field.

We define a microblog set as $W = \{ W_1, W_2, ..., W_N\}$, where W_i denotes the i-th microblog. The microblog field is determined by its promulgator. Assuming that a total of L microblog fields exist, $W_i \in F_j$ means that the i-th microblog message is in the j-th microblog field, where $i \in 1...N, j \in 1...L$.

Assuming that all microblog users belong to user set $U = \{ U_1, U_2, ..., U_M\}$, where U_i denotes the i-th user, $U_i \in F_j$ means that the i-th user is in the j-th field, where $i \in 1...M, j \in 1...L$.

We take the following assumptions when making recommendations in microblogs:

– Users are interested only in users and microblogs in their own field.
– Every user belongs to only one field.

When user recommendations are made, the input of the recommender system is the interest distribution of the target user U_i and all other users, and its output is the users to be recommended to U_i:

Input $= \{U, U_i\}$

Output $= Model(Input) = \{ U_j,$ where $j \neq i, and\ U_j \in F_k, U_i \in F_k, k \in 1...L\}$

When microblog recommendations are made, the input of the recommender system is the interest distribution of the target user and all the microblogs, and its output is the microblogs to be recommended to U_i:

Input $= \{W, U_i\}$

Output $= Model(Input) = \{ W_j,$ where $W_j \in F_k, U_i \in F_k, k \in 1...L\}$

---

[1] http://weibo.com/

4.2   TF-LDA

Because microblogs are very short and exhibit noise, directly applying LDA to microblog recommendation impairs model performance. Considering microblog platform users in the same field always focus on the same things and have similar interests, aggregating user microblogs in the same field reduces the impact of noise data. Moreover, given that some topics are more popular than others or a user may be interested in certain things in a certain period, microblogs are time-dependent.

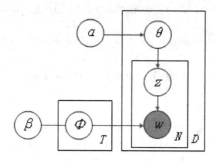

Fig. 2. Graphic model of TF-LDA

Based on these considerations, we propose time–field topic modeling method, we call it "TF-LDA". The graphical model of TF-LDA is shows in Fig. 2, where θ is the multinomial distribution of the time–field document (described in section 5.2) over topics, $\varnothing$ is the multinomial distribution of the topic over words, α and β are the Dirichlet priors of θ and $\varnothing$, T is the topic value, D is the number of time–field documents, N is the number of words in each document, Z is a certain topic drawn from θ and W is the number of words in each document.

Table 1. Generative process of TF-LDA

Choose $N \sim Poisson(\xi)$
For each topic
Draw a distribution over words $\varnothing \sim Dir(\beta)$
For each field
For each time slot
Draw a vector of topic proportions $\theta \sim Dir(\alpha)$
For each word
Draw a topic assignment $z \sim Mult(\theta)$
Draw a word $w \sim Mult(\varnothing_z)$

The basic idea is that the time-field documents are represented as random mixtures over latent topics, where each topic is characterized by a distribution over words. TF-LDA posits that each word of both the observed and unseen time-field documents is generated by a randomly chosen topic which is drawn from a distribution with a randomly chosen parameter. The generative process of TF-LDA is shown in Table 1.

4.3 Making Recommendations

To recommend users with interests similar to those of the target user and microblogs which the target user is interested in, we must know the interest distribution of all users and microblogs. This can be done by inferring the topic distribution of users and microblogs from the trained topic model.

Obtaining the interest distributions of users and microblogs enables the formulation of recommendations by computing the similarity of these distributions. We use the Kullback-Leibler (KL) divergence to compute the similarity in interest distributions:

$$D\left(p,q\right) = \sum_{j=1}^{T} p_j log \frac{p_j}{q_j} \tag{1}$$

$$KL\left(p,q\right) = \frac{1}{2}[D\left(p,q\right) + D(q,p)] \tag{2}$$

The specific methods for user recommendation are as follows:

- For a specific user A, supposing that his/her interest distribution is p, the symmetric KL divergence between p and the interest distribution of other users is computed.
- The symmetric KL diversity is sorted into ascending order, the same order as the similarity of the interests of other users with those of user A.

The pseudocodes of user recommendation are shown in Table 2.

Table 2. Pseudocodes of user recommendation

For each user
Compute user interest distribution based on the topic model
For each user
For each user
Compute KL divergence
Sort users according to their KL divergences

The specific methods for microblog recommendation are as follows:

- For a specific user A, supposing that his/her interest distribution is p, the symmetric KL divergence between p and the interest distribution of other microblogs is computed.
- The symmetric KL diversity is sorted into ascending order, the same order as that of the degree of interest of user A in all other microblogs.

The pseudocodes of microblog recommendation are shown in Table 3.

Table 3. Pseudocodes of microblog recommendation

```
For each user
  Compute user interest distribution based on topic model
For each microblog
  Compute microblog interest distribution based on topic model
For each user
  For each post
    Compute KL divergence
  Sort microblogs according to their KL divergence
```

5   Experiment Analysis

5.1   Dataset Description

Our experiment data set is obtained from Sina, the largest microblog platform in China. We crawl 197,810 microblogs posted by 396 certified users from 11 different fields within 150 d (from November 12, 2011, to April 9, 2012) by using the application programming interface of Sina[2]. The user fields are based on the field classification in Sina. The crawled user fields and user number are shown in Table 4.

Table 4. Number of users in each field

field	user number
sports	44
technology	49
real estate	31
geomancy	40
police	40
stock	35
entertainment	47
Chinese medicine	33
military	26
parenting	29
environment protection	22
total	396

We use open-source software IKAnalyzer to segment Chinese words. To obtain stable results, we use fivefold cross-validation.

5.2   Model Training and Analysis

The LDA-based modeling is described as follows:

---

[2] http://open.weibo.com/

- The microblogs in the training data set are preprocessed, and the data set is organized into training documents.
- The LDA model is trained using the training documents.

The USER-based modeling is described as follows:

- The microblogs in the training data set are clustered according to user (forming 396 documents in this experiment), and the documents are then preprocessed and organized into training documents.
- The USER model is trained using these training documents.

The TF-LDA-based modeling is described as follows:

- The microblogs in the training data set are clustered according to field (forming 11 field documents in this experiment).
- These field documents are divided according to period. One day is considered a period in this experiment, and 150 documents are formed in each field. These documents are preprocessed, and time–field documents are obtained.
- The TF-LDA model is trained using these time–field documents.

We use a symmetric Dirichlet prior and set the iteration number to 1000 during Gibbs sampling. We set the topic value to $[10, 50]$ and take a value every 5. Topic models achieve the desired performance when $\alpha = 50/T$ and $\beta = 0.01$, where T is the topic value [23].

We use the Jensen-Shannon (JS) divergence [24] to compute the similarity between two topics, as shown in (3) and (4). The smaller the JS divergence, the greater the similarity between the two topic distributions.

$$D_{JS} = \frac{1}{2}D_{KL}\left(P \parallel R\right) + \frac{1}{2}D_{KL}(Q \parallel R) \tag{3}$$

$$R\frac{1}{2}(P + R) \tag{4}$$

where $D_{KL}\left(A \parallel B\right)$ denotes the KL divergence between vectors A and B. This divergence is computed according to

$$D_{KL}\left(A \parallel B\right) = \sum_{n=1}^{M} \beta_{na} log \frac{\beta_{na}}{\beta_{nb}} \tag{5}$$

where M is the number of different words and β_{na} denotes the probability of the occurrence of word n in topic a.

In Table 5, we list the 30 most frequent words in one training data set of the fivefold cross-validation when $T = 20$. The order of the word corresponds to its probability of occurrence, and the higher such probability in a certain topic, the earlier the occurrence of the word. We can obviously see that this belongs to the police field, and the order of words varies with the modeling method. We compare the topic distribution with different topic values in Fig. 3, which indicates that the topic distribution significantly varies with the modeling method. In particular, the topic distribution of TF-LDA significantly varies with the other two methods, indicating the particularity of the proposed method.

Table 5. Distribution of high-frequency words with different modeling methods(T=20)

modeling method	high-frequency words
LDA	time, safe, railway, safety, mobile phone, public security, three, after, please, police station, phone, police, website, people's police, information, network, activity, web, online, traveler, car, Hangzhou, policeman, work, alert, proceed, Spring Festival travel, ticket, buy ticket, 12,
USER	railway, safe, public security, time, police station, safety, police, people's police, traveler, Spring Festival travel, alert, dont, ticket, buy ticket, after, phone, three, online, Hangzhou, everyone, alarm, please, police, real name, work, 12, prompt, book the ticket, train ticket, proceed
TF-LDA	railway, safe, public security, time, police station, police, people's police, safety, traveler, Spring Festival travel, alert, ticket, dont, alarm, buy ticket, online, three, phone, Hangzhou, policeman, real name, train ticket, 12, after, prompt, please, book the ticket, everyone, community, rail

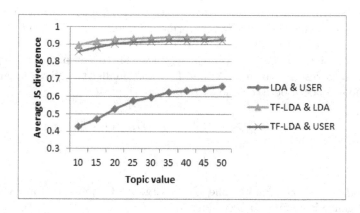

Fig. 3. Average JS divergence of three modeling methods with different topic values

5.3   Analysis of Recommendation Performance

5.3.1   Evaluation of User Recommendations.

We use accuracy to evaluate user recommendation performance. Supposing that M users exist in the field of target user A and N users exist in the top $2M-1$ users similar to user A, then the accuracy is

$$user\ recommendation\ accuracy = \frac{N}{M} \qquad (6)$$

5.3.2   Comparison of User Recommendations

We use three different topic modeling methods together with term frequency-inverse document frequency (TF-IDF) to show the user recommendation performance improvement produced by our TF-LDA method. The average accuracy of user recommendation with different topic values is shown in Fig. 4, which indicates that the user recommendation accuracy of TF-LDA is higher than that of the other two modeling methods. The user recommendation accuracy also becomes stable when the topic value exceeds a certain threshold (between 15 and 20). Thus, user recommendation accuracy is mostly determined by the modeling method rather than the topic value.

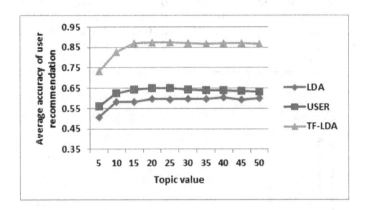

Fig. 4. Average accuracy of user recommendation with different topic values

The average accuracy of user recommendation with different methods under different fields is shown in Table   6. The user recommendation accuracies of LDA, USER, and TF-IDF under different fields significantly vary, whereas those of TF-LDA under different fields are stable. The user recommendation accuracies in 8 of the 11 fields exceed 80%, indicating excellent modeling performance in user recommendations.

5.3.3   Evaluation of Microblog Recommendations

We also use accuracy to evaluate microblog recommendation performance. Supposing that M microblogs exist in the field of target user A and N microblogs exist in the top $2M$ microblogs similar to that of user A, then the accuracy is

$$microblog\ recommendation\ accuracy = \frac{N}{M} \qquad (7)$$

Table 6. Average accuracy of user recommendation with different methods under different fields

field	LDA	USER	TF-LDA	TF-IDF
sports	0.5792	0.7773	0.9738	0.5671
technology	0.6917	0.7733	0.9472	0.4979
real estate	0.4269	0.4643	0.8490	0.5140
geomancy	0.5163	0.5613	0.7462	0.5699
police	0.9524	0.9809	0.7938	0.9415
stock	0.6114	0.6551	0.8128	0.6310
entertainment	0.6241	0.6314	0.8747	0.6445
Chinese medicine	0.6733	0.7053	0.8841	0.7218
military	0.3335	0.3646	0.7074	0.3237
parenting	0.5010	0.5096	0.8648	0.6055
environment protection	0.3835	0.4030	0.8325	0.3161
total	0.5721	0.6206	0.8442	0.5757

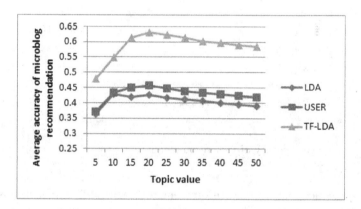

Fig. 5. Average accuracy of microblog recommendation with different topic values

5.3.4 Comparison of Microblog Recommendations

We also use the three different topic modeling methods together with TF–IDF to show the microblog recommendation performance improvement yielded by the proposed TF-LDA method. The average accuracy of microblog recommendation with different topic values is shown in Fig. 5. The microblog recommendation accuracy of TF-LDA is higher than that of the other two topic modeling methods, but lower than the user recommendation accuracy because microblogs are short and full of noise. In contrast to the accuracy of user recommendation, that of microblog recommendation is relatively sensitive to T: microblog recommendation accuracy increases with increasing T but decreases beyond a certain T threshold. Thus, microblog recommendation accuracy is determined by both the model and the topic value.

The average accuracy of microblog recommendation with different methods under different fields is shown in Table 7. The microblog recommendation ac-

Table 7. Average accuracy of microblog recommendation with different methods under different fields

field	LDA	USER	TF-LDA	TF-IDF
sports	0.2761	0.3678	0.5397	0.2612
technology	0.3199	0.3702	0.5226	0.2388
real estate	0.5081	0.5087	0.6640	0.3094
geomancy	0.4283	0.4791	0.6437	0.2983
police	0.7039	0.7526	0.8090	0.5844
stock	0.4371	0.4493	0.5706	0.1687
entertainment	0.4992	0.5011	0.6812	0.3406
Chinese medicine	0.4788	0.4060	0.6559	0.4330
military	0.3452	0.3747	0.5461	0.2481
parenting	0.4123	0.4533	0.7612	0.1785
environment protection	0.3060	0.2967	0.5349	0.2886
total	0.4263	0.4582	0.6306	0.3045

curacies of LDA, USER, and TF-IDF under different fields significantly vary, whereas those of TF-LDA are relatively stable in all fields and higher than those of the other three methods. Therefore, the proposed method also has good modeling performance in microblog recommendation.

6 Conclusions and Future Work

In this paper, we propose TF-LDA, an improvement of LDA, to make recommendations on microblogs, including recommendations on users with interests similar to those of the target user and microblogs which the target user is interested in. Experiments show that TF-LDA significantly improves user and microblog recommendation accuracy relative to those of TF-IDF, LDA, and USER.

Although TF-LDA achieves the desired recommendation performance, it ignores other useful information in microblog platforms, such as social trust networks and geographical location information. Our future work will focus on optimally using the rich information available in microblogs to improve recommendation performance.

Acknowledgments. This work is supported in part by the National Key Technology R&D Program (No. 2012BAH16F02), and the Natural Science Foundation of China (Grant No. 61003254), and the projects of Construct public services platforms for medium, small and micro enterprises in specialized towns (Grant No. 2012B040500020 and 2012B040500024).

References

1. Ramage, D., Dumais, S.T., Liebling, D.J.: Characterizing Microblogs with Topic Models. In: ICWSM (2010)
2. Lu, Y., Zhai, C.: Opinion integration through semi-supervised topic modeling. In: Proceedings of the 17th International Conference on World Wide Web. ACM (2008)
3. Salton, G., Wong, A., Yang, C.-S.: A vector space model for automatic indexing. Communications of the ACM 18(11), 613–620 (1975)
4. Ponte, J.M., Bruce Croft, W.: A language modeling approach to information retrieval. In: Proceedings of the 21st Annual International ACM SIGIR Conference on Research and Development in Information Retrieval. ACM (1998)
5. Deerwester, S.C., et al.: Indexing by latent semantic analysis. JASIS 41(6), 391–407 (1990)
6. Hofmann, T.: Probabilistic latent semantic indexing. In: Proceedings of the 22nd Annual International ACM SIGIR Conference on Research and Development in Information Retrieval. ACM (1999)
7. Blei, D.M., Ng, A.Y., Jordan, M.I.: Latent dirichlet allocation. The Journal of Machine Learning Research 3, 993–1022 (2003)
8. Blei, D.M., Lafferty, J.D.: A correlated topic model of science. The Annals of Applied Statistics, 17–35 (2007)
9. Griffiths, T.L., et al.: Integrating topics and syntax. Advances in Neural Information Processing Systems (2004)
10. Blei, D.M., Lafferty, J.D.: Dynamic topic models. In: Proceedings of the 23rd International Conference on Machine Learning. ACM (2006)
11. Blei, D.M., McAuliffe, J.D.: Supervised topic models. arXiv preprint arXiv:1003.0783 (2010)
12. Boyd-Graber, J., Blei, D.M.: Syntactic topic models. arXiv preprint arXiv:1002.4665 (2010)
13. Java, A., et al.: Why we twitter: understanding microblogging usage and communities. In: Proceedings of the 9th WebKDD and 1st SNA-KDD 2007 Workshop on Web Mining and Social Network Analysis. ACM (2007)
14. Sousa, D., Sarmento, L., Rodrigues, E.M.: Characterization of the twitter@ replies network: are user ties social or topical? In: Proceedings of the 2nd International Workshop on Search and Mining User-Generated Contents. ACM (2010)
15. Wu, X., Wang, J.: How about micro-blogging service in China: analysis and mining on sina micro-blog. In: Proceedings of 1st International Symposium on From Digital Footprints to Social and Community Intelligence. ACM (2011)
16. Naaman, M., Boase, J., Lai, C.-H.: Is it really about me?: message content in social awareness streams. In: Proceedings of the 2010 ACM Conference on Computer Supported Cooperative Work. ACM (2010)
17. Chen, C., Feng, H.: Microblog Recommendation based on user interaction. In: ICCSNT, pp. 2107–2111 (2012)
18. Li, Y., Zhang, Y.: A Hybrid Recommender System of Tencent Microblog
19. Wu, S., et al.: Making recommendations in a microblog to improve the impact of a focal user. In: Proceedings of the Sixth ACM Conference on Recommender Systems. ACM (2012)
20. Hong, L., Davison, B.D.: Empirical study of topic modeling in twitter. In: Proceedings of the First Workshop on Social Media Analytics. ACM (2010)

21. Ramage, D., et al.: Labeled LDA: A supervised topic model for credit attribution in multi-labeled corpora. In: Proceedings of the 2009 Conference on Empirical Methods in Natural Language Processing, vol. 1. Association for Computational Linguistics (2009)
22. Zhou, C.: Research on Recommendation in Microblogs Based on Topic Models. College of Computer Science, Zhejiang University, Hang Zhou (2012)
23. Griffiths, T.L., Steyvers, M.: Finding scientific topics. Proceedings of the National Academy of Sciences of the United States of America 101(suppl. 1), 5228–5235 (2004)
24. Lin, J.: Divergence measures based on the Shannon entropy. IEEE Transactions on Information Theory 37(1), 145–151 (1991)

A Computational Model for Trust-Based Collaborative Filtering

An Empirical Study on Hotel Recommendations

Qinzhu Wu[1], Anders Forsman[1], Zukun Yu[2], and William Wei Song[1]

[1] Dalarna University, Falun 791 88, Sweden
{h11qinwu,afm,wso}@du.se
[2] Zhejiang University, Hangzhou 310027, China
zukunyu@zju.edu.cn

Abstract. The inherent weakness of the data on user ratings collected from the web, such as sparsity and cold-start, has limited the data analysis capability and prediction accuracy in recommender systems. To alleviate this problem, trust has been incorporated in collaborative filtering approaches with encouraging experimental results. In this paper, we propose a computational model for trust-based CF with three different methods to infer trust in a social network, based on a detailed data analysis of hotel dataset. We apply these methods on users ratings of hotels and show its feasibility by comparing the testing results with conventional CF algorithm using evaluation metrics Mean absolute error (MAE) and prediction coverage. Our experimental results indicate that the use of trust can improve prediction accuracy if the definition of trust is reasonable enough.

Keywords: Trust, Collaborative filtering, Recommender systems.

1 Introduction

Recommender systems are software tools and techniques providing suggestions for items to be use of a user [1]. Although collaborative filtering has proven to be one of the most effective techniques to be incorporated into RS, it still suffers from the inherent weaknesses existed in raw data, such as data sparsity. For instance, in our case, a large number of ratings on hotels were collected from registered users of the well-known accommodations reservation website http://www.booking.com, however, only 5% of users in our datasets rated more than one hotel, the lack of prior ratings makes it difficult to find enough number of similar users and make accurate predictions for an individual with conventional CF method.

In this paper we propose a computational model with trust-based CF to alleviate the sparsity problem existed in our datasets. First, all hotels (items) were classified into different clusters based on their attributes with k-means clustering method and denoted by their cluster id. Secondly, for each testing user, we find a group of neighbors (k-nearest neighbor) who have similar preference based

Z. Huang et al. (Eds.): WISE 2013 Workshops 2013, LNCS 8182, pp. 266–279, 2014.

on their commonly rated clusters and prior rating values. Thirdly, predictions were made by using the data from their neighbors for each test user. At last, we evaluate and compare the performance of predictions by two metrics: mean absolute error (MAE) and prediction coverage. The results from our experiments have indicated that although the improvement of prediction accuracy is not very significant, the use of trust do really helps to improve the accuracy of predicted rating values, as long as the definition of trust is rational enough.

The remainder of this paper is organized as follows. Section 2 surveys existing research work on recommender systems, collaborative filtering and the rising interest to incorporate trust into CF. Section 3 provides details of descriptions on conventional collaborative filtering method, weight computation method for neighbors normally incorporated into CF, as well as our trust-enhanced CF method. In section 4 we introduce our hotel data sets and the sparsity problem with it, evaluation metrics and algorithm with regard to implementation steps, experimental results with detailed analysis. Section 5 provides a conclusion on our contributions and future work. The rest are our references and appendixes.

2   Related Work

2.1   Recommender Systems

Recommender systems (RS) [7] emerged as an independent research area since the appearance of collaborative filtering in the mid-1990s [8]. The first recommender system, Tapestry [6], originally designed to improve efficiency of E-mail filtering by incorporating other users opinions in the process, can be traced back to 1992. RS normally focused on giving suggestions on items towards individuals who may lack experiences before. Nowadays it is still a popular area to be developed, not only because it can address the information overload problem, but also owing to the far-ranging applications it has brought to us. Examples of such applications can be found everywhere: helping customers decide which products to purchase in an E-commerce website (Amazon.com [10]), recommending songs to music lovers in a radio website (Last.fm [5]), and mobile recommender systems using spatial data [11].

Usually recommender systems were classified according to techniques that have been incorporated into them. Based on this, we typically have three different types of recommender systems: collaborative filtering (CF), content-based and hybrid system. The main difference between collaborative filtering and content-based approach is that the former one recommends items that other similar users have liked by computing similarity values between users. As for content-based technique, we only recommend items which are similar to the items one user has liked in the past. One typical hybrid recommender system is Fab [3], by combining both techniques, it may alleviate some weaknesses found in each approach. A state-of-the-art introduction of recommender system can be found in [1].

2.2 Collaborative Filtering

Many literature reviews have indicated that collaborative filtering is one of the most well-known, successful and widely implemented techniques [1,4,13,14,19]. The biggest advantage of CF over content-based approach is that it only relies on opinions on items described by users [19]. Instead content-based systems require more detailed descriptions of each item, so as to generate similarities between items. Two general classes of CF algorithms were examined in [12]: Memory-based algorithm and model-based algorithm. Model-based algorithm can be viewed as calculating the expected value of a vote from a probabilistic perspective, based on what we know about the user. Related methods include cluster models and Bayesian networks. As for the memory-based algorithm, we will describe it explicitly in subsequent part of this paper.

However, CF approach still suffers from three fundamental challenges [20]: data sparsity, cold-start and scalability. Data sparsity refers to the situation that users only rate a small portion of the available items, thus resulted in a sparse user-item matrix where we can hardly find co-rated items between users. In cold-start problem, the lack of historical information occurs on new items or users consequently lead to a dumb state in RS, that the system fails to consider users with an empty file or items no one has previously rated. Scalability entails a large amount of computation when there are millions of users and items, which is usually the case in reality. In this paper we focused on data sparsity and proposed a model to alleviate this problem.

Several approaches have been adopted in previous work to cope with this challenge and received moderately good results. As we mentioned before, hybrid algorithm combing both CF and content-based techniques can alleviate weakness in both approaches. Dimensionality reduction methods, such as Singular Value Decomposition (SVD), Latent Semantic Indexing (LSI), reduce the dimensions of matrix by getting rid of unimportant users or items [22]. Huang et al [21] applied an associative retrieval framework and spreading activation algorithms to deal with the sparsity problem. Manos et al [17] used trust inference to alleviate such kind of problems.

2.3 Trust in RS

A rising interest in trust-enhanced recommender systems was found in recent research work [1,14,15,17,19]. Trust is a common concept in our daily life and it can be defined in various ways, B. Noteboom claims that trust is an expectation that things or people will not fail us, or the neglect or lack of awareness of the possibility of failure [23]. Another notion of trust was presented by P. Sztompka, It is a type of bet taken on the issue of uncertain future activities of other people[24]. For trust in recommender systems, there is no stationary definition for it. The main strength of applying trust into recommender systems is to quantify trust into numerical values and build a web of trust (WOT) for each user, using trust inference and trust propagation. Examples of major algorithms for building trust network are Moletrust [25] and Tidaltrust [26].

J. Wang [15] proposed a method to generate trust by incorporating the taste of users on choosing items. The tastes of users were implied from the classification of items, based on the intuition that users usually trust those who have similar taste with them. After that the trust metric is developed from the taste set of a user in all clusters of items. Then trust was propagated throughout a social network to include more similar users. Finally ratings were predicted by summing up all rating values from similar users. Results from experiments have indicated that the use of trust can decrease MAE and increase Coverage in a sparse dataset compared with User Similarity-based CF and Item Similarity-based CF.

3 Methodology

3.1 Conventional Method

Normally, the task in CF can be of two forms [13]: prediction and recommendation. Prediction is a numeric value expressing the predicted rating score on an item from a particular user (we will denote this user as the active user). Recommendation is to recommend a list of items the active user will like probably. We choose prediction as our task to implement with the hotel data set, i.e., predict rating values within the same scale (e.g., from 0 to 10) for the active user on hotels he or she has no experience before. Collaborative filtering usually follows two steps [27]: *1) Find neighbors who share the same rating pattern for the active user a; 2) Assign a weight for each neighbor found in the first step of user a and use their ratings to calculate predictions for user a.* We use the classical memory-based CF formula [18] as the basis of our algorithm to normalize the two steps:

$$p_{a,j} = \bar{r}_a + \frac{\sum\limits_{i=1}^{n} w(a,i)(r_{i,j} - \bar{r}_i)}{\sum\limits_{i=1}^{n} w(a,i)} \qquad (1)$$

where $p_{a,j}$ is the predicted rating of the active user a for item j. $\bar{r}_a$ and $\bar{r}_i$ is the mean rating score for user a and user i respectively. In Equation (1), n is the number of users in the collaborative filtering database with nonzero weights. $w(a,i)$ is the weights of n similar users and it can be decided by several different ways, such as K-nearest neighbor, Pearson Correlation Coefficient (PCC) and Cosine distance. PCC requires user a and user i have at least two co-rated items. In consideration of actual situation in our case, it is difficult to find more than one co-rated items between two users, so we choose k-nearest neighbor as weighting method due to its flexibility in defining neighbors.

To extend the scope of neighbors of users, we use k-means clustering to classify items into K clusters. K-means clustering is a term within the context of data mining, which aims to partition n observations into k clusters in which each observation belongs to the cluster with the nearest mean [28]. Here we partition the item set I into K clusters according to nine numerical attributes of each item: star level, number of total votes, average score, rating values corresponding to five aspects-clean, comfort, location, service, staff and value for money. We name this process as Fuzzification of items because all items were fuzzified into K clusters and users who have co-rated hotels in the same cluster can be correlated together. In this sense, much more neighbors can be found even when the active user has voted only one item. According to our data set, the scope of neighbors for an active user a can be defined as follow:

$$\begin{cases} ||C_a| - |C_i|| \leq \frac{K}{\theta_1} \\ |C_a \cap C_i| \geq \min\{|C_a|, |C_i|\} \times \theta_2 \xrightarrow{\ yields\ } i \in N_a \\ |\bar{r}_a - \bar{r}_i| \leq \theta_3, |\sigma_a - \sigma_i| \leq \theta_4 \end{cases} \tag{2}$$

Here $|C_a|$ is the number of C_a. θ_1 is a threshold parameter combined with K. $C_a \cap C_i$ is the intersection set of clusters that I_a and I_i falls in at the same time. θ_2 refers to a percentage parameter, e.g., 50%. θ_3 and θ_4 are two thresholds for the distance of mean value and standard deviation between two users.

3.2 Trust-Enhanced Method

After making rating predictions for the items used by users with conventional method, another question was triggered naturally: Can we make the predicted results more accurate? The answer is undoubtedly true. Past experiences in attempting to incorporate the concept of trust into recommender systems have shown encouraging results. In our case, trust inference is still a problem, because we just know the rating relations from users to items. Here we need to define trust value for a user i as $trust_i$ and it can be generated from three different angels based on our data sets:

1)Trust-1: $trust_i$ equals to the distance between the mean rating value $\bar{r}_i$ and the total mean rating value $\bar{t}_i$ for user i. As can be shown in Equation (3), we simply define $trust_i$ as the reciprocal of the absolute distance between $\bar{r}_i$ and $\bar{t}_i$ for user i.

$$trust_i = \frac{1}{|\bar{r}_i - \bar{t}_i|}. \tag{3}$$

The intuition behind this computation is that if user is actual rating value is nearly the same as the total rating value then user i is more trustworthy, i.e., $trust_i$ is allocated a relatively large value than other users. The total rating value t_j can be considered as the more truthful rating value for an item j. And the mean total rating value $\bar{t}_i$ can be defined as below:

$$\bar{t}_i = \frac{1}{|I_i|} \sum_{j \in I_i} t_j. \tag{4}$$

Trust-2: $trust_i$ is determined by the group type of user i, e.g., family with children or couple usually has higher trust value than group of friends. Stemmed from this idea, we assigned different values for each user according to their group type and listed them in Table 1.

Table 1. Trust value based on different group types and their percentage

Group type	Group id	$trust_i$	Percentage	Count
Family with young children	FY	70%	6.80%	7686
Family with older children	FO	70%	8.70%	9945
Group of friends	GF	40%	18.50%	21056
Young couple	YC	55%	21.30%	24276
Solo traveler	ST	50%	22.20%	25276
Mature couple	MC	60%	22.50%	25599
Total	-	-	100%	113838

From Table 1 we can see that users whose group type is family with children or mature couple were assigned a relatively big trust value, while group of friends and solo traveler were allocated a relatively small value. This is on the basis of our common sense that family with children usually needs to think about the childrens feelings and will probably give more objective and impartial ratings. Experienced people like mature couples judgment are also more trustworthy than young people.

Trust-3: $trust_i$ can be evaluated by the number of items that user i has voted $|I_i|$. We assume that users who have more experience should be more trustworthy. Hence we simple define $trust_i$ as $|I_i|$, as indicated in Equation(5):

$$trust_i = |I_i| . \tag{5}$$

The next step of out trust-enhanced method is simply to adjust weight computation measure by replacing w(a,i) with $trust_i$ in Equation (1). Thus we have a new Equation (6) which entails the effect of trust:

$$p_{a,j} = \bar{r_a} + \frac{\sum_{i=1}^{n} trust_i \left(r_{i,j} - \bar{r}_i \right)}{\sum_{i=1}^{n} trust_i} . \tag{6}$$

The intuition behind this computation is that users who have higher trust value will account for a greater proportion when giving suggestions to the active user a. In the former situation, w(a,i)=1 is a constant so that each neighbor account for the same proportion when giving suggestions to the active user a. Therefore we assume that this adjustment on weight computation will make the predictions more accurate.

4   Experiment

4.1   Datasets and Tools

The purpose of this section is to implement and compare the conventional method with trust-enhanced method presented in section 3, based on our hotel datasets. Our hotel datasets were generated from *Booking.com* (http://www.
(booking.com). We randomly selected a number of rating records from hotels

located in 8 cities in Europe from May, 2011 till July, 2012 to form the original dataset. These cities are Barcelona, Berlin, London, Paris, Prague, Rome, Stockholm and Zrich. After fundamental data analysis and processing, unimportant columns and duplicated rows were removed from original dataset, totally 123,296 ratings were obtained from 113,838 users and 5,291 hotels, ranging from 2.5 to 10.0. This leads to the sparsity problem that we have mentioned previously, because most users experience were not enough to generate a reasonably distributed dataset: 95% of all guests reviewed only one hotel, as indicated in Fig. 1.

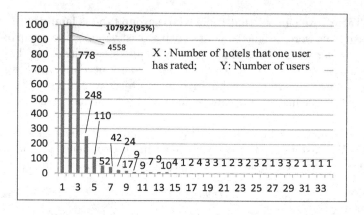

Fig. 1. Distribution of number of hotels that one user rated

4.2   Evaluation Metrics

For the purpose of evaluating and comparing the performance of each algorithm, we apply two metrics which are commonly used in the field of recommender systems to evaluate each algorithm: Mean Absolute Error (MAE) and Coverage [13, 14, 17, 19]. *1) MAE (Mean Absolute Error) is the average absolute deviation of the actual rating values to the predicted values.* Thus the lower the MAE, the more accurately the recommender algorithm because the predicted values do not vary very far from true ratings; *2) Coverage is another important metric to estimate recommender engines is coverage for rating predictions.* Higher coverage values indicate an algorithm can provide a relatively complete prediction for users.

4.3   Experimental Results

In this section we present our experimental results of applying both conventional method and trust-enhanced methods to implement the predictions and evaluate the results by using MAE and Coverage.

Performance of Different Prediction Methods. We implement the CF algorithm based on four different weight computation measures as described in methodology part. For each prediction method, we use training set to implement algorithm and predict rating values for hidden ratings in testing set. Parameters α, θ_2, θ_3, θ_4, K were not varied and a set of MAE values were generated for each method.

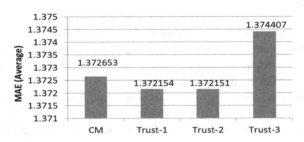

Fig. 2. Impact of the weight computation measure on collaborative filtering algorithm

It can be concluded from Fig. 2 that although the difference of performance between each measure is not very significant, the use of trust still affects the result. Trust-1 and Trust-2 proves to generate more accurate predictions than conventional method on average with our dataset. However, Trust-3 does not show advantage in improving prediction accuracy. This result indicates that if we inference trust value based on the difference between the actual rating value and total rating value (Trust-1) or based on group type of users (Trust-2), the prediction might be more accurate than using conventional weight computation method, although in some cases the conventional method proves to be the best one (see Table 2 in Appendix).

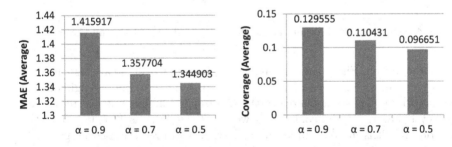

Fig. 3. Sensitivity of training ratio α on MAE and Coverage

Fig. 3 illustrates the average value of MAE and Coverage when α equals to different values. It can be observed from this figure that when $\alpha = 0.5$, the prediction result is more accurate on average but the prediction coverage is comparatively lower than in other conditions, i.e., a smaller proportion of hidden ratings can be predicted when α is lower. When α is set to 0.9, the Coverage is higher but this is at the cost of prediction accuracy.

Sensitivity of Training Ratio α. The first parameter we varied in our experiment is training ratio of experimental ratings α. Totally 15,229 ratings were selected as experimental data from 123,296 ratings. After that we set training ratio α as 0.9, 0.7 and 0.5 respectively, with a result of 1,363, 3,798 and 5,882 ratings hidden from experimental data. Then we find neighbors for the hidden users corresponding to the hidden ratings and make predictions for them using different methods.

Sensitivity of Threshold Parameters θ_2, θ_3, θ_4. The second parameters we varied in our experiments are threshold parameters that help to filter neighbors for testing users. As described in section 3, θ_2 represents the degree of similarity of two users when selecting items to use. Hence if θ_2 was set to a larger value, less neighbors can be found for testing users because it requires that two users should share a relatively big proportion of common clusters in items, i.e., they have strongly similar taste in choosing items to use. θ_3 and θ_4 are threshold parameters help to measure similarity of two users. θ_3 is threshold for the difference of mean rating values between two users and θ_4 is threshold for the difference of standard deviations of rating values. Hence if θ_3 and θ_4 were set to a smaller value, more users will be filtered out.

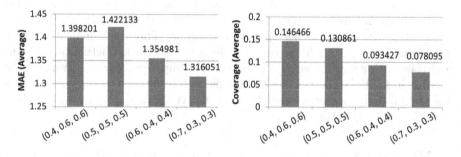

Fig. 4. Sensitivity of threshold parameters (θ_2, θ_3, θ_4) on MAE and Coverage

We can see from Fig. 4 that the average MAE and Coverage are also affected by this parameter. When we set (θ_2, θ_3, θ_4) as (0.4, 0.6, 0.6), more neighbors can be found for testing users therefore the Coverage is higher but the prediction accuracy is lower. On the contrary, if we set (θ_2, θ_3, θ_4) as (0.7, 0.3, 0.3), the prediction result is more accurate at the cost of high prediction coverage.

Sensitivity of Number of Clusters K. The third parameter we varied in our experiments is the total number of clusters for items K. Obviously K also influences the prediction accuracy and coverage as can be seen from Fig. 5. The Coverage becomes lower as K is set to be higher. This might be due to the reason that items were partitioned into smaller clusters thus making it difficult to find similar users who share the same proportion of clusters for items. However, there is no obvious pattern about how K affects the mean absolute error. When K = 30, MAE proves to be the least one but the Coverage is too low to generate reasonable predictions. When K = 10, though MAE = 1.37 is a little higher than MAE = 1.34 when K = 30, the Coverage = 0.17 is much better than that in any other conditions. Thus it can be concluded that it is better to set K as a relatively small number, e.g., K = 10.

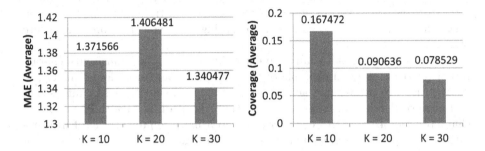

Fig. 5. Sensitivity of total number of clusters for items K on MAE and Coverage

We can see that the use of trust do really influence the prediction accuracy, though the improvement is not very significant here. Trust-2 proves to perform better than the other weight computation methods, which means the weight computation based on group type of users is better than the other weight computation methods. In general, rules from our analysis indicate that there exists a trade-off between the prediction accuracy and coverage, i.e., prediction accuracy is at the cost of prediction coverage and vice versa. However, when we set number of clusters K as 10, the Coverage (0.167472) is much higher than in any other conditions and the MAE is also better in Trust-2 (1.371566 < 1.372151).

5   Conclusion

5.1   Contributions

Our contributions in this paper are mainly focused on the following aspects. Firstly, we collected large amount of real data on hotel ratings and user information from a well-known accommodation booking website Booking.com. Secondly, we proposed a novel computational model incorporated with CF, k-nearest neighbor, k-means clustering techniques and three different definitions of trust to make rating predictions of items, and tested it with our hotel data sets to verify the feasibility of trust. Thirdly, we avoid using the conventional rating matrix to store data due to large amount of null values, instead we define new data structures like User, Item and Rating which helps to save memory.

One critical aspect of contributions in this paper is that we use k-means clustering to assign each hotel a cluster id. This innovation makes it easier for us to find the relevance of two users on their preference when choosing and rating items, on the basis of the common clusters of items that two users has voted, and their rating pattern on these clusters.

5.2 Future Work

Future work will be focused on the question: What will happen if we apply trust propagation into our model? What should be noticed here is the complexity of trust, which was denoted by Elizabeth Chang [16], that trust is composed by three fuzzy and dynamic characteristics: Implicitness, Asymmetry and Transitivity in trust. However, in our case, asymmetry and transitivity had not been taken into consideration thus this is something that we can improve in future work.

Trust propagation is actually the exemplification of the Transitivity characteristic of trust. A good example of trust propagation can be found in [17], in which trust was propagated according to a weighted sum of plus or minus sign and numerical values of users similarity. However, it didnt take the Asymmetry characteristic of trust into consideration. So a more improved way of incorporating trust propagation should consider both Transitivity and Asymmetry of trust.

References

1. Ricci, F., Rokach, L., Shapira, B.: Recommender Systems Handbook. Springer, Berlin (2011)
2. Adomavicius, G., YoungOk, K.: New recommendation techniques for multicriteria rating systems. IEEE Intelligent Systems 22(3), 48–55 (2007)
3. Balabanovic, M., Yoav, S.: Fab: content-based, collaborative recommendation. Communications of the ACM 40(3), 66–72 (1997)
4. Burke, R.: Hybrid recommender systems: Survey and experiments. User Modeling and User-Adapted Interaction 12(4), 331–370 (2002)
5. Levy, M., Klaas, B.: Music recommendation and the long tail. In: 1st Workshop on Music Recommendation and Discovery (WOMRAD), ACM RecSys, pp. 899–908. ACM, Barcelona (2010)
6. Goldberg, D., Nichols, D., Oki, B.M., Terry, D.: Using collaborative filtering to weave an information tapestry. Communications of the ACM 35(12), 61–70 (1992)
7. Resnick, P., Hal, R.V.: Recommender systems. Communications of the ACM 40(3), 56–58 (2005)
8. Adomavicius, G., Alexander, T.: Toward the next generation of recommender systems: A survey of the state-of-the-art and possible extensions. IEEE Transactions on Knowledge and Data Engineering 17(6), 734–749 (2005)
9. Schafer, J.B., Joseph, A.K., John, R.: E-commerce recommendation applications. Data mining and Knowledge Discovery 5(1), 115–153 (2001)
10. Linden, G., Brent, S., Jeremy, Y., Themistoklis, K.: Amazon.com recommendations: Item-to-item collaborative filtering. IEEE Internet Computing 7(1), 76–80 (2003)
11. Ge, Y., Xiong, H., Tuzhilin, A., Xiao, K., Gruteser, M., Pazzani, M.: An energy-efficient mobile recommender system. In: The 16th ACM SIGKDD International Conference on Knowledge Discovery and Data Mining, pp. 899–908. ACM, New York (2010)
12. Breese, J.S., David, H., Carl, K.: Empirical analysis of predictive algorithms for collaborative filtering. In: The Fourteenth Conference on Uncertainty in Artificial Intelligence, pp. 43–52. Morgan Kaufmann, San Francisco (1998)

13. Sarwar, B., Karypis, G., Konstan, J., Riedl, J.: Item-based collaborative filtering recommendation algorithms. In: The 10th International Conference on World Wide Web (WWW 2001), pp. 285–295. ACM, New York (2001)
14. ODoherty, D., Salim, J., Peter, V.R.: Trust-based recommendation: an empirical analysis. In: The Sixth ACM SIGKDD Workshop on Social Network Mining and Analysis (SNA-KDD). ACM, Beijing (2012)
15. Jing, W., Jian, Y., Yuzhang, L., Chuangguang, H.: Trust-based collaborative filtering. In: 2011 Eighth International Conference on Fuzzy Systems and Knowledge Discovery (FSKD), vol. 4, pp. 2650–2654. IEEE, Shanghai (2011)
16. Elizabeth, C., Farookh, H., Tharam, D.: Trust and reputation for service-oriented environments: Technologies for building business intelligence and consumer confidence. John Wiley & Sons (2006)
17. Papagelis, M., Plexousakis, D., Kutsuras, T.: Alleviating the sparsity problem of collaborative filtering using trust inferences. In: Herrmann, P., Issarny, V., Shiu, S.C.K. (eds.) iTrust 2005. LNCS, vol. 3477, pp. 224–239. Springer, Heidelberg (2005)
18. Resnick, P., Iacovou, N., Suchak, M., Bergstorm, P., Riedl, J.: GroupLens: an open architecture for collaborative filtering of netnews. In: The 1994 ACM Conference on Computer Supported Cooperative Work, pp. 175–186. ACM (1994)
19. Massa, P., Avesani, P.: Trust-aware collaborative filtering for recommender systems. In: Meersman, R. (ed.) OTM 2004. LNCS, vol. 3290, pp. 492–508. Springer, Heidelberg (2004)
20. Huming, G., Weili, L.: A Hotel Recommendation System Based on Collaborative Filtering and Rankboost Algorithm. In: The Second International Conference on Multimedia and Information Technology (MMIT), pp. 317–320. IEEE Computer Society, Washington, DC (2010)
21. Huang, Z., Hsinchun, C., Daniel, Z.: Applying associative retrieval techniques to alleviate the sparsity problem in collaborative filtering. ACM Transactions on Information Systems (TOIS) 22(1), 116–142 (2004)
22. Su, X., Taghi, M.K.: A survey of collaborative filtering techniques. Advances in Artificial Intelligence, 4:2 (2009)
23. Bart, N.: Trust: Forms, foundations, functions, failures and figures. Edward Elgar Publishing, Inc., Cheltenham (2002)
24. Sztompka, P., Kesselman, C.: Zaufanie: fundament spoleczenstwa. Znak (2007)
25. Massa, P., Paolo, A.: Controversial users demand local trust metrics: An experimental study on epinions. com community. In: The 20th National Conference on Artificial Intelligence, vol. 1, pp. 121–126. AAAI Press, Pittsburgh (2005)
26. Golbeck, J., James, H.: Filmtrust: Movie recommendations using trust in web-based social networks. In: 3rd IEEE in Consumer Communications and Networking Conference, vol. 1, pp. 282–286. IEEE Press, University of Maryland (2006)
27. Collaborative filtering, http://en.wikipedia.org/wiki/Collaborative_filtering
28. K-means_clustering, http://en.wikipedia.org/wiki/K-means_clustering

Appendix

Table 2. Notation and Terminology in this article

Sets:
U = set of all users in dataset denoted by i,   i = $\{1, \ldots, M\}$
I = set of all items in dataset denoted by j,   j = $\{1, \ldots, N\}$
R = set of all ratings in dataset denoted by k,   k = $\{1, \ldots, L\}$
I_i = set of items on which user i has rated
C_i = set of clusters to which I_i belongs
N_i = set of neighbors of user i
P_i = set of predicted items of user i
R' = set of experimental ratings from users whose $|I_i| > 1$
R'_t = set of hidden ratings with training ratio α from **R'**
U'_t = set of users whose ratings belong to R'_t
Variables:
t_j = total rating value of item j
$r_{i,j}$ = rating value of item j by user i
$p_{i,j}$ = predicted rating value of item j by user i
$\bar{t_i}$ = mean total rating value for user i
$\bar{r_i}$ = mean rating value for user i
σ_i = standard deviation of rating values for user i
$w(a, i)$ = weight between active user a and user i
P = number of predictions made by one algorithm
N = number of ratings expected to be predicted by one algorithm
Parameters:
K = total number of clusters for items set **I**
α = training ratio of experimental ratings set **R'**
$\theta_1, \theta_2, \theta_3, \theta_4$ = threshold parameters to filter neighbors for user i in equation (2)

Table 3. Complete experimental results on MAE and Coverage when choosing different parameters

Training ratio α	Threshold parameters $(\theta_2, \theta_3, \theta_4)$	Number of cluster K	MAE of CM	MAE of Trust 1	MAE of Trust 2	MAE of Trust 3	Coverage
0.9	(0.4, 0.6, 0.6)	10	1.35885	1.3606	1.35972	1.35919	0.23991
		20	1.50017	1.49752	1.49961	1.49702	0.146
		30	1.47728	1.47516	1.47709	1.48479	0.13353
	(0.5, 0.5, 0.5)	10	1.37709	1.37674	1.37782	1.37999	0.21717
		20	1.53767	1.53592	1.53734	1.53745	0.12546
		30	1.52705	1.52434	1.52665	1.52432	0.11519
	(0.6, 0.4, 0.4)	10	1.33374	1.33483	1.33469	1.33434	0.15334
		20	1.47678	1.47657	1.47651	1.476	0.08584
		30	1.42795	1.42739	1.4285	1.42783	0.0785
	(0.7, 0.3, 0.3)	10	1.28044	1.28159	1.28113	1.28131	0.12913
		20	1.37302	1.37211	1.37277	1.37163	0.06897
		30	1.32126	1.32096	1.32084	1.32246	0.06163
0.7	(0.4, 0.6, 0.6)	10	1.37691	1.37451	1.37537	1.38091	0.21037
		20	1.34935	1.34606	1.34654	1.35982	0.11532
		30	1.37676	1.37731	1.37537	1.38336	0.10532
	(0.5, 0.5, 0.5)	10	1.38256	1.37971	1.38101	1.38703	0.19484
		20	1.38783	1.38338	1.38503	1.39552	0.10321
		30	1.41474	1.41508	1.41332	1.41958	0.09189
	(0.6, 0.4, 0.4)	10	1.36404	1.36296	1.3629	1.36921	0.14797
		20	1.3419	1.33821	1.33961	1.34733	0.06925
		30	1.29522	1.29565	1.29384	1.29796	0.05977
	(0.7, 0.3, 0.3)	10	1.3495	1.3496	1.34949	1.35044	0.12428
		20	1.34179	1.3423	1.34154	1.3432	0.05635
		30	1.30595	1.30702	1.30572	1.30736	0.0466
0.5	(0.4, 0.6, 0.6)	10	1.42088	1.42178	1.42094	1.4206	0.17919
		20	1.42398	1.42334	1.42322	1.42439	0.10337
		30	1.29656	1.29741	1.29588	1.29697	0.08518
	(0.5, 0.5, 0.5)	10	1.44423	1.44491	1.44411	1.44475	0.16627
		20	1.44042	1.44061	1.44018	1.44088	0.09198
		30	1.28709	1.288	1.28689	1.28756	0.07174
	(0.6, 0.4, 0.4)	10	1.40063	1.40079	1.40049	1.40101	0.13176
		20	1.37934	1.37978	1.37932	1.37921	0.06528
		30	1.17372	1.17402	1.17354	1.1735	0.04913
	(0.7, 0.3, 0.3)	10	1.36532	1.36552	1.3652	1.36579	0.11544
		20	1.32714	1.32737	1.327	1.32742	0.05661
		30	1.17834	1.17851	1.17825	1.17853	0.04386
Average value			1.372653	1.372154	1.372151	1.374407	0.112212

How to Decide Upon Stopping a Heuristic Algorithm in Facility-Location Problems?

Xiangli Meng[*,**] and Kenneth Carling[*]

School of Technology and Business Studies,
Dalarna university, SE-791 88 Falun, Sweden
xme@du.se

Abstract. Solutions to combinatorial optimization, such as p-median problems of locating facilities, frequently rely on heuristics to minimize the objective function. The minimum is sought iteratively and a criterion is needed to decide when the procedure (almost) attains it. However, pre-setting the number of iterations dominates in OR applications, which implies that the quality of the solution cannot be ascertained. In this paper we compare the methods proposed previous literate of estimating minimum, and propose some thought of it.

Keywords: p-median problem, Simulated Annealing, discrete optimization, extreme value theory.

1   Introduction

Consider the problem of finding a solution to $\min_\Theta f(\Theta)$ where the large amount of data and potential solutions renders analytical solutions infeasible. For example, consider the p-median problem on the network. The problem is to allocate P facilities to a population geographically distributed in Q demand points such that the population's average or total distance to its nearest service center is minimized. Hakimi (1964) considered the task of locating telephone switching centers and showed later that, in a network, the optimal solution of the p-median model existed at the nodes of the network [1]. If N is the number of nodes, then the number of possible locations of facilities amounts to $\binom{N}{P}$, making the data set enormously large and rendering an enumeration of all possibilities infeasible.

To overcome that problem, much research try to use efficient (heuristic) algorithms to solve the p-median. In this work we will rely on a common heuristic known as Simulated Annealing. It is well described by Lenanova and Loresh [2]. The virtue of Simulated Annealing as other heuristics is that the algorithm will iterate towards a good solution, not necessarily the actual optimum.

---

[*] Kenneth Carling is a professor in Statistics and Xiangli Meng is a PhD-student in Micro-data analysis at the School of Technology and Business Studies, Dalarna university, SE-791 88 Falun, Sweden. We are grateful to partcipants at INFORMS Euro 2013 in Rome for useful comments on a previous version. Financial support from the Swedish Retail and Wholesale Development Council is gratefully acknowledged.
[**] Corresponding author.

Z. Huang et al. (Eds.): WISE 2013 Workshops 2013, LNCS 8182, pp. 280–283, 2014.

The overall aim of this paper is to provide a discussion of determining when a good solution is found and the algorithm may be stopped. While there is an ample literature on heuristic algorithms, only a few papers address the stopping criterion. Accordingly, the prevailing practice is to run the heuristic algorithm for a pre-specified number of iterations or until improvements in the solution becomes infrequent. Such practice does not lend itself to determine the quality of the solution in a specific problem and is therefore unsatisfactory.

This paper is organized as follows: in section two we review suggested methods for statically estimating the minimum of the objective function and add some further remarks on the issue. In the third section we compare statistical estimates of minimum. In section four we provide a intended computer experiment. At last, the fifth section gives a discussion of potential results.

2   Review of Previous Attempts

There have been quite a few researches on finding out the stopping rule when applying heuristics. Zhigljavsky and Hamilton [3] estimate the required time of each step for the solution to improve, and give the confidence interval. The heuristic process would stop when the confidence interval is small enough. The problem with that is the required time for getting improvement in the process is a variable, which increase the uncertainty of getting decent estimate, and it could not measure the quality of estimates.

More research goes to another direction, which depends on estimating the minimum and stops the process until it is close enough to the minimum. Before explaining them, we introduce the notations used throughout the paper:

z_p = feasible solution of locating P facilities in N nods, indexed by p, p = $1, 2, \dots, \binom{N}{p}$.

A = the set of all feasible solutions $A = \left\{ z_1, z_2, \dots, z_{\binom{N}{P}} \right\}$.

$g(z_p)$ = the objective function of solution z_p.

$\theta = \min_A g(z_p)$.

$\hat{\theta}$ = an estimator of θ.

$\tilde{x}_r^s$ = the heuristic solution in the rth iteration of the sth sample.

There are mainly two approaches that are proposed for estimating the minimum being the Jackknifing approach (hereafter JK) and extreme value theory approach (EVT). The JK-estimator is introduced by Quenouille [4].

$$\hat{\theta}_{JK} = \sum_{i=0}^{J} (-1)^i \binom{J+1}{i+1} g_{(i+1)}$$

where J is the order, $g_{(i)}$ is the ith smallest value in a random. Dannenbring [5] and suggest to use the first order, i.e. $J = 1$, for point estimating the minimum. Their argument is a bias of order n^{-2} and a mean square error being lower for the first order compared with higher orders as shown by Robson and Whitlock [6]. Nydick and Weiss also compare the case using other auxiliary information like heuristic solutions.

Derigs [7] discusses using EVT to estimate the optimum. In contrast to the JK-approach of choosing one random sample, he chooses S random samples and considers

$g_{(1)}$ of each sample an extreme value assumed to follow the Weibull distribution. The EVT-estimator of the minimum is the smallest value of the s extreme values, and Derigs [7] also derives a confidence interval for the minimum. Later Wilson, King and Wilson [8], referring to others work, employ the idea of substituting the extreme values obtained from a random sample by those produced as best solutions in s runs of a heuristics, i.e. $\tilde{x}_r^s$. In that case a $100(1 - e^{-s})\%$ confidence interval is found as $[\min(\tilde{x}_r^s) - \hat{b}, \min(\tilde{x}_r^s)]$, where $\hat{b}$ is the estimated shape parameter of the Weibull distribution. Consequently, the EVT approach offers a measure of uncertainty of its estimator in contrast to the JK approach.

3   Computer Experiment

We plan to use the problems in OR-lib to estimate the performance. The minimum θ of the 40 problems are known and the problems vary substantially in N and P.

Table 1. Illustration of the JK and EVT approaches on the 1st OR-lib problem

	Optimum	Estimator	St. Dev.	99.99%-CI
JK	5817	6650	68.26	[6445—6707]
EVT	5817	6339	157.52	[-1256—6339]

Table 1 gives an example of the two approaches by means of the first p-median problem in the OR-library presented in Beasley (1990). For the illustration we randomly picked z_p of size 100, computed the corresponding objective functions $g(z_p)$, and obtained $\hat{\theta}_{JK} = 2g_{(1)} - g_{(2)}$. To illustrate the EVT approach, we set $S = 10$ with each one based on a random sample of size $n = 100$ from A. The smallest value in each of $S = 10$ cases is used to estimate the parameters of the Weibull distribution. In line with Wilson et al. (2004), we used least squares estimation of the Weibull parameters with the Nelder-Mead simplex search procedure. For $s = 10$, the level of the confidence interval is presumed to be $100(1 - e^{-s})\% \approx 99.99\%$.

Neither of the approaches offers an estimate of the standard deviation of the estimator. We suggest the following methods to estimate their standard deviations and the 99% confidence interval for JK estimator. The bootstrap method is proposed to estimate it for the JK-estimator. Furthermore, we propose as a confidence interval $[\hat{\theta}_{JK} - 3\sigma^*(\hat{\theta}_{JK}), \min g(z_p)]$, where $\sigma^*(\hat{\theta}_{JK})$ is the standard deviation of $\hat{\theta}_{JK}$ obtained from bootstrapping. With the scalar 3, the level corresponds to 99.9% provided that the sampling distribution of the estimator being Normal. The quantities drawing on bootstrapping are shown in Table 1 as well as the standard deviation of the EVT-estimator obtained from the s sample-minima, and they are given in italics.

The JK approach is known to perform poorly, as also evident in this example with an estimator 10% off the actual minimum. The problem lays in the required size of the random sample. The objective function in p-median problems might be regarded as approximately Normal with a truncation in the left tail being the minimum θ. A good estimate of θ would require a random sample with some values near to θ. For θ far out in the tail, the required sample size to get such values would be huge. We show below that for many of the OR-library p-median problems, the minimum is at least some 6 standard deviations away from the mean requiring a sample size of $1/\Phi(-6) \approx 10^9$ (Φ is the standard Normal distribution function) to render hope of obtaining a random sample containing values close to θ. Such a computational effort is better spent at searching for the minimum by means of an effective heuristic.

4   Conclusions

The problems in large data set would increase the difficulty in estimating the minimum, thus the performance of different estimators would be deteriorated. But on the whole, EVT approach provides us with better performance in estimating minimum, but on the other hand, it will also require large sample size. Thus if we choose a large sample and use that sample to estimate the minimum, it will cost us more time. On the other hand, strategy like this would require more efficient results for stopping the heuristic process. However, if we choose to have a smaller sample to estimate the minimum, it will lead to a worse estimate of the minimum, but would save computational time. The saved time could be distributed to reaching for the minimum.

We have limited the study to location problems be means of the p-median problems with $g(z_p)$ being the average or total distance of the population to its nearest facility. Other combinatorial problems may imply objective functions of a more complicated. We are uncertain on how the two methods would work under such circumstances and, hence, further investigations are required along such lines.

References

1. Beasley, J.E.: OR library: Distributing test problems by electronic mail. Journal of Operational Research Society 41(11), 1067–1072 (1990)
2. Chiyoshi, F.Y., Galvão, R.D.: A statistical analysis of simulated annealing applied to the p-median problem. Annals of Operations Research 96, 61–74 (2000)
3. Dannenbring, D.G.: Procedures for estimating optimal solution values for large combinatorial problems. Management Science 23(12), 1273–1283 (1977)
4. Hakimi, S.L.: Optimum locations of switching centers and the absolute centers and medians of a graph. Operations Research 12(3), 450–459 (1964)
5. Hakimi, S.L.: Optimum Distribution of Switching Centers in a Communication Network and Some Related Graph Theoretic Problems. Operations Research 13(3), 462–475 (1965)
6. Kotz, S., Nadarajah, S.: Extreme value distributions, theory and applications. Imperial College Press (2000)
7. Levanova, T., Loresh, M.A.: Algorithm of ant system and simulated annealing for the p-median problem. Automation and Remote Control 65, 431–438 (2004)
8. Quenouille, M.H.: Notes on bias in estimation. Biometrika 43, 353–360 (1956)
9. Robson, D.S., Whitlock, J.H.: Estimation of a truncation point. Biometrika 51, 33–39 (1964)
10. Wilson, A.D., King, R.E., Wilson, J.R.: Case study on statistically estimating minimum makespan for flow line scheduling problems. European Journal of Operational Research 155, 439–454 (2004)
11. Zhigljavsky, A., Hamilton, E.: Stopping rules in k-adaptive global random search algorithms. Journal of Global Optimization 48(1), 87–97 (2010)

How Does Different Algorithm Work When Applied on the Different Road Networks When Optimal Location of Facilities Is Searched for in Rural Areas?

Pascal Rebreyend, Mengjie Han, and Johan Håkansson

Dalarna University, Sweden

Abstract. The p-median problem is often used to locate P service facilities in a geographically distributed population. Important for the performance of such a model is the distance measure. The first aim in this study is to analyze how the optimal location solutions vary, using the p-median model, when the road network is alternated. It is hard to find an exact optimal solution for p-median problems. Therefore, in this study two heuristic solutions are applied, simulating annealing and a classic heuristic. The secondary aim is to compare the optimal location solutions using different algorithms for large p-median problem. The investigation is conducted by the means of a case study in a rural region with a. asymmetrically distributed population, Dalecarlia. The study shows that the use of more accurate road networks gives better solutions for optimal location, regardless what algorithm that is used and regardless how many service facilities that is opt for. It is also shown that the Simulating annealing algorithm not just is much faster than the classic heuristic used here, but also in most cases gives better solutions.

Keywords: road network effect, p-median problem, simulated annealing heuristics, complex problem.

1 Introduction

1.1 Background

The facility location problem is a well-study problem (Farahani et al. 2012). A lot of works have been done in this area but most of them are not based on real road distances. Francis et al. (2009) gave an explicit summary on facility location problem. Among the 40 published articles, about half of them are studied on real data. Almost all of the distance measures are Euclidian distance and rectilinear distance.

The work in this study is followed by Håkansson et al. (2012) who investigated the optimal location of emergency hospitals on a network in a rural region, Dalecarlia in Sweden, with an asymmetric distributed population. To do so the p-median model was applied. It was shown that the use of Euclidean distance instead of other network based distance measures led to sub optimal location pattern of emergency hospitals.

Z. Huang et al. (Eds.): WISE 2013 Workshops 2013, LNCS 8182, pp. 284–291, 2014.

The road network in that study was limited to 1579 nodes. There was no investigation done of the effects on the suggested solutions by varying the density of the road network. However, differences in accuracy of the road networks could also affect the distance measures. Therefore, the primary aim of this paper is to analyze how the optimal location solutions vary, using the p-median model, when the road network is alternated. The investigation is conducted by the means of a case study in a rural region, Dalecarlia

In this study we increase the complexity of the road network that we use to find a optimal location in. Both the road networks we elaborate with in this paper are from the Swedish digital road system: NVDB (The National Road data Base). NVDB consists of the national roads and the local roads/street. The sparse road network is defined as the national roads and contains 1579 nodes. The dense road network is defined by adding local road/street to the national road network. This road network contains about 1.5 million nodes.

In this study we also increase the number of facilities to opt for. To do so we not only use emergency hospitals but also medical care centers in the region of Dalecarlia. The maximum number of facilities to be optimal located in this study is 34.

Several computer experiments using the p-median model was conducted. The p-median problem is NP-hard. The complexity depends both on the number of centers to be located and the number of demand points and the density of the road network. Since the exact optimal solution is difficult to obtain, the two heuristic solutions are compared. The experiments are conducted by a simulated annealing algorithm and a classical heuristic algorithm. This gives a secondary aim of the study that is to compare the optimal location solutions using different algorithms for large p-median problem.

To evaluate the effects of different road networks on the optimal location solutions we compare the results from the experiments with both algorithms in which we have alternate both the road networks and the number of facilities that are to be located. To evaluate the efficiency of the two algorithms we compare computing time and the optimal location solutions based on the same road networks and for the same number of located facilities. The best solution is the one that gives the smallest average distance for the population to travel to the closest service facility.

2   Literature Review

This p-median problem was first introduced by Hakimi (1964) The goal is to find p service centres which minimize the summed distances between demands and their nearest centres.

The p-median problem is NP-hard Kariv and Hakimi (1979). The complexity depends both on the number of centres to be located and the number of demand points. Therefore, for large number problems, the exact optimal solution is difficult to obtain. That why we have only a few studies examining the exact solutions (Hakimi, 1965; Marsten, 1972; Christofides, 1982; Galvão, 1980). More studies regarding p-median problem are heuristics and metaheuristics. See Ashayeri et al (2005); Rahman and Smith (1991); Kuehn and Hamburger (1963); Maranzana (1964); Crainic et al (2003) and Rolland et al (1996). One sub-class in metaheuristics is simulated annealing method , which we will examine in this paper. See Chiyoshi and Galvão (2000).

Although Euclidean distance is most widely used, the network distance is more accurate. The selection of distance measure does not only affect the optimal solution, but also affect the computational efficiency. Usually a denser network will also take more computing time to create the distance matrix. Peeters and Thomas (1995) examined the p-median problem for the different type of networks by changing the nature of the links. They only found the difference in optimal solutions but not in computational effort. Morris (1978) tested the linear programming algorithm for 600 random data sets, but the size is small and no real network is applied. Schilling et al (2000) examined the Euclidean distance, network distance and randomly generated network distance. Their conclusion is that it is much easier for the Euclidean and path network to obtain the optimal solution and less computational effort. However, neither did they make more comparison between the Euclidean network and the path network, nor did they provide the effect of network of different level of accuracy. When we are dealing with large (e.g. 1.5 million nodes), network approximation is an efficient way to decrease the computing speed. None of the previous studies provided any analysis of network approximation.

Therefore, the goal of this project is to handle real and accurate data for facilities localisation. Distances will be computed based on the real road network of different resolutions and Euclidean measure. Reaching excellent solutions is a challenge due to the size and complexity of data, which means both the accuracy of the optimal solution and computing time are affected by the number of facilities to be located and the number of possible locations. The accuracy and computing burden are contradicted to each other such that every algorithm aims at improving both of them. This paper, however, deals with extremely complex data set and it is very difficult to obtain the real optimal solution. Thus, two algorithms are suggested: one is time-consuming for huge data whereas the other one is flexible to control the stopping criteria.

3   Data

3.1   Road Network

The road networks are provided by the NVDB (The National Road Data Base). NVDB was formed in 1996 on behalf of the government and now operated by Swedish Transport Agency. NVDB is divided into national roads, local road and streets. The national roads are owned by the national public authorities, and the construction of them funded by a state tax. The local roads or streets are built and owned by private persons or companies or by local public authorities.

For comparison, experiments are executed under the sparse and dense road networks. The sparse road network only consists of the national roads, which contains 1,977 digital road segments and 1,579 nodes. The total road length is 5,437 kilometers. The dense road network is defined by adding local roads and streets to the national roads. The dense road network contains about 1.5 million nodes and 1,964,801 segments. The total length is 43431 kilometers. The extensions of the road networks used in the study is shown I figure 1a and 1b.

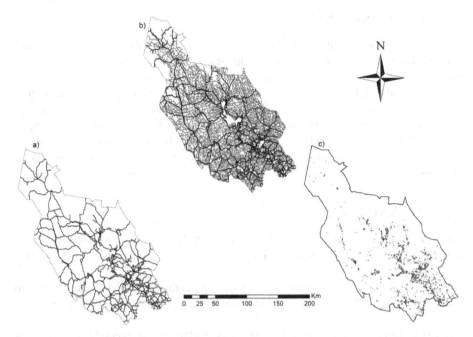

Fig. 1. a-c Map of Dalecarlia region showing 1a) the sparse road network (national roads), (1b) the dense road network (national and local roads/streets), (1c) and one-by-one kilometer cells where the population exceeds 5 inhabitants.

3.2   Facilities and Demand Points

In this paper, the emergency hospitals and care centers are considered as the facilities to be located. There are 5 hospitals in the region and there are 34 care centers. In the experiments we will find the optimal location pattern for 5, 8, 16 and 34 facilities.

The demand for health care is the population in 2002 in the region. The population is registered at squares by the size of 250m×250m. Each square is generalized to a point. Each point is weighted by the number of people living in each square. The population is then lives represented by 15,729 weighted points. The population data is from Statistics Sweden 2002 (www.scb.se). The total population number is 277,725. The distribution of the population is shown in figure 1c.

4   Algorithms

In case of a small number of facilities, an exhaustive search can be easily used. We have extracted in the Dalarna county the main nodes of the road network (around 1500 nodes) and we were able in less than 30 minutes to find optimal solution for 1 and 2 locations. The optimal solution for 3 locations has also been computed in few hours on a regular PC. In all cases, the location of each facility is on one the nodes of the network. But such approach cannot be used to the complexity of the problem when number of nodes or number of locations is much higher.

4.1   Classical Algorithm

A number of heuristic algorithms for p-median have been proposed (see literature review). Usually, two classes of such heuristics are suggested (Golden et al., 1980): construction algorithms and improvement algorithms. The myopic algorithm is a construction algorithm. The neighbourhood search and the exchange are improvement algorithm. The classical algorithm implemented in our paper consists of both of the two classes of heuristics. The idea is that the solution obtained by construction algorithm will not necessarily optimal; the improvement algorithms always take less computational burden given that the solution from construction algorithm is settled (Daskin, 1995).

4.2   Simulated Annealing

Since the localization problem is NP-complete, the algorithm proposed is a simulated annealing algorithm. This randomized algorithm has been chosen due to its flexibility and easiness to implement.

In our experiments, we are running a simulated annealing which either start from random solution either from the current solutions (only for cases with 5 or 34 locations).

Even if data are well preprocessed, an efficient algorithm is needed to compute solutions. Different algorithms exist for this kind of problem. In our case, the cost of evaluating a solution is rather high therefore we should focus on an algorithm which tries to keep the number of evaluated solutions low. This excludes for example algorithms such as genetic algorithm and to some extend Branch and Bound. On the other hand, we have or may have good starting point (based on current solutions or solutions pre-computed based on people localization). Therefore one good candidate is Simulated Annealing.

SA is like to cooling down some material from a high energy state to a low energy state. During this process, the particles are supposed to move to a steady configuration. The main problem is how to make this process best. If the cooling down speed is too fast, it would possibly cause sub-optimal solution. Otherwise, it will increase the annealing cost (such as time). Therefore, an appropriate controlling scheme is needed.

5   Experiment and Results

To make an explicit comparison, we run these two different algorithms on Euclidean distance, sparse network and the dense network. In Table 1 and Table 2, there are some results from the computer experiments using different road networks and different algorithms. The tables give information on the populations mean distance in the network to the closest located facility and the computing time. The results for 5, 8, 16 and 34 facilities are shown.

Table 1. Mean distance between population and nearest facilities for classical algorithm

centers	sparse network	dense network
5	21.97	20.25
8	14.99	14.62
16	9.51	9.70
34	6.11	5.43

Table 2. Mean distance between population and nearest facilities for simulated annealing algorithm

centers	sparse network	dense network
5	20.40	20.25
8	14.04	13.91
16	8.69	8.86
34	5.50	5.31

Firstly, we turn to the effect of using different road networks. In most cases a dense network gives a solution for the objective function that is about 4.54% better. However, depending on the number of facilities that have been located it can be more than 11% (the case with 34 facilities). From the table it could also be seen that the more facilities that are to be located the larger is the difference in the objective functions between the road networks. A last conclusion that could be drawn from the tables is that the improvement rates in the objective function, when the number of facilities to be located increases, is higher when a denser road network is used. For instance, the improvement when the number of facilities increases from 5 to 34 is 73% when the dense network is used, while it is 72% when the sparse network is used (75% to 74% for simulated annealing).

Turning to a comparison of the results produced by the two different algorithms, it is obvious that the use of simulating annealing algorithm gives much shorter computing times in general. Due to its structure, the computing time of the simulated annealing does not increase significantly when we increase the number of facilities. Simulating annealing also produce solutions with lower mean distances to travel to the closest facility regardless, network used and the number of facilities that are located. Further, it is also obvious that the when the simulating annealing is used together with an idea of where to begin the optimization process from in the space it can give better solutions compared to when the starting point is selected randomly. Lastly, for all cases, simulation annealing gets less improvement in the objective function when the road networks are alternated. This indicates that the solutions are more stable when the simulation annealing is used.

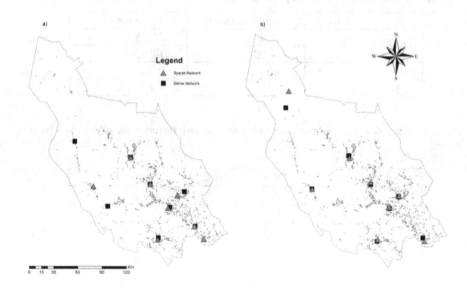

Fig. 2. Map of configurations for 8 hospitals: a) classical algorithm; b) simulated annealing algorithm

In Figure 2 the geographical configuration of best solution for 8 facilities are shown. When it comes to the configuration it is obvious that the use of different road network to opt at matters. For instance in the north western part of the county the solutions differ a lot. Another example that the road network has importance for the configuration could be seen in the more densely populated parts of the county. The visual difference might not be that large, however it involves a large part of the population in the county. Comparing Figure 2a with Figure 2b it is obvious that the use of different algorithms can give quit different solutions. Since the differences in configurations of facilities varies more depending on which road network that have been used when the classic algorithm for optimization have been used, it further indicates that classical heuristic of the kind used here is not as stable in its solutions as the simulating annealing algorithm.

6   Conclusion

This paper aims at examining the effect of road network density when facility location problem is studied. A first conclusion to draw from this study is that it is important to use as good road network as possible when a solution that gives as low mean distance for a population as possible to the closest facility is searched for. In this sense, we implement our experiment in a more realistic situation--optimizing the locations by travel time distance. We did not get worst solutions we a detailed network is used.

A second conclusion is that the use of simulating annealing gives better results when it comes to optimization. The results are also more stable and it is much faster, something needed when the complexity of the p-median problem increase.

References

1. Ashayeri, J., Heuts, R., Tammel, B.: A modified simple heuristic for the p-median problem, with facilities design applications. Robotics Comput.-Integrated Manufact. 21, 451–464 (2005)
2. Chiyoshi, F., Gao, R.: A statistical analysis of simulated annealing applied to the p-median problem. Annals of Operantions Research 96, 61–74 (2000)
3. Christofides, N., Beasley, J.: A tree search algorithm for the p-median problem. European Journal of Operational Research 10(2), 196–204 (1982)
4. Crainic, T., Gendreau, M., Hansen, P., Mladenović, N.: Parallel variable neighborhood search for the p-nedian. Les Cahiers du GERAD G 4 (2003)
5. Farahani, R.Z., Asgari, N., Heidari, N., Hosseininia, M., Goh, M.: Covering problems in facility location: A review. Computers and Industrial Engineering 62(1), 368–407 (2012)
6. Francis, R., Lowe, T., Rayco, M., Tamir, A.: Aggregation error for location models: survey and analysis. Annals of Operations Research 167, 171–208 (2009)
7. Galvao, R.D.: A dual-bounded algorithm for the p-median problem. Operations Research 28(5), 1112–1121 (1980)
8. Håkansson, J., Carling, K., Han, M.: Does euclidian distance work well when the p-median model is applied in rural areas? Dalarna University. Geographical Department (June 2012)
9. Hakimi, S.L.: Optimum locations of switching centers and the absolute centers and medians of graph. Operations Research 12(3), 450–459 (1964)
10. Hakimi, S.L.: Optimum distribution of switching centers in a communications network and some related graph theoretic problems. Operations Research 13, 462–475 (1965)
11. Kariv, O., Hakimi, S.L.: An algorithmic approach to network location problems. part 2: The p-median. SIAM J. Appl. Math. 37, 539–560 (1979)
12. Kuehn, A., Hamburger, M.: A heuristic program for locating warehouses. Manage. Sci. 9, 643–666 (1963)
13. Maranzana, F.: On the location of supply points to minimize transport costs. Oper. Res. 15, 261–270 (1964)
14. Marsten, R.: An algorithmic for finding almost all the medians of a network. Technical report 23, Center for Math Studies in Economics and Management Science, Northwestern University (1972)
15. Murray, A., Church, R.: Applying simulated annealing to planning-location models. Journal of Heuristics 2, 31–53 (1996)
16. Peeters, D., Thomas, I.: The effect of spatial structure on p-median results. Transportation Science 29, 366–373 (1995)
17. Rahman, S., Smith, D.: A comparison of two heuristic methods for the p-median problem with and without maximum distance constraints. Int. J. Open Product Manage. 11, 76–84 (1991)
18. Rolland, E., Schilling, D., Current, J.: An efficient tabu search procedure for the p-median problem. Eur. J. Oper. Res. 96, 329–342 (1996)

Multi-indexed Graph Based Knowledge Storage System

Hongming Zhu[1,2], Danny Morton[2], Wenjun Zhou[3], Qin Liu[1], and You Zhou[1]

[1] School of software engineering, Tongji University, China
{zhu_hongming,qin.liu}@tongji.edu.cn,
zyrusher@gmail.com
[2] Well-Being and Social Sciences, Bolton University, UK
dm3@bolton.ac.uk
[3] School of computer science, Tongji University, China
zhouwenjun77@hotmail.com

Abstract. With the rapid development of information technologies, knowledge management systems are facing the problem of how to manage the massive volume of data and make an efficient usage for the data. In this paper, we analyzed the current challenge of knowledge management system and proposed a multi-indexed graph based knowledge storage system to avoid the data duplication and optimized for parallel processing.

Keywords: Index, Storage System, Knowledge Management.

1 Introduction

With the development of information technologies, access to datasets from many different sources is an important part of any knowledge management process. It is still very difficult, however, to extract the exact meaning, or related attribute, of the knowledge within the dataset. This paper explores the framework for the management, coding, and analysis of large heterogeneous datasets.

In any knowledge management system, we usually find that the dataset comes from different sources with different formats, and varying degrees of structure. Some of the datasets are well structured, but there is also a lot of unstructured data arising from sources such as, wiki data, web data and social network data. The application of multiple sematic meanings to the same dataset, means that different applications may interpret or use the dataset in different ways. The objective of the research described in this paper was to design a framework of data storage, which would help overcome these problems in knowledge management systems.

2 Motivation

2.1 The Knowledge Management System Should Be Scalable and Optimized for Massive Dataset Analysis

With the massive explosion of data in knowledge management system, we have to handle large volumes of dataset during data analysis. How to avoid the data duplication

Z. Huang et al. (Eds.): WISE 2013 Workshops 2013, LNCS 8182, pp. 292–301, 2014.

in different knowledge analysis project and how to optimized for parallel process of the data becomes the key challenges in modern knowledge management system. A unified, scalable and parallel storage architecture is needed for knowledge management system.

2.2 Structured, Semi-structured and Unstructured Data Can Be Managed in the Same Way

In most of the knowledge management systems, the datasets will come from individuals or organizations. Some of these datasets will be well structured and based on the requirements of the originator, but it will not necessarily be very suitable for other analysis and processing around a different requirement. Indeed some datasets will be semi-structured and even unstructured, such as web data and social network datasets. The key is to design a storage and access system, which will work in the same way for all different types of dataset irrespective of their source and format.

2.3 Sematic Description Can Be Easily Added in the Dataset

In any knowledge management system, it is very difficult to define a proper schema for a data set and never change it. In different applications, we may focus on different schemas for the same dataset, and we may need to add more sematic meanings to the dataset during the process of analysis. For example, when dealing with a customer referral system, we may regard the address as a whole sentence but when dealing with a logistical application we may need to divide the address into countries, states, streets etc., in order to quantify the data. Within the storage system, one dataset may have several schemas depending on the application.

2.4 Sematic Meanings of Knowledge Can Be Easily Added in the Graph Based Knowledge Management System

In a knowledge management system, we will often have different definitions for the "knowledge". Knowledge is usually defined by certain properties and there may also be linkages between different parts of the knowledge dataset. In order to describe the different sematic meanings of "knowledge", we will regard a particular knowledge as a knowledge node type, atomic knowledge as an instance of a knowledge type node. For example, technical publications in a particular field can be regarded as a "knowledge node type"; a single publication in this field can be an instance of the node type. The "edge" is defined as the linkage between the knowledge nodes. For example, papers written by the same author. Thus we can build a heterogeneous graph for knowledge management problems. We will import the idea of a knowledge schema to describe the heterogeneous graph in the knowledge management system.

2.5 The Storage System Can Be Scalable and Have Good Performance in Knowledge Processing

With an increasing number of datasets within a knowledge management system, we have to think about the scalability, performance, and the processing of the data.

Distributed storage and processing is a potential solution for this problem. In order to get better performance, we do need to add some index in the distributed storage and process system. The index needs to be easily scaled. We can add and update an index based on graph schema, dataset schema, and the dataset. The index also needs to be processed in parallel for better performance. We will import the idea of index and delayed loading of a dataset into the knowledge management system.

3   Design Overview

The distributed storage system we proposed is based on the Google distributed file system GFS [6]. It contains four parts: data nodes, which contains the dataset; data schema nodes and graph knowledge schema nodes, which contain the dataset schema and graph schema; index nodes, which contain the index for the dataset; graph knowledge nodes, which contain the knowledge graph. Figure 1 shows the architecture of the proposed multi indexed knowledge management storage system.

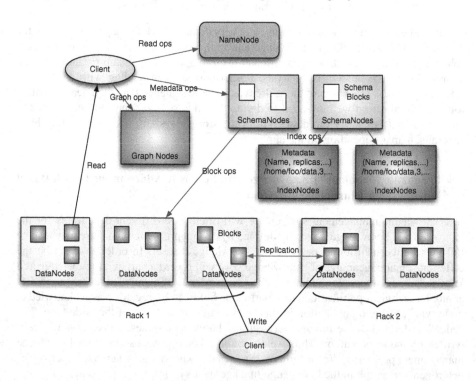

Fig. 1. The Logical Architecture of Multi-Indexed Storage System in Knowledge Management

The dataset is stored as a pure row data in the distributed file system based on Hadoop. Hadoop [7] is an open source software framework that supports data intensive distributed applications, is designed for big data processing, and supports the running of applications on large clusters of commodity hardware. We add index features in the Hadoop system to achieve the knowledge management system. We regard the dataset, no matter whether it is a structured data or unstructured data, as files, which will be stored in the Hadoop system as row files. During the processing, we also try to delay the read loading data of the dataset for better performance.

The data schema is the description about the dataset and the metadata of data index. One dataset may have more than one data schema. Each schema contains the self-described dataset structure and the metadata of the index. Since each row of data in the dataset has its own sematic meaning, the self-described dataset structure will present the position-sensitive or separate-sensitive meaning of the row data. The metadata of the index includes the availability of the index in each sematic meaning section of the dataset, the name, replicas, position of the index block. With the metadata of the index, we can easily find where is the index block. The data schema can be added when we import or first load the dataset, but we can also add more schemas after that.

The data index gives the metadata of the data blocks. With the index system, we can locate the exact position of the data blocks, so we can just start the minimal numbers of jobs to read the dataset, which reduces the total running jobs in the distributed storage and processing system. The data index can be built and updated dynamically, and based on the availability of the resource and the statistics of the query, we can choose how many indexes we need and update the index during the "off peak" time of the system.

The knowledge graph schema is very similar to the data schema. It is the description about knowledge heterogeneous graph and the metadata of the knowledge index. The information of the knowledge graph has three parts: node type, node and edge. Each category of the knowledge will be described as a node type; the instance of knowledge will be regarded as a knowledge node; and the edge will be the linkage of the two knowledge instances. The metadata of the knowledge index indicates whether the knowledge is indexed or not.

The knowledge graph node stores the knowledge graph. We regard knowledge as a heterogeneous graph; the knowledge graph node contains the knowledge atomic item and the linkage between knowledge atomic items. In order to avoid the duplication of data set, the knowledge node will only contains one or several pointers, which point to the dataset.

4   Details of Design

4.1   Name Node

The name node in our multi-indexed distributed knowledge management storage system is nearly the same as GFS name node. In GFS, the name node contain the metadata of the data node, but in our multi-indexed distributed knowledge management storage system, the index node contains the block metadata and a hash table of the logic block metadata and physical metadata. This means that in the event of hardware failure we do not need to update the index node.

4.2   Data Schema Node and Data Index Node

The data schema contains the semantic description of the data set. One dataset can have more than one schema. The schema is the description of the sematic meaning of the data set. It shows what kinds of the properties are in the data set, the metadata of the properties, the availability of index for each property and the metadata information of index for each property. A typical data schema file will contain six parts: dataset name, dataset description, property names, property description, property separation metadata and property index metadata. For the property separation metadata, it will support the separators, allies, the prefix and postfix, and the combination and iteration of the three. For the property index metadata, if the index is available, it will point to the data index block; if it is not available, it will point to the dataset block.

The data index contains the index information for each property; the index is full text index for the property. The value of the full text index is the data blocks for the key. The data index will be stored as a B+ tree for better search performance.

4.3   Knowledge Graph Schema Node

Nowadays, knowledge is interconnected and interacts, forming numerous, large, interconnected and sophisticated networks. We regard it as a heterogeneous graph. In our knowledge storage system, we also add the graph schema and graph index into the system.

The knowledge graph schema contains the sematic description of the knowledge. It includes the data schema to be used to support the knowledge, the property of the knowledge, the linkage between the knowledge and the linkage between the knowledge property and dataset property. A typical knowledge schema file will contain eight parts: knowledge names, knowledge description, proper names, property description, property metadata, linkage name, linkage description and linkage metadata. For the property metadata, it will contain the linkage between the knowledge property and the data schema property. For the linkage metadata, it will contain on which condition the node will have edge between and the direction of the edge.

4.4   Knowledge Graph Node

The knowledge graph node contains information about the knowledge schema, the knowledge itself and the linkage between them. In order to avoid the duplication of the dataset, we will only store the knowledge id, node/edge type and the serious pointers, which point to the related info of row data in each related dataset. There is no data duplication in the knowledge graph system. If there is a query by graph id, we can go to the dataset directly, if not, based on the knowledge graph schema, we will transfer the query to a serious data schema query. Since most of the knowledge graph is very sparse, we will use adjacency list to store the knowledge graph.

5   Query Process Analysis

Figure 2 shows a query process in multi-indexed storage system in knowledge management.

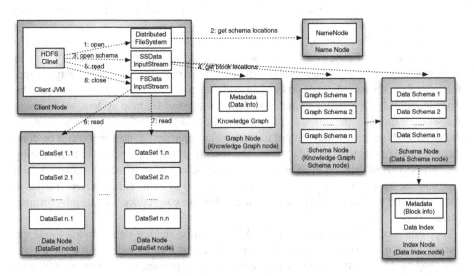

Fig. 2. Query Process in Multi-Indexed Storage System in Knowledge Management

The HDFS (Hadoop Distributed File System) Client first sends an open request to the distributed file system (step 1 in fig. 2), then the request goes to the Name Node (step 2 in fig. 2), depending on the open request sent to open a dataset or a graph, the name node returns the proper schema node based on the file name/graph name.

The HDFS Client then sends the query to the schema stream (SSData)(step 3 in fig. 2). The SSData queries the schema node for the block location of the dataset (step 4 in fig. 2). If it is a query for a graph, the graph schema node will follow the graph schema description; find the data schema node, then go to the data index to find the exact data block information. Alternatively it will find the block information directly if it is a query of graph node id. The data block information will then be returned to the HDFS Client.

After the HDFS Client gets the data block information, it will send the query to file stream (FSData)(step 5 in fig. 2). The FSData then goes to the exact data block to read all of the dataset it needs (step 6, 7 in fig. 2).

6   Performance Optimization

Distribution issues: the whole multi-indexed storage system is based on the Hadoop distributed file system. We add two new types of node, the schema node and index node. They act very similarly with the data node; they all need to report the heart beat to the name node. We still keep the Master/Slave architecture for the whole system. Different to some Lucene based index systems; we separate the index and schema from the original dataset for better scalability and control. Thus we can simply limit the volume of the index, also based on the statistical information of the query, we can dynamically change how much index we need and separate the update of index from the update of the dataset.

Performance of execution: The purpose of adding an index to the system is to reduce the total number of jobs running on the knowledge management system. We try to locate the exact block before the map-reduce job is started. We also try to delay the real loading of the dataset. A lot of processing such as set join, merge and difference can be done at the index level[8]. Compared to the non-indexed Hadoop system, we increase the work of building the index and find the block info in the schema-index system. As we described before, the building of the index is a separate job now and it can be done during the off-peak time of the system. The finding of the index will add data loading and process from schema node and index value before map-reduce is started, which will add the traffic of the internal network of Hadoop system. This is acceptable since the size of the load is small. If we hit in the index, we can reduce a lot of jobs for map processing.

Performance of building the index: We will add a default data schema to all the dataset, which marked as no attribute and all the blocks as index value. If we are querying an existing data schema with no index for a particular attribute, we will also add all the blocks of the dataset as its value. Through these, the index system can be work even if there is no index. So we can delay the building of index and based on the statistic info, we can build the index dynamically.

7   Experimental Evaluation

This new application is based on previous work relating to a transaction fraud detection system. In this application data is obtained from an internal transaction record system; data is also obtained from social networks and third party organizations that are related to the account holder. We then build a heterogeneous knowledge management system in order to analyze the historical data and find potential patterns for fraudulent transactions.

In the prototype of this system, we analyzed over 50,000 accounts related to over 2million transactions, combining the data with data from social network records, ip addresses and email addresses. The heterogeneous knowledge analysis was then undertaken for three different node types: Create Account, Cash Transaction and Credit Transaction. We add index to the transaction dataset and social network dataset. The x-axis of figure 3 and figure 4 is the paralleled query numbers; the y-axis is the execution time in Second. In figure 3, only 10% attributes are indexed and 80% indexed in figure 4.

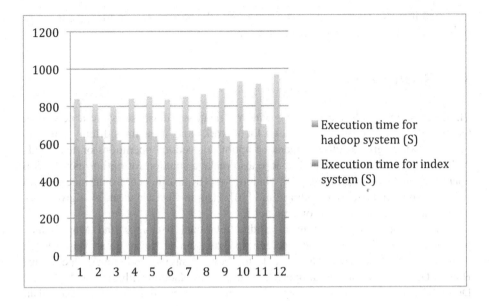

Fig. 3. The end-end execution time for parallelized query (10% indexed)

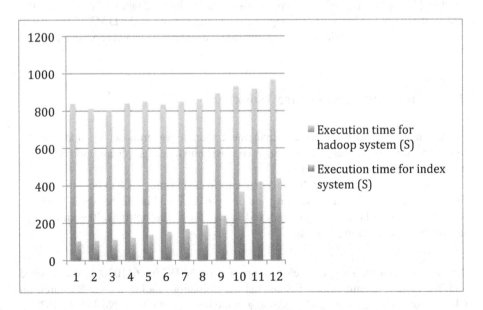

Fig. 4. The end-end execution time for parallelized query (80% indexed)

From the end-end execution time for parallelized query, we can see that in figure 3, because only 20% indexed, the performance of indexed system is not very different from the original Hadoop system. But in figure 4, the performance will be largely increased if the system overall load is not heavy, the heavier system load, the increase of the performance gain in not that significant.

8   Related Work

The integration of full-text indexing within a relational database is not a new idea; Oracle, IBM and Microsoft have done a lot of work along these lines. Jimmy Lin et al. [2] from twitter give a full-text index to optimize selection operations on text fields within records. M. Cafarella and C. R_e also make a solution for optimizes selection operations in Hadoop programs. [9] Hadoop++ [10] also injects trojan indexes into Hadoop input splits at data loading time [10]. Haojun Liao [1] et al. also give a R+ based full text index solutions on data node.

Some research is attempting to bridge relational databases and Map-Reduce programming models. Examples include an extension of the original Map-Reduce model called MapReduceMerge [3] to better support relational operations, HadoopDB[4], an architectural hybrid that integrates Hadoop with PostgresSQL, and Dremel[5], which takes advantage of columnar compression for large-scale data analysis.

Other research are adding index for graph system. Interval labeling [11] and 2HOP labeling [12] are the typical solutions on this field. The interval labeling approaches use min-post-labeling or pre-post-labeling on a spanning subtree of the DAG. In the 2HOP index, each node determines a set of intermediate nodes it can reach, and a set of intermediate nodes that can reach it.

9   Conclusion and Future Work

In the multi-indexed knowledge management system we propose, we add sematic meaning into the dataset, build heterogeneous knowledge graph and add index to optimize for the query performance.

In the future research, we will focus on performance turning such as how to improve the performance of the index building and delayed data load in the storage system; we will also focus on how to use the indexed storage system to optimize the knowledge management and sharing process.

Acknowledgement. This research is supported by NSFC No.61103006, the Science and Technology Commission of Shanghai Municipality funding for the Research on Cloud based Data Analysis and Processing in the internet of things (No.12510706200). We would like to express our sincere thanks to them.

References

1. Liao, H., Han, J., Fang, J.: Multi-dimensional Index on Hadoop Distributed File System. In: IEEE Fifth International Conference on Networking, Architecture and Storage (NAS) (2010)
2. Lin, J., Ryaboy, D., Weil, K.: Full-text indexing for optimizing selection operations in large-scale data analytics. In: Proceedings of the Second International Workshop on MapReduce and Its Applications (2011)
3. Yang, H., Dasdan, A., Hsiao, R.-L., Parker, D.S.: Map-Reduce-Merge: Simplified relational data, processing on large clusters. In: SIGMOD (2007)
4. Abouzeid, A., Bajda-Pawlikowski, K., Abadi, D., Silberschatz, A., Rasin, A.: HadoopDB: An architectural hybrid of MapReduce and DBMS technologies for analytical workloads. In: VLDB (2009)
5. Melnik, S., Gubarev, A., Long, J., Romer, G., Shivakumar, S., Tolton, M., Vassilakis, T.: Dremel: Interactive analysis of web-scale datasets. In: VLDB (2010)
6. Chang, F., Dean, J., Ghemawat, S., Hsieh, W.C., Wallach, D.A., Burrows, M., Chandra, T., Fikes, A., Gruber, R.: Bigtable: A distributed storage system for structured data. In: OSDI (2006)
7. Dean, J., Ghemawat, S.: MapReduce: Simplified data processing on large clusters. In: OSDI (2004)
8. Abadi, D.J.: Materialization strategies in a Column oriented DBMS, ICDE, Istanbul, Turkey, pp. 567–574 (2007)
9. Cafarella, M., Ré, C.: Manimal: Relational optimization for data-intensive programs. In: WebDB (2010)
10. Dittrich, J., Quiané-Ruiz, J.-A., Jindal, A., Kargin, Y., Setty, V., Schad, J.: Hadoop++: Making a yellow elephant run like a cheetah (without it even noticing). In: VLDB (2010)
11. Agrawal, R., Borgida, A., Jagadish, H.V.: Efficient management of transitive relationships in large data and knowledge bases. SIGMOD Rec. 18(2), 253–262 (1989)
12. Cheng, J., Yu, J.X., Lin, X., Wang, H., Yu, P.S.: Fast computing reachability labelings for large graphs with high compression rate. In: EBDT (2008)

A Novel Approach for Customer Segmentation Based on Biclustering

Xiaohui Hu[1], Haolan Zhang[2], Xiaosheng Wu[1], Jianlin Chen[1],
Yu Xiao[1], Yun Xue[1], and TieChen Li[1]

[1] School of Physics and Telecommunication Engineering,
South China Normal University, Guangzhou, China, 510006
Xiaohui_huhu@sina.com
[2] NIT, ZheJiang University, Hanzhou, P.R. China
Haolan.zhang@gmail.com

Abstract: The paper presents a novel approach for customer segmentation which is the basic issue for an effective CRM（Customer Relationship Management）. Firstly, the chi-square statistical analysis is applied to choose set of attributes and K-means algorithm is employed to quantize the value of each attribute. Then DBSCAN algorithm based on density is introduced to classify the customers into three groups (the first, the second and the third class). Finally biclustering based on FP-tree algorithm is used in the three groups to obtain more detailed information. Experimental results on the dataset of an airline company show that the biclustering could segment the customers more accurately and meticulously. Compared with biclustering based on Apriori, the Fp-tree is more efficient on the large dataset.

Keywords: customer segmentation, biclustering, Chi-square statistics, DBSCAN, FP-tree.

1 Introduction

In today's highly competitive business environment, customer relationship management (CRM) is a critical success factor for the survival and growth of businesses, which has been more widely used in some industries and areas, including tourism, catering, retail trade, network marketing, network services and other e-commerce, etc. Customer segmentation is the basic issue for an effective CRM due to its role in helping organizations to understand and serve existing customers better, and enabling the acquisition of profitable customers. Nowadays, data mining technology plays a more important role in the demands of analyzing and utilizing the large scale information gathered from customers.

Many studies in the literature have researched the application of data mining technology in customer segmentation, and achieved sound effectives. Alex. Berson used decision trees and clustering technology for customer segmentation [1]. Guillem Lefait presented a data mining architecture based on clustering techniques to help experts to segment customer based on their purchase behaviors[2]. Jaesoo Kim used

Z. Huang et al. (Eds.): WISE 2013 Workshops 2013, LNCS 8182, pp. 302–312, 2014.

neural networks in tourism industry customer classification[3], Meng Xiaolian, Yang Yu proposed a customer identifying model based on customer value in commercial banks[4].

Segmentation aims at to recognize groups of customers who share the same, or similar needs [5]. The K-Means clustering algorithm has been often selected [6], [7] to make the segmentation because of its simplicity and its efficiency. The use of clustering to automatically provide a segmentation has been done for two main objectives : 1) to identify groups of entities that share certain common characteristics and 2) to better understand consumer behaviors by identifying homogeneous groups [8]. However, there are different challenges when using clustering to perform the segmentation : which data to select, how many clusters to produce and how to evaluate the clustering results.

Thus, the customer segmentation has two main challenges. The first challenge is to formalize implicit data. The RFM values that represent respectively the Recency, the Frequency and the Monetary score of a customer are an example of derived information and is used in [9] and [10] to segment bank customers. A second challenge is to select a relevant subset of the available features to perform the clustering.

The paper proposes a novel approach for customer segmentation. Firstly, the chi-square statistical analysis is applied to choose set of attributes and K-means algorithm is employed to quantize the value of each attribute. Then DBSCAN algorithm based on density is introduced to divide the customers into three groups (the first, the second and the third class). Finally biclustering based on FP-tree compared with Apriori is used in the three groups to obtain more detailed information.

The rest of this paper is organized as follows. The proposed method is presented in Section 2. The results of the experiment are then presented and analyzed in section 3. Finally, the conclusion is made in section 6.

2   Customer Segmentation Architecture

Our objective is to produce detailed diverse and meaningful customer segmentations. These segmentations will be used to help experts to discover specificities in consumer behaviors. At first the raw data is preprocessed as following: Designate a attribute according to the business strategy, then analyze the correlation between the designated attribute and the other attributes, after that delete weak correlation and redundancy attributes . As far as the value of the attributes is concerned, K-means algorithm is applied to each attribute and each value is quantized according to its cluster. Secondly the customers are clustered by the DBSCAN algorithm, which are divided into three groups : the first class, the second class, the third class. At the third step, biclustering algorithm based on FP-tree is introduced for behavior feature clustering, which is compared with the algorithm based on Apriori. Finally, the final results are analyzed and the corresponding marketing strategy is put forward.

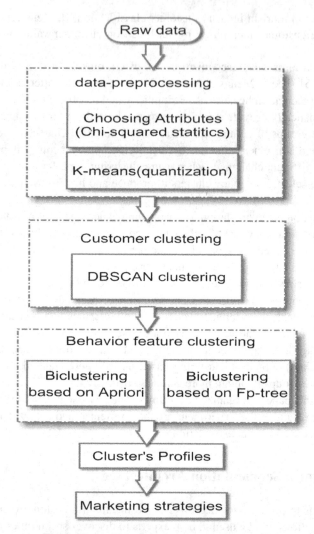

Fig. 1. The architecture of customer segmentation

2.1   Data-Preprocessing: Chi-squared Statistical Analysis and K-means Quantization

2.1.1   Chi-squared Statistical Analysis

In this paper we utilize the correlation of chi-square statistic[20] to measure the relevance between the arranged attribute and the rest attribute. The attributes are categorized in three levels: the strong correlation, correlation, and weak correlation. Remove redundancy attributes and attributes with the weak correlation, so the rest attributes are independent to each other.

The algorithm is stated as following:

1 Calculated the Chi-value K_i between the designated attribute C and the other attribute F_i.

2 Rearrange each attribute according to the results of 1.

3 Divide all the attributes into three categories, namely the strong correlation (Strong Relevant) subsets, the relevant subsets, the weak correlation subsets. Determine the Weakest-of-Strong-Relevant value FWoS and the Strongest-of-Weak-Relevant value FSoW.

4 Select the reference attribute Fi from the subset of strong correlation (SSR), iterate the other attributes F_j of the subset and calculate the Chi value K_{ij} between them.. If K_{ij} is greater than or equal to FWoS, then delete the attribute F_j, otherwise retain it. Put F_i into the subset of Reduction-of-Strong-Relevant (SRSR). If the SSR is not null, continue.

5 Calculate K_{ij} between the attribute F_i of the correlation subset and the attribute F_j of the Reduction-of-Strong-Relevant subset SRSR. If K_{ij} is greater than FSoW, then remove F_i; otherwise retain it and put it into the subset of Reduction- of-Relevant(SRR).

6 Delete the subset of the weakest correlation.

2.1.2   K-means Algorithm

K-means algorithm[11] is a classical algorithm to solve the clustering problem. The idea of specific algorithm is that the k sample points selected randomly are taken as the center of initialized cluster and then performing iterative operations. Clustering results are affected by the choice of initial point, and therefore the solutions obtained are always local optimum, not global optimum.

K-means algorithm is used to cluster the values of each attribute. The value is quantized according to its cluster, which means if it belongs to cluster 1 then its value is changed to 1 and if it belongs to cluster 2 then its value is 2, and so on. The Quantization procedure is shown as Fig2.

MemberID	A	B	C	D
M_1	a_1	b_1	c_1	d_1
M_2	a_2	b_2	c_2	d_2
...	...	...	...	..
M_n	a_n	b_n	c_n	d_n

MemberID	A	B	C	D
M_1	1	2	3	1
M_2	2	1	2	2
...	...	...	...	..
M_n	3	2	2	1

Fig. 2. Quantization of the values of attributes

2.2   DBSCAN

Density-based clustering algorithms find groups or regions with high densities which are separated by low density regions [12]. The density based spatial clustering of applications with noise (DBSCAN) algorithm classifies all available points as core points, border points, and noise points. Core points are those that have at least Minpts number of points in the Eps distance. Border points can be defined as points that are not core points, but are the neighbors of core points. Noise points are those that are neither core points nor border points. It has two parameters, a distance parameter Eps and a threshold MinPts. DBSCAN searches for clusters by checking the Eps of each point in the database. If the Eps of a point P contains more than MinPts, a new cluster with P as core object is created. DBSCAN then iteratively collects directly density-reachable objects from these core objects, which may involve the merge of a few density-reachable clusters. The process terminates when no new points can be added to any cluster.

The DBSCAN algorithm is given as following [12].

Algorithm: Basic DBSCAN Algorithm
1: Begin.
2: Arbitrary select a point p.
3: Retrieve all points density-reachable from p, set Eps and MinPts.
4: If p is a core point, a cluster is formed.
5: If p is a border point, no points are density-reachable from p and DBSCAN visits the next point of the database.
6: Continue the process until all of the points have been processed.
7: End.

In this paper, the customers are divided into three groups (the first, the second and the third) through the algorithm.

2.3   Biclustering Algorithm

Bicluster is a hot topic in data mining, which plays an important role in applications of the gene expression data. A bicluster is a sub-matrix in the given data matrix, which has certain consistency between its elements. However, bi-clustering clusters both rows and columns which is a NP hard problem. Besides traditional CC (Cheng and Church algorithm)[14] algorithm, there are few mature algorithms to solve it. We change the biclustering problem completely into mining the frequent patterns based on the association rules, so the mature algorithms in association rules can be used for biclustering.

Association rules mining seeks inter-relations hidden between data entries, its general objects are transaction databases. Hence we transform the original database into the transaction database after the first two steps.(Fig3.)

MemberID	A	B	C	D
M 1	1	2	3	1
M 2	2	1	2	2
...	...	...	...	..
M n	3	2	2	1

MemberID	Transactions
M 1	A1,B2,C3,D1
M 2	A2,B2,C2,D2
...	...
M n	A3,B2,C2,D1

Fig. 3. The transformation of the original database into the transaction database

2.3.1   Apriori

Frequent pattern mining forms a core component in mining association rules. A lot of methods have been proposed and developed for efficient frequent pattern mining. The most classical algorithm is Apriori algorithm. Apriori algorithm is a layered search iterative method based on frequency set theory ,the core idea is searching for (k+1) item sets through the k item sets , finding out the relationship between database project, in order to form the rules. This algorithm includes two steps: the first step is to identify all the frequent item sets, namely the support degree not less than the minimum support degree which the user specifies; The second step is to form rules form frequent items, guarantee the confidence not less than the minimum confidence user given.

But in practical applications, Apriori algorithm has many defects, such as: Multiple scanning databases makes expenses very large and each scan is executed on the entire database, which is very costly when the database is very large; May produce numerous candidate, causing algorithm's adaptability very poor in breadth and depth; When scanning databases, it needs to do pattern-matching with the candidate item sets and affairs, which wasting a lot of time.

2.3.2   Frequent Pattern Tree: FP-tree

Due to the defects of Apriori algorithm, j . Han put forward a frequent mode growing algorithm, which is FP-tree algorithm. FP-tree is a special prefix tree [13], it consists of a frequent item header table, one root labeled as "NULL", and a set of item prefix subtrees as the children of root. Each node in the item prefix subtree consists of four fields: node-name, node count, node-link and node-parent. Each entry in the frequent item header table (or Ftable for short) consists of three fields: item-name, item-sup and item-head, item-head is a pointer pointing to the first node in the FP-tree carrying the node name. Based on this definition, given a transaction database DB and a support threshold minsup, we have the following FP tree construction steps:

(1) Scan DB once. Collect L, the set of frequent items, and the support of each frequent item. Sort List in support-descending order as LF, the list of frequent items.

(2) Scan DB again. Select all frequent items in every transaction, sort them according to the order of LF then form the corresponding itemsets by combining the ordered frequent items in every transaction, and insert them to FP-tree respectively.

3   Experimental Results

The proposed method is validated through a dataset from the website of a domestic airline company which has 62988 members and 63 attributes and implemented on the computer with Win7 operating   and Matlab7.0 platform whose RAM is 4G and CPU is AMD Athlon II X4 645 . After data preprocessing, there are 7 attributes left and the value of each attribute is quantized as 1 , 2 , 3 representing low, medium and high level respectively. The left attributes are shown as table1.

Table 1. The explanation of the selected attributes

Attribute name	Explanation
EXPENSE_SUM	The total ticket price (the first year's ticket price + the second year's ticket price)
ELITE_POINTS_SUM	Sum of the elite points
FLIGHT_COUNT	Count number of flight
SEG_KM_SUM	The total segments distance of the flight(Km)
WEIGHTED_SEG_KM	The weighted total distance of the flight(Σdiscount$\times$segment distance)
Points_Sum	Sum of the points
BASE_POINTS_SUM	Sum of the base points

DBSCAN algorithm divide the customers into three classes(the first class, the second class and the third class).The following Table2,Table3,Table4 are biclusters of each class.

Table 2. Biclusters of the first class

Customers' number	EXPFNSE_SUM	SEG_KM_SUM	WEIGHTED_SEG_KM	Points_Sum	FLIGHT_COUNT	BASE_POINTS_SUM	ELITE_POINTS_SUM
42502	1	1	1	1	1	1	1
43308		1	1	1	1	1	1
43476	1			1	1	1	1
42555	1	1	1	1	1		
43631	1	1		1		1	1
42507	1	1		1	1	1	

It could be seen from Table2 that the biclusters that the attributes of the crowd are in the low level where the backslash means the corresponding attribute is not taken into account. These people are less involved in the flight consumption. The airline company need to improve its services to increase airline sales amount.

Table 3. Biclusters of the second class

Customers' number	EXPENSE_SUM	SEG_KM_SUM	WEIGHTED_SEG_KM	Points_Sum	FLIGHT_COUNT	BASE_POINTS_SUM	ELITE_POINTS_SUM
1823	2	2	2	2	2	2	1
1580	2	2	2	1	2	2	1
2318	2	2	2	2		2	1
1817	2	2	2	1		2	1
...	...	...	...	...	...	...	...
1907	2	2	2	2	2		
963	1	2	2	1			1
1889	2	2	2	1	2		
4772	2	2	2				
2518	2	2	2	2			
2136	2	2	2	1			

This is the middle class customer group(Table 3), who can be regarded as customers with potential value. Some of them could step to customers with high value. Each row represents the behavior with different characteristics.

For instance , the Points_Sum of the customers in the second row belongs to low level while the other attribute such as consumption, flight number, and flight distance have reached a good level.

Table 4. Biclusters of The Third Class

Customers' number	EXPENSE_SUM	SEG_KM_SUM	WEIGHTED_SEG_KM	Points_Sum	FLIGHT_COUNT	BASE_POINTS_SUM	ELITE_POINTS_SUM
138	2	3	3	2	3	3	
52	2	3	3	2	3	2	2
48	2	3	3	2	3	2	1
149	2	3	3	2	3	3	
233	2	3	3	2	3		
235	2	3	3	2			
37	2	3	2				

The accumulated points are not so important among the people of the class. Customers with low points gave much contribution to the air company as customers in the last three rows do. Therefore they should not be treated differently.

The base points of the customers in the third class (Table 4) have reached the highest level as well as the flight times and the flight distance. But there is still room for improvement considering about the elite points , the level of flight consumption and the total points.

The consumption level of this class should be the highest, while the consumption level of 295 customers (among total 331 customers) focused on the value of 2 (medium level). So it is necessary to give more preferential policies to stimulate their desire for consumption.

As the high-end users, most of the BASE_POINTS_SUM (points) are the medium level, thus the professional work for the basic point should be strengthened.

We also compared the biclustering on Apriori with the biclustering on FP-tree algorithm. The results is shown as Table5.

Table 5. The comparison between the Apriori and the FP-tree algorithm

Time \ Algorithm	Biclustering based on Apriori	Biclustering based on FP-tree
The First Class (331)	1s	1s
The Second Class (8962)	15s	14s
The third class (52946)	26mins52s	15mins03s

It could be obviously discerned from Table5 that FP-tree algorithm greatly reduces the number of database access and the searching cost as the data getting bigger, which greatly improved the efficiency.

4   Conclusions

In this paper, a novel approach for customer segmentation is proposed. Firstly, the chi-square statistical analysis is applied to choose set of attributes and K-means algorithm is employed to quantize the value of each attribute, then DBSCAN algorithm based on density is introduced to divide the customers into three groups (the first, the second and the third class), finally biclustering based on FP-tree compared with Apriori is used in the three classes to obtain more detailed information. Results of the experiment show that the biclustering could segment the customers more accurately and meticulously. A comparison was also made between the biclustering on Apriori and biclustering on FP-tree algorithm, which proved that the latter could be more preferable than the former.

Acknowledgements. The authors thank gratefully for the colleagues who have been concerned with the work and have provided much more powerfully technical supports. The work is supported by Guangdong Science and Technology

Department under Grant No.[2010]170,No.2009B010800051, No.2009B010900056, No.2009B090300336, No.2012B091100349; Guangdong Economy & Trade Committee under Grant No. GDEID2010IS034; Guangzhou Yuexiu District science and Technology Bureau under Grant No 2012-GX-004; Open Project Foundation of Information Technology Research Base of Civil Aviation Administration of China under Grant NO. CAAC-ITRB-201206.

References

1. Berson, A., Smith, S.J.: Building Data mining applications for CRM. Posts & Telecommunications Press, Beijing (2001) (in Chinese)
2. Lefait, G., Kechadi, T.: Customer Segmentation Architecture Based on Clustering Techniques. In: 2010 Fourth International Conference on Digital Society (2010)
3. Kim, J., Wei, S., Ruys, H.: Segmenting the Market of West Australian Senior Tourists Using an Artificial Neural Network. Tourism Managemen 24, 25–34 (2003)
4. Meng, X., Yu, Y.: The Study on the Customer Identifying Model Based on Customer Value in Commercial Banks. Value Engineering 7, 6–10 (2007) (in Chinese)
5. McDonald, M.: The role of marketing in creating customer value. In: Marketing from an Engineering Perspective (Digest No. 1996/172), pages 1/1–111 (November 1996)
6. Zhang, G.: Customer segmentation based on survival character. In: WiCom (September 2007)
7. Wu, J., Lin, Z.: Research on customer segmentation model by clustering. In: ICEC. ACM, New York (2005)
8. Punj, G., Stewart, D.W.: Cluster analysis in marketing research: Review and suggestions for application. Journal of Marketing Research 20(2), 134–148 (1983)
9. Aggelis, V., Christodoulakis, D.: Customer clustering using rfm analysis. Stevens Point, Wisconsin, USA, WSEAS (2005)
10. Niyagas, W., Srivihok, A., Kitisin, S.l.: Clustering e-banking customer using data mining and marketing segmentation. ECTI 2(1) (May 2006)
11. He, L., Wu, L.: Survey of Clustering Algorithms in Data Mining. Application Research of Computers 1, 55–57 (2007)
12. Tan, P.N., Steinbach, M., Kumar, V.: Introduction to Data Mining. Pearson Addison Wesley, Boston (2006)
13. Han, J., Pei, J., Yin, Y.: Mining frequent patterns without candidate generation. In: Proceedings of the 2000 ACM-SIGMOD International Conference on Management of Data, Dallas, pp. 1–12 (2000)
14. Cheng, Y., George, M.C.: Biclustering of expression data. In: Proceeding of the 8th International conference on Intelligent SystemS for Molecular Biology (ISMB 2000), pp. 93–103. The AAAI Press, MenloPark (2000)
15. Agrawal, R., Srikant, R.: Fast algorithms for mining association Rules in Large Databases. In: Proceedings of the 20th International Conference on Very Large Data Bases(VLDB 1994), Santiago de Chile, pp. 487–499 (1994)

16. Ceglar, A., Roddick, J.F.: Association mining. ACM Computing Surveys 38(2) (2006)
17. Han, J., Cheng, H., Xin, D., Yan, X.: Frequent pattern mining: current status and future directions. Data Mining Knowledge Discovery 15(1), 55–86 (2007)
18. Pandey, G., Atluri, G., Steinbach, M., Myers, C.L., Kumar, V.: An Association Analysis Approach to Biclustering. In: Proceedings of the 15th ACM SIGKDD International Conference on Knowledge Discovery and Data Mining, New York, pp. 677–686 (2009)
19. Han, J., Kamber, M.: Data Mining: Concepts and Techniques. Morgan Kaufmann, Burlington (2011)
20. Li, Y.: Applications of Chi-square test and contingency table analysis in customer satisfaction and empirical analyses. In: 2009 International Conference on Innovation Management (2009)

A Systematic Literature Review of Data Mining Applications in Healthcare

Olegas Niaksu[1], Jolita Skinulyte, and Hermine Grubinger Duhaze[2]

[1] Vilnius University, Institute of Mathematics and Informatics,
Akademijos str. 4, LT-08663, Vilnius, Lithuania
[2] AME International, GmbH
Hoyossgasse 5, Vienna 1040, Austria
Olegas.Niaksu@mii.vu.lt, Jolita.skinulyte@gmail.com,
h.grubinger@ame-international.com

Abstract. Data mining transforms clinical data into a new knowledge, providing novel highlights to the clinicians and to the patients. The semi-automated systematic literature review has been performed, utilizing semantic abstraction of MeSH controlled vocabulary. Publications indexed in Medline for the whole available period of time has been grouped by PubMed annotated MeSH terms. The trends of data mining related publications and public interest trends in the Data Mining topic is compared. Conclusions on the prevalence of topics, medical disciplines, data mining methods are provided and discussed.

Keywords: data mining applications, medical information systems, medical informatics, automated literature analysis.

1 Introduction

Data mining (DM) methods have been applied in different domains already for more than 40 years. The healthcare domain is known for its complexity, which is due to a variety of medical data standards, growing amounts of unstructured data, and ambiguous semantics [1, 2, 3]. Patient privacy constraints, legal regulations and restrictions make an effective medical knowledge discovery an evolving subject with a growing interest of academics and medical practitioners.

Currently many countries are on the way of national e-Health projects implementation [10], which in essence is a promise to benefit from the standardization, aggregation of patient clinical information and healthcare services by providing an instant access to that information. According to the report from the National Center for Health Statistics of USA [12], adoption of Electronic Health Record in the USA illustrates a linearly raising amount of data, reflecting patients' clinical data continuity together with the treatment and medication being used. It is becoming obvious that we are going to the point, where the research community will get a full set of a person's medical history from the moment of birth till he or she passes away. This anticipated scenario forecasts tremendous potential for machine learning and in particular for DM applications in healthcare.

Z. Huang et al. (Eds.): WISE 2013 Workshops 2013, LNCS 8182, pp. 313–324, 2014.

The amount of publications relevant to DM application in healthcare has been increasing since its accountable beginning till today. The relevant publications growth trends in Thomson Reuters Web of Science, Google Scholar and PubMed databases starting from 1997 to 2011 are shown in Fig. 1.

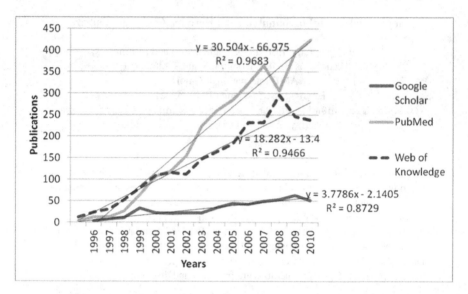

Fig. 1. Trend lines of DM applications in medicine related publications

It is worth mentioning, that in the early 90's up to 5 publications have been submitted during one year, and around 726 publications in year 2012. We could suppose DM usage penetration in healthcare facilities is increasing accordingly. However, our previous study [7] revealed, that a large number of research studies remains theoretical and has no clinical follow up and rarely goes beyond the institutions which were directly involved in the research. In the study we have compared the academic advances with practical achievements in the field. For the evaluation of the practical data mining usage, we have conducted a survey in 7 tertiary hospitals from 5 countries. The countries from diverse economic development regions were selected to cover tertiary hospitals with unlike economic potential. The survey revealed, that typically medical communities have either minimal or zero awareness of the DM practical usage and its potential possibilities. All the respondents from the largest university hospitals confirmed to be familiar with DM applications in healthcare, but only 29% were able to provide an example of practical DM usage.

In a nutshell, we have shown that DM perception and practical applications in healthcare are way beyond its continuous growth in the academic research field, and the currently applied interdisciplinary approach is not efficient enough.

Following the study [7], we have continued to explore the topics of DM impact in healthcare, its spread, and characteristics. The focus of this paper is an analysis of academic publications in the field of medical DM application.

There are a few known literature reviews [6, 8, 9] partly covering chosen subset of publications, e.g. publications related to predictive diagnosis data mining [6] or publications restricted to a limited time frame [3]. Additional information on these studies is provided in Section 3.

To our knowledge, there are no systematic literature reviews with semantic classification of all the publications related to the DM applications in healthcare. Therefore we have undertaken a systematic literature classification, aiming to understand which research topics are prevalent, which medical domains are more engaged, which DM methods are preferable, and hypothetically which medical specialties will benefit from DM in the nearest future.

Aiming to avoid misinterpretations, the generic concept of data mining used in this paper is explicitly defined here: data mining is a part of knowledge discovery process, using data analysis methods such as statistics, machine learning and artificial intelligence, and aiming to get new non-trivial knowledge, e.g. finding prediction values, hidden patterns, and dependencies.

The rest of the paper is structured as follows. Section 2 briefly summarizes the conclusions of our previous study. Section 3 presents our literature review approach and discusses other DM literature review studies. Section 4 describes the method of the literature review we had applied. The results of the study are outlined in Section 5. Section 6 adds additional perspectives of public interest on the topic of DM. Discussion and conclusions are presented in Section 7.

2   Data Mining Applications – Theory vs. Practice

In the study [7], we have combined the quantified results of published publications trends with the results of tertiary[1] hospitals' survey on the practical DM usage.

Thomson Reuters Web of Science, Google Scholar and PubMed databases have been used to analyze the number and distribution of scientific publications related to DM in medicine in the last decade. Tertiary hospitals were selected as a target audience for the conducted survey. Typically, tertiary hospitals are the first healthcare provider organizations which install clinical software systems, enabling to collect clinical and demographic patient data needed for DM applications.

We present certain differences between growing academic interest and practical usage of DM in healthcare facilities. Below are the main conclusions of this study:

o The survey revealed, that the greatest part of medical community of tertiary hospitals have either minimal or zero awareness of the DM practical usage and its potential possibilities. All the respondents from the largest university hospitals confirmed to be familiar with DM applications in healthcare, however only 29% of them were able to provide any example of practical DM usage.

---

[1] Tertiary hospital – a major hospital, providing wide range of high level specialized medical services. Commonly tertiary hospitals are university hospitals combining medical and academic activities.

o There is a noticeable confusion in differentiating *Data Mining* and *Statistics* among healthcare professionals. Hence, very rarely DM is treated by them as a practically valuable tool for clinical purposes.
o The respondents from healthcare facilities with a relatively recent adoption of ICT in the patient treatment process tend to mix statistical reporting and DM, hospital information systems, electronic medical record systems and decision support systems.
o The survey identified a considerable potential for a further DM penetration due to an increasing amount of patient clinical data collected in HCI and interest declared by hospitals' clinical representatives: 86% of respondents expressed their interest in DM and even more would like to participate in international DM research projects.
o Regardless of understanding and experience of DM, 86% of respondents expressed their interest in the DM topic and 93% would like to participate in international DM research projects as well as to be informed about utilization of DM techniques in the future.
o The process of information digitalization in the developing countries is still in the early phases and the lack of electronically available data is a stopping factor for the spread of exploratory DM in a poor economic area.

When considering the potential and benefits of knowledge discovery using DM tools in healthcare, it is clear that on the one hand more attention should be paid to the domain specific problems of successful DM application in healthcare [3, 5], emphasizing the usage of DM methods with self-explanatory models [2], and on the other hand there is a certain time delay till new methods will be widely applied in common practice.

3   Systematic Literature Analysis. Understanding the Current Research Domain

As it was concluded in the previous section, the real usage of novel technologies comes to healthcare organizations with a time lag. Certain time and effort are required until the technology becomes widely known and accepted in the community of the end users.

However, it is of great interest to understand, what are the hottest topics of academic medical data mining research, and how they do evolve. Knowing the answer, one can predict the future of DM developments in healthcare sector.

To tackle this question, we have chosen to analyze academic articles submitted to PubMed database. 2135 articles have been published to the date with MeSH [12] keyword *data mining*. Since the number of articles is too big for a manual review, a semantic semi-automated articles classification has been applied. Presuming, that MeSH tagging of the articles, which is mandatory in PubMed, gives a fair representation of the main topics covered by the articles, we have applied different hierarchical groupings to extract the largest, typical or non-typical groups of relevant publications.

3.1 Related Researches

There are a few known literature review studies highlighting DM usage in healthcare [5, 6]. Hian Chye Kob [5] et al. provides a high level overview of data mining applications in major areas such as predictive data mining, evaluation of treatment effectiveness, management of healthcare, customer relationship management, detection of fraud and abuse, identification of risk factors. Additionally, limitations and shortcomings of current DM application have been addressed and a case study example has been provided. However, the authors have not provided the reasoning behind: how they came to these certain topics, if selected topics have been prevailing in research studies, or there was an expressed interest from healthcare provider organizations.

Recent literature review of DM techniques used in healthcare databases is provided by Kocle E. et al. [6]. In the paper the authors presented an overview of the current research in the field of disease diagnosis and prognosis. The methodology used for this paper was the survey of journals and publications in the fields of computer science, engineering and health care. The authors have systematically reviewed 42 articles. The following most frequent DM algorithms have been identified: Decision Trees, Support Vector Machine, Artificial neural networks, Naïve Bayes, Fuzzy Rules.

Likewise to the previous article, the authors have not presented explicit article selection criteria, and hence it is not clear how the 42 articles have been chosen among other hundreds dealing with DM for diagnosis and prognosis.

Another group of articles [2, 4] explore unique problem areas of DM applications in healthcare. According to them, the most prominent of them are semantic data interoperability, patient privacy, unstructured data representation, noisy data, and missing values.

4 Methods

Our research strategy was designed in a way to identify the most relevant publications, where DM was applied or researched within healthcare domain. PubMed database was used, as the biggest medical database, having an explicit hierarchical semantic tagging system, called MeSH. Besides, as it was shown in [7], Pubmed has a largest number of relevant publications in comparison with Web of Knowledge and Google Scholar databases. The Pubmed database is comprised of more than 21 million citations for biomedical literature from Medline, life science journals, and online books. PubMed is operated by U.S. National Library of Medicine (NLM) and indexes all publications classifying its content with the help of MeSH structured vocabulary. The Medical Subject Headings (MeSH) is defined by NLM as a controlled vocabulary which is used for indexing, cataloging, and searching for biomedical and health-related information and documents.

The usage of MeSH vocabulary terms as a search parameter in Pubmed database guarantees that not only search wording matching publications will be found, but also its matching synonymic wording or previously used terms. MeSH term, classified as MeSH heading "*data mining*" is mapped to other similar concepts like "*text mining*".

"Data mining" as *a* term has been appended to the vocabulary only in 2010 and the former terms e.g. "Information Storage and Retrieval", previously used for the same or similar and related concepts, are mapped to the latest one. A simple search criterion "data mining" was used to retrieve a number of publications and books within the medical domain with assigned MeSH heading "data mining".

The whole search result data set with available attributes has been saved in XML format, and then transferred to a relational database. Complete MeSH controlled vocabulary is freely available and is provided by NLM in XML format. We have transferred MeSH data and joined with Pubmed search result datasets in the database.

Having MeSH vocabulary and the exported publications dataset in one database, allowed us to use semantic concept aggregation underlying in MeSH and to group articles on a higher abstraction layer.

A simplified hierarchical MeSH terminology structure can be presented as in the following entity relationship diagram.

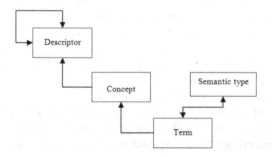

Fig. 2. A simplified MeSH Descriptor-Concept-Term ER diagram

NLM definitions of the entities are as follows. *Descriptors*, also known as *Main Headings*, are used to index citations in MEDLINE database, for cataloging of publications. Most *Descriptors* indicate the subject of an indexed item, such as a journal article, that is, what the article is about. MeSH *Descriptors* are organized in 16 categories, each of them is further divided into subcategories. Within each subcategory, Descriptors are arrayed hierarchically from most general to most specific in up to twelve hierarchical levels.

A *Descriptor* is broader than a *Concept* and consists of a class of concepts. *Concepts*, in turn, correspond to a class of *Terms* which are synonymous with each other. Thus MeSH has a three-level structure: *Descriptor* → *Concept* → *Term*. Every *Term* is assigned to one or more *Semantic Types*, which assign a broader meaning to a *Term*.

The MeSH structure allowed us to extract additional information from the keywords assigned to the articles. Hierarchical structure of the *Descriptors*, represented in MeSH tree, allows fetching the publication keywords filtered by disease groups, anatomy concepts, chemical and drug groups, phenomena and processes group, and information science categories.

The results of our investigations are presented in the next section.

5   Results

2135 publication items have been extracted from the PubMed search engine. The article number growth rate is uneven. The first publication is dated 1984, however, the second one appears only after 10 year interval in 1994. Since the last decade a steadily growing publication number has to be noted. Each publication in the resulting search dataset had in average 10 keywords, which we have mapped to Concepts, Descriptors and Semantic Types.

Top 10 of the most frequent publication keywords are presented below.

Table 1. The list of most popular keywords

Keyword	Number of articles
Humans	2135
Artificial Intelligence	699
Software Engineering	670
Software	670
Algorithms	549
Internet	460
Bio-Informatics	427
Computational Biology	427
Computational Molecular Biology	427
Gene Expression Profiling	342

By raising the abstraction level of the keywords to the *Descriptor* level, we have identified the following top 10 *Descriptors*.

Table 2. The list of most popular descriptors

Keyword	Number of occurrences
Humans	2708
Software	2010
Artificial Intelligence	1631
Computational Biology	1281
Reproducibility of Results	1050
Oligonucleotide Array Sequence Analysis	927
Information Storage and Retrieval	800
Databases, Genetic	726
Internet	690
Gene Expression Profiling	684

Grouping by semantic type gave the broadest available meaning as shown in Table 3.

Table 3. The list of most popular semantic types

Keyword	Number of occurrences
Intellectual Product	8450
Quantitative Concept	3263
Machine Activity	2382
Biomedical Occupation or Discipline	2064
Research Activity	2030
Qualitative Concept	1867
Manufactured Object	1804
Occupational Activity	1786
Biologically Active Substance	1685
Amino Acid, Peptide, or Protein	1667

More interesting results were obtained, grouping the subject area by specific MeSH tree brunches. Most frequent diseases groups being analyzed applying DM are presented in Table 4.

Table 4. The list of most popular disease groups

Disease group	Number of occurrences
Neoplasms	754
Nervous System Diseases	387
Pathological Conditions, Signs and Symptoms	233
Cardiovascular Disease	162
Substance-Related Disorders	137
Nutritional and Metabolic Diseases	75
Digestive System Diseases	53
Bacterial Infections and Mycoses	49
Musculoskeletal Diseases	48
Respiratory Tract Diseases	43
Wounds and Injuries	42
Virus Diseases	38
Hemic and Lymphatic Diseases	30
Male Urogenital Diseases	27
Congenital, Hereditary, and Neonatal Diseases and Abnormalities	22
Skin and Connective Tissue Diseases	19

At the end of this list rank Endocrine System Diseases and Disorders of Environmental Origin, which had no related publications, and Occupational Diseases – only 1 study found, and Animal Diseases - 7 studies found. Each group of diseases in MeSH tree is related to hundreds of specific diseases. Below we provide a top 10 list of mostly researched diseases in terms of DM application.

Table 5. The list of most popular diseases

Disease	Number of articles
Neoplasms	189
Breast Neoplasms	156
Alzheimer Disease	78
Drug Toxicity	76
Genetic Predisposition to Disease	52
Substance-Related Disorders	50
Chronic Disease	45
Heart Failure	42
Colorectal Neoplasms	36
Adenoma	35

Another highly profiled topic is the genetic research. High utilization of DM in the following areas has been identified.

Table 6. The list of most popular investigative techniques in genetics

Investigative technique (genetics)	Number of occurrences
Oligonucleotide Array Sequence Analysis	927
Gene Expression Profiling	684
Sequence Analysis, DNA	268
Gene Regulatory Networks	210
Promoter Regions, Genetic	196
Genetic Association Studies	172
Molecular Sequence Annotation	162
Epistasis, Genetic	144
Genes	138
Gene Library	108

Finally we provide a grouping from computer science perspective. We have to acknowledge that MeSH has a far from perfect *Term* set looking from computer science perspective, but even this limited information gives useful insights on the actuality and popularity of different methods and disciplines.

Table 7. The list of most computer science topics

Computer Science topics	Number of occurrences
Artificial Intelligence	1631
Bayes Theorem	325
Cluster Analysis	250
Decision Support Techniques	228
Pattern Recognition, Automated	220
Natural Language Processing	177
Neural Networks	104
Support Vector Machines	41
Knowledge Bases	29
Expert Systems	12

6   The Public Interest in Data Mining Topic

Another interesting projection is to evaluate the dynamics of internet community interest in DM topic, and to see if it correlates with the trends showed in Fig. 1. A publicly available tool Google Trends [11] was used for the purpose. Google Trends analyzes all search queries executed in Google search engine worldwide, combining searches in different languages coming from around the globe. Google Trends service has been collecting and mining data since 2004, and provides us with a summarized time-series analysis. To get a better understanding, we have compared the actuality of the *data mining* term to other disciplines: *artificial intelligence*, and *machine learning*.

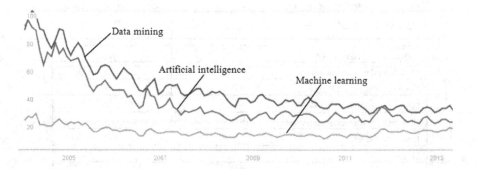

Fig. 3. Google Trends in DM, artificial intelligence and machine learning

Google trends is not providing absolute numbers of the searches performed, instead, the chart's data is scaled and normalized by the highest search activity, where 100 points meaning the peak search interest, in our case "data mining" term in year 2004.

As shown in Fig. 3, there is a general correlation among all the concepts analyzed: *artificial intelligence, machine learning* and *computer science*. A moderate decrease of the general public interest is noticeable in scientific topics over years.

By zooming in the results to the magnitude of one year, a reoccurring decrease of interest during summer months can be seen, which is a possible indication of summer holidays in the academic society. Hence, we can state, that search interest of these topics is arguably related to scholarly activities.

Summarizing Google Trends results, we can conclude that the peak popularity of "data mining" and "artificial intelligence" concepts has ended by year 2007 and afterwards it remains more or less stable. Remembering the growth tendency of DM related publications (Fig. 1) and combining it with decreasing public interest in the DM topic, we would assume, that *data mining* as a discipline has passed the fashion technology stage, and is currently on the way to its maturity.

7   Discussion and Conclusions

The main shortcoming of our research is the limited nature of MeSH keywords, which were used for the identification of publications topics. Although MeSH represents medical domain fairly well, it was not designed for computer science or data engineering. Therefore, in the future we plan to apply Information Retrieval techniques, for targeted text annotation and improved article tagging. Due to copyright and intellectual property restrictions, such an exercise, most probably, will be performed in a limited scope, using openly available article abstracts.

The results presented in 4th section are not homogeneous and do not allow to draw generic conclusion. Instead, we provide a few atomic conclusions.

1. **Oncology diseases**. Though it is not surprising that oncology diseases are on the top of the list, cardiovascular diseases are only on the third place after nervous system diseases (we are not counting pathological conditions ranking 3rd place in Table 4, as it represent a collection of different syndromes).
2. **Chronic diseases**. Noticeably, too little attention is paid to chronic diseases, which are believed to be the biggest challenge of modern healthcare systems because of the aging population (only 45 articles found, see Table 5).
3. **Genetics**. There are an outstanding number of keywords referencing to the topics in the field of genetic analysis, which reconfirms what is known in another domains, DM provides powerful arsenal of techniques for high volume data analysis.
4. **DM methods**. Interestingly, as presented in Table 7, methods based on *Bayes theorem* are 3 times more frequently used than *Neural Networks* and 5 times more frequent than *Support Vector Machines*. Regretfully, MeSH does not provide a comprehensive list of DM methods for a broader comparison. Therefore this aspect of analysis shall be continued using other methods, i.e. automated text annotation.

O. Niaksu, J. Skinulyte, and H.G. Duhaze

References

1. Bellazzi, R., Zupan, B.: Predictive data mining in clinical medicine: Current issues and guidelines. International Journal of Medical Informatics 77, 81–97 (2008)
2. Canlas Jr., R.D.: Data Mining in Healthcare: Current Applications and Issues (2009)
3. Chen, H., Fuller, S., Friedman, C., Hersh, W.: Medical Informatics. Knowledge Management and Data Mining in Biomedicine. Springer Science (2005)
4. Cios, K.J., Moore, G.W.: Uniqueness of medical data mining. Artificial Intelligence in Medicine 26, 1–24 (2002)
5. Kob, H.C., Tan, G.: Data mining applications in healthcare. Journal of Healthcare Information Management 19(2), 64–72 (2005)
6. Kolçe, E., Frasheri, N.: A Literature Review of Data Mining Techniques Used in Healthcare Databases (2012)
7. Niaksu, O., Kurasova, O.: Data Mining Applications in Healthcare: Research vs Practice (2011)
8. Pardalos, P.M., Boginski, V.L., Vazacopoulos, A.: Data mining in biomedicine. Springer Science (2007)
9. Satyanandam, N., Satyanarayana, C., Riyazuddin, M., Shaik, A.: Data Mining Machine Learning Approaches and Medical Diagnose Systems: A Survey
10. Stroetmann, K.A., Artmann, J., Stroetmann, V.N.: European countries on their journey towards national eHealth infrastructures. Final European progress report. European Commission. DG Information Society and Media, ICT for Health Unit (2011)
11. Google Trends. Web portal, http://www.google.com/trends/
12. Healthcare Information and Management Systems Society. Electronic Health Records. A Global Perspective. White paper. HIMSS Enterprise Systems Steering Committee and the Global Enterprise Task Force (2010)
13. National Library of Medicine – MeSH,
    http://www.nlm.nih.gov/mesh/meshhome.html
14. PubMed - database of references and abstracts on life sciences and biomedical topics,
    http://www.ncbi.nlm.nih.gov/pubmed/

Community-Based Scholar Recommendation Modeling in Academic Social Network Sites

JieMin Chen[1], Yong Tang[1,*], JianGuo Li[1], ChengJie Mao[2], and Jing Xiao[1]

[1] School of Computer Science, South China Normal University, Guangzhou, China
[2] Development and Planning Office, South China Normal University, Guangzhou, China
cjm_friends@126.com, {ytang,xiaojing}@scnu.edu.cn,
jianguoli@m.scnu.edu.cn, maochj@qq.com

Abstract. Academic social network sites (Asnss) have experienced rapid growth in recent years. Large amounts of users hope to make friends with other users for potential academic collaborations in Asnss. Though there are many scholar recommendation systems, they mainly consider the content similarity of users' profiles. In fact, the communities of Asnss can offer rich networking information to make recommendations. In this paper, we propose a community-based scholar recommendation model in Asnss. We firstly construct research-fields-based graphs, detect communities in the graphs by Louvain method and then make scholar recommendation by calculating friendship scores. We also implement the model on a real world dataset from an academic social network site called SCHOLAT. And the experimental results demonstrate that our approach improves the recommendations of core network members and outperforms the content-based user recommendation method.

Keywords: recommendation systems, academic social networks, community detection.

1 Introduction

In recent years social networking sites (SNSs) have experienced an unprecedented rapid development. Many popular social networking sites such as Facebook, QQ and Twitter have become increasingly popular. In addition, academic social network sites (Asnss) have emerged to meet the need of researchers, such as ResearchGate, Sciweavers, CiteLike, Academia.edu and SCHOLAT [1]. These Asnss are platforms to help users organize their research, collaborate with others online, discover the latest researches and build the complex academic relations [2].

In Asnss, users are often faced with an information overload and it is tough for them to find other users with similar research interests. Thus recommendation systems play an important role in Asnss. Most of these systems are based on the content similarity of users to make scholar recommendation. And it is neglected that the connection information of nodes in academic social networks[3].In fact, some users maybe have similar research interests but have less content similarity. At the same time,

Z. Huang et al. (Eds.): WISE 2013 Workshops 2013, LNCS 8182, pp. 325–334, 2014.

they always are the core network members in ASNSs. The core network members often have detailed profiles, make many friends and provide the information of their latest papers and projects. Other users always pay attention to them and like to make friends with them. It is a fact that these content similarity-based systems often forget to recommend these users. Consequently, in this paper, we propose a novel method to solve the problem. We construct a networking based on users' research fields, and then we detect communities in social network. A community in social network is defined as a group of people with common characteristics. In communities, we can calculate the similarities of users for recommending.

The rest of the paper is organized as follows. In Section 2, we briefly introduce the related work. In Section 3, we describe the dataset used in the experiments and community-based scholar recommendation modeling in ASNSs. In Section 4, we describe our experiments and analyze the results. Finally, we conclude in Section 5.

2   Related Work

A great variety of recommendation systems have been proposed since SNSs are hot research topics in recent years. Typically these systems can be divided into two types: the content-based filtering approach [4] [5] and the collaborative filtering approach [4]. Collaborative Filtering (CF) [6] has become one of the most popular techniques of personalized recommendation. It is based on the assumption that similar users share the same interest.

In ASNSs, a few systems use the communities. Lopes [7] presented an effective approach to recommend new partners to researchers for joint research based on the context of academic social network. TamaraHeck [6] combined social information to build networks of researchers and to recommend similar researchers to each other. Xu [8] proposed a two-layer network model to combine semantic and social network information together for recommendation. Nocera and Ursino [9] used information about user friendships and semantic information of tags for their recommendations. Sahebi [3] proposed community-Based recommendations to resolve the cold start problem. Liu Ji [10] improved the effects of collaborative recommendation by network cloud communities.

Additionally, scholars' research fields are distributed, always changing and crossing. Communities have often been linked to common characteristics of the community members. The aim of community detection is to find subgroups that the amount of interaction within group is more than the interaction outside of it [11]. Recently the community detection adopts multiple statistical and graph-based methods. The modularity-based method is a popular method in community detection [12].So in our work we construct users' networking with common research fields, detect communities by the modularity and recommend users by calculating their friendship scores in the same community.

3   Community-Based Scholar Recommendation Modeling

3.1   Background of SCHOLAT

SCHOLAT is an academic social network for professional scholars to share their research, which is developed by our research team in 2011. Since publishing SCHOLAT, the number of registered users with real names has risen to more than two thousand [13]. SCHOLAT contains many aspects of a social network, including friendships, groups, and publications. The registered users need to fill in some basic personal information, such as names, emails, research fields and biographies. In this paper, we mainly use the dataset that includes the research fields and profiles of users of SCHOLAT.

3.2   User Research Fields Modeling

Generally, we can extract users' information from their profiles, homepages and so on. But homepages of researchers do not always exist. Moreover, it would increase computational overhead. In this work, we utilize the users' research fields. Users in SCHOLAT must provide their research interests when they register. They can select the item contents from a list to fill in the field of research contents. These item contents are the statistics result of research fields from different universities and institutions. At a practical level, it can bring two benefits. Firstly, we are sure to obtain the information of users' interests that reflects the current and even the future research directions. Secondly, it is more convenient for us to build research-fields-based social networking.

Let G = (U,E,W) be an undirected weighted user-graph representing the academic social network, where U is the set of users and $u_i \in$ U represents the i-th user. E is the set of edges. $e(u_i,u_j) \in$ E represents the edge between u_i and u_j. The edge reflects that u_i and u_j have common research fields. W is the set of weight of edges, $w(u_i,u_j) \in$ W   represents the number of the same research fields between u_i and u_j.

We define the set of users $U = \{u_i\}_{i=1}^{I}$ and the set of tags of research fields $F = \{t_k\}_{k=1}^{K}$. In order to facilitate discussions in the following sections, we define a formula as follows:

T (u_i) = {t_j | t_j is a tag of research fields belonged to $u_i, t_j \in F$ }

We use WordNet to measure the similarities of tags. WordNet is a freely available lexical database for English whose design is inspired by current psycholinguistic theories of human lexical memory [15]. If $t_m \in T(u_i)$ and $t_n \in T(u_j)$ have a semantic similarity, we consider that u_i and u_j have the common research fields. Table 1 shows an example of research fields of users. For example, U_b have two tags and U_d have three tags. Obviously, U_a and U_c have a common research field that is social network analysis. In contrast, there is not any common research field between U_a and U_b.

Table 1. sample tags of four users

Name	Tags of research fields
U_a	Database, Computer Supported Cooperative Work, Cloud computing ,social network analysis
U_b	Artificial intelligence, Logic Programming
U_c	social network analysis
U_d	Database, CSCW, social network analysis

3.3   Research-Fields-Based Graph Construction

We generate an undirected weighted Research-fields-based graph G = (U, E, W). The nodes in the graph are users; the edge represents that two users have the common research interests; the weight of edge represents the number of common interests. Algorithm 1 shows the pseudo code of our method for generating a graph based on common research fields.

```
Algorithm1 Generate a research-fields-based graph.
  Procedure Research-fields-based graph(user,edge,weight)
Input: U = {u₁,…uᵢ ,…,uₙ}, uᵢ denotes the i-th user
        T(uᵢ),the set of research fields belonged to uᵢ
        F, the set of research fields
Output: Research-fields-based G(U,E,W)
for each name∈NameList
    add the node representing users' name to the graph G.
end for
for all uᵢ∈U do
  for all uᵢ₊₁ ∈U do
    for all tₘ∈ T(uᵢ)do
      for all tₙ∈T(uⱼ)do
        if tₘ∈ T(uᵢ) and tₙ∈ T(uⱼ)is semantic similarity then
          if e(uᵢ,uⱼ) not exists in G
          add the edge with uᵢ and uⱼ to the graph G
          w(uᵢ,uⱼ) = 1
          else
          w(uᵢ,uⱼ) = w(uᵢ,uⱼ)+1
        end if
        end if
      end for
    end for
  end for
end for
Return G(U,E,W)
```

Figure 1 demonstrates the Research-fields-based graph of table 1. We can find that U_a and U_d have common research fields on Database, CSCW and social network analysis. Accordingly, there is an edge between U_a and U_d and the weight is 3. Additionally, U_b does not have any common research fields with other users.

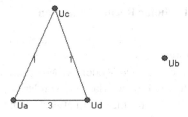

Fig. 1. The Research-fields-based graph of table 1

3.4   Research-Interest-Based Communities Detection

We define research-interest-based community as the group of academic social network participants with common research interests. And the community participants have a lot of internal connections but fewer connections with outsiders. Modularity has recently become quite popular as a way to measure the goodness of a clustering of a graph. It was designed to measure the strength of division of a network into communities. Networks with high modularity have dense connections between the nodes within communities but sparse connections between nodes in different communities [16].

We apply Louvain method to community detection in networks (D. Blondel, Guillaume, Lambiotte, Lefebvre 2008) [17].The Louvain method is a simple, efficient and easy-to-implement method for identifying communities in large networks and finds high modularity partitions of large networks in a short time. Let S denote a set of communities on Research-fields-based graph G. The modularity Q of the Louvain method for a division of the graph into s communities $\{s_1, \ldots ,s_s\}$ is given by Eq. (1):

$$Q = \frac{1}{2m} \sum_s \left(e_s - r * \frac{K_s^2}{2m} \right)$$

(1)

In the above, s is the communities (clusters), m is the number of edges in the graph and r is resolution parameter, default value 1 mean modularity as originally defined. Where k_s is the sum of degrees in community s, and is defined in Eq. (2).

$$K_s = \sum_{i=1}^{s} k_i$$

(2)

where e_s is 2 times the number of lines in community s, and is defined in Eq.(3)

$$e_s = 2 * \sum_{i=1}^{s} k_i \qquad (3)$$

The high values of the modularity correspond to good divisions of a network into communities.

3.5   Community-Based Scholar Recommendation

After detecting communities, we further propose a method to perform research-interest-based scholar recommendation. There is a classical method for calculating similarity between users: Vector Space Model (VSM) based TF/IDF method. TF/IDF method is a kind of basic method to calculate the similarity between two documents. Many users' profiles are simple and the core network members' profiles are rich in content. If we only depend on the content similarities of users' profiles, some core network members will be ignored. These members always play importance roles in research fields. So we propose the friendship score which is combined the classical method with features of communities to calculate users' similarities. Generally, the user's profile includes names, genders, the fields of scientific research, email, academic positions and so on. Firstly, we can calculate the content similarities of users' profiles using the Vector Space Model (VSM). A vector space represents a document or documents by the terms occurring in the document with a weight for each term. It can be defined as Eq. (4):

$$W_{i,j} = f_{i,j} \cdot \log \frac{N}{n_i} \qquad (4)$$

where $f_{i,j}$ is the term frequency of term T in document d (a local parameter), N is the total number of documents and n_i is the number of documents containing the term [19]. $W_{i,j}$ represents the weight of i-th term in document j.

Secondly, the similarity between u_i and u_j can be calculated by employing the cosine similarity [20]. The equation for calculating the similarity is as follows:

$$Sim(u_i, u_j) = cos(u_i, u_j) = \frac{\sum_{k=1}^{|T|} w_{k,i} \times w_{k,j}}{\sqrt{\sum_{k=1}^{|T|} w^2_{k,i}} \times \sqrt{\sum_{k=1}^{|T|} w^2_{k,j}}} \qquad (5)$$

where $sim(u_i, u_j) \in [0,1]$, the resulting similarity ranges from 0 to 1. If $sim(u_i, u_j) = 0$ we denote two users are independent. And 1 means exactly the same.

Additionally, the degree of nodes and the weight of edges can play an important role in recommendation. Thus, we propose the friendship score FS (u_i, u_j). The formula to calculate the similarity of two users is defined in Eq.(6):

$$FS(u_i, u_j) = \alpha * Sim(u_i, u_j) + \beta * D(u_j) + \gamma * W(u_i, u_j) \qquad (6)$$

where $D(u_j) = \text{degree}(u_j) / (g - 1)$, degree (u_j) is the number of direct connections of u_i and g is the number of the nodes in the community. $W(u_i,u_j)$ is the number of common interests between u_i and u_j. The sum of α, β and γ is 1.There parameters has been set empirically.

Finally, we rank the users by the friendship scores in the community and select the top k users for recommendation. If the user already has made friends with all other users in his/her community, we would recommend some users with the high similarity from other communities.

4   Experiments and Analysis

To evaluate our community-based scholar recommendation model, we conduct experiments with the users' profiles from SCHOLAT in July of 2013. In SCHOLAT, a user can make friends with other users who share similar research interests and delete friendships. Users are informed the latest information from his or her friends. In addition, a user is informed the list of users who have added him or her to their personal network, and a list of fans appears in this user's profile [13].

In SHCOLAT, we construct the Research-fields-based graph of SCHOLAT by Algorithm 1. Then we apply Louvain method to community detection in the graph. Figure 2 demonstrates communities of SCHOLAT sketched by Pajek software [21]. The details of communities of Figure 2 are given in table 2. In order to make the graph clear, the users' ID and the weight of edges are not shown here. Due to space limitation, figure 4 cannot show all nodes and edges at the same time. A large number of nodes and edges overlap.

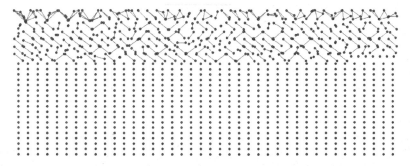

Fig. 2. The communities of SCHOLAT

Table 2. Details of communities of figure 2

NODES	COMMUNITIES	EDGES
2236	1542	1219

Obviously we can find that there are different communities. In the same community, users have same research interests. Figure 3 demonstrates a community which has 7 users.

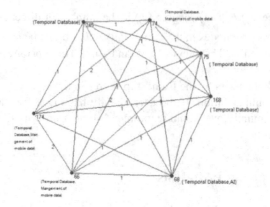

Fig. 3. An example community from Fig 2

We randomly choose two communities to make user recommendation. In the community a, we recommend scholars to user 203. The result is shown in Fig 4(a). User 17 has a great influence in the community a. The similarity between user 203 and user 17 is improved by calculating friendship score. We can see that the proposed model can improve the recommendation of the core network members. In Fig 4(b), it is improved that the similarity between user 245 and the core user 66. Although the core network members might have similar research interests, they always are poor at content similarity. We also test our method with the content-based recommendation method in communities. Generally speaking, our approach works better and is good at recommending the core scholars to users.

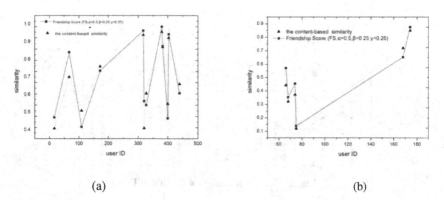

(a)   (b)

Fig. 4. (a) User Id, Similarity for community a, (b) User Id, Similarity for community b

5   Conclusion and Future Work

In this paper, we propose a novel approach for the scholar recommendations based on community detection. In this approach, we construct the graph based on users' research fields, detect the research- fields-based communities by Louvain method and implement scholar recommendation by calculating friendship scores. We implement the model on a real world dataset from SCHOLAT and get encouraging results. In future work, we would like to extract more useful research information from scholars, for example keywords from their papers, to improve the quality of recommendation. With the increasing number of nodes and edges in the social networks, it is necessary to extend our methods in large networks and improve the computing performance in the future.

Acknowledgment. This work was supported in part by the National High-Technology Research and Development Program ("863" Program) of China under Grand 2013AA01A212, the National Nature Science Foundation of China (No.61272067, 61202296, 60970044), Guangdong Province Science and Technology Foundation (No. 2011168005, 2011B090400145, S2012030006242) and Young Teachers Engagement Foundation of South China Normal university (No. 670203).Open Funding of Mobile Internet Application Middle Ware Technology and Engineering Laboratory from Shenzhen.

References

1. Li, J., Mao, C., Chen, J., Yu, J.: The Implementation of an Online Information Service Model based on Academic Social Network Systems. In: Proceedings of the 8th International Conference on Information Science and Digital Content Technology, Korea (South), pp. 223–226 (2012)
2. Li, J., Zhao, G., Rong, C., Tang, Y.: Semantic description of scholar-oriented social network cloud. The Journal of Supercomputing, Online First^{TM}, 1–16 (SCI) (January 21, 2011), doi:10.1007/s11227-010-0550-8
3. Sahebi, Shaghayegh, Cohen: William Community-Based Recommendations: a Solution to the Cold Start Problem. In: Workshop on Recommender Systems and the Social Web (RSWEB), ACM RecSys 2011, Chicago (October 23, 2011)
4. Mooney, R.J., Roy, L.: Content-based book recommending using learning for text categorization. In: Proceedings of the 5th ACM Conference on Digital Libraries, pp. 195–204 (2000)
5. Bezerra, B.L.D., de A.T. de Carvalho, F.: A symbolic approach for content-based information filtering. Information Processing Letters 92(1), 45–52 (2004)
6. Goldberg, D., Nichols, D., Oki, B.M., Terry, D.: Using collaborative filtering to weave an information tapestry. Commun. ACM 35 (December 12, 1992)
7. Lopes, G.R., Moro, M.M., Wives, L.K., de Oliveira, J.P.M.: Collaboration recommendation on academic social networks. In: Trujillo, J., Dobbie, G., Kangassalo, H., Hartmann, S., Kirchberg, M., Rossi, M., Reinhartz-Berger, I., Zimányi, E., Frasincar, F. (eds.) ER 2010. LNCS, vol. 6413, pp. 190–199. Springer, Heidelberg (2010)
8. Heck, T.: Combining social information for academic networking. In: Proceedings of the 2013 Conference on Computer Supported Cooperative Work, pp. 1387–1398 (2013)
9. Xu, Y., Hao, J.: A Personalied Resercher Recommendation Approach in Academic Contexts: Combining Social Networks and Semantic Concepts Analysis. In: Proceedings of the 2010 Pacific Asia Conference on Information Systems (2010)

10. Liu, J.: Aggregating collaborative recommendation method based on network cloud community. Computer Engineering and Applications 47(26), 21–24 (2011)
11. Girvan, M., Newman, M.E.J.: Community structure in social and biological networks. Proc. Ntl. Acad. Sci., USA 99(7821) (2002)
12. Clauset, A., Newman, M.E.J., Moore, C.: Finding community structure in very large networks. Physical Review E 70(6), 066111+ (2004)
13. Yang, A., Li, J., Tang, Y., Wang, J., Zhao, Y.: The Similar Scholar Recommendation in Schol@t. In: Proceedings of the 2012 IEEE 16th International Conference on Computer Supported Cooperative Work in Design, WuHan, China, pp. 666–670 (2012)
14. Nocera, A., Ursino, D.: An approach to provide a user with recommendations of similar users and potentially interesting resources. Knowledge-Based Systems 24(8), 1277–1296 (2011)
15. Fellbaum, C. (ed.): WordNet – An Electronic Lexical Database. MIT Press (1998)
16. Blondel, V.D., Guillaume, J.-L., Lambiotte, R., Lefebvre, E.: Fast unfolding of communities in large networks. J. Stat. Mech. 10008, 1–12 (2008)
17. http://en.wikipedia.org/wiki/Modularity_(networks)
18. Newman, M.E.J., Girvan, M.: Finding and evaluating community structure. Phys. Rev. E 69(2), 026113 (2004)
19. http://en.wikipedia.org/wiki/Tf%E2%80%93idf
20. http://en.wikipedia.org/wiki/Cosine_similarity
21. http://vlado.fmf.uni-lj.si/pub/networks/pajek/
22. Shen, Y., Li, S., Zheng, L., Ren, X., Cheng, X.: Emotion mining research on micro-blog. In: 1st IEEE Symposium on Web Society, SWS 2009, August 23-24 (2009)

A Privacy Protection Solution for the Balance of Performance and Security in Cloud Computing[*]

Ji Yi-mu[1,*], Kang Jia-bang[1], Liu Hai[2], Pan Qiao-yu[1], Sun Yan-peng[1],
Kuang Zizhuo[1], and Zhao Chuanxin[3]

[1] College of Computer, Nanjing University of Posts and Telecommunication, China
jim4njupt@gmail.com
[2] School of Computer, South China Normal University, GuangZhou, China
jim_love@163.com
[3] Department of Computer, Anhui Normal University, Wuhu, China
zcxonline@126.com

Abstract. In order to strengthen users' confidence to upload the private data to cloud platform, existing ways stressed too much on the security. However, cloud computing was an open and distributed environment, and it should provide highly robust, security and quality service to users. So it was necessary to balance the performance and security in cloud platforms, and one hybrid privacy protection solution was proposed with KP-ABE and CP-ABE. This way chosen different way to encrypt the privacy information based on user attributions according to cloud service business type. Finally, this hybrid solution was verified by the case of campus cloud environment.

Index Terms: Cloud Computing, ABE (Attribute-Based Encryption), Data Security, Privacy Protection.

1   Introduction

Cloud computing could help enterprises saving their costs in the fields of hardwires, platform and software services [1, 2]. However, security issues became more and more important when users or enterprises shared and stored theirs services relying on the third party cloud computing service providers, and privacy protection was the key issue [3, 4]. On one hand, user's identification should be verified and ensured the validation of its identification. On the other hand, the user privacy data stored at cloud platform should be ensured their security, so that cloud platform service providers or other customers could not get user's privacy data. Cloud service providers should take charge of the cloud data security and protect its validation and completeness of the privacy data, so that these data could not be destroyed and lost. Currently, the privacy data security could be protected with some technologies, and governments also made some rules and laws to restrict cloud service providers' behavior and obligation.

The technologies about privacy protection have been researched by many scholars. Ref. [5] proposed one public key encryption to authenticate user's identification. Ref.

---

[*] This work was supported by Projects of Jiangsu Industry Supporting (BE2010057), Jiangsu High School Natural Science Research (11KJB520013).

Z. Huang et al. (Eds.): WISE 2013 Workshops 2013, LNCS 8182, pp. 335–345, 2014.
© Springer-Verlag Berlin Heidelberg 2014

[6, 7] proposed the homomorphism encryption to ensure that cloud service providers could not read the contents of data when they executed the data computation for users. There was a fuzzy way to protect user's data [8], and user could code the data and then upload the handled data to cloud server. During the whole process, the server ender did not know user's real data.

Above researches stressed the data security and did not care the performance of the service provided and user's experience. So it needed a balance between the security and performance. Sahai and Waters proposed the conception of ABE (Attribute-Based Encryption) [9]. ABE made the cipher text and private key with relevance of one group of attributions, and user could decrypt the cipher text when user's private key matched the attributions of cipher text. This way could satisfy the balance between the platform performance and privacy protection. Based on ABE, KP-ABE(Key Policy ABE) and CP-ABE(Cipher Policy ABE) were proposed continuously, and these two ways could classify the attributions of user's sensitive data. One access control tree (ACT) would be created based on the classification levels [10]. In the following section, one solution would be given by combining the KP-ABE with CP-ABE for the balance.

2   Related Works

Goyal and its cooperators proposed KP-ABE solution based on ABE [11], and CP-ABE was given based on KP-ABE and ABE [12]. KP-ABE had the correlation among the same attribution set, and ABE could encrypt the attribution set. However, ABE could not decide who might access the data files encrypted. In KP-ABE, user key was connected with the ACT constructed by the same attributions tightly. Users could or not have the right to access and read the data files with relying on the third party key authority, and the right could not be decided by encrypted actor. On the contrary, in CP-ABE the data owner could encrypt the data by creating corresponding ACT and decide who could access the cipher text. Therefore, the accessing and controlling right lay on the data owner. The process of CP-ABE solution was as Fig.1 shown.

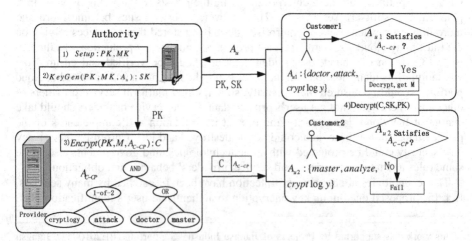

Fig. 1. The encryption and decryption process of CP-ABE

In Fig.1, A_{C-CP} meant the access policy of the cipher text and was described with the tree structure. A_{u_i} meant the set of attributes the number(i) customer's privacy data. Private Key was shortened to PK. Main Key was shortened to MK. And Session Key was shortened to SK. C meant the cipher text. There were four steps in the encryption and decryption process of CP-ABE, and they were <Set up>, <Key Gen>, <Encrypt>, and <Decrypt>. And there were three roles in CP-ABE system, which were customer, provider and authority. The detail work of each phase in Fig.1 would be introduced as following.

Phase 1 <Set up>: In this phase, PK and MK were created by authority firstly after customer requested and submitted A_{u_i} to the authority.

Phase 2 <Key Gen>: Authority generated the SK according to A_u, PK and MK. After this, authority would send the PK and SK to customer.

Phase 3 <Encrypt>: Provider used PK and A_{C-CP} to encrypt the customer data and generated cipher text C. And this phase could be marked as the expression $Encrypt(PK, M, A_{C-CP}): C$. Then provider sent the C and A_{C-CP} to the customer.

Phase 4 <Decrypt>: When customer received the C and A_{C-CP}, and then first judge if the A_u satisfied the policy of A_{C-CP}. If the condition was satisfied, customer could decrypt the cipher text. Otherwise, the customer could not decrypt the cipher text.

In order to describe the protection policy of cipher text more flexible and express more complex logical relationship, CP-ABE and KP-ABE would be integrated in the following solution for the balance of platform performance and privacy protection. In this solution, cloud customer's data would be shared more flexibly, and cloud platform would be more flexible, reliable and usable.

3   The Relationship of User Attributions and Access Control Policies

User privacy data in cloud could be classified into different levels according to different security requirements, so that the access control policy (ACP) based on the attributions would be designed according to different levels. The privacy data would be encrypted and then stored, and ensured user to open different level privacy data. Some data would be shared to other customers who had the rights, and some data would be owned by the owner. Therefore, this individual classification solution according to different security levels was more flexible and applicable. The mapping of access control policy and user privacy data level was shown as Fig.2.

The most important and difficult problem was to construct the ACT in Fig.2, and the leaf nodes in ACT were the privacy attributions. The parent nodes were logical operator, such as 'AND' and 'OR' operators. The sensitive data could be encrypted by ACT, and the encrypted data could be decrypted when the user's attributions satisfied with ACP. And there were three types of ACT in Fig.2, which were high secret level, middle secret level and low secret level.

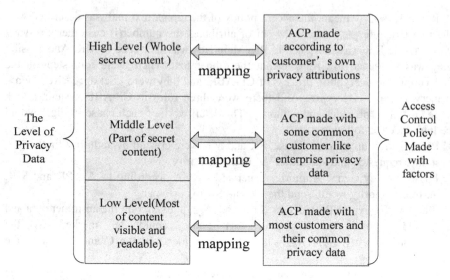

Fig. 2. The mapping between ACP and the level of customer privacy data

- **First type: High secret level**

To customer, the data with high secret level was the most sensitive and private information in cloud environment, such as user mailbox id and key, address, bank card id and key, and so on. These data could not be known by others. If someone satisfied with ACT as Fig.3., these sensitive and privacy data would be encrypted and read. In Fig.3, the user had to own the real name, department and member id, or own the real ID and KEY, and could decrypt the secret data. Otherwise, cloud platform would reject user's requirement. In this case, only valid user could access the data.

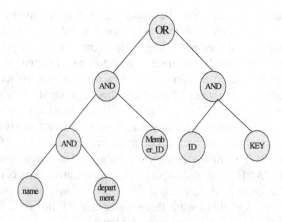

Fig. 3. Strict ACT structure sample

• Second type: Middle secret level

In this case, some users could access the same data, and they were considered to own the same right. Take an example of enterprise user, cloud service provider could set the ACT for the enterprise shown as Fig.4. Fig.4 showed that the manager of researcher, or business sales, or enterprise president could decrypt the encrypted data with middle secret level ACT.

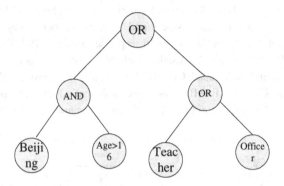

Fig. 4. Middle level ACT structure sample

• Third type: Low secret level

If the user data could be shared by most other users, such as the books, favorite videos, and etc, these type data should be shared in cloud platform and enhanced their usability. Then the service provider could set ACT to most users, and give them the rights to read and browser these data. This solution fit some different groups. Fig.5 was an example of this solution, which meant that in Beijing and age more than 16 years old, or teacher or office could visit the data. This type character was the data which was not the sensitive information.

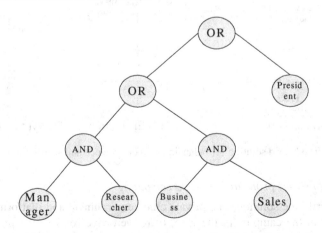

Fig. 5. Low level ACT structure sample

4   The Case of Privacy Protection and Its Implement

A. The hybrid solution for the balance of privacy protection in cloud computing

In order to balance the performance and security, a hybrid solution was proposed here, but this solution was different from Reference [13]. The dual solution in paper [13] used KP-ABE with user subjective attributions, and used CP-ABE with user objective attributions. Here the hybrid solution would choose CP-ABE or KP-ABE according to user customized business and balance the performance and security. If customers hoped that the business would response rapidly, KP-ABE would be chosen. Otherwise, CP-ABE would be used. In cloud computing, access control business needed high security and used CP-ABE, and query business needed high response performance and used KP-ABE [14], this idea called hybrid solution process as Fig.6(1) shown. The implement process of encryption and decryption in Fig.6(2).

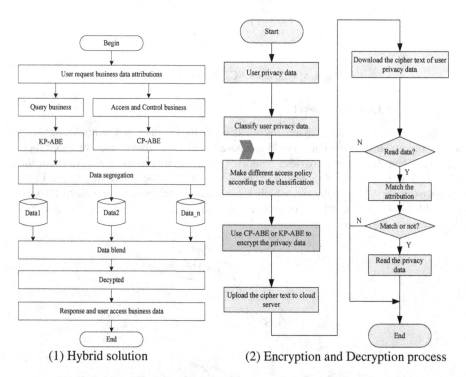

(1) Hybrid solution   (2) Encryption and Decryption process

Fig. 6. The hybrid solution for balancing the performance and security in cloud

B. The case of privacy protection in cloud computing

In order to verify the solution, one private cloud environment and platform was built and deployed in the campus. In the case, there were five roles in the private cloud environment, shown as Fig.7. They were cloud service provider, user, UDDI

(Universal Description, Discovery and Integration), key published center and key distributed center. After user uploaded the data, and got the key from the key distributed center. Cloud service provider both received user data and encrypted the privacy information with ACP. Cipher text C could be read or written when user could decrypt the privacy data with the private key.

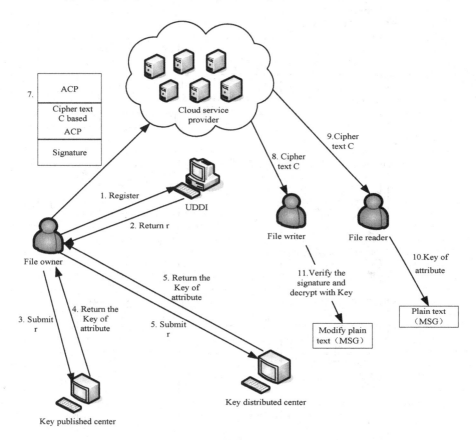

Fig. 7. The case of privacy protection structure in cloud computing

A CRM (Customer Relationship Management) cloud service oriented to Telecom was developed and deployed to the cloud environment as Fig.7 shown. User submitted personnel information which was encapsulated into messages, and these messages were sent to attribute based key distribution center. Then cloud environment fed back public Key and ACP to user, and then the cloud computing platform and cloud storage platform would utilized the CP-ABE and KP-ABE to encrypt user privacy data. The detailed interaction process between users and cloud platform was shown as Fig.8.

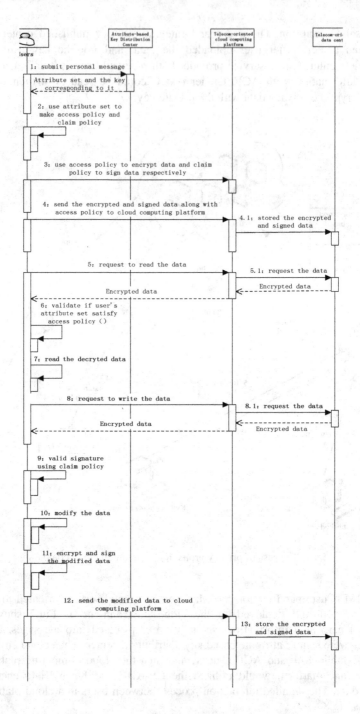

Fig. 8. The interaction process between users and cloud platform

C. The performance analyses of privacy protection solution in cloud computing

CP-ABE toolkit has been realized in reference [15], and KP-ABE toolkit was published in reference [16]. The innovation in the hybrid solution was to differentiate the cloud business service and choose KP-ABE or CP-ABE to encrypt privacy data with user attribution ACT. In order to discuss the performance of the hybrid solution, one CRM cloud service named customer lost analyzed was designed and developed as a product in cloud computing portal shown as Fig.9.

Fig. 9. Cloud service platform portal

The customer information could be accessed by those who had the right according to their attributions. In this case, the performance and security were both considered and implemented the hybrid solution, and this cloud service performance and security index was improved and balanced shown as Fig.10. Here performance index was counted with open cloud platform named Hadoop.

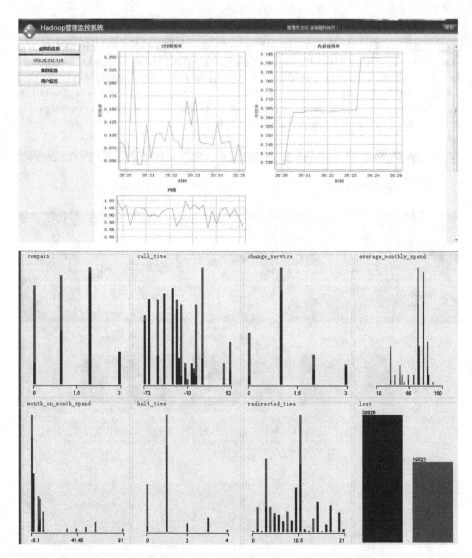

Fig. 10. Performance and security analyze with hybrid solution

The performance and security analyze shown as Fig.10 were realized by the CPABE toolkit. And cpabe-keygen, cpabe-en and cpabe-dec in CPABE toolkit had the line relationship with the number of attributions when they were deployed and run.

5   Conclusion

Although the hybrid solution looked like a rational way to balance the performance and security in cloud computing, the larger and more quantity of data were needed to verify the hybrid solution. The next work would focus on the big data in cloud computing, and continued to verify and optimize the hybrid solution.

References

[1] Demchenko, Y., Mavrin, A., de Laat, C.: Defining Generic Architecture for Cloud Infrastructure as a Service Provisioning model. In: CLOSER 2011 Conference, Nordwijk, Netherlands, May 7-9 (2011)

[2] Armbrust, M., Fox, A., Griffith, R., Joseph, A.D., Katz, R.H., Kon-winski, A., Lee, G., Patterson, D.A., Rabkin, A., Stoica, I., Zaharia, M.: Above the clouds: A berkeley view of cloud computing, University ofCalifornia, Berkeley, Tech. Rep. UCB-EECS (February 28, 2009)

[3] Gellman, R.: Privacy in the Clouds: Risks to Privacy and Confidentiality from Cloud Computing. World Privacy Forum (2009)

[4] Mowbray, M., Pearson, S.: A Client-Based Privacy Manager for Cloud Computing. In: COMSWARE 2009, June 16-19 (2009)

[5] Li, H., Dai, Y., Tian, L., Yang, H.: Identity-based authentication for cloud computing. In: Jaatun, M.G., Zhao, G., Rong, C. (eds.) Cloud Computing. LNCS, vol. 5931, pp. 157–166. Springer, Heidelberg (2009)

[6] Gentry, C.: A fully homomorphic encryption scheme. Ph.D. dissertation, Stanford University (2009), http://www.crypto.stanford.edu/craig

[7] Sadeghi, A.-R., Schneider, T., Winandy, M.: Token-based cloud computing. In: Acquisti, A., Smith, S.W., Sadeghi, A.-R. (eds.) TRUST 2010. LNCS, vol. 6101, pp. 417–429. Springer, Heidelberg (2010)

[8] Wroblewski, G.: General method of program code obfuscation, Ph.D. dissertation, Wroclaw   University   of   Technology   (2002), http://www.ouah.org/wobfuscation.pdf

[9] Sahai, A., Waters, B.: Fuzzy Identity-Based Encryption. In: Cramer, R. (ed.) EUROCRYPT 2005. LNCS, vol. 3494, pp. 457–473. Springer, Heidelberg (2005)

[10] Fang, W., Yang, B., Song, D.: Preserving Private Knowledge In Decision Tree Learning. Journal of Computers 5(5), 733–740 (2010)

[11] Bethencourt, J., Sahai, A., Waters, B.: Ciphertext-policy attribute-based encryption. In: IEEE Symposium on Security and Privacy, pp. 321–334 (2007)

[12] Goyal, V., Pandey, O., Sahai, A., Waters, B.: Attribute Based Encryption for Fine-Grained AccessConrol of Encrypted Data. In: ACM Conference on Computer and Communications Security (ACM CCS) (2006)

[13] Attrapadung, N., Imai, H.: Dual-Policy Attribute Based Encryption. In: Abdalla, M., Pointcheval, D., Fouque, P.-A., Vergnaud, D. (eds.) ACNS 2009. LNCS, vol. 5536, pp. 168–185. Springer, Heidelberg (2009)

[14] Yubin, G., Liankuan, Z., Fengren, L., Ximing, L.: A Solution for Privacy-Preserving Data Manipulation and Query on NoSQL Database. Journal of Computers 8(6), 1427–1432 (2013)

[15] http://hms.isi.jhu.edu/acsc/cpabe/

[16] http://sourceforge.net/p/kpabe/code/1/tree/com/zaranux/crypto/abe/kp/

Enhancing Modularity Optimization via Local Close-Knit Structures

Huajian Zhang[1], Youquan Wang[2], Changjian Fang[3], and Zhiang Wu[3]

[1] College of Internet of Things,
Nanjing University of Post and Telecoms, Nanjing,China
[2] College of Computer Science and Engineering,
Nanjing University of Science and Technology, Nanjing, China
[3] Jiangsu Provincial Key Laboratory of E-Business,
Nanjing University of Finance and Economics, Nanjing, China
zej@njupt.edu.cn, {youq.wang,zawuster}@gmail.com, jselab1999@163.com

Abstract. Discovering communities is crucial for studying the structure and dynamics of networks. Groups of related nodes in the community often correspond to functional subunits such as protein complexes or social spheres. The modularity optimization method is typically an effective algorithm with global objective function. In this paper, we attempt to further enhance the quality of modularity optimization by mining local close-knit structures. First, both periphery and core close-knit structures are defined, and several fast mining and merging algorithms are presented. Second, a novel Fast Newman (FN) algorithm named NFN incorporating local structures into global optimization is proposed. Experimental results in terms of both internal and external on six real-world social networks have demonstrated the effectiveness of NFN on community detection.

Keywords: Community Detection, Modularity Optimization, Fast Newman Algorithm, Close-knit Structures.

1 Introduction

Recent years, the theory and application of complex networks have attracted much attention, since many complex systems can be modeled as networks or graphs such as the World-Wide-Web, social and biological systems, and so on. Discovering community structures is crucial to understand the structural and functional properties of the networks [1]. Formally, this task can be formulated as a network community mining problem (NCMP), which aims to discover all communities from a given network [2].

To date, the existing methods addressing NCMP roughly fall into two categories, in terms of whether or not explicit optimization objectives are being used. The methods with explicit optimization objectives solve the NCMP by transforming it into an optimization problem and trying to find an optimal solution for different kinds of predefined objective functions, among which *modularity*

Z. Huang et al. (Eds.): WISE 2013 Workshops 2013, LNCS 8182, pp. 346–358, 2014.

(a.k.a. Q function [3]) is the most popular one. On the other hand, the methods without using explicit optimization objectives solve the NCMP based upon predefined properties of a node, a pair of nodes, or a group of nodes in a same community, a.k.a. *local close-knit structures*.

Local close-knit structures can give clear pictures about genuine communities, whereas the optimization for global objectives can easily obtain the partitions of all nodes in the network. In this paper, we aims to combine both *local* and *global* methods, that is, utilizing local close-knit structures for enhancing the effectiveness of the global optimization. Particularly, we first define periphery and core close-knit structures, and thus propose mining and merging algorithms for them to obtain all of local close-knit structures. We then take Fast Newman (FN) algorithm, a Q optimization method, as the baseline. Local close-knit structures are seamlessly incorporated into FN to finally obtain a novel algorithm named New Fast Newman (NFN). Experimental studies on six real-life social networks demonstrate that NFN outperforms FN in terms of both internal and external measures.

In the next section, we describe the related work. In section 3, we present the definition, mining and merging algorithms of periphery and core close-knit structures. In section 4, we introduce the algorithmic details of NFN and illustrate the difference FN and NFN by an example. Experimental results are given in section 5.

2   Related Work

Community detection can be traced back to graph partitioning methods, and it aims to minimize the number of edges cut to optimize the objective function, which is proven to be NP-hard. On the basis of this objective function scholars propose a series of heuristic algorithms, such as Kernighan-Lin algorithm, spectral averaging method, maximal flow and minimal cut method and so on. Girvan and Newman put forward Q function as optimization objective function in 2004 [4], and then proposed Fast Newman algorithm as a efficient Q optimization method [3].

Being different from the top-down style adopted by the optimization methods, a bottom-up strategy without global objective was also proposed. They often start by defining local close-knit structures, and then search within a whole network for the communities that hold the proposed definitions [5]. A network's global community structure is detected by considering the ensemble of communities obtained by looping over all of these local structures. For example, the method of k-clique percolation [6] is based on the concept of k-clique. Besides k-clique, a community could be regarded as a clique, a k-clan, a k-plex, an equivalent structures [5, 7]. Due to the limited space, it is difficult to include all the community detection methods in this paper, and we hope the cited review and book [1, 5] can point to some of those missing references.

3   Local Close-Knit Structure Mining and Merging

In this section, we classify the local close-knit structures into *periphery* and *core* close-knit structures, and thus present the mining methods for both two kinds of structures. Since connections naturally exist between two kinds of structures, we also explore several merging strategies to obtain disjoint close-knit structures.

3.1   Periphery Close-Knit Structure

In the literature, two kinds of special nodes, i.e., *hub* and *outlier*, have attracted more attention [8, 9, 10]. The hub node acts like a bridge which connecting different communities, whereas the outlier is often situated at the periphery of the network and connects to only one community with a single link. In other words, the communities of the outliers is fixed, and also lots of outliers might be connected to form the periphery close-knit structure. Formally, we define the outlier as follows.

Definition 1 (Outlier). *Given a graph $G = (V, E), v \in V$ is an outlier, iff one of the following three cases is satisfied: (1) $deg_G(v) = 1$; (2) if there exists a path $P = \{v_1, \cdots, v_f, w\}$ where $deg_G(v_j) = 2(1 \leq j \leq f)$ and $deg_G(w) \geq 2, v = v_j(1 \leq j \leq f)$; (3) $deg_G(v) = 2, \exists w \in N_v, deg_G(w) = 2, N_v \cap N_w \neq \emptyset$.*

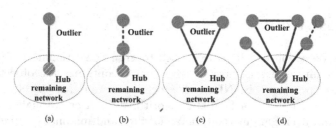

Fig. 1. Illustration of periphery close-knit structures.

Figs. 1(a)-(c) depicts three cases in the Definition 1. To be specific, case (1) represents the periphery isolated nodes, case (2) describes a outlier link, and case (3) corresponds to a outlier triangle. If the outliers are not a isolated part of the network, it will ultimately connected to a hub. Meanwhile, three outlier cases might probably be combined to form a more complex outlier case, as shown in Fig. 1(d). Therefore, four cases in Fig. 1 actually sketch out the periphery close-knit structures.

Definition 2 (Periphery Close-knit Structure). *A connected subgraph consists of a hub and several outliers.*

Next, our task is to mine all the periphery close-knit structures in the network. To this end, we put forward the PSMiner algorithm as shown in Algorithm 1. Case (1) can be regarded as the special case of (2), that is, if the path P in case

(2) contains only two nodes v and w, case (2) is altered to case (1). PSMiner traces back the path from the node with only one neighbor until discovering the hub, as shown in lines 4-15 of Algorithm 1. Then, lines 16-23 are responsible for mining case (3). Note that to mine the combination of three cases, an array $Line[n]$ is defined to record the sequence number in S_p of each node, and thus if the hub has been included by S_p, we put all outliers connected to this hub into the same line of this hub. Obviously, we can mine all periphery close-knit structures by traversing all nodes once, so the complexity of PSMiner is $O(|V|)$.

Algorithm 1. Mining Periphery Close-knit Structures of Graphs

---

1: **procedure** PSMINER(G)
2:     $curline \leftarrow 0$;
3:     **for** $v \leftarrow 1 : n$ **do**
4:         **if** $deg_G(v) = 1$ **then**
5:             $T = \{v\}, w = N_v$;
6:             **while** $deg_G(w) = 2$ **do**
7:                 $T = T \cup w, w = N_w/T$;
8:             **end while**
9:             **if** $Line[w] \neq 0$ **then**
10:                 $S_p \leftarrow$ ADDNODESTOLINE($T, Line[w]$);
11:             **else**
12:                 $S_p \leftarrow$ ADDNEWLINE($\{w\} \cup T$);
13:                 $curline + +, \forall k \in T, Line[k] = curline$;
14:             **end if**
15:         **end if**
16:         **if** $deg_G(v) = 2 \&\& \exists u \in N_v, deg_G(u) = 2, (w = N_v \cap N_u), w \neq \emptyset$ **then**
17:             **if** $Line[w] \neq 0$ **then**
18:                 $S_p \leftarrow$ ADDNODESTOLINE($\{u, v\}, Line[w]$));
19:             **else**
20:                 $S_p \leftarrow$ ADDNEWLINE($\{w, v, u\}$);
21:                 $curline + +, Line[i] \leftarrow curline, i = u, v, w$;
22:             **end if**
23:         **end if**
24:     **end for**
25:     **return** S_p;
26: **end procedure**

3.2   Core Close-Knit Structure

Core close-knit structure is a cohesive subgroup in which nodes are interacting more frequently with each other. An ideal cohesive subgroup is a *clique* [5]. In fact, community is strictly defined as a subgroup in which each pair of users has friendship [11]. This implies that nodes in the cohesive subgroup (e.g. clique) shall not be separated. In this paper, a clique containing k nodes is named k-clique. However, k-clique is a very strict definition, and it can rarely be observed in a huge size in real-life networks. This structure is very unstable as the removal of any edge in it will render it an invalid clique. Therefore, a number of cohesive subgroups relaxing clique have been proposed such as k-clan, k-plex, k-core, and so on. We then select k-clique, k-clan, k-plex as our core close-knit structures. Formally, we have following definitions.

Definition 3 (k-clique). *Given a graph $G = (V, E)$, if the subset $V' \subseteq V$ with k nodes satisfying $\forall v \in V' deg_{G[V']}(v) = k - 1$, V' is a k-clique.*

Definition 4 (k-clan). *Given a graph $G = (V, E)$, if the subset V' with k nodes satisfying $\forall u, v \in V', dis_{G[V']}(u, v) \leq k$, V' is a k-clan.*

Definition 5 (k-plex). *Given a graph $G = (V, E)$, if the subset V' with k nodes satisfying $\forall v \in V', deg_{G[V']}(v) \geq |S| - k$, V' is a k-plex.*

In Definitions 3-5, $G[V']$ denotes the extracted subgraph of G on V', i.e., $G[V'] = (S, E \cap V' \times V')$, and $dis_{G[V']}(u, v)$ denotes the length of the shortest part between u and v in $G[V']$. The search for the maximum cliques in a graph is typically a NP_hard problem. Since k-clan and k-plex are relaxed from k-clique, to mine both two structures might be even difficult. Therefore, mining core close-knit structures from large-scale networks might be infeasible, while the core close-knit structure can indeed improve the performance on community detection, which will be shown in section 5.

3.3   The Merging Strategy

Our task is to discover disjoint communities in the networks as similar as the most work in the realm of community detection [4, 3, 1]. However, the core close-knit structures defined by k-clique, k-clan or k-plex are often nested. For instance, every subgraph of k-clique is also a clique. Therefore, to obtain the close-knit structures as seeds, we have to handle the nested structures. To this end, we here present two strategies, i.e., Long-Structure-First(LSF) and Short-Structure-First(SSF). Taking LSF as an example, LSF first sorts the core close-knit structures in length-DESCENDING order, and then examines the structure one by one. If all of nodes in current structure are not selected, this structure is selected as a seed. Otherwise, the structure will be dropped. SSF is similar to LSF, but it sorts the core close-knit structures in length-ASCENDING order. Essentially, LSF assumes the larger structures are of much more interest, whereas SSF the smaller structures are of much more valuable.

After obtaining disjoint core close-knit structures, the following task is to merge the periphery and core structures. Note that since the case (3) of the Definition 1 is actually a 3-clique, we have to remove these 3-cliques from the set of core close-knit structures when it is defined as k-clique. Moreover, there is only one hub in each periphery structure, and this hub might be contained by at most one core structure. So the merging strategy is to consider the periphery and core structures that have intersecting hub node. Algorithm 2 shows the pseudocodes of the merging strategy.

Algorithm 2 first uses LSF or SSF to get the disjoint core close-knit structures, and then traverses the periphery close-knit structures set S_p. In line 4,

ExtractHub($S_p[i]$) is responsible for extracting hub node w in current periphery structure.Then, if w is contained by a core structure $DS_c[j]$, $S_p[i]$ and $DS_c[j]$ are merged. Finally, the structures that are not merged in S_p and DS_c are added into S to keep the completeness.

Algorithm 2. Merge Structures of Periphery and Core

1: **procedure** MERGE(S_p, S_c)
2:    $DS_c \leftarrow \mathrm{LSF}(S_c)$;
3:    **for** $i \leftarrow 1 : |S_p|$ **do**
4:        $w \leftarrow \mathrm{EXTRACTHUB}(S_p[i])$;
5:        **for** $j \leftarrow 1 : |DS_c|$ **do**
6:            **if** $(w \in DS_c[j])$ **then**
7:                $S \leftarrow S \cup (DS_c[j] \cup (S_p[i]/\{w\}))$, $DS_c \leftarrow DS_c/\{DS_c[j]\}$;
8:                **break**;
9:            **end if**
10:       **end for**
11:       $S \leftarrow S \cup S_p[i]$;
12:   **end for**
13:   $S \leftarrow S \cup DS_c$;
14:   **return** S;
15: **end procedure**

---

4   Modularity Optimization via Close-Knit Structures

In this section, we incorporate close-knit structures into the traditional FN algorithm to enhance its performance. The proposed algorithm is named New Fast Newman(*NFN* for short). We first introduce the algorithm details, and then give an example on `Karate` dataset to show the difference between NFN and FN.

4.1   The Algorithm Design

Generally, FN [3] is a modularity optimization method, which adopts an agglomerative hierarchical clustering strategy. FN starts by taking each node as a community, and then at each step merges two communities that contributes the largest increase of Q. The merging process will not stop until K communities are obtained. Now, we have mined close-knit structures, and we argue that taking these close-knit structures as seeds, i.e., communities at the beginning, will be better than taking every node as a community, because nodes in the close-knit structure essentially belong to the same community.

Along this line, the key part of NFN is to compute and update the Q function, which is determined by inner and inter edges among communities. Let $\mathbf{E}$ be a matrix, of which each element e_{ij} is the number of edges between community i and j. So, if $i = j$, e_{ij} denotes the number of inner edges in community i, and if $i \neq j$, e_{ij} denotes the number of inter edges between i and j. Based on $\mathbf{E}$, Q can be computed as follows.

$$Q = \sum_i (e_{ii} - a_i^2), \tag{1}$$

where a_i denotes the sum of edges between i and other communities, i.e., $a_i = \sum_{i, i \neq j} e_{ij}$. To find the largest $\triangle Q$, we need to compute $\triangle Q_{ij}$ for all community pairs. The advantage of NFN is that computing $\triangle Q_{ij}$, as shown in Eq. (2) only depends on community i and j.

$$\triangle Q_{ij} = e_{ij} + e_{ji} - 2a_i a_j. \tag{2}$$

Algorithm 3. New Fast Newman Algorithm

1: **procedure** NFN(G, S, K)
2:     $C \leftarrow$ CONNECTEDCOMP(G, L);
3:     **if** $K \leqslant C$ **then**
4:         **return** L;
5:     **end if**
6:     $l \leftarrow$ INITIALIZATION$(L, \mathbf{E})$;
7:     **while** $l > K$ **do**
8:         $\triangle Q_{ij}^{max} \leftarrow$ MAX$(\triangle Q)$;
9:         **for** $p \leftarrow 1 : n$ **do**
10:             **if** $L[p] = j$ **then**
11:                 $L[p] \leftarrow i$;
12:             **end if**
13:         **end for**
14:         $l - -$, UPDATE$(\mathbf{E})$;   ▷ update Matrix $\mathbf{E}$ by using Eq.(1) and Eq.(2)
15:     **end while**
16:     **return** L;
17: **end procedure**

If the graph is undirected, $\triangle Q_{ij} = 2(e_{ij} - a_i a_j)$, since $e_{ij} = e_{ji}$. NFN only needs to maintain the matrix $\mathbf{E}$ for modularity optimization. In particular, $\mathbf{E}$ is initialized according to the set of close-knit structures S, and then is updated as two communities are merged. To understand the updating details, assuming communities i and j are merged, $i < j$, the new community is labeled i, i.e., the smaller number. So we need to update the number of inner edges in i, the number of inter edges for i, and then delete the j-th line of $\mathbf{E}$. Eqs. (3) and (4) show both inner and inter edges update for i.

$$e_{ii}^{'} = e_{ii} + e_{jj} + 2e_{ij}, \tag{3}$$

$$e_{ir}^{'} = e_{ir} + e_{jr}(i, j \neq r). \tag{4}$$

Based upon the aforementioned computational details, the pseudocodes of NFN are depicted in Algorithm 3. As can be seen, lines 2-5 are to handle a special case

Table 1. Experimental network data sets

Datasets	$|V|$	$|E|$	$< k >$	C	K
Karate	34	78	4.588	0.571	2
School	69	227	6.580	0.468	6
Polbooks	105	441	8.400	0.488	3
Football	115	614	10.678	0.402	11
CMC05	23133	186878	16.157	0.633	-
Enron	1133	10902	19.244	0.220	-

of NFN. That is, if the graph is composed of C connected components and the number of communities set by user $K \leq C$, NFN will return C communities each of which is a connected component. If $K > C$, NFN initializes the matrix $\mathbf{E}$ and label vector L, where $L[i], 1 \leq i \leq n$, denotes the community ID for i-th node. Note that the variable $l = n - |S|$ indicates the number of seed communities. Lines 7-16 show the merging process of which the number of iteration is $l - K$. Although updating $\mathbf{E}$ as shown in Eqs. (3) and (4), it still traverse all nodes in the worst case. Therefore, the time complexity of NFN is $O(n(l - K)) = O(n(n - |S| - K))$.

4.2   An Example

Here we apply both FN and NFN on a small social network with ground truth. The purpose is to gain a direct comparison between FN and NFN both on process and performance. Karate [12] is a classic social network with 34 members in a Karate club of some university in USA. This club splits into two parties following a disagreement between an instructor(node #1) and an administrator(node #34), and constitutes two real communities. We apply NFN with k-clique as the definition of core close-knit structures and LSF as the overlapping removal strategy on Karate. Fig. 2 shows the ground truth of Karate, as well as two dendrograms obtained by FN and NFN, respectively. As can be seen, two dendrograms differed too much, and node #10 was misclassified by FN. However, the result of NFN perfectly matched the ground truth. Note that in the dendrogram of NFN the blue bold lines indicated the merging led by close-knit structures.

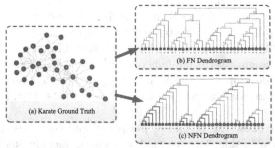

Fig. 2. Comparison between FN and NFN on Karate network

5 Experimental Results

In our experiments we utilized six network data sets: Karate, School, Polbooks, Football, CMC05 and Enron. Some characteristics of these data sets are shown in Table 1, where $|V|$ and $|E|$ indicate the numbers of nodes and edges respectively in the network, $< k > = 2|E|/|V|$ indicates the average degree, C indicates the average clustering coefficient, and K is the number of communities indicated by the ground truth. Note that two somewhat big data sets CMC05 and Enron do not have ground truth, and thus "-" are marked in K column.

Table 2. Results of periphery and core close-knit structures

Datasets		Karate	School	Polbooks	Football	CMC05	Enron
Periphery		1/2	1/2	0/0	0/0	1876/4925	129/282
	All	25/81	66/241	181/719	185/760	7576/31413	2045/7470
k-clique	LSF	4/15	11/44	14/59	18/110	1734/7772	121/492
	SSF	5/15	10/31	19/60	24/76	1988/6841	48/503
	All	8/87	58/540	145/2844	152/1737	7543/97962	1665/31054
k-clan	LSF	2/24	3/37	2/53	5/67	910/7361	35/419
	SSF	2/14	5/25	4/28	6/42	1133/5820	64/327
	ALL	273/926	589/2097	1809/7243	2465/8655	-	-
k-plex	LSF	4/17	10/48	18/76	16/109	-	-
	SSF	6/18	17/51	25/75	33/99	-	-

Note: x/y denotes there are y nodes in x structures.

Karate has been introduced in section 4.2. School [13]is a network of relationships which formed from students coming from six grades of some school in USA between 1994 and 1995. Every grade is a community, and friend relationships were obtained from student's self-reporting. Polbooks [14] contains 105 nodes representing books about US politics sold by Amazon.com, in which the edge indicates the pair of books were frequently bought together. Football [15] depicts a relationships graph of football games which are hold among different universities in USA in the 2000 season. In the graph there are 115 nodes, each of which represents a different team. Each edge of the graph means there is a contest between two teams, and eleven clubs compose eleven different communities. CMC05 [16] is a co-authorship network including all preprints posted between Jan.1, 1995 and Mar.31, 2005 on Cornell University Library. Each node of the graph is a author, and each edge of the graph means that two authors have co-authored at least one paper. Enron [17] is a communication network, nodes of the network are email addresses, if an address i sends at least one email to address j, there will be an undirected edge from i to j, and vice versa.

We use UCINET to mine three kinds of core close-knit structures [18], and use C++ language to implement PSMiner, LSF, SSF and merging algorithms. We develop the NFN based upon the open-source algorithm FN(http://cs.unm.edu/~aaron/research/fastmodularity.htm) which is also coded in C++.

First of all, we show the results of periphery and core close-knit structures on six data sets in Table 2. Note that a k-clique includes at least 3 nodes, while k-clan and k-plex contain at least 2 nodes. There are few periphery close-knit structures in small-scale networks, but indeed a great many in large-scale networks. For instance, there are 1876 periphery close-knit structures covering 4925 nodes in CMC05. Although each network includes lots of core close-knit structures, the number disjoint structures obtained by LSF or SSF are not too much. Due to the loose definition of k-plex, UCINET failed to mine them in two large networks, which leads to the missing data in Table 2.

5.1   Performance in Terms of the Internal Measure

Here, we investigate the improvement on the quality of discovered communities. Q is selected as the internal measure. Table 3 gives the overall results on k-clique, k-clan and k-plex, respectively. During the merging process of FN and NFN, the maximum Q value and its step were recorded. If the steps of maximum Q are different between FN and NFN, we also recorded the Q value of NFN as FN reached the maximum at this step. Meanwhile, it is easy to compute the number of discovered communities at each step, that is, $K = n - \#Step$. Note that the best one in each line is boldly marked.

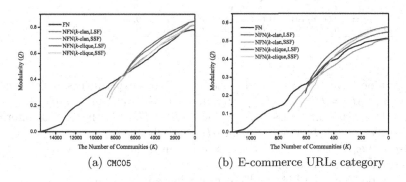

(a) CMC05   (b) E-commerce URLs category

Fig. 3. Q values along with the number of communities K

As can be seen, NFN outperforms FN in most cases, except selecting k-clan as core structures on School and Football. By comparing three definitions of three kinds of core structures, we find the k-clique achieved the best performance. Moreover, comparing LSF and SSF implies the LSF is better than SSF. Therefore, employing k-clique for defining core structures and LSF for removing overlapping nodes will be the best settings for NFN.

We then take a close look at the increasing of Q during each iteration. Fig. 3 shows the Q value along with K on CMC05 and Enron. The observations on Fig. 3 is similar to that on Table 3. That is, the performance of NFN is better regardless of settings, and also NFN with k-clique and LSF achieves the best performance.

5.2   Performance in Terms of the External Measure

In our experiment, four small data sets do have ground truth, which facilitates us to evaluate the performance on external measures. Many recent studies use the external measure: Normalized Mutual Information(NMI), to evaluate the

Table 3. Performance improvement on Q

(a) k-clique

Datasets	FN MaxQ/Step	NFN(k-clique, LSF) MaxQ/Step	Q/Step	NFN(k-clique, SSF) MaxQ/Step	Q/Step
Karate	0.3807/31	**0.4313/30**	0.4130/31	0.3787/31	-
School	0.5840/64	**0.6015/63**	0.6014/64	0.5566/63	0.5551/64
Polbooks	0.5020/101	**0.5364/100**	0.5364/101	0.5349/101	-
Football	0.5695/109	**0.6331/105**	0.6212/109	0.5206/109	-
CMC05	0.7818/15353	**0.8452/15451**	0.8441/15353	0.8194/15440	0.8185/15353
Enron	0.5130/1120	**0.5759/1122**	0.5757/1120	0.5724/1120	-

(b) k-clan

Datasets	FN MaxQ/Step	NFN(k-clan, LSF) MaxQ/Step	Q/Step	NFN(k-clan, SSF) MaxQ/Step	Q/Step
Karate	0.3807/31	**0.5409/31**	0.4133/32	0.4133/32	0.4091/31
School	**0.5840/64**	0.5707/64	-	0.4883/64	-
Polbooks	0.5020/101	**0.5610/100**	0.5607/101	0.4826/102	0.4820/101
Football	**0.5695/109**	0.5230/110	0.5143/109	0.4541/109	-
CMC05	0.7818/15353	**0.8467/15471**	0.8449/15353	0.8142/15451	0.8129/15353
Enron	0.5130/1120	**0.5187/1122**	0.5187/1120	0.5187/1122	0.5187/1120

(c) k-plex

Datasets	FN MaxQ/Step	NFN(k-plex, LSF) MaxQ/Step	Q/Step	NFN(k-plex, SSF) MaxQ/Step	Q/Step
Karate	0.3807/31	0.4290/31	-	**0.4326/31**	-
School	0.5840/64	**0.6240/64**	-	0.5770/65	0.5712/64
Polbooks	0.5020/101	**0.5634/100**	0.5622/101	0.5075/101	-
Football	0.5695/109	**0.6347/105**	0.6163/109	0.4207/111	0.4179/109

clustering performance [19]. we also use NMI in our experiments, which is computed as: $NMI = I(G, L)/\sqrt{H(G)H(L)}$, where the random variables G and L denote the cluster and class sizes, respectively, $I(G, L)$ is the mutual information between G and L, and $H(G)$ and $H(L)$ are the Shannon entropies of G and L, respectively. The value of NMI is in the interval: [0,1], and a larger value indicates a better clustering result.

As can be seen from Fig. 4, although FN has advantage over NFN with some settings, NFN with k-clique and LSF shows consistently higher quality than FN. However, other settings of NFN are not useful in all data sets. For example, NFN with k-plex and LSF obtained the best partitions on School and performed close to NFN with k-clique and LSF on Football.

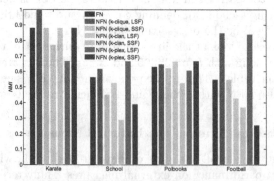

Fig. 4. The performance comparison on NMI

6   Conclusion

In this paper, we put forward a kind of community detection method based on modularity optimization and merging local close-knit structures. Firstly, based on definitions of hub and outlier, we give a definition of periphery close-knit structure, then propose a linear algorithm to mine the periphery close-knit structures. Secondly, a novel Fast Newman algorithm named NFN incorporating local structures into global optimization is proposed. Finally, experiments on six real-world social networks have demonstrated the effectiveness of NFN on community detection.

Acknowledgments. This research is supported by National Natural Science Foundation of China under Grants No.71072172, 61103229, Key Project of Natural Science Research in Jiangsu Provincial Colleges and Universities(12KJA520001); National Key Technologies R&D Program of China (2013BAH16F00); Natural Science Foundation of Jiangsu Province of(BK2012863).

References

[1] Fortunato, S.: Community detection in graphs. Phys. Rep. 486, 75–174 (2010)

[2] Yang, B., Liu, J., Feng, J.: On the spectral characterization and scalable mining of network communities. IEEE Transactions on Knowledge and Data Engineering 24(2), 326–337 (2012)

[3] Newman, M.: Fast algorithm for detecting community structure in networks. Phys. Rev. E 69(6), 66113 (2004)

[4] Newman, M.E., Girvan, M.: Finding and evaluating community structure in networks. Physical review E 69(2), 26113 (2004)

[5] Tang, L., Liu, H.: Community Detection and Mining in Social Media. Morgan & Claypool Publishers, California (2010)

[6] Palla, G., Derenyi, I., Farkas, I., Vicsek, T.: Uncovering the overlapping community structure of complex networks in nature and society. Nature 435, 814–818 (2005)

[7] Wasserman, S., Faust, K.: Social Network Analysis: methods and applications. Cambridge University Press (1994)

[8] Xu, X., Yuruk, N., Feng, Z., Schweiger, T.A.: Scan: a structural clustering algorithm for networks. In: Proceedings of the 13th ACM SIGKDD International Conference on Knowledge Discovery and Data Mining, pp. 824–833. ACM (2007)

[9] Lewis, T.G.: Network science: Theory and applications. John Wiley & Sons (2011)

[10] Papadopoulos, S., Kompatsiaris, Y., Vakali, A., Spyridonos, P.: Community detection in social media. Data Mining and Knowledge Discovery 24(3), 515–554 (2012)

[11] Everett, M.G., Borgatti, S.P.: Peripheries of cohesive subsets. Social Networks 21(4), 397–407 (2000)

[12] Zachary, W.W.: An information flow model for conflict and fission in small groups. J. Anthropol. Res. 33, 452–473 (1977)

[13] Zhao, Y., Levina, E., Zhu, J.: Community extraction for social networks. Proc. Natl. Acad. Sci. 108(18), 7321–7326 (2011)

[14] Newman, M.E.J.: Finding community structure in networks using the eigenvectors of matrices. Phys. Rev. E 74, 036104 (2006)

[15] Girvan, M., Newman, M.E.: Community structure in social and biological networks. Proceedings of the National Academy of Sciences 99(12), 7821–7826 (2002)

[16] Newman, M.E.J.: The structure of scientific collaboration networks. Proc. Natl. Acad. Sci. 98(2), 404–409 (2001)

[17] Leskovec, J., Lang, K., Dasgupta, A., Mahoney, M.: Community structure in large networks: Natural cluster sizes and the absence of large well-defined clusters. Internet Math. 6(1), 29–123 (2009)

[18] Borgatti, S.P., Everett, M.G., Freeman, L.C.: Ucinet for windows: Software for social network analysis (2002)

[19] Cao, J., Wu, Z., Wu, J., Xiong, H.: SAIL: Summation-based incremental learning for information-theoretic text clustering. IEEE Transactions on Cybernetics 43(2), 570–584 (2013)

Detecting Hotspots in Insulin-Like Growth Factors 1 Research through MetaMap and Data Mining Technologies

Shumei Yin[1], Chunying Li[1], Yigang Zhou[2], and Jun Huang[3]

[1] Peking University Health Science Library, Beijing 100191, P.R. China
{yinsm,licy}@bjmu.edu.cn, yingshumei@163.com
[2] Peking University Library, Beijing 100871, P.R. China
zhouyg@lib.pku.edu.cn
[3] Beijing Foreign Studies University, Beijing 100089, P.R. China
huangjbw@126.com

Abstract. Most digital information resources for readers of the medical library exist in the form of unstructured free text (journal papers). Therefore it has become the new direction of data mining research to extract keywords in the collection of medical literature and turn them into structured knowledge that is easily accessible and analyzable. MetaMap, a mapping tool from free text to the UMLS Metathesaurus developed by the U.S. National Library of Medicine, maps keywords to the normative UMLS thesaurus, and provides a rating for the mapping degree of every word. The present study extracts keywords from the English language literature of insulin-like growth factors 1 research, assigns weights to the keywords using the BM25F model, screens out groups of important keywords, carries out a cluster analysis of these keywords.

Keywords: Medical Data Mining, MetaMap, insulin-like growth factors 1, hotspot detection.

1 Introduction

Academic journals are publications that reflect latest academic developments. With every university or research institute being a subscriber to dozens of journal databanks, a researcher needs to go through the databanks one after one to obtain the information they need. Before a medical researcher decides on a research topic, they need to spend enormous time and effort to search for relevant literature, and induce hotspot research topics from them. For the time being, most of the digital information resources to which readers of medical libraries have access exist in the form of unstructured free text. Knowledge extraction[1] in its narrow sense means extracting keywords through analysis of free text, then transforming them into structured knowledge through statistical analysis for the purpose of further analysis and application. Therefore, the focus of the present study shall be how to extract hotspot keywords from collections of insulin-like growth factors 1 research, cluster those

Z. Huang et al. (Eds.): WISE 2013 Workshops 2013, LNCS 8182, pp. 359–372, 2014.
© Springer-Verlag Berlin Heidelberg 2014

important keywords to theme areas which are independent of each other and find emerging trends from those theme areas.

MetaMap is a mapping tool from free text to the Unified Medical Language System (UMLS) Metathesaurus developed by the U.S. National Library of Medicine. It carries out segmentation and semantic analysis of the free text, maps keywords to the normative UMLS thesaurus, and provides a rating for the mapping degree of every word. A higher rating suggests a higher degree in mapping accuracy and vise versa. The present study attempts to extract keywords from collections of insulin-like growth factors 1 literature (from Pubmed databank etc.) with the help of MetaMap. It will carry out a cluster analysis of these keywords, and display these keywords in graphical format to give a presentation of the hotspot keywords and their close relationships with other related keywords.

The rest of the paper is organized as follows: Section 2 summarizes the current major technical approaches in medical data mining; Section 3 presents methods and procedures of our analysis of insulin-like growth factors 1 research trends; Section 4 discusses the results of the analysis and the prospects of future research.

2   Major Technical Approaches in Medical Data Mining

The first successful attempt at detecting hotspots through data mining based on the Medline/Pubmed databank was made in 1986. Don R. Swanson from University of Chicago proposed the non-literature related knowledge discovery methods, and extracted two "hidden connections" successfully [2]. A survey of data mining systems used in the bio-medical research field within and without China was carried out in the present study. The following is a summary of the technical approaches adopted in medical data mining up to present.

Specific Term Extraction and Co-occurrence Analysis: For example, automated extraction of explicit and implicit biomedical knowledge from publicly available gene and text databases was carried out to create a gene-to-gene co-citation network of 13, 712 named human genes. The titles and abstracts in over 10 million Medline articles are processed with computer analysis to construct such a network. The undertakings are collectively known as "PubGene" [3]. Large-scale experiments also demonstrate that co-occurrence reflects biologically meaningful relationships, thus providing an approach to extract and structure known biology.

Natural Language Processing Technology: The Medstract [4] project of Brandeis University adopts UMLS as its normative thesaurus, and uses natural language processing technology to carry out parsing analysis, semantic type identification, re-rendering of semantic ontologies in analyzing specific terms in Medline literature. Named entities recognition and relation identification are realized through this approach.

Data Mining Methods: The knowledge discovery process consists of several key steps. (U. Fayyad, 1996)[5] These steps compose the basic procedure followed by most of the data mining software at present.

- Gaining familiarity with the application domain and identifying the ultimate goal of the application.
- Creating a target data set.
- Data cleaning and preprocessing.
- Data reduction and transformation: identifying useful features, standardization of the data, and reducing dimensionality of the data.
- Identifying which particular method (such as classification, clustering or association) is the most suitable to our goal.
- Choosing the mining algorithm(s) appropriate for the method chosen in the previous step.
- Data mining: search for patterns of interest, classification, clustering, etc.
- Evaluation of results and knowledge presentation: visualization, transformation, removing redundant patterns, etc.
- Use of discovered knowledge (U. Fayyad, 1996) [5].

Visualized Information Software Based on Scientific Literature Hotspots Detection: CiteSpace[6] is a visualized information software based on scientific literature hotspots detection. It was developed by the College of Information Science and Technology of Drexel University in the U.S. from 2003 to 2005. Its developers used this software for the analysis of two research fields: mass extinction (1981-2004) and terrorism (1990-2003). Through monitoring trends in visualized networks and combining it with consultations with domain experts, as well as discussions on practical application, Citespace is able to predict research challenges and opportunities in the future.

3   Methods and Procedures of Insulin-Like Growth Factors 1 Research Analysis

3.1   Data Set

The data set of the present study is obtained through searching the MeSH (Medical Subject Headings) headings "Insulin-Like Growth Factor I OR Insulin Like Growth Factor I" in the 1966-2012 data collections of Medline, Derwent Innovations Index (DII) and SciFinder Scholar. Documents from the three databanks are then matched. Articles with the same titles and authors are counted as one. The data set is comprised of 1085 articles altogether. The purpose of gathering data from Medline, DII, and SCI is to combine the document entry information resources of those databanks. For example, Medline keeps record of an article's MeSH headings and research fund number, while SCI records an article's frequency of being cited. Combining document information from those databanks will have their respective advantages integrated for the present research, and provide solid basis for further analysis.

3.2   Extracting Keywords

"MetaMap is a widely available program providing access to the concepts in the unified medical language system (UMLS) Metathesaurus from biomedical text."[7] It was developed by Dr. Alan Aronson at the National Library of Medicine (NLM). MetaMap uses a knowledge intensive approach based on symbolic, natural language processing (NLP) and computational linguistic techniques. It carries out segmentation and semantic analysis of the free text, maps keywords to the normative UMLS thesaurus, and provides a rating for the mapping degree of every word. A higher rating suggests a higher degree in mapping accuracy and vise versa. The present study attempts to extract keywords from collections of insulin-like growth factors 1 literature using the MetaMap tools. We collected the titles and abstracts of all the qualified documents and used these as input data for MetaMap (According to the requirements of MMTx, the data were put in text format, as is shown in figure 1.).

TI   - Exogenous insulin-like growth factor 1 enhances thymopoiesis predominantly through thymic epithelial cell expansion.

AB   - Insulin-like growth factor 1 (IGF-1) enhances thymopoiesis but given the broad distribution of IGF-1 receptors (IGF-1Rs), its mechanism of action has remained unclear. To identify points of thymic regulation by IGF-1, we examined its effects on T-cell precursors, thymocytes, and thymic epithelial cells (TECs) in normal and genetically altered mice. In thymus-intact but not thymectomized mice, IGF-1 administration increased peripheral naive and recent thymic emigrant (RTE) populations, demonstrating its effect on T-cell production, not peripheral expansion. IGF-1 administration increased bone marrow LSK (lineage(-), Sca-1(+), c-kit(+)) precursor proliferation and peripheral LSK populations, increased thymocyte populations in a sequential wave of expansion, and proportionately expanded TEC subpopulations and enhanced their chemokine expression. To separate IGF-1's effects on thymocytes and TECs, we generated mice lacking IGF-1R on thymocytes and T cells. Thymocyte and RTE numbers were decreased in these mice, but IGF-1 treatment produced comparable thymocyte numbers to similarly treated wild-type mice. We additionally separated thymic- from LSK-specific effects by demonstrating that IGF-1 increased thymocyte numbers despite impaired early thymic progenitor (ETP) importation in PSGL-1KO mice. These results indicate

---

Fig. 1. Format of input data for MetaMap

MetaMap processes the input data sentence by sentence, produces results in sentence units which mark the identification number of a concept word, the location of its source segment, the identification number of its source sentence, its semantic type etc. The figure 2 shows the results of applying MetaMap (the results shown here are for one search phrase).

The number before every concept word represents a score of rating based on the matching degree when the original phrase is mapped to a MeSH heading. It varies between 0 and 1000, with 1000 being an indicator of complete match. The phrase in the parenthesis is an alternative form of the concept word. The present study selects keywords according to the scores and the semantic types of the concept words. A set of keywords for every article is thus obtained and their location in the article is also recorded.

```
Processing 00000000.ti.1: Exogenous insulin-like growth factor
1 enhances thymopoiesis predominantly through thymic epithelial
cell expansion.

Phrase: "Exogenous insulin-like growth factor 1"
Meta Mapping (892)
    795 Exogenous [Functional Concept]
    913 Insulin-like growth factor 1 (Insulin-Like Growth Factor
I) [Amino Acid, Peptide, or Protein, Biologically Active
Substance]

Phrase: "enhances"
Meta Candidates (0): <none>
Meta Mappings: <none>

Phrase: "thymopoiesis predominantly"
Meta Candidates (0): <none>
Meta Mappings: <none>

Phrase: "through thymic epithelial cell expansion."
Meta Mapping (861)
```

Fig. 2. The results of applying MetaMap (the results shown here are for one search phrase)

The results from MetaMap need to be further screened according to their ratings and semantic types. In order to get the main concept words or phrases which can well express the main ideas of one paper, and also obtain newly appeared terms (words and word groups) which are not currently contained in UMLS, we developed a set of filtering rules as follows:

(1) The semantic units or subunits are kept as key words (or key word groups) if they got a score above 1000.

(2) If a semantic unit does not have exact correspondence in MeSH, and all its subunits have a score above 500, and the semantic unit does not include mathematical operators "=,>,<" in the original texts, then all MMTx-generated keywords or word groups will be kept.

(3) If a semantic unit contains mathematical operators "=,>,<", only the semantic unit from the original text will be kept, leaving out the MMTx-generated units.

(4) If a semantic unit does not have exact correspondence in MeSH, and the semantic type of its subunits (word or word groups) is "Age group", these subunits will be kept as key word or word groups.

(5) If a semantic unit does not have exact correspondence in MeSH, and its subunits (words or word groups) also do not have correspondence, the semantic unit will be segmented according to spaces in the original text. Only words with real meanings with will be kept as key words leaving out stop words and punctuations.

(6) Words or word groups that do not meet the above requirements are left out.

By using the MetaMap tools and the rules above, we get 188416 keywords from the title and abstact fields which come from the data sets.

3.3   Selection of Major Keywords

Although some words appear with high frequencies in the literature, they are not the focus of a research's discussion. To distinguish the keywords that truly reflect the focus of a research, and to eliminate the disturbance of pan-meaning words, the present study calculates weighted frequencies of the keywords using the BM25F model [8] proposed by Robertson et al. Major keywords are selected according to the weighted frequencies. The following is the BM25F model, as in (1).

$$wf_j(\bar{d},C)=\frac{(k_1'+1)tf_j'}{k_1'\left((1-b)+b\dfrac{dl'}{avdl'}\right)+tf_j'}\log\frac{N-df_j+0.5}{df_j+0.5} \qquad (1)[8]$$

Wherein, tf' refers to the frequency of the j-th weighted query words in document $\bar{d}$; dl' refers to the length of the weighted document; avd' refers to the average document length of the weighted documents; k_1' is the weighted free parameter.

Suppose in a given document d there are nF domains, f = 1, ..., nF, then the frequency of keyword j in domain f is $tf_{d,j,f}$, the length of the domain dl_f can be represented by the number of indexable words in the domain, that is

$$dl_f = \sum_{j\in V} tf_{d,j,f} \qquad (2)[8]$$

Wherein, V represents the collection of all indexable words in the collection.

Let the word frequency coefficients for each domain be W, the corresponding parameters in the the BM25F model are calculated as follows:

$$tf'_{d,j}= \sum_f W_f tf_{d,j,f} \qquad (3)[8]$$

$$dl' = \sum_f W_f dl_f = \sum_f \sum_j W_f tf_{d,j,f} = \sum_j tf'_{d,j} \qquad (4)[8]$$

$$avdl' = \frac{1}{N}\sum dl' \qquad (5)[8]$$

$$k_1' = k_1 \frac{atf_{weighted}}{atf_{unweighted}} = k_1 \frac{avdl'}{avdl} \qquad (6)[8]$$

This study carries out the screening of the collection of theme words to select the hidden subset of keywords that best reflects the main research content. The measurement of the weights of search terms in information retrieval and the measurement of the weights of keywords in literature keywords extraction are different applications of the same problem. From our analysis of the requirements of keyword selection and the weighted word frequency formula BM25F, it is believed that the BM25F probability model is suitable for weighted word frequency calculation based on source location (such as Title and abstracts, etc.). Firstly, the BM25F model guarantees that word frequency is not the only criterion in measuring the importance of a keyword in a document. Secondly, the model takes quite a few important factors into consideration, including word frequency, document frequency, document length, the average length of the document collection, etc. Moreover, added to the model are parameters that give different weights to keywords in different domains, which further ensures that the weighted word frequency of a keyword truly reflects its degree of contribution to the main content of the document.

The present study tested the effectiveness of the BM25F model through an experiment on a biological paper. After comparing the result of applying the formula in a weighted frequency analysis and the result of keywords extraction through manual reading, it's found that the two results are nearly identical. We take the following paper as an example to illustrated how keywords are extracted, "Locally produced insulin-like growth factor-1 by orbital fibroblasts as implicative pathogenic factor rather than systemically circulated IGF-1 for patients with thyroid-associated ophthalmopathy". 176 keywords are extracted from this paper, part of which are listed in the following table (in the order of weighted frequency).

Table 1. Keywords and the corresponding weighted frequencies in one document

keyword	weighted term frequency in one article
Troleandomycin	2199.46
IGF-1	1612.38
Orbital	899.72
OCT	894.29
Patients	784.32
Circulating	776.33
Fibroblasts	543.92
Ophthalmopathies, Thyroid Associated	527.47
somatostatin analogue	518.74
Secretion	494.74
......	......
tissue	93.07
methods	69.33
KIT	-134.19

Examining this ordering closely, we find that the important keywords that can reflect the main content of the paper have all been given rather high weighted frequency values, while the more general keywords have been given a lower value or even a negative value. As is shown through the example, with this weighted word frequency filtering method, the important keywords reflecting the main content of the target literature can be rather accurately extracted.

The values of coefficients in the formula are based on the Okapi[8] routine, the value of K_1 equals 2, the value of b equals 0.75. As to the values of term frequencies in different fields, wf | title, abstract, MJME, MIME |, the weight values are assigned according to the importance level of these fields in describing the focus of the research. wf | title, abstract, MJME, MIME | = {100, 60, 30, 10}。

Through the calculations above, the weighted term frequency values of every keyword in the data collection are obtained. The higher the value, the more significance the keyword bears in that data collection and the more representative it is of the research focus. Although the quantity of keywords extracted from the data set is enormous, it's neither plausible nor necessary to conduct analysis on every keyword. To reveal the hidden research hotspots in the data set, we only need to select major keywords according to the weighted term frequency values and carry out subsequent analysis.

By using BM25F model, We select 100 main keywords from 14516 keywords. The weighted term frequency values of 100 main keywords are more than 14059.The table 2 shows the top 20 main keywords and their weighted term frequency values.

Table 2. the top 20 main keywords and their weighted term frequency values

No.	Main keywords	weighted term frequency values
1	IGF1	105854.3
2	IGFI	98162.37
3	INSULIN-LIKE GROWTH FACTOR	61435.82
4	HUMAN	37915.99
5	MAMMAL	36632.26
6	INSULIN	36389.16
7	STEM CELLS	33720.13
8	BONE	30370.27
9	DIABETES	28610.45
10	APOPTOSIS	28413.28
11	POLYMER	25569.48
12	ANIMAL	25161.05
13	POLYNUCLEOTIDE	25018.02
14	MRNA	23067.11
15	BREAST CANCER	22521.03
16	OBESITY	22019.09
17	IGFBP3	21951.09
18	IGFBP1	21382.05
19	ANGIOGENESIS	21350.64
20	PROGENITOR CELLS	21311.71

3.4   Cluster Analysis of Keywords

Keywords are clustered according to their degrees of co-occurrence in the data set, thus forming a certain number of topic areas. The basic assumption about co-occurrence is that if two keywords are co-mentioned in the same document, there is a certain underlying relationship between them. The greater number of documents in which they both appear, the stronger the underlying relationship. As is known, a single keyword can not reflect the complete picture of a new trend in research. On the basis of the many keywords extracted from a data set, clustering of closely-related keywords needs to be conducted to form topic areas to represent new directions of research trends. Therefore, the clustering approach based on word co-occurrence enables us to identify close relationships among keywords within a topic area, while helps us to draw clear lines to separate independent topic areas.

Clustering means grouping data objects into classes or clusters. A number of approaches for clustering analysis exist at present. To meet the demand of the present study, which conducts clustering on the basis of degree of co-occurrence, the Partitioning Method is more suitable for the purpose here. The basic idea is to randomly select k centroids, one for each cluster. The next step is to associate each keyword to the nearest centroid. When no keyword is left, the first step is completed and an early groupage is done. At this point we need to re-calculate k new centroids as centers of the clusters resulting from the fist step. After we have these k new centroids, a new binding has to be done between the same keywords and the nearest new centroid. A loop has been generated. As a result of this loop the k centroids change their location step by step until no more changes take place. The present study adopts a quite typical algorithm in the Partitioning Method – K-means clustering algorithm. To measure the distances among keywords from the semantic perspective, the Salton Index of co-occurrence is used to indicate the closeness of relationships among the keywords. "S index can make two closely related keywords appear more closely, and two estranged keywords appear even more alienated "[9]. According to the definition of Salton Index, the following formula, as in (7), is developed to calculate the distance between keyword i and keyword j, or $distance\ (i, j)$:

$$dis\tan ce(i, j) = \begin{cases} n_{ij} / \sqrt{n_i * n_j} & n_{ij} \succ 0 \\ 10000 & n_{ij} = 0 \end{cases} \tag{7}$$

Wherein, n_i and n_j respectively denote the frequencies of keyword i and keyword j; n_{ij} represents the co-occurrence frequency of keywords i and j. When keywords i and j do not co-occur at all, the value of 10000 is assigned to indicate the farthest distance.

With the above clustering approach, we took all the eight clustering results with the value of k ranging from 3 and 15, and submitted these eight different clustering results to one professional researcher studying IGF and one subject librarian studying IGF for evaluation. After careful examination, their conclusion is that when the k value is 5 the clustering effect is the best, but if two approximate classes are merged, the results would be more in line with the real situation of present IGF study. Each of 5 clusters representing a hotspot research topic. Table 3 shows the 5 topic areas and main keywords.

Table 3. The 5 topic areas and main keywords

No.	Topic area	Main keywords
1	The signaling molecules, cytokines, kinases and others which are involved in apoptosis and carcinogenesis.	Cancer cell, apoptosis, mRNA, CD34, AKT, PCR......
2	IGF-related immune system diseases and cardiovascular system diseases	Psoriasis, breast cancer, rheumatoid arthritis, insulin-like growth factor I, atherosclerosis, prostate cancer, melanoma, ovarian cancer, skin, autoimmune disease, acromegaly, diabetic retinopathy......
3	Binding with specific cytokines and receptor, IGF affect bone cell metabolism, growth and development.	G-CSF, insulin-like growth factor I, IGFBP3, IGF1R, fusion protein, growth hormone, hematopoietic system cells......
4	IGF and IGF receptor	IGF, insulin-like growth factor I, EGFR......
5	The role of IGF in the cloning project and the nervous system diseases.	Stroke, bone, diabetes, progenitor cells, stem cell, Alzheimer's disease, regeneration, multiple sclerosis, myocardial infarction, cardiomyocyte, bone marrow, Parkinson disease......

3.5   Graphic Display and the Analysis of All Topic Areas

Finally, we also use the SPSS software for an analysis of multidimensional scaling matrix. Figure 3 shows multidimensional scaling matrix analysis of the 100 main keywords.

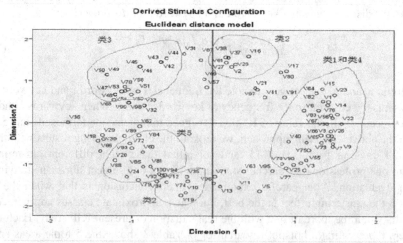

Fig. 3. multidimensional scaling matrix analysis of the 100 main keywords

The analysis of the 5 topic areas in researches on insulin-like growth factors 1is as follows:

(1)the role of the IGF and IGF receptor in apoptosis and carcinogenesis (Topic Area 1and Topic Area 4)

The keywords in Topic Area 1 represent the signaling molecules, cytokines, kinases etc, which are involved in apoptosis and carcinogenesis. The keywords in Topic Area 4 represent the IGF and IGF receptor. Through a multidimensional scaling matrix analysis, we found the keywords of Topic Area 4 are dispersed in the graph. That indicates a lower degree of cohesion within Topic Area 4. The keywords of Topic Area 1 are relatively concentrated, which indicates a higher degree of in-group similarity and cohesion. We also found a high co-occurrence rate between Topic Area 1 and Topic Area 4, therefore they are combined into one topic area in the analysis. Together, they represent the role of the IGF and IGF receptor in apoptosis and carcinogenesis.

(2) IGF-related immune system diseases, cardiovascular system diseases and neoplastic diseases (Topic Area 2)

The keywords of Topic Area 2 represent the IGF-related immune system diseases, cardiovascular system diseases and neoplastic diseases. Through a multidimensional scaling matrix analysis, we found the keywords of Topic Area 2 are relatively concentrated, which indicates a higher degree of similarity and cohesion within the group. The clustering results have higher reliability. The high frequency keywords in this topic are are breast cancer, prostate cancer, atherosclerosis, inflammatory diseases etc.

(3) Through conjoining with specific cytokines and receptor, IGF affects bone cell metabolism, growth and development (Topic Area 3)

The keywords of Topic Area 3 reflect the phenomenon of IGF affecting bone cell metabolism and growth and development through conjoining with specific cytokines and receptor. High frequency keywords of Topic Area 3 include granulocyte colony stimulating factor, insulin-like growth factor 1, insulin-like growth factor binding protein, growth hormone etc.

(4) The role of IGF in the cloning project and the nervous system diseases (Topic Area 5)

The keywords of Topic Area 5 reflect the role of IGF in the cloning project and the nervous system diseases. In the multidimensional scaling graph, the high frequency keywords include liver cells, progenitor cells, bone marrow, Parkinson's disease, regeneration. All the keywords of Topic Area 5 have a high rate of in-group co-occurrence. The clustering results have good reliability.

3.6   The Fluctuation in the Number of Articles in Each Topic Area

The present study extracts 5 topic areas from 1085 articles on insulin-like growth factor 1. The number of articles in each topic area in each of the years from 2006 to 2012 is calculated to make it possible to have a clear view of the emerging trends in insulin-like growth factor 1 research. Figure 4 shows the result of the calculation.

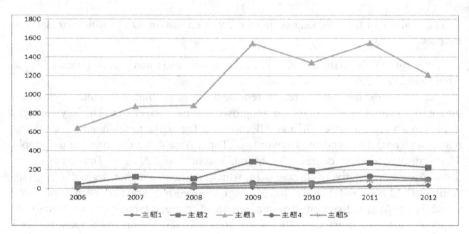

Fig. 4. The changing numbers of articles in each topic area in each of the years from 2006 to 2012

To make further analysis of the degree of hotness of each topic area, we drew comparison between the research volume of each topic area and the total research volume, calculating the percentage rate, as is shown in Equation 8.

$$ts_{ik} = \frac{p_{ik}}{p_k} \times 100 \qquad (8)$$

In the equation, ts_{ik} stands for the percentage of Topic Area i in Year k; p_{ik} stands for the number of research articles which include any of the keywords in Topic Area i; p_k stands for the number of research articles in Year k in the total collection. The fluctuation of percentage rates of 4 topic areas (Topic Area 1 and Topic Area 4 are merged.) in the recent 5 years is captured in Table4.

Table 4. Percentage rates of 4 topic areas in insulin-like growth factors 1 research

Year	Topic Area 1 and Topic Area 4	Topic Area 2	Topic Area 3	Topic Area 5
2006	3.2%	6.3%	88.8%	1.7%
2007	3.1%	14.4%	82.9%	2.1%
2008	4.6%	9.7%	84.1%	1.6%
2009	3.6%	14.7%	79.7%	1.9%
2010	4.8%	11.4%	80.7%	3.2%
2011	7.7%	13.1%	74.8%	4.3%
2012	7.9%	13.5%	73.4%	5.2%

From Table 4 we can see the following trends: The percentage rate of Topic Area 3 articles stays above 50% for seven years on end. However, the peak value didn't appear in the last two years. Based on these findings, it's claimed that Topic Area 3 is the most prominent topic area which has attracted the most articles in the area. Although it shows a tendency of decline in the recent two years, the number of articles in this topic area still forms the bulk part of the whole collection. Therefore, it is classified into the category of mature topic areas.

The percentage rate of Topic Area 2 articles shows a tendency of augmentation year on year. Furthermore, the annual growth rate stays above 10% unfailingly every year. Although articles in this topic area do not occupy a prominent position in the total collection, its tendency of growth is too strong to be dismissed as unimportant. Based on the above analysis, Topic Area 2 is classified into the category of emerging research hot spots.

The percentage rate of Topic Area 1 and 4 articles is below 10% in all seven years. However, it also shows a tendency of year on year growth. It is advisable to warn researchers in the related areas to be aware of this topic area.

The percentage rate of Topic Area 5 articles is relatively small. It awaits further monitoring in the future.

4   Conclusion

Through computer-based analysis of the research literature in the field of insulin-like growth factors 1 from 1966 to 2012, it's found that researches in this field concentrate into five topic areas. Topic Area 3 which research the role of IGF in bone cell metabolism and growth and development is the mature topic area. And Topic Area 2 which research IGF-related immune system diseases and cardiovascular system diseases and neoplastic diseases is the emerging trend. The keywords of each topic are valuable references for doctors and researchers as well in the field.

Through data mining on the English language literature of insulin-like growth factors 1 research, the present study is able to extract significant research topics to provide convenient information service for doctors and researchers in the field.

The limitations of this study are:

(1)The characteristics of the trends in medicine research are manifold. The techniques proposed by this study should be combined with a variety of information resources for comprehensive judgment. Due to time and access constraints, the paper only examined English medical publications for detecting IGF research trends.

(2) As in many other researches, the treatment of synonyms and polysemy still needs improvement.

(3) The interpretation of the semantics of the keywords largely relies on the UMLS.

(4) Several key procedures in the study heavily involve human judgment, such as the number of clusters, the amount of keywords to be selected, the filtering of general words. Although these are done by or under the guide of professional IGF researchers, a certain degree of subjectivity is still unavoidable.

Based on the research findings, it is proposed that further research in detecting IGF research trends can be pursued in the following directions:

(1) Compare more results from computer analysis and from evaluation done by professionals, find problems and inspirations through the differences and make corresponding improvement to the technique.

(2) Find more medical experts to help correct the parameters that need human judgment, so that the results of computer analysis will come closer to the results of expert evaluation after enormous amount of medical literature reading.

(3) Expand the data sources for analysis. Information resources on the Internet and other related medicine professional databases can also be included.

(4) Further explore all kinds of technical applications in key parts of the analysis, draw lessons from feasible technical solutions in other related fields, and come up with better schemes for practice on the basis of what we have found.

Acknowledgments. The paper is supported by National Social Science Fund of China (Grant No. 12CTQ004). We thank the National Library of Medicine for access to MEDLINE and the ISI (Institute for Scientific Information) Web of Knowledge for access to SCI. We also thank the National Library of Medicine for access to MetaMap.

References

1. LOD2 EU Deliverable 3.1.1 Knowledge Extraction Extraction from Structured Sources, http://static.lod2.eu/Deliverables/deliverable-3.1.1.pdf
2. Swanson, D.R.: Fish oil, Raynaud's syndrome, and undiscovered public knowledge. Perspect. Biol. Med. 30(1), 7–18 (1986)
3. Jenssen, T.K., Laegreid, A., Komorowski, J., Hovig, E.: A literature network of human genes for high-throughput analysis of gene expression. Nat. Genet. 28(1), 21–28 (2001)
4. Pustejovsky, J., Castaño, J., Saurí, R., Rumshinsky, A., Zhang, J., Luo, W.: Medstract: creating large-scale information servers for biomedical libraries. In: Pustejovsky, J., Castaño, J., Saurí, R., Rumshinsky, A., Zhang, J., Luo Medstract, W. (eds.) BioMed 2002 Proceedings of the ACL 2002 Workshop on Natural Language Processing in the Biomedical Domain, vol. 3 (2002)
5. Fayyad, U., Piatetsky-Shapiro, G.: Knowledge Discovery and Data Mining: Towards a Unifying Framework. In: Proceedings of the Second International Conference on Knowledge Discovery and Data Mining. AAAI, Portland (1996)
6. Chen, C.: CiteSpace II: Detecting and Visualizing Emerging Trends and Transient Patterns in Scientific Literature. Journal of the American Society for Information Science and Technology 57(3), 359–377 (2006)
7. Aronson, A.R., Lang, F.M.: An overview of MetaMap: historical perspective and recent advances. Journal of the American Medical Informatics Association 17(3), 229–236 (2010)
8. Robertson, S.E., Walker, S.: Some simple effective approximations to the 2-Poisson model for probabilistic weighted retrieval. In: SIGIR 1994 Proceedings of the 17th Annual International ACM (1994)
9. 梁立明,武夷山. 科学计量学：理论探索与案例研究. 北京: 科学出版社 (2006)

An Integrated Biomedical Ontology Mapping Strategy Based on Multiple Mapping Methods

An Fang, Na Hong, Sizhu Wu,
Jianli Zheng, and Qing Qian

Institute of Medical Information
Chinese Academy of Medical Sciences, 100020 Beijing, China

Abstract. In investigating relevant ontology mapping methods, this study focuses on the integration method of ontology mapping. Many resources such as PubMed and UMLS are used for designing the multi-dimensional calculation parameters of ontology mapping, with consideration for morphology, semantics, attributes, and background knowledge. Furthermore, we develop a study on biomedical ontology mapping methods based on multiple strategies, as well as experimentally validate the proposed ontology mapping framework.

1 Introduction

Along with the study and practice of ontology techniques, the identification of various types of domain knowledge ontologies that are application oriented has been undertaken by IT researchers. Despite the breadth of effort devoted to such studies, ontological heterogeneity remains a challenging problem, especially among the vast ontological resources in the biomedical field. This heterogeneity is due to the differences in coding formats, cognitive differences (i.e., knowledge base) between institutions and programmers, semantic granularity, languages, terms, and other similar factors. These heterogeneous resources should be mapped and integrated because biomedicine is characterized by a knowledge hierarchy of close internal relations. Ontology mapping is the basis of semantic interoperability, and the mapping relation between ontologies facilitates across-dataset inquiry submission, data conversion, and knowledge inference for multiple heterogeneous resources.

Focusing on the characteristics and status quo of ontological resources in the biomedical field, this paper consolidates ontology mapping concepts and methods, and puts forward an approach that is suitable for the biomedical field. The proposed method can support most biomedically related ontology mapping tasks and serves as basis for the integration of biochemical resources, the semantic interoperability of heterogeneous resources, and the sharing and application of distributed resources. The method also serves as technical support for large-scale biochemical knowledge sharing, integration, release, and semantic research on knowledge organization systems and other upper-level biomedical applications. These requirements reflect the considerable significance of studying biomedical ontology mapping.

Z. Huang et al. (Eds.): WISE 2013 Workshops 2013, LNCS 8182, pp. 373–386, 2014.
© Springer-Verlag Berlin Heidelberg 2014

2   Related Work

2.1   Current Ontology Mapping Techniques

As summarized by Euzenat and Shvaiko, who expressed form in accordance with method granularity or input data, current ontology mapping techniques comprise mainly two methods: element- and structure-level methods. The former is divided into syntactic- and external-base methods, whereas the latter is classified into structure rule-, external structure-, and semantic-based methods (Fig.1).

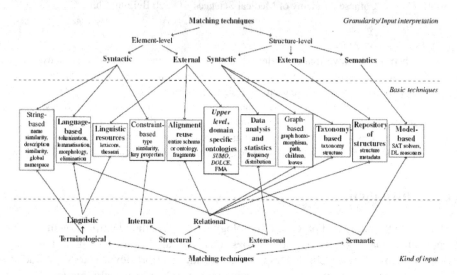

Fig. 1. Classification of current ontology mapping techniques [1]

From the perspective of input data type, ontology mapping techniques can also be divided into term (linguistics)-, structural information-, ontology extension information-, and semantic information-based methods.

2.2   Research Progress for Ontology Mapping Methods

The directions adopted by researchers in studying ontology mapping are described as follows.

(1)   Through the concept similarity calculation method, the similarity between mapping objects is determined to identify the relation between heterogeneous ontologies. Rodriguez et al. [2], for example, developed a concept similarity calculation method on the basis of concept definition, in which ontological concepts are classified into the synset of presentation concepts, feature set of characterization concepts, and semantic relationship set of concepts. Using these three components for similarity calculation enables the determination of the mapping relation between concepts.

(2) The structural similarity between heterogeneous ontologies is analyzed, and the mapping relation is identified through the compilation of mapping rules. Sunna et al. [3] proposed the ontology mapping method, which uses an ontology structure chart as contextual information. Aside from referring to node information, father, child, and grandchild nodes, as well as and other multi-level information, are also considered in the analysis.

(3) With ontological examples, machine learning and other techniques are implemented to determine the mapping relation between ontologies. A typical example is the GLUE system proposed by Doan et al. [4] at the University of Washington. This method comprehensively considers various heterogeneity issues of ontology and classifies concept examples through machine learning. The joint distribution probability of concept examples is used to calculate the similarity between concepts. The mapping relation is then determined through the combination of domain constraints and heuristic knowledge.

(4) Ontology mapping is achieved by integrating various methods. Shailendra et al. [5] developed a mixed ontology mapping engine, which combines syntactic-, background knowledge-, and structure-based ontology mapping algorithms. The engine also executes mapping in multiple aspects and dimensions. Maximizing the advantages of various methods compensates for their disadvantages.

The achievements discussed above not only indicate the tremendous significance of studying ontology mapping, but also serve as useful reference for research conceptualization and technique selection. However, various factors influence ontology mapping and adopting only one analytical method may be restricted by algorithm angle, incomplete calculation information, and other similar issues. These result in imbalanced mapping. To minimize the limitations of various methods, we compensate with such disadvantages with multiple strategies to achieve a more satisfactory mapping effect. Given the complexity of ontological structures and the complex heterogeneity between ontologies, current studies on ontology mapping remain inadequate, especially those on the integration of mapping similarity indices. The commonly used similarity integration algorithm is based on the weighted linear combination algorithm or support vector machine (SVM) algorithm. These algorithms are easy to implement but suffer from the following problems:

(1) The weight of each similarity index is difficult to determine—an important issue because the systematicity with which weight is established directly influences the final effect of an integration algorithm.

(2) An integration algorithm can only be implemented as each similarity index is calculated. Some similarity indices can basically determine the establishment of term semantic similarity. The calculation of other indices increases computational cost.

3   Design of Multi-strategy-Based Biomedical Ontology Mapping Techniques

3.1   System Framework

On the basis of the investigation on ontology mapping theories, methods, and tools, as well as on the analysis of biomedical ontology, we design a system framework for multi-strategy-based biomedical ontology mapping techniques (Fig. 2).

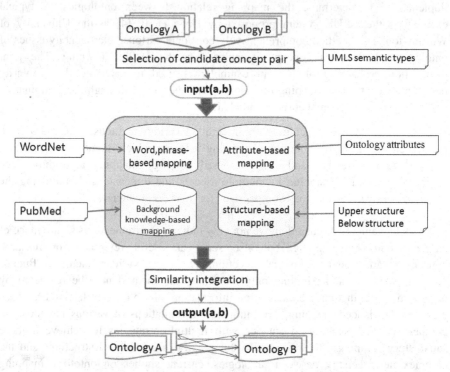

Fig. 2. System framework of multi-strategy-based biomedical ontology mapping

The basic idea of multi-strategy-based biomedical ontology mapping is discussed as follows.

(1) Extraction of the elements used in ontology mapping.The concepts in ontologies A and B are taken as input, and the calculation of the mapping relation between the concepts in a heterogeneous ontology is calculated.

(2) Selection and calculation of a single mapping method.Useful external resources are collected during mapping calculation; various strategies and methods are selected on the basis of concept name, background knowledge, ontology attribute, and ontology structure. Various resources are then used to calculate the similarity between concepts.

(3) Similarity integration.For multiple single-similarity values, the rule based algorithm is adopted. The rule evaluation method is used to calculate the overall similarity and provide the integrated mapping results in accordance with the individual calculation parameters.

3.2   Core Technology Solutions

3.2.1   Selection of Candidate Concept Pair

Small samples of FMA and NCI provided by OAEI are selected for testing. Out of these samples, 3,696 FMA concepts, 6,488 NCI concepts, and 23.97 million pairwise mapping concepts are derived. If the calculation indicates near-synonyms, hypernyms, hyponyms, and other factors, more concept pairs are involved in the calculation, translating to huge time costs. To effectively select candidate concepts for the calculation, we use semantic types in the semantic network of the Unified Medical Language System (UMLS) to screen concepts.

UMLS was developed by the National Library of Medicine (NLM) in 1986. It mainly includes three components: Metathesaurus, Semantic Network, and SPECIALIST Lexicon and Lexical Tools. The semantic network is an important component of UMLS, which is composed of semantic types and semantic relations. Currently, UMLS has 133 semantic types and 54 semantic relations. Semantic network classifies all the concepts in the UMLS super thesaurus and clearly presents their relations. Semantic types are the nodes in the semantic network, and their relations are combined to form the semantic network. Semantic types are grouped into organisms, anatomic structures, physiological functions, chemical substances, events, physical objects, and concepts. UMLS features an extensive coverage of semantic types, thereby enabling the semantic classification of terms in multiple fields. Each concept in the super thesaurus has at least one semantic type, usually the one that most accurately fits a concept in the semantic type level. For example, the semantic type of concept *Macaca* is *Mammal*. In the UMLS semantic network, the granularity of semantic types changes in accordance with specific conditions—a feature that is considerably significant for the understanding of the concept of the super thesaurus.

In calculation during ontology mapping, the concepts in different general classes or categories should never have the same or similar concepts. In calculation during concept matching, we adopt UMLS semantic types to filter the candidate concepts involved in the calculation. Concepts *a* and *b* are derived from Vocabularies A and B, respectively. If they belong to the same UMLS type, then they are involved in the calculation of concept similarity; otherwise, they are set aside for the identification of relevant relations at a later stage.

3.2.2   Word- and Phrase-Based Mapping Strategies

The concept name-based mapping strategy starts from a linguistics aspect, in which the morphology, and semantics of concept names in two ontologies are analyzed. The mapping strategy for concepts is implemented. The mapping method is detailed as follows.

(1) Mapping method based on string matching

The mapping method based on string matching is the first step in the preliminary mapping of concepts. This method hypothesizes that mapping objects belong to the same subject area and that homonymy rarely occurs. The selected mapping objects, namely, FMA and NCI, are biomedical constructs. We therefore hypothesize that the words with the same font are characterized by the same connotation. Therefore, this method matches only the concepts with the same font and considers that such concepts can be preliminarily evaluated with the same concept.

However, some ontology concepts with mapping relations are synonyms and near-synonyms with different fonts. These characteristics increase the likelihood of failure in calculating the similarity between concepts when the pure string matching algorithm is used. In genetic mutation and genetic variation, for example, "mutation" and "variation" are synonyms, but have different fonts. Thus, accurate calculation results cannot be obtained by the font matching algorithm. In the implementation process, lead-in terms and synonyms of concepts are included in matching, aside from the string matching of concept names. The mapping results are scored at different levels, falling in the range [0, 1]. For the pair input (a, b) of the input candidate concept, the scoring of the parameter value of string matching, string_sim(a,b), is described thus:

- If concepts a and b completely match, then string_sim(a,b)=1.
- If the lead-in terms of concepts a and b or the lead-in terms of concepts b and a completely match, then string_sim(a,b)=0.9.
- If the synonyms of concepts a and b or those of concepts b and a completely match, then string_sim(a,b)=0.8.
- If neither concepts a and b match of if neither their lead-in terms and synonyms are mutual, then string_sim(a,b)=0

Except for concept names, lead-in terms, and synonyms, no other corpora resources are required by the mapping method based on string matching. It also presents a direct and convenient calculation. Although it suffers from a certain loss rate, its accuracy is relatively high, making it a widely applied method.

(2) Mapping method based on lexical analysis

The mapping method based on lexical analysis adopts the two-layer lexicon-similarity algorithm of letter-based edit distance similarity and head-word-and-modifier-based word matching similarity. This method performs similarity calculation on the candidate concepts of pairwise-ontology combination. The results are regarded as the bases for evaluating concept mapping in ontology. The results of the algorithm are also taken as the standard similarity that indicates involvement in the mapping strategy based on the ontology structure discussed in the succeeding section.

The principle of the mapping strategy is that the closer a modifier is to the head word of a concept, the more the weight contributes to the similarity calculation. Thus, the levels of similarity between concepts can be more objectively embodied. The formula below is the distribution function of similarity weight, which derives the uniform weight distribution of the head words and modifiers of concepts. In this manner, we can obtain the similarity calculation formula on the basis of lexical analysis as follows:

$$LS(t_1, t_2) = \frac{\sum_{i=0}^{|t_1|-1} (\max_{j=0}^{|t_2|-1} sim(w_{t1i}, w_{t2j}).Weight(w_{t1i}, w_{t2j}))}{\sum_{l=0}^{\max(|t_1|,|t_2|)-1} \frac{1}{l+1}}$$

where $t1$ and $t2$ represent the concept pair of similarity calculation, and $sim(w_{t1i}, w_{t2j})$ represents the similarity value (edit distance) between word i in concept $t1$ and word j in concept $t2$. The Porter Stemmer algorithm can be used to obtain the stem representation of words. The edit distance between words is derived using the Jaro-Winkler distance algorithm. $Weight(w_{t1i}, w_{t2j})$ represents the distributed similarity weight of $wt1i$ and $wt2j$, acquired according to the distance between the head words of concepts. The value range of l in the denominator falls in the range [0, max (|t1|, |t2|)]. That is, the lower limit is 0 and the upper limit is the maximum of the word number of concepts $t1$ and $t2$.

3.2.3   Background Knowledge-Based Mapping Strategy

The background knowledge-based mapping strategy starts from the context of concepts, in which the language environment and knowledge background of concepts in two ontologies are analyzed. The mapping strategy is then applied to the concepts. This method usually requires external corpus resources. Considering that PubMed is an open-access database and contains authoritative resources on the biomedical field, we use it as the external resource for concept mapping. The detailed mapping method is described below.

(1) Mapping method for PubMed distance

The mapping method for PubMed distance implements calculations in accordance with the recorded number of retrieval hits in the PubMed library based on concepts. We refer to Google Distance [6] as the calculation method for the retrieval term semantic similarity and introduce it into biomedical application. Given that PubMed is a specialty literature database and Google is a universal search engine, the calculation for PubMed presents more convergence and better effect than do that for Google in the similarity calculation of concepts in semantic information.

The reformulated mapping method for PubMed distance uses the hit record number of PubMed retrieval to calculate the semantic distance between concepts. The smaller the distance, the closer the semantic relation between two concepts. The concepts in the ontology are retrieved as the retrieval term. As an example, for concepts X and Y from two ontologies, the PubMed distance NPD (x, y) between X and Y can be expressed as

$$NPD(x, y) = \frac{\max\{\log f(x), \log f(y)\} - \log f(x, y)}{\log M - \min\{\log f(x), \log f(y)\}}$$

where $f(x)$ represents the PubMed hit number of retrieval term x; $f(y)$ represents the PubMed hit number of retrieval term y; $f(x, y)$ denotes the PubMed hit number of retrieval pair term x and y; and M is the total literature in PubMed.

(2) Mapping method of PubMed co-occurrence double checking

Aside from the calculation based on retrieval record number, some concept similarity algorithms are based on search result summary. Hsin-Hsi [7] proposed the CODC method in the comprehensive phraseology similarity calculation method based on search engines.

We propose the use of the PubMed CODC method for analyzing PubMed biomedical literature. A literature summary is a text segment of the condense description of hit literature in the process of retrieval. This summary provides the local context of retrieval terms. We introduce the context of concepts into calculation:

$$CODC(P, Q) = \begin{cases} 0 & \text{if } f(P@Q) = 0 \\ e^{\log[\frac{f(P@Q)}{H(P)} \times \frac{f(Q@P)}{H(Q)}]^\alpha} & \text{otherwise} \end{cases}$$

where $f(P@Q)$ represents the frequency of occurrence of concept P in a high-ranking text segment (composed of title, keywords, and abstract) of concept Q in PubMed. $H(P)$ denotes the record number of retrieval P; a represents a constant value in the model, usually set as 0.015. The output results of PubMed CODC fall between interval [0, 1]. Under the extreme condition that f(Y@X)=0 OR f(X@Y)=0, then PubMed CODC(X,Y)=0; f(Y@X)=f(X) and f(X@Y)=f(Y), then PubMed CODC(X,Y)=1. The ranking of retrieval results in PubMed follows relevancy, time, and other similar factors. To balance effect and complexity, we select the top 100 PubMed studies as the high-ranking text segment inquiry.

3.2.4   Attribute-Based Mapping Strategy

The more adequate the description of concept attributes in ontology, the more helpful it is to the evaluation of concept similarity. The strong coincidence between the attribute values of two concepts indicates that these concepts are similar. The concept similarity, obtained by assessing the similarity level of the corresponding attributes of concepts, is important information provided by ontology. The basic principle of concept similarity calculation through attribute information is as follows. If the attributes of two concepts are the same, then these concepts are similar; if the attributes of two concepts are similar, then these concepts are also similar.

Using the obtained attribute information as basis, we adopt the description attributes of concepts in the concept mapping process, and propose a mapping strategy based on ontology attributes.

Cosine similarity is adopted to calculate the similarity of concept description text. This calculation reflects the similarity between two concepts with the value of text similarity. The cosine similarity [8] algorithm reflects the level of similarity between vectors, with a cosine-included angle between two n-dimensional vectors. For two given attribute vectors $W1$ and $W2$, cosine similarity θ can be expressed as

$$Sim(D_1, D_2) = \cos\theta = \frac{\sum_{k=1}^{n} W_{1k} \times W_{2k}}{\sqrt{(\sum_{k=1}^{n} W_{1k}^2)(\sum_{k=1}^{n} W_{2k}^2)}}$$

where $W1k$ and $W2k$, represent the weights of feature item K of text $D1$ and $D2$, respectively; $1<=k<=N$ [9].

In text matching, the attributes of vectors $W1$ and $W2$ are usually the frequencies of concept occurrence in documents. Cosine similarity calculation results fall in the interval $[-1, 1]$, where -1 indicates that the two vectors are completely opposing; 0 indicates that the two vectors are mutually independent; and 1 shows that the two vectors completely consistent. The frequency of word occurrence cannot be a negative number; thus, the cosine similarity value falls in the interval $[0, 1]$ and the included angle between term frequency vectors does not exceed $90°$.

3.2.5   Structure-Based Mapping Strategy

Ontology is usually expressed in a tree-like structure, reflecting the generalized, narrow, and allele relations between concepts. The combination of the hypernym and hyponym concepts and the allele concept into ontology mapping contributes to the deep semantic relation between concepts. The ontology structure-based mapping strategy proposed in this paper requires the inclusion of a standard similarity in the calculation. We refer to the descendant's similarity inheritance (DSI) algorithm and the sibling's similarity contribution (SSC) algorithm [10] proposed by Sunna and Cruz, who regarded the similarity value of lexical analysis as the standard similarity.

(1) DSI mapping method

The DSI method involves the generalized structure (father node and superior node) information of concepts in the calculation based on lexical analysis. A premise of this method is that concept similarity is influenced by the similarity of the father node, as well as that of the grandfather and other superior nodes. The more similar the superior nodes of a and b, the larger the possibility of concept similarity between concepts a and b. This influence contributes partial values to concept similarity. The specific calculation is

$$mcp \times word\_sim(a,b) + \frac{2(1-mcp)}{n(n+1)} \sum_{i=1}^{n} [(n+1-i) \times word\_sim(parent_i(a), parent_i(b))]$$

where $n = \min(path\_len\_root(a), path\_len\_root(b))$

in which *word_sim(a,b)* represents the concept similarity based on lexical analysis. *Mcp* usually takes the empirical value 0.75.

(2) SSC mapping method

The SSC method involves the allele structure information (brother node) of the concept calculation based on lexical analysis. A premise of this method is that concept similarity is influenced by the similarity of the brother node. The more similar the brother nodes of *a* and *b*, the larger the possibility of concept similarity between concepts *a* and *b*. This influence contributes partial values to concept similarity. The specific calculation is

$$mcp \times word\_sim(a,b) + \frac{1-mcp}{n} \sum_{i=1}^{n} \max(word\_sim(S_i, S_1^{'})....word\_sim(S_i, S_m^{'}))$$

where $n = sibling\_count(a), m = sibling\_count(b)$

The value of *Mcp* is the same as in the DSI mapping method.

3.2.6   Similarity Integration

The above-mentioned seven methods begin from the perspectives of morphology, semantics, attributes, and background. They are also initiated with consideration for their advantages and disadvantages. If the advantages of these algorithms can be integrated, the evaluation of ontology mapping can generate ideal results. To this end, we validate the following multiple integration schemes: the weighted average method, SVM-based machine learning method, and rule-based judgment method. After comparing and analyzing the effects of the methods, we found that

(1) The weight of the weighted average method should be set by an expert because subjectivity may considerably influence results.

(2) The automatic classification method of SVM-based machine learning method substantially depends on the quality of training sets and the integrity of test data. However, the calculation results of this technique do not correspond with data results. Not all concepts, for example, have description attributes; thus, the similarity calculation based on description attributes is characterized by null results. Using machine learning to resolve these null objects is inconvenient and may easily cause errors.

(3) The rule-based judgment method in this paper causes optimal effects. Therefore, this method can directly reflect the effective relation of concepts.

The basic procedure and pseudo-code of the rule-based similarity integration is shown in Fig. 3.

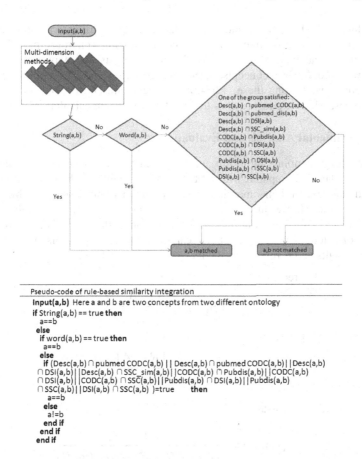

Fig. 3. Process of rule-based similarity integration algorithm

4   Experiment and Results

We include the small version of ontology, NCI and FMA, in the 2012 Biomedicine Group Competition in Ontology Alignment Evaluation Initiative as the test data for carrying out system development. We use OAEI and the NCI-FMA mapping results in UMLS as the standards of comparison; we also combine these standards with the expert verification mode for validating and evaluating the effects.

4.1   Data Pre-processing

The factors in the extraction process of ontology mapping are the premise of the imputing-specific mapping algorithm. The ontology factors included in the algorithm calculation are concept name, attribute, and hypernym and hyponym structure information. Those factors have been extracted in the pre-processing stage and calculated as the input parameter or condition of the next step.

According to the UMLS semantic types, the concepts are filtered and the candidate concept pair that is most likely to generate a mapping relationship that enables inclusion in the calculation is selected. Through analysis and experimentation, we come up with 3,696 FMA concepts, 6,488 NCI concepts, and 23.97 million pairwise mapping concepts. Among these, 4,634,082 concepts are consistent with the UMLS semantic types, which are regarded as the input set of system calculation.

4.2   Experimental Analysis and Evaluation

For the ontology mapping algorithm and consistency assessment of the system, one reference standard is compared with UMLS and the quality of the calculation results is assessed. To develop benchmarking, we adopt the mapping results of UMLS as the comparison standard. Because UMLS contains only the mapping results of exact matching, we choose these findings for comparison with the calculation results of UMLS. Consistency measurement is carried out: A represents the similarity calculation results and R represents the mapping results of UMLS.

(1) Precision

$$P(A,R) = \frac{|R \cap A|}{|A|}$$

(2) Recall

$$P(A,R) = \frac{|R \cap A|}{|R|}$$

(3) F-measure

$$M_\alpha(A,R) = \frac{P(A,R) \cdot R(A,R)}{(1-\alpha) \cdot P(A,R) + \alpha \cdot R(A,R)}$$

Here, α was allocated with value 0.5. The evaluation of our individual method and integrated method is shown in Table 1.

Table 1. Comparation with UMLS standard

Methods	Precision	Recall	F-measure
String matching	0.991	0.491	0.657
Word and phrase analysis	0.666	0.864	0.752
Similarity of concept description	0.354	0.203	0.504
DSI	0.998	0.447	0.617
SSC	0.550	0.370	0.442
PubMed CODC	0.538	0.259	0.349
PubMed distance	0.559	0.430	0.485
Rule based integrated similarity	0.759	0.619	0.682

The F-score values obtained in rule based integrated method up to 68%, precision and recall values achieve a relative better balance than just evaluate any one of other methods.in all these methods, PubMed CODC and PubMed distance cost much in time complexity, for the reason that it need submit many query to access PubMed database. Furthermore, the performance of PubMed CODC and PubMed distance is not very good and this indicates the complexity has not brought ideal precision and recall. Therefore, these methods are not good for use in seperately view, but they are help for judge from different mensions in integrated view.

5   Conclusion

Focusing on the characteristics and status quo of ontological resources in the biomedical field, we consolidate ontology mapping concepts and methods, as well as propose a method suitable for biomedical applications. This method can support most ontology mapping tasks in the biomedical field. From the perspectives of morphology, semantics, attributes, and background resources, we select measurement indices and combine them with beneficial resources, PubMed and UMLS, to improve the analysis. Finally, we realize comprehensive ontology mapping from multiple aspects. FMA and NCI are selected as experiment ontologies for the testing and evaluation of the algorithm. The extensive investigations and experiments confirm the validity of the proposed method. Nevertheless, certain limitations should be noted. For example, the semantic analysis method based on WordNet exhibits weak accuracy. The accuracy of the PubMed-based mapping method should also be improved. The hypothesis of UMLS-based filtering and the reference mechanism cannot be established even though these methods are characterized by strong operability. If medical ontology cannot be found in UMLS, the screening scheme for candidate words cannot be used. At the same time, the concept mapped by UMLS also presents the possibility of semantic conflicts. These problems should be the focal points of future research.

Acknowledgments. This work is jointly funded by the National social science fund project (NSSF), "Research on discovering methods of underline knowledge relations from Linked Data", China. Project Number is 11CTQ016, National Twelfth Five-Year Technology Support Program, "Developing of collaborative work systems and tools for scientific and technological knowledge organization system" China. Project Number is 2011BAH10B02, and National Twelfth Five-Year Technology Support Program, "Shared services platform for scientific and technological knowledge organization system", China. Project Number is 2011BAH10B03-1.

References

1. Euzenat, J., Euzenat, J., Shvaiko, P.: Ontology matching. Springer (2007)
2. Rodríguez, M.A., Egenhofer, M.J.: Determining semantic similarity among entity classes from different ontologies. IEEE Transactions on Knowledge and Data Engineering 15(2), 442–456 (2003)

3. Sunna, W., Cruz, I.F.: Structure-based methods to enhance geospatial ontology alignment. In: Fonseca, F., Rodríguez, M.A., Levashkin, S. (eds.) GeoS 2007. LNCS, vol. 4853, pp. 82–97. Springer, Heidelberg (2007)
4. Doan, A., et al.: Ontology matching: A machine learning approach. In: Handbook on Ontologies, pp. 385–403. Springer, Heidelberg (2004)
5. Singh, S., Cheah, Y.-N.: Hybrid approach towards ontology mapping. In: 2010 International Symposium Information Technology (ITSim), vol. 3. IEEE (2010)
6. Normalized Google Distance, http://en.wikipedia.org/wiki/Normalized_Google_distance
7. Chen, H.-H., Lin, M.-S., Wei, Y.-C.: Novel association measures using web search with double checking. In: Proceedings of the 21st International Conference on Computational Linguistics and the 44th Annual Meeting of the Association for Computational Linguistics. Association for Computational Linguistics (2006)
8. Monge, A.E., Elkan, C.: The Field Matching Problem: Algorithms and Applications. In: KDD (1996)
9. Cohen, W.W.: Data integration using similarity joins and a word-based information representation language. ACM Transactions on Information Systems (TOIS) 18(3), 288–321 (2000)
10. Sunna, W., Cruz, I.F.: Structure-based methods to enhance geospatial ontology alignment. In: Fonseca, F., Rodríguez, M.A., Levashkin, S. (eds.) GeoS 2007. LNCS, vol. 4853, pp. 82–97. Springer, Heidelberg (2007)

Generation of Semantic Data from Guidelines for Rational Use of Antibiotics

Qing Hu[1,2], Zhisheng Huang[3], and Jinguang Gu[1,2]

[1] Faculty of Computer Science and Engineering, Wuhan University of Science and Technology, Wuhan 430065, China
[2] Key Laboratory of Intelligent Information Processing and Real-time Industrial System of Hubei Province, Wuhan 430065, China
[3] Department of Computer Science, VU University Amsterdam, The Netherlands

Abstract. Rational use of antibiotics has become an important issue in medical practice and health care. Clinical guidelines are one of the most useful knowledge resources for rational use of antibiotics. As the monitoring of rational use of antibiotics involves complex knowledge of guidelines analysis and management process, traditional way of human intervention is not sufficient to monitor rational use of antibiotics effectively. Therefore, we introduce the semantic technology to semi-automatically transform the knowledge contained in the clinical guidelines and get the semantic data. In this paper, we firstly investigate how to obtain the semantic data from the guidelines knowledge which are described in natural language, then propose an approach to transformation of guidelines knowledge into semantic data, which can be loaded into SeSRUA, a Semantically-Enabled System for Rational Use of Antibiotics. Finally we report how to implement the proposed approach in SToGRUA, a system of Semantic Transformer of guidelines for Rational Use of Antibiotics, as a tool of SeSRUA.

Keywords: Semantic Technology, Antibiotics, Rational use of drug, Knowledge Acquisition.

1 Introduction

Rational use of antibiotics is an important issue in medical practice and health care. However, only relying on human intervention is not sufficient to monitor rational use of antibiotics effectively. Therefore, in the monitoring process, a semantically-enabled system for knowledge management can be adopted to generate the monitoring knowledge with the semantic data format. Then the monitoring knowledge will be used in the management of the medical information systems to realize the automatic monitoring of the rational use of antibiotics.

The medical authorities have published the guidelines for rational use of antibiotics. In China, the main medical professional organizations(i.e. The Chinese Medical Association, Pharmacy Administration Commission of Chinese Hospital Association, and Hospital Pharmacy Committee of Chinese Pharmaceutical Association) have promulgated the clinical guidelines for rational use of antibiotics

Z. Huang et al. (Eds.): WISE 2013 Workshops 2013, LNCS 8182, pp. 387–400, 2014.

in 2008[1]. The guidelines have become one of the most important knowledge resources for rational use of antibiotics. Therefore, the key issue here is how to transform the guidelines in natural language into semantic knowledge, so that they can be used in a semantically-enabled system.

Computerized Clinical guidelines, alternatively called Computer-Interpretable guidelines (CIGs), implement the guidelines in computer-based decision support systems. Although several formalisms of computer-interpretable guidelines, such as PROforma[2], Asbru[3], EON[4], and GLIF[5], have been proposed to formalize clinical guidelines. Those CIGs rely on an independent system of reasoning and processing. In this paper, we are more interested in a lightweight approach to accommodating guidelines knowledges. Taking into account of the description format of the guidelines being transformed is relatively fixed and the scale of the guidelines knowledge being preprocessed is not so large, we can preprocess the knowledge contained in the guidelines manually to obtain a set of rules with the pattern "if ..., then ...", so that they can be processed by using DCG (Definite Clause Grammar)[1] in the logic programming language Prolog. DCG is a lightweight tool to parse natural language text. With DCG, we can obtain semantic data, without relying on complex natural language processing tools.

In order to get the semantic knowledge contained in the guidelines that can be used in a semantic-enabled system for rational use of antibiotics, a series of work have been done, which include: i) distinguishing three levels of knowledge rules, ii) transforming rules at different levels, and iii) use the semantic data of guidelines in the Semantically-enabled System for Rational Use of Antibiotics system SeSRUA[6].

The rest of this paper is organized as follows: Section2 analyzes the guidelines. Section3 proposes the transformation methods between different levels rules in guidelines and presents the System of Transformer guidelines for Rational Use of Antibiotics(SToGRUA). Section4 evaluates the transformation results. Section5 make the conclusions.

2   Analysis of Knowledge in the Guidelines

Since the diseases caused by bacterial infections are found in various clinical sections, antibiotics become one of the most commonly used drugs in clinical application. While universal use of antibiotics save the lives of many patients, the adverse reactions caused by the abuse of antibiotics appear gradually. Therefore, main medical professional organizations have promulgated the clinical guidelines to manage and monitor the rational use of antibiotics.

In this paper, we will focus on the guidelines for rational use of antibiotics in China[1]. The guidelines in Chinese consist of four parts. Part I mainly describes the basic principles of clinical use of antibiotics in therapeutic application, prophylactic application and special pathology or patient physiological conditions application. Part II enacts the management rules of clinical use of antibiotics. Part III emphasizes the corresponding indications and precautions on concrete

---

[1] http://en.wikipedia.org/wiki/Definite_clause_grammar

antibiotic drugs. Part IV elaborates the treatment principles and pathogen treatment of various types of antibiotic infections.

Those four parts describe the main functions of clinical guidelines for rational use of antibiotics, which include on what kinds of condition a medical professional should use what kinds of antibiotics, on what kinds of clinical indications an antibiotic drug can be used and how to use. These relatively simple knowledge of clinical guidelines are relatively fixed and well structured. For example, the following statement excerpted from the clinical guidelines points out the diagnosis indications for deciding whether or not to use an antibiotic drug.

```
Example 1: According to the patient's symptoms, signs, and blood,
urine and other laboratory examination results, the patient is
preliminarily
diagnosed as bacterial infections and through the pathogen examination
the patient was preliminarily diagnosed as  bacterial infections with
indications for use of antibiotics.
```

It is rather easy for a human to understand the meaning of the guidelines in natural language text, like those in Example 1. However, it is rather difficult for computers to understand those guidelines. Considering the fact that those guidelines are quite limited, we can convert those knowledge contained in the guidelines into a format so that they can be handled by computer systems more easily. Thus, an easy and simple solution is to generate a set of rules with the pattern "if ..., then ..." by manual. For example, the text in Example 1 can be transformed into the rules, which are shown in Example 2.

```
Example 2: According to the patient's symptoms, signs, and blood,
urine and other laboratory examination results, the patient is
preliminarily diagnosed as suspected bacterial infections, then
do the followings.

1.If the patient has blood laboratory test results and has been
preliminary diagnosed as bacterial infections and pathogenic
diagnosed as bacterial infections, then he indeed has indication
to use antibiotics.

2.If the patient has urine laboratory test results and has been
preliminary diagnosed as bacterial infections and pathogenic
diagnosed as bacterial infections, then he indeed has indication
to use antibiotics.
```

The description format of Example 2 represents the logical relationship clearly. However, in the specific diagnosis process, without the specific indication values which can be checked in patient data, those knowledge are insufficient for a judgment whether or not an antibiotic should be used. So we do further processing to transform the knowledge in Example 2 into one with concrete values in patient data, like those shown in Example 3.

Example 3: According to the patient's symptoms, signs, and blood, urine and other laboratory examination results, the patient is preliminarily diagnosed as suspected bacterial infections, then do as follows:

1.If the patient has blood laboratory test, according to concrete item and its value(which refer to the patient examination report), and has been preliminary diagnosed as bacterial infections and pathogenic inspection report show that item and its value (with refer to the patient examination report), then he indeed has indication to use antibiotics.

2.If the patient has urine laboratory test, according to concrete item and its value(which refer to the patient examination report), and has been preliminary diagnosed as bacterial infections and pathogenic inspection report show that item and its value (with refer to the patient examination report), then he indeed has indication to use antibiotics.

The work converting the rules from Example 1 into Example 3 is called the preprocessing of the guidelines. The main purpose of this preprocessing is to convert the guidelines knowledge into a set of concrete rules which can be used to check the patient data directly. After that preprocessing, we can finally get the fixed format of "if...then..." to describe the clinical guidelines knowledge, just like those with the format of Example 3. After we obtain a set of concrete rules with the pattern "if ..., then ..." in natural language text, we can use DCG in the logic programming language Prolog to parse the preprocessed guidelines knowledge to obtain their semantic data.

In order to distinguish the guidelines rules in every preprocessing stage, we classify the guidelines rules into three different levels of rules, i.e., abstract rules, concrete rules, and semantic rules. The task of the SToGRUA system is to generate the semantic rules that can be used in SeSRUA, a semantically-enabled system for raitonal use of antibiotics.

Abstract Rules. Knowledge in the guidelines provides the rules to guide the rational use of antibiotics, so the knowledge in the guidelines that cannot be used to guide our actions directly are called *abstract rules*. In the guidelines, the guide-makers made those abstract rules for professionals only. For this, knowledge in the guidelines described by natural language requires extracting and form-transformation into concrete rules.

By screening the contents of the guidelines, we extract the knowledge and preliminary transform them into "if ...then ..." form, which can be dealt by a computer. We define the "if ... then ..." form of knowledge as Abstract Rules. Example 1 is an example of abstract rules. First, make sure knowledge can be converted into the "if ... then ..." form.

Concrete Rules. Concrete rules are relative to abstract rules. It means to make abstract rules in the guidelines more concrete so that hyponymy, entailment and other logical relationship between the knowledge will become more clear. The extracted abstract rules include No-doing rules, How-to-do rules and Experience-based rules. It is obvious that the first two rules are instructive, while the third one is not so instructive, namely, the concrete index values are not clearly stated in the rules. In such kind conditions, the participation of medical experts will be needed to make the rules more concrete so that they can be used for a checking with computers. The concrete processed rules are called concrete rules.

With the participation of medical professionals, based on the values in hospital examination reports and the relationship between the values (such as "and" or "or" relationship), the abstract rules can be specified. Concrete rules are basic for the description of logical relationship.

Semantic Rules. Semantic web technology provides a common framework for data sharing and reusing. The experience of antibiotics selection need be shared. There are enormous amount of accumulated medical and experiential data in antibiotic selection. These scattered information resources in different hospital system are beyond practitioners' learning ability and it is impossible for practitioners to fully acquire them. Thus, hospitals have to rely on computera to process the data. In order to help the computer to understand the knowledge, semantic web technology can be used to deal with the representation of those knowledge and data.

The community of the semantic technology has developed several international standards for the knowledge representation language of semantic data, such as RDF (Resource Description Framework) and OWL (Web Ontology Language), which have been found many applications in biomedical domains. Therefore, in order to achieve automatic monitoring of rational use of antibiotics, those standards (e.g. RDF/RDFS) will be used to describe pharmacological knowledge and pharmacokinetics-based rational antibiotic-use method. The natural language description in documents and guidelines that related to rational use of antibiotics can be transformed into their semantic description. By transforming, hyponymy, entailment and other logical relationship between the semantic knowledge will become so clear that they can be mapped to corresponding ontology knowledge graph[7].

Semantic rules are knowledge description that transformed from concrete rules. Knowledge described in nature language will be transformed into semantic technology-based descriptions that can be handled by computer directly.

3   Semantic Transformer of Guidelines for Rational Use of Antibiotics (SToGRUA)

SToGRUA is the system of semantic transformer of guidelines for rational use of antibiotics. Through the SToGRUA system, we get the semantic rules of the knowledge in the guidelines of rational use of antibiotics. Of course, it is not the case that all of the guidelines knowledge can be represented as a RDF/OWL data. Some of those knowledge may need a higher level of knowledge representation language, like those in rule-based language. In this paper, we will focus on the knowledge which can be represented in those lightweight languages, i.e., RDF/RDFS/OWL. We leave the rule-based formalisms of the guidelines knowledge in the future work.

In order to get those semantic data (i.e., semantic rules of the guidelines), firstly, we transform the abstract rules into concrete rules. Then we transform the concrete rules into semantic rules.

3.1   Transformation from Abstract Rules to Concrete Rules

Abstract rules in the guidelines contain many instructional rules for using antibiotics rationally and the rules expression form is in the "if...then..." format. With the help of medical experts, this form of knowledge can be further transformed into concrete rules in following two steps:

Some of the abstract rules are specified while some are not. The specified abstract rules are concrete rules. Therefore, the first step is to distinguish the concrete rules from abstract rules. For instance, if we extract the indication knowledge in the guidelines, the abstract rules will be specified and do not need transformation. However, as Example 2, we need the participation of medical experts since they can turn the abstract medical test results into concrete medical rules. Based on corresponding values on the medical examination reports, we can then transform the abstract rules into the concrete rules in the format of "if ... then ...".

3.2   Design for Semantic Transformation of Concrete Rules

A considerable part of the knowledge in the guidelines involves indications and contraindications in the antibacterial instructions. For instance, "If infection caused by hemolytic streptococcus, then penicillin should be used" and "If infection caused by Streptococcus pneumoniae, then penicillin should be used". These knowledge can be used directly in detecting the data on the electronic medical records. There exist some well-known pharmacological and pharmaceutical semantic data set, such as Drugbank[2], which are usually represented as the RDF Ntriple format. For example, the description of a drug's indications uses a predicate (e.g. Indication) followed by the indication descriptions in natural language as follows:

```
<http://www4.wiwiss.fu-berlin.de/drugbank/resource/drugs/DB00007>
<http://www4.wiwiss.fu-berlin.de/drugbank/resource/drugbank/indication>
"For treatment of prostate cancer, endometriosis, uterine
fibroids and premature puberty" .
```

---

[2] http://www.drugbank.ca/

Obviously, we need more fine-grained knowledge about indications, because the indication knowledge in a text cannot be used directly in the system. We have to transform them into the semantic data. Hence, a particular predicate "indications" is introduced to represent the set of all the indications.

Meanwhile, for each disease symptom description involves its causes description, we introduce the predicate 'CausedBy' and the additional parameters predicate 'Modifier' in the Indication description to cover various conditions. Therefore, a complete indication of semantic rules should be like the followings:

```
<http://ontoweb.wust.edu.cn/medicine#ZSH121216D6369005>
<http://www.w3.org/1999/02/22-rdf-syntax-ns#type>
<http://ontoweb.wust.edu.cn/medicine#DrugBook>.
# The above triple description set an internal concept
# identifie for certain drug (e.g. penicillin)

<http://ontoweb.wust.edu.cn/medicine#ZSH121216D6369005>
<http://wasp.cs.vu.nl/apdg#Concept>
<http://www.ihtsdo.org/SCT_6369005>.
# The above triples map the concept into the medical ontology SNOMED

<http://ontoweb.wust.edu.cn/medicine#ZSH121216D6369005>
<http://ontoweb.wust.edu.cn/medicine#Indications>
<http://ontoweb.wust.edu.cn/medicine#id_hzs121216g6369005>.
# The above triples define a collection of indications

<http://ontoweb.wust.edu.cn/medicine#id_hzs121216g6369005>
<http://ontoweb.wust.edu.cn/medicine#Indication>
<http://ontoweb.wust.edu.cn/medicine#id_hzs121216g6369005_1>.
#The above triples define the first indication description

<http://ontoweb.wust.edu.cn/medicine#id_hzs121216g6369005_1>
<http://ontoweb.wust.edu.cn/medicine#Symptom> "infection" .
<http://ontoweb.wust.edu.cn/medicine#id_hzs121216g6369005_1>
<http://ontoweb.wust.edu.cn/medicine#CausedBy> "Hemolytic streptococcus".
```

Of course, some concrete rules, especially those involving multiple steps detections of antibiotics clinical rational use, cannot be simply described in RDF Ntriples. We need to put the knowledge into a clinical diagnosis decision support system and describe them in higher-level rules (such as rules description about time and event). Because RDF is not expressive enough to represent the temporal knowledge and the event knowledge, more powerful and expressive formalism should be used to formalize that kind of higher-level rules. The workflows built on the LarKC Platform [8] can be used to solve the problem partially.

3.3   Rules Parsing through DCG in The SToGRUA System

The concrete rules have a unified "If ... then ..." format. That is a fixed format of "premise and conclusion" and can be defined into a template easily. Hence, based on the templates they can be automatically transformed into semantic rules without relying on a complex natural language processing tool.

The reasons why we are using the logic programming language Prolog for the processing are based on its distinguished features. Prolog is a rule-based language. It can be used to describe and generate knowledge representation for rules[9,10]. Prolog provides DCG support and then it can be used as a convenient syntactic parsing tool. Comparing with the natural language processing system, parse of DCG is relatively simple, it works quite well to deal with the concrete rules with a fixed format rules paring. Using Prolog, we implement the SToGRUA system (Semantic Transformer of guidelines for Rational Use of Antibiotics). First, we load the specified guide knowledge as a text file into the Prolog system, then it will be parsed by the SToGRUA system with DCG. Finally, corresponding semantic triples are generated. The main process is just as follows:

```
start :- initial_id_number(N),
        working_on_drug(Drug),
        working_on_ontology(Ontology),
        file_name(File), open(File, read, In),
        output_file_init(Drug, Ontology, Out),
        set_stream(In, encoding(utf8)),
        rules_processing(In, Out, N, M),
        close(In), close(Out),
        format('~w rules have been processed.~n',[M]).
```

The predicate *rules_processing* realizes the DCG processing, i.e. Using the following rules to get the corresponding information of cause-result-state-drugname. The corresponding triples are generated by the predicate *write_ntriples*.

```
rule_processing(Line, Out, N):-
        phrase(rule(Cause Result, Status, Drug), Line, Rest),
        atom_codes(Cause1, Cause),
        atom_codes(Result1, Result),
        atom_codes(Drug1, Drug),
        atom_codes(Rest1, Rest),
        write_ntriples(Out, N, Cause1, Result1, Status, Drug1, Rest1).
```

The DCG rule parsing process is as follows: the corresponding parameters are obtained by matching condition and result in concrete rules. We get the causes and symptoms from the condition and get the status and drug name parameter from the result.

```
rule(Cause, Result, Status, Drug)  -->
        condition(Cause, Result),
        separators,
        conclusion(Status, Drug).
```

We use the following DCG rules to parse conditions of different concrete rules:

```
condition(Cause, Result) -->
             causal_condition_header,
             cause(Cause),
             lead_to,
             result(Result).


condition(Cause, Result) -->
             condition_header,
             goal_operator(Goal),
             result(Result),
             goal_end,
             {Cause = [goal(Goal)]}.

condition(Cause, Disease) -->
             condition_header,
             disease(Disease),
             patient_operator,
             goal_operator(Goal),
             {Cause =[goal(Goal)]}
```

We use the following DCG rules to parse results of different concrete rules:

```
conclusion(indication, Drug) -->
             conclusion_header,
             indication_operator,
             drug(Drug).
......
conclusion(operation(Operation), Disease) -->
             conclusion_header,
             disease(Disease),
             patient_operator,
             operation(Operation).
.....
conclusion(drug_property(sameas), Drug) -->
             conclusion_header,
             drug_pointer,
             drug(Drug).
```

4 Implementation and Experiments

4.1 A Semantically-Enabled System for Rational Use of Antibiotics

SeSRUA is a semantically-enable system for rational use of antibiotics[6]. It is built on the top of the LarKC[8], a platform for scalable semantic data

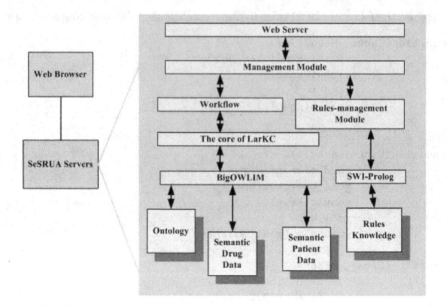

Fig. 1. Architecture of the SeSRUA system

processing[3]. LarKC uses OWLIM to store and manage semantic data and provides many plug-ins to handle semantic data processing and reasoning. Users can use a Web browser to access the data in the JSON format, which return from the SPARQL endpoint. The user interface of SeSRUA[6] transforms these JSON data into the corresponding visual data and displays them in a user-friendly interface. Therefore, any SeSRUA user will be able to use it even if he/she has no any background knowledge of the semantic technology. We use the APDG (Advanced Patient Data Generator)[11] to generate ten thousand patient data of chronic bronchial in Hubei Province. Those virtual patient data are loaded into the SeSRUA system for the test. APDG uses the domain knowledge to generate virtual patient data, so that the generated patient data look like real ones.

The architecture of SeSRUA is shown in Figure 2.

We have implemented the proposed approach in this paper in the system SToGRUA. STOGRUA is designed to be a tool of SeSRUA for its data integration. Semantic rules generated by SToGRUA are used in SeSRUA. The relationship between SToGURA and SeSRUAas is shown in Figure 2.

The right frame in Figure 2 is the SToGRUA system. The management component in SToGRUA calls the logic programming language SWI-Prolog to generate semantic rules. The concrete rules are loaded into SToGRUA in the form of text. DCG rules called by the SWI-Prolog system are used to parse concrete rules. Semantic rules of guidelines knowledge which are generated by SToGRUA are loaded into the SeSRUA system, through matching the semantic guidelines data and the patient data to realize the monitoring of rational use of antibiotics.

---

[3] http://www.larkc.eu

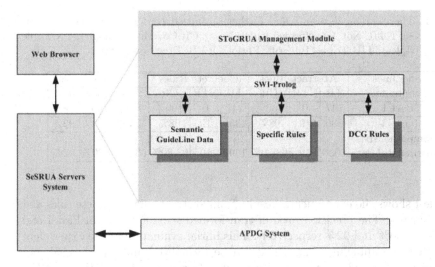

Fig. 2. the Relationship Between SToGURA and SeSRUA

4.2 Experiments and Evaluation

In the first experiment, we focus on the generation of the semantic data of the guidelines for rational use of antibiotics[1]. We have converted the knowledge of Part I and Part IV of the knowledge in the guidelines into a set of rules. We would not deal with Part II of the guidelines, because that part of the guidelines concerns only the procedure of hospital management for using antibiotics, which is not the focus of our system. We have not yet converted Part III of the guidelines, because most content of Part III has been covered by the drug manuals of antibiotics, for which its semantic data has been available, by converting the XML-based files into RDF NTriples. Furthermore, some of them have been available at DrugBank. We have used the system SToGRUA to generate the semantic data from those concrete rules.

For the evaluation of the experiment, we firstly assess the quality of transformed abstract rules and concrete rules. We count how many rules have been obtained and how much of the content have been covered by the transformed rules, which is called the coverage ratio (CR), for the assessment of the rule extraction process. We consider a single sentence of the guidelines as the basic unit of the coverage measurement. Thus, the coverage ratio (CR) is the percentage of that transformed rules (TR) with respect to the total number of the sentences number (SN) in the corresponding contents. Namely,

$$CR = TR/SN.$$

The precision of the semantic rules is measured through the amount of the integrated properties in RDF Ntriples. A summary of the experiment is shown in table Table1.

The evaluation results are shown in Table1.

Table 1. The exprement results and further optimized contents. TR: Transformed Rule (pieces); NTR: Not Transformed Rule(pieces); CR:Covering Ratio(%); TN:Triple Number (triples); TIR:Triples Integrity Ratio(%); PR: Precision Ratio;

guidelines contents	Abstract Rules			Concrete Rules			Semantic Rules		
	TR	NTR	CR	TR	NTR	CR	TN	TIR	PR
Part I	147	0	100%	247	0	100%	988	100	100%
Part IV	889	19	98%	1351	19	98%	5340	98.80%	92%
Comprehensive experimental data	1036	19	98.80%	1598	19	98.80%	6328	98.80%	92%

Table 1 shows the experimental results from abstract rules, concrete rules and semantic rules. The precision ratio of transformed semantic rules in Part I and Part IV is 100% and 92% respectively. This initial evaluation of the experiment shows that the guidelines knowledge can be formalized and transformed into its semantic data. Those generated semantic data are useful for the SeSRUA system. The experiments of the SeSRUA system show that it can judge the 78% percent of the cases for rational use of antibiotics, and 55% percent of the cases for correctly selecting what kinds of antibiotics should be used[6]. A screenshot of the monitoring of rational use of antibiotics in the SeSRUA system is shown in Figure 3.

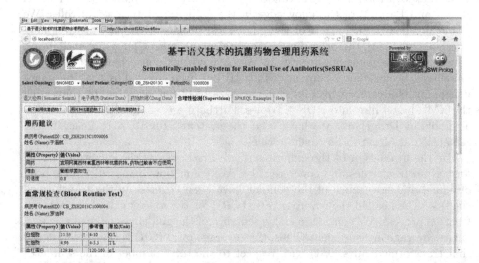

Fig. 3. the Screenshot of Monitoring in SeSRUA

5   Conclusions

In this paper, a systematic approach to transforming the guidelines for rational use of antibiotics in natural language into corresponding semantic data has been proposed. In this transforming process, we convert the text into a set of rules in natural language text, then use the DCG tool in Prolog to generate the corresponding semantic data automatically. These two-step transformation approaches make the system able to handle the vast majority of knowledge in the guidelines and provides basic semantic data for SeSRUA.

These generated semantic data are actually structured knowledge that can be used in the monitoring system of rational use of antibiotics. Using inference engine and workflow management process provided by a semantic platform (e.g. LarKC), the knowledge make it possible to judge and monitor the rational use of antibiotics in terms of various patient data in electronic medical records. Hence, processing and managing the knowledge of rational use of antibiotics automatically and semi-automatically by using the semantic technology.

Based on the existing work, the next work that we will do is to use some new methods to reduce the degree of human intervention in the process of rules' transformation. Currently, the transformation from natural language text to rule is done by the manual works. In the future, we will use the tools of natural language processing for semantic annotation of the guidelines text and develop a system so that we can obtain concrete rules automatically or semi-automatically.

Acknowledgments. This work was partially supported by the following projects: The projects of Natural Science Foundation of China under grant number 61272110 and 61100133, the key projects of National Social Science Foundation of China under grant number 11ZD&189 and the project of the State Key Lab of Software Engineering Open Foundation of Wuhan University under grant number SKLSE2012-09-07.

References

1. Chinese Medical Association, Pharmacy Administration Commission of Chinese Hospital Association, Hospital Pharmacy Committee of Chinese Pharmaceutical Association: Clinical guidelines for rational use of antibiotics. Technical report (2008)
2. Fox, J., Johns, N., Rahmanzadeh, A., Thomson, R.: Proforma, approaches for creating computer-interpretable guidelines that facilitate decision support. In: Proceedings of Medical Informatics Europe, Amsterdam (1996)
3. Shahar, Y., Miksch, S., Johnson, P.: The asgaard project: a task specific framework for the application and critiquing of time oriented clinical guidelines. Artif. Intell. Med. 14, 29–51 (1998)
4. Tu, S., Musen, M.: A flexible approach to guideline modeling. In: Proceeding of 1999 AMIA Symposium, pp. 420–424 (1999)
5. Peleg, M., Boxwala, A., Ogunyemi, O., et al.: Glif3: The evolution of a guideline representation format. In: Proceedings of AMIA Annu. Fall Symp., pp. 645–649 (2000)
6. Hua, X., Chen, C.; Huang, Z., Hu, Q.: Intelligent monitoring on use of antibacterial agents based on semantic technology. Journal of China Digital Medicine 8, 12–15 (2013)

7. Cheptsov, A., Huang, Z.: Making web-scale semantic reasoning more service-oriented: The large knowledge collide. In: Proceedings of the 2012 Workshop on Advanced Reasoning Technology for e-Science (ART 2012) (2012)
8. Fensel, D., van Harmelen, F., Andersson, B., Brennan, P., Cunningham, H., Della Valle, E., Fischer, F., Huang, Z., Kiryakov, A., Lee, T., School, L., Tresp, V., Wesner, S., Witbrock, M., Zhong, N.: Towards LarKC: a platform for web-scale reasoning. In: Proceedings of the IEEE International Conference on Semantic Computing (ICSC 2008). IEEE Computer Society Press, CA (2008)
9. Wielemaker, J., Huang, Z., van der Meij, L.: SWI-Prolog and the web. Journal of Theory and Practice of Logic Programming 8(3), 363–392 (2008)
10. Wielemaker, J., Schrijvers, T., Triska, M., Lager, T.: Swi-prolog. Journal of Theory and Practice of Logic Programming 12(1-2), 67–96 (2012)
11. Huang, Z., van Harmelen, F., ten Teije, A., Dentler, K.: Knowledge-based patient data generation. In: Riaño, D., Lenz, R., Miksch, S., Peleg, M., Reichert, M., ten Teije, A. (eds.) KGC 2013 and ProHealth 2013. LNCS, vol. 8268, pp. 83–96. Springer, Heidelberg (2013)

Design and Implementation of Visualization Tools for Advanced Patient Data Generator

Minghui Zhang[1,2], Zhisheng Huang[3], and Jinguang Gu[1,2]

[1] Computer Science and Technology, Wuhan University of Science and Technology,
Wuhan 430065, China
[2] Hubei Province Key Laboratory of Intelligent Information Processing and
Real-time Industrial System, Wuhan 430065, China
[3] Department of Computer Science, VU University Amsterdam, Amsterdam 1081hv,
The Netherlands

Abstract. APDG (Adanced Patient Data Generator) is a tool for knowledge-based patient data generation. However, the existing APDG has not yet provided any visualization tool to define patient data. This paper proposes a visualization approach to make the APDG system more feasible to developers and end-users of medical information systems. This paper investigates the design of the visualization interface tool for APDG, and discusses how the proposed approach is implemented by using the C# in the dot NET platform.

Keywords: Semantic Technology, Advanced Patient Data Generator, Electronic Medical Records, Visual Interface.

1 Introduction

During the research and development of medical information system, a lot of patient data are needed for system validation, performance evaluation and other major processing. However, due to legal and many other reasons, access of those patient data is strictly restricted, even within a hospital. As to the medical information system companies, to get the authorization is extremely hard. However, without those patient data, it is quite difficult for the developers to make experiments with the medical information systems for the evaluation and others.

In order to solve that problem, the Advanced Patient Data Generator (APDG)[5] is designed to provide an effective solution. While a variety of scientific evidence collected from the group of patients, the APDG system can automatically generate patient data by using those collected knowledge or evidences. Those knowledge can be collected from medical literature (such as PubMed, medical textbook, etc.), and web resources (such as Wikipedia and medical websites). The APDG system can generate virtual patient data efficiently, which looks exactly realistic as real ones, and avoid the problem of the access restriction of real patient data.

The APDG system uses the Patient Data Definition Language(PDDL), an XML-based language, to define the patient data format, the relation of a variety of relevant scientific evidence to generate virtual Electronic Health Records

Z. Huang et al. (Eds.): WISE 2013 Workshops 2013, LNCS 8182, pp. 401–414, 2014.

(patient data) or Clinical records (CRs). Currently, APDG has not yet provided any visual user interface. Thus, it is still inconvenience to most users, who have very limited knowledge to use an XML file. To benefit APDG users, in this paper, the visual interface with a user-friendly PDDL editor is designed for APDG. We have implemented the visual tool for the APDG system by using .Net platform. We have used the visual tool of the APDG system to generate large scale patient data and used those generated patient data in the System SeSRUA, a semantically-enable system for Rational Use of Antibiotics[4].

The rest of this paper is organized as follows: Section 2 provides a brief introduction to the APDG system. Section 3 presents the design of the visual tool for the APDG system. Section 4 reportes the experiments with the visual tool for the APDG system, Section 5 makes a conclusion of the paper.

2   The APDG System

2.1   The Architecture of the APDG System

The major function of APDG system is to generate virtual patient data, which should meet the medical statistics requirements and can be used as test datasets in the developing process of medical systems. In particular, we are interested in the generation of semantic patient data, i.e., those patient data with the format of RDF Ntriple or others, because they can be used in a triple store, a platform for semantic data processing by using semantic technology.

The APDG system consists of the editing system of the Patient Data Definition Language (PDDL), and the patient data generating system. The architecture of the APDG system is shown in Figure 1. The PDDL editing system is used to define the patient data, based on the collected medical knowledge. The patient data generating system is used to generate the corresponding virtual patient data.

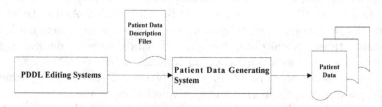

Fig. 1. The architecture of the APDG system

2.2   Patient Data Description File

To initiate APDG system, the patient data description file is the firstly constructed in accordance with the characteristics of a variety of medical records. In order to standardize the patient data description file, a PDDL language had been designed to define it.

2.2.1 The PDDL Language

The PDDL language is designed to be an XML-based language, which defines the patient data format. The APDG system introduces the archetype-based patient data structures, like those have been used in Openpatient data[2]. The general structure of patient data in PDDL consists of the hierarchy of session-archetype-slot. To ease the design of the visual editing interface, the PDDL language labels are properly refined. The XML Schema structure of PDDL is shown in Figure 2. Namely we define the four labels of PDDL, i.e., Archetype, Slot, Condition and Distribution.

- Archetype: used to describe a medical model, the basic archetype consists of several slots or archetypes.
- Slot: used to describe a data value of the patient, such as age, blood pressure, etc. Archetypes and slots can be further combined to form a new archetype.
- Condition: used to describe the distribution of Slot values under certain conditions. Its attribute expression is used to describe the corresponding condition. A condition may contain a number of Distributions.
- Distribution: describing specific distribution of the attributes and their values

In order to facilitate the querying and reasoning support of the semantic data which are associated with some ontologies, such as SNOMED[6], The attributes "ontology" and "conceptid" are introduced to be additional ones for Archetypes, Slot and Distribution. These two attributes are associated with the specified value of the name and the identifier of the corresponding ontology.

2.2.2 Construction of the Archetype

Through the PDDL language, we can build an archetype according to the needs of medical records. For example, for the systolic and diastolic blood pressure in a patient record, we can use the following PDDL statement to define an archetype of blood pressure.

```
<Archetype concept="BloodPressure">
  <Slot name="Systolic" type="integer"/>
  <Slot name="Diastolic" type="integer"/>
</Archetype>
```

Archetypes and slots can be further combined to build a new archetype. For example, we can integrate temperature, pulse, blood pressure to build a new archetype as follows:

```
<Archetype concept="Examination">
  <Slot name="BodyTempature" type="decimal" decimaldigits="1"/>
  <Slot name="Pulse" type="integer"/>
  <Archetype concept="BloodPressure">
    <Slot name="Systolic" type="integer"/>
    <Slot name="Diastolic" type="integer"/>
  </Archetype>
</Archetype>
```

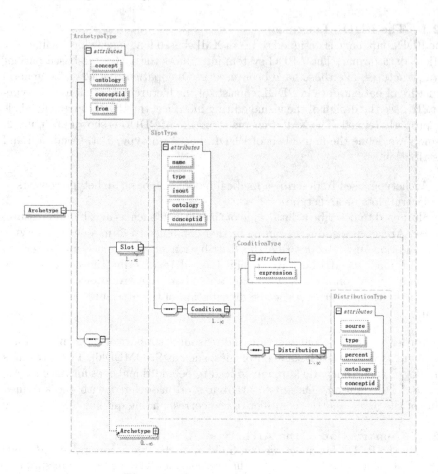

Fig. 2. PDDL XML Schema diagram

In order to construct a re-usable archetype that can be referred in the other PDDL file, we introduce the attribute "from" in an archetype. For example, the archetype "examination" can be saved in a file named "Examination.xml", then through the "from" attribute in archetype, we can build a new archetype, which is shown below:

```
<Archetype concept="Patient">
    <Slot name="name" type="string"/>
    <Slot name="Gender" type="string"/>
    <Archetype concept="Examination" from="Examination.xml">
</Archetype>
```

2.2.3   Slots

The label Slots are used to describe the value in a domain. The attribute "type" in a Distribution defines the way of getting value. PDDL provides a rich varieties of distributions, such as prescribed value, the arithmetic expression, uniform distribution within a set, normal distribution within a set, uniform distribution on the interval, normal distribution on the interval,etc. The attribute "source" in a Distribution defines the way of getting data which can be described in the form of single value, a set, an interval, and an expression.

- **Prescribed value**
  If in the generated data,the percentage of male is 50% and the female has the same percentage,then we can define the domain of gender as follows:

```
<Slot name="Gender" type="string">
  <Condition>
    <Distribution type="PrescribedValue" source="male" percent="0.5"/>
    <Distribution type="PrescribedValue" source="female" percent="0.5"/>
  </Condition>
</Slot>
```

- **Uniform distribution within a set**
  In the above example,the percentage of male and female are the same, so it can also be described as follows:

```
<Slot name="Gender" type="string">
  <Condition>
    <Distribution type="SetUniform" source="male,female" percent="1"/>
  </Condition>
</Slot>
```

- **Uniform distribution on the interval**
  If the generated data for the age from 10 to 60 years old is uniform distribution, then it can be defined as follows:

```
<Slot name="Age" type="integer">
  <Condition>
    <Distribution type="IntervalUniform" source="10~60" percent="1"/>
  </Condition>
</Slot>
```

- **Normal distribution on the interval**
  In the above example, if the data of age meets the (0,1) normal distribution, then it can be defined as follows:

```
<Slot name="Age" type="integer">
  <Condition>
    <Distribution type="IntervalNormal" source="10~60" percent="1"/>
  </Condition>
</Slot>
```

2.2.4   Relationship between the Slots

Between different slots, there exist a variety of relationships which can be expressed by a condition. For example, as the statistics of the examination data of one unit shows that the percentage of having Hypertension is 2.84% when the age is between 20 and 30, while the percentage is 4.32% when the age is between 30 and 40. If the normal value of systolic is ranged between 110 and 140, and that of diastolic is ranged between 60 and 90. The value of systolic in Hypertension is ranged between

110 and 140, and that of diastolic is ranged between 90 and 100. Based on the above data, the archetype can be built as follows:

```
<Archetype concept="Patient">
   <Slot value="Age" type="integer">
      <Condition>
         <Distribution type="IntervalUniform" source="20~30"
                       percent="0.5"/>
         <Distribution type="IntervalUniform" source="30~40"
                       percent="0.5"/>
      </Condition>
   </Slot>
   <Archetype concept="BloodPressure">
      <Slot value="Systolic" type="integer">
         <Condition expression="$Age &gt;= 20 AND $Age &lt; 30">
            <Distribution type="IntervalUniform" source="110~140"
                          percent="0.9716"/>
            <Distribution type="IntervalUniform" source="140~160"
                          percent="0.0284"/>
         </Condition>
         <Condition expression="$Age &gt;= 30 AND $Age &lt; 40">
            <Distribution type="IntervalUniform" source="110~140"
                          percent="0.9568"/>
            <Distribution type="IntervalUniform" source="140~160"
                          percent="0.0432"/>
         </Condition>
      </Slot>
      <Slot value="Diastolic" type="integer">
         <Condition expression="$Age &gt;= 20 AND $Age &lt; 30">
            <Distribution type="IntervalUniform" source="60~90"
                          percent="0.9716"/>
            <Distribution type="IntervalUniform" source="90~100"
                          percent="0.0284"/>
         </Condition>
         <Condition expression="$Age &gt;= 30 AND $Age &lt; 40">
            <Distribution type="IntervalUniform" source="60~90"
                          percent="0.9568"/>
            <Distribution type="IntervalUniform" source="90~100"
                          percent="0.0432"/>
         </Condition>
      </Slot>
   </Archetype>
</Archetype>
```

As showed in the above example, using the method of adding a prefix "$" at the slot name to define a variable. We introduce the operators (such as 'AND','<'(less than), '>'(greater than)) to describe the relationship.

2.3 Virtual Patient Data

After defining the patient data description file by using PDDL, the APDG system can generate the virtual medical data. The format of the output data can be selected to be RDF Ntriple/Turtle. For example, part of generated patient data in the format of RDF Turtle are shown following.

```
@prefix  apdg:   <http://wasp.cs.vu.nl/apdg#>
@prefix  rdf:    <http://www.w3.org/1999/02/22-rdf-syntax-ns#>
@prefix  rdfs:   <http://www.w3.org/2000/01/rdf-schema#>
apdg:VMRBP_MHZ100000   rdf:type  adpg:VirtualMedicalRecord.
apdg:VMRBP_MHZ100000   apdg:has Archetype   apdg:VMRBP_MHZ100000_A1.
apdg:VMRBP_MHZ100000_A1   rdfs:label   "Patient".
apdg:VMRBP_MHZ100000_A1   apdg:hasSlot   apdg:VMRBP_MHZ100000_A1S1.
apdg:VMRBP_MHZ100000_A1S1   rdfs:label   "Age".
apdg:VMRBP_MHZ100000_A1S1   apdg:value
        "36"^^<http://www.w3.org/2001/XMLSchema#integer>.
apdg:VMRBP_MHZ100000_A1   apdg:has Archetype   apdg:VMRBP_MHZ100000_A1A1.
apdg:VMRBP_MHZ100000_A1A1   rdfs:label   "BloodPressure".
apdg:VMRBP_MHZ100000_A1A1   apdg:hasSlot   apdg:VMRBP_MHZ100000_A1A1S1.
apdg: VMRBP_MHZ100000_A1A1S1   rdfs:label   "Systolic".
apdg: VMRBP_MHZ100000_A1A1S1   apdg:value
        "116"^^<http://www.w3.org/2001/XMLSchema#integer>.
apdg:VMRBP_MHZ100000_A1A1   apdg:hasSlot   apdg:VMRBP_MHZ100000_A1A1S2.
apdg:VMRBP_MHZ100000_A1A1S2 rdfs:label   "Diastolic".
apdg:VMRBP_MHZ100000_A1A1S2 apdg:value
        "77"^^<http://www.w3.org/2001/XMLSchema#integer>.
```

By the way of generating patient data automatically, enough electronic medical records data can be generated and can be provided as test data sets in a semantically-enabled medical information system.

3 Visual APDG System

3.1 Editing Patient Data Description File

On the .NET platform, the visual APDG system is implemented through C# language. The interface of patient data description files is shown in Figure 3. With the visual interface, for the users who are not familiar with the XML language, they can complete the patient data description file easily.

3.1.1 The Editing Interface

The patient data description file has actually a tree structure, .NET TreeView control is used to present the tree structure. As shown in Figure 3, the left panel (TreeView control) displays the entire structure of the patient data description file. Each node represent a label, as described in the previous section,i.e., Archetype, Slot, Condition and Distribution. The right panel (ProertyGrid control) displays specific attribute values belong to these four kind of labels, for which the users can modify the attribute values for each labels as they want.

The toolbar at top of the interface provides two kind specific functions; The first kind is for patient data description files, "Open", "New" and "Save" operation. Second kind used to edit labels, "Add", "Remove" operation.

In order to facilitate the users who want to check the generated XML codes of the patient data description file, also provides the description file in XML, users can view it by clicking "XML Source Code" tab. The interface is shown in Figure 4.

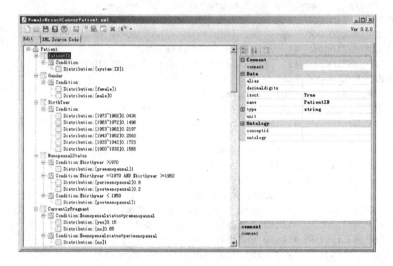

Fig. 3. Describes the document editing interface patient data

3.1.2   Patient Data Editing

The patient data editing functions mainly provide the two operations.One is to add and remove labels by calling the add and remove method of TreeView control. Another editing function is to edit label attributes, this function is achieved through ProertyGrid control. In order to edit attribute values of these labels, a class is defined for each defined label. For example, Archetype, the label has concept, ontology and conceptid three attributes, which is defined as follows:

```
class ArcheTypeProperty {
    private string _concept, _form _ontology, _conceptid,;
    public string concept {
       get { return _concept; }  set { _concept = value;}}
    public string form {
       get { return _from; }  set { _from =from;}}
    public string ontology {
       get{return _ontology;} set {_ontology = value;}}
    public string conceptid {
       get{return _conceptid;} set{_conceptid = value;}}}
```

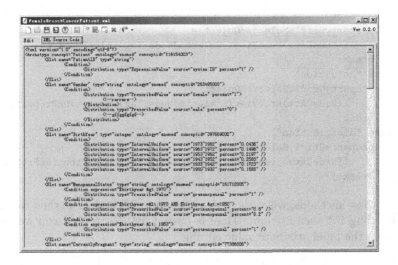

Fig. 4. Describes patient data XML source file

While a class established, we just need to assign the instances of the class to "SelectedObject" attribute of ProertyGrid controls then instance attribute values can be edited.

In the same way, we can establish Slot, Condition and Distribution of the three labels class SlotProperty, ConditonProperty and DistributionProperty.

While a node in the TreeView control express the four defined label, for easy data processing, we define the node data class NodeData, which is defined as follows:

```
class NodeData {
    public string nodeType;
    public ArcheTypeProperty archeTypeProperty;
    public SlotProperty slotProperty;
    public ConditionProperty conditionsProperty;
    public DistributionProperty distributionProperty;}
```

In the NodeData class, nodeType mainly used to indicate the dedicate node type, whose value is the "archetype", "slot", "condition" and "distribution" of four. So that when the user clicks on the different nodes,"AfterSelect" event of the TreeView control is triggered. The "AfterSelect" event coded is defined as follows:

```
private void treeView1_AfterSelect(object sender, TreeViewEventArgs e){
    string nodeType = ((NodeData)treeView1.SelectedNode.Tag).nodeType;
    switch (nodeType) {
        case "archetype":
            propertyGrid1.SelectedObject =
                ((NodeData)treeView1.SelectedNode.Tag).archeTypeProperty;
            break;
```

```
case "slot":
  propertyGrid1.SelectedObject =
      ((NodeData)treeView1.SelectedNode.Tag).slotProperty;
  break;
case "condition":
  propertyGrid1.SelectedObject =
      ((NodeData)treeView1.SelectedNode.Tag).conditionProperty;
  break;
case "distribution":
  propertyGrid1.SelectedObject =
      ((NodeData)treeView1.SelectedNode.Tag).distributionProperty;
  break;}}
```

Through these methods, when the user clicks on a different node then the node corresponding instance attribute label is passed to ProertyGrid controls, thus completing the label attribute value editing.

3.1.3   Processing Conditional Expressions

Within patient data description file Condition label, "expression" attribute describes Slot value distribution under certain conditions, to facilitate the user to set the condition, the condition expression editor designed and shown in Figure 5. The user can select the name from the slot list and the value under this slot and operators($>, >=, =, <, <=$ and AND) to compose a variety of conditions.

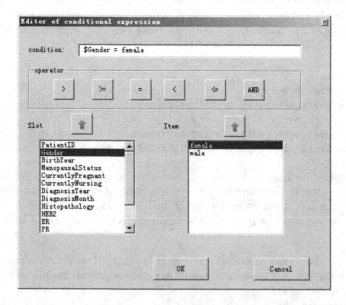

Fig. 5. Conditional expression editor

3.1.4   TreeView and XML Conversion

While patient data description file is composed in XML language, so the completed results should be convert into XML language. Briefly, the data presented in the TreeView control need to be translated into XML format expression. Reversely, the editing system needs to parse the XML language to convert it to TreeView control data to present to the user when open a patient data description file.

Because the patient data description file is defined as a nested structure, in the TreeView with XML mutual conversion can easily accomplish by recursive method.Two recursive method are defined in the implementation to accomplish this process.

3.2   Generation of Virtual Patient Data

When the patient data description file editing is complete, you can generate virtual patient data according to the definition, virtual data generation interface is shown in Figure 6. To avoid duplicated data generated by different users, the system through user input DiseaseID (disease identification), CreatorID (creator logo) and the SessionID (generation time identification) to build virtual data. To generate valid virtual data, the first step is to detect fault in the file, and the second step is to generate correct data against defined rule.

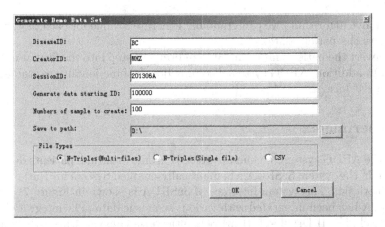

Fig. 6. Patient data virtual data generation interface

3.2.1   Detecting Patient Data Description Files

For fault detecting in a patient data description file, mainly from the following aspects will be dealt with:

1)determine the legality of the conditional expression, is mainly detected match between operators and operands, and whether to use a slot while undefined.

2) Verify total ratio of the same conditions, the ratio accounted for a variety of distribution should be 1. This test can traverses Distribution tab "percent" attribute value of the Condition label to complete. Until these tests passed, data can be generated.

3.2.2   Patient Data Generation

In order to facilitate the generation of virtual data, take advantage of TreeView control to generate the data, and avoid directly deal with the obscure XML code. In the implementation, through the following two steps to complete the task:

1) First, the value generated gradually for each Slot. Specific generate Slot value algorithm is as follows :

```
For each Condition in Slot
   If (Condition.expression is True)
      R=Random(0,1)  //Get (0,1] random number between
      P=0
      For each Distribution in Condition
         P=P+Distribution.percent
         IF(R<=P)
            Result=GetValue(Distribution.type,Distribution.source)
         End if
      End For
   End If
End For
```

By the above algorithm , we can gradually generate a value for each Slot, which constitutes the patient data.

2) Convert the patient data generated in previous step into the format of RDF Ntriple. In addition, APDG system also provides the functionality to storage the data in CSV format.

4   Experiments

We use the APDG system to generate 10,000 chronic bronchial patients data and use them in the system SeSRUA,a Semantically-enabled System for Rational Use of Antibiotics[4]. The system interface of SeSRUA is shown in Figure 7.

SeSRUA has been integrated with various semantic data. The integrated data sources includes: i) Drugbank[1], ii) Semantic rules converted from the clinical guideline for rational use of antibiotics[7], iii) the semantic data converted from the drug manuals of antibiotics, iv) the semantic patient data generated by APDG. The total number of triples is up to 4 millions in the existing SeSRUA system.

SeSRUA is built on the top of LarKC (Large Knowledge Collider)[1], a platform for scalable semantic data processing[3,8]. With the built-in reasoning support for large-scale RDF/OWL data of LarKC, SeSRUA is able to provide various reasoning and data processing services for rational use of antibiotics, which include

---
[1] http://www.larkc.eu

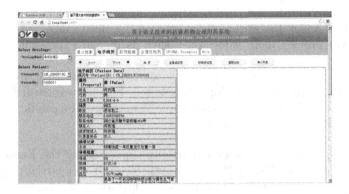

Fig. 7. The system interface of SeSRUA

antibiotics query and the usage recommendation for patient against corresponding personal information.

According these practice experience and results, the APDG tool is a valuable one, which makes the generated data have no difference with real data, and avoid the access restriction for real patient data.

5 Conclusion

In this paper, we have presented the visual APDG system, which defines the patient data description file, then generates the corresponding patient data. The main feature of the visual ADPG system are:

- Flexible patient data definition. The patient data description file in XML language, with strong representation capabilities to define the archetype. During the design, Archetype label support the nested label. Also, expression, value range, and else features enable users to easily build flexible structures to describe the various diseases.
- Integration of semantic data set. The APDG system can generate the triples data, and associate the concepts in an ontology. It provides a foundation for further semantic data processing and reasoning/querying by using a semantic platform (e.g. the LarKC Platform).
- Friendly user interface. The visual APDG system provides a user-friendly interface and the detection system to find various pre-defined errors, with those tools, users, even for those who have no any XML knowledge, can define patient data description files easily.

Currently the APDG system is still being optimized. The followings are future work for the visual APDG system:

- More operators of the conditional expression representation. The current system only supports the AND operator. Further work will provide the OR, and NOT operators.

- Value definition. In the current system, the way of getting value includes prescribed value, the arithmetic expression, specified ranges value. Further work will provide more value ways, such as regular expression for values setting, etc.
- Improved ontology association. In the current system, associated concept names in an ontology are done by manual. Further work will include an automatic or semi-automatic search over an ontology for a candidate concept name and concept identification.

Acknowledgments. This work is partially supported by the European 7th Framework Project (FP7-ICT-2011-7, Grant288048). It was partially supported by a grant from the NSF (Natural Science Foundation) of China under grant number 61272110 and 61100133, the Key Projects of National Social Science Foundation of China under grant number 11ZD&189. It was partially supported by NSF of educational agency of Hubei Prov. under grant number Q20101110, and the State Key Lab of Software Engineering Open Foundation of Wuhan University under grant number SKLSE2012-09-07.

References

1. Drugbank 3.0. Technical report (2011)
2. Beale, T.: Archetypes: Constraint-based domain models for future-proof information systems. In: OOPSLA 2002 Workshop on Behavioural Semantics (2002)
3. Fensel, D., van Harmelen, F., Andersson, B., Brennan, P., Cunningham, H., Della Valle, E., Fischer, F., Huang, Z., Kiryakov, A., Lee, T., School, L., Tresp, V., Wesner, S., Witbrock, M., Zhong, N.: Towards LarKC: a platform for web-scale reasoning. In: Proceedings of the IEEE International Conference on Semantic Computing (ICSC 2008). IEEE Computer Society Press, CA (2008)
4. Hua, X., Chen, C., Huang, Z., Hu, Q., Gu, J.: Towards intelligent monitoring on use of antibacterial agents by using semantic technology. Chinese Digital Medicine 8(4), 12–15 (2013)
5. Huang, Z., van Harmelen, F., ten Teije, A., Dentler, K.: Knowledge-based patient data generation. In: Riaño, D., Lenz, R., Miksch, S., Peleg, M., Reichert, M., ten Teije, A. (eds.) KR4HC 2013/ProHealth 2013. LNCS (LNAI), vol. 8268, pp. 83–96. Springer, Heidelberg (2013)
6. Spackman, K.: Managing clinical terminology hierarchies using algorithmic calculation of subsumption: Experience with snomed-rt. Journal of the American Medical Informatics Association (2000)
7. The Chinese Medical Association, P. A. C. of Chinese Hospital Association, and H. P. C. of Chinese Pharmaceutical Association. the clinical application guideline for rational use of antibiotics. Technical report (2008)
8. Witbrock, M., Fortuna, B., Bradesko, L., Kerrigan, M., Bishop, B., van Harmelen, F., ten Teije, A., Oren, E., Momtchev, V., Tenschert, A., Cheptsov, A., Roller, S., Gallizo, G.: D5.3.1 - requirements analysis and report on lessons learned during prototyping. Larkc project deliverable (June 2009)

Semantic Approach for Rational Use of Antibiotics: A Perspective from Clinical Research

Xiaoli Hua[1], Zhisheng Huang[2], Rui Yang[4], Chen Chen[1], Qing Hu[3], Dongsheng Chen[1], and Jinguang Gu[3]*

[1] Department of Pharmacy, Wuhan Union Hospital Affiliated with Tongji Medical College, Huazhong University of Science and Technology, Wuhan 430022, China
[2] Department of Computer Science, VU University Amsterdam, Amsterdam 1081hv, The Netherlands
[3] College of Computer Science and Technology, Wuhan University of Science and Technology, Wuhan 430065, China
[4] Department of General Surgery, Tongji Hospital Affiliated with Tongji Medical College, Huazhong University of Science and Technology, Wuhan 430030, China

Abstract. Antibiotic abuse has potentially serious effects on health. Rational use of antibiotics has become a basic principle in medical practice. In this paper we propose a semantic approach for rational use of antibiotics, by introducing the semantic technology into the monitoring on the use of antibiotic agents. In particular, we investigate the problem from the perspective of clinical research. The proposed approach has been implemented in a prototype system named SeSRUA, a Semantically-enabled System for Rational Use of Antibiotics. This semantic system with the support of data interoperability provides a basic infrastructure for the intelligent monitoring on the use of antibiotics.

Keywords: semantic technology, antibiotics, rational use, intelligent monitoring.

1 Introduction

In recent years, antibiotics abuse leads to the high-rate of bacterial resistance to antibiotics and the world widespread of "super bacteria"[1]. The development of new antibiotics requires longer cycle and higher cost. All these will threaten the human health, and even the survival. Antibiotics abuse in China has been increasingly fierce. Faced with severe situation, the Chinese Ministry of Health with other four healthcare authorities jointly launched a national campaign against the antibiotics abuse in 2011.

Using the semantic technology to solve the problem in biomedical area is a hot topic in recent years. The semantic technology provides a common framework for network data sharing, reuse and interoperability. Linked Life Data (LLD)

---

* Corresponding author.

Z. Huang et al. (Eds.): WISE 2013 Workshops 2013, LNCS 8182, pp. 415–428, 2014.

and Bio-medical data in Linked Open Data (LOD)[2], such as Drugbank[3] and SNOMED-CT (Systematized Nomenclature of Medicine-Clinical Terms)[4], provide rich data resources for the data interoperability to solve the problem of heterogeneous medical data in the existing medical information systems.

In this paper, we will investigate the problem of the development of a system for rational use of antibiotics from the perspective of clinical research. Furthermore, we will propose a semantic approach for rational use of antibiotics, by introducing the semantic technology into the monitoring on the use of antibiotics. We have implemented a prototype named SeSRUA (Semantically-enabled System for Rational Use of Antibiotics). This semantic system with the support of data interoperability provides a basic infrastructure for the intelligent monitoring on the use of antibiotics.

The contributions of this paper are:

- We analyze the present situation of the information management for antibiotics. The key points for antibiotics management and the difficulties of its hospital management are also discussed.
- We propose a semantic approach for rational use of antibiotics by introducing the semantic technology, which has been widely used in the Semantic Web and Ontology Engineering.
- We present the system of SeSRUA and discuss the initial implementation of the system.

2   Rational Use of Antibiotics and Semantic Technology

2.1   Research Problem and Analysis

The health authorities have published the guidelines for rational use of antibiotics. It aims at further strengthening the management of clinical rational use of antibiotics, effectively controlling antibiotic resistance and ensuring medical quality and safety.

However, the status of antibiotics application in China is still not optimistic. The irrational use of antibiotics is still a serious problem[5,6]. All the data suggested that the use of antibiotics in China is still far away from the rational level. Due to the limit time and heavy task caused by domestic strained medical resources, along with all kinds of medical information exploding and long-term drug habit, medication errors maybe easily occurred.

Antibiotics have the following characteristics:

1. *Particularity.* Antibiotics acts on pathogen, rather than the human tissues and organs. The relationship among infected body, antibiotics and pathogens, as shown in Figure 1, which requires multiple knowledge containing not only clinical pharmacy but also microbiology and diagnosis on infectious diseases
2. *Universality.* Infectious diseases, especially the bacterial infections are the most common diseases in clinical, so that the antibiotics is one of the drugs most widely applied in clinical.

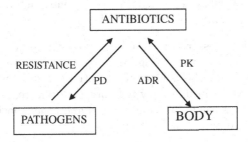

Fig. 1. Schematic diagram of antibiotics- pathogens - body relationship.PD:pharmacodynamics ;PK:pharmacokinetic; ADR:adverse drug reaction

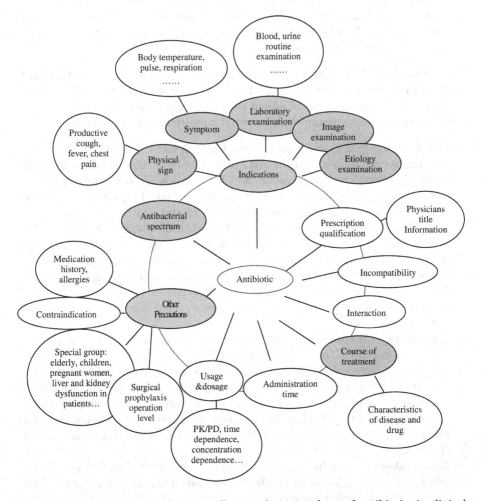

Fig. 2. Schematic diagram of factors affecting the rational use of antibiotics in clinical

3. *Complexity.* As shown in Figure 2, there are so many factors effecting rational use of antibiotics in all aspects of clinical.

For example, it is necessary to exercise caution for the risk of kidney damage from antibiotics as shown in Figure 2. According to dispensatory, when using antibiotics, it should be paid more attention for dose and renal function monitoring, such as renal insufficiency patients, children (renal function not yet mature), senile patients (renal function decline) and other special groups. There are different kinds of damage for kidney:

1. Basic diseases such as hypertension, diabetes, hyperlipidemia and systemic lupus erythematosus often complicated with nephropathy;
2. Some drugs have renal toxicity themselves, such as cyclosporine, tacrolimus, aminoglycosides, vancomycin, non-steroidal anti-inflammatory drugs;
3. Some drugs cleared by the kidney. While taking these drugs combined with kidney-harmful drugs, then the probability of renal injury will increased along with the higher blood concentration in kidney.

Some laboratory parameters are closely related to the renal function and valuable to determine whether renal injury. Once the parameters fluctuating abnormally, the clinician should adjust the dosage regimen in time.

Common laboratory parameters for renal impairment are as follows:

1. *Blood uric acid*: uric acid is an independent risk factor for renal dysfunction. The risk is even higher than the urine protein volume. Rise of serum uric acid is closely related to renal disease, which involve acute uric acid nephropathy, uric acid nephrolithiasis and chronic uric acid nephropathy, etc. Normal serum uric acid values are $149\sim417\mu mol/L$ (male) and $89\sim357\mu mol/L$ (female) for the adults; $250\sim476\mu mol/L$ (male), $190\sim434\mu mol/L$ (female) for elderly (>60 years old). The value above $420\mu mol/L$(7.0 mg/dl)for male or $360\mu mol/L$(6.0 mg/dl) for female are diagnosed as hyperuricemia.
2. *Proteinuria*: normal urine protein is <40mg/24h, adult ceiling 150mg/24h. Pathological proteinuria is common in all types of kidney diseases, such as primary and secondary glomerular disease, renal disease and interstitial nephritis, etc.
3. *Hematuria*: It is common in acute or chronic glomerulonephritis, acute cystitis, pyelonephritis and renal calculi, etc.
4. *Blood urea nitrogen* (BUN): BUN is mainly filtrated through glomerular with urine. When the kidney function is impaired, glomerular filtration rate will reduced along with serum urea nitrogen increased. BUN has a certain reference value in reflecting the filtration function of glomerular. Normal reference value is $3.2\sim7.5$mmol/L for adult; $1.8\sim6.5$mmol/L for infants and children.
5. *Serum phosphorus* (Pi): normal reference value is $0.97\sim1.62$mmol/L for adult, $1.29\sim1.94$mmol/L for children. Elevated Pi is common in chronic kidney disease, multiple myeloma.

6. *Serum creatinine* (Scr): Normal reference value is 53~106 μmol/L for male, 44~97 μmol/L for female, and 44~70μmol/L for the elderly (>60 years old). Reduced glomerular filtration function caused by kinds of factors can lead to a rise in Scr, which is more sensitive than BUN to reflect the situation of the renal function. Endogenous creatinine clearance rate (Ccr) is a sensitive parameter for glomerular damage. The normal value is 90pm10 ml/min. The clinical significance of Ccr as follows:

   – below the reference value of 80% or less implies glomerular filtration hypofunction;
   – 50~70 ml/min value means mild renal function damage;
   – 31~50 ml/min value implies moderate renal damage;
   – below 30 ml/min value means severe renal damage;
   – 11~20 ml/min value means early renal inadequacy;
   – 6~10 ml/min value means advanced renal inadequacy;
   – below 5 ml/min value means end-stage renal failure.

In addition, imageological examination is another common method for the diagnosis of renal function, including:

1. Ultrasound imaging of the urinary tract, which is helpful to rule out possibilities of urinary tract obstruction and chronic renal inadequacy;
2. CT examination, which shows the existence of stress-related expansion. If there is sufficient reason to doubt the obstruction, then retrograde or descending pyelography could discover some recurrent urinary tract infection factors such as urinary tract stones, obstruction, reflux or deformities;
3. CT angiography, MRI or radionuclide examination, which are helpful to determine the presence of occlusive vascular disease;
4. Renal angiography, which help make a definitive diagnosis of renal inadequacy.

In summary, in the application of antibiotics treatment, when faced with complex disease, just for renal function, there are many things need for caution. Doctors must make a thoughtful therapeutic schedule considering all information, such as contraindication, drug interaction, various laboratory parameters and examination reports etc. In addition to this, close monitoring of kidney function and real-time adjust regimen are necessary. Doctors exercise extreme caution as mild negligence may cause serious consequences, for which the doctor and the patient have to pay a terrible price. In clinical, far more than antibiotics or renal function should be cautious about. All these brought great pressure for doctors. So it is urgent to effectively reduce the professional burden on doctors and avoid medication risk.

Compared with general drugs, the supervision of antibiotics is more difficult and the situation is more urgent as its irrational use may do greater harm to humans. So it is not enough for clinical antibiotics management only depending on rules, regulations and manual intervention of Medical Management[7,8]. Network management based on advanced information technology becomes the inevitable choice for rational use of antibiotics. The information technology which able to integrate and interoperate all kinds of information flow will enable monitoring of antibiotics more intelligent and more suitable for clinical practice requirements.

To reduce the risk of the patient's medication and make up the lack of professional knowledge structure, both clinicians and clinical pharmacists are in urgent need of specialized system solutions for technical and resource support[9,10]. Foreign software for the rational use of drugs has many restrictions in the domestic large-scale hospital application due to the difference of language habits, number of patients and medical model. In nearly a decade, the rational drug use system embedded in HIS system is developing rapidly in China. With the application in some hospitals, the software achieved good clinical effect in rational drug use and provided valuable experience and ideas for the use of information means to control the clinical medication.

But the existing system of rational drug use still has some drawbacks:

1. The collected information is poor, which only covered drug information but no the important clinical information, such as "medical indications", "diagnosis" and so on (see the gray part of Figure 2).
2. What the system checked and warned real time mainly covered the irrational use between drug and drug, such as interaction, incompatibility, repeated use, etc.But the irrational use between drug and disease are omitted.
3. Some systems can warn for some irrational drug use such as allergies, Pathophysiology changes, but require doctors filling out online, which cost lots of time but obtain limited information.

This situation brought problems for the management of rational drug use:

1. We can only rely on software to realize partial but not overall control for clinical rational drug use.
2. To judge whether clinical factors like medication indications was reasonable or not, we couldnt obtain the real-time warning results by linkage analysis from massive information, but need input the medical record number for inquiries in different information systems, such as PACS (medical image storage and transmission system), LIS (inspection information system), EMR (electronic medical record system), etc.

Seen from Figure 3, when the irrational drug use occurred, current domestic antibiotics supervision software unable automatically extract patients clinical information or provide optional dosage regimen for physician, but only requiring physician's manual input (left) or artificial distinction(right), which may increase the burden on doctors.

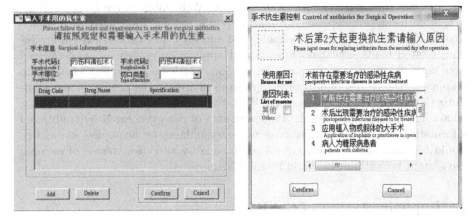

Fig. 3. Common interface diagram of current domestic antibiotics supervision software

In short, there are many areas in need of improvement to achieve efficient and intelligent network management. Confront the complex clinical condition, current system failed to achieve real time monitoring of rational drug use for actual individuals.

One reason is that the process monitoring methods of existing rational drug use systems are based on the structured document. But lots of important clinical information is a semi-structured or non-structured data form, such as electronic medical records (text), imaging results like X ray (picture). In result, clinical data among different disciplines, such as clinical medicine, pharmacy, laboratory science and medical imaging, could not be combined analysis. For example, any name of drug or dis-ease should only be input or query in a unique code, even if their names are synonymous. So it is necessary to introduce semantic technologies to change the current situation.

2.2 Semantic Approach

In fact, all experience of antibiotics use should be shared. In the Semantic Web, web content can not only be understood, but also be easily processed or inferred by machines. Due to the application of antibiotics has accumulated huge amount of information and valuable empirical data which distributed in kinds of systems, it is impossible to fully grasp for practitioners. Only by recombining and processing upon the computer technology, can these scattered, isomeric, numerous, inconsistent and dynamic resources be understood by computer. This exceeds the traditional information-process systems function and must rely on the new semantic technology.

The community of the semantic technology has developed several international standards for data representation language based on semantics, such as resource description framework (RDF) and the Web Ontology Language (OWL), so that data can be independent from the specific system. Pharmaceutical knowledge was described with the technology of ontology. The rational use of antibiotics related management documents and application guidelines are converted from natural language to semantic description, which has more clear relationship mapped to the corresponding ontology graph in order to realize intelligent monitoring and knowledge management. With the help of semantic web technology, knowledge management for the large amounts of data generated by traditional information system will become easy, while redundancy or incomplete knowledge would be effectively overcome. As a result, quality and effectiveness of rational use system for antibiotics would be further improved.

3   Implementation of SeSRUA

Based on the analysis above, we propose the approach of semantic technology to realize intelligent monitoring on rational use of antibiotics. We have implemented SeSRUA, a Semantically-enabled System for Rational Use of Antibiotics. The architecture of SeSRUA is shown in Figure 4. SeSRUA is built on the top of LarKC[11], a platform for scalable semantic data processing[1]. OWLIM is used to be the basic data layer of LarKC. The platform has a pluggable architecture in which it is possible to exploit techniques and heuristics from diverse areas such as databases, machine learning, cognitive science, the Semantic Web, and others. LarKC provides a number of pluggable components: retrieval, abstraction, selection, reasoning and deciding. In LarKC, massive, distributed and necessarily incomplete reasoning is performed over Web-scale knowledge sources.

3.1   Knowledge and Semantic Patient Data

At present, there exist several pharmaceutical data sets, such as DrugBank[3], which is developed by University of Alberta, and RxNorm[12], which is developed by US National Library of Medicine. Those data sets provide the basic knowledge of drugs and become basic data sources for the application of semantic technology in medical pharmacy. However, many of drug properties have still not yet been refined to meet comprehensive needs of knowledge for applications. For example,in Drugbank, multiple indications of a drug are described in a natural language text, which is not easy to be processed directly in a medical information system, because they are not structured data. So we should make the design of semantic data, so that they are suitable for the practice for monitoring antibiotic use.

We use APDG (Advanced Patient Data Generator)[13], a knowledge-based patient data generator, to generate ten thousand of virtual patients of chronic

---

[1] http://www.larkc.eu

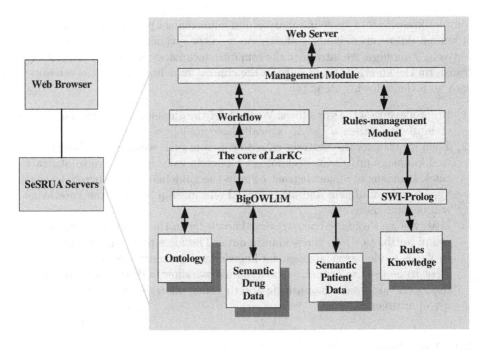

Fig. 4. The Architecture of SeSRUA

bronchial in Hubei Province, China. Those virtual patient data are loaded into the SeSRUA system for the test. APDG uses domain knowledge to generate virtual patient data, so that the generated patient data look like real ones.

Table 1 shows the integrated data sets in SeSRUA, which include drug data sets, patient data, and generated data sets of the Chinese guidelines for rational use of antibiotics.

Table 1. The number of triples in the SeSRUA system

Group	Numbers	Triple number for each	Triple Numbe
Guidelines	247 rules	4	988
Patient Data	10,000 patients	350	3,500,000
Antibiotics	88 drugs	31	2,728
DrugBank	6,689 drugs	79	528,431
Total			4,032,147

3.2 Guidelines and Rules

Clinical guideline are one of the most useful knowledge resources for rational use of antibiotics. As the monitoring of rational use of antibiotics involves complex knowledge of guideline analysis and management process, traditional way of human intervention is not sufficient to monitor rational use of antibiotics effectively. Therefore, we introduce the semantic technology to semi-automatically transform the knowledge contained in the clinical guideline and get the semantic data with the following steps[14]:

1. Preprocessing of the guidelines. We transfer the guideline in natural language style to "if ..., then ..." style, we call these guidelines abstract rules.
2. Then we transfer the abstract rules to concrete rules with pattern based natural language processing technology. Concrete rules are relative to abstract rules. It means to make abstract rules in the guideline more concrete so that hyponymy, entailment and other logical relationship between the knowledge will become more clear.
3. Last, we use Prolog to convert some knowledge in the guidelines for rational use of antibiotics into the semantic data. The logic programming language Prolog is a rule-based language for knowledge representation. It is also convenient to be used to formalize the dynamic workflow, a distinguish feature to realize the automatic monitoring and dynamic management for the rational use of antibiotics.

3.3   User Interface

Figure 5 shows the graphic user interface of SeSRUA. The figure shows the result of monitoring over a patient on her routine blood test. Users can use web browser to visit the data in JSON form, which return from the SPARQL server. The user interface of SeSRUA transforms these JSON data into corresponding visual data and displays them in a user-friendly interface. Therefore, any SeSRUA user will be able to use it even if he/she has no any knowledge of the semantic technology. The SPARQL server returns the data in the JSON format, which can be accessed by the users. Because the JSON format data is accessed by the user through user-friendly interface of the SeSRUA system.

The SeSRUA system is expected to make effectively use of the mass clinical information. This semantic data interoperability platform can finely reduce clinical doctors?professional burden and finally realize the intelligent supervision of antibiotics.

4   Evaluation

Currently we have developed SeSRUA system framework for the initial study, and obtained preliminary results:

1. Integrated DrugBank and Chinese semantic data of nearly 100 kinds of present antibiotics used in China hospitals;

Fig. 5. The SeSRUA system frame diagram

2. Integrated semantic patient data of ten thousand virtual patients with chronic bronchitis;
3. Transformed the knowledge of the guidelines of clinical use of antibiotics, which are expressed in natural language, into one in a semantic language, namely, to generate the corresponding semantic data of the guidelines.
4. Evaluated the clinical application effects of the experimental system of SeSRUA.

Table 2. Clinical Evaluation of Overall Results

Projects of evaluation	Correct Medical Records Total	Ratio
Whether to Use Antibiotics	93	93%
What Antibiotics to Use	55	55%
Total Evaluation	55	55%

Clinicians and clinical pharmacists together selected the first 100 copies of medical records and estimated the automatic results of SeSRUA which contain "Whether to use antibiotics" and "What antibiotics to use" (see Tab. 2). The medical records are divided into five groups based on their common character evaluated, the detailed results see Figure 6, which is also mentioned in Table 3.

Group	Number of Medical records	Indications of drug use	Whether to use antibiotics		What antibiotics to use		Overall evaluation	Main problems for improvement*
			Systematic Review	Whether correct	Systematic Review	Whether correct		
1	38	Fever, Abnormal blood test results	No enough reason to use	Yes	No, did not find any bacterial infection	No	No	2 (1,3)
2	24	None	No enough reason to use	Yes	No, did not find any bacterial infection	Yes	Yes	(1,3)
3	14	Fever, Abnormal blood test results, etiology check for bacterial infection	Probably should use	Yes	Bacterial test positive, recommend using certain types of antibiotics	Yes	Yes	4,5(1,3)
4	17	etiology check for bacterial infection	Probably should use	Yes	Bacterial test positive, recommend using certain types of antibiotics	Yes	Yes	5(1,3)
5	7	Fever	No enough reason to use	No	No, did not find any bacterial infection	No	No	2(1,3)
Total	100							

*The details see Table 3.

Fig. 6. Groups of Medical records

Table 3. Groups of SeSRUA for Improvement

Group	Main problems for improvement
1*	The present history description should be improved. It will be perfect if the content of diagnostic description be more accurate. For example, the out-patients' chest radiograph should include variety of situations such as chest infection and pulmonary thicker texture without infection etc. It is necessary to increase cases of chronic bronchitis in relieving stages besides acute stages appropriately.
2	For patients with acute exacerbation of chronic bronchitis (AECB), if there are any signs of infection, such as symptoms or examination results, then there is a possibility to choose antimicrobial drugs for prophylaxis based on experience. Even though the bacteriological examination report did not find any bacterial infection, as inspection reports may be false-negative results.
3*	Further expand the content to cover more medication indications, such as sputum color (yellow-green represents infection), antimicrobial susceptibility test results, erythrocyte sedimentation rate (ESR), C-reactive protein (CRP) and other indicators.
4	The pathogens of acute exacerbation of chronic bronchitis (AECB) coverage should be: Haemophilus influenzae, Streptococcus pneumoniae, Moraxelle catarrhalis, Mycoplasma pneumoniae, Chlamydia pneumoniae and Klebsiella pneumoniae etc. The variety of Pathogens in SeSRUA should be increased.
5	The dose schedule provided should be more accurate and comprehensive. For example?What specific drugs is the third-generation cephalosporin? Is there any alternative medicine to choice in addition to the preferred drugs?

* Group 1 and 3 happens highly in all the medical records

5 Conclusion and Future Work

5.1 Conclusion

In this paper, the problems and necessities in antibiotics management were analyzed. A noted technical method using semantic technology to monitor rational use of antibiotics was put forward. We designed the system framework of the rational use of antibiotics of semantic technology system based on SeSRUA, introduces the basic technology of module of SeSRUA system, including the use of LarKC massive se-mantic data processing platform as the basis of the data processing core, and adopts the logic programming language Prolog as the rules for dynamic language data work-flow description language, the realization of the basic functions of SeSRUA system. Experimental system of SeSRUA realized linkage analysis of electronic medical records, routine blood tests and pathogens inspection reports. It directly search drug indications for doctors and offer dose regimen with a comprehensive analysis based on advanced semantic technology. It has solved the "Why" and "How" questions of using antibiotics, which is more intelligent than the existing other systems, which have been used in China hospitals. However, due to SeSRUA is still in its prototype, there is still much future work for improvement.

5.2 Future Work

1. Improvement of the system. Due to SeSRUA is still in its prototype, there are still lots of work needed for improvement. According to the existing evaluation results, Improvement for SeSRUA are expected to be done in five groups (see Tab.3).
2. Tests of SeSRUA in a medical practice. We will test the system in some small clinics in China for one year. After that, we will exploy SeSRUA in some medium-sized hospitals in China for further improvement.

Acknowledgement. This work was partially supported by a grant from the NSF (Natural Science Foundation) of China under grant number 60803160 and 61100133, the Key Projects of National Social Science Foundation of China under grant number 11ZD&189. It was partially supported by the State Key Lab of Software Engineering Open Foundation of Wuhan University under grant number SKLSE2012-09-07.

References

1. Zhang, R., Eggleston, K., Rotimi, V., Zeckhauser, R.J.: Antibiotic resistance as a global threat: evidence from china, kuwait and the united states. Globalization and Health 2(6), 1–14 (2006)
2. Bizer, C., Heath, T., Berners-Lee, T.: Linked data - the story so far. International Journal on Semantic Web and Information Systems 5(3), 1–22 (2009)

3. Knox, C., Law, V., Jewison, T., Liu, P., Ly, S., Frolkis, A., Pon, A., Banco, K., Mak, C., Neveu, V., Djoumbou, Y., Eisner, R., Guo, A.C., Wishart, D.S.: Drugbank 3.0: a comprehensive resource for 'omics' research on drugs. Nucleic Acids Research 39(suppl. 1), 1035–1041 (2010)
4. Stearns, M.Q., Price, C., Spackman, K.A., Wang, A.Y.: Snomed clinical terms: overview of the development process and project status. In: Proc AMIA Symp., pp. 662–666 (2001)
5. Heddinia, A., Carsb, O., Qiangc, S., Tomsond, G.: Antibiotic resistance in china-a major future challenge. The Lancet 373(9657), 30 (2009)
6. Xiao, Y.H., Giske, C.G., Wei, Z.Q., Shen, P., Heddini, A., Li, L.J.: Epidemiology and characteristics of antimicrobial resistance in china. Drug Resistance Updates 14(4-5), 236–250 (2011)
7. Sun, Q., Santoro, M.A., Meng, Q., Liu, C., Eggleston, K.: Pharmaceutical policy in china. Health Affairs 27(4), 1042–1050 (2008)
8. Xiao, Y., Li, L.: Legislation of clinical antibiotic use in china. The Lancet Infectious Diseases 13(3), 189–191 (2013)
9. Bignardi, G.E., Hamson, C., Chalmers, A.: Can we use electronic prescribing to reduce prescription errors for antibiotics? Journal of Infection 61, 427–442 (2010)
10. Soleymani, F., Abdollahi, M.: Management information system in promoting rational drug use. International Journal of Pharmacology 8(6), 586–589 (2012)
11. Fensel, D., van Harmelen, F., Andersson, B., Brennan, P., Cunningham, H., Della Valle, E., Fischer, F., Huang, Z., Kiryakov, A., Lee, T., School, L., Tresp, V., Wesner, S., Witbrock, M., Zhong, N.: Towards LarKC: a platform for web-scale reasoning. In: Proceedings of the IEEE International Conference on Semantic Computing (ICSC 2008). IEEE Computer Society Press, CA (2008)
12. Bennett, C.C.: Utilizing rxnorm to support practical computing applications: Capturing medication history in live electronic health records. Journal of Biomedical Informatics 45(4), 634–641 (2012)
13. Huang, Z., van Harmelen, F., ten Teije, A., Dentler, K.: Knowledge-based patient data generation. In: Riaño, D., Lenz, R., Miksch, S., Peleg, M., Reichert, M., ten Teije, A. (eds.) KR4HC 2013/ProHealth 2013. LNCS (LNAI), vol. 8268, pp. 83–96. Springer, Heidelberg (2013)
14. Hu, Q., Huang, Z., Gu, J.: Generation of semantic data from guideline for rational use of antibiotics. In: submit to STeH 2013 (2013)

Using Semantic Technology for Automatic Verification of Road Signs

Dan Xu[1], Qinghua Liu[1], Zhisheng Huang[2],
Diming Zhang[1], Jiangli Zhang[1], and Ning Li[1]

[1] School of Computer Science and Engineering,
Jiangsu University of Science and Technology, China
[2] Department of Computer Science, Faculty of Sciences,
Vri je University of Amsterdam, Holland
xudan.zj@gmail.com, {giant_liu,tkh4}@163.com, huang@cs.vu.nl
zhangdiming@sina.com, jiangli@just.edu.cn

Abstract. Road signs play an important role in traffic. The transportation authorities have published some guidelines and regulations about the design and implementation of road signs. However, along with rapid development of road networks, existing road sign system faces with the problem of constantly revision and update. In the paper we propose a semantic approach to check if existing road signs abide the guidelines. The main advantage of the semantic technology is that the verification of road signs can be achieved by automatic reasoning and data processing services provided by a semantic system. We have integrated multi-source geographic data and developed a semantically-enabled road sign management system, which is built on the top of the LarKC, a platform for scalable semantic data processing. The experiments show that our system can successfully find the road signs which are set improperly.

Keywords: Semantic technology, Intelligent transport system, National guidelines, Road sign management.

1 Introduction

With the rapid development of the economy, China's vehicle amount ascends 20% annually. In large cities like Shanghai and Beijing, where are densely populated, vehicles are comparably concentrated. The traffic flow is heavy and complicated, which results in traffic problems of congestion and unsafety in the urban [1,2].

Besides the factor that rapid increment of vehicle amount, road sign is another key factor for traffic. Road signs are used to regulate traffic, warn drivers, and provide useful information to help make driving safe and convenient [3,4]. National guidelines set the detailed rules about the classification, appearance of road signs and where and how to install. The China national guideline of road traffic signs and markings was first released in 1986 [5]. Along with the development of traffic, the revisions were implemented in 1999 and 2009 [6,7]. The guidelines are the foundation

Z. Huang et al. (Eds.): WISE 2013 Workshops 2013, LNCS 8182, pp. 429–438, 2014.

of road sign setting and our main work is to verify whether the existing road signs obey the guidelines.

One challenge for road sign management is that road network and POI (point of interest) of China change frequently, which leads to the modification of road signs correspondingly [2]. Nowadays, management and maintenance of traffic sign system are mainly dependent on manual record and checking, which is a complex work for traffic management departments [8]. Human beings tend to make mistake in such repeated and heavy task. Therefore, it is necessary to develop a road sign management to maintain and update road signs automatically [9].

We are constructing a semantically-enabled system of road sign management called SeRSM which includes verification of road signs, examination of road sign consistency, automated sign generation and routing planning. In this paper, we present our efforts toward the first part of the system, i.e. verifying whether the existing road signs conform to the national guidelines [7]. Some existing data such as Open Street Map (OSM), Point of interest (POI) data and road sign data are integrated by mediation ontologies in the system [10]. Then LarKC platform[1] is used for semantic data processing and reasoning in our road sign management system [11,12]. In addition, the guidelines should be first extracted and then expressed with SPARQL query which can be supported by the SPARQL endpoint in the LarKC platform. The overview of our work is shown in Fig.1.

Contributions. The contributions of our paper include: 1) A semantic management system of road signs is proposed, 2) road sign guidelines of China are expressed by SPARQL queries, 3) an ontology of road sign is built for the system.

The paper is organized as follows: Section 2 analyses existing problems of road signs. Section 3 describes the proposed method in detail. The implementation and results are given in Section 4, and conclusions are given in Section 5.

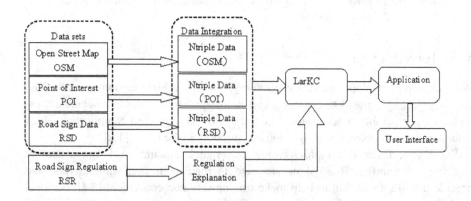

Fig. 1. Overview of our system

---

[1] http://www.larkc.eu

2   Motivation

As we know, Chinese cities grow and evolve much faster than many other cities in the world. POIs may move, new roads may be built, and road signs may be changed accordingly [13]. There may be some road signs don't be changed timely. In addition, many signs don't follow the national regulation and are set at liberty.

Fig. 2. Information overloading

There are four kinds of problems in road signs setting. The first one is information overloading. As shown in Fig.2, there are fifteen and nine destinations in two guide posts respectively. However, the guideline requires that the number of destinations in a single road plate should not be more than six.

(a)   (b)

Fig. 3. Unsuitability apposition

The second kind of problems is about apposition of several signs. As shown in Fig.3 (a), eight signs are set in the same place. The number should be less than four according to the guideline. Fig.3 (b) shows another example of improperly apposition, where stop sign should be set alone.

(a)   (b)

Fig. 4. (a) Inconsistency of guide signs, (b) Irregular signs

The third one is inconsistency of guide signs. As shown in Fig.4 (a), there are two indications to international trade city, however, one to right (marked by red circle) and another to forward (marked by blue circle). The last one is irregular signs, as shown in Fig.4 (b), the yield sign should be inverted triangular rather than circular.

In the paper, we focus on the first three kinds of problems only, because the fourth one concerns the shape or color of the signs may be checked by more complicated pattern recognition technologies. There have been several researches which investigate the problems of road sign management by using the semantic technology. In [14], semantic technology is used to check the consistency of the guide signs in Seoul. Our system is different from the one of Seoul in that we concern about all kinds of road signs (warning, prohibition, indicative and guide) and verify whether they are set according to national regulations. To the best of our knowledge, there is no similar research about road sign verification.

3   Approach

3.1   Data Integration

Data used in the system includes road network data from Open Street Map (OSM, http://www.openstreetmap.org), Point of Interest (POI) data from Baidu map and the road sign data collected by our group. All the data are integrated by several mediation ontologies [15]. Ontologies related to the consistency checking of guide signs are same with the ones used in Seoul road sign management system, including Node Element (POIs and road signs), Link Element, Way Element and Road Element [14]. In our system, we consider not only guide signs but also warning, prohibition and indicative signs. Therefore, we introduce more concepts about road sign classification and

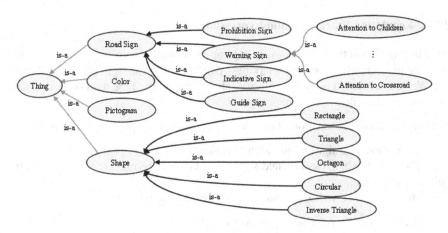

Fig. 5. Ontology of road sign

description in the ontology, as shown in Fig.5. Due to space limitations, color and pictogram are not described in detail in the figure.

There are four kinds of main road signs, prohibition signs, warning signs, indicative signs and guide signs. Every road sign can be described by color, shape and the pictogram of the sign. Take sign "attention to children" for example, the sign consists of triangle shape, yellow and black color and children pictogram.

In addition, the setting of the road signs associate with the grade of the road. For example, the regulation "when a branch road intersecting vertically with a primary road, a yield sign should be set in the branch road" describes the relationship between road grades and sign setting. Our road network data is acquired from OSM, whose grades of way are different from the ones in China. It is necessary to create ontology to express the mapping between them, as shown in Fig.6.

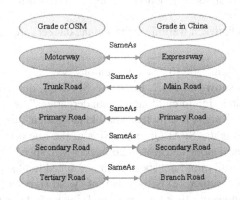

Fig. 6. Concept mapping between OSM and China road grades

3.2   Regulation Extraction and Expression

Regulation Extraction. The current regulation of traffic sign of China is national standard of road traffic signs and markings--part 2: road traffic signs (GB 5768.2-2009) [7]. We have extracted more than 60 rules about the setting of the road signs, and these rules can be classified into 5 categories.

(1) Rules about the location of the road signs. Some examples are listed as follows:

a. There should be signs of attention to children near kindergartens.

b. There should be crossing yield signs in one end of the narrow roads where difficult to pass for cars.

c. There should be walking signs in both ends of pedestrian streets.

(2) Rules about the relationship between signs.

a. Release of no passing sign should appear with no passing sign in pairs.

b. Minimum speed limit sign should not be used alone and always co-occurs with speed limit sign.

(3) Rules about the content of the road signs.

a. The total number of destinations of a guide sign should not be more than six.
b. The value of a speed limit sign should not be less than 20km/h.

(4) Regulations when more than one signs are set in the same place.

a. There should not be more than four signs in a road sign plate.
b. If more than one warning signs are needed, only the most important one is reserved.

(5) Regulations about the distance between signs and places they refer to.

a. The prediction signs of junctions should be set 300 to 500 meters before the junctions.

b. The distances between warning signs and the dangers are dependent on designed speed of the road.

Regulation Expression. Due to space limitations, we only show some examples of SPARQL query, as shown in Fig.7. (a) is the SPARQL query of the rule of "there should be signs of attention to children near kindergartens". In the query, we find the "attention to children" signs nearby the "Dadi kindergarten", the rule is not obeyed if the result is null. (b) is the SPARQL expression of the rule of "minimum speed limit sign should not be used alone and always co-occurs with speed limit sign". We find all the road sign plates with minimum speed limit and speed limit separately and compare whether they are set together. (c) is the query of "yield sign should be set alone". We first select all the yield signs, then for every yield sign we judge whether there are other signs in the same place. (d) is the expression of "number of all the destinations of a guide sign should not be more than six". In the first step, all the guide signs are selected, and then destinations of every sign are computed. If the counting function is provided by the LarKC platform, the expression of the rule will be much easier.

```
SELECT ?rsp_lat ?rsp_long ?poi_lat ?poi_long
WHERE
{ ?rsp rdf:type its:RoadSignPlate.
  ?rsp wgs:lat ?rsp_lat.
  ?rsp wgs:long ?rsp_long.
  ?rsp its:hasRs ?rscode.
  ?rscode rdf:type its:RoadSign.
  ?rscode its:label 'attention to children'
^^xmls:string.
  ?poi rdf:type its_POIType:kindergarten.
  ?poi wgs:lat ?poi_lat.
  ?poi wgs:long ?poi_long.
  ?poi its:label 'Dadi kindergarten'
^^xmls:string.
  FILTER(?rsp_lat>?poi_lat-0.005
&& ?rsp_lat<?poi_lat+0.005
&& ?rsp_long>?poi_long-0.005
&& ?rsp_long<?poi_long+0.005). }
```

(a)

```
SELECT DISTINCT ?rsp2 ?rsp2_lat ?rsp2_long
WHERE
{?rsp1 rdf:type   its:RoadSignPlate.
  ?rsp1 wgs:lat   ?rsp1_lat.
  ?rsp1 wgs:long  ?rsp1_long.
  ?rsp1 its:hasRs ?rscode1.
  ?rscode1   its:label     'speed    limit'
^^xmls:string.
  ?rsp2 rdf:type its:RoadSignPlate.
  ?rsp2 wgs:lat   ?rsp2_lat.
  ?rsp2 wgs:long  ?rsp2_long.
  ?rsp2 its:hasRs  ?rscode2.
  ?rscode2  its:label  'minimum   speed    '
^^xmls:string.
  filter(rsp1_lat != rsp2_lat || rsp1_long !=
rsp2_long}
```

(b)

```
SELECT ?rsp ?rscode1 ?lat1 ?long1
WHERE
{?rsp rdf:type its:RoadSignPlate.
  ?rsp wgs:lat    ?lat1.
  ?rsp wgs:long   ?long1.
  ?rsp its:hasRs ?rscode1.
  ?rscode1 its:label 'yield'^^xmls:string.
}
SELECT ?rsp ?rscode
WHERE
{?rsp rdf:type its:RoadSignPlate.
  ?rsp  wgs:lat ?rsp_lat.
  ?rsp  wgs:long ?rsp_long.
  ?rsp its:hasRs ?rscode.
  filter(?rsp_lat = lat1 && ?rsp_long =
long1).}
```

(c)

```
SELECT ?rsp ?rscode ?lat1 ?long1
WHERE
{?rsp rdf:type its:RoadSignPlate.
  ?rsp wgs:lat    ?lat1.
  ?rsp wgs:long   ?long1.
  ?rsp its:hasRs ?rscode.
  ?rscode   its:label    'guide    sign'
^^xmls:string.}
SELECT ?rsp ?destination
WHERE
{?rsp rdf:type its:RoadSignPlate.
  ?indicate rdf:type its:RoadSignIndicate.
  ?rsp ?indicate ?destination.
  ?rsp wgs:lat ?rsp_lat.
  filter(?rsp_lat = lat1 &&?rsp_long =
long1 ).}
```

(d)

Fig. 7. SPARQL query of guidelines

4   Implementations and Results

We choose the city of Zhenjiang which is growing and evolving like other Chinese cities as our experimental sample. The data set contains about five million triples. 1 million triples describe the streets, and are directly extracted from OSM. 3 million triples describe POIs related to road signs and come from Baidu map. 0.3 million triples describe road signs and collected by our group[2].

The architecture of the system is shown in Fig.8. All the triples are imported into Dataload Server of the LarKC platform. National guidelines are expressed by SPARQL language which can be processed by the query endpoint of the LarKC. ITS-JUST is our application program which is built on the Jetty Server and users can visit the application by web browser.

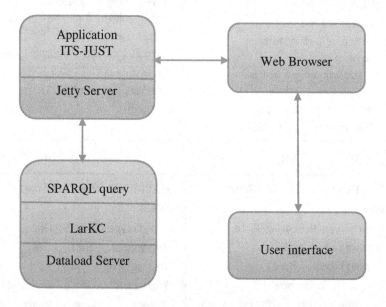

Fig. 8. Architecture of our system

During experiment, four roads are considered: Xuefu road, Zhengdong road, Mengxi road and Tianqiao road, in which Xuefu road and Tianqiao road were constructed a few years ago and Zhengdong and Mengxi road are old roads more than ten years. There are 215 road sign plates include 384 road signs in these roads, among which 46 plates are set inappropriately. As shown in Tab.1, our system successfully finds 42 problematic plates and misses 4 of them. The missing plates include signs with irregular shape or color which can't be verified by our system, or signs involve in the height information which absent in the existing data. Tab.2 shows the different kinds of problems and the corresponding plate number.

---

[2]   Ntriple data of Zhenjiang can be obtained from website

http://jisuanji.just.edu.cn/iit.

The code to implement the system is java and the simulation platform is 2.59GHZ Pentium machine. The whole system is expected to satisfy real-time practice with the average response time of 1.3s.

Table 1. Results of our system

Number of plates	Problematic plates	Successfully detected	Missing
215	46	42	4

Table 2. Kinds of problems and the corresponding plate number

Problems	Number
Information overloading	8
Unsuitability apposition	26
Inconsistency of guide signs	8
Irregular signs	4

5   Conclusions and Future Work

In the paper, we propose a method for road sign verification based on semantic technology. Firstly, road network data from OSM, POI data from Baidu map and road sign data collected by our group are integrated by median ontologies. Secondly, national guidelines of road signs are classified into five categories and expressed by SPARQL query. Finally, the LarKC platform is used for semantic data processing and reasoning. We have tested our system in some roads of Zhenjiang and the results show that our method can successfully detect three kinds of problematic road signs.

There are several related works along our research. In [14], semantic technology is used to develop road sign management for Seoul, the system pays attention on validation checking of guide signs. In [16], a route planning service in mobile environments is provided for city of Milano. The system employs history traffic data and real data from Linked Open Data Cloud to predict traffic flow and plan the best route.

The novelty of our system is: it can verify the existing road signs according to China national guidelines by using a semantic platform (e.g., the LarKC platform). In future work, we will construct more comprehensive ontology which would cover not only various road signs, but also various concepts concerning the transportation and traffic. In addition, we will develop more reasoning support for our road sign management system.

References

1. Wang, J.: Research of scheme to unban traffic congestion in China. Shandong Normal University (2011) (in Chinese)
2. Guo, R., Wei, Z., Li, Y.: Study on encoding technology of urban traffic signs based on demands of facilities management. In: AFTC 2011 (2011)
3. Fang, C.Y., Chen, S.W., Fuh, C.S.: Road-sign detection and tracking. IEEE Transactions on Vehicular Technology 52(5), 1329–1341 (2003)
4. Seifert, C., Paletta, L., Jeitler, A.: Visual object detection for mobile road sign inventory. In: Mobile Human-Computer Interaction, MobileHCI 2004, pp. 491–495 (2004)
5. GB 5768-1986. Road traffic signs and markings. Standards Press of China (1986) (in Chinese)
6. GB 5758-1999. Road traffic signs and markings. Standards Press of China (1999) (in Chinese)
7. GB 5768.2-2009. Road traffic signs and markings– Part 2: Road traffic signs. Standards Press of China (2009) (in Chinese)
8. Maintenance and management manual of traffic sign setup and installation. China Communications Press (2008) (in Chinese)
9. Rasdorf, W., Hummer, J.E., Harris, E.A., et al.: IT issues for the management of high-quantity, low-cost assets. Journal of Computing in Civil Engineering 23(2), 91–99 (2009)
10. Battle, R., Kolas, D.: Enabling the geospatial semantic web with Parliament and GeoSPARQL. Semantic Web 3(4), 355–370 (2012)
11. Huang, Z., Fang, J., Park, S., et al.: Noisy Semantic Data Processing in Seoul Road Sign Management System. In: Proceedings of the 10th International Semantic Web Conference (ISWC 2011), Bonn, Germany, p. 10 (2011)
12. Fensel, D., van Harmelen, F., Andersson, B., et al.: Towards LarKC: a platform for web-scale reasoning. In: 2008 IEEE International Conference on Semantic Computing, pp. 524–529. IEEE (2008)
13. Jin, J.: A comparative study of the urban transportation system in Beijing and Seoul, Beijing Jiaotong University (2009) (in Chinese)
14. Lee, T., Park, S., Huang, Z., et al.: Toward Seoul road sign management on the larkc platform. In: Posters and Demos of ISWC (2010)
15. Zhang, C., Li, W., Zhao, T.: Geospatial data sharing based on geospatial semantic web technologies. Journal of Spatial Science 52(2), 35–49 (2007)
16. Huang, Z., Zhong, N.: Scalable semantic data processing platform, technology and applications. Higher Education Press, Beijing (2012)

A Semantically-Enabled System for Road Sign Management

Liu Qinghua[1], Qian Qiang[1], Xu Dan[1], Zhang Xiaofei[1], Li Ning[1],
Wang Dongsheng[1], Wang Zhi[1], and Huang Zhisheng[2]

[1] Faculty of Computer Sience and Engineering,
Jiangsu University of Science and Technology, China
[2] Computer Science Department, Vrije University Amsterdam, the Netherlands

Abstract. The road sign is an important facility which manages the road traffic safety and eases the road traffic congestion. This paper proposes a Semantically-enabled System for Road Sign Management (SeRSM). The SeRSM system is built based on LarKC, which is a platform for scalable semantic data processing. In the SeRSM system, the users can select the corresponding operations through the interface integrated with a map service. These operations are sent to Jetty server for corresponding processing. They include sending some SPARQL query to invoke the corresponding workflow in the LarKC platform and to retrieve and reason the massive data stored in the data layer of LarKC and to return the result to the Jetty server. The paper made a full description of technical points such as the design objective, data sources, data integration, noisy data processing, detection of road consistency effectiveness. It also describes the system's user interface and basic functions in the end. The SeRSM has great value and social significance for improving traffic efficiency and traffic safety through successful applications in Zhenjiang and Yiwu in China.

Keywords: Semantic technology, Road sign management, LarKC.

1 Introduction

The road sign is the marker which is set to warn, prohibit, limit or indicating the road user in most countries. It passes the clear, intuitive, easy to understand and the standard visual information to the traffic participants to meet the fast and convenient travel requirements. The road sign is an important facility which manages the road traffic safety and eases the road traffic congestion. The information of road sign guides the direction of the traffic flow. Clear and accurate road sign information plays an important role in reducing traffic congestion and improving traffic safety. However, with the continuous expansion of the city size and the continuous development of urban construction, road sign system is also facing the problem of constantly revised and updated. Many problems existed in road sign system such as inconsistencies, out-of-date, non-standardization and lack of road sign information and so on. When the system needs to be extended and redesigned, developers will spend more manpower

Z. Huang et al. (Eds.): WISE 2013 Workshops 2013, LNCS 8182, pp. 439–451, 2014.

and resources in order to fully research the original data format. Therefore, the traditional information system development methods are not suitable for the expansion of the system's function and the interoperability and reuse of existed data between the different systems. There are also a lot of other problems such as the lack of automation and reasoning ability, insufficient capability of mass data processing in traditional system [1].

With the development and maturity of the semantic technology in recent years, it provides an effective technical means to solve such problems. We are able to use the international standardized description of the data through semantic technology so that data are independent of specific application. So a road sign system is easy to be updated and expanded, and also easy to integrate of existing public semantic data source. The Semantic technology provides an easy expansion platform of the reasoning knowledge integration for the road sign management system. Our system adopts B/S design mode based on the LarKC platform and solves the problem such as wrong road sign indication or inconsistent and lack of reach information or nonstandard road sign in traditional road sign management system. This system base semantic multi-source data to avoid data duplication and thus has a high application value and social significance[2].

The rest of this paper is organized as follows: Section 2 introduces Semantic Web and its application in intelligent transportation, Section 3 presents design objective and scheme of our system, SeRSM dataset such as OSM, LGD, POI are described in Section 4, the approaches and the user interface of the system are discussed in Section 5 and Section 6. Section 7 presents the discussion and conclusions.

2   Semantic Technologies and Its Applications in Intelligent Transportation

Intelligent Transportation System referred to as ITS is to effectively integrate advanced information technology, communication technology, sensor technology, control technology and computer technology, applied to the entire transportation management system. So ITS is a real-time, accurate and efficient integrated transport and management system which plays a wide range and round role. Such as vehicle control, traffic monitoring, traffic information services etc are functions which intelligent transportation system provides. Along with the accelerated progress of China's urbanization, a series of problems such as infrastructure construction speed backward, traffic congestion, exhaust emission and pollution, serious traffic safety situation are to be solved. Research in Intelligent Transportation Systems are still facing a lot of challenges, such as a large number of "isolated islands of data" in existing transportation system, repeated development in development framework and infrastructure components of traffic application software, and some difficulties in flow, distribution and integration of data between equipments and peoples. To solve these problems, we require a new integrated data sharing method, high performance infrastructure, new information platform and software tools. The semantic technology offers the possibility for all above.

2.1   Semantic Technology

The Semantic Web is a collaborative movement led by the World Wide Web Consortium (W3C). The standard promotes common data formats on the World Wide Web. By encouraging the inclusion of semantic content in web pages, the Semantic Web aims at converting the current web dominated by unstructured and semi-structured documents into a "web of data". The Semantic Web is based on the W3C's Resource Description Framework (RDF). According to W3C, The Semantic Web provides a common framework that allows data to be shared and reused across application, enterprise, and community boundaries. The term was coined by Tim Berners-Lee, the inventor of the World Wide Web and director of the W3C, which oversees the development of proposed Semantic Web standards [3]. He defines the Semantic Web as a web of data that can be processed directly and indirectly by machines. The applications of Semantic Web in industry, biology and human sciences research have already proven the validity of the original concept.

The establishment of the Semantic Web is greatly involved in the part of artificial intelligence area, to coincide with the concept of Web 3.0 intelligent network, so the initial realization of Semantic Web is also viewed as an important feature of Web 3.0. But Semantic Web still needs long-term research if it is to be super brain on the network.

This means the realization of the Semantic Web will occupy an important part of the Web's development process, continue several Internet generations, and gradually transform into intelligent Web.

The Semantic Web has become a hot research field of the computer from the date of its birth. W3C is the main movers and standard-setter of the Semantic Web, Stanford University, University of Maryland, University of Karlsruhe, Victoria University of Manchester, Vrije University in the Netherlands and other educational institutions has carried out extensive and in-depth study of the Semantic Web. It has been developed a series of the Semantic Web technology development and application platform and information integration and query, reasoning and ontology editing system such as Jena, KAON, Racer, Pellet and LarKC [4-7]. China attaches great importance to the Semantic Web research. As early as 2002, Semantic Web is listed as a key support project by the National 863 Program. Tsinghua University, Southeast University, Shanghai Jiaotong University, Beijing University of Aeronautics and the Chinese People's University are research center of the Semantic Web and its related technologies.

2.2   LarKC

The aim of the EU FP 7 Large-Scale Integrating Project LarKC is to develop the Large Knowledge Collider (LarKC, for short), a platform for massive distributed incomplete reasoning that will remove the scalability barriers of currently existing reasoning systems for the Semantic Web. The core idea of LarKC is the use of a portfolio approach to achieving massive semantic data processing. LarKC Platform is a massive semantic data processing platform through the basic plug-ins can be combined. It has abandoned the traditional knowledge based inference engine which requires reasoning system to be absolute correct and complete technical constraints. The introduction of non-complete and non-absolutely correct reasoning techniques, of which LarKC can be extended to meet the requirement of semantic web reasoning massive semantic data. The specific design objectives of LarKC are: to design a pluggable massive data processing platform, including a full-featured platform based on plug-in settings. And these plug-in of different fields can be seamlessly integrated to achieve full integration of heterogeneous fields such as logical reasoning, databases, machine learning, cognitive science and other fields [8,9].

The huge advantage of LarKC is that semantic technology developers can use directly standard inference engine to reason complex mass data, and do not need to spend a lot of manpower and resources to design a special inference engine to integrate data. So far, the LarKC platform in intelligent transportation, urban computing, biomedical information retrieval, genetic research and other fields have achieved a wide range of applications[11]. The official web address of LarKC project is http://www.larkc.eu.

2.3   Applications of the Semantic Technology in Intelligent Transportation

Intelligent transportation is a specific application of urban computing , it involves many aspects of the acquisition, conversion, storage, integration, organization, processing, services and their interface design of traffic-related mass data to specific city etc. Some of the existing traffic information software development has an important flaw , that is isolation. In general, neither the integration of existing software nor data resources are considered, as well as who will need to integrate them on the future. All these cause 'the islands of data'.

The Semantic Web Technology is used in intelligent transportation because it is suitable for multi-source, massive data objects. For massive data processing, it includes a variety of processing mode such as parallel distributed computing, heuristic methods and anytime behavior. The Semantic Web can provide strong support not only for macro data analysis and knowledge management and reasoning, but also decision making system based on traffic information. A lot of related research in the field of Semantic Web has been carried out at home and abroad. There are some successful cases abroad such as Milano, Italy, Traffic flow forecasting system based on Semantic Web, and Seoul, South Korea, Traffic road sign management system. Domestic data processing method in the field of intelligent transportation has applied traditional development methods of information system.   Application of the semantic technology is still in its infancy. However semantic technology has great application prospect with the rapid development of China's economy and the urgent demand for intelligent traffic because of sharp increasing of car ownership.

3   Design Objective and Design Scheme

3.1   Design Objective

Our road sign management is designed to be able to fully integrate the advantage of semantic technology and the powerful features of the LarKC platform. Our system can solve many problems which cannot be solved by traditional information processing technology such as confusion of road sign's location, inconsistence of landmark information, non-standardization and lack of road sign. For processing data format in system, we apply the formulation of international standardization, RDF and OWL, in order to expand and integrate the existing data and the function of the future. In the system we has integrated the existing public open data sources as much as possible, such as Wikipedia semantic data, geo-semantic data, Baidu POI data etc. in order to reduce the consumption of human and material resources for the duplication of information collection.

3.2   Design Scheme

We adopts Browser/Server mode as system structure, Jetty as server, browser as UI to interact with the system. The system is based on LarKC 2.5. In this version of the platform, the system can use the RSM reasoner to bind the RSM workflow in order to complete the corresponding process flow.

The users select the corresponding operations through the web browser interface integrated with map service. These operations are sent to Jetty server for corresponding processing. They include sending some SPARQL query to invoke the corresponding workflow in the LarKC platform, and to retrieve and reason the massive data stored in the data layer of LarKC, and to return the result to the Jetty server.

SeRSM based on the LarKC v2.5 has configured corresponding RSM decider, RSM identifier, RSM transformer, the RSM selecter and RSM reasoner as LarKC workflows. RSM data sources can be easily obtained from the World Wide Web including the Open Street Map data, POI data provided by Baidu Map and the RSD data provided by the city traffic management department. The architecture of the system is shown in Figure 1.

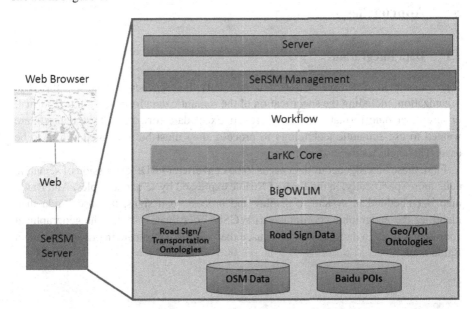

Fig. 1. Overview of the system

4   SeRSM Dataset

The timely and accurate acquisition and maintenance data of urban transportation is quite large in traditional information system method. And these data is also very easy to form a "islands of data", cannot be exchanged and reused between data from other systems. The use of semantic technology can be very easy to access urban traffic information from the World Wide Web. Such as Open Street Map (OSM) to provide a free map of the world that allows anyone to edit, linked geographic data to be extracted from the OSM relational database and converted to form large-scale geographic semantic data, Baidu map service to provide the Chinese cities POI data and the traffic management department to own all road sign information on existing roads for a common average city. So the present RSM includes the related data sets, such as shown in table 1.

Table 1. SeRSM dataset

Dateset	Features
Open Street Map (OSM)	the open street data of the WGS84 coordinate
Linked geo-data(LGD)	WGS84 coordinate triplet data Including English POI data
Baidu POI(POI)	Baidu POI data in a specific format with road sign
Traffic management department data(TMD)	specific format
Intermediary ontology (IO)	associated with OSM, LGD,POI,TMD, etc.

5   Approaches

5.1   Data Integration

Data source in SeRSM datasets are generally heterogeneous data on the data organization, including the specification of the semantic data format, plain text format, or any other data format such as Microsoft Excel data format. If these datasets are wanted to use semantic technology to process, they must be integrated before to be used. This includes two aspects:

First, these heterogeneous data needs to be converted to RDF expression of semantic data, more specifically, in the form of Ntriple expressed by semantic triples. And Baidu map is embedded in system to display and process road signs, because Baidu map identifies the geographic coordinates as WGS84 coordinates, so that the geographical coordinates of each data set should be used the WGS84 coordinate in order to locate in Baidu map.

Second, the datasets are very large in the size which are designed in SeRSM system, so these massive data require the use of ontology technology integration to form a unified whole. The core of data integration is the SeRSM intermediary ontology. We have applied the entities and axioms provided by SeRSM intermediary ontology to unify the huge amounts of data in each data source on the semantic level.

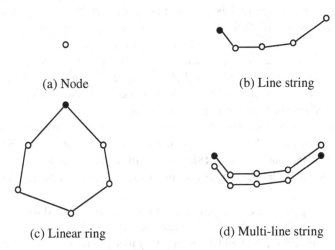

(a) Node   (b) Line string

(c) Linear ring   (d) Multi-line string

Fig. 2. Typical spatial data types

In our intermediary ontology, road sign generally is represented with various elements. The most important objects to construct road network are roads and junctions in a city. These objects will be represented as the data types shown in figure 2. First, we need to analyze Node which is the basic element of all data in the system. Each Node has a node identifier (ID) and coordinates (lat and long). Road sign nodes, Baidu POI nodes and nodes of common scenic spots are a subclass of the Node. Both Line string and Linear ring are composed of multiple nodes. They expressed a continuous direction of the road and a ring road. Multi-line string expressed a road more direction. The variety of relationships between roads, like disjoint, intersects, touches, crosses, will be calculated based on intermediary ontology. Then, these roads, junctions, and relation between them will be stored into LarKC as RDF triples and be processed.

5.2   Noisy Data Processing

In the SeRSM data source, the most important information includes the node, the link and POI information. In general, the node includes ID, the latitude and longitude coordinates, the link includes the ID and the information of start node and end node, POI is a special point, includes information such as ID, location and interest types. We generally think that the following types of data for noisy data: 1) junction data loss.

Two intersecting roads in the map plane may intersect or interchange be due to reasons such as bridges or tunnels in a real geographical environment. Interchange is junction where roads pass above or below one another. Whether intersect of roads is very important information for the SeRSM path choice, but in some of the data source, the information is missing. 2) Erroneous data. In some cases due to reasons such as real-time, data in sources may be outdated and incorrect. While in other cases it may appear road crossing the POI or meaningless road connection error messages etc. 3) Repeat data. Different geographic coordinates of nodes may own the same ID. These types of data are generally considered to be a noisy data. We can see in the definition of the noisy semantic data that mainly includes two types: The missing and inconsistency. In noisy data processing, in order to remain consistence, it is necessary to remove some of the data and also add some corresponding data.

The SeRSM system can make the right treatment for these noisy data. The user sends operations command such as road signs checks, noisy data check to the SeRSM server through a webpage interface. The RSM server will send corresponding SPARQL query to the processing endpoint. These endpoints load SeRSM workflow on the LarKC platform.

Given starting point of a road and the corresponding the SeRSM data source, we can through the following method to calculate the path: 1) Select the relevant data. 2) Refine noisy data. We adopt added directly way to solve for missing intersection data, use the remove wrong rule processing for error road data, adopt the method of allocation uniqueness ID correction for repeated data. 3) Select Path. Its basic idea is from the starting point, choosing the nearest path to the end for every step, so recursively until it reaches the end or retrospective.

5.3   Consistency Verification of Road Signs

Because some SeRSM data source use the semi-automatic method to achieve transformation, the semantic data contains a large number of inconsistencies and missing phenomenon[12,13] The system needs to make the correct and effective treatment for these data, especially needs to make accurate discriminated reasoning for road sign continuous effectiveness[14] The discriminated reasoning function is the missing of the traditional RSM system [12].

In order to achieve intelligent logic reasoning capabilities to deal with the inconsistency of the road sign or landmark identification error, our SeRSM should detect the continuous validity of road signs. Most cities in China are facing road sign error such as road sign disorder, the sign point to contradictions, non-standardization of road sign setting due to the increase of the rate of urban growth and urban scale. These errors require the appropriate methods and techniques to solve.

We need to take full account of the situation in China for the reasoning mechanism settings of the road sign effectiveness detection. In the LarKC Platform reasoning mechanism we achieve China's national standards specification, that is "road traffic signs and markings-- part 2: road traffic signs"(GB 5768.2-2009) [15]. Reasonable set and audit of road sign information also need to consider the road layout such as whether crossings etc., which need to consider the information on the surrounding road, that is geo-spatial information. With the development of computer technology and the World Wide Web, in particular, constantly improve of city maps and road information system such as OSM, it is easy to incorporate into geo-spatial information into a signpost management system.

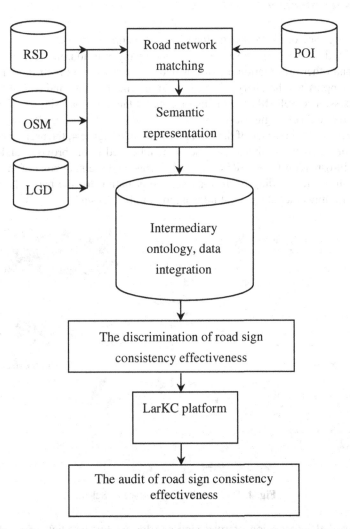

Fig. 3. Flow chat of road consistency effectiveness detection

The principle of road sign consistency effectiveness is that the layout must be continuous corresponds to a particular destination signpost guide, corresponding signs should be set to echo before a signpost direct for turn at the intersection ahead, and if the continuous road signs for a destination are suddenly interrupted, it means that the destination has been reached, or we can see the next destination signpost if we go straight some distance. It is shown in Figure 3. The SeRSM has applied the LarKC Platform for logical reasoning to obtain the results for consistency effectiveness.

6   User Interface

The user interface of SeRSM combined with the actual situation in China, embedded map provided by the Chinese search engine company -- Baidu, in order to display the position and other information of various nodes , link, way and road sign. The system provides support for the query of city road sign semantic data and audit of road sign effectiveness. The SeRSM features include path planning, road sign error correction, signpost find and new signpost set.

The overall user interface of the system is shown in Figure 4, the user could perform the appropriate action in the area of the map embedded in the browser, and could get feedback information from SeRSM in the left zone and the map zone of the webpage. Figure 4 shows the finding of all road sign information for the particular road. The results of findings include general information of all road sign.

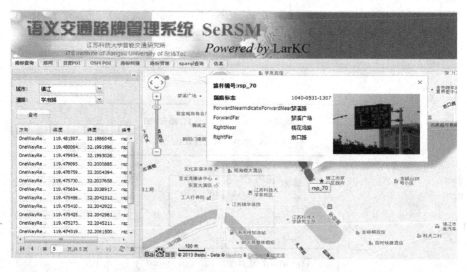

Fig. 4. The overall user interface of SeRSM

The detailed information of road sign can be get by the click of corresponding marker in map as shown in Figure 5. This figure shows the name, type and relevant picture of the road sign.

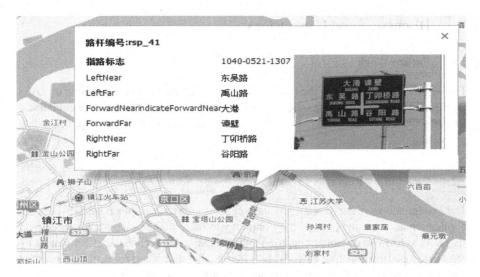

Fig. 5. The detailed information of road sign

Fig. 6. The construction of new road

The set of new road sign requires setting up new road first, then automatically reasoning the supporting road sign's attribute such as location, type etc. The construction of new road is achieved by setting starting node and end node, as shown in Figure 6.

7   Discussion and Conclusions

7.1   Future Work

The work we would study in the future includes the following several aspects: utilizing high quality of integrated semantic data, road sign verification according to guidelines, adopting OGC geo-SPARQL , to achieve better user experience and large scale data processing.

7.2   Concluding Remarks

The system adopts massive open semantic multi-source data as data base to avoid data duplication and uses the intermediary ontology to make the massive multi-source road sign data to form an organic integration and automatically detects the effectiveness by the LarKC platform to find effectively unreasonable and incorrect settings in a road sign system, which facilitates the transport sector to update its data.

The application of the semantic technology in the system have the advantages of multiple-source data integration and reasoning and noisy data processing compared with traditional information system. The system has been successfully applied in Zhenjiang and Yiwu city of China. SeRSM has great value and social significance for improving traffic efficiency and traffic safety.

References

[1] Fang, C.Y., Chen, S.W., Fuh, C.S.: Road-sign detection and tracking. IEEE Transactions on Vehicular Technology 52(5), 1329–1341 (2003)

[2] Tresp, V., Huang, Y., Bundschus, M., et al.: Materializing and querying learned knowledge. In: Proc. of IRMLeS (2009)

[3] Berners-Lee, T., Hall, W., Handler, J., et al.: A Framework for Web Science. Foundations and Trends in Web Science 1(1), 1–130 (2006)

[4] Lee, T., Park, S., Huang, Z., et al.: Toward Seoul road sign management on the larkc platform. In: Posters and Demos of ISWC 2010 (2010)

[5] Kindberg, T., Chalmers, M., Paulos, E.: Guest Editors' Introduction: Urban Computing. IEEE Pervasive Computing 6(3), 18–20 (2007)

[6] Huang, V., Tresp, M.: Multivariate Structured Prediction for Learning on the Semantic Web. In: Proceedings of the 20th International Conference on Inductive Logic Programming (ILP 2010) (2010)

[7] Huang, Y., Tresp, V., Bundschus, M., Rettinger, A., Kriegel, H.-P.: Multivariate prediction for learning on the semantic web. In: Frasconi, P., Lisi, F.A., et al. (eds.) ILP 2010. LNCS, vol. 6489, pp. 92–104. Springer, Heidelberg (2011)

[8] Huang, Y., Nickel, M., Tresp, V., et al.: A scalable kernel approach to learning in semantic graphs with applications to linked data. In: Proc. of the 1st Workshop on Mining the Future Internet (2010)

[9] Huang, Z., et al.: Evaluation and revision of reason plug-ins, LarKC deliverable D.4.7.3 (September 2011), http://www.larkc.eu/deliverables/

[10] Assel, M., Cheptsov, A., Gallizo, G., et al.: Large knowledge collider: a service-oriented platform for large-scale semantic reasoning. In: Proceedings of the International Conference on Web Intelligence, Mining and Semantics, p. 41. ACM (2011)

[11] Huang, Z., Bal, H., Chezan, M., et al.: Final Evaluation and Revision of Plug-ins Deployed in Use-cases, LarKC Deliverable D4.7.3 (2011)

[12] Huang, Z., Fang, J., Park, S., et al.: Noisy Semantic Data Processing in Seoul Road Sign Management System. In: Proceedings of the 10th International Semantic Web Conference (ISWC 2011), Bonn, Germany, p. 10 (2011)

[13] Dell'Aglio, et al.: 5th periodic report on data and performances, LarKC Delieverable D6.11 (2011)

[14] Tresp, V., Bundschus, M., Rettinger, A., Huang, Y.: Towards machine learning on the semantic web. In: da Costa, P.C.G., d'Amato, C., Fanizzi, N., Laskey, K.B., Laskey, K.J., Lukasiewicz, T., Nickles, M., Pool, M., et al. (eds.) URSW 2005 - 2007. LNCS (LNAI), vol. 5327, pp. 282–314. Springer, Heidelberg (2008)

[15] Ng, J.C.W., Sayed, T.: Effect of geometric design consistency on road safety. Canadian Journal of Civil Engineering 31(2), 218–227 (2004)

[16] GB 5768.2-2009. Road traffic signs and markings– Part 2: Road traffic signs

Interface Design of Semantic System
for Road Sign Management

Ning Li[1], Zhisheng Huang[2], Dan Xu[1], Xiaofei Zhang[1], Dongsheng Wang[1],
Zhi Wang[1], Qinghua Liu[1], Jiangli Zhang[1], and Diming Zhang[1]

[1] Institute of Intelligent Transport System, School of Computer Science and
Engineering, Jiangsu university of Science of Technology
Zhenjiang, 212003, P.R. China
[2] Department of Computer Science, Vrije Universiteit Amsterdam, The Netherlands
{tkh4,wds_ict,Giant_liu,DMZhang}@163.com, huang@cs.vu.nl,
xudan.zj@gmail.com, {julychang,cw,jiangli}@just.edu.cn

Abstract. The semantic technology has provided an effect and efficient solution for the data interoperability in various applications. Semantic technology has played an important role in intelligent transport systems. In this paper, we investigate the interface design on semantic systems of road sign management. We present a user modeling by introducing a classification of various users in the system, and analyzing the user's knowledge requirement. Based on the user modeling, we propose an interface design for different use cases of semantic systems for road sign management, and discuss the implementation of the interface for semantic systems with different application scenarios.

Keywords: Semantic technology, User interface, Road sign management.

1 Introduction

Transportation is the civilized sign and living basis of modern societies, and is also the important connection among infrastructures of social economies. Economic de-velopment enriches the obvious increase of the transport needs. With the development of the informational technology, more and more people tend to solve transport problems by information technology. Semantic technology is the very active content of research and development. Through the combination of achievements of linguistics and computer technology, realizing the understanding of vocabulary at the semantic level[1]. Road signs are the signs of transport, which are used to inform the vehicles and passengers the road information. On each road board, one or more road signs can be fixed. Present road board systems often show problems as follows: incorrect road boards, mutual contradiction of road boards, road changes without corresponding changes of road signs[2,3]. For these problems, a transport system of road boards is required to administrate all the road boards. We apply the semantic technology to the transport system of road sign, and realize the management of semantic transport of road sign

Z. Huang et al. (Eds.): WISE 2013 Workshops 2013, LNCS 8182, pp. 452–460, 2014.

when based on the analysis of users types, users cases. This system is called semantically-enabled system of road sign management. This system is composed of searching road sign, searching road, correcting road sign, SPARQL search, simulation, searching POI and managing system.

Some investigators applied the semantic technology to solve transport problem. Li Xiang, researcher of the Chinese University of Hong Kong, analyzed the develop-ment of Location Based Services (LBS) and Intelligent Transportation Systems, and then he raised the concept of Cooperative Intelligent Transportation Systems (CITS) [4]. Li Yang, researcher of Dalian Maritime University, built the three leveled structure of ontology system composed of basic ontology, field ontology and applied ontology, when facing the semantic integration problems of CITS of China [5]. Huang Geping, researcher of Tongji University, built the transport ontology of cities against the research and applied background of city transport, using the knowledge of ontology model to show technology[6].

The rest of this paper is organized as follows. Section 2 requirement analysis, section 3 realization of system, section 4 conclusions.

2   Requirement Analysis

2.1   Type of Users

Users of system can be classified into three types: ordinary users, users of developing, administrator. Ordinary users are the final users in charge of the practice in this sys-tem. Ordinary users can use some basic functions. Developing users are the developers of this system. Users of developing can use some functions that are related to devel-oping. Administrator is those final users who take charge of the whole system. Ad-ministrator can set right and set basic parameters.

Knowledge required by different users can be seen in Figure 1. Ordinary users do not need relevant knowledge concerning semantics. Since ordinary users need prac-ticing tasks, they are asked to own intermediary knowledge of transport. Ordinary users only need the interface of operational system, so their knowledge of computer only needs to be low. Developing users have to design and develop the whole system, so they are required to master the intermediary level of semantic knowledge. These users do not need to know a lot about transport

users knowledge	Ordinary users	Developers	Administrators
Knowledge of semantics	zero	medium	low
Knowledge of transportation	medium	low	medium
Knowledge of computer	low	high	low

Fig. 1. Knowledge required for different users

knowledge, but have to master much higher level of computer knowledge. Administrators need low level of semantic knowledge. Administrators need to take charge of whole system, so they have to own knowledge of intermediary level. And their knowledge of computer just needs to be low.

2.2 Use Cases

Use cases cover searching road sign, searching road, correcting road sign, SPARQL searching, POI searching, simulation, system management. Road sign searching use case is based on city names and road names, searching all the road signs information of these roads, which are displayed on the maps. Road searching use case searches all the points of the roads based on city names and road names, connecting all these points into a road on the map. POI searching use case searches corresponding POI (the abbreviation of Point of Interest) according to the key words typed in, which could be displayed on maps. Simulation use case refers to the fact that if setting up the starting point and ending point, the vehicles' running process can be displayed on maps. System management use case includes rights management and perimeter set. Rights set means the setting of basic perimeters of some systems.

Use cases of users can be shown in Figure 2. Ordinary users can use road sign searching, road searching, road sign correcting, poi searching, and simulation. De-veloping users can use any cases but system management. Administrators can use any case.

use cases \ users	Ordinary users	Developers	Administrators
searching road sign	√	√	√
searching road	√	√	√
correcting road sign	√	√	√
SPARQL using	×	√	√
Searching Poi	√	√	√
simulation	√	√	√
System management	×	×	√

Fig. 2. Accessible use cases for different users

3 Development of System

3.1 Architecture of System

The whole system can be classified into three levels, of which, the lowest level is data level which submit data to the higher level through LarKC platform.

The aim of the EU FP 7 Large-Scale Integrating Project LarKC is to develop the Large Knowledge Collider (LarKC, for short, pronounced lark), a platform for massive distributed in-complete reasoning that will remove the scalability barriers of currently existing rea-soning systems for the Semantic Web[7,8]. The intermediary level is the application support level, including Web server, Tomcat server and JVM. The highest level is the system application level which includes function models of searching road sign, searching road, correcting road sign, SPARQL search, simulation, searching POI and managing system etc. Architecture of system can be shown in Figure 3.

When using application level of the system to search data, it sends SPARQL searching languages to LarKC of data level through applicable supportive level. After receiving the request, LarKC would act out the SPARQL language and give back the result to the application level.

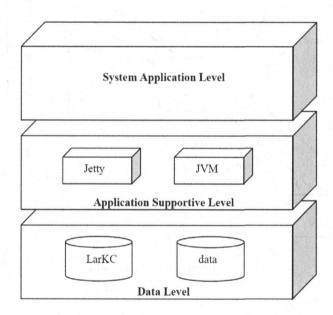

Fig. 3. System architecture

3.2 Architecture of Application

We use Struts2 as MVC framework, and use ExtJS as front web tier framework. The front web page is html page, thus we can separate java code with page code. Architecture of application can be shown in Figure 4.

At first, we open the navigator and input the URL to access the html page. StrutsPrepareAndExecuteFilter of Struts2 framework will get the page access request, it will get the html page and return to the Navigator. Then we will see the html page in the navigator. When we press the button in the html page or trigger event of other controls in the html page, It will send request to StrutsPrepareAndExecuteFilter of Struts2. When StrutsPrepareAndExecuteFilter get the request, it will execute the Action. The Action will call the function of business logic in model component. When model component receive the request, it will execute business code and return result to Action. When Action receives the result, it will convert the result to JSON format. At last, the JSON data will be sent to Navigator.

Base on the AJAX, we will not see the process of refresh page. We only see the change of data in the page.

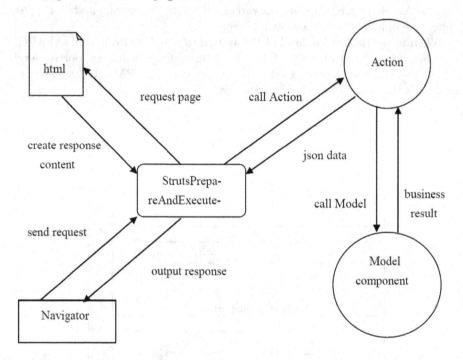

Fig. 4. Architecture of application

3.3   Data of System

Data includes road sign data, road data, POI data, ontology data.

Road board refers to boards directing ways. On boards, there are many instruc-tions about roads and directions. Road sign refer to signs of transport on boards. Data of road boards include roads boards belong to, longitude of road boards, latitude of road boards, how many signs on each board, types of road signs, and content of road signs.

Roads offer infrastructures of various trolleybus and pedestrians. Data of roads include names of roads, longitude and latitude of each point of roads, directions of roads.

POI is the abbreviation of Point of Interest. Data of POI include types of POI, name of POI,longitude and latitude of POI.

Ontology defines basic vocabulary and their relations, making up for vocabulary of theme field, and combines them to be system of roles, including targets, property and relevance. Here, targets represent entity of concepts or knowledge. Property reveals the specialty and value of targets, or certain limits of targets. Relevance represents the relation among targets of entity, including concepts, relations of equality and synonyms, hierarchy, relations. The relevance connects ontology to be an organic integrity of semantic meaning [9]. Ontology includes roads, road boards, POI etc.

This system uses GPS equipment to locate coordinate of each road sign, recording the direction of road sign and the road the sign belongs to , which form the road sign data. The road data include road names and all the coordinate of each road point. Each point has its own direction and could be single or two way directions. All these data come from OSM. Open Street Map (OSM for short) is a coordinate plan of internet map, aiming at creating a world map of free content and can be edited by all people. POI data come from Baidu map.

There are two free web maps that we can use. One is Google map, the other is Baidu map. But in China, we can't access Google map stably. So, we choose Baidu map to display data of transportation. Baidu provides Baidu map API for us to program on Baidu map. Baidu API is a series of application interface programmed by JavaScript. Map display means directly calling Baidu map and API, which can insert the map into the web pages. Through API of Baidu atlas, we can set up road sign marks, drawing road points and drawing roads on the maps.

3.4   Road Sign Searching

Selecting the roads need to be searched, then all the information of the road sign on the road could be searched, including the direction of each road sign, information of the longitude and latitude, the directing information of the road signs. The road signs searched out would display itself in bubbles, after being clicked, it can display the directing information and photos of the related road signs.

This application uses ExtJS as front web tier framework. ExtJS is a pure JavaS-cript application framework that works everywhere from IE6 to the latest Chrome. It enables you to create the best cross-platform applications using nothing but a browser, and has a phenomenal API. In ExtJS, there are a lot of controls to use. We can program event function for those controls.

Interface of road sign search can be shown in Figure 5. The page is a html file. We use several ExtJS controls to design this page. The map of the right of the page is from Baidu map. The page is embedded Baidu API. When Navigator displays this page, Baidu API will access server of Baidu and load map in this page.

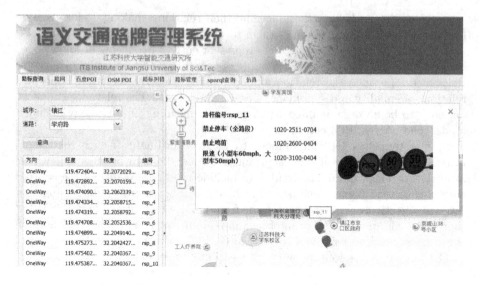

Fig. 5. Interface of road sign searching

3.5   Development of Other Functions

Road searching can searches the route of the roads based on city names and road names. Selecting the roads needed to be searched, all the information of the road can be searched, including every direction of the point, information of the longitude and latitude. The points searched out can display on the maps and be connected through lines. Interface of road searching can be shown in Figure 6.

POI searching can searches corresponding POI according to the key words typed in. POI is the short form of Point of Interest. Typing in the key words of POI, then all the information of POI in this city can be found out, including every term, longitude and latitude of each POI. The POI being searched out can be displayed in the form of bubbles. Interface of POI searching can be shown in Figure 7.

Typing in SPARQL language which can be delivered directly to LarKC, and after being acted out, the results can be found out.

Simulation can show the vehicles' running process base on setting up the starting point and ending point. To select the starting point on the map, and type in the destination, after being stimulated, there would be a car at the starting point on the map, and the car would move towards the destination. And the route of the moving process is deduced according to the road sign.

System management can set up the basic perimeters of some systems. System management includes perimeters, designation of users rights limits. The perimeters include cities users are in and the levels of the map display proportions.

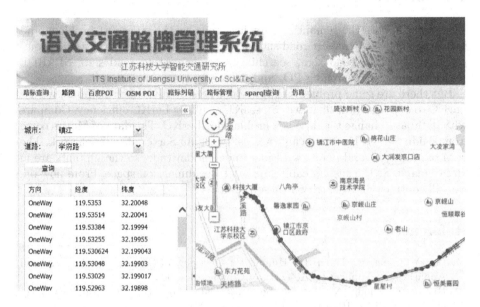

Fig. 6. Interface of road searching

Fig. 7. Interface of POI searching

4   Conclusions

This paper applies the semantic technology to solve the transport problem, and realize a semantic transport road sign management system. This system is composed of searching road sign, searching road, correcting road sign, SPARQL search, simulation, searching POI and managing system.

But there are some problems that are not be solved yet. For example, we use LarKC to deposit data, then, we can search result by LarKC efficiency. Compare with database, change the data is a problem for LarKC. The data of Map is come from Baidu Server. If system can't access the Baidu Server, it will not work. The data of road is several points with longitude and latitude, so these points are in an x-y plane. So the system can't support three dimension space. From now on, we will continue do research on these problems.

References

1. Lin, Y., Song, B., Duan, H., Huang, F.: Overview of Semantic Technology and Applications. Application Research of Computers (2005)
2. Huang, Z., Zhong, N.: Scalable Semantic Data Processing Platform,Technology and Applications. High Education Publisher (2012)
3. Jin, J.: A comparative study of the urban transportation system in Beijing and Seoul. Beijing Jiaotong University (2009)
4. Li, X., Lin, H., Sheng, D.: Discovery of Cooperative Intelligent Transportation Systems. Transportation and Computer (2004)
5. Li, Y., Zhai, J., Chen, Y.: Using ontology to achieve the semantic integration of the intelligent transport system. Information Technology (2005)
6. Huang, K., Jiang, C.: Analyzing and Reasoning Knowledge of Urban Transportation: Based on Ontology. Computer Science (2007)
7. Huang, Z., Fang, J., Park, S., et al.: Noisy Semantic Data Processing in Seoul Road Sign Management System. In: Proceedings of the 10th International Semantic Web Conference (ISWC 2011), Bonn, Germany (2011)
8. Fensel, D., van Harmelen, F., Andersson, B., et al.: Towards LarKC: a platform for web-scale reasoning. In: 2008 IEEE International Conference on Semantic Computing, pp. 524–529. IEEE (2008)
9. Liu, Z.: Ontology and Semantic Web. Research of ChongQing Map (2006)
10. LarKC Consortium, Explanation of Reasoner plugins, including the SPARQLQuery-Evaluation Reasoner, http://wiki.larkc.eu/LarkcProject/WP4/ReasoningPlugins

A Linked Data-Based Framework for Personalized Services Information Retrieval in Smart City

Dehai Zhang[1], Tianlong Song[2], Jin Li[1], and Qing Liu[1]

[1] School of Software, Yunnan University, Kunming City, China
{dhzhang,lijin,liuqing}@ynu.edu.cn
[2] School of Engineering, Univ. of Melbourne, Parkville, VIC, Australia
egmont.tl.song@gmail.com

Abstract. Recently, personalized services finding in Smart City or Digit City is a hotspot in research area. City and urban areas contain plenty of services but some of them are difficult to extract and retrieval to people. Furthermore, with the development of the Semantic Web, more and more datasets are represented as RDF format and become part of the Linked Data, which provides a fundamentally new venue for personalized urban services retrieval in smart city applications. In this paper, we propose a personalized urban services retrieval framework which is performed by using ontology and comparing RDF-based user profiles with dataset in relation to civic services on web of data. To extract hidden information, the domain specific ontology is involved for linking entities on the web of data. The cases we envisage will show that the proposed framework can effectively return services resources with respect to the user's interests.

Keywords: Linked Data, Personalized Urban Service Retrieval, Semantic Cities, Ontology.

1   Introduction

With the explosion of the cities information on the Web, people's requirement for cities services retrieval is strongly growing. However, it is difficult to review the semantics of multiple services in a city, since people are used to exploit high-level semantic concepts to retrieve information [1]. In general, the current technologies can only handle one type of scattered content, like isolated locations and name of facilities, which creates a wide gap between semantic concepts of services and user's interest. This semantic gap makes implementation of smart city a major problem in future research.

For example, if a person holding a doctor's prescription to find a drugstore to sell these drugs, as in cities, drugstores may be relatively small unit, and it is difficult to find them in city map or Web. As we well known, the hospital is usually relatively large units in the city and its information will be very plenty. According to our life experience or common sense, we know that drugstores usually can be found near to hospital. So the person's search will find the hospital firstly, and then looking through the drugstores near to the hospital. This process requires the semantic link between the hospitals and drugstores, which is the current problem of a Smart City

Z. Huang et al. (Eds.): WISE 2013 Workshops 2013, LNCS 8182, pp. 461–473, 2014.

encountered. For these reasons, we use ontology [2] to fill the semantic gap in Smart City, which will improve the effect of urban services information retrieval.

On the other hand, in recent years, the Web has evolved from a global information space of linked documents to Linked Data [3], which have been adopted by an increasing number of data providers over the last few years. According to the statistics of ESW wiki[1], the Web of Data consists of 4.7 billion RDF triples, which are interlinked by around 142 million RDF links by May 2009.

In this paper, we present a framework for personalized services retrieval based on Linked Data and ontology, which uses a novel RDF graph-based matching algorithm to extract the semantics from user profiles defined as RDF graphs and the dataset of service provided in Linked Open Data. Technically, Linked Data uses RDF [4] to make typed statements that link arbitrary things in the world. For these reasons, the Linked Data opens up new possibilities for personalized services retrieval in smart cities. However, some hidden information is distributed in the Linked Data, and they are linked in instance-level, which means the links not contain concept relations in multiple level. Hence, we involve domain ontologies to deal with this kind of semantics, which can use high-level semantic concepts of services to integrate multiple services in a city, while providing related information to users. Moreover, Linked Data cannot provide space semantic reasoning. Therefore, the LBS (Location Based Service) [5] modular is involved in our framework to provide locational relations.

2   Related Work

There are numerous of organizations working on the publication of Linked Data. Linking Open Data (LOD) provides the possibility to link many RDF datasets on the Web [6]. One of the datasets is Linked Movie Database (LinkedMDB) [7], it contains hundreds of millions RDF triples through the properties (like actors, director, country, etc.). Guo and Lu[8] proposes an approach to handle recommendation issues of one-and-only items in e-government services, which integrates the techniques of semantic similarity and the traditional item-based collaborative filtering. Paper[9] proposes a conceptual framework for governments to provide personalized services to their citizens, and the framework combines several recommendation techniques that use several data sources i.e. citizen profile, social media citizen's interactions, users profiles databases and services databases. Paper [10] proposes a Service Oriented Architecture implementation based on multi-agent systems. They take advantage of the mobility features of software agents and developed a solution that intended to be applicable to different smart space scenarios. In paper [11], Sabou and his colleagues reflect on a set of challenges that semantic technologies are likely to face in smart products. Ferragina and Gulli [12] implement an open source and personalized search engine based on web-snippet hierarchical clustering using given variable length query statement to perform searching. The keywords-based search engines as we known today (like Google [13]) exploit user's personalized requirements by analyzing web-browsing history. But keywords-based information retrieval is hard to reflect personalized

---

[1] http://esw.w3.org/topic/TaskForces/CommunityProjects/
LinkingOpenData/DataSets/LinkStatistics

information. A graph-based query can enables the IR process with additional seman-tics. Kasneci et al. [14] present a semantic search engine NAGA. It extracts informa-tion from several sources on the web and support graph-based query, but user has to learn all the relations linked two entities and a specific query language.

3   Preliminaries

Linked Open Data (LOD) has interlinked entities from different areas, and given huge scale of datasets. However, these datasets are interlinked on instance level, which means they has linked similar instance to themselves without subclass relations.

For the purpose of retrieval services information, a system needs relations between the service providers and information providers (e.g. drugstore and hospital, respec-tively). For instance, a patient will need to buy medicines after a doctor gives a prescription to him, but Linked Data has no linking which describes the relevance between hospital and drugstore. Therefore, the patient cannot get drugstore informa-tion from the hospital. To fix this issue, a domain specific ontology which contains this relation will be involved. Based on the ontology, we can find the semantic link between two entities in Smart City, and do some semantic reference about them.

In this particular example, the link will be described as shown in Figure 1.

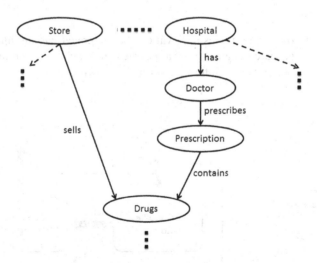

Fig. 1. Links provided by ontology

In the framework proposed in this paper, we provide a further process after filter the Linked Data datasets by tracking the links described by ontologies. Personalised services retrieval by which we mean returning services provider information with respect to user's profiles. A user profile can be used to describe the personalized in-formation of individuals. It contains basic information of individuals like name, gend-er, height, weight etc. or social information of individuals like career, specialty, title etc., as well as hobby information such as favorite movies, music, food etc.

For illustration, we present an example of user profile represented in RDF graph showed in Figure 2.

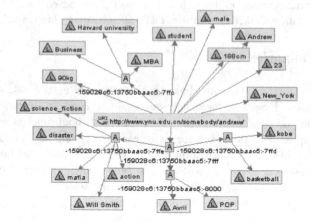

Fig. 2. A RDF graph for an example of a user profile

4   Framework

4.1   Overview

The framework of urban services retrieval can be integrated into an information provider system (e.g. search engine), so that people can search service information conveniently.   The entire view of information flow is shown in Figure 3.

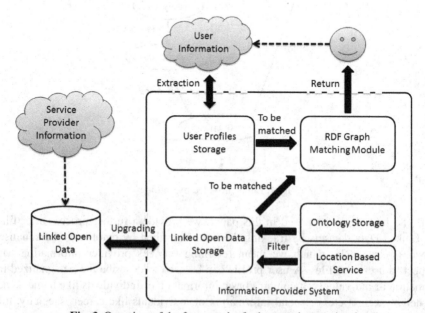

Fig. 3. Overview of the framework of urban services retrieval

As shown in the overview, Linked Open Data is generated from original service provider (like drugstore) information. They are distributed on the web data. Consequently, our framework use ontology to filter these datasets. User profiles are generated from user information which describes user basic and special information.

Our framework is established on the information flow shown in Figure 3, the main part can be integrated into an information provider system, like hospital system which is available to patients to obtain useful pathway after their consultation.

There are five main modules in this framework, the first module is related to the storage of Linked Data, it will continue upgrade the dataset from Linked Open Data to refresh the services information. The second part is ontologies storage, in this module, all ontologies which generate hierarchical links describing the hidden semantic relations between information providers and service providers will be storied. The third part is Location Based Service (LBS), it will be combined with ontology to filter Linked Open Data by providing locational relations, and then find services provider addresses for further recommendation. The fourth part is user profiles storage. The purpose of user profiles generation is to transform original information to RDF format. The final part is the RDF graph matching algorithm, which will be furthered in section 3.3.

4.2   The Process of Personalized Urban Services Retrieval

The personalized of personalized urban services retrieval process is shown in Figure 4, and described as follows:

Step1: original urban services data will be extracted from LOD. In this step, the linked data will be captured within three levels, which means the generated Linked Data datasets will have a three depth, in terms of avoiding useless information.

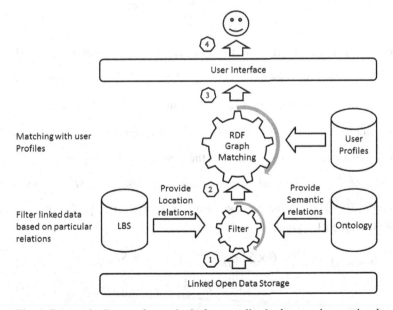

Fig. 4. Schematic diagram for method of personalized urban services retrieval

Step2: Utilize the links which provides by ontologies in figure 1 to find the labels which tracked by the links in the dataset. At the same time, use LBS to find the service providers locations.

Step3: Match user profile to the set of RDF graphs, and then calculate the similarity to determine the matching extent, finally return a ranked list according to the similarity.

Step4: Return the service provider information to users.

4.3   RDF Graph Matching Based on Similarity

The nature of RDF graph similarity calculating is the core algorithm in our approach. There are still some effective related graph matching algorithms, such as Similarity Flooding [15], which relies on the intuition that elements of two distinct models are similar when their adjacent elements are similar. Moreover, Zhu [16] integrates similarities between nodes and similarities between arcs to construct similarity between graphs. But these algorithms cannot be used in our method directly, because the real RDF graphs has its own characteristics that many nodes in RDF graphs are URIs.

Consequently, our RDF graph matching algorithm takes the linguistic similarity and structural similarity of triples in RDF graph into account. In order to measure the features in RDF graphs.

The formula to calculate similarity of two graphs is as follows:

$$Sim(G_U, G_R) = \frac{\sum_{i=1}^{n} [Sim_{statement}(s_R^i, s_U^{i\_max}) \times Deg(s_R^i)]}{\sum_{i=1}^{n} Deg(s_R^i)} \tag{1}$$

where G_U is the RDF graph of user profile, and G_R is the RDF graph which describes the information resource, $Sim_{statement}(s_R^i, s_U^{i\_max})$ is the similarity between triple (also called statement) i in G_R (represented by s_R^i) and the triple in G_U that has maximum similarity with triple i in G_R (represented by $s_U^{i\_max}$), and the $Deg(s_R^i)$ is the degree of s_R^i which as the weight of triple in graph.

We denote the similarity between statements use $Sim_{Statement}(t^u, t^r)$ that defined in formula (2), where t^u is the statement comes from user profile and t^r comes from the resource RDF graph.

$$Sim_{Statement}(t^u, t^r) = \theta \times Sim_{Triple}(t^u, t^r) + \gamma \times Sim_{Structural}(t^u, t^r)$$
$$(\theta + \gamma = 1) \tag{2}$$

The $Sim_{Triple}(t^u, t^r)$ and $Sim_{Structural}(t^u, t^r)$ are labels similarities and structural similarity between t^u and t^r respectively, θ and γ are references of weights.

For the purpose of reducing computation complexity, we take a triple as the smallest element when calculate the similarity. The similarity between two triple is defined as follows:

$$Sim_{Triple}(s_R^i, s_U^j) = \frac{Sim_{label}(s_R, s_U) + Sim_{label}(p_R, p_U) + Sim_{label}(o_R, o_U)}{3} \quad (3)$$

Where $Sim_{label}(s_R, s_U)$, $Sim_{label}(p_R, p_U)$ and $Sim_{label}(o_R, o_U)$ is the linguistic or string similarity of the subjects, properties and objects in information resource and user profile.

For calculating the linguistic similarity between triples, we use WordNet [17] to measure the semantic distance between words in two nodes or arcs in RDF graph. For those strings of labels do not exist in WordNet, Levenshtein [18] algorithm is used to calculate the string distance of the labels.

The structural similarity between statements is the weighted sum of upper set similarity and lower set (shown in Figure.5) similarity of the distinct statements. The formula is shown in Equation 4.

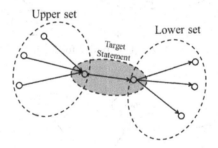

Fig. 5. The Upper set and lower set of a statement

$$Sim_{Structural}(t^u, t^r) = \alpha \times Sim_{upper}(t^u, t^r) + \beta \times Sim_{lower}(t^u, t^r) \quad (4)$$
$$(\alpha + \beta = 1)$$

The upper set similarity between t^u and t^r is defined as follows:

$$Sim_{upper}(t^u, t^r) = \frac{\sum_{j=1}^{k} \max(Sim_{1j}, Sim_{2j}, Sim_{3j}, \dots, Sim_{dj})}{k} \quad (5)$$

Where the Sim_{dj} presents the similarity between the two corresponding statements in user profile and target graph. The lower set similarity can be defined in the same way, and denoted by $Sim_{lower}(t^u, t^r)$.

5   Simulation

At the present time, there has no suitable dataset for us to test our framework. Therefore, we generate a case below for further implementation.

In the first place, we generate two user profiles, which contain different personal information of these two patients (John and Jim), as shown in Figure 6 and Figure 7.

John

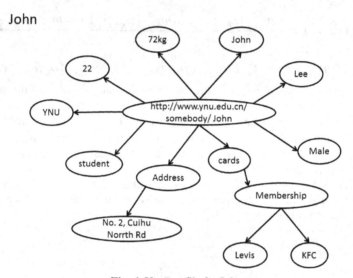

Fig. 6. User profile for John

Jim

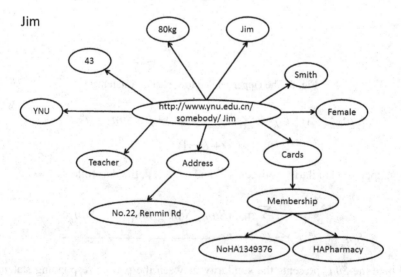

Fig. 7. User profile for Jim

After a normal treatment process for the patient, the doctor will give them the prescriptions. The patients will buy medicine (azithromycin) based on the prescription. They can enter the keywords of the medicines into hospital information system or even do nothing, and then the framework will track the links which is generated from ontology to find services provider. Finally, the framework will locate three drugstores (D1, D2 and D3). All these stories sell azithromycin which is involved in their prescription. The RDF graph fragments are shown in Figure 8, Figure 9 and Figure 10.

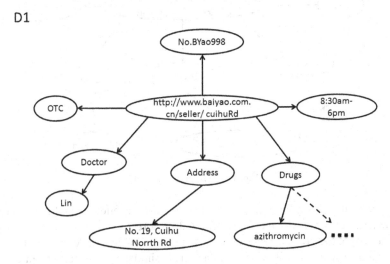

Fig. 8. RDF graph for D1

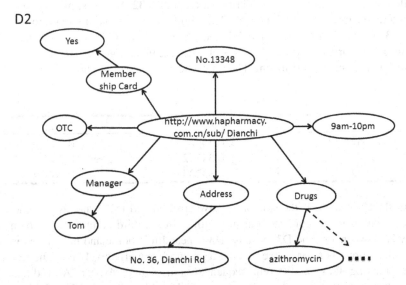

Fig. 9. RDF graph for D2

D3

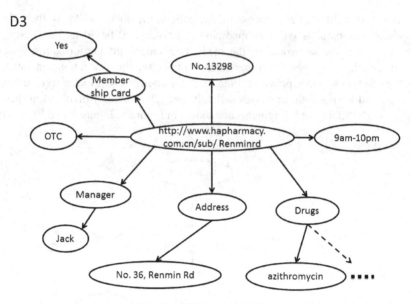

Fig. 10. RDF graph for D3

After that, the user information of the patient, such as etiology and the home location, will be compared with the details of the drugstores.

In this stage, the process relies on the calculated similarities. As we set, D1 is near John's home (their addresses are similar). The similarity between statements "address→No.36, Cuihu North Rd" and "address→No.2 Cuihu North Rd" is 0.932. While the rest of statements similarities are about 0.32. So the similarity of address plays a major factor in matching task. This similarity is Jim has a membership card of D2; D3 is near Jim's home, and D2 and D3 belong to the same company, which means Jim's card is valid in D3 as well. After calculation, the framework recommends D1 to John and D3 to Jim. The final calculating result is shown in Table1.

Table 1. Similarities Result

	John	*Jim*
D1	0.35987	0.32008
D2	0.34322	0.34898
D3	0.34234	0.36044

As shown in table 1, the similarity between John and D1 is the biggest one in the three comparisons. It confirms our pre-setting. In the third column, the maxim similarity is between Jim and D3, because D3 is near Jim's home and may have discount. This simulation, therefor, prove that the framework can effectively rank the result and return ranking lists in different sequence as user may expect. Accordingly, our framework can also be used in other cases which are described briefly below.

(1) When the housewives need to pay for a common bill, but cannot find the location and method of payment immediately. At this time, the framework will match the user information and the keywords input by users associated with the bill to determine the address and manner of payment.

(2) When international students come to a new country, they need to rent rooms. However, due to he is unfamiliar to the new place, and he cannot immediately find the right one. At this time, the framework can recommend nearby and cheap room according to his school address, income and the extra requirement described by keywords.

6 Complexity Analysis

The time complexity of our algorithm lead the main complexity cost in our framework and can be expected to the number of comparison between the nodes and arcs in RDF graphs, which lies around n^2. Figure 11 show the running time of our algorithm in different size of target RDF graphs (The size of user profile RDF graph is around 2k).

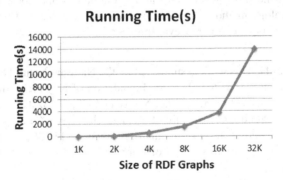

Fig. 11. Running Time

The existing graph isomorphism based algorithms are inefficient and the others ignored semantic characteristics of RDF graph. So we need an efficient and semantic similarity based RDF matching algorithm to meet the requirements. The proposed algorithm is based on similarity measure, which takes semantic characteristics and structural features into account while matching RDF graphs. In our method, the similarity calculation is divided into different levels, and various possible scenarios of label of nodes or arcs be fully considered. The experimental results show that the proposed algorithm can effectively measure the similarity between RDF graphs in various situations.

We will keep optimizing this algorithm in the future work, make it more effective and try to meet the requirements of Semantic Web.

7   Conclusions and Future Work

In our framework, the process of retrieval urban services data which is annotated with Linked Data principle provides a feasible method to match particular service information to user's demand. It transfers a new idea of personalized information retrieval in Linked Data environment. We show that how the process retrieve urban services and personalize the return lists according the user profile. The simulation shows the applicability of the framework. There are two main contributions in our framework. The first one is using ontology to address the hidden semantic relations between information providers and service providers, meanwhile, using LBS to provide locational relations in order to locate the near service provider. Secondly, our novel personalised RDF graph matching algorithm is certified in the simulation section, and it can effectively return ranking lists as user expected. Finally, the proposed framework can be utilized on smart cities application with the enrichment of urban services triples in Linked Data.

Based on this framework, we will aim to further integrate the modules of ontology, LBS and RDF graph matching. We will focus on the implementation of this framework, improving the links generation through ontologies and coordinating the LSB method with ontology method. Primarily, we will use real data to verify our personalized urban service information retrieval framework.

Acknowledgements. This work is supported by the National Natural Science Foundation of China (Grant No. 61263043) , the Foundation of Key Program of Department of Education of Yunnan Province (Grant No. 2011Z020, 2013Z049) , the Key Discipline Foundation of School of Software of Yunnan University (Grant No.2012SE103), the Natural Science Foundation of Yunnan Province (2011FB020), and the Foundation of the Key Laboratory of Software Engineering of Yunnan Province (2012SE303).

References

1. Rowley, H., Baluja, S., Kanade, K.: Human Face Detection in Visual Scenes. In: Advances in Neural Information Processing Systems 8 (Proceedings of NIPS), Denver, USA, pp. 875–881 (November 1996)
2. Uschold, M., Gruninger, M.: Ontologies: Principles, Methods and Applications. The Knowledge Engineering Review 11(2) (1996)
3. Berners-Lee, T.: Linked Data, DesignIssues (July 27, 2006),
   http://www.w3.org/DesignIssues/LinkedData.html
4. Klyne, G., Carroll, J.J.: Resource description framework (RDF):Concepts and Abstract:syntax. In: The World Wide Web Consortium (W3C) (2004)
5. Schiller, J.H., Voisard, A.: Location-based services. Morgan Kaufmann (2004)
6. Bizer, C., Heath, T., Ayers, D., Raimond, Y.: Interlinking Open Data on theWeb (Poster). In: 4th European Semantic Web Conference (ESWC 2007), pp. 802–815 (2007)
7. Hassanzadeh, O., Consens, M.P.: Linked Movie Data Base. In: Proceedings of the WWW 2009 Workshop on Linked Data on the Web (2009)

8. Guo, X., Lu, J.: Intelligent e-government services with personalized recommendation techniques: Research Articles. International Journal of Intelligent Systems 22(5), 401–417 (2007)

9. Abdellatif, A., Amor, N.B., Mellouli, S.: An intelligent framework for e-government personalized services. In: Proceeding of the 14th Annual International Conference on Digital Government Research, pp. 120–126. ACM, New York (2013)

10. Marsa-Maestre, I., Lopez-Carmona, M.A., Velasco, J.R., Navarro, A.: Mobile agents for service personalization in smart environments. Journal of Networks 3(5), 30–41 (2008)

11. Sabou, M., Kantorovitch, J., Nikolov, A., Tokmakoff, A., Zhou, X., Motta, E.: Position paper on realizing smart products: challenges for Semantic Web technologies. In: 2nd International Workshop on Semantic Sensor Networks 2009 (SSN 2009) at ISWC 2009, Washington, D.C., USA (October 26, 2009)

12. Ferragina, P., Gulli, A.: A Personalized Search Engine Based on Web-Snippet Hierarchical Clustering. In: International World Wide Web Conference Committee (IW3C2), Chiba, Japan, May 10-14 (2005)

13. Sherman, C.: Google Personalized Search Leaves Google Labs. Search Engine Watch.com (November 10, 2005)

14. Kasneci, G., Suchanek, F.M., Ifrim, G., Ramanath, M., Weikum, G.: Naga:Searching and ranking knowledge (2008)

15. Melnik, S., Garcia-Molina, H., Rahm, E.: Similarity Flooding: A Versatile Graph Matching Algorithm. In: Proceedings of the 18th International Conference on Data Engineering (ICDE), San Jose, CA (2002)

16. Zhu, H., Zhong, J., Li, J., Yu, Y.: An Approach for Semantic Search by Matching RDF Graphs. In: Proceedings of the Fifteenth International Florida Artificial Intelligence Research Society Conference, Pensacola Beach, Florida, May 14-16, pp. 450–454 (2002)

17. Fellbaum, C.: WordNet: An Electronic Lexical Database (Language, Speech, and Communication). The MIT Press (1998)

18. Levenshtein, I.V.: Binary codes capable of correcting deletions insertions and reversals. Cybemetics and Control Theory 10(8), 707–710 (1966)

Taxi Travel Purpose Estimation and Characteristic Analysis Based on Multi-source Data and Semantic Reasoning — A Case Study of Beijing

Yang Si[1], Jiancheng Weng[1], Zhihong Chen[2], and Yueyue Wang[1]

[1] Beijing University of Technology, Transportation Research Center, Beijing, China
{siyang,youthweng,wangyueyue}@emails.bjut.edu.cn
[2] Beijing Transportation Information Center, Beijing, China
chenzhihong@bjjtw.gov.cn

Abstract. Taxi is an important part of urban public transportation which meets the demands of special people to travel from door to door. Taxi trip characteristics are influenced by districts location and travel purposes. This paper extracts the time and location information of taxi alighting based on the taxi meter data and taxi GPS data. Based on the point-of-interest (POI) and searching popularity of the POI from online map data, this paper also utilizes the semantic reasoning methods to predict the purpose of taxi travels, and taxi trips are grouped into three most popular types: commuting travel, business travel and external travel. Then, multi-source data analysis models are proposed to calculate the characteristic parameters of taxis trips including average travel mileage, travel time, regional travel intensity of three types of taxi trips. The case study of Beijing selects three typical areas of different land use types. The analysis result shows that trip characteristics of different areas are various and the travel distance in resident area is shortest, and the travelers leave for external transportation hub usually have lower sensitivity to travel mileage; and the taxi travel mileage of business areas are almost same with resident areas, however the travel time is more longer. The analysis results of taxi trips characteristics of different areas revealed in this paper provide significant reference for acquiring the taxi travel demand and travel characteristics, the taxi stations planning, the estimation of the reasonable amount of the taxis and the operation of the intelligent Taxi Dispatching System (TDS).

Keywords: Intelligent Transportation System (ITS), Taxi, Travel Purpose, Travel Characteristics, GPS Data, Taxi Meter Data.

1   Introduction

Taxi system is an important supplement of urban public transportation as a part of urban passenger transport system. The taxi can provide more convenient, comfortable and personalized travel service than traditional public transport services. Exploring the taxi travel characteristics is the foundation of taxi management and service

Z. Huang et al. (Eds.): WISE 2013 Workshops 2013, LNCS 8182, pp. 474–492, 2014.

improvement. However, the methods based on sampling surveys or empirical models are generally adopted in the former studies and planning of taxi pick-up stops, taxi demand analysis and the taxi scheduling system at present. These methods lack the analysis of systematic characteristics based on the actual taxi travel. Besides, there's a significant difference in the occurrence time, space and characteristics during the trip for different travel purposes, including commuting, shopping, or external travel, etc. The definition of the average trip distance, travel time and regional attraction intensity is important for the administrative department to master the characteristics of taxi travel demand. Acquiring the taxi trip characteristics including the time-space characteristic and service quality evaluation can promote the industry management level.

A series of studies have been conducted in the analysis of taxi operation characteristics and reached related conclusions. In previous studies, Hu established the taxi operation management database by organizing the taxi GPS data including the functional parameter such as single taxi cycling index, overall indices, spatial and temporal distribution and OD distribution [1]. Deng put forward indicator of utilization of vehicle and operating revenue to evaluate the taxi operation efficiency of Beijing [2]. Chi developed the method of floating car data processing and analysis [3]. The paper extracted and analyzed the number of taxi ride point and the durations of passenger in the central area of Shanghai through the floating car data processing, and the analysis results reflected the taxi travel demand of a certain area. Li established the indicator system and analysis method of the taxi trip characteristics, the travel time distribution and space distribution based on the taxi OD data analysis [4]. Weng analyzed the parameters including travel mileage, virtual mileage ratio, time-space distribution on the road-network and the labor intensity of drivers by using the urban floating car data collection system [5]. Kamga analyzed the taxi travel distance on different TOD (time-of-day) [6].

A lot of studies obtained data from GPS. Tong carried out cluster analysis on the GPS data and extracted popular regions of taxi travel and determined travel purposes by the popular spots, but the analysis only focused on the macro regional purpose of taxi trips, it ignored specific analysis on a single trip travel purpose [7]. Jean used GPS data loggers to collect travel data in personal vehicles and demonstrated that it is feasible to derive trip purpose from the GPS data by using a spatially accurate and comprehensive GIS [8]. Murakami used the GPS receiver to capture vehicle-based daily travel information [9]. Wolf used GPS to supplement traditional data elements collected in paper or electronic travel diaries [10]. Bohte demonstrated that GPS-based methods provide reliable multi-day data including trip purpose [11].

With the development of the intelligent transportation system and the improvement of the data collection system, the existing meter data and GPS data record the spatial and temporal distribution of taxi operation process, and become important data source for the analysis of taxi characteristics. It joints analysis of GPS data and meter data to obtain GPS location information and utilizes the semantic logic identification to determine the point-of-interest and the popularity of the POI. The paper finally takes Beijing as an example to analyze the characteristics of taxi travel including the travel times, trip distances of different trip purposes, and attraction intensities of various areas.

2   Data Foundation

The data used in this study contain taxi meter data, taxi GPS data and semantic data. Taxi meter data provide the operational information for analyzing the operating characteristics of different travel purposes. Taxi GPS data contain the real-time location information of the vehicle. It could support the association analysis of point-of-interest and travel purpose. Semantic data mainly refer to the location, description, categories of the point-of-interest, as well as the popularity of the point-of-interest extracted from the online system. The trip purposes of different starting point and ending point in different time interval can be predicted by the categories of point-of-interest. Based on the joint analysis of three kinds of data above, we can differentiate the trip purposes of taxi travels and analyze the different trip characteristics of them.

2.1   Taxi Meter Data

Taxi meter is installed on the taxi to record the operation status and process. It produces a record at a time after every taxi trip. The meter data mainly contains the passenger boarding and alighting time, waiting time of a trip, the transaction amount, mileage etc. The meter data is an important basis of a deal, it is accurately record all information of a taxi travel, but it still has the following four errors sometimes: (1) Vehicles registered don't match the meter records; (2) The alighting time is recorded before the boarding time; (3) A single running time is too long (more than a few hours); (4) A single operating distance is 0.

The amount of data in those four cases accounts for about 0.2%. These data are fault data, which need to be eliminated during data pretreatment. The sample data of meter data is shown as table 1:

Table 1. The sample data of taxi meter data

CAR_CODE	TRANS_AMOUNT	DEAL_TIME	WAIT_TIME	TRAVEL_MIL	UNTRAVEL_MIL	DAY_TIME
BK6093	25	2012/11/5 8:58:15	16	7	2.7	8:27:38
BK6081	68	2012/11/5 6:53:07	4	25.5	2.5	6:26:03

2.2   Taxi GPS Data

The taxi uploads GPS data according to the time interval system set. Taxi GPS data contains basic information such as time, longitude, latitude, direction angle, and it can also transmit state information(e.g.no-load, full-load, parking, off-stream etc.) according to the events during the operation(e.g., boarding, alighting, locking the door, opening the door etc.). The sample data of taxi GPS data is shown as table 2:

Table 2. The sample data of Taxi GPS data

CENTER_NAME	TAXI_CODE	GPS_TIME	LONGITUDE1	LATITUDE1	SPEED	DIRECTION_ANGLE
JYJ	BN3974	2012/11/6 23:28:33	116.48	40.01	10	334
JKSX	BH0479	2012/11/5 21:25:58	116.54	39.91	32.4	238

Taxi GPS data can be matched with taxi meter data at the same time, then we can obtain the time and location of every starting point and ending point that the taxi meter data provided.

In Beijing, all the taxis (about 67,000 vehicles) are equipped with GPS module. Taxis upload the information of the latitude and longitude coordinates at predefined time interval (between 30 to 60 seconds), which provides a reliable data for the relevant analysis of travel characteristics.

2.3 Semantic Data

Semantic data is mainly acquired through obtaining the location and search times information about the point-of-interest in online maps. Point-of-interest (POI) records many described information about city site, which including famous buildings, scenic spots, traffic facilities, shops, companies, markets and units in this city, and every POI contains PoiID, PoiName, PoiType, Longitude and Latitude.

At present, more than 130,000 point-of-interests are involved in this study, they were divided into more than 100 types such as catering, companies, residential property, entertainment, office blocks and so on. The sample data of semantic data is shown as table 3:

Table 3. The sample data of semantic data

ID	NAME	TYPE	Longitude	Latitude
11447352825	Baijialou Bridge	Landbridge, Traffic Facility	116.55	39.93
17651930122	Jin Qianding Supermarket	Supermarket, Shopping	116.42	39.90

The search times of a point-of-interest in unit time means the popularity of this POI. It can be acquired through the public information facilitators which provide search capabilities. The more search times means the higher popularity degree.

The type information is reduced to three most popular taxi travel types: commuting travel, business travel and external travel in this paper. We calculate the probability of different categories of travel and identify the purpose of this travel by extracting the location and popularity information of the POI around the trading place.

2.4   The Process of Taxi Trip Characteristics Extraction

Extract the location information from taxi GPS data and the carrying mileage, boarding time, alighting time information from taxi meter data. Then use semantic technology to estimate travel purpose, and analyze the trip characteristics of different types. The detailed process is shown as the figure 2:

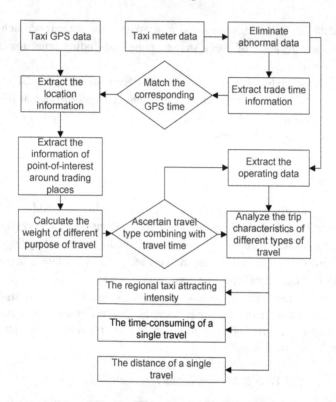

Fig. 1. Process of taxi trip characteristics extraction

3   Indicators of the Taxi Travel Characteristics

The indicators of the taxi travel characteristics reflect the differences in different travel types. The regional attraction intensity, the time-consuming of a single travel and the distance of a single travel are defined as the three kinds of indicators.

3.1   The Regional Attraction Intensity

The regional attraction intensity refers to the total number of taxis arriving in one popular region per unit area per unit time with a certain trip purpose. This index reflects the attraction intensity of taxis with different trip purposes in this area.

The higher value of the attraction intensity indicates the higher frequency of taxi trips for one certain purpose in this area. The equation is:

$$I_a = N_t/A \tag{1}$$

Where I_a is the regional attraction intensity with a certain purpose probability, the unit is the taxi number per square kilometer per day. N_t is the arriving number of taxis with one certain purpose, the unit is the taxi trips. A is the area of the zone; the unit is square kilometer(s).

3.2   The Time Consuming of a Single Travel

The indicators include the average travel time, the median travel time and the distribution of travel time. The time-consuming of a single travel refers to the average consuming time of one category of the travel purposes. The median travel time of a single travel refers to the value in the middle position when all the time-consuming of one category of the travel purposes are arranged in order of size. The value eliminates the effects of the external series and improves the representative of distribution series. The distribution of travel time refers to collect and classify the data of a certain trip purpose. The time-consuming of a single travel will be included when it falls into one certain time interval. Finally the statistics of the distribution number in each interval will be obtained. It can reflect the travel time distribution of some category of trip purposes.

3.3   The Distance of a Single Travel

The indicator is similar with the time-consuming of a single travel. It includes the average travel distance, the median travel distance and the distribution of travel distance.

The median travel distance of a single travel refers to the value in the middle position when all the distances of one category of the travel purposes are arranged in order of size. The distribution of the distance refers to collect and classify the data of a certain trip purpose according to the distance. The distance of a single travel will be included when it falls into one certain distance interval. Finally the statistics of the distribution number in each interval will be obtained. This indicator can reflect the acceptance for the distance within different categories of travel purposes. For example, the acceptance for the distance of the commuting travel is relatively shorter than that of the external travel.

4   Taxi Trip Purposes

Spatial distribution of residents travel usually has certain regularity, such as the passengers with different travel demands will arrive in different locations, for example, a large residential area, commercial region and entertainment site. These places centralized with passengers can be regarded as a popular region which has many points of interest (POIs), and different POI has different popularity degrees. According to the points of interesting properties and the popularity degrees around the taxi destination coordinates, the travel purpose can be judged.

4.1   Trip Purposes Classification

For taxi trip purposes classification, nearby POIs which used the taxi destination coordinates should be obtained and the travel purpose is judged according to the popularity of POI and a combination of travel time. Combined with urban land type and purpose of travel, the travel category is divided into commuting travel, business travel, and external travel. Table 4 shows the category.

Table 4. Trip purposes category

Travel Category	Trip Purpose	POI Category	Representative Region
Commuting Travel	Go to Work, Go Home	Residence Zone, Office Building	Wangjing
Business Travel	Entertainment, Shopping	Park, Marketplace	Xidan
External Travel	Inter-cities Travel	Railway Station, Motor Station, Airport	Beijing Railway Station

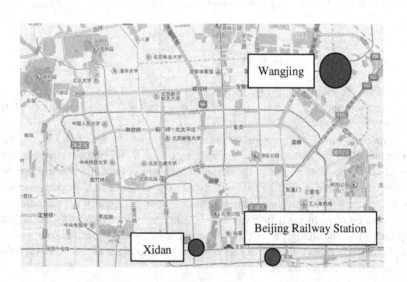

Fig. 2. Representative regional locations in the Beijing

Different areas will present different characteristics. For example, business travel is the main travel purpose in Xidan area; and there're different purposes in the same area. This is because there're kinds of buildings in the same area; and the travel purpose will be different at different times. If the taxi arrives before 9:30 AM, it will be judged as the commuting travel and judged as business travel after 9:30 AM in the same area.

This paper selects Wangjing, Xidan and Beijing Railway Station as three typical areas and selects 7:00 AM to 10:00 PM of November 5, 2012 (Monday), November 7 (Wednesday) and November 10 (Saturday) to analysis. Three red pots show the regional positions on Figure 2.

4.2   Travel Purpose Predict Based on Semantic Technologies

The core idea of the semantic technology is to make computer automatically processing information content on the network. Using the semantics of the data on the network related to the GPS data and the meter data can predict the travel purpose rapidly. Steps as follows:

(1) Pick up the coordinates of the destination of taxi trip as a red circle on FIGURE 3.

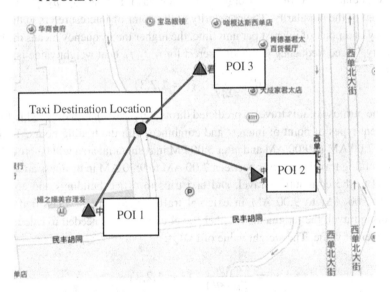

Fig. 3. The example of destination and POIs

Taking the Zhongshui Building as an example, transforming the point into semantic expression:

```
<http://www.w2t-waas.com/uc#POIID-baidu11447352836>
<http://www.w3.org/1999/02/22-rdf-syntax-ns#type>
    <http://www.w2t-waas.com/uc#CPOI>.
    <http://www.w2t-waas.com/uc#POIID-baidu11447352836>
<http://www.w2t-waas.com/uc#id> "11447352836".
```

```
    <http://www.w2t-waas.com/uc#POIID-baidu11447352836>
<http://www.w2t-waas.com/uc#POISource> "Baidu".
    <http://www.w2t-waas.com/uc#POIID-baidu11447352836>
<http://www.w2t-waas.com/uc#name> "Zhongshui Building"@en.
    <http://www.w2t-waas.com/uc#POIID-baidu11447352836>
<http://www.w2t-waas.com/uc#POIClass> "Office Building"@en.
    <http://www.w2t-waas.com/uc#POIID-baidu11447352836>
<http://www.w2t-waas.com/uc#ParentClass> "Business Building"@en.
```

(2) Select nearest three points of interest as POI 1, POI 2, POI 3 on above figure according to trading location coordinates, then assign them to the different categories(A means commuting travel, B means business travel, and C means external travel). Distance of POI and trading location respectively for d_1, d_2, d_3, and the corresponding distance weights for α_1, α_2, α_3, the value of the weight higher follows the shorter distance. Weight value for the distance is:

$$\alpha_i = \frac{\frac{1}{d_i}}{\sum_1^3 \frac{1}{d_i}} \quad (i = 1,2,3) \tag{2}$$

(3) Calculate the different weight value for each POI as β_1, β_2, β_3 using the assessment of the popularity. The popularity of the point-of-interest refers to the search frequency of a point of interest per unit time, the higher the frequency means the higher popularity. Three frequency points of interest for f_1, f_2, f_3, heat weight value is:

$$\beta_i = \frac{f_i}{\sum_1^3 f_i} \quad (i = 1,2,3) \tag{3}$$

(4) The purpose of this travel is predicted through the calculation of weighted values of different types of point of interest and combined with the trading hours. Taxi trips between 7:00 AM to 9:00 AM and after 5:00 PM in residential area will be brought into the commuting travel, taxi trips between 7:00 AM to 9:30 AM in business areas will be belonged to the commuting travel, and taxi trips to office buildings and companies between 7:00 AM to 9:00 AM in external traffic areas will be classified into the commuting travel, the judgments of other travel categories is needed to calculate each type of weight value. The weight value of POI is:

$$\gamma_i = \frac{\alpha_i \times \beta_i}{\sum_1^3 (\alpha_i \times \beta_i)} \quad (i = 1,2,3) \tag{4}$$

Then sum the weight values of the same category. Commuting travel result is γ_A, business travel result is γ_B, and external travel result is γ_C. If $\gamma_A > \gamma_B$ and $\gamma_A > \gamma_C$, then this trip is predicted to be commuting travel; if $\gamma_B > \gamma_A$ and $\gamma_B > \gamma_C$, then this trip is predicted to be business travel; and if $\gamma_C > \gamma_A$ and $\gamma_C > \gamma_B$, then this trip is predicted to be external travel. Take Figure 3 as an example, the judgment of POI information and travel purpose corresponding to the taxi destination location as the following table:

Table 5. Match the POI information and travel purpose

	NAME	TYPE	Distance to Destination	Search Count	α	β	γ
POI 1	Zhongshui Building	Office Building, Business Building	50m	500	0.37	0.25	0.26
POI 2	Xidan north China unicom business hall	Telecom Company	69m	200	0.26	0.10	0.07
POI 3	Grand Pacific Mall	Comprehensive Market, Shopping Center	50m	1300	0.37	0.65	0.67

POI 1 and POI 2 are both POI of commuting travel, POI 3 is POI of business travel, because of γ3>γ1>γ2, so this trip could be regarded as business travel.

5   Taxi Trip Characteristics Analysis for Different Purposes

Calculated three typical areas in the three days of data according to the steps above, and predict trip purpose. The results will be analyzed by dividing into different regions and different travel purposes.

5.1   The Taxi Travel Features of Different Areas

(1) The regional attract intensity

Areas can be divided into residential district, business zone and external traffic area, put Wangjing, Xidan and Beijing Railway Station as an example. The area of Wangjing area is 6.218 km^2, Xidan is 0.4503 km^2, and Beijing Railway Station is 0.1525 km^2. Attract intensity of different areas as follows:

Table 6. Attract strength of different areas(trips/km^2/day)

Attract intensity / Day	Wangjing		Xidan		Beijing Railway Station	
	Commuting	Business	Commuting	Business	Commuting	External
Mon.	359	214	433	3304	98	8641
Wed.	698	402	371	5905	170	13670
Sat.	339	252	524	3835	216	8681

There are quite differences of trip intensity of different purposes in different regions. Commuting travel is the main travel type in Wangjing area, accounting for about 60% of the total trips; Xidan area are mainly composed of business travel, which accounts for about 90% of the total travel; the external travel attracts the highest intensity in Beijing station area which accounts for about 98% of the total amount of travel, this is due to the number of external travel trips to Beijing railway station is higher, and it's more convenient for the people with heavy luggage get to the train station by taxi.

(2) The time consuming of a single travel

There're differences in the travel times of different areas, the average and median travel time are shown in table 7:

Table 7. The mean and median of travel time in different areas (min)

Areas	Wangjing		Xidan		Beijing Railway Station	
	Mean	Median	Mean	Median	Mean	Median
Commuting travel	18.2	14.8	22.5	19.6	24.9	21.4
Business travel	16.9	13.8	23.5	20.7	—	—
External travel	—	—	—	—	24.0	21.7

The durations of the taxis which destinations are in Beijing railway station area are significantly higher than other areas. The external travel takes the longest time. The time durations of the taxis trips toward Wangjing area are lower than other areas. The duration distributions of different areas are shown as follows:

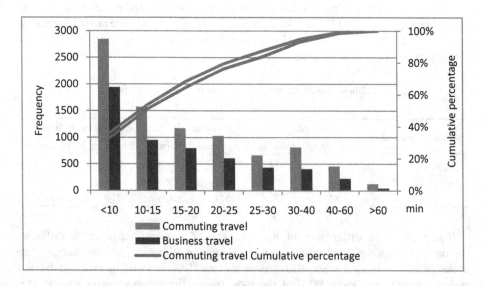

A) Wangjing Area

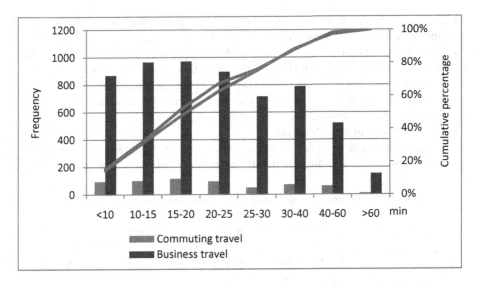

B) Xidan Area

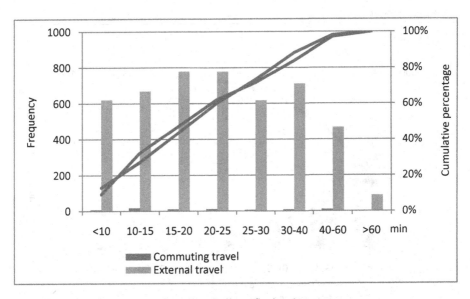

C) Beijing Railway Station Area

Fig. 4. Time consuming distribution of three sample areas

The distribution diagram shows, the travel time distribution of Wangjing area are close to the negative exponential distribution. The percentage of short distance travel under 10 minutes is the highest, other areas are close to normal distribution. The external travel time distributions in Beijing railway station area mainly concentrate in

15-25 minutes. In Xidan area, the travel time distributions mainly distribute in 10-20 minutes. As a residential area, the percentage of short distance travel in Wangjing is obviously higher than other areas, the trips for a short time are significantly higher than other areas. Some trips heading for the rail transport and commuting travel in a short distance, etc. For different travel purposes in the same area, the characteristics of frequency distribution of the travel time are generally consistent. There are no significant differences between them.

(3) The distance of a single travel

The travel distance of different areas can also reflect the difference of trips, the mean and median of travel distance in different areas are shown in table 8.

Table 8. The mean and median of travel distance in different areas (km)

Trip Purposes	Wangjing		Xidan		Beijing Railway Station	
	Mean	Median	Mean	Median	Mean	Median
Commuting travel	7.9	5.5	7.6	6.5	10.4	8.25
Business travel	7.6	5.3	7.9	6.5	—	—
External travel	—	—	—	—	10.2	9.1

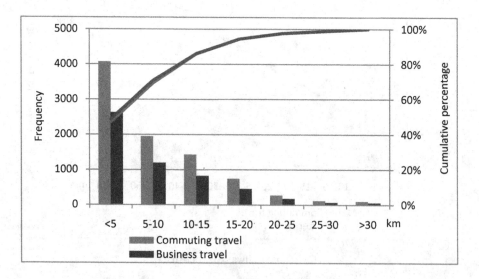

A) Wangjing Area

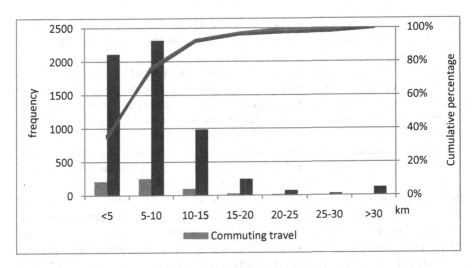

B) Xidan Area

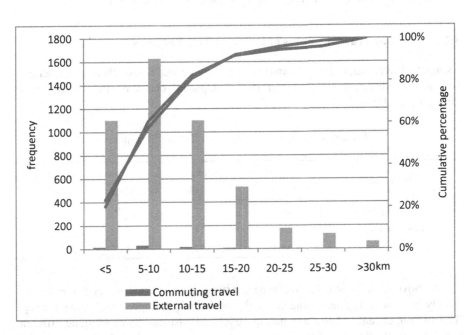

C) Beijing Railway Station

Fig. 5. Travel distance distributions of three sample areas

Table 8 shows that the taxi travel distance of Beijing railway area is the longest for the lower sensitivity to taxi trip distance of the train passengers with big luggage. Though the average trip distance of Xidan area close to Wangjing area, the median value of travel distance of Wangjing area is shorter significant than the Xidan area, the main reason is that there is a connection close commuter rail transportation and close to travel.

Take Wangjing area and Xidan area as example, the commuting travel distances in the two areas have little difference, but on the travel time, travel time-consuming to Xidan is about 30% higher than Wangjing area, this is mainly due to the poor traffic conditions in the urban center like Xidan, which leads to a single trip takes longer time. Travel distance distribution of different areas as follow:

The travel distance distribution is similar with the travel time distribution. In the distribution characteristics, the frequency curve of travel distance distribution of Wangjing area has obvious differences with the other two areas. The percentage of short distance travel is the highest in Wangjing area which reaches 45%. The short distance travels mainly happen in residential areas with relatively large areas. The percentage of short distance travels is higher in the areas and some taxi trips connection rail transit is also included. The Beijing railway station area is an external transport hub, some long-distance travelers also choose taxi as a traffic mode. The percentage of traveling more than 15km travel accounts for nearly 20%.

5.2   The Taxi Travel Features of Different Trip Purposes

Using the travel purpose as a standard and carrying out the synthetically fractional analysis for different samples and then comparing characteristic differences of different travel purposes.

Table 9. The mean and median of different trip purposes

Trip Purposes	Time Consuming/min		Travel distance/km	
	Mean	Median	Mean	Median
Commuting travel	18.5	15.1	7.9	5.7
Business travel	20.3	17.6	7.7	6.0
External travel	24.0	21.7	10.2	9.1

As above table shows that the time consuming of external travel is the longest, mainly because of the increasing demands for taxi of passengers with heavy luggage. The average distance of the commuting travel and business travel are quite different, while the median value of the commuting travel is lower than the business travel, which indicates that commuting travel mostly is given priority to short distance travel.

Time consuming distribution and haul distance distribution of different trip purposes as follow:

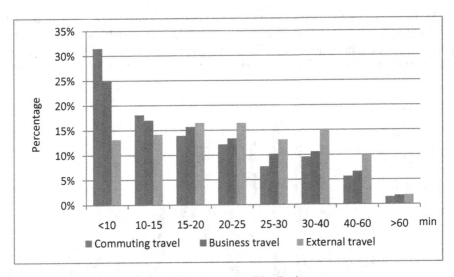

A)   Time Consuming Distribution

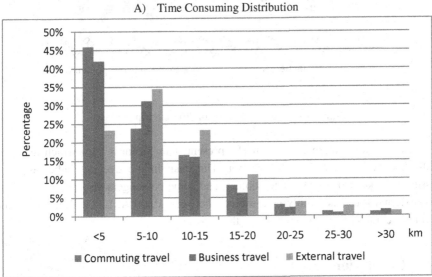

B)   Travel Distance Distribution

Fig. 6. Travel distance distribution of different trip purposes

From the graph above, the business travel distribution and the commuting travel distribution present the characteristics that distribution frequency decreases gradually with longer distance and time. It's approximately according with negative exponential distribution. The travel distance is less than 5 kilometers; the percentage of travel time below 10 min is higher. The external travel distribution tends to obey the normal distribution, the travel distances are mainly concentrated in the 5-10 kilometers, and the travel time is concentrated in the 15-25 minutes.

As the commuter travel mainly concentrated in the morning and evening peak, and its stronger regularity of time, therefore, the statistics and analysis throughout the period of all day can be done to business trips and external trips, and the regularity is finally analyzed. Travel time distribution as showed in figure 7:

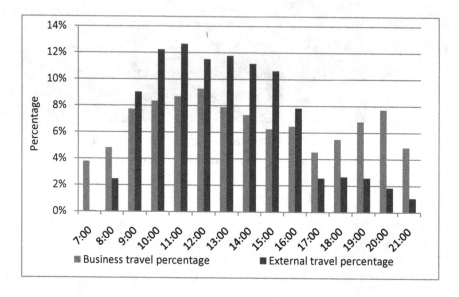

Fig. 7. Taxi trips distribution of different trip purposes

Figure 7 shows there are two peaks presented in business trip, which at 11:00 AM-12:00 AM and 7:00 PM-8:00 PM. The peak in the evening indicates some passengers take taxi to eat out for dinner, and some passengers go shopping by taxi. And external travel is mainly concentrated between 10:00 AM-3:00 PM, this period of time accounts for more than 60% of the trips.

6   Conclusions

Take the characteristics analysis of taxi travel as a goal, the paper processed the taxi meter data and the taxi GPS data, combined with the semantic information including the POI data and search popularity of the POI from the online map data, established the method to distinguish the taxi trip purposes by using the semantic reasoning techniques. According to the comprehensive analysis on characteristics of different trip purposes of taxi travel from different types of areas, the conclusions can be draw as follows:

1) Based on the Semantic data the POI information and search popularity of the POI, and combined with the spatial-temporal data of the taxi travel, the taxi trip purpose can be estimated rather accurately.

2) There is considerable diversity in the taxi trip intensity of the areas with different land use types and locations. Compared with the residential and commercial areas, the external transportation hub area has the maximum taxi trip intensity.

3) The taxi travel distance and travel time is the longest in the external transportation hub areas, and reached 10.2km and 24 minutes respectively, and 60% external travel aimed taxi travel is concentrated during the 10:00 AM to 3:00 PM.

4) The short distance travel proportion in residential area is much larger, the proportion of below 10 minutes is almost 35%; and the travel distance and travel time presents the Negative Exponential Distribution, the distribution characteristics of commercial areas and external transportation hub areas are both close to the Normal Distribution.

5) With the travel distance and time becomes longer, the frequency distribution of business travel and commuting travel gradually become smaller, the taxi travel within 5km trip distance and below 10min time cost account for a high proportion; distribution of the external travel is about Normal Distribution, trip distance are concentrated in 5-10 km, trip time cost are between 15 to 25 minutes.

The paper proposed a sound research method for the taxi trip purpose estimation and characteristics analysis. However, the number of POIs selected in the trip purpose identification still need to be completely tested, and more applicable semantic reasoning rules also should be discussed to acquire more accurate trip purposes in the future work. Additionally, further expansion analysis of more typical regions should be conducted, and dynamic monitoring of the taxi travel characteristics of the whole city will provide effective support for the planning and design of taxi stops, the taxi operation management and scheduling.

Acknowledgements. The authors would like to show great appreciation for the support from the Ministry of Industry and Information Technology of P. R. China under the Major Program of national science and technology with No. 2013ZX01045-003-002.

References

1. Hu, Z.W., Yu, Q., Shao, C.Q., Rong, J., Wang, J.G.: Beijing Taxi Operation Condition Analysis System Development. Road Traffic and Safety 7(4), 45–55 (2007)
2. Deng, Y.H., Ou, G.L.: Taxi Utilization Efficiency Evaluation and Analysis. Comprehensive Transportation 6, 54–59 (2009)
3. Chi, G.H.: The Taxi Operation Characteristics Analysis Based on Floating Car Data. Transportation World (20), 84–85 (2011)
4. Li, Y.H., Yuan, Z.Z., Xie, H.H., Cao, S.H., Wu, X.Y.: Analysis on Trips Characteristics of Taxi in Suzhou Based on OD Data. Journal of Transportation Systems Engineering and Information Technology 7(5), 85–89 (2007)
5. Weng, J.C., Zhao, Y.Q., Zhao, X.J., Rong, J.: Floating Car Data based Taxi Operation Characteristics Analysis in Beijing. In: 2009 World Congress on Computer Science and Information Engineering, Los angle, USA, p. 3 (2009)

6. Kamga, C., Yazici, M.: Abhishek: Hailing in the Rain: Temporal and Weather-Related Variations in Taxi Ridership and Taxi Demand-Supply Equilibrium. In: Transportation Research Board 92nd Annual Meeting, Washington, D.C. (2013)

7. Tong, X.J.: Analysis of Residents' Behavior Based on the Taxi GPS Data, China. Central South University, Changsha (2012)

8. Wolf, J., Guensler, R., Bachman, W.: Elimination of the Travel Diary: Experiment to Derive Trip Purpose from Global Positioning System Travel Data. Transportation Research Record (1768), 125–134 (2001)

9. Murakami, E., Wagner, D.P.: Can Using Global Positioning System (GPS) Improves Trip Reporting. Transportation Research Part C: Emerging Technologies 7, 149–165 (1999)

10. Wolf, J.: Using GPS Data Loggers to Replace Travel Diaries in the Collection of Travel Data. Georgia Institute of Technology, Georgia (2000)

11. Bohte, W., Maat, K.: Deriving and Validating Trip Destinations and Modes for Multi-day GPS-based Travel Surveys: An Application in the Netherlands. Transportation Research Part C 17(3), 285–297 (2009)

12. Mu, C., Zhao, X.M.: Simulation for the 24-Hour Features of Cruising Taxi Operation System. Applied Mechanics and Materials, 639-644 (195-196): 639-644

Author Index